TOWN, COUNTRY, AND REGIONS IN REFORMATION GERMANY

STUDIES IN MEDIEVAL AND REFORMATION TRADITIONS

History, Culture, Religion, Ideas

VOLUME CVI

TOM SCOTT

TOWN, COUNTRY, AND REGIONS IN REFORMATION GERMANY

TOWN, COUNTRY, AND REGIONS IN REFORMATION GERMANY

BY

TOM SCOTT

BRILL
LEIDEN · BOSTON
2005

This book is printed on acid-free paper.

Library of Congress Cataloging-in-Publication Data

Scott, Tom, 1947-
Town, country, and regions in Reformation Germany / by Tom Scott.
p. cm. — (Studies in medieval and Reformation traditions, ISSN 1573-4188 ; v. 106)
Includes bibliographical references and index.
ISBN 90-04-14321-1 (alk. paper)
1. Rhine River Region—Economic conditions. 2. Cities and towns—Rhine River Region. 3. Group identity—Rhine River Region. 4. Reformation—Germany. 5. Peasants' War, 1524-1525. I. Title. II. Series.

HC288.R66S36 2005
943'.031—dc22

2004062924

ISSN 1573-4188
ISBN 90 04 14321 1

PRINTED IN THE NETHERLANDS

CONTENTS

ACKNOWLEDGEMENTS

For permission to reproduce four essays in the volume I am grateful to Hodder Arnold (no. 7), Cambridge University Press (no. 8, in a revised and expanded version), Peter Lang A. G. (no. 9), and the editors of *German History* (no. 14). Translations from the German originals of essays 3, 4, 5, 6, 10, 11, 12, 13, and 15 are by the author.

In the preparation of the volume I have incurred numerous debts. My thanks go to Margaret Farrington for preparing several of the essays for publication; to Alan Rogers for advice and support on matters of computing and computer-generated graphics; to Andrew Gow, the editor of *Studies in Medieval and Reformation Traditions*, for accepting these essays with enthusiasm for his series; and not least to Tom Brady, who initially endorsed the notion of compiling this volume and who at an early stage volunteered to write an Introduction. My thanks go also to Dr Irene van Rossum and Boris van Gool at Brill Academic Publishers for their help in seeing the volume through the press with courtesy and efficiency.

My greatest debt goes to those colleagues and friends who have sustained and supported me in recent years. They shall remain anonymous, but to be able to thank them now from a Scottish address is suitable consolation.

Tom Scott
University of St. Andrews
Summer 2004

LIST OF ILLUSTRATIONS, MAPS, AND TABLES

Illustrations

Maps

Tables

NOTE ON USAGE

Place-names are spelt in accordance with modern political frontiers, though in eastern Europe the German names precede the Slav ones. All variants are cross-referenced in the index. In the German-speaking lands, only the commonest English usages have been retained: Munich, Cologne, Nuremberg (but Basel, Bern, Braunschweig, Konstanz, Luzern). In the case of two Swiss lakes the English form has been retained (Lake Constance, Lake of Lucerne) since their German names—Bodensee, Vierwaldstättersee—do not translate directly into English. The lands east of the river Elbe are referred to collectively as 'east Elbia'.

To avoid confusion, Estates (social corporations, political associations) are distinguished from estates (lands) by the use of an initial capital for the former. Similarly, the religious Reformers and the Reformation of the sixteenth century are given initial capital letters in order to differentiate them from general movements of reform within the Holy Roman Empire in the fifteenth and sixteenth centuries.

Unless otherwise indicated, all measurements and distances are metric. One German mile equates to 4.6 statute miles (7.4 kilometres). The imperial coinage was denominated in guilders or florins (abbreviated fl.).

AUTHOR'S PREFACE

The articles collected in the present volume reflect themes which have preoccupied the author since his doctoral dissertation more than thirty-five years ago, and which have found expression in three monographs. The reasons for choosing to collect the following selection of essays fall under three headings. Many of the pieces, especially the most recent, have appeared in German, often in relatively obscure locations. For English-language readers, and especially for students, it seemed desirable to make them available more accessibly and conveniently in translation. The articles, moreover, although written over a long span and for very differing occasions (invitations to conferences, contributions to Festschriften and exhibition catalogues) deal thematically with issues which are perhaps less familiar to those whose own historical interests do not involve fragmented polities such as the Holy Roman Empire, with its distinct local identities and peculiarities. The essays, addressing in large part issues that lie at the borders of historical regional studies, economic politics, and historical geography, always seek to emphasize that these questions cannot be examined without reference to power, politics, and indeed social or class formation—an approach which, in the German context, requires above all a sensitivity towards the interplay of local, regional, territorial, and national or imperial interests, structures, and identities. A final motive concerns methodology, for the *cantus firmus* of these essays remains the conviction that local and regional history, if it is to have wider meaning and application and not fall into the trivial, episodic, picturesque, or adventitious, needs to be underpinned by theoretical approaches which, while honouring the diversity and quiddity of historical experience, must yet offer frameworks for understanding which not only make that experience logically intelligible in itself but also provide opportunities for comparison and contrast. Hence, many of the essays interrogate theories of location in order to illuminate particular configurations of society, economy, politics, and cultural identity at regional level. Such methodologies, of course, should not be allowed to distort the historical record: they are the handmaidens of history, not its governesses.

The tradition of historical regional studies (*geschichtliche Landeskunde*) is a long and honourable one in German history, even if it has been sullied at various times over the last century by being pressed into nationalistic service as the ostensible validation for pan-Germanness and *Lebensraum*, issues which acquired a particular resonance on the western borders of the German lands, with which the present essays are chiefly concerned. Since World War II, however, the tradition of historical regional studies has been able to bring together scholars across regional frontiers and international boundaries—both on the Upper Rhine, embracing Germany, Switzerland, and Alsace, as well as in a major academic research project on the historical landscape between the rivers Rhine and Maas/Meuse, initiated at the University of Trier, but involving scholars from Germany, Luxemburg, France, and Belgium. Such initiatives, born of a spirit of European cooperation across traditional divides, are the best testimony, if testimony be needed, to the vitality, validity, and value of interdisciplinary regional history.

The essays remain as written. In translating from German, I have allowed myself to phrase freely, preferring idiom to literalness. Where necessary, I have silently emended a few factual errors and typographical slips. The sequence of footnote referencing has been retained in order to permit easy cross-checking, except in essay 1, where parts 1 and 2 of the text have been run together, and the footnotes accordingly through-numbered, and in essay 8 on 'Town and Country in Germany, 1350–1600', where the original text and footnotes have been restored to their full length and extent. References to literature that has appeared subsequently, and to English-language publications of German works originally cited, have been incorporated into the existing footnotes. Otherwise, the author hopes that it is neither arrogance nor delusion on his part to believe that the essays do not require major revisions or corrections. It is inevitable that there are overlaps (mostly quite modest) between some of the essays. Rather than apologize for subjecting readers to the tedium of repetition, I urge them to regard it as an opportunity to spot discrepancies and inconsistencies in my arguments.

One source of confusion, however, may arise from the use of the term 'Reformation Germany'. The chronological boundaries of many of the essays are certainly not confined by the age of the Reformation. The common alternative—to speak of 'between late Middle Ages and early modern times'—is one which can only irritate the economic historian, for whom the year 1500, or the early decades of the Reformation, mark no fundamental divide or epochal shift in underlying economic or social structures. This is a view which even some historians of religion and culture now regard with inchoate sympathy. Until historians can agree on a better overarching term, then 'Reformation Germany' it shall be. *Verbum sapienti sat est.*

INTRODUCTION

Thomas A. Brady, Jr

The German Lands in the Early Modern Era, 1300–1600: A Journey with Tom Scott

More delicate than the historians' are the map-makers' colours.
Elizabeth Bishop (1911–89)

Some of the historian's most creative work takes place in landscapes from which history itself has blasted once-accepted understandings and explanations, leaving only question-marks and mysteries in their places. For a generation after 1945, German history was such a landscape. Gradually, since around 1960, the wreckage of old master-narratives and once-potent symbols has been cleared away, and the work of regaining understanding and reconstructing explanations has gone forward. One of its richest lodes has been the era between 1300 and 1600, which constitutes the earlier part of what is now called 'the early modern era'. Its special value lies in a great spurt of documentation about societies which were not yet undergoing the great transformation of the eighteenth century—sustained growth of populations and economies—and its major consequences: the power of the sovereign state, the revolutionary power of the market, and the cultural hegemony of science.

How the special difficulties of understanding this era, at once post-medieval and pre-modern, affect our understanding of Europe generally is suggested by the uncertainties that currently swarm around all of its classic organizing categories: Renaissance, Reformation, Scientific Revolution, Absolutism, and Enlightenment. Multiply these difficulties by removing the national narratives (long the most important spinal cords, overt or covert, of European historiography), and one adds a second impediment to understanding the history of Germany, which has never had an uncontested idea of nationality and national development. Posit, furthermore, a third impediment to understanding posed by the lack of any centre to German history comparable to those that give Anglo-British, French, and Russian—though not Italian or Dutch—histories their appearance of continuity. Finally and most seriously, think away nearly all alleged continuities between the political organization of the Holy Roman Empire, dissolved in 1806, and any part of modern Germany, and the magnitude of the problem becomes most oppressive. Medieval European history may be organized by reference to the continuity of the Church, but modern European history is organized in terms of countries, and there was no country of Germany until 1871.

One can gain some notion of the difficulty of writing the histories of the German lands before Napoleon by poring over the Holy Roman Empire in the guise of Elizabeth Bishop's delicate 'map-makers' colours' at almost any time in this polity's history. It is a colourful rag-bag of alien shapes and names. A few names, true, are familiar. There is an Austria, but it looks nothing like the dwarfish Republic of Austria we know. Here is a slimmed-down Bavaria, there a fatter Saxony, and Prussia exists, though it is a small principality on the Baltic coast, not a large one centred on Berlin, as we know it should be. Moreover, since 1947 Prussia no longer exists. Beyond these largest entities, whose names are at least familiar, the empire's map displays spaces limned helpfully in mapmaker's colours but offering few points of recognition outside of the rivers, mountain ranges, and major cities. Strewn across its landscapes are many things called 'ecclesiastical territories', all coloured in purple as though they were mere specifications of the same polity. Among them are scattered the bright red pimples for the imperial free cities. They are relatively easy to recognize, but if we dig deeper yet, we uncover a riot of wildly strange, unidentifiable petty polities: imperial free abbesses and prince-provosts, heads of military-religious orders and free knights, and even some free peasants, such as the thirty-nine free villages and hamlets on the Leutkirch Heath in Upper Swabia, whose folk appointed their sheriffs and judges and owned no lord but the emperor.

To dwell on the mapmaker's delicate colours alone, and not on the far more messy realities they feebly represent, is to gain some inkling of the dismaying task faced by those who research, write about, and seek to understand and explain the economic, social, political, cultural, and religious realities of the German lands—the unifying term 'Germany' hardly existed before the sixteenth century—during the centuries before, say, the eighteenth. The Scottish historian Tom Scott, who has few rivals as guide to these old German landscapes, has constructed a new way to map them. It is the region, an entity both economic and political, which grew into a historical unity without necessarily becoming coterminous with any state. They appear on no map in mapmaker's colours.

I

Town, Country, and Regions in Reformation Germany brings together fifteen studies published by Tom Scott between 1978 and 2004 in historical journals and collective volumes. The volume ranges temporally from 1350 (the era of the Black Death) to 1600 (the eve of the Thirty Years War), a period named in the book's title according to the best current usage as the era of the Reformation. Spatially, *Town, Country, and Regions* ranges over the lands stretching from the Central Alps northward down the Rhine basin to around Frankfurt, reaching into the Upper Danube basin as well. This is the old 'German southwest' as it existed before its fairly recent dissection into Switzerland, France, Germany, and Austria. Inside this large area, which has supported some of the most innovative recent research on post-medieval German history, Scott's home ground is the Upper Rhine valley from Lake Constance to the zone where Alemannic and Swabian give way to Franconian dialects along the east-line of the River Main from Nuremberg to Frankfurt. The characteristics of Scott's chosen lands help to explain the diversity of his themes. First, they were densely populated lands of farming (and some pastoralism) dotted and tied together economically by their numerous small cities, towns, and markets. Second, they were lands of radical political fragmentation, which lacked dominant principalities and supported the empire's richest fabric of local self-government both in the towns and on the land. Third, they were central sites of the greatest disruptions of the age, the German Peasants' War and the Protestant Reformation. Nowhere in the German lands was the fragmentation of authority and power that hardened during the decades after 1350 more—and the forces of unification and centralization less—successful.

The chapters of this volume are grouped in three parts, the subjects of which reflect the master themes of Tom Scott's oeuvre. Part I focuses on events, the Reformation and the Peasants' War; Part

II on structures and economic regionalism; and Part III on institutions and culture, regional identities and characteristics. All three subjects appear already in Scott's first book, a study of the middling town of Freiburg im Breisgau at the end of the Middle Ages, which bears the sub-title, *Town-Country Relations in the Age of Reformation and Peasants' War*.[1]

II

Each of Part I's six chapters explores an aspect or a setting of the great events in the German south-west—the Peasants' War and the preliminary revolt called the 'Bundschuh', the early Reformation, and political collaboration between burghers and peasants (chs 1–6). Scott's belief in an objective conflict of economic interests between farmers and burghers led him to develop a sceptical attitude toward the thesis advanced many times since 1975 that burghers' and peasants' communal institutions formed a solid basis for political collaboration between them in the upheavals of the early sixteenth century.[2] To Scott, for whom structural factors are more powerful in shaping history than are human mentalities, what has been called the 'Revolution of the Common Man' in 1525 emerged as one possible outcome of earlier rural conspiracies (ch. 5), while political collaboration between burghers and revolutionary peasants turns out to have rested more on opportunism than on solidarity (ch. 6).

Scott brings the same measured scepticism to bear on the argument—advanced, again, by Peter Blickle—that burghers and peasants participated in a common 'Communal Reformation', which sought to bring theological criticism to serve their desire to communalize the Church. Scott's initially negative view of the possibil-

[1] Tom Scott, *Freiburg and the Breisgau: Town-Country Relations in the Age of Reformation and Peasants' War* (Oxford, 1986); idem, *Regional Identity and Economic Change: The Upper Rhine, 1450–1600* (Oxford, 1997); and the important volume by Peter Ainsworth and Tom Scott (eds), *Regions and Landscapes: Reality and Imagination in Late Medieval and Early Modern Europe* (Oxford/Bern/Berlin/Brussels/Frankfurt am Main/New York/Vienna, 2000).

[2] See on this controversy Thomas A. Brady, Jr, 'German Burghers and Peasants in Reformation and Peasants' War: Partners or Competitors?', in Michael W. Maher, SJ, and Charles H. Parker (eds), *Between the Middle Ages and Modernity: Individual and Community in the Early Modern World. Studies in Honor of James D. Tracy* (forthcoming).

ity of religious solidarity and the role of theology (ch. 1) has softened somewhat, though he contends—against Blickle—that 'it was possible to achieve a Communal Reformation without the introduction of evangelical religion' (ch. 2). It is not that Scott denies the historical significance of religion and religious ideas—he is the author of a study on Thomas Müntzer, the radical theologian of the German Peasants' War[3]—but he doubts that religious motives are reducible to socio-political interests or that they exhaust themselves in the particular contexts in which they become visible. Above all, he insists on the multiple possibilities every complex of historical forces contains and therefore rejects the portrayal of the religious Reformation as either the inevitable outcome of the evolution of serfdom and communal liberties in general or of a late medieval agrarian crisis in particular.

III

The five chapters in Part II display Tom Scott's command of the subject on which his most creative work has focused, the regional character of relations between town and country in early modern Germany. Though he can draw on an older literature about economic regionalism, the current concept of an economic region with respect to the early modern German lands is largely Scott's creation. He revived the subject of economic regionalism (ch. 7) practically from the dead, or from the limbo in which it languished for a century. His concept subtly meshes natural with historical elements. The former, most stable, are defined by geology, geography, or climate, on which divisions of colonization, settlement, and ethnic and linguistic identities were later superimposed. Only in the era after 1300 did regional identities become increasingly shaped by economic and political factors to create the distinctive economic landscapes of early modern Germany: agrarian, mixed agrarian and manufacturing, and mining and industry. These fundamental units arose from the interplay, often highly complex, of both natural and historical factors.

In the following chapters Scott applies this concept to the German lands as a whole (ch. 8), to the southern stretch of the Upper Rhine

[3] Tom Scott, *Thomas Müntzer: Theology and Revolution in the German Reformation* (Houndmills, Hants/London, 1989).

valley (chs 9–10), and to the single city of Freiburg im Breisgau and its hinterland (ch. 11). Scott believes that town–country relations in the German lands were more varied than in any other part of Europe. They ranged from the economically modest but politically fully fledged city-states of the Swiss Confederation to the economically powerful but politically weak cities of the southern Low Countries. All cities strove to bring the surrounding countryside into a hierarchy of influence or dependence, but they also collaborated with other cities to create the great urban leagues of the later Middle Ages. In his analysis of town–country relations, as in all other subjects on which he has written, Scott affirms the possibility of plural outcomes from similarly structured situations. He argues that the size of a city's territory, for example, is no guide to how its economic power shaped relations with the countryside. Once again, similarity of structure does not dictate a similarity of destinies.

A consistent strength of Tom Scott's work on cities is his attention to the middling and the small places as well as to German metropolises such as Nuremberg, Cologne, and Augsburg. He is, indeed, virtually the only non-native speaker of German among the social historians who have recently revitalized the ideas of central-place and urban networks as keys to understanding the structures and fates of economic regions. Scott examines the southern Upper Rhine valley, the region in which he is most at home, to distinguish the elements of competition and collaboration among towns in the formation of economic regionalism. Unsurprisingly, he finds that the existence of particular structures supplies no reliable guide to the economic fates of regions. We can be sure, he concludes, 'that that the terms "urban landscape" or "urban network" contain no inherent explanatory capacity; even as descriptors they are neither unequivocal nor unambiguous' (ch. 10).

IV

The four chapters of Part III form the most varied section of *Town, Country, and Regions*. They contain his contributions to an entire generation's debates on the political fates of the large and extremely variegated southwestern sector of the Holy Roman Empire. Chapter 12 bridges Parts II and III by examining the place of Alsace in the histories and historiographies of the German-speaking south-west. Scott's chief goal is to extricate the historical Alsace from modern misconstructions of its past in order to examine what role it did play in the Upper Rhine region during the fifteenth and sixteenth centuries. He strips away modern conceptions of several kinds: the characterization of Alsace as a 'bridging landscape' in the promotional rhetoric of the European Union; the twentieth-century German nationalist idea of Alsace as a German bastion west of the Rhine; and older, quaint Swiss detachment of what is now northwestern Switzerland from the Upper Rhine region, of which it forms a natural and historical part. In the place of these artificial constructions, Scott builds a picture of Alsace's regional embeddedness with materials from his extensive and original research on the region.

Chapters 13–15 bear directly on issues of current interest in the political historiography of the German-speaking south-west. In chapter 13 he takes on one of the most intriguing and difficult texts from the time around 1500, the *Booklet of One Hundred Chapters* of an unknown author who goes under the modern name of the 'Revolutionary of the Upper Rhine'. Building on a recent identification of the author as a Habsburg official and not a confused and mystically minded priest, Scott explores the book's combination of strong partisanship for the Habsburg dynasty with a belief that the author's native Alsace lay at the heart of a revitalizing empire. Scott's study is an object lesson in the importance of context to the interpretation of a text.

The final two chapters explore issues of liberty and community in the German-speaking south-west. His study of medieval Switzerland (ch. 14) takes off from the wave that occurred in the 1990s of debunking the traditional narratives of the steady rise of the Confederation as a free, peasant polity since 1291. Against the argument that the formation of Switzerland was essentially a movement to suppress violence, Scott contends that feuding violence was an integral part of the Swiss political experience, and that, in the longer run, peasant liberties, even in the Swiss bastion of freedom, proved no match for the city-states' military power.

The final study (ch. 15) is a conversation between the two reigning masters of the late medieval and early modern south-west. Scott reviews Peter Blickle's central argument about the political uses and abuses of serfdom in the German-speaking south-west, which holds that by 1600 serfdom had run its course, having lost its economic utility with the overcoming of the agrarian crisis and its political utility with the territorialization of the smaller lordships. Serfdom, now degenerated into a formula, nevertheless survived just because it had outlived its purpose. Scott's goal is to test how far this picture of serfdom can be generalized for other German lands. Looking over research on other lands, he concludes that the southwestern story is but one of a whole spectrum of configurations of the relationship between legal unfreedom and genuine subjection of peasants to their lords. It is not possible, therefore, to write the history of German serfdom as a master narrative of the fortunes of popular freedom and unfreedom.

V

This volume of studies by Tom Scott is unusual for the consistent felicity of its prose, the clarity of its conceptions, and the unity of its themes. Its readers are advised to read also his general social and economic history of the German lands from 1300 to 1600, in which he demonstrates the need for a general history of the subject to be rooted in a command of the particulars of a single region.[4] This book, the finest study of the subject in any language, illustrates how the mid-century collapse of narratives based on the histories of the state and the nation have since the 1960s dispersed social historians of early modern Germany into the myriad houses of regional history. New narratives, arising from new assumptions, are building on new research combined with the best of the old.

The importance of building new pictures of early modern German history rests on two considerations. The first is that the German past has been freed from the nationalist myth only to fall prey to accounts of German history in which all roads lead to Adolf Hitler. The second is that the German lands present an important set of variants on general European patterns of social history. The absence of strong states and the lack of a political or a cultural centre allowed many European forms to flourish in the German lands far into the more

[4] Tom Scott, *Society and Economy in Germany, 1300–1600* (Houndmills, Hants/New York, 2002).

densely documented early modern era. The early modern history of the German lands, like the modern history of Germany, was fully European and can be understood in no other context. We are fortunate to have Tom Scott's guidance through the regional structures and events that lie beneath the map-maker's colours.

PART I

TOWN AND COUNTRY BETWEEN REFORM AND REVOLT

CHAPTER ONE

REFORMATION AND PEASANTS' WAR IN WALDSHUT AND ENVIRONS: A STRUCTURAL ANALYSIS

At the heart of all revolutionary theory stands the relationship of ideas to action: what part does ideology play in the genesis of social protest?* How far can it transform local uprisings into a general revolt? To what extent can it convert specific demands for the rectification of individual grievances into a radical programme for the overthrow of the social order as a whole? How far can it reconcile the conflicting aims of different social groups by forging an overriding sense of solidarity through which the downtrodden will unite in a common struggle against their oppressors? Does the radicalization of social protest in fact depend upon the impact of an egalitarian ideology which, by asserting fundamental principles of social justice, transcends the particular circumstances of protest, or is radicalization instead an immanent consequence of those circumstances themselves?

These are questions that touch the mainsprings of the German Peasants' War. Can the eruption of widespread revolt in 1524 after decades of isolated uprisings be explained without recourse to the potent ideology and unifying impetus of the Protestant Reformation? These arguments have aroused fierce controversy in east and west.[1]

* Dedicated to Erich Hassinger on his 70th birthday.

Archives are cited by the following abbreviations:

FWWA	Fürstlich von Waldburg-Wolfegg'sches Gesamtarchiv, Schloß Wolfegg
GLA	Badisches Generallandesarchiv, Karlsruhe
HKA	Hofkammerarchiv, Vienna
HSA	Württembergisches Hauptstaatsarchiv, Stuttgart
SASh	Staatsarchiv Schaffhausen
SAZh	Staatsarchiv Zürich
StAA	Stadtarchiv Augsburg
StAFr	Stadtarchiv Freiburg im Breisgau
StAWt	Stadtarchiv Waldshut
TLA	Tiroler Landesarchiv, Innsbruck

[1] On the present state of debate between east and west over the Peasants' War and the Reformation see Rainer Wohlfeil (ed.), *Reformation oder frühbürgerliche Revolution?* (nymphenburger texte zur wissenschaft, modelluniversität 5) (Munich, 1975); idem

Both are agreed that there is a strong current of anticlericalism and Reforming sentiment in the peasants' demands, but opinions differ greatly about their character, function, and significance. Marxist historians have developed the concept of a 'People's Reformation' (*Volksreformation*) led by Thomas Müntzer, whose radical religious doctrines incited the peasantry of central Germany to challenge the legitimacy of the existing feudal order. Western ('bourgeois') historians, on the other hand, and especially Reformation scholars, in arguing that even the more radical preachers were concerned primarily with theological and spiritual ends, have been reluctant to accept that these teachings were designed to transform the peasant uprisings into a revolutionary movement.

Recent scholarship has begun to overcome this impasse by focusing more on the structural significance of the Reformation rather than on its ideological impact. It is now recognized, for example, that Reforming preaching first helped to create the broad public audience without which the Twelve Articles of the Upper Swabian peasantry could never have been disseminated so widely or so rapidly.[2] Similarly, the striking correspondence between the radical Swiss congregationalists' demands for a recasting of church organization and the peasants' demands for village autonomy in agricultural, legal, and religious matters has encouraged a reassessment of the Anabaptists' role in the Peasants' War.[3] A structural approach to the Reformation, however, also requires that the role of the towns in peasant upris-

(ed.), *Der Bauernkrieg 1524–26. Bauernkrieg und Reformation* (nymphenburger texte zur wissenschaft, modelluniversität 21) (Munich, 1975); Peter Blickle (ed.), *Revolte und Revolution in Europa. Referate und Protokolle des Internationalen Symposiums zur Erinnerung an den Bauernkrieg 1525 (Memmingen, 24.–27. März 1975)* (*Historische Zeitschrift*, Beiheft 4 (new series)) (Munich, 1975). For a convenient summary see Peter Blickle, *Die Revolution von 1525*, 1st edn (Munich, 1975); 3rd edn (Munich, 1982); Engl. as *The Revolution of 1525. The German Peasants' War from a New Perspective*, transl. and ed. Thomas A. Brady, Jr and H. C. Erik Midelfort (Baltimore, MD/London, 1981). For a specific analysis of the historiography of the German Democratic Republic see Joseph Foschepoth, *Reformation und Bauernkrieg im Geschichtsbild der DDR* (Historische Forschungen, 10) (Berlin, 1976).

[2] Hartmut Boockmann, 'Zu den geistigen und religiösen Voraussetzungen des Bauernkriegs', in Bernd Moeller (ed.), *Bauernkriegs-Studien* (Schriften des Vereins für Reformationsgeschichte, 189 [vol. 82,2/83]) (Gütersloh, 1975), pp. 26–7.

[3] James M. Stayer, 'Die Anfänge des schweizerischen Täufertums im reformierten Kongregationalismus', in Hans-Jürgen Goertz (ed.), *Umstrittenes Täufertum 1525–1975. Neue Forschungen* (Göttingen/Zürich, 1975), pp. 28–9. See now also James M. Stayer, 'Radikaler Frühzwinglianismus: Balthasar Hubmaier, Fabers "Ursach" und die Programme der Bauern', *Mennonitische Geschichtsblätter*, 42 (1985), pp. 43–59.

ings be re-examined. Reforming preaching was concentrated in the towns, whence it spread outwards to the surrounding countryside. How far, therefore, did the towns act as rallying-points of resistance to which the peasants looked for inspiration, leadership, and support?

One town in particular has long attracted historical attention. From 1521 until his flight four years later, the little Habsburg community of Waldshut on the *Hochrhein* (the Upper Rhine above Basel) had as its preacher Balthasar Hubmaier, one of the most eminent radical theologians of the Reformation. In defiance of the Austrian authorities and the bishop of Konstanz, Hubmaier introduced Zwinglian and later Anabaptist reforms to Waldshut. The town's refusal to abandon its preacher and his teachings under duress brought it into alliance with the rebellious peasantry of south-west Germany. The following analysis of Waldshut's relations with the surrounding countryside before and during the Peasants' War is designed to trace the origins and nature of this alliance. How far did Hubmaier's preaching impinge upon the rural population? Are his teachings reflected in the peasants' grievances and actions? Did they serve to make the peasants' demands more radical? Did the peasantry regard Waldshut as a champion of its cause? What were the circumstances that led to the alliance? What were its aims? How long did it last? Did it constitute a revolutionary movement which embraced the common man in town and country?

To some of these questions there can be no satisfactory answer, since the sources are often too sparse or too ambiguous. But only detailed investigation of local circumstances can hope to counteract the facile assumptions that are sometimes made about the revolutionary potential of revolts in which religious radicalism and social protest coincide.

I

At the beginning of the sixteenth century Waldshut's situation had two features in common with the surrounding countryside that affected relations between them in the Peasants' War. One was its involvement with the Swiss; the other, its conflicts with monastic institutions in the neighbourhood. Although Waldshut belonged to Austria, it lay within the orbit of the Swiss Confederation. As part of the settlement after the Swiss Wars the latter had acquired rights of protection and military occupation over the four Austrian Forest Towns on the *Hochrhein*.[4] These rights mirror the extensive influence which some northern Swiss cities already exercised over parts of the south-west German countryside. To the east of Waldshut, the landgraviate of the Klettgau had come under the protective jurisdiction of Zürich because its lord, count Rudolf von Sulz, head of the Upper Austrian government in Innsbruck, held burgher's rights there.[5] Schaffhausen, too, whose territory formed a Swiss bridgehead on the north bank of the Rhine, had seigneurial rights in several Austrian villages, while its burghers held land in both the Klettgau and the Hegau at the western end of Lake Constance.[6] These political connections not only created favourable circumstances for the reception of Zwinglian and other Swiss Reformers' ideas in south-west Germany, but were also of decisive consequence in 1524/25, because they repeatedly deterred the Habsburg authorities and the Swabian League from taking effective action against Waldshut and the neighbouring peasantry lest it lead to war with the Confederation. Indeed, the threat of intervention by Zürich on behalf of the Klettgau peasants enabled them and their ally Waldshut to continue to defy the authorities long after the other peasant armies in the south-west had been defeated.[7]

Tensions between Waldshut and the religious houses revolved around the privileges and jurisdictions which they possessed there. The advowson of Waldshut's two parishes was held by the Swiss

---

[4] The *Waldstädte* comprised Rheinfelden and Laufenburg on the left bank, and Säckingen and Waldshut on the right bank of the Rhine upriver from Basel (known properly as the *Hochrhein*, to distinguish it from the *Oberrhein*—the Upper Rhine proper—below Basel). In 1526 the Austrian military commander of the Four Towns and bailiff of Laufenburg, Ulrich von Habsberg, protested to archduke Ferdinand that, despite repeated penalties, the inhabitants of Laufenburg had often held the town gates open overnight, so that the Swiss had been able to enter. HKA, Reichsakten, Faszikel 79, fo. 99v.

[5] Franz Ludwig Baumann, 'Die Eidgenossen und der deutsche Bauernkrieg bis März 1525', *Sitzungsberichte der philosophisch-philologischen und der historischen Classe der königlich bayerischen Akademie der Wissenschaften zu München*, 1896, pp. 116–17.

[6] Paul Herzog, *Die Bauernunruhen im Schaffhauser Gebiet 1524/25* (Aarau, 1965), p. 33; Arnold Elben, *Vorderösterreich und seine Schutzgebiete im Jahre 1524. Ein Beitrag zur Geschichte des Bauernkriegs* (Stuttgart, 1899), p. 38.

[7] For Zürich's attempts at mediation see Franz Ludwig Baumann, 'Die Eidgenossen und der deutsche Bauernkrieg seit dem Märze 1525', *Sitzungsberichte der philosophisch-philologischen und der historischen Classe der königlich bayerischen Akademie der Wissenschaften zu München*, 1899, 1, pp. 58–64. Baumann argues forcefully that Zürich never contemplated military intervention. Ibid., p. 44.

nunnery of Königsfelden in canton Aargau, and although the two could choose vicars for the parishes their appointment had to be ratified by the nunnery.[8] In return, Königsfelden was required to provide for the maintenance of the two parish priests. When Hubmaier arrived in Waldshut he and his fellow-priest, Konrad Armbroster, petitioned the nunnery to augment their competency, which it only agreed to do after the bishop of Konstanz had intervened on their behalf.[9] This parsimony stands in marked contrast to Königsfelden's earlier attempts to secure its revenues whilst evading any fiscal and legal obligations within the town. In 1487 the nunnery had become involved in a dispute with some Waldshut burghers who were refusing to pay it tithes from lands which they claimed were free-of-tithe. The town council quickly saw a chance of using the case to press its own complaints against the nunnery. These included refusal to pay the excise on wine and corn, and the tax on land, as well as the refusal by the steward of the nunnery's estates in Waldshut to swear allegiance to Austria or to bear arms for the town's defence.[10]

How far such rancour persisted into the 1520s is impossible to tell, but in any case it is overshadowed by Waldshut's running battle with the abbey of St Blasien in the Black Forest over the latter's rights in the town. Unlike Königsfelden, St Blasien was a corporate burgher of Waldshut, but the abbey showed little inclination to accept the duties and responsibilities incumbent upon a burgher. In particular, the abbey was accused of endangering the citizens' livelihood (and the council's revenues presumably) by selling wine in the immediate vicinity, and of buying up property in the town. To put a stop to these and other abuses the council signed a treaty with St Blasien in 1504;[11] its effect is unknown, but conflict continued over quite different claims. For decades the abbey had been trying to tighten its control over those of its subjects who left the land to settle in Waldshut. St Blasien demanded that they should still swear fealty to the abbot, submit to his jurisdiction, and render him boon-service

[8] Torsten Bergsten, *Balthasar Hubmaier. Seine Stellung zu Reformation und Täufertum 1521–28* (Acta Universitatis Upsaliensis: Studia Historico-Ecclesiastica Upsaliensa 3) (Kassel, 1961), p. 95. (An abbreviated version now exists in English: Torsten Bergsten, *Balthasar Hubmaier. Anabaptist Theologian and Martyr*, ed. W. R. Estep (Valley Forge, PA, 1978), but all references below are taken from the German original.)

[9] GLA 11/509. 19 March 1522; Bergsten, *Hubmaier*, pp. 95–6.

[10] StAWt, Urkunden VI/1. 5 Feb. 1487.

[11] GLA 11/511. 22 May 1504; cf. GLA 67/1208, fo. 19v–23v.

and other servile dues. In 1495 Waldshut managed to have some of these obligations abolished,[12] but the abbey refused to abandon its seigneurial claims upon several men and women, some of whom, by their own account, had lived in Waldshut for thirty years or more without any legal demands upon their person by St Blasien. In 1509 Waldshut succeeded in establishing the freedom of those bondmen long resident in the town by agreeing to pay a lump sum to discharge all claims upon them, but had at the same time to concede the abbey's right to uphold its jurisdiction over any who moved to Waldshut after the settlement of 1495.[13] That the town remained at loggerheads with St Blasien during the critical years of 1524/25 can be seen from a dispute over the abbey's right as mortgagee of the Austrian village of Gurtweil a few miles east of Waldshut. There, as it protested to the Upper Austrian government in March 1524, a burgher of Waldshut, Hans Ulrich Gutjahr, was seeking to obstruct the abbey in the exercise of its rightful jurisdiction.[14] What seems at first merely a private quarrel becomes more ominous on learning that Gutjahr was not only magistrate of Waldshut but Hubmaier's earliest and most influential supporter.

Waldshut's grievances against St Blasien coincide with the culmination of a much more prolonged and bitter struggle by the Black Forest peasants, the free men of the lordship (afterwards county) of Hauenstein, to withstand the abbey's attempts to reduce them to serfdom.[15] In 1369 and again in 1412 the Hauensteiners had risen against the abbey and plundered it.[16] Although the Austrian Forest doom of 1467 reaffirmed the peasants' rights, St Blasien continued to encroach upon them.[17] After renewed complaints in 1522 that

---

[12] StAWt, Urkunden I/2, 15. 22 (*recte*: 28) March 1495; cf. GLA 11/510; GLA 67/1208, fo. 1r–3v.

[13] GLA 11/510. 6 Aug. 1509; cf. GLA 67/1208, fo. 4r–7v.

[14] HSA, B 17, 1*, fo. 22r–v. 14 March 1524; ibid., fo. 22v. n.d. (14 March 1524).

[15] Emil Müller, *Der Bauernkrieg im Kreise Waldshut* (Ettikon, 1961), pp. 13–14. Cf. Karl Friedrich Wernet, 'Die Grafschaft Hauenstein', in Friedrich Metz (ed.), *Vorderösterreich. Eine geschichtliche Landeskunde*, 2nd edn (Freiburg im Breisgau, 1967), pp. 437, 458. See now fundamentally Claudia Ulbrich, *Leibherrschaft am Oberrhein im Spätmittelalter* (Veröffentlichungen des Max-Planck-Instituts für Geschichte, 58) (Göttingen, 1979), pp. 59 f.

[16] Müller, *Bauernkrieg im Kreise Waldshut*, p. 17.

[17] Wernet, *Grafschaft Hauenstein*, p. 458; Paul Rothmund, 'Aus der Geschichte', in Norbert Nothelfer (ed.), *Der Kreis Waldshut* (Stuttgart/Aalen, 1975), p. 91; Ulbrich, *Leibherrschaft*, pp. 93–4.

their customary rights were being infringed,[18] the abbey's Black Forest subjects in May 1524 summarily declared their refusal to render henceforth any servile dues, demanding instead to be as free as the peasants in other districts.[19] The common opposition to St Blasien in town and country provided a bond of mutual interest between Waldshut and its northern hinterland, a bond strengthened by the solidarity which the town displayed towards the abbey's subjects in asserting the freedom of its inhabitants in the face of abbatial interference.

It is against the background of involvement with the Swiss on the one hand, and hostility towards the religious houses on the other, that the content, impact, and extent of Hubmaier's preaching before the outbreak of the Peasants' War must be assessed. From the beginning of his sojourn in Waldshut until early 1525 Hubmaier's development as a Reforming theologian was shaped and stimulated by his close contacts with the Swiss Reformers, above all with Huldrych Zwingli in Zürich. Although their first meeting did not take place until May 1523,[20] Hubmaier had already begun earlier that year to introduce Reforming doctrines in Waldshut according to Zwinglian precepts. Hubmaier clearly drew strongly upon Zwingli's Sixty-Seven Articles, composed for the first Colloquy of Zürich in January 1523, when formulating his own Eighteen Axioms for a debate with the clergy of Waldshut and environs in April 1524.[21] His undoubted acceptance of the Zwinglian Reformation during 1523/24 cannot, however, disguise the fact that Hubmaier was aware of the radical, dissenting voices amongst Zwingli's followers, who demanded that the congregation have a greater say in the constitution and administration of the Reformed Church. During the second Colloquy of Zürich in October 1523 it became clear that Hubmaier in fact shared some of the congregationalist opinions of men such as Vadian from St Gallen and Hofmeister from Schaffhausen when he argued that

---

[18] Müller, *Bauernkrieg im Kreise Waldshut*, p. 17.

[19] Johann Heinrich Schreiber (ed.), *Der deutsche Bauernkrieg. Gleichzeitige Urkunden* (*Urkundenbuch der Stadt Freiburg im Breisgau*, Neue Folge), 3 vols (Freiburg im Breisgau, 1863–66), 1, pp. 1–2, no. I.

[20] Bergsten, *Hubmaier*, p. 110.

[21] Ibid., p. 109. For dating and chronology see Gunnar Westin and Torsten Bergsten (eds), *Balthasar Hubmaier. Schriften* (Quellen und Forschungen zur Reformationsgeschichte, 29: Quellen zur Geschichte der Täufer, 9) (Gütersloh, 1962), pp. 69–71.

decisions (such as the removal of images from churches) could be taken by the community as a whole, provided that it had been properly instructed in the evils of idolatry, rather than being left to the discretion of the magistracy.[22]

But above all it is essential to know whether Hubmaier sided with the radicals on the one issue that was to bring about a lasting rift between them and Zwingli: the payment of tithes to holders of benefices. The Reformers' teaching on tithes assumed a crucial importance in the Peasants' War, because the wrath of the peasantry was frequently directed against the exactions and extortions of religious houses and cathedral chapters, which had commonly incorporated parish benefices. Refusal to pay tithes was, of course, nothing new, but after 1517 the incidents increased, particularly in northern Switzerland around Zürich and Schaffhausen.[23] In several villages belonging to Zürich from 1522 onward radical Reformers such as Simon Stumpf and Wilhelm Reublin, who were demanding autonomy for the rural parishes with corresponding control of church revenues, declared that tithes need not be paid to indolent, good-for-nothing monks. Zwingli, on the other hand, whose reforms depended on the political support of the Zürich government (which had for long controlled the administration of benefices and tithes in the city), found himself obliged to defend the payment of tithes on the grounds that it was the Christian's duty as a citizen to pay them if the council so demanded.[24]

As early as February 1524—that is to say, even before Hubmaier had begun to introduce the main Zwinglian church reforms in Waldshut, and a full year before his contacts with the Zürich radicals had led him to embrace Anabaptist doctrines—the bishop of Konstanz had sent 'articles' by Hubmaier (in reality, a list of charges against him) to the Outer Austrian government in Ensisheim, in which he was accused, *inter alia*, of having preached that no one need henceforth pay rents, tithes, and interest-charges, or owe any

[22] Stayer, 'Anfänge', p. 34.
[23] See Herzog, *Bauernunruhen*, pp. 13–30.
[24] Stayer, 'Anfänge', pp. 29–31; see also idem, 'Reublin and Brötli: The Revolutionary Beginnings of Swiss Anabaptism', in Marc Lienhard (ed.), *The Origins and Characteristics of Anabaptism* (International Archive of the History of Ideas, 87) (The Hague, 1977), pp. 83–102.

obedience or obligation to his lord.[25] Several of the accusations were repeated in 1528 by Johann Fabri, the vicar-general of the bishop until 1523, who alleged that Hubmaier had inveighed against feudal dues in a sermon preached to a band of peasants who had marched upon the town (probably the Klettgau peasants in late January 1525).[26]

Hubmaier himself later denied these charges after his flight to Nikolsburg in Moravia in 1526. In his tract A Short Apology he declared that he had always taught that a Christian should give a fifth or even a third of his goods, never mind a tenth, rather than sow discord; he claimed never to have uttered the slightest condemnation of tithes and interest-charges.[27] That his attitude towards the latter was at the very least ambivalent is demonstrated, however, by another tract, On Brotherly Punishment, which he composed in Nikolsburg. In it he castigated the Pope for permitting religious institutions to charge interest contrary to the Word of Christ; lay persons, too, had subsequently adopted the practice, which was spreading like a cancerous growth throughout society.[28] Although, as Bergsten has shown, Hubmaier upheld the Christian's duty to obey divinely sanctioned worldly authority,[29] this passage at least suggests that he

---

[25] TLA, Pestarchiv, XVIII, 55, fo. 12r. Printed in Carl Sachsse, *D. Balthasar Hubmaier als Theologe* (Neue Studien zur Geschichte der Theologie und der Kirche, 20) (Berlin, 1914; repr. Aalen, 1973), p. 231.

[26] Johann Fabri, *Ursach warumb der widertewffer Patron vnd erster anfenger Doctor Balthasar Hubmair zu Wien auff den zehenden tag Martÿ Anno 1528 verbrant sey. Gedruckt zu Dressden durch Wolffgang Stoeckel, M.D.xxviii*, fo. A iiii recto. Fabri does not specify which peasants, but since his next two sentences mention Hubmaier's contacts with the peasants during Lent and Waldshut's support for the Klettgauers against count Rudolf von Sulz, it is reasonable to assume that he was referring to the Klettgauers' march to Waldshut on 29 Jan. 1525.

[27] Westin and Bergsten, *Hubmaier. Schriften*, p. 277; Bergsten, *Hubmaier*, p. 238.

[28] Westin and Bergsten, *Hubmaier. Schriften*, p. 341; cf. Wilhelm Mau, *Balthasar Hubmaier* (Abhandlungen zur mittleren und neueren Geschichte, 40) (Berlin/Leipzig, 1912), p. 19. On the Reformers' attitude towards tithing see also Gunter Zimmermann, *Die Antwort der Reformatoren auf die Zehntenfrage. Eine Analyse des Zusammenhangs von Reformation und Bauernkrieg* (Europäische Hochschulschriften, 3rd series: Geschichte und ihre Hilfswissenschaften, 164) (Frankfurt am Main/Bern, 1982).

[29] In his last Nikolsburg treatise, On the Sword, Hubmaier took his stand against the pacifist doctrines of those Anabaptists who rejected secular authority out of hand. Although the work was dedicated to two Moravian noblemen who acted as his patrons and protectors there, Hubmaier states explicitly in his introduction that he had already preached obedience to the ruler, whether good or evil, from the pulpit in Waldshut. Westin and Bergsten, *Hubmaier. Schriften*, pp. 432–3, 435. See Bergsten, *Hubmaier*, pp. 297–300, who argues further that Hubmaier's conception of Christian obedience came closest to Zwingli's.

objected strongly to what that obedience might at times entail. Bergsten himself admits that in all probability Hubmaier rejected the small tithe but accepted the great (from corn, wine, timber, etc.), for which there was scriptural authority in the Old Testament.[30] It is certainly worth noting that up to 1525 Waldshut was receiving wine and corn from the nunnery of Königsfelden for the maintenance of its priests.[31] But whether Hubmaier did preach against tithes must also be judged in the light of events in and around Waldshut before and during 1524. Some of Waldshut's burghers, it will be recalled, had withheld tithes dues to Königsfelden as far back as 1487 on practical, not religious, grounds. In 1524 in the neighbouring Forest Town of Rheinfelden the burghers were blocking tithes to the chapter of St Martin.[32] It is surely no coincidence that Rheinfelden's preacher during the previous autumn had been Johann Eberlin von Günzburg, in whose vision of a perfect Christian society the congregation should elect its own priests, who were forbidden to receive tithes or enjoy any privileges denied to other citizens.[33] Given these circumstances, there is no reason to think that Hubmaier would have gone out of his way to defend the payment of tithes. If they were demanded by a lord who showed himself to be un-Christian by laying too heavy a burden upon his subjects, then to levy them was an abuse, according to Hubmaier. He may well have rejected the small tithe altogether. Certainly he seems to have condemned the taking of interest. How far he rejected all feudal obligations must remain undecided. The bishop of Konstanz's charges were in any case based on hearsay, and some are fairly implausible.[34]

After his return from the second Colloquy of Zürich Hubmaier resumed his preaching of Zwinglian doctrines with fresh vigour.

---

[30] Ibid., pp. 236–7, 284–5.

[31] Ibid., pp. 239, 273–4.

[32] TLA, An die fürstl. Durchlaucht, 1523–25, fo. 200v. 18 June 1524; ibid., fo. 199r–200r. 20 June 1524.

[33] The description of a Christian Utopia, called Wolfaria, is contained in the two concluding pamphlets of Eberlin's Fifteen Confederates, published in 1521. An analysis of its religious and secular programme is given in Steven E. Ozment, *The Reformation in the Cities. The Appeal of Protestantism to Sixteenth-Century Germany and Switzerland* (New Haven, CT/London, 1975), pp. 91–108, esp. p. 99.

[34] Bergsten, *Hubmaier*, pp. 238–9. Herzog accepts the bishop of Konstanz's allegations *in toto*, and those of other contemporary chroniclers such as Andreas Lettsch, who saw Hubmaier as the instigator of the Peasants' War, but he makes no attempt to evaluate the credibility of these sources. Herzog, *Bauernunruhen*, p. 32.

Within six weeks, on 5th December, an imperial deputation consisting of the deputy Outer Austrian governor, Hans Imer von Gilgenberg, and the bailiff of Laufenburg, Ulrich von Habsberg, had arrived in Waldshut with instructions to investigate why the town had ignored the commands of the emperor and the bishop of Konstanz by tolerating a heretical priest in its midst whose false preaching was causing great disturbance in Waldshut and the neighbourhood. From the reception they received it is clear just how rapid and profound an impact Hubmaier's preaching had achieved.[35] The town council brusquely dismissed the charges against him, declaring that Hubmaier had simply preached the unadulterated truth, and it challenged the two emissaries to enquire of Hubmaier himself or the congregation whether he had defied the authorities. Among the population there was much excitement. News of the council's deliberations with the emissaries was apparently leaked to Hubmaier within the quarter-hour. One inhabitant wished to have von Gilgenberg and von Habsberg dumped in the sea [i.e. Lake Constance], whilst another would have struck them down if he had known the purpose of their visit.[36] Waldshut was given two weeks to reconsider its decision, but after only six days the council informed the Outer Austrian government that it had interrogated Hubmaier and found the charges against him groundless. It was therefore not prepared to surrender its preacher to the Austrian authorities, but would be willing to allow Hubmaier to appear before the bishop of Konstanz, if given

[35] The sources for these events are located in TLA, Pestarchiv, XVIII, 55, fo. 1r–20r. This folder contains two distinct items: 1. Ulrich von Habsberg's report to the Outer Austrian government, 2 June 1524 (fo. 1r–2v), which is printed in extract by Wilhelm Stolze (ed.), 'Akten zur Geschichte der Stühlinger Erhebung des Jahres 1524', *Zeitschrift für die Geschichte des Oberrheins*, new series 42 (1928), pp. 276–8; 2. a series of copy letters sent with a covering letter by the Outer Austrian government to the archduke, 29 Feb. 1524 (fo. 17r–20r). These copies comprise: a) Waldshut's reply to the Outer Austrian government, 11 Dec. 1523 (fo. 3r–7v), printed by Johann Loserth, 'Die Stadt Waldshut und die vorderösterreichische Regierung in den Jahren 1523–1526. Ein Beitrag zur Geschichte des Bauernkrieges und der Reformation in Vorderösterreich', *Archiv für österreichische Geschichte*, 77 (1891), pp. 95–9; b) Hans Imer von Gilgenberg's report to the Outer Austrian government, n.d. (after 5 Dec. 1523) (fo. 9v–10r); c) Ulrich von Habsberg's report to the Outer Austrian government, 4 Jan. 1524 (fo. 9v–10r); d) the bishop of Konstanz's articles against Hubmaier in a letter to the Outer Austrian government, 20 Feb. 1524 (fo. 10v–12r). The events are discussed in Loserth, 'Stadt Waldshut', pp. 13–17; Bergsten, *Hubmaier*, pp. 121–4.

[36] TLA, Pestarchiv, XVIII, 55, fo. 10r.

a safe-conduct. This defiant stand marks the beginning of Waldshut's long political and military struggle to survive in Catholic Austria.

That the council would scarcely have taken such a stand unless it had been confident of the overwhelming support of the inhabitants goes without saying; that it did so at all must largely be attributed to the Reforming convictions of the magistrate, Hans Ulrich Gutjahr.[37] He was, for instance, reported as having eaten meat with Hubmaier during the ember days in December 1523,[38] and appears to have remained his foremost champion until the late summer of 1524. The Austrian authorities were particularly worried that Gutjahr's Swiss connections would encourage the latter to look to Zürich for protection and defence.[39] But strong though Hubmaier's following amongst council and commons might be, it was neither unwavering nor unanimous. During May 1524 Waldshut underwent a crisis of political will which was only resolved in favour of the Reformation by the expulsion of the remaining Catholic priests and by Gutjahr's rallying of support within the town.

The crisis was precipitated by the expiry at Whitsun of the time-limit set by the Upper Austrian government for Hubmaier's expulsion, and was intensified by the decision of the Outer Austrian Diet at Breisach on 23rd May to condemn all Lutheran and Reforming teaching and to punish its adherents. The possibility of his expulsion provoked the women of Waldshut to gather on Whit Monday at the town hall, clamouring for the council not to let Hubmaier go; in the wake of this demonstration eight of the town's twelve priests were forced to leave and seek refuge in St Blasien.[40] When

---

[37] Bergsten, *Hubmaier*, p. 125 describes Gutjahr as burgomaster of Waldshut, but all the available documents and chronicles describe him as magistrate: TLA, Pestarchiv, XVIII, 55, fo. 10r; ibid., fo. 19r; HSA, B 17, 1*, fo. 22v; J. Huber (ed.), *Heinrich Küssenbergs Chronik der Reformation in der Grafschaft Baden, in Klettgau und auf dem Schwarzwalde* (Archiv für die schweizerische Reformations-Geschichte, 3) (Solothurn, 1875), p. 415. It appears that there was no office of burgomaster in Waldshut. See Karl Schib, 'Die vier Waldstädte', in Metz, *Vorderösterreich*, p. 383.

[38] TLA, Pestarchiv, XVIII, 55, fo. 10r.

[39] Ibid., fo. 19r (Feb. 1524); fo. 1r (June 1524). Gutjahr had relations in Zürich and Schaffhausen, ibid., fo. 19r. Huber, *Küssenbergs Chronik*, p. 419 states that Gutjahr was the only burgher who dared contradict Hubmaier, but this must refer to their quarrel in late 1524. Bergsten, *Hubmaier*, pp. 133, 208–9.

[40] Fabri, *Ursach*, fo. A iii r–v; Huber, *Küssenbergs Chronik*, p. 420. Cf. Bergsten, *Hubmaier*, pp. 132–3. All eight priests returned to Waldshut around 13 July; a ninth had previously gone to Konstanz and stayed there. Huber, *Küssenbergs Chronik*, p. 420.

Waldshut's three representatives at the Breisach Diet returned home a week later they found the town in a state of agitation. The town's armourer, Veltin Frick, went to Ulrich von Habsberg to inform him that Hubmaier, Gutjahr, and their followers might be driven by fear of Austrian reprisals to call on Zürich for help; two hundred men, he said, had sworn to protect their preacher at all costs.[41] Despite the genuine loyalty which Hubmaier enjoyed there are indications, therefore, that the political difficulties caused by his remaining encouraged some (above all those on the council), even if they were sympathetic to his reforms, to wish for his departure.

What made the Austrian authorities so keen to muzzle Hubmaier was not merely his heretical preaching in Waldshut but the pressing fear that his influence and example would incite the surrounding district to rebellion against both Church and state. If, as Ulrich von Habsberg warned in June 1524, matters were let slide, Laufenburg and Säckingen would soon be in revolt and the Black Forest peasants would follow suit; Rheinfelden was already seized by turmoil.[42] In December 1523 the Austrian emissaries in Waldshut had accused Hubmaier of attending the second Colloquy of Zürich as a representative of all four Forest Towns and the Black Forest,[43] a charge which was repeated by the bishop of Konstanz a few months later.[44] Both Hubmaier and the Waldshut council strenuously denied the allegation and Hubmaier immediately appealed to Zürich for a document testifying to the nature of his participation at the Colloquy.[45] It is scarcely likely that he would have done so unless he had been sure of his ground. In any case, a further passage from the bishop's 'articles' makes the charge seem well-nigh absurd. In it Hubmaier was alleged on his return from the Colloquy to have invited a dozen or so Swiss to Waldshut to debate with him in his own house, at which meeting not a single member of the Waldshut clergy or anyone else from the diocese of Konstanz was present.[46]

---

[41] TLA, Pestarchiv, XVIII, 55, fo. 1r; Stolze, 'Akten', pp. 276–7; cf. Bergsten, *Hubmaier*, pp. 134–5.

[42] TLA, Pestarchiv, XVIII, 55, fo. 1v; Stolze, 'Akten', p. 277; cf. idem, 'Die Stühlinger Erhebung des Jahres 1524 und ihre Gründe', *Historische Zeitschrift*, 139 (1929), p. 296.

[43] TLA, Pestarchiv, XVIII, 55, fo. 3v ff.; Loserth, 'Stadt Waldshut', pp. 95 ff.

[44] TLA, Pestarchiv, XVIII, 55, fo. 12r.

[45] SAZh, A. 184, 1, no. 131. 7 Dec. 1523; Loserth, 'Stadt Waldshut', pp. 93–4.

[46] TLA, Pestarchiv, XVIII, 55, fo. 11r. This fact was, of course, intended to discredit Hubmaier by showing that he was in league with the Swiss.

By the spring of 1524, however, Hubmaier was clearly concerned to broadcast his religious beliefs beyond the confines of a small community. Towards the end of April he invited the clergy of the entire rural deanery of Waldshut to debate the Reforming principles set forth in his Eighteen Axioms.[47] It can of course be assumed (though there is no confirming evidence) that the peasantry from the surrounding district flocked to Waldshut to hear such an inspiring preacher, just as the Strasbourg Reformers or Jakob Otter in Kenzingen drew large crowds to their sermons from the neighbouring villages. Whether Hubmaier took his preaching into the countryside is not known. In August 1524 he is said to have preached the Gospel around Hallau and Trossadingen in Schaffhausen's territory,[48] but the constant risk of capture by the authorities must have deterred him from venturing far beyond the walls of Waldshut.

II

By midsummer 1524 the situation in the sweep of countryside directly to the north of Waldshut, the southeastern Black Forest and its foothills, was far from settled. Towards the end of May the subjects of St Blasien, their patience exhausted, gave the abbot notice of their refusal to render him feudal dues;[49] on midsummer's eve count Sigismund von Lupfen's peasants in the landgraviate of Stühlingen assembled to complain about the infringement of their ancient village customs and rights, an event which led the St Blasien peasants in the neighbouring villages of Ewattingen and Bettmaringen to revolt as well;[50] and around that time the Schaffhausen peasants rallied at

---

[47] Westin and Bergsten, *Hubmaier. Schriften*, p. 69; Bergsten, *Hubmaier*, p. 130. This information is contained in a letter from the Upper Austrian government to Waldshut on 4 May 1524, which Bergsten claims is no longer traceable; ibid., p. 130, n. 50. It is to be found in HSA, B 17, 1*, fo. 24v–25v, along with a corresponding letter to the bishop of Konstanz, 4 May 1524, ibid., fo. 24r–v.

[48] Loserth, 'Stadt Waldshut', p. 30.

[49] Schreiber, *Bauernkrieg*, 1, p. 1, no. I.

[50] Ibid., p. 3, no. III; Günther Franz (ed.), *Quellen zur Geschichte des Bauernkrieges* (*Ausgewählte Quellen zur deutschen Geschichte der Neuzeit*, ed. Rudolf Buchner, 2) (Darmstadt, 1963), pp. 85–6. Accounts principally in Stolze, 'Stühlinger Erhebung', pp. 273–302; Günther Franz, *Der deutsche Bauernkrieg*, 12th edn (Darmstadt, 1984), pp. 98 ff. See now also Hiroto Oka, *Der Bauernkrieg in der Landgrafschaft Stühlingen und seine Vorgeschichte seit der Mitte des 15. Jahrhunderts* (Konstanz, 1998), pp. 234 ff. The St Blasien peas-

Hallau to voice a series of radical religious demands, declaring that they would have no lord but God.[51] Of these assemblies the least radical in intent was that of the Stühlingen peasants, who wished no more than to negotiate with their lord over their rights and who made no attempt to challenge his authority in principle on religious or on other grounds. Yet it is the Stühlingen uprising which marks the onset of widespread rebellion in south-west Germany which developed into the Peasants' War.[52]

In the negotiations which followed between the Stühlingers and the counts of Lupfen envoys from all four Forest Towns (i.e. including Waldshut) and the Black Forest tried to bring about a settlement, but to no avail.[53] When negotiations were resumed in the

ants are mentioned only in Heinrich Hug's chronicle, but there seems no reason to doubt its accuracy. Franz, *Quellen*, p. 89.

[51] Schreiber, *Bauernkrieg*, 1, p. 3, no. III. The nature of the Hallauers' demands (hitherto believed not to have survived, see Stolze, 'Stühlinger Erhebung', p. 299), is set forth in a letter from Veit Suter, the Austrian roving ambassador, to the archduke, 14 July 1524. TLA, Oberösterreichische Hofregistratur, Reihe A (1520–64), laufender Faszikel 12, Position 30 (Bauernkrieg, 1525–26). Translation in Tom Scott and Bob Scribner (eds), *The German Peasants' War. A History in Documents* (Atlantic Highlands, NJ/London, 1991), p. 81, no. 5.

[52] The explanation of this apparent paradox is largely that the Stühlingen uprising threw up one of the most resolute and radical of the peasant leaders, Hans Müller from Bulgenbach near Bonndorf, a former mercenary. As he himself later admitted, however, he had received active support from the Hallauers, though this may refer only to the summer of 1525. Schreiber, *Bauernkrieg*, 3, p. 78, no. CCCCIX; cf. Stolze, 'Stühlinger Erhebung', p. 299. Stolze argued that although the Stühlingers' demands were in themselves moderate, the collapse of negotiations with the counts of Lupfen, and the continued unrest in the landgraviate can only adequately be explained by the influence of Reforming doctrines, which encouraged the peasants' intransigence, ibid., pp. 276–7. In part this argument is correct, and Stolze's criticism of Elben, *Vorderösterreich*, pp. 14–20 for failing to distinguish between the individual phases of the Stühlingen uprising is partly justified. But at least Elben recognized the crucial point that the Stühlingers were split between a moderate group, and a radical group led by Hans Müller; idem, *Vorderösterreich*, pp. 48 f. Stolze dismissed this distinction as unimportant because of the undisputed fact that the uprising began as a concerted action by the peasantry of the county as a whole. Stolze, 'Stühlinger Erhebung', p. 278. The split came later, probably in the wake of Müller's election as military leader (he was, after all, a St Blasien, not a Stühlingen, subject).

[53] Ibid., p. 280; Bergsten, *Hubmaier*, p. 146. According to Bergsten, Waldshut denied having taken the part of the Stühlingers; rather, it had begged both sides to be allowed to attend the negotiations, to which the two Austrian emissaries, von Gilgenberg and von Habsberg, had given their assent. This most unlikely story rests on a misreading of the sources. In its written defence to the Swabian League six months later, from which Bergsten quotes, Waldshut claimed that it had helped to mediate, and that it had also begged von Gilgenberg and von Habsberg to try to

second half of July at Tiengen, close by Waldshut, the two Austrian emissaries, Ulrich von Habsberg and Hans Jacob von Landau, suggested setting up a commission of arbitration, but the Stühlingers insisted that half its members be chosen by the peasants and comprise two from the Black Forest, and one each from the four Forest Towns. Count Sigismund rejected this proposal because he feared the Black Forest and Waldshut representatives would be *parti pris*.[54] As a result the parties agreed on 24th July to a moratorium of thirty days, during which time neither side was to engage in hostilities. Despite this agreement six hundred Stühlingers thereupon marched to Waldshut and quartered there for three days.[55]

The circumstances of this encounter are by no means clear. The Stühlingers, Stolze argued, had nothing to fear from the authorities as long as negotiations continued; in entering the town they had in effect broken the undertaking at Tiengen by committing what was bound to be construed as an act of aggression. From that he concluded that only a deep sense of solidarity could have driven them to act against their interest,[56] but other explanations are possible. It is fairly clear that the Stühlingers came to Tiengen in a truculent mood. Instead of despatching a handful of delegates, they apparently turned up *en masse* and under arms, a rudimentary fighting force already under the captaincy of Hans Müller from Bulgenbach, the former mercenary whose single-minded and unflagging efforts to organize the peasants militarily helped transform a local uprising into widespread insurrection.[57] It is little wonder that the negotiations

---

bring about an amicable settlement in order to avert any injury to the archduke's territory or subjects. Text printed in idem, *Hubmaier*, pp. 503–8, here at pp. 505–6.

[54] Schreiber, *Bauernkrieg*, 1, p. 17, no. XV. Cf. StAA, Literaliensammlung 1524, fo. 276r–v; Stolze, 'Akten', pp. 283 f., 287.

[55] TLA, An die fürstl. Durchlaucht, 1523–25, fo. 240r–v. 31 July 1524. Stolze, 'Stühlinger Erhebung', p. 287; Bergsten, *Hubmaier*, pp. 146–7.

[56] Stolze, 'Stühlinger Erhebung', p. 298.

[57] In his letter to Freiburg on 25 Aug., which is admittedly often very sketchy about times and places, count Sigismund quite clearly sets the Stühlingers' election of a captain (i.e. Hans Müller) before the Tiengen negotiations, possibly even before the first negotiations of all. Schreiber, *Bauernkrieg*, 1, pp. 16–17, no. XV. The contemporary chronicle of Andreas Lettsch, the abbot of St Blasien's notary, which mentions Müller's election as captain, places it simply in the time between the first uprising and the (second) march to Waldshut in September. Franz, *Quellen*, pp. 86–7. On 19 July the bishop of Konstanz's official, Dr Johann Raming (or Raminger), wrote to his superior from Konstanz to inform him. Schreiber, *Bauernkrieg*, 1, p. 6, no. V. Some confusion surrounds this letter. Did Raminger mean Tengen in the

quickly foundered. The moratorium that followed gave the Stühlingers valuable time to continue the military preparations already begun; of these, one of the most important was the search for allies. The march to Waldshut fits logically into this context: the Stühlingers knew of Waldshut's struggle against the Austrian government and the St Blasien peasants may well have told them of the town's disputes with the abbot; their request for Waldshut's participation in any arbitration had just been brusquely rejected; the town lay only a few miles away from Tiengen. What was more natural than to cock a snook at the authorities by marching thither in the hope of forging an alliance? Stolze is quite right to see the march as a 'demonstration', as a calculated act of defiance.[58]

For its part, the town seems to have been ready enough to let them in.[59] Waldshut's situation in the summer months was highly precarious. It could not hope for protection from the Swiss,[60] and

---

Hegau or Tiengen in the Klettgau? At first glance Tengen does seem more likely, since Konstanz's proximity to the Hegau should have prevented him from confusing the two place-names. Moreover, the spelling 'Tengen' for Tiengen is very uncommon indeed. Archduke Ferdinand, it is true, refers to Tiengen as 'Tengen', but his geographical ignorance (or that of his officials in Innsbruck) is underlined by his describing the lordship of Stühlingen as lying in the Hegau. Ibid., p. 7, no. VII. It is the case that the counts of Lupfen and Stühlingen were also the rulers of the lordship of Hewen in the Hegau, with its town of Engen, which they held as a mortgage from Austria. See now Rolf Köhn, 'Der Hegauer Bundschuh (Oktober 1460)—ein Aufstandversuch in der Herrschaft Hewen gegen die Grafen von Lupfen', *Zeitschrift für die Geschichte des Oberrheins*, 138 (1990), pp. 99–141. But since the Hegau peasants remained at peace until October 1524, Tiengen in the Klettgau must be meant.

[58] Stolze, 'Stühlinger Erhebung', p. 298. On this point for the Peasants' War in the south-west as a whole see now Hans-Martin Maurer, 'Der Bauernkrieg als Massenerhebung. Die Dynamik einer revolutionären Bewegung', in Kommission für geschichtliche Landeskunde in Baden-Württemberg (ed.), *Bausteine zur geschichtlichen Landeskunde von Baden-Württemberg* (Stuttgart, 1979), pp. 255–95, here at pp. 268 ff.

[59] In its letter to the archduke on 31 July, the Innsbruck government complained bitterly that Waldshut had admitted the Stühlingers, whereas shortly before it had refused entry to a group of Austrian noblemen with ten horses on their way to a campaign. TLA, An die fürstl. Durchlaucht, 1523–25, fo. 240r–v; cf. Stolze, 'Stühlinger Erhebung', p. 287.

[60] Bergsten, *Hubmaier*, pp. 145–6. In the summer of 1524 the evangelically-minded Confederates were in a minority and hard pressed by their Catholic counterparts, who blamed Reforming preaching for the Thurgau peasants' attack on the charterhouse of Ittingen in July. At the Confederate Diet in Baden (AG) during mid-August the Swiss Estates renounced any intention of aiding Waldshut and expressed their displeasure that two of the ringleaders in the attack on Ittingen had found refuge there. *Amtliche Sammlung der älteren Eidgenössischen Abschiede*, 4, 1a, ed. Johannes Strickler (Brugg, 1873), p. 473.

was probably glad of support from whatever quarter it might come. But there is no indication that Waldshut concluded any formal alliance with the peasants. The town may well have encouraged them to stay as reinforcements for its garrison, but it is not so clear that the peasants saw their own interests best served by being cooped up in a beleaguered town, and after three days they left.

During August the Stühlingers' military preparations continued apace. They made a red, white, and black banner and with it scoured the countryside for support. By the middle of the month, the Austrian authorities, who feared that both the Black Forest and the Schaffhausen peasants would join the rebels, recognized that the Stühlingers were preparing for war as soon as the truce expired on 24th August.[61] Count Sigismund von Lupfen had already appealed to archduke Ferdinand for help, since Stühlingen was an Austrian protectorate.[62] Accordingly, an emergency commission of Austrian officials and local nobles was appointed and detailed to meet in Radolfzell on 31st August to plan the suppression of both the Stühlingen and Waldshut revolts. There was no doubt in the minds of Austrian officials that the Stühlingen and Black Forest peasants were already in league with Waldshut.[63] This belief became a self-fulfilling prophecy, for the imminent danger to the rebels had two startling consequences. On 29th August Hubmaier left Waldshut for Schaffhausen. A few days later eight hundred Stühlingen peasants entered Waldshut under their banner and pledged an alliance of mutual protection.

There has been considerable argument about the dating and interpretation of both events. It is now certain that Hubmaier did indeed leave Waldshut before the peasants arrived, and can have played no active part in bringing the alliance about.[64] The town later claimed

---

[61] TLA, An die fürstl. Durchlaucht, 1523–25, fo. 254v–255v. 20 Aug. 1524. Cf. Stolze, 'Akten', p. 292; idem, 'Stühlinger Erhebung', p. 292. The Innsbruck government saw the banner as the signal for a new Bundschuh uprising, like those which had convulsed the Upper Rhine between 1493 and 1513.

[62] Schreiber, *Bauernkrieg*, 1, pp. 12–13, no. XII; Bergsten, *Hubmaier*, p. 147.

[63] See archduke Ferdinand's instructions to the commission at Radolfzell, 30 Aug. 1524. Franz Ludwig Baumann (ed.), *Akten zur Geschichte des deutschen Bauernkrieges aus Oberschwaben* (Freiburg im Breisgau, 1877), p. 9, no. 17. TLA, An die fürstl. Durchlaucht, 1523–25, fo. 261r. In this letter of 1 Sept. 1524 the Innsbruck government expressly included the Black Forest peasants: *wie sich E. f. g. vngehorsamen vnnderthanen zu waldshuet mit sambt vil vnnderthanen am Swartzwald gegen denselben* [Stühlinger] *paurn eingelassen haben* . . .

[64] Bergsten, *Hubmaier*, p. 147, n. 18.

that Hubmaier had begged the council to be allowed to go, but also that it had expelled him in order to demonstrate its loyalty to Austria. But although Hubmaier chose or was forced to leave, Waldshut as a community still refused to disavow his Reforming doctrines.[65] In its extremity the town could only hope for immediate and effective resistance from the Stühlingen peasants, whose armed troop had been amassing since July. Even though their aims and interests differed, it is argued, the peasants and Waldshut combined in emergency for mutual defence in the face of a common enemy.[66]

But was this alliance supported by the Stühlingen peasants as a whole? Their armed troop, with Hans Müller almost certainly at its head,[67] entered Waldshut in full military array after 1st September,[68] and yet on 7th September twenty-two emissaries from thirty-five Stühlingen villages had begun fresh peace negotiations in Schaffhausen with the Austrian commissioners.[69] Both Waldshut and the Stühlingen peasantry seem strangely caught between appeasement and defiance. The puzzle deepens when it is remembered that the authorities were unable to muster a fighting force for lack of money,[70] thereby presenting the Stühlingers with a fine opportunity to press home their military advantage.

The answer is that both parties were split. Bergsten has convincingly argued that Hubmaier's departure allowed those in Waldshut who were uneasy about the political consequences of his religious innovations to reassert themselves. There are signs that such voices had already been raised that summer.[71] The grovelling behaviour of the three Waldshut councillors in front of the Austrian commissioners at Radolfzell on 12th September does indeed suggest that the

---

[65] Ibid., p. 152; Schreiber, *Bauernkrieg*, 1, p. 73, no. XLVIII; ibid., p. 88, no. LIV.

[66] Bergsten, *Hubmaier*, p. 149, n. 23. The argument has been recently restated by Walter Elliger, *Thomas Müntzer. Leben und Werk*, 2nd edn (Göttingen, 1975), pp. 644–5.

[67] The military organization suggests this, but there is no documentary proof.

[68] Bergsten, *Hubmaier*, p. 148, n. 21.

[69] Schreiber, *Bauernkrieg*, 1, p. 27, no. XXII; ibid., p. 31, no. XXV; ibid., pp. 42–3, no. XXXII. Elben, *Vorderösterreich*, pp. 39 f., Bergsten, *Hubmaier*, p. 148.

[70] Baumann, *Akten*, p. 11, no. 20; Schreiber, *Bauernkrieg*, 1, pp. 28–9, no. XXIII; Elben, *Vorderösterreich*, pp. 36 f.

[71] I.e. the clamour to expel Waldshut's Catholic priests in May. Their quiet readmittance less than two months later suggests that some members of the town council were *politiques*.

town's political leaders were trying to retrieve a desperate situation.[72]

Meanwhile, on 10th September the Schaffhausen town council had managed to bring about a settlement between count Georg von Lupfen and the twenty-two Stühlingen emissaries. When news of it spread, there was uproar amongst the many peasants from the surrounding area who had flocked to market day in the town. Some of them, the Austrian commissioners reported in alarm, were fresh from the armed troop and would gladly have disrupted the negotiations.[73] This can only refer to the armed Stühlingen detachment that had marched to Waldshut's aid. On 12th September, the day appointed for the peasants to gather unarmed at Stühlingen castle to surrender their flag and swear renewed fealty,[74] seven of their emissaries appeared before count Georg and the Austrian advisers in considerable agitation to complain that the other Stühlingers from the armed troop were heaping threats and curses upon them and intended to reject the treaty, even though the emissaries had been given full powers to conclude it.[75]

Discussions and negotiations dragged on fruitlessly until the end of the month, partly because the counts of Lupfen refused to budge from the provisions of the original treaty, but largely because the peasants' representatives were now prevented from reaching any agreement with their lords without first referring matters back to the armed troop, which defiantly rejected all demands to surrender its banner.[76] Most of the peasants, the authorities reckoned, and especially the village notables (*Ehrbarkeit*) wanted to come to terms, but a truculent minority, egged on by Hans Müller, was holding out and intimidating the majority.[77]

---

[72] Bergsten, *Hubmaier*, pp. 152–4; cf. ibid., pp. 209–10; Schreiber, *Bauernkrieg*, 1, pp. 70–1, no. XLVII. One of the demands of the Austrian commissioners before the Swabian League at Ulm in mid-November was that those who had fled Waldshut because of the troubles should be allowed to return and resume their citizen's rights. StAA, Literaliensammlung 1524, fo. 473v.

[73] Schreiber, *Bauernkrieg*, 1, p. 55, no. XXV: . . . *dann es sind gestern neu vom Huffen komen, die hätten gern alle Unruh erst in den Handel geworffen*. Elben, *Vorderösterreich*, p. 43.

[74] Schreiber, *Bauernkrieg*, 1, pp. 55–6, no. XXV; Elben, *Vorderösterreich*, p. 44.

[75] Schreiber, *Bauernkrieg*, 1, p. 56, no. XXVI: . . . *wie die Andern, so by dem Huffen liegen, sie hoch schelten, drayen ihnen, sie zu erwürgen, wollen den zugesagten Vertrag, wiewol sie ihnen den zu beschliessen allen Gewalt geben, nit halten*. Elben, *Vorderösterreich*, p. 44.

[76] Schreiber, *Bauernkrieg*, 1, p. 59, no. XXXVIII; ibid., p. 64, no. XLIV; Franz, *Quellen*, p. 90; Elben, *Vorderösterreich*, pp. 45–50.

[77] Schreiber, *Bauernkrieg*, 1, pp. 68–9, no. XLVII: . . . *und sonderlich dieweil die Baurn*

In the light of these circumstances the alliance with Waldshut takes on a new significance. It was not a gesture of defensive solidarity by the Stühlingen peasants as a whole towards a town with which they had nothing in common except the fight for survival: it was a calculated attempt by the militant wing of the Stühlingen peasantry to forge an active alliance with an urban community in order to widen the basis of resistance and so transform a local rural uprising into a general revolt.[78] Indeed, according to the Marxist historian M. M. Smirin, the peasants' march on Waldshut had an ulterior purpose. They had come to found an Evangelical Brotherhood with a town which had embraced Zwinglian Reforming doctrines; the alliance was a conscious union between like-minded religious radicals in town and country.[79]

But why, in that case, was the alliance so ineffective and short-lived? In the first place, the notion that it was an Evangelical Brotherhood cannot be sustained.[80] Certainly the attraction to Hubmaier's centre of activity was not accidental, but Hubmaier had left and the town was in confusion. As Smirin himself admits, Waldshut's allegiance to Hubmaier was, at least until November 1524, a commitment to 'Zwinglian iconoclasm', not 'social revolution'.[81] In the second place, it became impossible to reconcile the aims and

under ihnen selbst getailt, gantz irrig, verwirrt und erschrockhen sein, dann etlich und sonderlichen die Erberkhait, dergleichen die Baurn von Sandt Blasy ob dem Wald, die wellen solchem Vertrag nachkhomen, die übrigen, der nit über 200 auf diesen Tag sein, wellen nit halten. Ibid., p. 66, no. XLV: . . . *wie die Buren noch der Meynung syen, den Vertrag nit anzunemen, und sey der Hauptmann vast Ursächer.* Elben, *Vorderösterreich*, p. 48.

[78] The authorities were quite right to fear another Bundschuh, for it was precisely the attempt to establish links between the peasantry and the towns which characterized the revolutionary Bundschuh conspiracies of Joß Fritz on the Upper Rhine in 1502, 1513, and 1517. The discrepancy in numbers between those who marched on Waldshut (800) and the later minority (200) who would not surrender can be attributed to the initially enthusiastic response to Müller's military leadership, which began to crumble as the negotiations wore on. The sources record the figure 200 'on this day' (16 Sept.), and suggest that much of his earlier following had been coerced.

[79] M. M. Smirin, *Die Volksreformation des Thomas Münzer und der grosse Bauernkrieg*, transl. Hans Nichtweiss (Berlin, 1952), pp. 401–2, 405.

[80] It had already been established by the edition of Heinrich Hug's Villingen chronicle in 1883 that the phrase 'Evangelische Bruderschaft' was a later gloss on the original text. Elben, *Vorderösterreich*, p. 155, n. 3.

[81] Smirin, *Volksreformation*, p. 440. On Hubmaier's return the iconoclasm was resumed. StAFr, B 5 XI, 12, fo. 232v. 2 Nov. 1524: *wie sÿ Irn doctor widervmb zu Inen hinein gen Waldtzhut genomen vnd kurtzlich vil bilder In der kirchen zerschlagen haben sollen . . .*

expectations which each party cherished of the alliance. The militant Stühlingen peasants looked on the town as a strategic base for operations and a stronghold to which they could withdraw. Waldshut, on the other hand, saw the peasants as reinforcements for its meagre garrison. But the peasants could not afford to remain quartered in a town on the defensive, as Müller, the ex-mercenary, well understood. They must continue to harry the countryside, attract or coerce support, forestall or defeat counter-attack, in other words, be on the offensive.

That is why in late September, as the new deadline for its surrender was about to expire, Waldshut appealed in desperation to the Black Forest peasants for mercenaries to defend the town.[82] On their arrival they swore to remain at least thirty days, and it took repeated exhortations and dire warnings from the Austrian authorities to induce them to leave.[83] Waldshut was saved from subsequent attack only by the arrival on 3rd October of 170 armed volunteers from Zürich.[84] At the end of that month Hubmaier returned from Schaffhausen to resume his work of reforming Waldshut's religious life.

By that time the scene of active peasant revolt had shifted away from Waldshut. In the east the Hegau peasants, who had hitherto remained at peace, rallied at the Hilzingen church-ale on 2nd October to demand the restoration of their ancient rights.[85] Within days a Stühlingen detachment under Hans Müller—which included subjects

[82] Christian Roder (ed.), *Heinrich Hugs Villinger Chronik von 1495 bis 1533* (Bibliothek des Litterarischen Vereins in Stuttgart, 164) (Tübingen, 1883), p. 102. Once in Waldshut they began to build bastions and other defence works. Smirin, *Volksreformation*, p. 401 erroneously dates the contract with the Black Forest peasants before the Stühlingers' second march on Waldshut.

[83] At the Diet of the Swabian League in Ulm in mid-November, the Austrian commissioners accused Waldshut of having allied itself with the Stühlingen rebels and the Black Forest peasants. Karl Klüpfel (ed.), *Urkunden zur Geschichte des Schwäbischen Bundes (1488–1533)*, 2 (Bibliothek des Litterarischen Vereins in Stuttgart, 21) (Stuttgart, 1853), p. 282. For the correct dating of the Diet see Bergsten, *Hubmaier*, p. 220, n. 6. In A Truthful Apology Waldshut mentioned the Black Forest mercenaries, but passed over the Stühlingen alliance in silence. Loserth, 'Stadt Waldshut', p. 116. For dating of A Truthful Apology see Bergsten, *Hubmaier*, p. 199, n. 32. In its reply to the Swabian League Waldshut again admitted recruiting mercenaries from the Black Forest, but denied any involvement in peasant rebellion. Ibid., pp. 505–6 (dating, p. 503). Schreiber, *Bauernkrieg*, 1, p. 106, no. LXX. Cf. Elliger, *Müntzer*, p. 645.

[84] Bergsten, *Hubmaier*, pp. 157 f.

[85] Elben, *Vorderösterreich*, pp. 72–8; Franz, *Bauernkrieg*, pp. 106–7. Cf. Elliger, *Müntzer*, pp. 646–7.

of St Blasien from the same villages that had joined the midsummer rising, along with new recruits from the territories of the counts of Fürstenberg—embarked upon an audacious expedition northwards over the Black Forest and the Baar in order to rally further support.[86] Waldshut took no part; not until the end of January 1525 was it again in league with the south-west German peasant rebels.

III

During the autumn of 1524 the peasantry of the landgraviate of the Klettgau, immediately to the east of Waldshut, and the Black Forest peasants in the lordship of Hauenstein and from the territories of St Blasien in the hills to the north of the town became increasingly restive and threatened to revolt. The circumstances and grievances of the peasantry in these districts, as we have already argued, had much in common with those of Waldshut and its inhabitants. Yet during 1524 neither the Klettgauers nor the Hauensteiners made any sustained attempt to seek support from, or enter into alliance with, the town.[87] This apparent indifference towards the town as a partner in rebellion compels one to ask whether the peasants on Waldshut's doorstep regarded it as a natural ally or champion of their cause, and whether the origins of unrest and the articulation of demands in those areas were influenced or inspired by the town's adherence to the Zwinglian Reformation.

The behaviour of the Klettgauers is particularly striking. At the beginning of October they had been urged by Hans Müller to join the Stühlingers' march north and threatened with reprisals if they refused. Thereupon the Klettgauers appealed to count Rudolf von Sulz's bailiff, Hans Jakob von Heidegg, to get Zürich, as protector of the landgraviate, to order Müller and his men to leave them in peace. The city government willingly complied, on condition that the peasants and their lord obey the true Word of God, although it recognized that the uprising had largely been provoked by the

---

[86] Franz, *Quellen*, pp. 90–1; Elben, *Vorderösterreich*, pp. 78–81; Franz, *Bauernkrieg*, p. 107.

[87] The recruitment of mercenaries from the Black Forest indicates only that the peasants were prepared to help Waldshut in a common defensive struggle against Austria, not that they regarded its cause as their own.

preaching of the Gospel.[88] The Klettgauers gladly accepted Zürich's demands, but when they assembled again at the end of the month they announced their refusal to render any dues or services to count Rudolf unless he showed them deeds and titles thereunto with seals.[89] Both the Austrian authorities and the Zürich council made efforts to mediate during November and December, not without some success, for on 28th December the Klettgauers, while rejecting any new impositions, promised to pay all tithes and rents to count Rudolf as before.[90]

Most scholars have argued that the Klettgauers' sudden challenge to their lord's authority can only have resulted from the insidious impact of Zwinglian doctrines that Zürich insisted they adopt. A close reading of the sources, however, makes this view hard to uphold. Until mid-October, Zürich declared, the Klettgauers had not voiced any complaint against count Rudolf von Sulz, though that does not mean that they harboured no grievances.[91] And other evidence suggests that the Klettgauers were no strangers to anti-Catholic and anticlerical protest. In the years before 1525 the inhabitants of Grießen, the most important village of the Klettgau, had witnessed a protracted quarrel between their local priest and the abbey of St Blasien (as collator of the benefice) over the decline in the former's competency, in which they had acted as mediators.[92] Then in April

[88] SAZh, A. 192, 1, no. 112. n.d. (11 Oct. 1524); cf. Schreiber, *Bauernkrieg*, 1, pp. 115–17, no. LXXXI (dated Nov. 1524); *Eidgenössische Abschiede*, 4, 1a, p. 527; Baumann, *Akten*, pp. 22–3, no. 40; idem, 'Eidgenossen bis März 1525', pp. 128–9; Otto Schiff, 'Thomas Münzer und die Bauernbewegung am Oberrhein', *Historische Zeitschrift*, 110 (1913), p. 70. Elben, *Vorderösterreich*, pp. 101–3 expressed astonishment that Zürich should ascribe the revolts to the impact of the Reformation, when none of the peasants' articles of grievance displayed any trace of religious influence. That may be true, but the persistent refusal of the Stühlingen peasants to accept a negotiated settlement suggests, as Stolze observed, that the origins and course of the revolts should not be interpreted simply in terms of the peasants' formal grievances or demands.

[89] SAZh, A. 192, 1, no. 114. 1 Nov. 1524. Cf. *Eidgenössische Abschiede*, 4, 1a, p. 527; Baumann, 'Eidgenossen bis März 1525', p. 129; Schiff, 'Münzer', p. 71; Elben, *Vorderösterreich*, pp. 103–4.

[90] Baumann, 'Eidgenossen bis März 1525', p. 131; idem, *Akten*, p. 25, no. 46; p. 27, no. 49; Elben, *Vorderösterreich*, pp. 104–5.

[91] Schreiber, *Bauernkrieg*, 1, p. 116, no. LXXXI: *Und so sie sich ab ihrem Herrn, dem Grafen von Sultz, bissher nüt klagt, sich auch Niemants Handlungen zu beladen Willens syent*... The articles of grievance which the Klettgauers presented to Zürich in March 1525 all concerned persistent infringement of customary rights which clearly had been taking place long before the spring of 1525. Cf. Franz, *Quellen*, pp. 226–31.

[92] SAZh, A. 192, 1, no. 122, 14 Jan. 1525: ... *das Sich verschinen Iarn Ain span*

1524 von Heidegg had reported to Zürich that on von Sulz's orders anyone who ate meat in Lent should be thrown into gaol, which he had done.[93] Antagonism towards count Rudolf, therefore, was nothing new, although Zürich's intervention may well have strengthened the Klettgauers in the righteousness of their cause by suggesting that they were acting in accordance with the Scriptures. Nevertheless, the peasants' actions were hesitant and cautious. The refusal to acknowledge von Sulz's rights without written authority was, of course, a secular application of the Zwinglian principle of Scriptural justification, but the peasants had not yet gone so far as to judge the legitimacy of von Sulz's authority itself according to divine law contained in the Scriptures.[94] As long as the Klettgauers looked to Zürich for political protection and religious inspiration they had no need to contemplate hazardous alliances with rebellious peasants or beleaguered towns, even if they had grievances and beliefs in common. The crux of the matter was how far Zürich would be willing to defend the peasants against count Rudolf and the abbot of St Blasien, both of whom were burghers of the city, since the rights and revenues which its inhabitants enjoyed in the Klettgau gave the city a vested interest in upholding seigneurial obligations, not assisting in their abolition. The peasants' adherence to Zürich was contingent and friable, and it is no great surprise that towards the end of December a detachment of Klettgauers under Clewi Maier from Grießen set out to join Hans Müller on his second march north over the Black Forest.[95]

In the last three months of 1524, meanwhile, the peasantry from the southern valleys of the Black Forest began to renew the threats which they had first uttered in May. Rumours (quite implausible)

---

zwuschen gedachtem minem gnedigen herren von Sant Blasien vnd der von griessen Seelsorgern begeben vmb den abgang der pfründ Als an opfer vnd Anderm.

[93] SAZh, A. 192, 1, no. 123. 2 April 1524.

[94] Schiff, 'Münzer', p. 71. To equate the principle of Scriptural justification directly with the appeal to God's law, as Schiff does, blurs an important distinction and obscures the fact that the Klettgauers' insistence on sticking to the letter of seigneurial documents does indeed echo Reforming convictions. On the Klettgauers' subsequent commitment to godly law see now Peter Blickle and a Berner Arbeitsgruppe, 'Die Vorstellung des göttlichen Rechts im Klettgau. Zürichs Anteil am deutschen Bauernkrieg', *Zeitschrift für die Geschichte des Oberrheins,* 133 (1985), pp. 81–101.

[95] Baumann, 'Eidgenossen bis März 1525', p. 130. On 28 Dec. they were ordered home by Zürich—not by count Rudolf—which was arrogating to itself his rights of seigneury.

that Waldshut and its Swiss auxiliaries were about to attack the abbey of St Blasien prompted its subjects east of the Schwarza river[96] to offer their services in defence. This kind of assistance the abbot felt he could do without, but thought it best to invite them and the Hauensteiners to send to Waldshut for information. The Hauensteiners declined, saying that they had already been to the town, which had told them that it had no designs upon the abbey. The Schwarza peasants, however, did so, but whatever they discovered they did not divulge to the abbot. Thereupon the Hauensteiners held an assembly, during which they abrogated their oath of allegiance and renounced their serfdom and all servile dues. On 1st November two hundred of them marched on the abbey, where they were joined the next day by three hundred men from east of the Schwarza and another two hundred miscellaneous peasants from the surrounding districts.[97] The assembled company invoked the Stühlingers' example, demanding that the abbot do away with all new impositions and let them live by their old rights and customs. After three days' board and lodging at the abbey's expense the peasants were making ready to depart peacefully when the abbot learned that some of them were threatening to damage the church furnishings and plate. When he called upon the peasants' leaders to get these unruly elements to disperse, it transpired that they belonged to the two-hundred-strong miscellany who had flocked to St Blasien of their own accord from the district round Waldshut. The assembly of Hauensteiners ordered them to go home forthwith, which they did, destroying the wayside shrines as they went. The remaining Hauensteiners and Schwarza peasants left the next day, 4th November.[98]

---

[96] I.e. from the lordship of Blumegg, the bailiwick of Gutenburg, and the administrative district of the Wutach valley, all bordering on the landgraviate of Stühlingen belonging to the counts of Lupfen.

[97] Schreiber, *Bauernkrieg*, 1, pp. 121–2, no. LXXXVI; ibid., p. 119, no. LXXXIII; Franz, *Quellen*, pp. 88–9. The Hauensteiners later claimed that the abbot had invited their military support. Ibid., p. 99.

[98] Schreiber, *Bauernkrieg*, 1, pp. 122–3, no. LXXXVI: . . . *dass ettlich unter ihnen und nemlich die gegen Waldshut zu sigen und selbs zugeloffen, willens, den Kilchengezird Schaden zu thun*. According to rumours reaching the Austrian commissioners in Stockach, the Hauensteiners intended to occupy the four Forest Towns and join forces with the rebellious subjects of margrave Ernst of Baden. Lina Beger, *Studien zur Geschichte des Bauernkriegs nach Urkunden des Generallandesarchivs zu Karlsruhe*, 1 (Forschungen zur deutschen Geschichte, 21) (Göttingen, 1881), p. 585; cf. Elben, *Vorderösterreich*, p. 110, n. 1. It is hard to make much sense of these reports: the margravial peasants were not even in revolt.

Three weeks later, however, the Hauensteiners called another assembly which reiterated their refusal to render servile dues unless the abbot could provide title-deeds to his claims attested by a notary. When he enquired who was to act as notary, they put forward the name of Waldshut's notary, though the abbot's own secretary was to be allowed to attend if he wished. For their part the Schwarza peasants threatened to stop all taxes and tithes unless the abbot agreed not only to adopt the provisions of the Stühlingen settlement of 10th September, but also to grant them rights of military occupation in Gutenburg castle. In the meantime, the abbot's subjects in the lordship of Gurtweil, next door to Waldshut, had also proclaimed their intention to withhold taxes.[99] The abbot asked for time to consider the peasants' demands, but this delaying tactic availed little, for in the first week of December there were fresh rumours that the Hauensteiners were about to launch a second attack on St Blasien. On 10th December the Outer Austrian Estates called upon the peasantry to abandon such plans and offered instead to arbitrate between the abbot and his subjects.[100] Despite this warning the Hauensteiners rallied again on 12th December, apparently in order to ward off any danger from the latest rebellion on their borders, which had succeeded in uniting peasants from many jurisdictions in the Baar and the northern Black Forest.[101] Although the Hauensteiners

---

[99] Schreiber, *Bauernkrieg*, 1, pp. 123–4, no. LXXXVI.

[100] Ibid., p. 142, no. CIII. Elben, *Vorderösterreich*, p. 111, n. 1 was at a loss to understand why the Estates warned the peasants not to attack the abbey when the previous day (9 Dec.) they had reported in haste to Laufenburg, Säckingen, and Rheinfelden that the peasants had already done so. But the letter states no more than that the peasants were apparently contemplating another attack, not that it had taken place. Schreiber, *Bauernkrieg*, 1, p. 139, no. CI.

[101] On 14 Dec. Laufenburg reported to Freiburg that on Monday evening, 12 Dec., its 'neighbours from the Forest' (i.e. the Hauensteiners) had risen up, even though that same morning the Forest bailiff and one of the eight captains of the Hauenstein communes (*Einungen*) had appeared before the three Forest Towns (excepting Waldshut) to explain that the communes of Schönau and Todtnau, the two valleys to the north of St Blasien which were attached to the *Einungen*, had informed them in alarm that they had received repeated warnings (after the assault on St Trudpert, it seems) of an imminent attack, though by whom they did not know. The bailiff and captain appealed for support, which Laufenburg was willing to give, provided that the peasants' military preparations were not directed against Austria or its subjects. It also agreed to send emissaries the following Wednesday (21 Dec.) to Steinbach to help arbitrate.

Laufenburg went on to complain of Waldshut's pliable loyalties: it had treated with the peasants, despite its previous undertaking to stand by Laufenburg, and had

approached Waldshut for help, the town remained at peace, secure in the knowledge, as its magistrate was reported to have boasted, that the Swiss had undertaken to defend it against any aggression.[102]

Several points emerge from these events. In their encounters with St Blasien the Black Forest peasants displayed a sense of rugged determination and sturdy independence which suggests that they were confident enough of their rights not to need the example and encouragement of neighbouring revolts or the broader justification of freedom contained in radical interpretations of the Scriptures. For the Hauensteiners, it should be remembered, the events of 1524–26 were only part of a five-hundred-year struggle against the abbey, a struggle between two conflicting principles of political organization in the Black Forest—the communal and the territorial.[103] Some of St Blasien's subjects, especially those east of the Schwarza, did identify with the Stühlingers and take part in several of their campaigns, but the subsequent invocation of the Stühlingen settlement by the bulk of the abbey's peasants should be attributed less to its ostensible demonstration of the fruits of popular rebellion than to the fact that its provisions largely coincided with their own grievances. Despite the countless incidents of anticlericalism in the surrounding districts on both sides of the Rhine, it is quite remarkable that the Black Forest peasants showed so little inclination to couch their protests against the abbey in religious terms or to commit acts of violence against church property. Even the Schwarza peasants' threat to withhold tithes did not imply an attack on their legitimacy as such; it was simply a means of forcing the abbot to produce written evidence of

---

not replied to the latter's most recent appeal for help. Ibid., pp. 151–2, no. CXVII; ibid., p. 153, no. CXVIII. A partial account of these complicated events is given by Müller, *Bauernkrieg im Kreise Waldshut*, pp. 64–5, who suggests that the peasants' demands at the meeting on 14 Dec. for the abbot of St Blasien to return home to help protect them became garbled, so that it was rumoured they had driven him out in the first place. Müller may well be right in assigning the Hauensteiners' articles of grievance (printed by Franz, *Quellen*, pp. 98–101, and dated by him to Jan. 1525) to these mid-December negotiations.

[102] Schreiber, *Bauernkrieg*, 1, p. 153, no. CXVIII: *Die von Waldshut sind ohn diess; doch haben sie vom Schultheissen daselbst erfaren, dass er ihnen gesagt: ob sie schon den Eidgenossen nit mit Pflicht verwandt, allein haben dies die Eidgenossen ihnen zugesagt, sie by Recht zu handhaben, dess sie sich vermessen.*

[103] Wernet, 'Grafschaft Hauenstein', p. 458; cf. Ulbrich, *Leibherrschaft*. For the subsequent Saltpetre revolts of the eighteenth century see now David M. Luebke, *His Majesty's Rebels. Communities, Factions and Rural Revolt in the Black Forest, 1725–45* (Ithaca, NY/London, 1997).

his right to receive them. Above all, the brusque dismissal of the peasants from around Waldshut who wished to get their hands on the church plate makes it plain that the Hauensteiners, at least, were perfectly capable of distinguishing between their own practical grievances against St Blasien and the religiously inspired fervour of the Waldshuters. It also suggests that the impact of Hubmaier's preaching and the Waldshut Reformation had not reached very far into the surrounding countryside by the winter of 1524.

There is no doubt that the peasants regarded Waldshut as a potential ally in the struggle for self-determination within Austrian territorial overlordship, or that an awareness of common grievances against St Blasien encouraged them to react sympathetically to the town's appeals for help by sending mercenaries to man its garrison, but an active alliance was inhibited not only by the Hauensteiners' strong feeling of corporate identity, but also by Waldshut's own ambivalent attitude towards the peasantry. During the last quarter of 1524 the town had by no means thrown in its lot with the rebellious south-west German peasantry; it still hoped to come to some accommodation with Austria. This explains Waldshut's frequent entreaties to Freiburg for support in late September, even though the latter's unremitting loyalty to Austria and the Catholic faith made any compromise inconceivable.[104] Once troops had arrived from Zürich at the beginning of October the situation eased. But growing political tension between the Protestant and Catholic Swiss cantons forced Zürich on 4th December to withdraw its men from Waldshut, though a small contingent refused to return.[105] Nevertheless, the town continued to look primarily to the Swiss for protection. At negotiations in Rheinfelden on 15th November, for instance, Basel and Schaffhausen, as well as Zürich, lent Waldshut their counsel and support; the same three cities appeared again on Waldshut's behalf in Konstanz at the end of January 1525 during negotiations with the Swabian League.[106] To rely on the Swiss and to play on Austria's fear of war with the Confederation was clearly a far better strategy for a small and relatively powerless community than pinning its hopes on the shifting constellations of peasant revolt.[107] Even so the town

[104] Schreiber, *Bauernkrieg*, 1, pp. 93–4, no. LX.

[105] Bergsten, *Hubmaier*, pp. 206–7.

[106] Ibid., pp. 196–7, 222; Baumann, *Akten*, p. 91, no. 71.

[107] At the end of November it transpired that Waldshut had contracted a bond

appears to have kept its options open, for at the very end of December reports reached the Austrian authorities that a burgher of Waldshut was helping to stir up trouble in the Klettgau and elsewhere.[108]

Towards the end of November Thomas Müntzer, the fieriest champion of the Radical Reformation, came to the Klettgau, where he spent eight weeks during which—in his own words—he composed certain articles on government according to the Gospel, from which others made further articles.[109] There has been endless argument about Müntzer's stay in south-west Germany and the possible identity of these articles. Did Müntzer meet and influence Hubmaier? Can the greater cohesion and adamancy of the peasant leagues after the winter of 1524 be attributed to the radical preaching of Müntzer and his new disciple Hubmaier? Are the so-called Constitutional Draft and Letter of Articles found amongst Hubmaier's belongings after his flight from Waldshut in November 1525 those referred to by Müntzer in his confession? Were they emended, or even originally composed, by Hubmaier, and how far were they adopted as part of the rebels' programme? There is no room here to expatiate upon this venerable debate, which in any case has always been hamstrung by a lack of conclusive evidence. Recent scholarship, nevertheless, has managed to establish certain points with greater authority. The Constitutional Draft clearly betrays Müntzer's influence in both concept and terminology, though Elliger's attempt to equate it directly with the Klettgau articles is not altogether convincing.[110] The Letter

of mutual assistance with the village of Bülach, north of Zürich. Herzog, *Bauernunruhen*, p. 34. In itself Bülach was of no importance, but it could have provided men for Waldshut's garrison.

[108] HSA, B 17, 1*. fo. 44v. 30 Dec. 1525 (i.e. 1524): *Als ain genannt Iunghanns zu waldshuet im kleckgew vnd sonnst allenthalben vil practicka in disem aufruerigen wesen hin vnd wider vben vnd prauchen sol* . . . Was this the Waldshut councillor, Junghans Schaller, who had been sent to Zürich in October to obtain military reinforcements? See Bergsten, *Hubmaier*, p. 159.

[109] See now Peter Matheson (ed.), *The Collected Works of Thomas Müntzer* (Edinburgh, 1988), pp. 433–4. The German edn is by Günther Franz (ed.), *Thomas Müntzer. Schriften und Briefe, Kritische Gesamtausgabe* (Quellen und Forschungen zur Reformationsgeschichte, 33) (Gütersloh, 1968), p. 544. The dating of Müntzer's arrival in the Klettgau is uncertain; it cannot have been before 10 Nov. (Bergsten, *Hubmaier*, p. 201), but Elliger, *Müntzer*, p. 634 suggests *circa* 10 Dec., since Müntzer probably did not leave Nuremberg for Basel until mid-November: ibid., p. 629. However, Elliger's chronology of Müntzer's sojourn in southern Germany, while correct in outline, is vague and conjectural in detail.

[110] Ibid., pp. 653–72. For text see Fabri, *Ursach*, fo. a iiii r–b i r; transl. in Tom Scott, *Thomas Müntzer. Theology and Revolution in the German Reformation* (Houndmills,

of Articles reveals an undeniable dependence upon the contents of the Constitutional Draft, though its purpose—an exhortation by the Black Forest peasants under Hans Müller to join their Christian Union, not a programme of political demands—lends it a more urgent and hostile tone than the Draft. Because the Constitutional Draft does not survive as an original document (its title is an historian's invention), but only in Fabri's tendentious paraphrase, a version may have been in circulation before the Letter of Articles was sent to Villingen on 8th May. Bergsten has gone to great lengths to show that Hubmaier was author of neither document, but the invocation of the secular ban in the Letter of Articles as the penalty for refusal to join the Christian Union of the Black Forest so closely resembles Hubmaier's doctrine of the spiritual ban that Bergsten's depiction of them as no more than simultaneous phenomena deriving from a common New Testament source looks like special pleading.[111] Who else was supposed to have instructed the peasants in the meaning and application of such passages from Scripture?

The Constitutional Draft remained no more than a blueprint, but the Letter of Articles was adopted by the combined Black Forest peasants, who began a new military campaign in April 1525.[112] Up

Hants/London, 1989), pp. 133–4. (German: Franz, *Müntzer*, pp. 231–2.) Elliger's ascription depends upon construing one sentence, which refers to the duke of Lorraine's slaughter of the Alsatian peasantry at Saverne on 16 May 1525, as a later gloss, possibly added by Hubmaier himself. Although challenged as too contrived by Peter Blickle, 'Thomas Müntzer und der Bauernkrieg in Südwestdeutschland. Bemerkungen zu Walter Elliger, *Thomas Müntzer. Leben und Werk . . .*', *Zeitschrift für Agrargeschichte und Agrarsoziologie*, 24 (1976), pp. 79–80, it has been accepted by Scott, *Müntzer*, pp. 134–7, not least in the light of Gottfried Seebaß, *Artikelbrief, Bundesordnung und Verfassungsentwurf. Studien zu drei zentralen Dokumenten des südwestdeutschen Bauernkrieges* (Abhandlungen der Heidelberger Akademie der Wissenschaften, philosophisch-historische Klasse, 88, 1) (Heidelberg, 1988), pp. 165 ff. Seebaß accepts that the Constitutional Draft contains, in some form or other, Müntzer's articles on how to govern, and ascribes the Letter of Articles to Hubmaier. Ibid., pp. 165 f., n. 77 f.

[111] Bergsten, *Hubmaier*, pp. 285–301, esp. 289–93. He argues that because Hubmaier's chief aim was the renewal of the Christian Church he can have had no interest in the secular ban which served a quite different purpose. So it did, but Bergsten himself acknowledged that Hubmaier took a benevolent attitude towards the rebellious peasantry, even if he was not its active champion.

[112] Elliger, *Müntzer*, p. 112 has suggested that the much less overtly religious content of the Letter of Articles may point to one of the peasants' leaders, possibly Hans Müller himself, as author. That cannot be ruled out, but it ignores the context in which the Letter (as it survives) was first presented, namely in the exhortation to Villingen on 8 May. Schreiber, *Bauernkrieg*, 2, pp. 87–9, no. CCXVII. He prints (but Franz, *Quellen*, p. 235 omits) the Letter's preamble, in which the peasants

till then, however, there is no trace of such ideas amongst the population of those very areas exposed to the preaching of the two Reformers, Waldshut and the Klettgau. At the very least this implies that Müntzer, and through him Hubmaier, had failed to turn Waldshut into 'the organizational and ideological centre of the peasants in the southern Black Forest' by the end of 1524.[113] Yet within a month the situation in town and country had changed again.

IV

Throughout December 1524 and January 1525 the Austrian authorities attempted to negotiate a series of settlements with the Stühlingen, Hegau, Klettgau, and Baar peasants, but their success was largely ephemeral: the peasants were in no mood to compromise.[114] It is tempting to explain this greater truculence by citing Müntzer's activities in the area and duke Ulrich of Württemberg's seditious propaganda amongst the peasantry, designed to gain its support for his campaign to reconquer his duchy. Neither argument is particularly convincing. There are no signs that Müntzer's sojourn had any immediate effect in radicalizing the peasantry, whilst both the Hegauers and the Klettgauers refused at first to have anything to do with duke Ulrich's plans.[115] It is much more likely that the continuing and patent inability of the authorities to take any effective military action against the peasants heightened their confidence and encouraged them to exploit a favourable situation. At the beginning of January the commissioners in charge of negotiations in Stockach were lament-

ask for Villingen's help in establishing divine justice and the Holy Gospel of Christ. These religious appeals, rather than the Letter of Articles, are repeated in the Christian Union's subsequent correspondence and treaties with south-west German towns. Schreiber, *Bauernkrieg*, 2, p. 89, no. CCXVIIa; pp. 100–1, no. CCXIX; pp. 103–5, no. CCXXXIII; p. 109, no. CCXXXVIII; p. 113, no. CCXXXXIII; p. 120, no. CCLX; pp. 131–3, no. CCLX; pp. 133–5, no. CCLXI; pp. 145–6, no. CCLXXIII; pp. 203–4, no. CCCXXX. It should be pointed out, however, that two central features of the Letter of Articles, the secular ban and the notion of a Christian commonweal, are also repeated in the peasants' negotiations with the towns.

113 Smirin, *Münzer*, p. 406. He believed that Müntzer composed the Letter of Articles and Hubmaier the Constitutional Draft!

114 Elben, *Vorderösterreich*, pp. 141–8.

115 Ibid., pp. 119–20.

ing that the peasants were seeking help from Zürich, Basel, and Schaffhausen, as well as Waldshut.[116]

During the first week of January fresh talks between Waldshut and the Swabian League had been arranged in the nearby town of Tiengen. As the League's representatives made their way thither, they learned that the Klettgauers were refusing to allow Tiengen to be used for the negotiations, which had to be postponed.[117] In the end it was agreed to meet in Konstanz on 23rd January. The Klettgauers, it transpired, were at last in open revolt. They were variously reported to have marched on Schaffhausen in harness with the Hallau peasants, to have laid siege (or at least blocked access) to the Küssaburg, the seat of von Sulz's bailiff, Hans Jakob von Heidegg, and to be in active alliance with the Todtnau peasants, who before Christmas had helped sack the abbey of St Trudpert in the western foothills of the southern Black Forest.[118] About their intentions there was some confusion. In reply to Zürich's earnest enquiry von Sulz's subjects from the entire landgraviate[119] sent a letter on 23rd January venting their grievances. In it they reaffirmed their willingness to fulfil all obligations to count Rudolf which conformed to Scripture, provided that he in turn allowed them to follow the Word of God and obey His divine justice. The letter did not elaborate their specific grievances, but it reassured Zürich of their intention to pay rents and tithes to count Rudolf.[120] On 27th January their captain, Clewi Maier from Grießen, who in December

---

[116] Loserth, 'Stadt Waldshut', p. 74. It is not clear whether all, or only some, of the rebellious peasantry was involved. The appeal to Waldshut, Bergsten argues, implies that its contact with the peasantry from the previous summer had not been broken off. Bergsten, *Hubmaier*, p. 235. That may well be so, but there is no evidence that the formal alliance with the Stühlingers still held.

[117] Ibid., p. 220.

[118] Herzog, *Bauernunruhen*, pp. 45–6; Baumann, *Akten*, pp. 88–9, no. 69; Wilhelm Stolze, *Der deutsche Bauernkrieg. Untersuchungen über seine Entstehung und seinen Verlauf* (Halle an der Saale, 1907), p. 54; Elben, *Vorderösterreich*, p. 133. Cf. SAZh, A. 192, 1, no. 122. 14 Jan. 1525.

[119] I.e. the landgraviate of the Klettgau itself, alongside the Küssaberg valley and the town of Tiengen, both mortgaged to the counts of Sulz by the bishop of Konstanz. Though Tiengen was an enclave lying within the Austrian landgraviate of Stühlingen, it acted as the administrative centre of the Klettgau.

[120] Schreiber, *Bauernkrieg*, 2, pp. 3–5, no. CXLIV. At the end of the letter the Klettgauers offered to draw up articles of grievance; these presumably became the Forty-Four Articles of March (?) 1525. Ibid., 1, pp. 179–84, no. CXL (undated); Franz, *Quellen*, pp. 226–31 (March 1525).

had led a detachment of Klettgauers to join Hans Müller, was reported to be waiting in Schaffhausen, along with other peasant military commanders, for duke Ulrich's campaign to begin.[121] Two days later, however, the Klettgauers, carrying a blue and white banner aloft, marched on Waldshut, whose inhabitants joyfully flung open the town gates to let them in.[122]

Simultaneously with these events, the long-standing dispute with the abbey of St Blasien over the village priest of Grießen was still smouldering on. On 14th January the villagers answered Zürich's charge that they were withholding tithes from the abbot, claiming that they had begged him to be allowed to retain the tithe because of widespread damage in the neighbourhood and on account of the priest, but this request had been turned down. However, they had not prevented the abbot from already carting away one hundred stooks of corn: they were only asking to keep the remaining fifty or so.[123] This news displeased Zürich, which upbraided the villagers and ordered them to release the tithe or else argue the matter out before the city council.[124] In its reply on 31st January Grießen showed its hand more plainly. The villagers declared that they were without a priest; several times they had requested the abbot to appoint a replacement who would preach the pure and unadulterated Word of God, but he had refused. For these reasons they were unwilling to sur-

---

[121] Baumann, *Akten*, pp. 92–3, no. 75. Clewi Maier is certainly identical with the Claus Maier from Grießen, 'captain in the Klettgau', mentioned in the Klettgauers' letter to Zürich, 25 March 1525. Schreiber, *Bauernkrieg*, 2, p. 32, no. CLXVII; Franz, *Quellen*, pp. 225–6. He is, in addition, presumably the same person as Claus Wagner (i.e. a cartwright by trade?), named as the Klettgauers' captain in Huber, *Küssenbergs Chronik*, p. 426. Cf. Schiff, 'Münzer', p. 85, n. 2.

[122] StAA, Literaliensammlung, 1524, fo. 486v; Karl Walchner and Johann K. Bodent, *Biographie des Truchsessen Georg III. von Waldpurg* (Konstanz, 1832), p. 249, Appendix X. Whether Clewi Maier was at their head is not recorded, but it must be assumed that he was.

[123] SAZh, A. 192, 1, no. 121. 14 Jan. 1525: *uwer schriben vnd pytt hand wir wol verstanden von des zehenden wegen vnsers g. h. von sant blásien, so wir in gebetten fruntlich, vnss dem lÿchen vnd gůtlich verlangen lassen von wegen des landtprůsts, so ÿetz nit allein bÿ vnss, sunder allenthalb ist, welchs pÿtt er vnss abgeschlagen. Ist vnser meinung gsin, vnd nach, er sÿ so gůttig vnd gnedig, lass vnss das noch verlangen, wan wir nit allein von des sellsorgers, sunder von des landtprust wegen vnd s. g.en zů zimlichen zÿtten bezalen. Ouch hand wir im den zehenden nit gar geschult, dan er hatt wol bÿ hundertt stucken hinweg; habend wir im nutt ingeredt, vnd trÿft sich noch bÿ funzig oder sechzig stucken, die im noch gehóren. Ist vnser . . . pÿtt, . . . wellend den erwirdigen . . . herren Enstlich pÿtten, vnss das lassen verlangen . . .*

[124] Schreiber, *Bauernkrieg*, 2, p. 5, no. CXLV. 28 Jan. 1525.

render the remaining tithe, and were relying on Zürich to persuade the abbot to install a new preacher.[125]

The events in Grießen and the march on Waldshut have been widely regarded as evidence that the introduction of Zwinglian Reforming doctrines into the landgraviate drove the peasants inexorably to challenge temporal authority on the basis of Scripture: by January 1525 radical reform and social protest had coalesced in the Klettgau, a conjunction which created a bond of solidarity between the peasantry and a town defiantly committed to its Reforming preacher and which was exemplified by their new alliance. There is truth in this argument, but the sources simply do not support the notion that there was any causal connection between the events in Grießen and the activities of the Klettgau peasantry as a whole.[126] Zürich certainly did not see any. Its correspondence with the combined Klettgau peasants was concerned solely with their grievances against count Rudolf von Sulz, whilst its letters to Grießen refer only to the village's dispute with the abbot of St Blasien. Indeed, at exactly the same time as Grießen was withholding tithes from the abbot, the Klettgau peasantry as a whole was promising Zürich to render count Rudolf all his rents and tithes. At the very least this demonstrates that the Klettgauers were not rejecting tithes on principle;[127] it also suggests that they regarded their complaints against an ecclesiastical and a secular lord as separate and distinct. To discern behind these events the hidden hand of Müntzer or Hubmaier, rousing the peasants against their lords with egalitarian slogans extracted from Scripture, will not do. The conflict in Grießen had not broken out suddenly, and the villagers' demand for an evangelical preacher was no more than the logical outcome of Zürich's desire to spread the Zwinglian Reformation to its dependent territories. It is true that during his stay on the Upper Rhine Müntzer apparently made Grießen his headquarters.[128] But there is nothing in the dispute with

[125] SAZh, A. 192, 1, no. 132. 31 Jan. 1525; Schreiber, *Bauernkrieg*, 2, pp. 5–6, no. CXLVI.

[126] Schiff, 'Münzer', p. 71 implies that the two phenomena were connected. Bergsten wrongly conflates the correspondence between Grießen and Zürich and that between the entire Klettgau peasantry and Zürich, and ignores Grießen's letter of 14 Jan. altogether. Idem, *Hubmaier*, pp. 239–40.

[127] Grießen never maintained that it was withholding tithes on principle; on the contrary, it gave perfectly understandable practical reasons for doing so.

[128] Schiff, 'Münzer', p. 85; Bergsten, *Hubmaier*, p. 201.

St Blasien that suggests that the political impact of his preaching on the village was anything other than nugatory.[129] On the other hand, the military commander of the Klettgauers, Clewi Maier, who was clearly committed to a general uprising, came from Grießen.[130] But even if he was influenced by Müntzer it proves very little, since the Klettgauers as a whole throughout 1525 showed no signs of adopting a revolutionary programme and some reluctance to join their neighbours in a common military campaign.[131]

What, therefore, were the circumstances behind the Klettgauers' march to Waldshut on 29th January? After the negotiations in Konstanz, which had ended in stalemate three days earlier, Waldshut found itself isolated once more. The remaining Zürich auxiliaries were recalled, and as Bergsten rightly points out the town desper-

---

[129] It is worth noting that St Blasien not only held the advowson of the parish benefice, it also exercised rights of lesser jurisdiction in Grießen. The villagers did not attempt to challenge these rights: on the contrary, in the face of Zürich's plan to hear their dispute before the city council sitting in court session because it supposed that there was no court in the village, the Grießeners proudly retorted that they indeed had a weekly court, presided over by the abbot's legal officer. Schreiber, *Bauernkrieg*, 2, p. 6, no. CXLVI. 31 Jan. 1525.

[130] This can be deduced from his march to join Hans Müller in Dec. 1524, and his subsequent intrigues with duke Ulrich of Württemberg. He may also have instigated the march on Schaffhausen at the beginning of January 1525. In a further fragment of his confession (under torture), Müntzer claimed to have discussed with the peasants of the Klettgau and the Hegau whether they would join forces with the Thuringian rebels, 'to which they said that if they were paid for it they would come'. Matheson, *Müntzer*, p. 438. This statement (even if reliable) has often been taken as an indication of the Klettgauers' principled commitment to Müntzer's cause. In fact, in a region famous for the recruitment of mercenaries, it suggests exactly the opposite.

[131] The march on Schaffhausen is exceptional, and the Klettgauers appear to have taken over none of the Hallauers' radical congregationalist demands. It is a cardinal error to equate the appeal to divine justice with a revolutionary challenge to the existing order. As the Forty-Four Articles made abundantly plain, the Klettgauers invoked God's law and God's Word, but then proceeded to list a series of specific local grievances—infringements of their customary rights—which made no attempt to call the foundation of von Sulz's authority into question. Over the payment of the small tithe they meekly requested instruction from Zürich. Certainly the appeal to divine justice did in some instances have momentous implications as a legitimation of revolutionary change, but that was not a consequence drawn by the Klettgauers, who remained steadfastly committed to the precepts of the Zwinglian Reformation. See SAZh, A. 192, 1, no. 157. 4 Aug. 1525; SASh, Korrespondenzen V, no. 165. 26 Oct. 1525. Cf. Schreiber, *Bauernkrieg*, 3, pp. 170–1, no. CCCCLXX; Herzog, *Bauernunruhen*, p. 41. For the view that the Klettgauers were guided by a revolutionary commitment to divine justice see now Blickle *et al.*, 'Vorstellung des göttlichen Rechts', pp. 81–101.

ately needed allies to deter an Austrian attack.[132] Of the surrounding peasantry only the Klettgauers were at that moment in active revolt, and their allegiance to the Zürich Reformation must have given them a ready sympathy with Waldshut's predicament. If, as seems likely, the town appealed to them for help, it is not surprising that they should willingly respond. There is, admittedly, no record of a formal alliance being sealed, but it would be odd to assume otherwise: the circumstances were quite different from Müller's demonstration marches the previous year. That is not to say, however, that the peasants had no reasons of their own for wishing to enlist Waldshut's help. During the Konstanz negotiations a deputation of Hegau peasants from Hilzingen had arrived to canvass Waldshut's support, though they likewise approached Zürich, Basel, and Schaffhausen, as well as the Black Forest and Klettgau peasants, not to mention duke Ulrich![133] There is no doubt that the peasants on the southern fringes of the Black Forest continued to look upon Waldshut as a natural ally in the defensive struggle against Austria, or that its survival against the odds evinced their admiration.[134]

Whether they regarded Hubmaier as their mentor is another matter. Fabri alleged that Hubmaier had delivered a sermon to the Klettgauers after their arrival, in which he had preached that game, fish, fowl, wine, pasture, and wood were all free, that is, common property.[135] That is perfectly possible—Hubmaier himself later admitted in Zürich that he had looked favourably upon the peasants' aspirations—but it scarcely bears out the image of Hubmaier as a great fomenter of rebellion, since such assertions were by then the common stock of peasant demands.[136] There is no reason to doubt that Hubmaier lent the Klettgauers moral support, but their subsequent articles of grievance contain almost no trace of his doctrines, unless their questioning of the small tithe is included. Only Hans Müller's Christian Union seems actively to have embraced authentic Hubmaier teachings.

---

[132] Bergsten, *Hubmaier*, pp. 223, 239.

[133] StAA, Literaliensammlung 1524, fo. 488r; cf. Bergsten, *Hubmaier*, p. 235.

[134] As the authorities were well aware. Ibid., p. 239.

[135] Fabri, *Ursach*, fo. a iiii r; cf. Bergsten, *Hubmaier*, p. 238.

[136] See, for example, the articles of the Brigach valley peasants of 18 Nov. 1524. Scott and Scribner, *German Peasants' War*, p. 82. Cf. Baumann, *Akten*, p. 97, no. 82; Franz, *Quellen*, pp. 96–7.

Despite its pact with the Klettgau peasantry Waldshut could not afford to ignore the sharp change in the international situation which followed upon the French defeat at Pavia on 24th February. Duke Ulrich's campaign to recapture Württemberg collapsed abruptly as his Swiss mercenaries, on hearing of Charles V's victory, turned tail and headed home. As a result, archduke Ferdinand was at last free to proceed energetically against the rebellious peasantry of south-west Germany and the renitent town of Waldshut.[137] At the beginning of March Waldshut sought further help from Zürich. It pleaded to be taken under the city's civic jurisdiction, in the same manner as the landgraviate of the Klettgau which, by virtue of count Rudolf von Sulz's burgher's rights, already enjoyed Zürich's protection. But the city was in no position to comply. The defeat at Pavia had left the Swiss to deal with a revived Habsburg Austria, and the Protestant cantons had little room for manoeuvre. Zürich must in any case have been angered by Waldshut's involvement with the Klettgauers, since it had felt obliged to take the part of its burghers—the abbot of St Blasien and count Rudolf von Sulz—against the peasants. All in all, Waldshut could no longer count upon the Protestant Swiss, whose ideological support began in any case to crumble during April as Hubmaier set about anabaptizing his hitherto Zwinglian congregation. From that point onwards the town's fate depended entirely upon making common cause with the rebellious peasantry.[138]

During the first quarter of 1525 the many efforts to bring about a settlement between the south-west German lords and their subjects had no more than temporary and limited success, since the militant wing of the peasantry under Hans Müller was party to none of the agreements. At the end of February Müller and 150 followers had deserted duke Ulrich on his march northwards, ostensibly for lack of pay, and had returned home.[139] Throughout March Müller

---

[137] Bergsten, *Hubmaier*, p. 245. Cf. Baumann, 'Eidgenossen bis März 1525', p. 140; Franz, *Quellen*, p. 112.

[138] Bergsten, *Hubmaier*, pp. 246–7. Loserth's view in 'Stadt Waldshut', p. 76 (repeated by Herzog, *Bauernunruhen*, p. 37) that Waldshut asked to join the Swiss Confederation as a constituent member is mistaken. In any case, the Swiss were not prepared to put the precarious balance of their internal and external relations at risk by extending their territory any further north of the Rhine. Baumann, 'Eidgenossen bis März 1525', pp. 117–18. For Zürich's reaction to Waldshut's request see SAZh, A. 184, 1, no. 154. 4 March 1525.

[139] Schreiber, *Bauernkrieg*, 2, p. 16, no. CLXVII.

began sowing the seeds of a new and more ambitious campaign, a war of general liberation in town and country.[140] To this end he appears to have made contact with the Upper Swabian peasants, who by then had broken into open revolt. Under his leadership the Black Forest and Hegau armies adopted the Twelve Articles and styled themselves a Christian Brotherhood or Union, just as the combined troops of the Baltringen, Allgäu, and Lake Constance peasants had done. At the beginning of April the latter, faced with impending attack from Truchseß Georg von Waldburg and the forces of the Swabian League, called on Müller to come to their aid: he was to occupy Tiengen and Waldshut and then bring the Black Forest under his control.[141] Müller, however, did nothing of the kind. Around 8th April he began to assemble his army at Bonndorf, whence, it was rumoured, he planned to march westwards over the Black Forest into the Breisgau and the Upper Rhine valley.[142] But after reaching Neustadt the peasants suddenly backtracked to Hüfingen, which they took on 13th April.[143]

Müller's apparent vacillation requires some comment. That his ultimate strategy was indeed directed towards the Upper Rhine is evidenced by his victorious march into the Breisgau in May. In mid-April, however, there was pressing danger on his eastern flank. The Hegau peasants, who were as alarmed as their neighbours on the north shore of Lake Constance at the approach of Truchseß Georg, had already taken up arms and were threatening to march on Hüfingen and Bräunlingen.[144] Müller seems to have waited at Hüfingen

---

[140] Blickle, *Revolution of 1525*, pp. 127 ff. (German 1st edn, pp. 182 ff.; 2nd and 3rd edns, pp. 198 ff.).

[141] Johann Heinrich Schreiber, 'Balthasar Hubmaier. Stifter der Wiedertäufer auf dem Schwarzwalde', *Taschenbuch für Geschichte und Altertum in Süddeutschland*, 2 (1840), pp. 204–5, n. 1: *Die Buren haben Rabensburg ingenommen und besetzt, dessglichen Tettnang, Mörsburg und Markdorf, und liegen jetzund vor Ueberlingen; haben auch Hans Müller von Bulgenbach, so jetzt zu Bonndorf sitzt, zugeschrieben, er sölle mit sinen Buren uf syn, so wöllen sie Thiengen und Waldshut innemen und besetzen, dessglichen den Schwarzwald auch innemen.* Cf. StAFr, C 1, Militaria 100. Laufenburg to Freiburg, 7 April 1525. The interpretation of this passage is hampered by poor syntax; Bergsten, *Hubmaier*, p. 278 takes it to mean that the Upper Swabian peasants specifically asked Müller to occupy Tiengen and Waldshut, though why they should have done so he does not explain.

[142] Schreiber, *Bauernkrieg*, 2, pp. 36–7, no. CLXXI; ibid., pp. 37–8, no. CLXXII; ibid., p. 38, no. CLXXIII.

[143] Ibid., p. 38, no. CLXXIV; ibid., pp. 40–1, no. CLXXVII; ibid., p. 41, no. CLXXVIII.

[144] Ibid., pp. 34–5, no. CLXX.

to join forces with them and recruit further support from the Black Forest.[145] Then the peasants moved steadily eastwards, gradually consolidating their defences by besieging and capturing the Baar and Hegau towns. On 19th/20th April they were encamped before Engen;[146] by the beginning of May they had reached Möhringen and were about to attack Tuttlingen.[147] The need for caution vanished, though, when an urgent summons from the Austrian government of occupation in Stuttgart compelled the Truchseß to head northwards into Württemberg to exact revenge for the massacre at Weinsberg. Thereupon the peasants followed suit, until news that the beleaguered garrison at Radolfzell had used their withdrawal to sack the surrounding villages caused the Hegauers to turn back.[148] The Black Foresters under Hans Müller then sent from their camp at Vöhrenbach a summons to Villingen to join their Christian Union, before driving on into the Breisgau. By mid-May 1525 the whole of southwest Germany seemed at the peasants' mercy.

Waldshut actively participated in these undertakings, but its help was necessarily limited. Its small population was already fully stretched by the need for constant manning of the town's defences, so that it could spare no more than a token force for the peasant armies. Envoys had been sent to the peasants at Hüfingen on 13th April, and the next day three troops of 'Swiss' arrived—supposedly a contingent of Klettgauers and two detachments from Waldshut. However, a few days later the Hauensteiners reported that a mere fifteen men from Waldshut had joined Hans Müller's forces.[149] At the beginning

[145] On 13 April another 1200 peasants from the Black Forest arrived in Hüfingen. Ibid., pp. 40–1, no. CLXXVII. That Hans Müller's troop and the Hegauers did unite can be inferred from duke Ulrich's letter to Schaffhausen on 29 April. Ibid., p. 69, no. CC.

[146] Ibid., p. 52, no. CLXXXVIII. On 19 April the entire Hegau contingent at Engen sent a plea for 7000 reinforcements to the Neckar Valley-Odenwald band at Heilbronn on account of the redoubled danger from the Swabian League forces after the treaty of Weingarten with the Lake Constance peasants on 17 April, which had left the Truchseß free at last to suppress the revolt in the Hegau. Baumann, *Akten*, p. 249, no. 237. On 16 April the Hegauers had already sought military assistance from Stammheim and other Thurgau villages. Herzog, *Bauernunruhen*, p. 47.

[147] FWWA, Archiv Wolfegg, 9890x. 1 May 1525. Cf. Baumann, *Akten*, p. 257, no. 251.

[148] Franz, *Bauernkrieg*, p. 138; cf. Baumann, 'Eidgenossen seit dem Märze 1525', pp. 47–8.

[149] Schreiber, *Bauernkrieg*, 2, p. 41, no. CLXXVII; ibid., p. 41, no. CLXXVIII. StAFr, C 1, Militaria 100. The eight *Einungsmeister* of the lordship of Hauenstein to Freiburg, 19 April 1525. Cf. Karl Hartfelder (ed.), 'Urkundliche Beiträge zur

of May, when the threat from Truchseß Georg's troops seemed most immediate, Waldshut sent another thirty men and some light artillery to the peasant armies in the Hegau.[150] Compared with the thousands of peasants who thronged to the rebels, Waldshut's contribution was numerically negligible; even the weapons it brought were too few to have made much difference. Its geographic position, moreover, made it strategically irrelevant to Müller's plans (which may explain why he ignored the Swabian peasants' call to occupy it). Its real usefulness to the peasants lay in the propaganda which they could derive from boasting of its support. Müller was in any case eager to win as many towns as possible for his Christian Union, both as a means of broadening his basis of action and of gaining a series of military strongholds,[151] but the support of a town which had successfully defied the authorities for so long in adhering openly to radical Reforming doctrines implied vindication of their cause, justification for their demands, and, not least, a powerful reassurance and attraction for the timorous and hesitant. Müller's invocation of the Letter of Articles should be seen in this context. But whatever Waldshut's ideological significance for the peasants' armed struggle may have been, its modest and subordinate role in the actual campaigns gave it little opportunity to exert any practical influence on Müller's aims and strategies.

Geschichte des Bauernkrieges im Breisgau', *Zeitschrift für die Geschichte des Oberrheins*, 34 (1882), p. 414. Amongst the Waldshuters was the town's magistrate, Hartmann vom Hof, though he was presumably leading the envoys, not the combatants. Schreiber, *Bauernkrieg*, 2, p. 43, no. CLXXXI. Cf. Bergsten, *Hubmaier*, p. 279.

[150] Karl Schib (ed.), *Hans Stockars Jerusalemfahrt 1519 und Chronik 1520–1529* (Quellen zur Schweizer Geschichte, new series 1, 4) (Basel, 1949), p. 114. Cf. Roder, *Heinrich Hugs Villinger Chronik*, p. 114; Huber, *Küssenbergs Chronik*, p. 424. Hug mentions 50 men and 10 arquebuses. Only Stockar records that the Waldshuters were making for the peasants encamped at Radolfzell. These comprised a separate Hegau contingent under Heinrich Maler, which was besieging the town, not the main Hegau troop under Hans Bienckler, which had joined forces with Hans Müller. Waldshut was rumoured to be sending troops to the latter as well, then encamped at Möhringen. Baumann, *Akten*, p. 257, no. 251. From a letter from Schaffhausen to Zürich on 29 April it appears that some Waldshuters and Black Foresters were already among the Hegau forces at Radolfzell before 1 May. SAZh, A. 190, 1, no. 49. Its contents refer to negotiations which had taken place the previous day at Pfullendorf between Truchseß Georg and the peasants who were besieging Radolfzell. Baumann, 'Eidgenossen seit dem Märze 1525', p. 48.

[151] Hüfingen, for instance, had been forced to send three of its inhabitants to accompany Müller's troops 'in order that they may say that the Hüfingers are with them'. Schreiber, *Bauernkrieg*, 2, p. 40, no. CLXXVII.

This ineffectualness stands in striking contrast to the initiative shown by Waldshut in its active support for the Hauenstein peasants in campaigns which were quite independent of the mass uprising led by Müller. While the latter was raising an army in the north, the Hauensteiners in the south continued their own war of attrition against the abbot of St Blasien. On 5th April the peasants had announced their refusal to negotiate any further, and demanded yet again that the abbot furnish evidence of his rights and privileges at the next communal assembly.[152] At the end of April the Black Forest peasants beyond the Schwarza left Müller's army in the Hegau and returned home, but that was no sign of willingness to capitulate.[153] On the contrary, it enabled them to redirect their energies exclusively against St Blasien.[154] The abbot himself had long since taken refuge elsewhere, but a monk, brother Fridolin, reported to him on 2nd May his fears of an imminent attack. He had tried to fend off the peasants' importunate demands by pointing to the abbot's absence and had arranged, as instructed, for the removal of the abbey's holy relics and valuables to its priory at Klingnau in canton Aargau.[155]

His fears were well grounded. Within days the Hauensteiners, hand-in-glove with Waldshut, had dealt the abbey a fourfold blow. They made good their threats of the previous November by taking Gutenburg castle and the neighbouring village of Gurtweil on the Schwarza river, and installing a garrison of fourteen men under the command of Hans Giller, a member of the Waldshut town council.[156]

---

[152] Ibid., p. 33, no. CLXIX. The abbot offered to present his deeds in Säckingen or Laufenburg, but the peasants turned him down flat.

[153] Ibid., p. 74, no. CCV. A monk of St Blasien, brother Fridolin, believed that Truchseß Georg's call to disband had caused the Schwarza peasants to quit. At all events, on 1 May they received an urgent appeal from Müller to rejoin his army in even greater numbers.

[154] In the meantime, however, the eight *Einungsmeister* of the lordship of Hauenstein had written to Freiburg on 19 April reiterating their loyalty to Austria. StAFr, C 1, Militaria 100; Hartfelder, 'Urkundliche Beiträge', pp. 413–14. This apparent paradox is explained by the Hauensteiners' tenacious but erroneous belief that their avowed status as free subjects of Austria would oblige archduke Ferdinand to intervene on their behalf against the abbey.

[155] Schreiber, *Bauernkrieg*, 2, p. 74, no. CCV; cf. Müller, *Bauernkrieg im Kreise Waldshut*, p. 65. Abbot Johann had already requested Freiburg the previous autumn to take custody of St Blasien's seals, title deeds, documents, and jewels. Schreiber, *Bauernkrieg*, 1, p. 13, no. XIII; ibid., p. 40, no. XXX.

[156] GLA 74/4563, fo. 17r–v. Brother Fridolin Rats to the abbot of St Blasien, 5 May 1525. Copy: . . . *die von waldshüt Das schloss gütennberg mitsambt gurtwil ingenomenn,*

On 4th May the eight captains of the Hauenstein communes, together with Waldshut, compelled brother Fridolin to agree to appear before them with the full authority of the abbot to answer their demands of 6th April.[157] Meanwhile, the peasants at large had rallied at Waldkirch, just north of Waldshut, determined to attack the abbey. Despite attempts to dissuade them, six hundred Hauensteiners fell upon St Blasien at the beginning of May and ravaged it for six days, breaking windows, images, and furniture, and carousing in the abbot's cellar.[158] Then Waldshut seized the consignment of relics and ornaments from the abbey as it was being transported through the town on its way to Klingnau, hidden in wine casks. The valuables, however, were neither sold nor destroyed, but stored in safe-keeping until they were eventually released in the autumn.[159]

These actions speak for themselves. Waldshut's alliance with the Hauensteiners was conceived in a different spirit from its involvement in Hans Müller's campaigns. The latter was a tactical commitment; the former an expression of solidarity born of common

schwarlichenn beschediget vnnd noch zum tag besitzenn . . . Huber, *Küssenbergs Chronik*, p. 424. Presumably the Schwarza peasants just returned from Müller's army were in the forefront of this attack. Loserth, 'Stadt Waldshut', p. 78 maintained quite incorrectly that the garrison under Hans Giller was part of Hans Müller's Black Forest army, and even Bergsten, *Hubmaier*, p. 279 argues that the occupation of Gutenburg castle implied that Waldshut had joined the Christian Union.

157 GLA 74/4563, fo. 17v: . . . *vnnd vff obgemelt anforderung vnns mit denen vonn waltzhüt vnnd viii mannenn vom wald vff ÿetz verschinen donnstag be zwungenlichenn ver annlasst, müssenn zu sagenn, mit vnnserem vollenn gewalt aldo erschinenn vnnd Enntlichen handlen bÿ Ia oder nein* . . .

158 Ibid., fo. 17v: . . . *Ein vfflüff vonn waldpurenn mit dem sturm gonn waldkilch gerottet vnnd vber das gotshuss ziechenn furgenomenn, biss schire gonn heche schwannd* [Höhenschwand] *zügerachet, vnnd doch durch etwas heimlichss verstanndts durch ir oberkeit vnnd derenn vonn waltzhüt geschwinde krÿg dissmal verhindert abgestelt* . . . Müller, *Bauernkrieg im Kreise Waldshut*, pp. 66–8. As well as various Swiss authorities, therefore, it appears that Waldshut had also tried to prevent the peasants plundering the abbey. This does not mean that the town did not actively support their demands, but it may reflect Hubmaier's condemnation of destructive aggression, as opposed to legitimate defence, against constituted authority.

159 Ibid., p. 66. Waldshut's reluctance to interfere with the abbey's valuables should be contrasted with the progressive introduction of Anabaptist doctrines by Hubmaier from April 1525 onwards, one of whose most significant features was the casting out of images and relics from the town's two churches. Bergsten, *Hubmaier*, pp. 302 f.; Loserth, 'Stadt Waldshut', pp. 62–3. On 3 June the abbot of St Blasien complained to Schaffhausen that the Hauensteiners were thwarting his attempts to sell the abbey's bells to a Zürich and a Schaffhausen burgher. Schreiber, *Bauernkrieg*, 2, pp. 170–1, no. CCC.

grievances. That is not to say that Waldshut had any idea of withdrawing its troops from Müller's army; on the contrary, they fought with it to the bitter end.[160] It was not long in coming. After his triumphs in the Breisgau Müller marched back eastwards to bring reinforcements to the Hegau troop which was still vainly besieging Radolfzell. During the first half of June the peasants confidently dismissed all offers of arbitration by the Swiss, but as the troops sent by the Swabian League and archduke Ferdinand at last closed upon the Hegau in the third week of June the peasants' mood changed drastically. Urgent cries for help went out to the northern Swiss villages, to the Protestant Swiss cities, to the Confederate Diet at Baden, and even to that arch-Catholic redoubt, Freiburg im Breisgau.[161] On 26th June the peasants abandoned their siege; the next day the relieving army under Marx Sittich von Ems entered Radolfzell. Within days the peasants' resistance was ruthlessly crushed; over twenty Hegau villages were razed to the ground. Thereupon the Baar and Stühlingen peasants surrendered without further hostilities.[162] Many peasants fled over the border into Switzerland, hoping to rally support from the Schaffhausen villages. Hallau, in particular, was eager to avenge the Foresters' and Hegauers' defeat, but the widespread unrest throughout the Swiss countryside discharged itself in a rebellion against Schaffhausen which did not spill over into southern Germany.[163] Hans Müller escaped, only to be captured by Ulrich von Habsberg in mid-July along with two henchmen from Waldshut. The latter were released, but Müller was tortured to extract a confession. During his imprisonment he asked for no mercy and was shown none. After forty days he was beheaded.[164]

---

[160] On 3 June the Hegau troops rejected Schaffhausen's proposed arbitration on the grounds that it could not act alone without the knowledge and consent of *vnser brůderschafft, versamlung vnd huffen, mit Namen Schwartzwald, Sungow, Prÿssgow, Elsseÿss, Waltzhůt, vnd ander mit vnss verpflichten Stetten vnnd Lendern.* SASh, Korrespondenzen V, no. 157; cf. Schreiber, *Bauernkrieg*, 2, pp. 171–2, no. CCCI.

[161] Herzog, *Bauernunruhen*, p. 48; Bergsten, *Hubmaier*, p. 281; Schreiber, *Bauernkrieg*, 2, pp. 245–6, no. CCCLXII; ibid., pp. 246–7, no. CCCLXIII; ibid., pp. 235–6, no. CCCLIII; Baumann, 'Eidgenossen seit dem Märze 1525', pp. 52–4.

[162] Ibid., pp. 56–7.

[163] Herzog, *Bauernunruhen*, pp. 49–50, 52 f.

[164] TLA, Oberösterreichische Hofregistratur, Reihe A (1520–64), laufender Faszikel 12, Position 30 (Bauernkrieg, 1525–26). Christoph Fuchs von Fuchsberg to Dr Jakob Frankfurter, 14 July 1525. Schreiber, *Bauernkrieg*, 3, pp. 78–9, no. CCCCIX; Müller, *Bauernkrieg im Kreise Waldshut*, p. 79.

V

Although Müller's defeat signalled the end of the Peasants' War as a mass movement in south-west Germany, it failed to herald the rapid downfall of Waldshut and its closest allies, the peasants from Hauenstein and the Klettgau.[165] Indeed, it made the search for new allies all the more pressing. After their communal assembly at Steinbach on 13th July the Hauensteiners, along with Waldshut, made approaches to the peasants in the lordship of Rheinfelden and the three margravial territories of Rötteln, Sausenberg, and Badenweiler, who were already in league with one another. The authorities certainly believed that the Forest Towns were not yet safe from rebellion within or without their walls.[166] In fact, peace negotiations in Basel during the summer averted the danger of a fresh conflagration in the south-west, but the Hauensteiners did not finally submit until 15th November, when the eight captains were made to swear a new oath of loyalty before Gutenburg castle.[167]

During the summer and autumn of 1525, therefore, Waldshut was effectively thrown back upon its alliance with the Klettgau peasants, who were long spared the fate of their neighbours in the Hegau and the Black Forest on account of Austria's fear lest a campaign against

---

[165] Waldshut's particular ties with the Black Forest and the Klettgau are reflected in Stumpf's chronicle: *Ouch hattend sy sich zu den puwren ab dem Schwartzwald und uss dem Kleckow mit ettwas vereynungen verlybt.* Ernst Gagliardi, Hans Müller, and Fritz Büsser (eds), *Johannes Stumpfs Schweizer- und Reformationschronik* (Quellen zur Schweizer Geschichte, new series 1, 5) (Basel, 1952), p. 290.

[166] TLA, Oberösterreichische Hofregistratur, Reihe A (1520–64), laufender Faszikel 12, Position 30 (Bauernkrieg, 1525–26). Ulrich von Habsberg to the Austrian commissioners in Radolfzell, 24 July 1525: . . . *Vnd seyn von Stund an mit sambt denen von Waltzhut zu den puren Inn die herrschafft Reynfelden Ir bottschafft vnd zu den Marggraffischen geschickt, Sich do vff eÿn news mit eynander zuuerpflichten* . . .

. . . *So Nun die handlung dermossen stet, das mann sich zu den puren Inn den drÿen Stetten nichts guts versehen soll, Sonder gwertig ist nacht vnd tag, die abzusteigen oder abzulauffen, So were fur war gut, das f. dt. Ordnung geb, das Sÿ bass besetzt wurden* . . . The rest of the letter recounts, *inter alia,* the unsettled conditions in and around Rheinfelden; the Forest Towns' declaration at Steinbach to afford the Hauensteiners no further protection; and the latter's continued refusal to pay the abbot of St Blasien a single penny. Loserth, 'Stadt Waldshut', p. 79 gives a partial and misleading account of this letter.

[167] Wernet, 'Grafschaft Hauenstein', p. 448. Even then the Hauensteiners' resistance was not broken. At Easter 1526 they took revenge for the execution of their leader, Kunz Jehle, by storming the abbey and sending it up in flames. As a result, Austria was forced to restore their ancient rights and customs, but the abbey took twelve years to recover. Ibid., pp. 448, 459.

the landgraviate unleash a full-scale war with the Swiss Confederation. Waldshut thus continued to enjoy, albeit indirectly, the benefits of Zürich's protection, even though its own relations with that city had rapidly deteriorated upon Hubmaier's introduction of Anabaptist reforms. These had begun at Easter when Wilhelm Reublin, the pastor at Witikon near Zürich, came to Waldshut to rebaptize Hubmaier and sixty of his followers. Over the next few days Hubmaier himself set about rebaptizing three hundred of his congregation.[168] Most of Waldshut's population, council and commons alike, accepted Hubmaier's reforms readily enough, but a minority which resisted the innovations was apparently forced to leave the town.[169] How far Waldshut's conversion to Anabaptism left its mark on the surrounding countryside is less certain. Both Reublin and Hubmaier were reported to have carried out baptisms in the area around the town, whilst the latter on his own admission led several burghers of Waldshut to a nearby village and there anabaptized them.[170] Yet despite its proximity to Waldshut on the one hand, and to the northern Swiss Anabaptist communities on the other, there were few traces of Anabaptist sentiment in the Klettgau. Above all, the rebellious Klettgau peasantry never ceased to proclaim its loyalty to the tenets of the Zwinglian Reformation.[171] By definition, therefore, Waldshut's alliance with the Klettgauers in the second half of 1525 lacked the common commitment to the Zürich Reformation that had helped to sustain it in January 1525. Indeed, the survival of the alliance would have been fundamentally jeopardized if Hubmaier had tried to enforce those Anabaptist doctrines in Waldshut which repudiated the use of the sword and the holding of public office. As it was, both his own position within the town and its beleaguered stand against Austria

[168] Bergsten, *Hubmaier*, pp. 304, 306.

[169] Christian Meyer, 'Zur Geschichte der Wiedertäufer in Oberschwaben, 1: Die Anfänge des Wiedertäuferthums in Augsburg', *Zeitschrift des Historischen Vereins für Schwaben und Neuburg*, 1 (1874), p. 246; Bergsten, *Hubmaier*, p. 305.

[170] Ibid., p. 319. Emil Egli (ed.), *Aktensammlung zur Geschichte der Zürcher Reformation in den Jahren 1519–1533* (Zürich, 1879), p. 431, no. 911.

[171] In its letter to Zürich of 1 Nov. 1525 the Klettgau peasantry implored the city's help in the face of imminent attack in order to protect the Word of God: *darmit wir by inhalt euwer Christenlichen mandaten vnd gotz wort bleiben mögen* ... SAZh, A. 192, 1, no. 176. Of course, the letter is *parti pris*: in appealing to Zürich the peasants were bound to manifest their loyal support for its Reformation. Nevertheless, there is not a scrap of evidence to suggest that this was not their genuine conviction. See now Blickle *et al.*, 'Vorstellung des göttlichen Rechts'.

made the adoption of pacifist and apolitical beliefs quite unthinkable.[172] Not surprisingly, perhaps, Hubmaier's own brand of Anabaptism consequently encountered opposition in Waldshut from those who considered themselves true believers. One in particular, Jakob Groß, was expelled from the town because he refused to carry arms or join the expeditionary force sent to Radolfzell.[173] But, by the same token, Hubmaier's introduction of Anabaptism to Waldshut created no serious rift with the Klettgau peasantry, since any doctrinal differences were far outweighed by a common antagonism, fuelled by a general Reforming religious fervour, towards the Catholic Austrian authorities.

Towards the end of June the threat of an early attack from the Swabian and Austrian armies approaching the Hegau had prompted the Klettgauers to try to take possession of Küssaburg castle, von Heidegg's headquarters and the only fortress of any significance in the landgraviate.[174] Zürich immediately urged the peasants to withdraw,[175] and was able on 29th June to bring about a two-month truce until 1st September. The peasants, however, could only be persuaded to accept the truce and withdraw their occupying forces from the castle by Zürich's agreeing to install four of its own burghers in the Küssaburg as guarantors of the truce.[176] The Swiss presence in the Klettgau, together with the fear that the rebels who had fled across the Rhine would hasten back to help their comrades, deterred the Austrians from mounting an attack upon the recalcitrant peasantry.[177]

---

[172] Bergsten, *Hubmaier*, pp. 320–1. He rightly emphasizes that Hubmaier's close cooperation with the town council had given him a position akin to Zwingli's vis-à-vis the Zürich council. Unlike most Anabaptists, therefore, who found themselves excluded from political power *ab initio*, Hubmaier had successfully wielded a dominant influence in Waldshut for more than two years. After his return from Schaffhausen, it was alleged, he had taken part in every session of the town council. Loserth, 'Stadt Waldshut', p. 56.

[173] Bergsten, *Hubmaier*, p. 322. Strictly speaking, Groß was willing to help guard and dig defences, but was not prepared to kill an enemy.

[174] Schreiber, *Bauernkrieg*, 2, p. 238, no. CCCLV. Their written summons to von Sulz and von Heidegg was signed: *Grafschaft Cleggew mit sambt der ganzen Bruderschaft und Zugewandten*. This suggests that they had been acting in concert with Müller's Christian Union, though active support seems to have come only from subjects of Zürich and Schaffhausen. Baumann, 'Eidgenossen seit dem Märze 1525', p. 58.

[175] Schreiber, *Bauernkrieg*, 2, pp. 238–9, no. CCCLVI.

[176] Ibid., pp. 251–2, no. CCCLXVII.

[177] Bergsten, *Hubmaier*, p. 332. TLA, Oberösterreichsiche Hofregistratur, Reihe A (152–64), laufender Faszikel 12, Position 30 (Bauernkrieg, 1525–26). Christoph Fuchs

In spite of the truce the Klettgauers remained restive. In July they refused to render tithes to count Rudolf, and showed little inclination to accept the results of Zürich's mediation with the Austrian commissioners in Radolfzell on 25th/28th July, which would have entailed a capitulation scarcely less abject and ominous than that of the Hegauers and Foresters.[178] When further attempts by Zürich to gain some concession for the Klettgauers proved futile, it gradually dawned on the peasants how grave their predicament was. They began to change tack by declaring their readiness to acquiesce in the terms of surrender, provided that they were not forced to return to the old religion.[179] This placed Zürich in an awkward dilemma. It could only reply that the peasants had transgressed against the true Word of God by taking part in campaigns of rebellion.[180] The Klettgauers naturally took exception to Zürich's response and began looking instead for support from the Swiss countryside where, it was reported, several hundred Thurgauers were ready to join them.[181] At the same time Zürich appealed to its Protestant Swiss neighbours to lend their weight to renewed efforts to reach some agreement with the Austrian authorities. When negotiations resumed at Radolfzell on 15th August, however, the Swiss managed to secure no more than formal changes to the wording of the treaty of surrender, which was duly presented to the Klettgauers for them to accept or reject by 22nd August. But the peasants, who remained steadfast in their attachment to Reforming doctrines, saw no glimpse of compromise therein and turned the treaty down. In consequence, when the truce expired at the beginning of September, Zürich withdrew its burghers from the Küssaburg and left the Klettgauers to their fate.[182]

The Klettgauers' intrepid refusal to surrender has been attributed to the insidious influence of their ally Waldshut, whose preacher, Balthasar Hubmaier, was determined to impose his revolutionary

von Fuchsberg to archduke Ferdinand, 29 July 1525. This is presumably the letter which Bergsten, *Hubmaier*, p. 332, n. 32 could not trace.

178 Baumann, 'Eidgenossen seit dem Märze 1525', pp. 59–60.

179 Ibid., pp. 60–1; cf. Schreiber, *Bauernkrieg*, 3, p. 71, no. CCCC.

180 Baumann, 'Eidgenossen seit dem Märze 1525', pp. 61–2.

181 Schreiber, *Bauernkrieg*, 3, p. 79, no. CCCCX. By guarding the Rhine crossings, however, Zürich ensured that no more than a handful of Swiss peasants managed to reach the Klettgau.

182 Baumann, 'Eidgenosen seit dem März 1525', pp. 62–4.

ideas upon the whole of southern Germany.[183] Certainly Waldshut had a stake in the Klettgauers' continued defiance, since that contributed to the town's own chances of survival, but the sources simply do not support the contention that the peasants were dancing to Waldshut's tune. The decision to reject the original treaty at the end of July, as the Klettgauers themselves declared on 4th August, was reached only after sounding out their compatriots in the entire landgraviate.[184] And in his letter to Zürich on the same day, which refers quite openly to Waldshut's active support for the peasants, von Heidegg nowhere implies that the town had incited or was encouraging their adamancy.[185]

Meanwhile, count Rudolf's efforts to muster an army to put down his subjects' rebellion had been extraordinarily ponderous: two whole months elapsed without any attempt at action.[186] Finally, at the beginning of November, the attack was launched. In their extremity the Klettgauers appealed once more to Zürich, but it was too late.[187] Yet the Klettgauers did not fight alone. Waldshut sent men and guns, and many Swiss peasants rallied to their defence.[188] On the evening of 4th November the Klettgauers and their allies met the Austrian troops under von Sulz and von Fuchsberg at Grießen. In the ensuing slaughter three hundred peasants fled into the churchyard, only giving themselves up in the early hours of the morning.

---

[183] Herzog, *Bauernunruhen*, p. 35. This, admittedly, was a view shared by the authorities. Cf. Schreiber, *Bauernkrieg*, 3, p. 173, no. CCCCLXXII.

[184] SAZh, A. 192, 1, no. 157. 4 Aug. 1525.

[185] SAZh, A. 192, 1, no. 156. Hans Jakob von Heidegg to Zürich, 4 Aug. 1525: *Wiewol zu ledst vff put miner herren von Zurich vnd schaffhusen sandbotten Inen viertag vff hindersich bringen Irer gmeinden verdannkh zü gelassen ist, Nicht destoweniger ettlich sich lassen merken, das sy den vertrag nit annemen wellen. Darzü sich ouch die von Waldshüt, die vormals mit Irm geschutz vnabgesagt vnd bewart Ir eren minem gnedigen herrn fur sein hus gezogen, vählich vnd kriegisch gehanndelt, Sich mit denen, so an andern enden von vngehorsami wegen vertriben, vast stecken.* This is the letter on which Herzog principally bases his assertions.

[186] Baumann, 'Eidgenossen seit dem Märze 1525', p. 64. On 12 Sept. archduke Ferdinand had promised military support to defend Küssaburg castle, should it again be besieged. Schreiber, *Bauernkrieg*, 3, pp. 131–2, no. CCCCLIV. He erroneously gives the recipient of the letter as count Sigismund von Lupfen!

[187] SAZh, A. 192, 1, no. 176. The landgraviate of the Klettgau to Zürich, 1 Nov. 1525. Both Zürich and Schaffhausen tried to avert the impending bloodshed, but to no avail. Baumann, 'Eidgenossen seit dem Märze 1525', p. 65.

[188] Roder, *Heinrich Hugs Villinger Chronik*, p. 148. The Swiss villages which lent the most active support to the Klettgauers were, significantly, those in the northernmost tip of canton Zürich, on the right bank of the Rhine—Rafz, Wil, and Hüntwangen—whose proximity to the Klettgau clearly stimulated their sympathy for the peasants' cause. Cf. SAZh, A. 192, 1, nos 184, 185, 186.

Several Waldshuters were killed and two were taken prisoner, whilst the priest of Grießen, Johannes Rebmann, an arch-supporter of the peasants who had gone there from Waldshut after its Catholic priest had fled, had his eyes put out.[189]

The immediate danger which now faced Waldshut itself brought to the surface the latent conflicts within the town over its religious and political course. During November Hubmaier was a sick man, and the leaders of Waldshut's community appear to have used his illness to treat with the Austrian authorities over his head.[190] Several young burghers fled to Laufenburg, von Habsberg's headquarters, and begged for mercy, whilst Waldshut's military commander, Hans Gerber, let it be known that if he were assured of a pardon he and seventy others would abandon the town and its defences.[191] On 5th December Hubmaier called his congregation together at the town hall, where he revealed that the town had at last agreed to surrender. Because he could not tolerate the inevitable restoration of the Catholic religion there was nothing left for him but to flee. Hubmaier made his way across the Rhine into Switzerland, and many of his sympathizers followed. That evening an army of nobles acting in the

---

[189] TLA, Oberösterreichische Hofregistratur, Reihe A (1520–64), laufender Faszikel 12, Position 30 (Bauernkrieg, 1525–26). Count Rudolf von Sulz and Christoph Fuchs von Fuchsberg to archduke Ferdinand, 9 Nov. 1525. Cf. SAZh, A. 192, 1, no. 181. The four Zürich envoys at Grießen to Zürich, 4 Nov. 1525. An unsatisfactory account is given in Loserth, 'Stadt Waldshut', pp. 80–2, documents pp. 121–2. After Grießen several burghers of Tiengen fled with their cattle to Waldshut. Despite his support for the peasants, the Zwinglian Rebmann later received a benefice near Zürich, which disposes of any notion that he might have entertained Anabaptist sympathies. Bergsten, *Hubmaier*, p. 347. It is also further testimony to the negligible impact of Anabaptism in the Klettgau.

[190] HKA, Reichsakten, Faszikel 78, fo. 600v. Christoph Fuchs von Fuchsberg to archduke Ferdinand, 22 Nov. 1525. Copy. *Hewt frue egg von Reyschach mir antzaigt, wie diss teg zwen von waltzhut des Rats bey Im zu weyler gewesen vnnd in vnder anderm bericht, das Rat, gericht vnnd gemaind sich zusamen gethon vnd Iren doctor erfordert, Ime mit ainer lanngen materi antzaigt, wie er sich allweg berembt, sein handlung mit Recht vnd wol wissen zuuerantwurten, der beger, was gemiets er noch sey*... Cf. Bergsten, *Hubmaier*, pp. 349, 351. This is the letter which Bergsten was unable to trace. Ibid., p. 349, n. 94.

[191] HKA, Reichsakten, Faszikel 78, fo. 604r. Cf. archduke Ferdinand to Christoph Fuchs von Fuchsberg, 2 Dec. 1525. TLA, Pestarchiv, XVIII, 115; cf. Loserth, 'Stadt Waldshut', pp. 124–7; Bergsten, *Hubmaier*, p. 349. Further evidence of the divisions within Waldshut is given in a letter from one of its burghers, Friedrich Rieder, to Freiburg, 31 Dec. 1525:... *da mit die warheit an dag keme, dan der Doktor baldesser hůb meÿer hat ein soliche Irrung vnd wider werdykeit vnder vns zů walcz hůt gemacht, das billich alle cristenlichen menschen dar zů důn soltend*... StAFr, C1, Militaria 99.

name of the archduke entered the town and occupied it without bloodshed.[192] The Reformation in Waldshut was at an end.

VI

Without its defiant commitment to Reforming doctrines Waldshut would never have become so deeply involved in the Peasants' War in south-west Germany. But how far that commitment determined the pattern of Waldshut's alliances with the peasantry is another matter. Enough has been said to suggest that it is essential to distinguish between the impact of Hubmaier's preaching upon the peasants and their willingness to ally with Waldshut, for these alliances were shaped by the complex interaction of several variables, structural as well as ideological. What made the origins, character, and course of the alliances so disparate was, not least, the marked divergence of aims within and between the rural and urban populations. On the one hand, the peasantry was split into radical and moderate factions, whilst for its part Waldshut was caught between the desire for religious Reform and the need for political engagement. On the other, the expectations which both sides entertained of the alliances frequently conflicted. This makes it difficult to typify the alliances, but they can nevertheless be divided into two broad categories: communities of action and communities of interest. The former arose in response to external dangers; they were leagues of mutual protection between allies whose situation and interest might differ. The latter entailed active commitment to a common cause between partners whose circumstances and aims coincided.[193]

All the alliances between Waldshut and the rebellious peasantry up to May 1525 were essentially the product of immediate and

---

192 Bergsten, *Hubmaier*, pp. 350–1.

193 See now Tom Scott, 'The German Peasants' War: A Historiographical Review', part 2, *Historical Journal*, 22 (1979), pp. 955 ff.; idem, 'Bemerkungen zum Begriff "Gemeiner Mann": Das Stadt-Land-Verhältnis zur Zeit des Bauernkreigs', in Fridolin Dörrer (ed.), *Die Bauernkriege und Michael Gaismair* (Veröffentlichungen des Tiroler Landesarchivs, 2) (Innsbruck, 1982), pp. 289–92; and most recently Tom Scott, 'Südwestdeutsche Städte im Bauernkrieg. Bündnisse zwischen Opportunismus und Solidarität', in Bernhard Kirchgässner and Hans-Peter Becht (eds), *Stadt und Revolution* (Stadt in der Geschichte. Veröffentlichungen des Südwestdeutschen Arbeitskreises für Stadtgeschichtsforschung, 27) (Stuttgart, 2001), pp. 9–36. [Engl. version in this vol.]

specific political and military exigencies, not of any deep-rooted sense of common interest between town and country. Hans Müller, it is true, looked to Waldshut for ideological and strategic support for his Christian Union, but the nature of his campaign and his ultimate ambitions in effect relegated Waldshut to the role of a useful adjunct rather than an equal partner. Only Waldshut's alliance with the Hauensteiners and to a lesser extent with the Klettgauers in the summer of 1525 can justly be described as a genuine community of interest, born of common grievances and sustained by common goals, in which the town took an active and leading part. Yet it was precisely these two groups of peasants which showed such small ideological dependence on, or derived so little inspiration from, Waldshut as the headquarters of Hubmaier's Reformation, notwithstanding their proximity to the town. This illustrates the double hurdle that faced Hubmaier in spreading his doctrines. As long as he clove to Zwinglian Reforming doctrines, Waldshut could not compete with Zürich as the natural focus of Reforming allegiance in the southwest (as the attitude of the Klettgauers amply demonstrated),[194] whilst his subsequent Anabaptist beliefs seemingly made little headway outside Waldshut, largely, it may be argued, because Anabaptism's intrinsic appeal lay in its identification with village autonomy, an appeal which depended upon the direct efforts of Anabaptist preachers in the countryside, rather than upon the remote example of urban congregationalism.[195]

The key to Waldshut's active involvement with the Hauenstein and Klettgau peasants is undoubtedly to be found in the common antagonism towards St Blasien on the one hand, and the common dependence upon the northern Swiss cities on the other.[196] But it must not be overlooked that this structural parallelism only led to a

[194] The notion that the rebellious peasants around Waldshut made Hubmaier their adviser and leader dies hard. See Manfred Hannemann, *The Diffusion of the Reformation in South-Western Germany, 1518–1534* (University of Chicago Research Paper, 167) (Chicago, 1975), p. 100; cf. p. 44.

[195] See now Stayer, 'Reublin and Brötli'.

[196] As Hannemann, *Diffusion*, p. 44 recognizes: '... the entire area immediately north of the Swiss-German border was oriented towards, and existed in a socio-economic equilibrium with Zurich, which served as an economic, cultural and religious central place'. See the map of Zürich's and Schaffhausen's market area in Peter Schöller, 'Der Markt als Zentralisationsphänomen', *Westfälische Forschungen*, 15 (1962), p. 91.

community of interest in mid-1525. In the winter of 1524 the Hauensteiners had rebuffed those peasants from the vicinity of Waldshut who wished to mount an iconoclastic attack on St Blasien, whilst Waldshut's alliance with the Klettgauers in January 1525 did nothing to dissuade the latter from pursuing peace negotiations with Zürich. Why, therefore, was the bond of solidarity so long in the making? One reason is that Waldshut's relations with the surrounding countryside were caught in a cross-play of cooperation and conflict. Their common political interests could not conceal that Waldshut and the other Forest Towns, like so many German communes at the turn of the fifteenth century, were the victims of economic competition from the countryside. Village craftsmen were stealing the towns' trade; country salt stores were eroding their revenues; and the local lords were encouraging their subjects to buy direct rather than from the urban markets.[197]

What, therefore, happened during 1525 to bring about an active alliance between Waldshut and the surrounding peasants? And how far did this alliance constitute a revolutionary movement of the common man in town and country? Both the Hauensteiners and the Klettgauers, it should be noted, had achieved nothing by negotiation; those whom they regarded as their rightful protectors—Austria and Zürich—had dashed their expectations; and they could hardly hope for support from Hans Müller's Christian Union of the Black Forest, which had other fish to fry. By the summer of 1525 Waldshut was the only natural ally left. Nevertheless, the Klettgauers remained essentially committed to the rectification of their own specific grievances, whilst the Hauensteiners, despite acts of violence against St Blasien, were fighting to uphold their ancient liberties, rather than to extirpate the abbey as a feudal lord. Only Hans Müller saw an alliance with Waldshut as a means of forging a general revolt in which town and country would unite in ideological solidarity against the existing social order.

In other words, the complex pattern of Waldshut's relations with the peasants suggests that the origins of alliances between town and

---

[197] StAFr, C 1, Landstände 3. Particular complaints of the Breisgau towns at the Austrian Diet in Innsbruck, compiled 14 March 1518, presented 4 May 1518: no. 7: complaints of the four Forest Towns. See now generally Tom Scott, *Freiburg and the Breisgau. Town-Country Relations in the Age of Reformation and Peasants' War* (Oxford, 1986); idem, *Regional Identity and Economic Change. The Upper Rhine, 1450–1600* (Oxford, 1997).

country in the Peasants' War and their contribution to its radicalization depended less upon the impact of an overriding extraneous ideology than upon the circumstances in which those alliances were formed. What is needed now is a rigorous analysis, not so much of the preconditions and programmes of the various rebellions, but of their internal dynamics.[198] The aetiology of the Peasants' War as a mass movement has only just begun.

[198] A stimulating preliminary investigation which draws upon a wide range of literature on the theory of revolution has been carried out for Würzburg by Hans-Christoph Rublack in section 3 of Jürgen Bücking and Hans-Christoph Rublack, 'Der Bauernkrieg in den vorder- und oberösterreichischen Ländern und in der Stadt Würzburg. Ansätze zu einer Theorie des Bauernkriegs', in Moeller, *Bauernkriegs-Studien*, pp. 58–68; cf. esp. 64–8. Elliger, *Müntzer*, p. 642 acknowledges the 'immanent consequence' which led peasants from seeking to withstand the unjust demands of their lords to calling into question the legitimacy of lordship as such.

CHAPTER TWO

THE COMMUNAL REFORMATION BETWEEN TOWN AND COUNTRY

The Communal Reformation as a designation of the overriding characteristic of enthusiasm for religious renewal in the early 1520s has provoked lively and vigorous debate. The present paper cannot hope, and does not aim, to review the range of arguments put forward in criticism of Peter Blickle's thesis.[1] It takes as read the objections both to his chronology (that the defeat of the Peasants' War marked the end of communal religious aspirations and opened the way to a magisterial Reformation) and to his geography (that his typology is hardly valid for areas of the empire beyond Upper Germany and the Alpine valleys).[2] It also goes beyond the critique put forward in my review article on the common people in the German Reformation, which concentrates on issues of communal solidarity and self-perception,[3] to investigate the laity's understanding of 'reformation' as such. That task cannot properly be divorced from a discussion of popular religiosity on the eve of the Reformation, but since a later session addresses itself to that question, my remarks here will be selective and brief.[4]

My purpose, rather, is limited and precise: to enquire whether the concept of a Communal Reformation, in Blickle's own definition, is fully applicable to his chosen area of Upper Germany and Switzerland.

---

[1] Expanded and revised version of my paper given in Washington D.C. on 27 Sept. 1990. For critical comments on Graubünden I am very grateful to Randolph Head of the University of Virginia, Charlottesville.

[2] See the review article by Mark U. Edwards Jr, 'Gemeindereformation als Bindeglied der mittelalterlichen und der neuzeitlichen Welt', *Historische Zeitschrift*, 249 (1989), pp. 95–103. Further references may be found in Peter Blickle, 'Die Reformation vor dem Hintergrund von Kommunalisierung und Christianisierung', in idem and Johannes Kunisch (eds), *Kommunalisierung und Christianisierung. Voraussetzungen und Folgen der Reformation 1400–1600* (*Zeitschrift für Historische Forschung*, Beiheft 9) (Berlin, 1989), p. 13 nn. 7, 9–11.

[3] Tom Scott, 'The Common People in the German Reformation', *Historical Journal*, 34 (1991), pp. 183–192.

[4] Regrettably, discussion of popular religion was drastically curtailed. Therefore I have elaborated my remarks in the text below.

To that end, I shall restrict myself to two case-studies, one on the countryside, the other on the towns. The former will examine the situation in Graubünden and the Inner Swiss cantons, the latter events in certain Alsatian imperial free cities and territorial towns. At the outset it may be helpful to recall that Blickle's argument rests upon two leitmotivs. He points to the singular convergence (which can hardly be accidental) between areas of strong communal traditions and widespread enthusiasm for religious change along communal-congregational lines. Indeed, such areas, he argues, had been engaged for much of the fifteenth century in a determined attempt to extend secular communal rights into the ecclesiastical and religious domain, a process which he terms 'Christianization'. In the early 1520s this political struggle became ideologically supercharged with the advent of evangelical beliefs; they furnished the necessary theological legitimation for the break with the old Church, which in turn allowed communal aspirations to achieve their fullest and final expression. The Communal Reformation, therefore, presupposes a large degree of compatibility and identity between the laity's understanding of Reform and the religious intentions of the Reformers themselves. Without that shared commitment, Blickle insists, we should not speak of a Communal Reformation.

Yet it is no secret that enthusiasm for the new doctrines was at best patchy, at worst seemingly altogether absent, in three areas of Upper Germany and the Alps which had avowed and entrenched traditions of communal liberty at local level and even of political representation in Diets at territorial level—the Austrian Tirol, parts of Graubünden, and the Inner Swiss cantons. In acknowledging this point Blickle counters, quite correctly, that a genuine Reforming movement did spread throughout Tirol, only for it to be suppressed by the Austrian authorities in the wake of the peasants' defeat in 1526. However, in the other two regions (which, *en passant*, were not affected by the Peasants' War), strong communalism did not serve as the precursor of a broad Reforming movement.[5] Swiss historiography, he notes, has not yet provided a coherent and plausible explanation for this apparent 'failure'.[6] In Inner Switzerland, especially in

[5] Blickle, 'Reformation', pp. 22–3.

[6] But see Hans R. Guggisberg, 'The Problem of "Failure" in the Swiss Reformation: Some Preliminary Reflections', in E. I. Kouri and Tom Scott (eds), *Politics and Society*

Uri, Schwyz, Unterwalden, Zug, and Glarus, the rural communes had often wrested rights of presentation to livings from their collators in the course of the fifteenth century; by extension, they had acquired the right to dismiss their parish priests, and in some instances they carried out annual re-elections to benefices.[7] Such efforts exactly mirrored the spirit of rugged independence and communal autonomy for which the Alpine valleys were long famous. Accordingly, Blickle ponders: 'It is seductive . . . to speculate whether a causal connection exists between the profusion of communal advowsons and the relative indifference towards Zwingli's doctrines evident in the Inner Swiss cantons.'[8] This is a question which Blickle cannot afford to evade, for the very strength of communal traditions is critical to his argument about the receptivity of the common people to evangelical doctrines: the examples of Inner Switzerland and Graubünden cannot be brushed aside as peripheral curiosities. It is a challenge which Blickle faces honestly, and to which he gives an ingenious yet simple solution. Because the communalization of the Church had already largely been achieved, he argues, there no longer existed in the heart of the Swiss Confederation any need for the Reformation: the Reformers could offer the inner cantons nothing which they did not already have.[9] Despite the apparent paradox, he concludes, the successful process of communalization in the later Middle Ages, far from rendering the Catholicism of the inner cantons inexplicable, in fact helps to explain why they remained Catholic.[10] Communalism can explain more than it might seem. I agree. Whether this line of argument can be squared with Blickle's view of the theological and religious motives behind communalism, however, is another matter.

---

in Reformation Europe. Essays for Sir Geoffrey Elton on His Sixty-Fifth Birthday (Houndmills, Hants/London, 1987), pp. 188–209.

[7] Blickle, 'Reformation', p. 21; idem, *Gemeindereformation. Die Menschen des 16. Jahrhunderts auf dem Weg zum Heil* (Munich, 1985), pp. 181–2. [Engl. *Communal Reformation. The Quest for Salvation in Sixteenth-Century Germany*, transl. Thomas Dunlap (Atlantic Highlands, NJ/London, 1992), pp. 166–7.] The evidence is drawn from Dietrich Kurze, *Pfarrerwahlen im Mittelalter. Ein Beitrag zur Geschichte der Gemeinde und des Niederkirchenwesens* (Forschungen zur kirchlichen Rechtsgeschichte, 6) (Cologne/Graz, 1966), p. 315 *et passim.*

[8] Blickle, *Gemeindereformation*, p. 182 (my translation); idem, *Communal Reformation*, p. 167.

[9] Idem, 'Reformation', p. 23.

[10] Ibid., p. 24.

I

Let us turn first to Graubünden. There is widespread agreement amongst scholars that religious opinion radicalized in the valleys of the three Leagues (Grey League, League of Ten Jurisdictions, League of the House of God) between the composition of the First Ilanz Articles on 4th April 1524 and the proclamation of the Second Ilanz Articles on 25th June 1526.[11] The articles of 1524 have been described as 'moderate and cautious';[12] in essence, they demanded that the priest be resident in his benefice, and that ecclesiastical courts should not be invoked in civil cases, barring marriage and clerical claims for rents.[13] By contrast, the Second Ilanz Articles two years later demanded complete communal-congregational control of the clergy (the right of appointment and dismissal, the regulation of competency, the cancellation of the small tithe, and the disposition of the large tithe), together with the abolition of all episcopal and clerical jurisdiction,[14] in effect a clarion to the secularization of the bishopric and the creation of a free Alpine republic of Graubünden.[15] Behind the markedly sharper tone of the 1526 articles, it is held, lurk the influence of the Twelve Articles of Upper Swabia and the intrigues of Michael Gaismair in neighbouring Tirol and in the Prättigau.[16] Given the constitutional situation of the three Leagues, all subject in large measure to the temporal as well as the spiritual authority of the bishop of Chur, it comes as no surprise that a series of secular grievances—at bottom a struggle over the payment of tithes and feudal renders to the bishop Paul Ziegler, and to various convents

[11] Constanz Jecklin (ed.), *Urkunden zur Verfassungsgeschichte Graubündens*, 2: *Zeit der Entstehung der einzelnen Bünde und ihrer Verbindungen (bis zum Ende des 15. Jahrhunderts)* (Chur, 1883), pp. 78–83, 89–95.

[12] Benjamin R. Barber, *The Death of Communal Liberty. A History of Freedom in a Swiss Mountain Canton* (Princeton, NJ, 1974), p. 51.

[13] Jecklin, *Urkunden*, pp. 78–79, 80; cf. Barber, *Death of Communal Liberty*, p. 51.

[14] Jecklin, *Urkunden*, pp. 89, 91–93.

[15] See Blickle, *Gemeindereformation*, pp. 52–4; idem, *Communal Reformation*, pp. 34–6; Barber, *Death of Communal Liberty*, p. 51; Oskar Vasella, 'Die Entstehung der bündnerischen Bauernartikel vom 25. Juni 1526', *Zeitschrift für schweizerische Geschichte*, 21 (1941), p. 73 speaks of an attempt to create a territorial constitution.

[16] See Jecklin, *Urkunden*, pp. 97–8; Barber, *Death of Communal Liberty*, p. 52; Peter Stadler, 'Eidgenossenschaft und Reformation', in Heinz Angermeier (ed.), *Säkulare Aspekte der Reformationszeit* (Schriften des Historischen Kollegs: Kolloquien 5) (Munich/Vienna, 1983), p. 98; Vasella, 'Entstehung der Bauernartikel', p. 68.

and clerical foundations within Graubünden—should have spilled over into a general campaign of political liberty. In that sense, the radicalization of opinion was immanent within the logic of the peasants' demands. Yet the radical thrust of the Second Ilanz Articles betokened no ostensible willingness to break with the Catholic faith. A casual reading of article 4, which demanded an end to payments for requiem masses and chantries to convents or churches, might suggest disillusion with the nature and efficacy of sacramental religion;[17] on closer inspection, however, the demand is located squarely in the context of others which excoriated the financial rapacity of the Church, especially its monastic houses.[18]

Moreover, it is not the case that more overtly religious or theological demands emerged from earlier purely secular ecclesiastical grievances. On the contrary, as Oscar Vasella showed half a century ago, such demands were present from the outset in Graubünden.[19] Indeed, the call for Scripture to be the sole authority for a Christian, and for evangelical preaching in conformity with it, characterized the early months of unrest, only to be overshadowed by political and social agitation against ecclesiastical lords throughout 1525.[20] There was, in other words, no steady or straightforward progression from moderate to radical demands (or from secular to religious), and the preaching of the Gospel in individual Graubünden communes did not lead everywhere to the adoption of the Reformation.[21] Rather, opinion in the valleys of the three Leagues remained cautious and uncertain. It was the prolonged and violent campaign of disobedience against the feudal power of church lords which made it imperative to restore civil and religious stability in Graubünden. That purpose underlay the convocation of the Leagues' deputies to a colloquy at Ilanz on 7th/9th January 1526. Had the colloquy been stage-managed by the sympathizers of Reform, as was previously the case in Zürich, the outcome might have favoured the evangelical cause. But far from being influenced by representatives of the city

[17] Jecklin, *Urkunden*, pp. 90–1.

[18] See ibid., pp. 90–2, §§ 2, 3, 5, 9–12. An appendix to the articles, however, expressly drew a distinction between the question of mass-payments and the handling of other rents and dues accruing to churches. Ibid., p. 95.

[19] Oscar Vasella, 'Bauernkrieg und Reformation in Graubünden 1525–1526', *Zeitschrift für schweizerische Geschichte*, 20 (1940), p. 4.

[20] Ibid., pp. 27–32.

[21] Ibid., p. 4, n. 8.

of Chur, where a genuine Reforming movement had grown up under the leadership of Johannes Comander, a disciple of Zwingli, the colloquy was dominated by powerful deputies from the rural communes (*Landschaft*) hostile to the new doctrines, and the meeting broke up without agreement.[22]

The Diet which assembled at Chur in March 1526 reflected the division of opinion manifest at the Ilanz Colloquy. It resulted, however, in a remarkable compromise, which recognized the existence of both religious positions (to talk of confessions would be premature). On the one hand it offered explicit protection for the central tenets of Catholicism—the Mass, veneration of the Virgin Mary and the saints, infant baptism, confession, and penance—yet on the other it defended (rather than merely acquiescing in) preaching by the light of Scripture alone.[23] In my view, it would be wrong to regard the outcome of the Diet either as a victory for toleration or as a demonstration of hopelessly irreconcilable and contradictory religious stances. On the contrary, the deputies apparently believed evangelical preaching to be quite compatible with Catholic doctrine. It might be objected that the deputies were simply buying time, temporizing between two factions before deciding firmly in favour of Reform, in a manner similar to the city fathers in Basel, Bern, and Strasbourg, or even Zürich itself. The comparison, I would assert, is askew, for the magistrates in those cities sat at the pinnacle of a social hierarchy, fearful of dissent and unrest amongst the common citizenry and were accordingly keen to maintain civic peace and protect their own patrician interests, whereas the deputies at Chur were not rulers but delegates, answerable to their fellow-citizens and attuned to their views.[24]

Nor did those delegates vacillate, for the direct result of the colloquy and the Diet was the formulation of the Second Ilanz Articles which took the secular ecclesiastical grievances of the Graubünden Leagues to their logical (and radical) conclusion—albeit leaving their adherence to Catholicism intact. The singular provisions of the Diet

[22] Ibid., p. 45. On the Reformation in Chur see Martin Bundi, Ursula Jecklin, and Georg Jäger, *Geschichte der Stadt Chur*, part 2 (Chur, 1986), pp. 313–18.

[23] Vasella, 'Bauernkrieg und Reformation', p. 50.

[24] Vasella himself alludes to the example of Basel, though he takes a more indulgent view of the motives of the city fathers. Ibid., p. 51, n. 130. He also points out that it was the powerful leaders of the three Leagues who sought to hinder the promulgation of the Articles from March 1526 onwards, and who were opposed to their radical provisions. Vasella, 'Entstehung der Bauernartikel', p. 70.

of Chur had afforded an opening to the spread of evangelical doctrines, yet that opportunity was not seized in Graubünden for another decade, and then only in part. In the longer term the upshot was that Catholic and Reformed congregations co-existed within one community, even in one instance, that of Churwalden, sharing the same church.[25] That outcome should occasion no surprise, for the Second Ilanz Articles had enshrined a commitment to grass-roots control of the Church in a network of largely autonomous *Kirchgemeinden*, regardless of confessional allegiance.[26] How vital that system remains has been demonstrated in our own day by the extraordinary events in the diocese of Chur which followed the appointment of a new bishop, Wolfgang Haas—civil disobedience by his flock, some of whom lay down in his path during the inauguration ceremony, in protest at Haas being imposed upon Chur by pope John Paul II, against the express wishes of the faithful.

The reasons for the reluctance of much of Graubünden to embrace Reformation have received no more than perfunctory attention. From the vantage-point of mid-century it is possible to see how political and diplomatic ties came increasingly to bear upon confessional allegiance. The equation of Austria with Catholicism and France with Protestantism survived even the massacre of St Bartholomew's Day in 1572![27] But this alliance of foreign politics and religion was much less clear-cut in the 1520s. Vasella has pointed to the fact that the bishopric of Chur (if not its bishop, Paul Ziegler, who fled his see in 1524) enjoyed the support of rural potentates who profited from employment in episcopal service and were well on their way to becoming a peasant aristocracy.[28] Similarly, as a land of mountain passes Graubünden was particularly dependent upon mercenary service, even more so than cantons such as Zürich, where Zwingli had championed the abolition of foreign military employment.[29] It is also true, as Peter Blickle has reminded us, that the *Landschaft* lacked a charismatic evangelical preacher of the stamp of a Comander.

---

[25] Barber, *Death of Communal Liberty*, p. 54.
[26] Ibid., pp. 53–4.
[27] Ibid., p. 53.
[28] On this point see most recently Paul Eugen Grimm, 'Die Anfänge der Bündner Aristokratie im 15. und 16. Jahrhundert' (Diss. phil. Zürich, 1981); Vasella, 'Bauernkrieg und Reformation', pp. 36–7.
[29] Ibid., p. 37.

Important though such considerations are, they cannot be regarded as entirely compelling. Conversions to Protestantism did after all occur, but with an appreciable delay.[30] The proper question, therefore, turns on why there was doctrinal conformity and continuity in the 1520s but some readiness to change in the 1530s. What Graubünden shows is an initial willingness to carry through far-reaching reform of the Church as *ecclesia*, but a reluctance to break with the Church as *doctrina*. That this distinction is neither capricious nor artificial may be evinced by a subsequent example. The canton of the Valais, no less committed to communal control of the Church than its counterpart east of the Gotthard, several decades later stripped the bishop of Sion/Sitten of the last vestiges of his judicial authority (in what appears almost as a replay of the Second Ilanz Articles), yet remained then and thereafter staunchly Catholic.[31]

II

Let us look now at the Inner Swiss cantons. Two papers on this subject by Peter Blickle were not available to me in advance of my comments here, but my thoughts, it transpires, partly take up where he leaves off.[32] Three preliminary observations need to be made in order to show that Inner Switzerland was not immune from influences at work elsewhere.

1. As Hans Guggisberg has alerted us, all areas of the Confederation experienced certain beginnings of Reforming propaganda, however

---

[30] In 1530 Comander reported to the St Gallen Reformer Vadian that the Graubünden valleys still displayed considerable resistance or uncertainty towards the new doctrines: the Mass was abolished and then reintroduced 'at will' ('*nach Belieben*'). Bundi, Jecklin, and Jäger, *Geschichte der Stadt Chur*, p. 316.

[31] Stadler, 'Eidgenossenschaft', p. 98.

[32] 'Antiklerikalismus um den Vierwaldstättersee 1300–1500. Von der Kritik der Macht der Kirche' (Tucson, AZ, September 1990), now printed in Peter A. Dykema and Heiko A. Oberman (eds), *Anticlericalism in Late Medieval and Early Modern Europe* (Studies in Medieval and Reformation Thought, 51) (Leiden/New York/Cologne, 1994), pp. 115–32; and 'Eidgenossenschaften in reformatorischer Absicht oder: Wie begründet ist die Kritik an der "Gemeindereformation"?' (Washington, DC, September 1990), now printed in Hans R. Guggisberg and Gottfried G. Krodel (eds), *Die Reformation in Deutschland und Europa. Interpretationen und Debatten* (*Archiv für Reformationsgeschichte*, Sonderband) (Gütersloh, 1993), pp. 159–74.

muted, in the 1520s.[33] The Forest cantons should certainly not be viewed as backward, inward-looking, or isolated. Apart from their exposure to—and control of—traffic crossing the Alpine passes,[34] two of the five inner cantons grouped around the Lake of Lucerne were city-states—Luzern itself, and Zug (though the latter was undeniably diminutive). In both Luzern and Zug the city councils moved to intervene against proponents of Reform, in Luzern's case as late as 1528.[35]

2. The groundswell of anticlericalism, so evident in Graubünden, which many historians regard as the tide carrying late medieval disaffection with the Church and its servitors onto the farther shores of Protestantism,[36] may have surged less violently in the inner cantons, but there were still rocks for it to break on. Contrary to the commonly held, but superficial, opinion, the heart of the Confederation was not bereft of powerful ecclesiastical foundations—Engelberg, Einsiedeln, Interlaken, Disentis, Seedorf. The inner cantons may not have been a *Pfaffengasse* like Alsace, but the abbey of Engelberg controlled a quasi-independent territory sandwiched between Unterwalden and Uri. (Disentis, by contrast, in the *Vorderrhein* valley was already swayed by its commune.) Certain preconditions which led peasants elsewhere—for instance, in Upper Swabia—to embrace the Gospel as a potent weapon in their struggle against secular feudal monastic lordship were therefore present in the inner cantons.[37]

3. The Catholic inner cantons did not doubt that the Church was in need of reform, though their hopes remained pinned upon the

[33] Guggisberg, 'Problem of "Failure"', p. 192.

[34] I am, however, well aware of H. S. Offler's mordant comment: 'To allow due weight to localism is not to deny the capital influence exerted on the making of Switzerland by the long-distance routes across the Alps. There is no paradox here: international roads are not necessarily destructive to the particularisms through which they pass . . .; it cannot reasonably be alleged that the railway which created Crewe has endowed its inhabitants with a breadth of outlook superior to that of other communities.' Edgar Bonjour, H. S. Offler, and G. R. Potter, *A Short History of Switzerland* (Oxford, 1952), pp. 9–10.

[35] Guggisberg, 'Problem of "Failure"', pp. 193–7.

[36] See most recently Hans-Jürgen Goertz, *Pfaffenhaß und gross Geschrei. Die reformatorischen Bewegungen in Deutschland 1517–1529* (Munich, 1987).

[37] Guggisberg, 'Problem of "Failure"', p. 196 points to the ironic exception of the convent of Kappel near Zug. Some of Zug's citizens in the summer of 1524 were eager to attack the convent in retaliation for the peasants' storming of the Charterhouse at Ittingen, for Kappel under its abbot Wolfgang Joner and the young Heinrich Bullinger was a patron of Reforming ideas!

convocation of a General Council.[38] When the five inner cantons concluded the Concordat of Faith with Fribourg in 1525, they agreed to discipline lax clergy and to act jointly against abuses in the Church.[39] The fact that such a course of action was deemed necessary at least permits the hypothesis that there would have been trouble had no action been taken.

At first sight, therefore, there seem to be few good reasons why the Reformation made so little headway in the inner cantons, and, if communalism is seen as the driving force, every reason why it should have. There is no need to rehearse the well-known explanations, in particular the dependence upon mercenary service, which have so often been adduced. All such theories, however pertinent, run the danger of reductionism. It is striking how far recent historians have been at pains to stress that real religious and theological motives were in play. For Blickle these underlay the struggle in the inner cantons to extend secular political autonomy into the ecclesiastical sphere, to 'Christianize' the commune,[40] whilst for Guggisberg the rejection of the Reformation was shaped by ideas and mentalities as well as by obvious material considerations.[41] He cites a highly instructive letter from Bern to Zürich in June 1529, in which the former conceded that the inner cantons wished to remain true to Catholicism 'from real piety' (*uss rechter fromheit*).[42] Since the reality of that piety is now accepted (if imperfectly understood), it becomes even harder to explain why, in *theological* terms, the rural population in certain areas embraced the Reformation at all. In an almost despairing comment Peter Blickle has written: 'Why people wanted to see the Host in 1515 but hear the pure Word of God in 1525—to discover why remains a fascinating because unanswered question.'[43] Yet in posing the question in that form we may perhaps discern the glimmerings of an answer.

---

38 Vasella, 'Bauernkrieg und Reformation', p. 41, n. 102.

39 Guggisberg, 'Problem of "Failure"', p. 193.

40 Blickle, 'Reformation', p. 21. This view is underscored by Rosi Fuhrmann, 'Dorfgemeinde und Pfründstiftung vor der Reformation. Kommunale Selbstbestimmungschancen zwischen Religion und Recht', in Blickle and Kunisch, *Kommunalisierung und Christianisierung*, pp. 77–112, here at p. 105.

41 Guggisberg, 'Problem of "Failure"', p. 201.

42 Ibid., pp. 201–2.

43 Blickle, 'Reformation', p. 24 (my translation).

In a recent article Charles Zika has drawn attention to a significant shift in late medieval pious practices to a marked emphasis on veneration of the Host and demands for its display: 'Emphasis on the host as Christ's sacramental presence focuses on the act of producing the host and the role of those responsible for its production. In other words, the host is decisively located *within the context of priestly power* [my emphasis] and the locally approved church and liturgy.'[44] He concludes that 'the host seemed to assume a religiosity which could be kept within the control of the clergy'[45] (which is why the Church promoted it).

The transference of pious cults to those which required clerical mediation may at last put some flesh on the bare bones of the concept of the 'burdensomeness of late medieval religion'. If dependence upon the clergy for access to apotropaic religion fused with long-standing secular disaffection with the Church, it becomes possible to envisage how outwardly orthodox manifestions of popular religiosity might suddenly capsize into hatred and disavowal. A metaphor may help to make the point clear: when the too tautly drawn bow (a too energetic pious devotion) snaps, it cannot readily be restrung. At last we may discern a link between hostility to *ecclesia* and rejection of *doctrina*—provided that the latter is not understood as the final stage of a gradual estrangement. Whatever pressures for change had built up, their discharge was sudden, violent and above all conscious. Men and women did not stumble into the new faith unaware of the significance of their actions. The soteriological break was not a velleity but a volte-face.

With these thoughts in mind, let us return to the loyalty of the Inner Swiss cantons to the old faith. If their steadfast Catholicism is not held to have resided in a different configuration of pious practices (a most unlikely supposition), then may it not have lain in their very success in communalizing the Church and thereby gaining control of the mediators of salvation? What elsewhere was a potential burden could here become an actual boon. Let us be quite clear: the communalization of the Church had not stripped the Catholic clergy of its necessary power of mediation; but whilst that power

[44] Charles Zika, 'Hosts, Processions and Pilgrimages: Controlling the Sacred in Fifteenth-Century Germany', *Past and Present*, 118 (1988), pp. 25–64; quotation at p. 58.

[45] Ibid., p. 59.

remained, in terms of theology and salvation, absolute, its foundations, in ecclesiastical terms, had been undermined, inasmuch as the clergy's ability to exercise that power had become contingent upon communal-congregational consent. Such an argument, I am perfectly aware, does not get to the heart of what constituted late medieval popular piety or why Catholicism was so persistent in the inner cantons, but it does suggest a way out of the impasse. In this context it is worth recalling the sardonic comment of the Luzern town clerk, Renward Cysat, in the second half of the sixteenth century, that the pious practices of Reformed Protestants barely differed from those of the Catholics: 'Indeed they provide for special masses and divine worship, make the Mass a sacrifice, give pious offerings to the Church, donations, alms . . .; and this they do clandestinely out of fear of punishment by their overlords.'[46] This observation, however jaundiced, throws open once again the issue of just how far the laity's understanding of the essential Reforming message actually ran.

III

Finally I wish to consider the situation in the cities and towns of Alsace. The dominant mood of townsfolk in Alsace on the eve of the Reformation was a pervasive and long-standing anticlericalism, which in the 1520s found active expression in a widespread desire to domesticate the clergy.[47] Yet among the Alsatian free cities (leaving aside the anomalous case of Mulhouse)[48]—notwithstanding their

[46] Renward Cysat, *Collectanea Chronica und denkwürdige Sachen pro Chronica Lucernensi et Helvetiae,* vol. 2, 2: *Observationes contra Haereticos* (Quellen und Forschungen zur Kulturgeschichte von Luzern und der Innerschweiz, 5, 2) (Luzern, 1977), p. 571: *Ja sie bestellen auch sonderbare messen und gottesdienst, thun opfer under der mess, gottsgaben an die kirch, spendt, allmusen*...; *und dieses thun sie verborgenlich auss forcht vor der straf ihrer oberkeit.* Cited in Therese Bruggisser, 'Frömmigkeitspraktiken der einfachen Leute in Katholizismus und Reformiertentum. Beobachtungen des Luzerner Stadtschreibers Renward Cysat (1545–1614)', *Zeitschrift für Historische Forschung,* 17 (1990), p. 15.

[47] See the programmatic title of William S. Stafford's book, *Domesticating the Clergy. The Inception of the Reformation in Strasbourg, 1522–1524* (American Academy for Religion Dissertation Series, 17) (Missoula, MT, 1976).

[48] In Mulhouse anticlerical disturbances followed rather than preceded the introduction of the Reformation. As early as July 1523 an evangelical preaching ordinance had been promulgated (see Blickle, *Gemeindereformation*, pp. 92, 104; idem, *Communal Reformation*, pp. 74–5, 83–4), and the city, protected by its treaty of external association with the Swiss Confederation, thereafter remained in the Reformed

schools, printing presses, and humanist circles—only Strasbourg initially embraced Reform to the point of breaking with Catholicism and even then it did so with some hesitation, back-sliding, and doctrinal uncertainty. Elsewhere, especially in Colmar and Sélestat, the struggle to domesticate the clergy, where it was successful, restored the authority of the city magistrates and preserved the Catholic faith. Obernai is the exception which proves the rule, for there it was the council's reluctance to accede to communal demands to discipline the clergy which drove many citizens into the peasants' arms in 1525; the city might well have turned evangelical, had the peasants' rebellion not been defeated.[49]

In Alsace, once again, ecclesiastical grievances did not lead necessarily to adoption of the Reformation. Colmar illustrates this point exactly. The Thirteen Articles of December 1524 combined a clear commitment to preaching the Word of God with demands to subordinate the clergy to civic jurisdiction.[50] Although they did not go as far as demanding communal election of priests or control of tithing, the evangelical tenor of the Articles is unmistakable.[51] Yet they were to be overshadowed (though not abandoned) by the airing of purely secular grievances against the city's clergy and ecclesiastical foundations in the civic unrest of the following spring,[52] which culminated in what one historian has dubbed a 'revolutionary crisis' during the Peasants' War.[53] Once that danger had passed, peace was restored,

camp, though with some oddities. The history of the Reformation in Mulhouse is bedevilled by a paucity of sources.

[49] Franziska Conrad, *Reformation in der bäuerlichen Gesellschaft. Zur Rezeption reformatorischer Theologie im Elsaß* (Veröffentlichungen des Instituts für Europäische Geschichte Mainz, Abteilung für abendländische Religionsgeschichte, 116) (Stuttgart, 1984), pp. 145–6. See now Tom Scott, 'Südwestdeutsche Städte im Bauernkrieg. Bündnisse zwischen Opportunismus und Solidarität', in Bernhard Kirchgässner and Hans-Peter Becht (eds), *Stadt und Revolution* (Stadt in der Geschichte. Veröffentlichungen des Südwestdeutschen Arbeitskreises für Stadtgeschichtsforschung, 27) (Stuttgart, 2001), p. 25. [Engl. version in this volume.]

[50] Günther Franz (ed.), *Der deutsche Bauernkrieg. Aktenband* (Munich/Berlin, 1935; repr. Darmstadt, 1968), pp. 186–8.

[51] Kaspar von Greyerz, *The Late City Reformation in Germany. The Case of Colmar 1522–1628* (Veröffentlichungen des Instituts für Europäische Geschichte Mainz, Abteilung für abendländische Religionsgeschichte, 98) (Wiesbaden, 1980), p. 62.

[52] Ibid., pp. 53–4. See now also idem, '"Liber ortę seditionis inter nonnullos contra senatum . . ." Die Colmarer Unruhen von Dezember 1524/Januar 1525 aus der Sicht des Stadtschreibers Johannes Hummel', in Heinrich R. Schmidt, André Holenstein, and Andreas Würgler (eds), *Gemeinde, Reformation und Widerstand. Festschrift für Peter Blickle zum 60. Geburtstag* (Tübingen, 1998), pp. 371–89.

[53] Georges Bischoff, 'Colmar et la crise révolutionnaire de 1524–1525', *Annuaire de la Société d'Histoire et d'Archéologie de Colmar*, 1975/76, pp. 43–54.

the council reasserted its authority, and the Catholic religion was left in place, though under magisterial supervision. In Sélestat, a set of Eight Articles, very similar to those of Colmar, had been submitted to the council in October 1524; they had been drafted on the advice of one of the city's Reforming clerics, Paul Phrygio, and also included a demand for free preaching of the Gospel.[54] Although the council sought to buy time by declaring that the other members of the Decapolis should be consulted, the weakness of its position became increasingly apparent by the end of the year, as Reforming agitation led by Phrygio and the rector of the Latin school, Johann Sapidus, gathered pace. To retrieve its position the council entered into a compact with a newly constituted guild committee in April 1525. The enraged citizens demanded the immediate destruction of the convents, but the council was only willing to suspend their judicial immunity and to order an inventory of clerical property.[55] After the city had received (evangelically inspired) advice from Strasbourg on how to proceed, a further guild committee was established on 13th May which pledged itself to deal with the convents according to the Gospel and the Word of God.[56] Yet that decision, far from being a prelude to the introduction of Reformed worship, led to the citizens closing ranks with the council against the peasants, the expulsion of the fractious *evangelical* clerics, and to the consolidation of the old faith. In their subsequent religious mandates after 1525 the councils of both Sélestat and Colmar were clearly inclined to equate evangelical fervour with the threat of social unrest.[57]

An accurate assessment of the remaining Alsatian cities is hampered either by the sparseness of sources (as for Rosheim, Munster, or Turckheim), or because Reforming movements, in whatever guise, were suppressed by outside agency (as was the case in Kaysersberg[58] and Wissembourg),[59] though events in Haguenau seem to have con-

[54] Lina Baillet, 'Deux Villes de la Moyenne Alsace: Sélestat et Colmar, face aux conflits religieux et sociaux', in Alphonse Wollbrett (ed.), *La Guerre des Paysans 1525* (Société d'Histoire et d'Archéologie de Saverne et Environs: Études Alsatiques, supplément 93) (Saverne, 1975), p. 95.

[55] Ibid., p. 99.

[56] Conrad, *Reformation in der bäuerlichen Gesellschaft*, pp. 146–7.

[57] von Greyerz, *Late City Reformation*, p. 67.

[58] Conrad, *Reformation in der bäuerlichen Gesellschaft*, p. 148.

[59] Ibid., p. 141.

formed to the pattern of Colmar and Sélestat.[60] But, in any case, no sharp distinction ought to be drawn, as Franziska Conrad has sought to argue, between the cities of the Decapolis and the situation in the territorial towns of Alsace.[61] Size, social structure, and economic activity mattered far more in determining their response to the new doctrines than any formal constitutional status. *Landstädte* may have been willing, as she contends, to identify with a specifically peasant understanding of the Gospel, whose political-ethical function as the norm or law of human society was expressed in the precepts of the commonweal and good neighbourliness, but in the region of Upper Alsace the more important territorial towns—Belfort, Ensisheim, Altkirch, Ferrette, possibly also Thann—displayed a very limited openness to the new doctrines.[62] At the same time, it is well attested that the countryside in the Sundgau was riddled with hedge-priests, all trumpeting evangelical beliefs.

Between widespread Reforming enthusiasm in the countryside, linked to a vision of Christian liberty from serfdom and feudal oppression, and commitment to the new faith in larger, more complex and sophisticated cities—with higher rates of literacy, better educational provision, and greater civic self-consciousness—there existed a band of middling towns and cities in Alsace which were either suspicious of the new doctrines, or else saw their aspirations satisfied in the rectification of manifest secular ecclesiastical abuses. It is worth noting, moreover, that very similar circumstances prevailed on the right bank of the Rhine, where enthusiasm for Reform occurred throughout the countryside and in the lesser towns of the Breisgau but left the middling towns such as Freiburg, Breisach, or Waldkirch largely untouched. There were, of course, obvious external constraints. The pervasive presence of the Habsburgs in Alsace, as territorial princes and as sovereigns of the imperial bailwick of Alsace with its seat in Haguenau, may well have deterred a more open commitment to Reform. Likewise, the presence of powerful ecclesiastical foundations—one thinks of the abbey of Munster looming over the tiny imperial city in the remote valley of the Fecht, or of the prince-abbacy of

---

[60] von Greyerz, *Late City Reformation*, p. 55 n. 76.

[61] Conrad, *Reformation in der bäuerlichen Gesellschaft*, p. 149.

[62] Claudia Ulbrich, 'Geistliche im Widerstand? Versuch einer Quantifizierung am Beispiel des Sundgaus', in Peter Blickle (ed.), *Zugänge zur bäuerlichen Reformation* (Bauer und Reformation, 1) (Zürich, 1987), pp. 237–65, here at p. 250 and n. 65.

Murbach and Lure as feudal lord of Guebwiller—inhibited the growth of a Reforming movement.[63] Just as with the Inner Swiss cantons, however, such prosaic reasons are unlikely to tell the full story. The mentality of these middling towns and cities, caught between fear of the surrounding peasantry (for instance, the threat of economic competition)[64] and distrust of powerful civic neighbours, such as Basel or Strasbourg (the parallel between Luzern and Zürich comes to mind), requires more investigation than it has yet received.

At all events, whatever variations in the pattern of communal Reformation may have existed between town and country, it is clear that the line of demarcation did not run neatly between urban communes, circumvallated and enfranchised, and village communes, subject to feudal dominion.[65] Rather, it ran between rural-agrarian society as a whole, including peasant burgher towns, on the one hand, and the guild or mercantile communities on the other. Conrad has stressed the peculiar permeability of Alsatian society, in a region of population density and commercialized agriculture, in which the distinction between town and country was blurred;[66] however true that may be, there were also conflicts of interest, culture, and mentality which imprinted themselves from the outset upon the differing pattern of Reform.

IV

In conclusion I wish to make four points.

1. The Communal Reformation is not *explanans* but *explanandum*. It identifies a vital, perhaps the salient, strand in the tangle of motives which drove men and women in town and country to embrace the new doctrines in the early 1520s. It draws attention to late medieval efforts to 'Christianize' the Church, but the links between the secu-

---

[63] This point has also been made by Bob Scribner, 'The Reformation Movements in Germany', in *New Cambridge Modern History*, 2, 2nd edn, ed. G. R. Elton (Cambridge, 1990), p. 84 with reference to the empire as a whole.

[64] See Tom Scott, *Freiburg and the Breisgau. Town-Country Relations in the Age of Reformation and Peasants' War* (Oxford, 1986).

[65] Not least because in Alsace some villages were walled, and others exceeded the smaller towns in population.

[66] Conrad, *Reformation in der bäuerlichen Gesellschaft*, pp. 49 ff.

lar motives behind a prevailing desire to bring the Church back into the community (to domesticate the clergy) and the theological-religious assumptions of the participants are by no means clearly understood, and certainly not adequately explained by invoking the concept of a *Gemeindereformation.* Moreover, the manifestations of a Communal Reformation are so diverse—both Hans-Jürgen Goertz and Bob Scribner speak not of one Reforming movement but of many—that to use the term as an overarching explanatory category may well press it to bear more weight than it can support. There is a danger of the concept buckling and collapsing if treated as explanation rather than description. Certainly, the ideal-typical character accorded to the commune in Blickle's analysis tends to conceal the enormous disparities between various types of commune.[67] Most recently Bob Scribner has put forward yet another model of the urban communal Reformation, namely that of an *amtsstädtische Reformation,* or administrative-town Reformation, which occurred in the subject communes of the territorial principalities, thus complicating the search for single archetypes still further.[68]

2. The Communal Reformation is not an event but a process. As such, it should be subjected to a phase-analysis. But from the examples discussed here there can be no doubt that the successive phases of communal Reforming endeavour contain no teleology. Ecclesiastical grievances, usually of long standing, do not necessarily engender a conscious decision to break with the theological core of Catholic doctrine. Moreover, apparently Reforming (i.e. religious-theological) demands—for preaching of the pure Gospel, or for the Word of God as the template of human behaviour—not only, in some cases, precede, rather than evolve from, secular ecclesiastical demands, they also, in other instances, betoken no fundamental commitment to evangelical religion as propounded by the Reformers themselves. Instead, they are regarded as compatible with the old faith. It is questionable, therefore, whether demands for local or parish control of the clergy and of preaching form the essential bridge or clasp between secular anticlericalism and commitment to the new theology.

Indeed, I am only willing to accept Blickle's bipartite model—originally advanced for peasant society, whereby one set of demands

---

[67] Robert W. Scribner, 'Paradigms of Urban Reform: Gemeindereformation or Erastian Reformation?', in Leif Grane and Kai Hørby (eds), *Die dänische Reformation vor ihrem internationalen Hintergrund* (Göttingen, 1990), pp. 111–28.

[68] Ibid., p. 122.

(for the pure Gospel, communal election of pastors, and decision on true preaching) is somewhat procrusteanly assigned to 'theology', in contrast to another set (calling for clerical residence, a 'cheap' church, and abolition or restriction of church courts), which is assigned to 'ecclesiology'—provided that the 'theological' category is not pre-emptively subsumed under the heading of an (evangelical) *Reformationsverständnis.*[69]

3. The limited development (or even virtual absence) of a fully-fledged Reforming movement should not be deemed a *failure.* A phase-analysis of the Communal Reformation reveals differing levels of evangelical Reforming conviction and suggests different perspectives on what 'a', let alone 'the', Reformation might entail. For some of those who succeeded in bringing the Church back into their community and in domesticating the clergy, that achievement was adequate to, and corresponded with, their aspirations at that time. Behind their endeavour there did indeed lie a communal Reforming commitment, even though it stopped short of a decisive theological break. Those perceptions and aspirations could, of course, change. What was adequate for the Graubünden Leagues in the 1520s no longer sufficed for some valleys in the 1530s.[70] Colmar and Haguenau converted to Protestantism two generations later, under much altered circumstances.[71]

My argument, therefore, is quite different from Rublack's on the south German episcopal residential cities.[72] It differs, too, from von Greyerz' analysis of the 'late city Reformation' in Colmar,[73] as well

---

[69] Peter Blickle, 'Die bäuerliche Reformation und ihre spätmittelalterlichen Grundlagen', in Ferdinand Seibt (ed.), *Gesellschaftsgeschichte. Festschrift für Karl Bosl zum 80. Geburtstag,* 1 (Munich, 1988), pp. 295–304, here at p. 296. English version (with some modifications) as 'Communal Reformation and Peasant Piety: The Peasant Reformation and its Late Medieval Origins', *Central European History,* 20 (1987 [appeared 1990]), pp. 216–28.

[70] The official introduction of the Reformation in Graubünden in 1527 by Johannes Comander must not be equated with actual conversion to Protestant beliefs in the Alpine valleys.

[71] If there was a 'failure' in Colmar in the 1520s, it lay in the terms of the treaty of 27 Sept. 1528 with the bishop of Basel, which rescinded the ecclesiastical innovations of 1525 and restored the *status quo ante.* Von Greyerz, *Late City Reformation,* pp. 65–6.

[72] Hans-Christoph Rublack, *Gescheiterte Reformation. Frühreformatorische und protestantische Bewegungen in süd- und westdeutschen geistlichen Residenzen* (Spätmittelalter und Frühe Neuzeit. Tübinger Beiträge zur Geschichtsforschung, 4) (Stuttgart, 1978). See also idem, 'Reformatorische Bewegungen in Würzburg und Bamberg', in Bernd Moeller (ed.), *Stadt und Kirche im 16. Jahrhundert* (Schriften des Vereins für Reformationsgeschichte, 190) (Gütersloh, 1978), pp. 109–24.

[73] von Greyerz, *Late City Reformation, passim.*

as from Guggisberg's on certain Swiss cantons.[74] It is also distinct from Scribner's well-known analysis of Cologne, for there the communal disturbances of 1525, which demanded the clipping of the clergy's wings and the preaching of the pure Word of God, were actively suppressed by the city council.[75] On the contrary, my argument is concerned not with failure or defeat but with success. By that token it departs fundamentally from Blickle's analysis which affirms that there could be no Communal Reformation without widespread theological acceptance and understanding on the part of the laity. In a sentence, I believe that it was possible to achieve a Communal Reformation without the introduction of evangelical religion.

4. In the subtitle of his book *Gemeindereformation* Blickle describes the people of the sixteenth century as being *auf dem Weg zum Heil* (on the path to salvation). From his own evidence on patterns of communal religiosity in the later Middle Ages, however, it is clear that the people of the fifteenth century also considered themselves to be on the path to salvation. We must at least entertain the possibility, therefore, that some of these people were confident that, with the 'Christianization' of their community, they had indeed achieved the prospect of salvation, without recourse to Reformation theology. If that be the case, then the search for an explanation of what we call 'Reformation' should no longer lead us along the highway of a proud, self-assertive, and altogether stylized late medieval communalism, which presents us with a picture of the commune attaining an almost Buddha-like equilibrium and repose,[76] but down the byways of early modern popular religion. There, if we allow religious anthropology, not political science, to be our guide, we may well be disconcerted by what we find.

---

[74] Guggisberg, 'Problem of "Failure"', *passim*.

[75] R. W. Scribner, 'Why was there no Reformation in Cologne?', *Bulletin of the Institute of Historical Research*, 48 (1975), pp. 217–41; reprinted in idem, *Popular Culture and Popular Movements in Reformation Germany* (London/Ronceverte, WV, 1987), pp. 217–41, esp. 235–6.

[76] Blickle's highly idealized view of the commune ignores, in the case of the Inner Swiss cantons, for instance, the social tensions arising from overpopulation and consequent periodic emigration into mercenary service. It reminds one uncomfortably of the classic studies of village life in the West of Ireland which, in painting a rosy picture of communities subsisting in frugal but benign harmony, entirely concealed the massive overseas emigration from those areas! See for west Clare Conrad M. Arensberg and Solon T. Kimball, *Family and Community in Ireland* (Cambridge, MA, 1940; revised edn 1968), and the devastating critique of their approach in J. J. Lee, *Ireland 1912–1985. Politics and Society* (Cambridge, 1989), p. 651.

CHAPTER THREE

THE 'BUTZENKRIEG': THE ROUFFACH REVOLT OF 1514

Throughout 1513 and 1514 almost all areas of south-west Germany were seized by popular rebellions. The Bundschuh uprising of 1513 in Lehen in the Breisgau, organized by Joß Fritz, soon spilled over onto the left bank of the Rhine, while the so-called Poor Conrad revolt in the duchy of Württemberg the following year engulfed the entire principality. Although they had differing preconditions and goals, these regional rebellions had certain structural features in common—careful preparation, a coherent programme, and a comprehensive legitimation. In the case of the Poor Conrad, the revolt even led to a provisional political victory, enshrined in the Treaty of Tübingen, which duke Ulrich, however, subsequently sabotaged.*

If one compares the unrest in 1514 in the Upper Mundat of Alsace, which belonged to the ecclesiastical territory of the bishops of Strasbourg, with these contemporary regional revolts, it is hard to see that it amounted to anything more than a locally confined and spontaneous reaction against arbitrary seigneurial rule, examples of which can be found in the preceding decades all over Upper Germany—short-lived uprisings without a broader manifesto. Seventy years ago Günther Franz remarked: 'All these small revolts, disturbances, and conflicts . . . are in themselves petty local events, altogether trivial.'[1] Even recent research on the Peasants' War has accorded these so-called local 'pre-revolts' (a misleading term by any standard) under the banner of the 'old law' little importance. One exception is Peter Blickle, who compiled a fundamental survey of

* Archives are cited by the following abbreviations:
AAEB: Archives de l'Ancien Évêché de Bâle, Porrentruy
ADBR: Archives Départementales du Bas-Rhin, Strasbourg
ADHR: Archives Départementales du Haut-Rhin, Colmar
AMRf: Archives Municipales de Rouffach
GLA: Badisches Generallandesarchiv, Karlsruhe
HHSA: Haus-, Hof- und Staatsarchiv, Vienna
SABs: Staatsarchiv des Kantons Basel-Stadt

[1] Günther Franz, *Der deutsche Bauernkrieg*, 1st edn (Munich/Berlin, 1933), p. 32.

late mediaeval peasant revolts in Germany, as well as offering an analytical overview in his *Unruhen in der ständischen Gesellschaft 1300–1800* (*Enzyklopädie Deutscher Geschichte*, vol. 1).[2] But as long as these uprisings are regarded as deficient in revolutionary quality because they lacked an ideological perspective, the path remains blocked to a deeper understanding of the revolts, whose impact cannot simply be read off in positivistic fashion from their subjective demands and goals, but must rather be analyzed pragmatically in terms of their objective unfolding and the historical circumstances which conditioned them. An approach to the revolts which stresses their underlying dynamic allows the participants to step forth as actors on the political stage, who in decisive phases of the revolt are presented with several possible courses of action, only some of which are structurally predetermined, and which therefore offer the rebels real alternatives.[3]

If, according to Franz, the inhabitants of the Upper Mundat sought only 'their old freedom' and 'the old law',[4] the efforts of the authorities throughout the southern Upper Rhine to bring about a settlement as quickly as possible would be well-nigh incomprehensible. For it was not simply the bishop of Strasbourg as the territorial ruler of the Upper Mundat who intervened in the negotiations, but the bishop of Basel, the Outer Austrian government in Ensisheim, as well as the Outer Austrian Estates and the city of Basel. Attempts at arbitration were undertaken both by a commission comprised of four councillors from the Ensisheim government, representatives of the abbey of Murbach, the lords of Hattstatt, and the imperial city of Colmar,[5] and also by the magistracy of Basel. Of itself, this flurry

---

[2] Peter Blickle, 'Bäuerliche Erhebungen im spätmittelalterlichen Reich', *Zeitschrift für Agrargeschichte und Agrarsoziologie*, 27 (1979), pp. 208–31 [Engl. as 'Peasant Revolts in the German Empire in the Late Middle Ages', *Social History*, 4 (1979), pp. 223–39]; idem, *Unruhen in der ständischen Gesellschaft 1300–1800* (*Enzyklopädie Deutscher Geschichte*, 1) (Munich, 1988). On the Poor Conrad revolt see now Andreas Schmauder, *Württemberg im Aufstand. Der Arme Konrad 1514. Ein Beitrag zum bäuerlichen und städtischen Widerstand im Alten Reich und zum Territorialisierungsprozeß im Herzogtum Württemberg an der Wende zur frühen Neuzeit* (Schriften zur südwestdeutschen Landeskunde, 21) (Leinfelden-Echterdingen, 1998).

[3] See most recently the exemplary study by Andreas Suter, *Der schweizerische Bauernkrieg von 1653. Politische Sozialgeschichte—Sozialgeschichte eines politischen Ereignisses* (Frühneuzeit-Forschungen, 3) (Tübingen, 1997).

[4] Franz, *Bauernkrieg*, pp. 31 f.

[5] GLA 79/1644, 2 Aug. 1514.

of activity makes plain how alarmed the authorities were lest local grievances in the Upper Mundat unleash a conflagration throughout the Upper Rhine. Their attitude was clearly shaped by the example of the Lehen Bundschuh and the revolt in Württemberg. But to attribute the rattled behaviour of the Alsatian officials—which was quite out of proportion to the actual grievances and events in the bailiwicks and administrative town of the Upper Mundat—to their experience of severe unrest in other parts of the Upper Rhine obscures the existence of long-standing tensions between the bishop of Strasbourg and Outer Austria over the territorial integrity of the Upper Mundat, tensions which were played out on the backs of the episcopal subjects. Against this background, the Rouffach revolt acquires a rather different political dimension: what counted was less the aims of the rebels themselves than the opportunities which presented themselves for the ominous intervention of third parties.

I *The Course of the Revolt*

At the outset it is necessary to give a brief account of the events in and around Rouffach, since the discovery of new sources has supplemented and refined our knowledge. According to the main source, the Anonymous Chronicle of the Milan Wars from 1507 to 1516, compiled by an unknown Basel chronicler, in the weeks before the feast of St Lawrence (10th August) the common people in the countryside and in the town of Rouffach rose together against the episcopal bailiff and the town council. Thereupon the latter took refuge in the bishop's residence, Isenbourg Castle, above the town, only to be besieged by armed peasants. What directly provoked the uprising was the high-handed behaviour of the magistrate as leader of the council: he was alleged to have molested several female citizens. When their husbands protested, he had threatened them with imprisonment. In addition, he had illegally and exorbitantly raised the episcopal tax and other excises without the bishop's permission. While the bishop, Wilhelm von Honstein, remained at a safe distance, venturing no nearer to Rouffach than Marckolsheim, thirty kilometres away, the city of Basel sent two of its aldermen, the former burgomaster Wilhelm Zeigler and the former guild-captain Hans Trutmann, to Rouffach to settle the dispute, where they were cordially received. The nobility in the Upper Mundat, however, was suspicious of Basel's initiative, fearing that the city, which had been admitted to the Swiss Confederation in 1501, would exploit the opportunity to encourage the common people to join the Confederation.[6]

Although the Basel chronicler was clearly *parti pris*, his account is broadly confirmed—or perhaps simply rehearsed—in a short entry in the Guebwiller Chronicles of Hans Stolz and his continuator Seraphin Dietler. But here the benevolent intervention of Basel is couched in blander terms: 'Thus many lords of the region and many other pious folk intervened, so that the matter was brought to arbitration.'[7] The impression that the revolt was confined merely to the episcopal enclave within Outer Austrian territory must, however, be qualified in the light of correspondence emanating from the Outer Austrian chancery and of the proceedings of the third Estate of Alsace. In their missive to the Upper Austrian government in Innsbruck on 2nd August the Ensisheim authorities enclosed a detailed report on the course of events, according to which 1500 peasants first rallied and then on 29th July entered Rouffach in order to persuade the inhabitants to follow them to a church-ale in a nearby village. Instead, the inhabitants of Rouffach took the opportunity to seize the town gates and keys as a prelude to accusing the council of gross malfeasance and demanding a public reckoning of the accounts. The Ensisheim government was at the same time well aware that the revolt might spread to other lordships (which is why it had despatched four councillors to Rouffach to act as intermediaries), and was determined 'that we, unless our Lord of Strasbourg desires otherwise, should rally to his Grace with subjects of his Imperial Majesty under our authority, so far as lies within our power, to punish the peasants and bring them to obedience, as an example to other subjects to desist from such enterprises'.[8] The self-confident tone was intended

[6] *Basler Chroniken*, 6, ed. August Bernoulli (Leipzig, 1902), pp. 63 f. In the town of Rouffach alone five nobles had residences.

[7] Johan von Schlumberger (ed.), *Die Gebweiler Chronik des Dominikaners Fr. Seraphin Dietler* (Guebwiller, 1898), p. 98: *Also legten sich vill herren des landts, vndt sonst vill frome leith darein, das die sach also vergetädiget wurde.* Up to 1545 Dietler's material is taken from Hans Stolz's Chronicle. Ibid., Introduction, p. xxix.

[8] HHSA, Maximiliana 32/1, fo. 23r–v, here fo. 24r–v: *das wir, so es anders vnser herr von Straburg* [!] *begert, mit Kaÿ. Mt. Vndtertanen in vnnsers regiments verwaltung, souil das wir an den gehaben mugen, sein gnaden zueziehen vnd die pawrn mit der tat straffen vnd zugehorsame bringen wellen, andern vndtertanen zü ainem exempel sich vor solcher . . . handlung . . . zuerhueten.*

to convince the Innsbruck government of the Ensisheim administration's competence and alertness—the former usually regarded the latter as country cousins and hopeless bunglers. But four weeks later, long after the Rouffach revolt had ended in defeat, the Outer Austrian Estates in Alsace were warning of further unrest, 'for they are credibly informed that in some administrative districts of the Sundgau [i.e. on Austrian territory] 1500 men were shortly to rally at a church-ale, including many from the [Upper] Mundat'.[9] Although the figure of 1500 men echoes the number given for those who were to assemble in the Upper Mundat at the end of July at a church-ale, the members of the third Estate were close enough to the common man to be reliably informed about such stirrings, so that it may indeed be the case that a fresh subversive conspiracy was afoot.

We are also informed about events in the Upper Mundat from the negotiations between the episcopal councillors and the rebellious communes. At the end of his comprehensive report detailing the communes' articles of grievance the clerk includes a description of events from the viewpoint of the Rouffachers themselves, clearly intended as exculpation. Six weeks previously, they claimed, the bailiff, magistrate, and council had begun to undertake defensive works at the town walls for no very obvious reason, as if the town were about to be attacked. When the commons raised the matter, the council left them none the wiser. The bailiff, however, had forbidden the inhabitants to visit to the church-ale at 'Irßwiler' (Orschwihr by Guebwiller).[10] It was then that the officials and councillors had removed themselves to Isenbourg Castle. In their absence the commons took it upon themselves to be responsible for guard-duty and weapons, affirming that 'their intention was none other than to maintain the honour of the town, until my Grace's arrival and instructions'.[11]

[9] ADHR, 1 C 7, 164: *diewill sy dann gloublich annlanngt, das inn ettlichenn ammpterenn Sungkews inn kurtzem vff einer kirchwyhy by dem funffzehennhunndert mannen, deßglich ettlich vß der Montat zu den selbigenn khommen solltend.*

[10] Until the middle of the 16th century St Martin's was the parish church of Orschwihr. J. M. B. Clauss (ed.), *Historisch-topographisches Wörterbuch des Elsaß* (Saverne, 1895–1914), p. 827. Neither his saint's day (11 Nov.) nor his translation (4 July) fit the narrative of events well, unless one supposes that the stirrings of discontent in the Upper Mundat had already begun in late June or early July, which is entirely possible.

[11] Günther Franz (ed.), *Der deutsche Bauernkrieg. Aktenband*, 2nd edn (Darmstadt, 1968), pp. 124 f., following ADBR, 1 G 122/3, fo. 37v–38r: *Und sey ir furnemen nit anders gewest, dann die stat also in eren zu halten, biß uf m. g. h. zukunft und wytern bescheid.*

It is improbable that the Rouffachers simply invented the authorities' defensive measures and the prohibition on visiting the church-ale at Orschwihr. Rather, it is likely that rumours had reached the episcopal bailiff that the commons from various lordships were bent upon rallying at Orschwihr, which lay within the bishop of Strasbourg's territory. Therefore the unrest seems hardly to have been restricted to the Upper Mundat. Whether the intention was to mount a general uprising remains entirely in the dark, but there are two clues which point in this direction. In its report to Freiburg im Breisgau at the beginning of August on the progress of the arbitration talks, the Outer Austrian government complained that the negotiators 'can come to no equitable settlement with the rebels', since the latter insisted upon submitting articles which were intolerable to any constituted authority.[12] This statement can hardly be squared with the articles of grievance of the individual communes, which have survived in good number, since they contain neither general demands nor ideological slogans. Moreover, a stipendiary priest in Rouffach seems to have given encouragement to the rebels, since he was subsequently required to account for his actions before the bishop of Basel, Christoph von Utenheim. The latter reported to his colleague in Strasbourg on 11th August that he 'had had discussions concerning his priest in Rouffach, with a report of the deeds which the same priest had committed in the unrest and uprising, . . . whereupon he had brought the priest to stand question-and-answer, who was ready to account for himself'.[13] These sparse hints should not be overinterpreted, but they make plain that the articles of grievance, to which we shall now turn, must be set in a wider context.

II *The Grievances of Town and Country in the Upper Mundat*

The grievances of the town of Rouffach and the communes of the Upper Mundat are contained in a folder which was discovered and printed by Günther Franz. The folio sequence of the folder, however, does not correspond to the order of the printed articles; more-

---

[12] GLA 79/1644, 2 Aug. 1514: *dheyn billicheit by den vffrurigen erlangen mogen . . .*

[13] AAEB, Missiven 332, fo. 334r–v: *sins lutpriesters halb zu Ruffach red gehalten, und in darby der handlung, so sich der selb lutpriester der uffruwen und empörung geprucht, . . . ouch uff solichs den lutpriester zu red gestalt, der sich zuuerantworten begert.*

over, the response of the bailiff, magistrate, and council to the grievances of the Rouffach commons was not included.[14] The grievances of the Rouffach commons and those of the 'common countryside' (*gemeine Landschaft*), including the complaints of individual villages, were submitted separately, but display many common features. In Rouffach complaints were voiced over the arbitrary conduct of the civic administration, as well as over its excessive cost, unlawful imprisonment without right of appeal, and over restrictions on communal usufructs. These complaints can all be found—with the usual variations in detail—in the grievances of the individual rural communes, above all in the articles of the commune of Soultz, which also had an urban charter. But in addition there were tensions between the subordinate communes and the Rouffach council, which were expressed in the general grievances of the 'common countryside'. Here the authoritarian attitude of the magistrate and council towards the countryside was denounced. The latter had been refused inspection of its custumals; Rouffach's share of the territorial tax at the annual apportionment had been set or suspended without prior consultation; and in contentious pleas for debt the cases had been referred to the Rouffach town court rather than to the bishop's territorial court, as was the custom in appeals over inheritance and property disputes. The arrogant style of rule on the part of the town council was therefore not only evident in its dealings with its own commons but with the rural communes beyond the town gates as well. This created the essential preconditions for common cause between the urban and rural rebels against the oligarchical urban government, which ran the risk of degenerating to nothing more than the executive arm of the episcopal bailiff.

Though not revealed in the articles themselves, this tendency can be discerned well before 1514. In his sketch of the history of Rouffach Theobald Walter pointed out: *la véritable cause en était l'impôt sur le pain, la viande, le bois, le vin, le sel etc., établi en 1498 déjà, mais relevé depuis quelque temps ainsi que l'augmentation du soi-distant mauvais denier et surtout la suppression de la plupart des poëles de tribus (en 1511) que surexcitèrent les masses.*[15] This view, advanced in 1920 by a local historian of repute, can no longer be verified against the sources that survive

[14] ADBR, 1 G 122/3, fo. 27v–30v.

[15] Theobald Walter, *Abrégé de l'histoire de la ville de Rouffach* (Colmar, 1920), p. 19.

today. But it is indirectly borne out in the Rouffach articles, which complain at the exclusion of the guildmasters from important decisions, especially from the annual accounting. Whether a majority of the guilds had in fact already been suspended in 1511 appears questionable, since the final article talks of a curfew for all guild members after 10 pm in the guild parlour. The penultimate article also complains that grievances presented earlier on behalf of the commons as a whole had still not been addressed. Instead, the bailiff had become even harsher in his dealings with the inhabitants. During the original arbitration the bishop had even promised to relieve the magistrate of his office; this presumably refers to the long-serving Erhard Schneeberger, who was already installed in 1502 and, despite his humiliating flight in 1514, still held office in 1516.[16]

In their response, the bailiff, magistrate, and council did not give an inch, strikingly presenting themselves as a closed leadership clique. No differences of interest are discernible between the episcopal bailiff on the one hand and the magistrate and councillors on the other. In a brief addendum the bailiff merely reiterated his loyalty to the bishop, at whose behest he had always acted.[17] This closing of ranks makes it hard to pin down the exact nature of the Rouffach revolt. Against whom was it directed—against the ruling council of Rouffach itself or against the episcopal administration of the Upper Mundat altogether? The rebels had every interest in denouncing the shortcomings of the civic administration, rather than exposing themselves as perjured subjects of the bishop. The articles of the individual rural communes, by contrast, were largely concerned with the transgressions of the episcopal bailiff; only the grievances of the 'common countryside' and of the Soultzmatt valley are directed against the Rouffach council.[18] To assume a straightforward antagonism between rural subjects and episcopal officials would none the less be wide of the mark. In some communes it was the village lord who was the target of peasant resentment. Junker Claus von Schauenburg in Jungholtz Castle, for instance, was accused of various infringements of the law: in Soultz he had blocked access to streams within the

[16] ADBR, 1 G 122/3, fo. 3v–4v; Franz, *Aktenband*, pp. 115, 117. On Schneeberger see Theobald Walter, 'Der alte Adel der Stadt Rufach', *Jahrbuch für Geschichte, Sprache und Literatur Elsaß-Lothringens*, 16 (1900), p. 66.

[17] ADBR, 1 G 122/3, fo. 27v–30v, 31r.

[18] Ibid., fo. 8r–9v, 24r–25r; Franz, *Aktenband*, pp. 117 ff., 122.

civic lands; in Wunheim he had committed illegal acts against several citizens; and in Rimbachzell he had denied access to a common pasture and its drove-road. Again, Junker Hans Wilhelm Waldner of Hartmannsweiler was arraigned for failing to observe a deed of arbitration between himself and the villagers, handed down by the bishop of Strasbourg.[19] Acts of lordly high-handedness do not to make up the bulk of the grievances, but they do indicate that what was at stake in the Upper Mundat was on occasion a triangular relationship, in which the peasants might not necessarily regard the bishop as territorial lord and potential protector with hostility.

How the territorial nobles of the Upper Mundat in their capacity as feudal lords treated the peasants of the bishop of Strasbourg's territory is a question which has been neglected in existing scholarship. Hans Wilhelm Waldner presumably belonged to the Waldner von Freundstein dynasty, which had estates in Upper Alsace and whose members were vassals both of the Habsburgs and of the bishops of Strasbourg. Nothing more is known about him. But the researches of Georges Bischoff have allowed Claus von Schauenburg to step out of the shadows. Like the Waldner, he held fiefs from Austria and from the bishopric of Strasbourg which lay on the boundary between the Upper Mundat and Outer Austria. His seat, Jungholtz Castle, was of strategic importance, since it was situated on the southern edge of the Upper Mundat above the little town of Soultz, which in any case was an exclave of the Upper Mundat, separated from the rest of the territory around Rouffach by a narrow strip of Outer Austrian land. Claus von Schauenburg's father, Reinhard, who was already a vassal of the bishop, had been invested with Jungholtz Castle in 1482 by archduke Sigismund of Tirol. Austria succeeded thereby in gaining control of one of the best-fortified castles of Upper Alsace;[20] that, in turn, provides the broader political context within which the events in the Upper Mundat in 1514 must be analyzed.

---

[19] ADBR, 1 G 122/3, fo. 18r–20r, 21r, 22v, 33v–34v; Franz, *Aktenband*, pp. 120 f., 124.

[20] Georges Bischoff, 'La guerre du Haut-Mundat. Un épisode oublié de l'histoire d'Alsace', *Annuaire de la Société d'Histoire des Régions de Thann-Guebwiller*, 13 (1979–80), pp. 83 f.

III *Austria's Threat to the Upper Mundat*

Seventeen years before the Rouffach revolt a passage-of-arms had occurred in the Upper Mundat, provoked by Claus von Schauenburg's acts of violence. In the summer of 1497 Claus von Schauenburg and his varlets physically assaulted a citizen of Soultz together with his day-labourer on the former's field, which he held in tenancy from the prior of Thierenbach. Von Schauenburg, however, maintained that the field lay within the jurisdiction (*Zwing und Bann*) of Jungholtz Castle. Having thrown the Soultz citizen into the dungeon at Jungholtz Castle, von Schauenburg 'together with some varlets on several occasions criminally approached the gates of Soultz under arms, heaping upon the citizens arrogant threats and provocations'.[21] Thereupon on 8th September several citizens of Soultz took revenge upon von Schauenburg and his retinue by assaulting them during divine worship at Thierenbach, killing one varlet and wounding von Schauenburg himself, who was seized and dragged off to Isenbourg Castle in Rouffach in captivity. The Outer Austrian governor in Ensisheim, Kaspar von Mörsberg, who had already intervened in the affair at the beginning of September by proposing arbitration through the Lower Union, immediately demanded his release, since he had been taken by force and without permission through Outer Austrian sovereign territory on his passage from Soultz to Rouffach. This demand was soon revealed as a pretext for the incursion of Outer Austrian troops into the Upper Mundat.[22]

When his request was refused, von Mörsberg declared a feud upon the bishop of Strasbourg and issued a call to arms. The campaign that ensued was directed first against Soultz, which surrendered without much resistance, and then Hartmannsweiler, Wunheim, and Jungholtz Castle, before turning northwards. Only the marshalling of a Palatine army to come to the rescue of the bishop of Strasbourg, Albrecht of Bavaria, a Wittelsbach cousin of the elector Palatine, prevented a prolonged siege of Rouffach by Austrian troops, which was abandoned after two days. Members of the Lower Union were in fact able to bring about a provisional truce in Colmar, but the

---

[21] Ibid., p. 78 n. 5, following ADHR, 3 G 58: *mitsampt ettlichen knechten mit gewerter hanndt zu mermalen fur das thor gen Sultz . . . frevenlich genehert, den burger daselbs manigvaltig üppig trowort unnd reitzung zugefugt.*

[22] Bischoff, 'Guerre du Haut-Mundat', pp. 79 f.

animosities continued, neither side trusting in the other's good faith, until the conflict was laid before the imperial Diet in Freiburg im Breisgau in November 1497. But despite a resolution being reached, Soultz was not relieved until the following summer.[23]

As Bischoff correctly observed, the governor Kaspar von Mörsberg could have achieved his goal by other means, not least by negotiations. His decision to resolve the dispute by force of arms—a unique occurrence in the relations between Outer Austria and its neighbours in the years before and after 1500—must therefore have been driven by deeper motives. His action can only be understood in the light of emperor Maximilian's efforts in the early 1490s to revive the Lower Union, which had been formed as a defensive or protective alliance against Burgundy's penetration of the Upper Rhine, as an instrument of Habsburg dynastic politics in the west after the original treaty had expired in 1484.[24] Von Mörsberg, whose ancestors had carved out careers in Austrian service, now planned to give this vision of Habsburg hegemony concrete expression by proposing the construction of a unified Austrian territory on the Upper Rhine. To achieve this goal required the extinction of all sovereign lordships in an area which was stamped by advanced territorial fragmentation, or else their subordination to Austrian overlordship and therewith integration into a new 'kingdom', as he put it.[25]

Although von Mörsberg's blueprint never became reality, the incursion into the Upper Mundat represented a reckless attempt to make capital out of confused feudal loyalties in order to abet Outer Austrian expansion. At least from the time of archduke Sigismund's infeudation in 1482 the boundaries of the Jungholtz jurisdiction over against the land of the town of Soultz were hazily defined;[26] a further complication resulted from Reinhard von Schauenburg's already holding estates in feoff from the bishop of Strasbourg. Both the double

---

[23] Ibid., pp. 80–3.

[24] See Thomas A. Brady, Jr, *Turning Swiss. Cities and Empire 1450–1550* (Cambridge, 1985), pp. 49 ff.

[25] Dieter Mertens, 'Reich und Elsaß zur Zeit Maximilians I. Untersuchungen zur Ideen- und Landesgeschichte im Südwesten des Reichs am Ausgang des Mittelalters' (Diss. habil. Freiburg im Breisgau, 1977), pp. 234 f.

[26] Before Sigismund's enfeoffment boundary disputes had occurred between the then owner of Jungholtz Castle, Wersich Bock von Stauffenberg, and the commune of Soultz, which were only finally settled by treaty in 1493. Bischoff, 'Guerre du Haut-Mundat', p. 84.

vassality of the von Schauenburg and the disputed demarcation between the two jurisdictions presented sufficient opportunity for the Ensisheim governor to intervene, particularly since the nobles of the Upper Mundat were already inclined towards Austria on account of their family and financial connections. The provisional agreement in September 1497 in Colmar reveals this blurring of interests very clearly, since its terms provided for a restitution of the fiefs of the episcopal vassals that had been alienated to Austria.[27]

Although von Mörsberg must be regarded beyond question as the aggressor in an incident which verged on warfare, he was acting in perpetual fear of a Confederate incursion in the Sundgau from the south as well as against the background of the current threat to the abbey and imperial city of Wissembourg from the Palatinate in the north—a foretaste of the rivalry between Habsburg and Wittelsbach which discharged itself in the Bavarian War of Succession in 1504. It is at all events striking that von Mörsberg was not reprimanded by Maximilian for his resort to force. Rather, he remained in office until he took over in 1504 the administration of the imperial bailiwick of Haguenau, which had just been reclaimed from the Palatinate.[28]

The treaty which was finally concluded at the imperial Diet in Freiburg in the summer of 1498 accorded the Habsburgs important military rights in the Upper Mundat: safe-conduct for Austrian troops marching through the territory, military support in an emergency, and the right of access (*Öffnungsrecht*) at Soultz, that is, unfettered admission to the town. Claus von Schauenburg, moreover, was restored to his fiefs.[29] But for the subjects of the Upper Mundat the treaty could on no account be deemed a satisfactory solution to the conflict, since it embraced the risks inevitably attached to the passage of troops, above all the danger that Austrian soldiers or indeed mercenaries would hold the population to ransom on their way through. Nor was an end put to the local wrangles between von Schauenburg and the burghers of Soultz over their respective jurisdictions. It is therefore no surprise that the hostilities continued. Between 1501 and 1507 they were the subject of an exhaustive

---

[27] Ibid., pp. 83 ff.

[28] Ibid., pp. 83 f.; Mertens, 'Reich und Elsaß', p. 165.

[29] Bischoff, 'Guerre du Haut-Mundat', p. 88. Claus von Schauenburg died in 1540. See P. E. Lehr (ed.), *L'Alsace noble, suivie de la Livre d'Or du patriciat de Strasbourg*, 3 (Paris, 1870), p. 115.

enquiry, which likewise failed to achieve a resolution, since the points of contention reappear undiminished in the rebels' articles of grievance in 1514.[30]

It is beyond doubt, therefore, that the population of the bailiwick of Soultz felt a permanent sense of legal insecurity. But that sense of insecurity was not confined to the southern exclave of the Upper Mundat, both because of the concessions which had been made to Austria, and also because Maximilian was still toying with the idea of incorporating the Upper Mundat into Outer Austrian Upper Alsace. Maximilian used his visit to the pilgrimage church of St Valentine in Rouffach in March 1511 as a pretext to put out feelers about exchanging territory between lands on the left and right banks of the Rhine. The territorial bailiwick of the Ortenau with its imperial cities Offenburg, Gengenbach, and Zell, he intimated, might be swapped for the Upper Mundat. Despite the bait dangled before the bishop—the prospect of taking ownership of three imperial cities—the balance of advantage would have lain decisively with Maximilian, who at a stroke would have removed a considerable territorial irritant within Outer Austria and simultaneously have gained an agriculturally and viticulturally rich landscape. The bishop of Strasbourg understandably demurred.[31]

The fact that the 1514 articles contained no grievances about a possible Austrian intervention in the Upper Mundat, let alone its annexation, should not be misconstrued to imply that Wilhelm von Honstein as Albrecht of Bavaria's successor in the see of Strasbourg had dispelled such fears by his rejection of Maximilian's overture. The resentment of feudal lords who irresponsibly put their estates at risk or, as so often in Alsace, mortgaged them, was ingrained in the common man, as the protests of subjects in the Outer Austrian lordship of Ferrette against their mortgagee lords, the Reich von Reichenstein, in these same years make perfectly clear.[32] What confidence could the subjects of the Upper Mundat have that the bishop as their territorial ruler would always defend them against claims from outsiders? After all, he had been unable to prevail against

[30] Bischoff, 'Guerre du Haut-Mundat', p. 88.

[31] Walter, *Abrégé*, p. 18.

[32] See Georges Bischoff, 'Les grèves anti-seigneuriales de Ferrette. Les habitants d'un baillage du Sundgau et leur seigneur au début du XVIe siècle', *Revue d'Alsace*, 105 (1979), pp. 35–52.

Claus von Schauenburg. His cunctatory behaviour during the revolt itself—following the course of events from a safe distance in Marckolsheim—does not stand as eloquent testimony of courageous decisiveness. We must therefore enquire whether his subjects may subliminally have been hoping to find other sources of legitimation.

IV *The Ideological Context of the Revolt*

In a recent essay on the programmes of the Bundschuh conspiracies on the Upper Rhine under the leadership of Joß Fritz, Gunter Zimmermann has sought to demonstrate that the distinction made by Günther Franz for revolts before the Peasants' War between those which embraced the 'old' or the 'godly' law cannot be sustained. According to Zimmermann, all uprisings of the common man before 1524/25 aimed at restoring the old social order (which was ordained, of course, by God). The demand for 'godly law' in Joß Fritz's Bundschuh revolts is, on closer inspection, a chimera. The slogans which occasionally seem to point in this direction were not part of a revolutionary undercurrent among the common people, stretching back to Hus and Wyclif, but simply indicated that the participants regarded their undertaking as pleasing to God and in accordance with Scripture. The connection between grievances under the old law at feudal oppression and an overarching legitimating principle derived from the Gospel, containing explosive revolutionary potential, only came to pass in the Peasants' War with the invocation of Reforming doctrines. The Bundschuh conspiracies on the Upper Rhine instead took as their model the republican freedom of the Swiss.[33]

Without necessarily accepting Zimmermann's argument in full, one can acknowledge that appeals to the Confederation or the possibility of allying with the Swiss run like a red thread through the statements and confessions of the Bundschuh participants. The glorious victory of the Confederates over Maximilian's imperial army in the Swiss War of 1499 had undoubtedly stiffened the resolve of the common man to 'turn Swiss' (in Tom Brady's phrase) when the opportunity arose.[34] This aspiration was by no means confined to the

[33] Gunter Zimmermann, 'Die Grundgedanken der Bundschuhverschwörungen des Joß Fritz', *Zeitschrift für die Geschichte des Oberrheins,* 142 (1994), pp. 142, 149, 154 f.

[34] Brady, *Turning Swiss, passim.*

frontier area below Basel, which had the closest political and economic links to the Swiss Confederation, but extended into the north of Lower Alsace, as the report of the participant Klaus Fleckenstein from Riedseltz reveals, according to which the conspirators around Haguenau and Wissembourg in 1517 intended to send emissaries to the Swiss with a request for counsel and support.[35] It is unlikely that there was any thought of annexing lordships on the Upper Rhine to the Confederation: the territorial integrity of the region was to remain intact. But it is probable that the conspirators had a vision of transforming existing lordships into a confederation on a corporative basis without secular or ecclesiastical overlords.[36]

There is no doubt that in planning the Lehen Bundschuh of 1513 in the Breisgau Joß Fritz had sought contacts in Alsace. Whether his clandestine recruitment had gained followers in the Upper Mundat is impossible to tell from the scanty sources. Nothing in the language of the 1514 grievances points in that direction but the course of the arbitration talks displays some suggestive oddities. As already noted, the initial efforts of the negotiators from neighbouring lordships and towns came to naught as a result of the rebels having presented intolerable demands. The Ensisheim government, which had sent four of its councillors to the talks, was so concerned at the situation that it sent a detailed report to its superiors in Innsbruck, warning of the danger of the revolt spilling over into Outer Austrian territory.[37] The Upper Austrian councillors by no means regarded the affair as a bagatelle, for they instructed Ensisheim to make further investigations.[38] To the imperial chancellor Zyprian von Serntein they observed that it might be difficult to keep the Outer Austrian subjects under control if they were ordered to help suppress the revolt.[39]

One can, of course, regard this excitable attitude as a natural reaction to the previous Bundschuh conspiracy and to the Poor Conrad in Württemberg, rather than as a correct assessment of the

[35] Zimmermann, 'Grundgedanken', p. 155, following Albert Rosenkranz (ed.), *Der Bundschuh. Die Erhebungen des südwestdeutschen Bauernstandes in den Jahren 1493–1517*, 2: *Quellen* (Schriften des Wissenschaftlichen Instituts der Elsaß-Lothringer im Reich, 12, 2) (Heidelberg, 1927), p. 308.

[36] Zimmermann, 'Grundgedanken', p. 153.

[37] HHSA, Maximiliana 32/1, fo. 23r–24v, 2 Aug. 1514.

[38] Ibid., fo. 159r–v, 16 Aug. 1514.

[39] Ibid., fo. 160r, 16 Aug. 1514.

subjective intentions of the Rouffach rebels. But it can just as easily be explained by the failure of the first round of negotiations, which was seemingly broken off abruptly, since Ensisheim could report the depressing outcome to Freiburg as early as 2nd August, even though the revolt had only begun on 29th July. Moreover, some time elapsed before a second round under Basel's supervision could be arranged, for the entry in the Basel weekly expenditure ledger of the expenses of its former burgomaster and former guild-captain is only dated Saturday after St Lawrence (12th August).[40] This arbitration, as we have seen, elicited resistance on the part of the Upper Mundat nobility, who scented the danger of their subjects 'turning Swiss'. The prehistory of the Rouffach rising shows that the nobles had every reason to be concerned, since the basis of their social and legal superiority—the guarantee of protection in return for their subjects' tribute—had been jeopardized by their willingness on occasion to abandon their vassal allegiance to the bishop in favour of more advantageous ties to Austria, thereby treating their lordships as a commodity to be bought or sold.

It becomes difficult, therefore, to interpret the revolt as a movement directed exclusively against the oligarchical magistracy of Rouffach or against the episcopal bailiff. The slippery feudal loyalties of the territorial nobility of the Upper Mundat must also be included in the equation. Perhaps the Outer Austrian government did not go so wrong in assuming that the revolt could burst the boundaries of the episcopal enclave. The decision to call upon Basel to mediate cannot have been an easy one for the bishop, and certainly would not have been greeted with approbation in Ensisheim. But in contrast to the first round of negotiations, the Basel councillors do seem to have succeeded in reaching an amicable resolution of the conflict, since after the end of August 1514 we hear of no further incidents in the Upper Mundat, apart from rumours circulating at the Alsace Diet. How this resolution was achieved we do not know. Writing to the cathedral chapter on 29th August, which had thanked him for information on the course of the Poor Conrad revolt, Wilhelm von Honstein merely admitted that an uprising had taken place in the Upper Mundat, and that he was now in the process of punishing the rebels and hunting for further suspects in

[40] SABs, Finanz G 13, 225.

other administrative districts of the bishopric.[41] Had the terms of the settlement precluded a more energetic pursuit of the rebels?

These reflections should on no account be reduced to a hypothesis that the rebels in the Upper Mundat were seeking a peasant republic on the Swiss model; they are simply intended to demonstrate the framework within which the rebels acted and what perspectives could have been opened to them. We should in any case recall that a love of Swiss freedom in principle cannot necessarily be assumed on the part of the common man on the Upper Rhine. In this regard, the petition of the Ferrette subjects of the mortgagee lords Jakob and Marx Reich von Reichenstein to Maximilian in 1513 deserves to be cited, in which they reminded the emperor in the light of the Swiss raids in recent wars

> that the Baselers and other Swiss have plundered us severely, and even the Solothurners, our neighbours; the Baselers on one side, and the inhabitants of the bishopric of Basel, who joined the Swiss campaigns, on the other, and those of Mulhouse as a third group who are our immediate neighbours, so that we cannot raise our heads without risk, and sit here as if trussed up in a sack.[42]

Georges Bischoff accordingly speaks of *une antipathie des habitants du baillage pour les dangereux voisins*,[43] but plays down the context, which shows the subjects hell-bent on proclaiming their loyalty to Maximilian as their territorial ruler.

Within the Swiss Confederation, however, the horizontal configuration of lordship—the balance between urban and peasant interests—permitted more harmonious forms of conflict resolution. When Solothurn's rural territory was seized by considerable unrest in 1513 on account of servile taxes and *corvées*, Bern, Basel, Fribourg, and Biel offered their services as intermediaries out of good neighbourliness. The deed of arbitration which they sealed in 1514 accorded the rural subjects palpable concessions which amounted to a rescission

---

[41] Jean Rott (ed.), 'Documents inédits sur le "Bundschuh" et la Guerre des Paysans en Alsace', *Revue d'Alsace*, 105 (1979), p. 63.

[42] Franz, *Aktenband*, p. 40: *daz die von Basel und ander Schweitzer vast nach uns gehaust, auch die von Solothurn, unser anstößer, die von Basel zu ainer seitn und ains bischofs von Basel gebiet, so mit den Schweitzern reysen, zu der andern seiten und die von Mülhausen zu dem dritten unser allernegst nachpaurn seind, deshalb wir nit fröhlich die höpter daran aufheben, sitzen, als ob wir in ainem sack verstrickt.*

[43] Bischoff, 'Grèves anti-seigneuriales', p. 42.

of serfdom itself.[44] As the anonymous Basel chronicler at the end of his account pithily remarked: 'Who seeks at first too much afterwards commonly receives too little. So the matter was laid to rest; those in the town [Solothurn] had to bite the bullet, and then everyone went home.'[45] Basel's mediation in the Rouffach revolt would never have been able to reach a similar result on account of the quite different structure of lordship.

V *'Butzenkrieg' and Peasants' War*

The Peasants' War gave rise to fresh discord in Rouffach, and in the articles of grievance drawn up by the commons the influence of Reforming doctrines is manifest. The clergy should be answerable before the town court in civil matters and give up its judicial immunities. Above all, it was the commons' 'desire that a learned pastor be here appointed to assure and instruct the common folk to the salvation of our souls and that the same should receive his proper competency'.[46] If we compare these demands with the foundation deed for a brotherhood of tailors, weavers, bathhouse-keepers, clothiers, and other craftsmen of May 1520, whose wording is couched in the language of conventional late mediaeval Catholic lay piety,[47] we can see that Reforming precepts had only recently made headway in Rouffach. Yet the ideological legitimation for a general campaign of liberation of the common man which they might have provided did not lead in Rouffach's case to an alliance with the rural population of the Upper Mundat, as had occurred in 1514. Apart from a few hot-headed apprentices who rushed to join the peasants' camp at Issenheim, the town's inhabitants laid their griev-

---

[44] Franz, *Aktenband*, pp. 70 f.

[45] *Basler Chroniken*, 6, p. 63: *Wenn man aber ze vil wil, wird eim hindernach gern zu wenig. Also wart die sach gestillet, musten die in der stat die nusz bissen, fur yederman wider heym.*

[46] Theobald Walter (ed.), *Urkundenbuch der Pfarrei Rufach nebst einem Anhange: Kurze Pfarrchronik von Westhalten* (Rouffach, 1900), pp. 126 f. (no. 120): *beger, das man ein gelerten Pfarrer allhie verordne, dadurch das gemein volk zu vnser selen heil gewißt und gelert werde vnd das derselb auch sein zimliche Narung hab.*

[47] Ibid., pp. 120–4 (no. 118). The brotherhood was founded amongst other reasons in order to avoid *die pin deß gruselichen fegfüres,* and venerated the *Jüngkfrowe Marie, die dann ein sonder gnadherwerberin ist aller sünder.* Ibid., p. 120.

ances against the council and the clergy before a representative of the bishop in the guild parlour 'zum Bürgelen' (one of the two parlours of the winegrowers' guild). As the Alsatian peasant army drew near, the town gates were shut and a strengthened watch posted on the town walls. All offers of negotiation by the rebellious peasants were turned down.[48]

From the revolt of 1514 both the commons and the town government of Rouffach had clearly learned lessons. Internal differences were resolved by mutual agreement; by contrast, a pact with the peasants would have raised the spectre of a general rebellion with a corresponding destabilization of episcopal rule in the Upper Mundat and would thereby have vitiated any chance of a settlement confined to the town itself. Rouffach, indeed, was not the only Alsatian small town that recoiled from fraternizing with the rebellious peasants in 1525.[49]

If grievances under the 'old law' in 1514 had been no hindrance to town and country making common cause against their lords (albeit that we can only speculate about echoes of 'Swiss freedom' in the Upper Mundat), the appeal to 'godly law' as Reforming doctrines spread to Rouffach did not ineluctably lead to a comprehensive rising based on general principles. The experience of 1514 conditioned the stance of 1525.

The revolt in and around Rouffach, the so-called 'Butzenkrieg', was by no means a trivial affair, since it lived on in popular memory.[50] When the council and commons in 1544 came to blows with the episcopal bailiff, Wilhelm Böcklin von Böcklinsau, it was the slogan of the 'Butzenkrieg' that was bandied about, not the Peasants' War, during which, after all, the town had remained calm. In its minute-book the council rejected the bailiff's defamation in the following terms:

---

[48] Idem, *Abrégé*, p. 19.

[49] Tom Scott, 'The Communal Reformation between Town and Country', in Hans R. Guggisberg and Gottfried G. Krodel (eds), *Die Reformation in Deutschland und Europa. Interpretationen und Debatten* (*Archiv für Reformationsgeschichte*, Sonderband) (Gütersloh, 1993), p. 187 [repr. in this volume].

[50] 'Butze' in the sense of a bogey, mannekin, or mask (cf. carneval mask: *Fastnachtsbutze*), or else of an evil child. E. Martin and H. Lienhart (eds), *Wörterbuch der elsässischen Mundarten*, 2 (Strasbourg, 1907), pp. 128 f.; Hermann Fischer (ed.), *Schwäbisches Wörterbuch*, 1 (Tübingen, 1904), pp. 1569 ff.

> It lies heavily on our hearts that many times rash words were spoken by our lord [the bailiff] or in his presence about the treaty which ended the revolt and about the Butzenkrieg; and such was put before us and raised many times, as if we too were of like opinion (which God forfend), for our predecessors the council of Rouffach were innocent of any involvement; rather, they have always acted towards your Princely Grace's . . . ancestors and the bishopric honourably and well. And no one can in truth gainsay that in the recent peasant rebellion we acted as honest persons and would therefore in justice wish to be spared these words about the Butzenkrieg.[51]

But the bailiff was not to be put off: 'It is true that on occasion I spoke of the Butzenkrieg, for I encountered from those who had been against the authorities in the Butzenkrieg just such ignominy, contempt and the like.'[52] The events of the 'Butzenkrieg' were therefore still vivid after thirty years and gave the surviving participants ammunition with which to take pot-shots at the bailiff. The council, however, maintained that only one participant was still alive, and he was old, ill, and stooped.[53] The 'Butzenkrieg' had become a legend. Had the power of the legend in the meantime overtaken the reality?

The present investigation argues consequently for an approach to peasant revolts that does not disavow from the outset their revolutionary potential simply on account of a lack of an overt ideological direction. The remembrance of heroic resistance—the *locus classicus* being the legend of Wilhelm Tell in the origins of the Swiss Confederation—can also be seen as a legacy of the 'Butzenkrieg', given that its events were still fresh in the mind in 1544. It is true that in Rouffach the threshold to a genuine revolutionary situation was never crossed: for that Basel was ultimately to be thanked, whose

---

51 AMRf, BB 3, fo. 260v, 22 July 1544: *So gedt vnns auch nit wenig zuhertzen, das vielmalen durch vnsern junckhern ettwan vnbesonnenn wort beÿ ime oder vmb ine ist von dem vertrag der emperung vnnd dem bütz kriege geredt wurdt; vnnd wurdt vns der viel malen, als ob wir auch der meynung seÿent, für geschlagen vnnd vff geheptt, das sich, ob gott will, nÿmer befÿnnden soll, dann vnser vorfarn ein Rath von Ruffach darann nit schuldig, darinn nie gehalten haben, sonder jder zeit beÿ E. F. G. . . . vorfarn vnnd stifft erlich vnnd woll gehalten, anders nÿmants mit warheit redden kann noch mag, denn wir inn nechsterer burischer vffrur auch vnns wie fromben sich gehalten, vnnd wurden pillich diser wort des butzen kriegs vberhebt wöllen.*

52 Ibid., fo. 264r: *Das ich sollte vnder weÿlenn vonn dem butz krieg geredth haben, ist wor, dann mir der gleich von den jhennigen, so im butzenn krieg wider die oberkeit gewessen, schmocheit, ferachtung vnnd anders begegnet.*

53 Ibid., fo. 270r.

intervention compensated just in time for the parlous behaviour of the targeted authorities. For that reason it is all the more remarkable that in the Peasants' War in Rouffach the rebels failed to match the achievements of 1514 in terms of organization or solidarity. The legitimizing slogans derived from Reforming doctrines were unable to reawaken, let alone to reinvigorate, the tradition of resistance in the Upper Mundat. And that confirms the starting-point of this analysis, namely that the aetiology of any revolt must include a consideration not only of its subjective aims but of its objective unfolding and of its historical framework as well.

CHAPTER FOUR

FREIBURG AND THE BUNDSCHUH

I *The Situation of the Town Around 1500**

On the threshold of the sixteenth century Freiburg im Breisgau had weathered more than a hundred years of economic and demographic decline.[1] Efforts to restore the civic finances and to boost the urban economy, however, provoked occasional resistance on the part of the citizenry. An exhaustive enquiry in 1476 had proposed cuts in the civic budget and in the number of civic officials as well as their remuneration, but had not called into question the regressive character of the town's taxation system, which was staggered unequivocally in favour of the well-off.[2] Hints of authoritarianism (*Obrigkeitsdenken*), moreover, can be discerned in the enquiry, which found their expression in the increasing rigidity of the council oligarchy. These tensions came to a head in the council elections of 1492, when representatives of the commune led by a political outsider and troublemaker, Konrad Walzenmüller, staged a partial coup. In the long run, his clique did not prevail, after Walzenmüller himself had been killed in suspicious circumstances.[3] From the so-called Walzenmüller

---

* Archives are cited by the following abbreviations:
AAEB: Archives de l'Ancien Évêché de Bâle, Porrentruy
ADHR: Archives Départementales du Haut-Rhin, Colmar
AMS: Archives Municipales de Strasbourg
GLA: Badisches Generallandesarchiv, Karlsruhe
StAFr: Stadtarchiv Freiburg im Breisgau

[1] Tom Scott, *Freiburg and the Breisgau. Town-Country Relations in the Age of Reformation and Peasants' War* (Oxford, 1986), pp. 114–54; Dieter Mertens, Frank Rexroth, and Tom Scott, 'Vom Beginn der habsburgischen Herrschaft bis zum "Neuen Stadtrecht" von 1520', in Heiko Haumann and Hans Schadek (eds), *Geschichte der Stadt Freiburg im Breisgau*, 1: *Von den Anfängen bis zum "Neuen Stadtrecht" von 1520* (Stuttgart, 1996), pp. 215–78.

[2] Tom Scott (ed.), *Die Freiburger Enquete von 1476. Quellen zur Wirtschafts- und Verwaltungsgeschichte der Stadt Freiburg im Breisgau im fünfzehnten Jahrhundert* (Veröffentlichungen aus dem Archiv der Stadt Freiburg im Breisgau, 20) (Freiburg im Breisgau, 1986), pp. xxv–xxvii, 53, 61–8.

[3] Idem, 'Der "Walzenmüller-Aufstand" 1492. Bürgeropposition und städtische

revolt, however, the council drew lessons, which culminated in 1495 in a general 'reformation of the guilds'. The guild ordinances then renewed largely took account of the desire of the craftsmen for an economic policy that was protectionist and hostile to entrepreneurialism.[4]

At the same time, the demography of the town seems to have regained its balance; from a nadir of around 6135 inhabitants in 1450 the population gradually recovered to around 6500 by 1500.[5] The explanation is to be sought in the foundation of the university in 1457 and the arrival of dons and students, who constituted a not inconsiderable additional group of consumers of civic goods and services. On the other side of that coin, though, lay the legal immunities of members of the university, which gave rise to repeated friction with the population and civic administration. Quarrels with the ecclesiastical foundations and convents, who enjoyed similar immunities, seem by contrast to have eased by 1500. There had been sharp conflicts in the 1490s with the convents over their advantageous citizen's rights, whereby they paid merely a composition fee (*Satzbürgerrecht*), but these had been mitigated, though not entirely resolved, through the intervention of king (later emperor) Maximilian. Attempts at a thorough reform of the mendicants, however, never really got off the ground; Observants and Conventuals were perpetually bickering, without either side ever gaining a clear ascendancy.[6] By way of comparison, in Basel the Observants triumphed, thereby strengthening their prestige among the citizenry, whereas in Strasbourg the Conventuals retained the upper hand, ensuring that the mendicant orders continued to be denounced as hypocrites, with

---

Finanzen im spätmittelalterlichen Freiburg im Breisgau', *Zeitschrift des Breisgau-Geschichtsvereins ('Schau-ins-Land')*, 106 (1987), pp. 69–93.

[4] StAFr, A 1 VI e α, 21 Feb. 1492, 14 Apr. 1497, 30 Oct. 1499, n.d. (1495); Scott, *Freiburg and the Breisgau*, p. 141.

[5] Ibid., pp. 123–5, 127–8; Rosemarie Merkel, 'Bemerkungen zur Bevölkerungsentwicklung der Stadt Freiburg zwischen 1390 und 1450', *Zeitschrift des Breisgau-Geschichtsvereins ('Schau-ins-Land')*, 108 (1989), pp. 83–91. See now also Horst Buszello, 'Krise, Reform und neuer Aufschwung. Die Stadt Freiburg am Ende des 15. Jahrhunderts', in Hans Schadek (ed.), *Der Kaiser in seiner Stadt. Maximilian I. und der Reichstag zu Freiburg 1498* (Freiburg im Breisgau, 1998), pp. 274–312.

[6] Scott, *Freiburg and the Breisgau*, pp. 133–5; Hans Schadek and Jürgen Treffeisen, 'Klöster im spätmittelalterlichen Freiburg. Frühgeschichte, Sozialstruktur, Bürgerpflichten', in *Geschichte der Stadt Freiburg*, 1, pp. 449–57; Petra Rohde, 'Freiburger Klöster zwischen Reformation und Auflösung', in Heiko Haumann and Hans Schadek (eds), *Geschichte der Stadt Freiburg im Breisgau*, 2: *Vom Bauernkrieg bis zum Ende der habsburgischen Herrschaft* (Stuttgart, 1994), pp. 427–32.

the result that they were immediately dissolved on the introduction of the Reformation.[7] Traces of deep-rooted anticlericalism in Freiburg on the eve of the Reformation, nevertheless, are signally lacking.

Dynastically, the town was irrevocably tied to the house of Habsburg, since its political influence on the Upper Rhine was attributable to the pre-eminence which it enjoyed within the community of Outer Austrian subjects, as long as the seat of government of the 'outer lands' remained in the otherwise insignificant small Alsatian town of Ensisheim. In the territorial Diets Freiburg's was beyond peradventure the leading voice amongst the third Estate of towns and administrative districts. But the town's loyalty to Austria, which also precluded any deviation from Catholicism, turned out to be its undoing during the Reformation and the Peasants' War. Even before the Peasants' War, the leading role that Freiburg on occasion assumed by default within Outer Austria soured its relations with the surrounding peasantry. For a territorial town it was in any case quite unusual for its sphere of influence in the immediate hinterland to have been buttressed by the admission of both noble and peasant outburghers, a policy which Freiburg had successfully pursued over the preceding two centuries.

Although the town's outburgher policy brought it strategic and financial advantages, as well as gaining peasant outburghers as obedient subjects on account of their preferential legal status, it cannot be ignored that towards the end of the fifteenth century Freiburg had had to shed its largest and most prosperous outburgher communities in the Kaiserstuhl as a result of bitter resistance on the part of the village nobility.[8] By then the focus of Freiburg's foreign policy had in any case shifted to the construction of a rural territory in the Dreisam valley, which was intended to secure the turnpikes over the Black Forest and the transit tolls accruing from them.[9]

---

[7] Bernhard Neidiger, *Mendikanten zwischen Ordensideal und städtischer Realität. Untersuchungen zum wirtschaftlichen Verhalten der Bettelorden in Basel* (Berliner Historische Studien, 5: Ordensstudien, 3) (Berlin, 1981), pp. 211–18; Francis Rapp, 'Die Mendikanten und die Straßburger Gesellschaft am Ende des Mittelalters', in Kaspar Elm (ed.), *Stellung und Wirksamkeit der Bettelorden in der städtischen Gesellschaft* (Berliner Historische Studien, 3: Ordensstudien, 2) (Berlin, 1981), pp. 85–102.

[8] Scott, *Freiburg and the Breisgau*, pp. 94–7.

[9] Idem, 'Die Territorialpolitik der Stadt Freiburg im Breisgau im ausgehenden Mittelalter', *Zeitschrift des Breisgau-Geschichtsvereins ('Schau-ins-Land')*, 102 (1983), pp. 7–24. [Engl. version in this volume.]

The first serious incident took place at the Ebringen church-ale in August 1495, when a group of Freiburg apprentices was set upon by villagers, in which one apprentice was stabbed to death and several sustained severe injuries. Hatred of the Freiburgers seems to have derived from a recently introduced customs duty on produce brought to the town. But it was the unbridled reaction of the town itself which was truly startling. News of the bloody 'Ebringen Disgrace' provoked such a storm of protest that many citizens planned to take revenge that same evening. When an armed posse headed by the burgomaster rode out the following morning to the village to take several peasants hostage, it was accompanied by seven hundred men—almost a third of the entire adult male population of the town! When they found Ebringen deserted, the burgomaster had difficulty in restraining his troops from attacking the village and ransacking it. During the subsequent interrogation of those present at the church-ale, the inhabitants of the Breisgau villages gave vent to their resentment of the town in no uncertain terms. It turned out that several Freiburg outburghers from Merdingen had abetted the Ebringers in their acts of violence.[10]

The deterioration in relations between Freiburg and its hinterland, however, went back much further in time. When the council agreed in 1476 to pursue its enquiry by sending the town clerk on a journey lasting five weeks to towns and cities throughout Upper Germany to gather information on administrative practices and economic policies, it summed up the town's precarious situation in the following lapidary words:

> Whereas the town of Freiburg out of willing obedience has always hitherto staked its life, property, and wealth in every situation which has arisen, be it war or peace, for the sake of our gracious lord, although burdened with great debts, nevertheless it has suffered a grievous decline in its commercial livelihood and necessities of trade by virtue of the fact that trades and crafts have all burgeoned in the countryside.[11]

---

[10] Idem, *Freiburg and the Breisgau*, p. 112.

[11] Idem, *Die Freiburger Enquete*, p. 4: *Wie ein statt Fryburg uß williger gehorsami allweg bißhar zü anligenden geschäfftten unser gnedigen herrschaft beide in frids und kriegs löiffen ir lib und güt und alles vermögen geseczt . . .*, *wiewol sy mit mercklichen schulden beladen, und dennocht an gewerben, nuczlichem züfarn mercklich zü abgang komen sigen durch das, das alle gewerb und handtwerck uff dem land geuffet werden.*

The sparse sources hardly permit an informed verdict on the extent and consequences of this rural competition. But the foundation of new markets in the margraviate of Baden as an integral part of a consciously espoused policy of autarky can at all events be attested from the beginning of the fifteenth century.[12] These village markets certainly diverted trade from the long-established Outer Austrian market towns, though it was the smaller territorial towns which chiefly suffered, as market conflicts from the mid-sixteenth century onwards demonstrate. Whether Freiburg was affected is more open to question.[13] The rise of rural handicrafts and trading is even harder to pin down, apart from repeated complaints by the craft towns themselves, especially at the Outer Austrian territorial Diets. But we should recall that in this period territorial guilds embracing craftsmen in town and country were spreading rapidly. Whether organized regionally (as with several fraternities spanning the whole of the Upper Rhine) or territorially by lordships (as in the case of guilds in the margraviates of Baden) the legal confirmation of their status serves in itself as proof of the existence of rural crafts.[14]

Although this economic war of attrition hardly affected relations between Outer Austria and Baden on a diplomatic level before 1500, the political barometer on the Upper Rhine in the later Middle Ages was pointing decidedly towards storm. Burgundy's advance to the Rhine from the west, which culminated in the mortgaging of Alsatian Austria together with the fortress of Breisach on the right bank of the river in 1469, heralded the danger of a complete territorial upheaval on the Upper Rhine. The Burgundian threat was in the end averted with the help of the Swiss Confederates, but the situation remained critical, for the Upper German authorities began to suspect the Swiss themselves of harbouring expansionist designs to the north. The fears were greatly exaggerated, but contributed all

[12] Idem, 'Economic Conflict and Co-operation on the Upper Rhine, 1450–1600', in E. I. Kouri and Tom Scott (eds), *Politics and Society in Reformation Europe. Essays for Sir Geoffrey Elton on His Sixty-Fifth Birthday* (Houndmills, Hants/London, 1987), pp. 210–31, esp. 222. See also Jürgen Treffeisen, 'Aspekte habsburgischer Stadtherrschaft im spätmittelalterlichen Breisgau', in idem and Kurt Andermann (eds), *Landesherrliche Städte in Südwestdeutschland* (Oberrheinische Studien, 12) (Sigmaringen, 1994), p. 214.

[13] Tom Scott, *Regional Identity and Economic Change. The Upper Rhine, 1450–1600* (Oxford, 1997), pp. 122–52.

[14] Ibid., pp. 102–21.

the same to a general sense of political insecurity and encouraged the common man to entertain notions of throwing off the yoke of feudalism by following the example of 'Swiss freedom'.[15] In this regard the imperial Diet held at Freiburg in 1497/98 had fateful consequences, inasmuch as the Swiss emissaries, who had arrived to present their grievances, were rudely told where they could get off. The failure of negotiations with the Swiss emissaries over the Common Penny, the imperial tax agreed at the Diet of 1495, as well as over the competence of the imperial court of chancery, provided the backdrop to the outbreak of the Swiss War of 1499, which threw the Upper Rhine into turmoil.[16] The victory of the Swiss over an imperial army mustered by Maximilian was hailed in the contemporary propaganda literature not only as a military but also as a political triumph. It led to the final severance of the Confederation *de facto* from the empire, and prompted Basel to join the Confederation as a full member in 1501. In the Bundschuh conspiracies on the Upper Rhine the example of Swiss valour and courageous independence was to find a lively echo.

II *The Beginnings of the Bundschuh Movement*

At the end of the fourteenth century we hear for the first time of a popular movement described as a Bundschuh. But the chronicler in question was not using the image of the peasant's laced boot as a designation of a peasant revolt; instead, he was offering a commentary on the defeat of the Lower Rhenish Town League in 1398: 'Therewith the great Bundschuh came to an end.'[17] In the following decades the Bundschuh was still regarded as an emblem of local resistance to foreign troops, discharged mercenaries, or irregulars,

---

[15] Thomas A. Brady, Jr, *Turning Swiss. Cities and Empire 1450–1550* (Cambridge, 1985); idem, 'The Common Man and the Lost Austria in the West. A Contribution to the German Problem', in Kouri and Scott, *Politics and Society*, pp. 154–5.

[16] Hermann Wiesflecker, *Kaiser Maximilian I. Das Reich, Österreich und Europa an der Wende zur Neuzeit*, 1 (Vienna, 1971), pp. 293–4. On the Swiss War and its propaganda effect see now Regierungsrat des Kantons Solothurn (ed.), *'an sant maria magtalena tag geschach ein grose schlacht.' Gedenkschrift 500 Jahre Schlacht bei Dornach 1499–1999* (Solothurn, 1999) [also *Jahrbuch für solothurnische Geschichte*, 72 (1999)].

[17] Günther Franz, 'Zur Geschichte des Bundschuhs', *Zeitschrift für die Geschichte des Oberrheins*, 86 (1934), pp. 1–23, here at p. 5: *domit nam der grosse buntschuoch ein ende.*

rather than as a symbol of peasant struggle for liberation against feudal oppression. Such defensive leagues embracing town and country were directed against the irruption of French and Burgundian troops in Strasbourg in 1439, in the Westrich north-west of Frankfurt in 1443, and in Säckingen on the *Hochrhein* (the Upper Rhine above Basel) a year later.[18] At the same time they exposed the shortcomings of the authorities in fulfilling their duty of protection towards their subjects, so that the term Bundschuh quickly came to imply a barely concealed threat to feudal lords who had neglected their responsibilities. Out of militias popular movements developed which set their sights on both secular and ecclesiastical lordships. On the Upper Rhine peasants had risen in 1443 in Schliengen in the Markgräflerland (the southern margraviate of Baden) in a Bundschuh against their lord, the bishop of Basel. In 1460 in the Hegau at the western end of Lake Constance an uprising occurred in the lordship of Hewen which called itself a Bundschuh. In reality—against the older historiography—this was not a regional revolt abetted by the Swiss, but simply an uprising by subjects of the lordship's villages who combined with the town of Engen against their lords, the counts of Lupfen.[19] According to the chronicles, the rebels are supposed to have desecrated the Host in a church and to have cut off the fingers of the priest who tried to stop them.[20] Even if the tenor of this account is coloured by the patently anti-Helvetic stance of the revolt's noble antagonists, who sought to defame the Bundschuh rebels and the Swiss as enemies of Christendom,[21] a virulent hatred of the clergy was to become a leitmotiv of the later Bundschuh revolts.

Anticlericalism is—notoriously—one of the most familiar commonplaces of the late mediaeval 'critique of Estates' (*Ständekritik*), whether one thinks of John Wyclif in England or Jan Hus in Bohemia. The Upper Rhine, however, the 'parsons' lane' (*Pfaffengasse*) of the empire, with its innumerable convents and ecclesiastical foundations,

---

[18] Albert Rosenkranz, *Der Bundschuh. Die Erhebungen des südwestdeutschen Bauernstandes in den Jahren 1493–1517*, 2 vols (Schriften des Wissenschaftlichen Instituts der Elsaß-Lothringer im Reich, 12) (Heidelberg, 1927), 1: *Darstellung*, pp. 14–15.

[19] Rolf Köhn, 'Der Hegauer Bundschuh (Oktober 1460) – ein Aufstandsversuch in der Herrschaft Hewen gegen die Grafen von Lupfen', *Zeitschrift für die Geschichte des Oberrheins*, 138 (1990), pp. 99–141.

[20] Günther Franz (ed.), *Quellen zur Geschichte des Bauernkrieges* (Darmstadt, 1963), p. 62; idem, 'Zur Geschichte des Bundschuhs', p. 11.

[21] Köhn, 'Hegauer Bundschuh', p. 122.

seems to have been particularly susceptible to anticlericalism. Above all, the appeal to ecclesiastical courts in civil suits, especially those for debt, gave rise to repeated grievances. In 1488 the Outer Austrian governor in Ensisheim was even moved to warn the bishop of Basel of the consequences of costly appeals to his courts, for they burdened the common man so onerously that they were being driven from their farms. If things did not change for the better, he opined, the hatred which had built up against the clergy would discharge itself in violent rebellion.[22] From the point of view of the secular authorities, therefore, the grievances of the common man were, in this respect at least, entirely justified.

An older school of research accordingly saw in the Bundschuh revolts an autonomous tradition of rebellion, which by the end of the fifteenth century had begun to take on unambiguously revolutionary traits. This 'ascending path of class struggle' (to use Marxist parlance) on the Upper Rhine contained such an explosive force because it combined a stark anticlericalism with the overarching legitimating slogan of 'godly justice', which bound peasants and townsfolk together in a broad alliance under a common ideological banner to achieve the general liberation of the common man. These Bundschuh risings—1493 in Sélestat, 1502 in the bishopric of Speyer, 1513 in Lehen in the Breisgau, and 1517 throughout the Upper Rhine as a whole—allegedly departed from the general pattern of local revolts in Upper Germany at this time, which only pursued the restricted goal of restoring the 'old law'.[23] This distinction has long been called into question,[24] most recently by Gunter Zimmermann. In his judgement, before the Peasants' War of 1525, whose articles of grievances were indebted to the new Reforming doctrines since they appropriated the divine justice of the Gospel, no revolutionary undercurrents can be detected which invoked the precept of godly law. Any such invocation in the Bundschuh revolts around the turn of the century merely reveals on closer inspection that the participants regarded their enterprise as pleasing to God and in accor-

---

[22] AAEB, Extradita Wien 42, ad 27g, 24 March 1488.

[23] Rosenkranz, *Bundschuh*, 1, pp. 12 f.; Günther Franz, *Der deutsche Bauernkrieg*, 8th edn (Darmstadt, 1963), pp. 41 f.

[24] Tom Scott, 'Relations between Freiburg im Breisgau and the Surrounding Countryside in the Age of South-West German Agrarian Unrest before the Peasants' War' (PhD Cambridge, 1973), pp. 414 f.; idem, *Freiburg and the Breisgau*, pp. 167–8.

dance with Scripture. Instead, Zimmermann argues, the Bundschuh on the Upper Rhine took its inspiration from the republican freedom of the Swiss Confederates.[25]

This argument has some points in its favour, apart from the unconvincing attempt to reserve revolutionary quality to the Peasants' War alone, and it does show that the leading ideas of the subsequent Bundschuh movement on the Upper Rhine can much more plausibly be explained by proximity to the Swiss than by regarding them as a continuation of radical religious currents reaching back to the age of Hus and Wyclif.

III *The First Bundschuh Conspiracies on the Upper Rhine*

The Bundschuh of 1493 around the Lower Alsatian imperial city of Sélestat had radical overtones both on account of its organisation as a secret conspiracy and on account of its plan to bring peasants and townsfolk together in a common cause. But the hallmarks of revolutionary intent observable elsewhere—the demand for the abolition of all feudal dues and recourse to an ideological legitimating principle—were completely lacking. Instead, the grievances of the Lower Alsatian villages centred around violations and abuses of the law before the ecclesiastical courts of the bishop of Strasbourg, particularly in cases of debt (as we have already encountered in the bishopric of Basel's courts), and before the imperial court of justice in Rottweil. Acting on these grievances, the village magistrate of Blienschwiller, Jakob Hanser, sought support for a general uprising from a close relative in Sélestat, the former burgomaster Hans Ulman. His role was to incite the inhabitants of the city to join the rebellion, although the imperial cities could invoke their *jus de non appellando* to avoid appeals to foreign courts, so that their citizens were usually spared such anguish. At Ulman's urging, the catalogue of grievances was extended to include the demand that the Jews be expelled and that all tolls, excises, and the territorial tax (*Bede*) be abolished. For his part, Hanser proposed restricting clerics to a

[25] Gunter Zimmermann, 'Die Grundgedanken der Bundschuhverschwörungen des Joß Fritz', *Zeitschrift für die Geschichte des Oberrheins*, 142 (1994), pp. 141–64, here at pp. 142, 149, 154–5.

single benefice with an annual income of no more than fifty fl.; priests who resisted should be put to death. But this demand, with its echo of earlier anticlerical sentiments, apparently found no support, for it was dropped.[26]

Tactically it was agreed in the first instance to recruit captains from various lordships and if necessary to appeal to the Swiss for military assistance. Only after Sélestat had been taken was it planned to hoist the Bundschuh flag and spread the campaign of liberation northwards to smaller imperial cities of Alsace such as Rosheim and Obernai. At the end of March 1493, however, the conspiracy was discovered, and the leaders captured, condemned, and executed. Only Jakob Hanser managed to escape and to disappear forever.[27] What prompted Hans Ulman to take part in a peasant conspiracy remains unknown. His failure to be re-elected to the Sélestat council in 1492 may have embittered him. At all events, he emerges as a turbulent and divisive figure who out of chagrin was driven to subversive designs:[28] the parallels with the simultaneous machinations of Konrad Walzenmüller in Freiburg are quite striking. Whether a genuine sense of solidarity between the participants in town and country under a common programme ever existed must remain arguable.

The Sélestat Bundschuh, however, had a sequel which affected Freiburg directly. After the conspiracy had been exposed, one of the captains, Ulrich Schütz from Andlau, fled across the Rhine to Ebnet, where he found shelter in the household of the village lord, David von Landeck. When the Freiburg council got wind of this, it sent an armed party to take Schütz prisoner, but David von Landeck refused to hand him over, until he was finally compelled by the Outer Austrian government. There then ensued a protracted legal battle over jurisdictional competence, during which the continuing tensions between the town and the nobility of the Breisgau brought about by the former's outburgher policy resurfaced. In the end Schütz was sentenced to have his oath fingers cut off.[29] The hard line which Freiburg took in the face of von Landeck's opposition demonstrated

---

[26] Albert Rosenkranz, *Der Bundschuh*, 2: *Quellen*, pp. 6, 10–11, 15–16; Scott, *Freiburg and the Breisgau*, pp. 168–9.

[27] Rosenkranz, *Bundschuh*, 1, pp. 80 f.; Scott, *Freiburg and the Breisgau*, p. 170.

[28] Rosenkranz, *Bundschuh*, 1, pp. 41–2.

[29] Ibid., pp. 50–1, 108–10; StAFr, B 2 4, p. 144; Scott, *Freiburg and the Breisgau*, p. 172.

the councillors' fear of the slightest trace of social unrest. But this attitude was to rebound upon it in full measure during the Bundschuh revolts of 1513 and 1517.

With the conspiracy in the lands of the bishop of Speyer on the right bank of the Rhine in 1502 the Bundschuh movement on the Upper Rhine entered a new phase. Both its organization and its programme were the work of a single individual, one of the most cunning and experienced agitators before the Peasants' War, an episcopal serf from Untergrombach near Bruchsal by the name of Joß Fritz, who was also to be responsible for the conspiracies in 1513 and 1517. Unfortunately, very little is known about him, although his strategic farsightedness suggests a period of service in a Swiss mercenary army. At any rate, the support of the Confederates and the example of Swiss freedom lay at the core of his revolutionary vision.

Traditionally, the financial and administrative mismanagement of the bishopric under its incumbent Ludwig von Helmstädt was regarded as the principal cause of the Bundschuh conspiracy of 1502. But this assumption has been seriously questioned in recent years. The bishop's oft-denounced forest ordinances, which curtailed his subjects' usufruct of wood and pasture, were intended to preserve and renew the stock of woodland over time, which had been jeopardized by excessive felling. The bishopric's grave indebtedness, which had led to tithes, tolls, and taxes being increased, was only partly the bishop's fault, since a feud by the Swabian League in 1490 and a wave of price rises up to 1500 had afflicted the territory.[30] But the objective difficulties under which the bishop laboured were not apparent to his subjects, who gave free rein to their hostility towards the bishop and his diocesan clergy.

According to the report compiled by the famous humanist and chronicler, abbot Johannes Trithemius of Sponheim, the Bundschuh participants were demanding the suspension of all ecclesiastical privileges and immunities, the expropriation of church property, and its transfer into peasant hands. Moreover, the rebels demanded a

[30] Lawrence Gerald Duggan, *Bishop and Chapter. The Governance of the Bishopric of Speyer to 1552* (Studies presented to the International Commission for the History of Representative and Parliamentary Institutions, 62) (New Brunswick, NJ, 1978), pp. 176 f., 263–4.

reduction in the number of clergy and control over their appointment and remuneration, as well as compelling them to return to apostolic poverty. Trithemius, of course, was no dispassionate observer, and in any case his account is garbled and unreliable, but he does identify a vision of a communally controlled Church that was to recur in the Peasants' War.[31] Yet the conspiracy also targeted secular lordship: seigneurial rights of common along with hunting and fishing privileges were to be put at the disposal of the commonweal and administered by the local village communes. Indeed, all feudal burdens were to be abolished—and that would have meant serfdom, too.

On joining the conspiracy the participants had to recite on their knees the rosary and the Hail Mary five times. Their password ran, 'God greet you, good fellow! How fares the world?' To which the reply was, 'We cannot rid ourselves of the plague of parsons.' A variant response, however, included the feudal lords alongside the priests.[32] On the flag (which was not ready when the Bundschuh was betrayed) Christ crucified and the Gregorian man of sorrows were to be depicted on one side, and on the other two laced boots with a peasant kneeling between them, his hands folded in prayer, and above his head the inscription 'Nothing save the justice of the Lord'.[33] The religious cladding of the revolt is therefore unmistakable. Whether the slogan on the flag should be readily equated with a principled commitment on Joß Fritz's part to godly justice as the overarching source of legitimation is, none the less, a moot point, since the actual demands of the Bundschuh and the testimonies of captured participants make no mention of it.[34]

From the outset Joß Fritz contemplated a campaign of liberation throughout the entire bishopric. First, the episcopal castle in Obergrombach was to be attacked, then the town of Bruchsal captured (where four hundred citizens were allegedly standing by), and latterly the episcopal palace at Udenheim (Philippsburg). After that,

---

31 Rosenkranz, *Bundschuh*, 2, pp. 89–92; Scott, *Freiburg and the Breisgau*, p. 174.

32 Rosenkranz, *Bundschuh*, 1, pp. 188, 191.

33 Ibid., p. 200. His interpretation needs to be corrected in the light of Ulrich Steinmann, 'Die Bundschuh-Fahnen des Joss Fritz', *Deutsches Jahrbuch für Volkskunde*, 6 (1960), pp. 243–84.

34 See Zimmermann, 'Grundgedanken', p. 157. However, he does not deal with the problems surrounding the flag in 1502.

the rebels intended to march eastwards from the bishopric into the margraviate of Baden-Durlach, probably heading for Pforzheim. Simultaneously, initial feelers were to be put out to the Swiss.[35] But the plans came to naught, since a mercenary who had been signed up confessed the conspiracy to the bishop. Although the participants were rapidly arrested, ten executed, and many more banished, Joß Fritz himself managed to escape. Despite an intensive manhunt, he apparently continued his agitation undeterred, for reports reached king Maximilian at the end of July that Fritz was planning an incursion into the Alsatian imperial bailiwick of Haguenau.[36]

IV *The Bundschuh in Lehen in the Breisgau*

For ten years Joß Fritz disappeared without trace, until he cropped up as a field-watch in the village of Lehen by Freiburg. What brought him to Lehen is unknown, though perhaps the proximity to a town whose capture lay at the heart of his strategic revolutionary thinking was more than a coincidence. It is remarkable that he was able to go to ground anonymously in Lehen. But at all events he found himself in a situation which was grist to his mill. The 'crisis of feudalism', which Peter Blickle has designated as the decisive factor in the outbreak of the Peasants' War, was reflected in exemplary fashion in the village. Rights of lordship were shared between two noble families, whose possessions and jurisdictions, moreover, often fluctuated. Rights of landlordship lay in 1513 with the von Ankenreut dynasty, while jurisdictional authority was exercised by the deeply indebted Balthasar von Blumeneck, who resided in the village's moated castle. But in Lehen there also lived serfs of foreign lords, one of whom, Kilian Meiger, had borne testimony to the arbitrary rule and acts of violence of his lord, Gabriel von Bollschweil, from the old Freiburg patrician dynasty of von Snewlin, in an extensive court case in 1511.[37] This had turned upon von Bollschweil's attempts with threats to

[35] Scott, *Freiburg and the Breisgau*, pp. 174–5.
[36] ADHR, E 657. Maximilian to count Wolf [von Fürstenberg], 25 June 1502.
[37] GLA 229/8577, § 24, n.d. (1511). For critical remarks on the 'crisis of feudalism' see now Tom Scott, 'The German Peasants' War and the "Crisis of Feudalism". Reflections on a Neglected Theme', *Journal of Early Modern History*, 6 (2002), pp. 265–95.

force free peasants into his servile jurisdiction. It is worth noting that von Bollschweil, who was a noble outburgher of Freiburg, received support from the town council.[38] In Lehen Meiger was subsequently one of the first to be inducted into the Bundschuh conspiracy by Joß Fritz, and served thereafter as his right-hand man.

The conflict with Gabriel von Bollschweil demonstrates that in Lehen the tinder for a peasant rebellion was to hand. The court case involving von Bollschweil is also significant because the Bundschuh itself, in conformity with its character as a conspiracy, produced no written articles of grievance of its own. The causes and aims of the movement can only be inferred from the subsequent interrogations of captured participants. Their statements largely tally with the complaints we have already encountered in 1493 and 1502: grievances against restrictions on the usufruct of common, against usurious rates of interest, and against the competence of ecclesiastical courts to hear suits for debt. The demands to limit the competency of the clergy and those in regular orders as well as prohibiting sinecures also recur. But the Lehen Bundschuh added another aim so extraordinary that it must have derived from Joß Fritz himself. The conspirators were to acknowledge no lord but the pope, the emperor, and above all God. This revolutionary demand for the abolition of all feudal intermediary authority would of course have led to the rescission of serfdom. But the intention to retain the feudal heads of Church and state also shows that Joß Fritz's thinking scarcely anticipated Reforming doctrines, and his vision of a peasant republic, moreover, can only partly be squared with the Swiss Confederation. Older views, which suggested that Fritz articulated a sense of imperial loyalty, can no longer be sustained.[39]

In the spring of 1513 Fritz began secret agitation in the neighbourhood. At a gathering on the Hardmatte west of the village the first adherents were sworn in, but the sources give no reliable indication of the spread of the conspiracy in the following months.[40] During his interrogation, Marx Stüdlin from Munzingen claimed that Fritz's recruitment had won over many peasants in the Kaiserstuhl, in the march of Buchheim, and also in the Glotter valley.[41] But

[38] StAFr, B 5 XI, 8, fo. 206v–207r, 3 April 1512.
[39] Zimmermann, 'Grundgedanken', p. 149.
[40] Rosenkranz, *Bundschuh*, 2, p. 192.
[41] Ibid., p. 151.

Stüdlin asserted at the same time that half the Freiburg guildsmen were in the conspiracy—an improbable claim, which the Freiburg council briskly rejected.[42] It is more likely that Joß Fritz in the light of his experiences in the bishopric of Speyer went about his recruitment cautiously. After careful preparation the Bundschuh flag was to be hoisted at the Biengen church-ale on 9th October as the signal for revolt, a good six months after the first overtures in Lehen. In the course of his agitation Fritz now played down the religious language that had reflected the situation in the bishopric of Speyer. Because the Breisgau was largely a district of secular lordships, it made sense to seek a more general slogan. The password's response, therefore, was no longer 'We cannot rid ourselves of this plague of parsons', but simply 'In all the world the common man can find no comfort'. On joining the conspiracy the rebels were only sworn to secrecy; they were not required to recite religious litanies.

The flag, which Fritz retained in safekeeping after the 1502 revolt, albeit unfinished, was now completed with its striking symbols. What motto was inscribed is not entirely clear. According to Jakob Huser of Lehen it read, 'Lord, stand by thy godly justice' (as had been intended in 1502), but he admitted not having seen the flag himself.[43] His fellow-villager Kilian Meiger maintained instead that the blue and white flag depicted a white cross, the images of emperor, pope, the Virgin Mary, St John the Baptist, the wounds of Christ, and a kneeling peasant, and not least a laced boot as the symbolic representation of their intentions—but nothing at all about a motto. But Meiger too had not actually seen the flag in person![44]

At the Biengen church-ale Fritz hoped at a stroke to recruit two hundred peasants, whereupon the Bundschuh would be unleashed as an armed revolt. His strategy was to march first to the smaller towns such as Burkheim and Endingen, whose capture would secure the rebels strongholds and arsenals, then to turn south to seek military aid from the Swiss, for only with their help could an assault upon the larger and better-defended towns of the Breisgau—Freiburg and Breisach—be contemplated. St Martin's Day (11th November) was set as the date for the attack on Freiburg, during the large

[42] Ibid., p. 139. Zimmermann regards the conspiracy as being effectively confined to Lehen and Betzenhausen. Idem, 'Grundgedanken', p. 144.

[43] Rosenkranz, *Bundschuh*, 2, p. 193.

[44] Ibid., p. 197.

Martinmas fair after the wine harvest, when many peasants would be lodging in the town. Before that support for the Bundschuh was in any case to be garnered from among the craftsmen. In other words, Fritz was thinking less of besieging the town directly than of taking it by stealth. That a siege by a relatively modest array of troops could have taken the town was to be demonstrated by the rebels in the Peasants' War, as the combined forces of the Black Foresters, and peasants from the Markgräflerland, Kaiserstuhl, and Ortenau—altogether no more than 6000 men—cut off the town's water supply. But it seems to have lain in Joß Fritz's temperament to prefer conspiratorial agitation and clandestine subversion. The Martinmas fair provided him with a golden opportunity, for he planned to create panic by an arson attack, whereupon the commons would rush to arms and topple the council in a coup. And indeed on the eve of the fair a furniture-maker started a fire around midnight in the tavern 'zum Kiel' next door to the town hall.[45] But when the alarm sounded, the guilds mustered on the Minster Square in orderly and obedient fashion.

In any case, the conspiracy by then had long been betrayed. During the summer a painter in Freiburg by the name of Theodosion had alerted the council that a peasant acting on Joß Fritz's behalf had surreptitiously approached him about the Bundschuh flag, though he was unable to give any details.[46] Not until early October was the entire plan of revolt disclosed to margrave Philipp of Baden at Rötteln Castle by one of the participants, Michael Hanser from Schallstadt. The margrave immediately informed Freiburg and other authorities in the district, who set about hunting down the conspirators.[47] Joß Fritz, the leader and 'true author' (*rechter Houptsecher*) of the Bundschuh,

---

[45] Zimmermann maintains that the plan to use arson to create panic in Freiburg is a later interpolation, ostensibly confirmed by the fact that fire had indeed been laid in the tavern 'zum Kiel' on 10 Oct. Idem, 'Grundgedanken', p. 144 n. 12. Four years later, however, the furniture-maker arsonist admitted having passed information about the situation in the town to the Bundschuh leaders, so that there is an indisputable connection. Arson was in any case one of the preferred means of intimidation used in the general Upper Rhine Bundschuh of 1517. Scott, *Freiburg and the Breisgau*, p. 187; Rosenkranz, *Bundschuh*, 2, pp. 268, 284.

[46] Ibid., p. 195. A Theodosius Kaufmann, painter and sculptor, is recorded in the Freiburg tax lists from 1490 until his death in 1521. See Hans Rott (ed.), *Quellen und Forschungen zur südwestdeutschen und schweizerischen Kunstgeschichte im XV. und XVI. Jahrhundert*, 3: *Oberrhein*: *Quellen I (Baden, Pfalz, Elsaß)* (Stuttgart, 1936), pp. 102–3.

[47] Rosenkranz, *Bundschuh*, 1, pp. 323 f.

together with his closest associates from Lehen, Kilian Meiger and Jakob Huser, escaped, but the latter two were captured on their way to Switzerland. Only Fritz himself managed to slip away.

Even after the Lehen Bundschuh had collapsed, the Upper Rhine remained disturbed. In Alsace, where Fritz had made contacts, the stirrings of unrest continued. The authorities there, including the Outer Austrian government in Ensisheim, were alarmed lest the revolt in late July 1514 in the territory of the bishop of Strasbourg around Rouffach, the so-called Upper Mundat, burst the frontiers of that lordship and escalate into a regional conflagration.[48] In the same year the territorial rising of the Poor Conrad broke out in the duchy of Württemberg, spinning off a smaller namesake in the Ortenau at Bühl.[49]

In the Breisgau, by contrast, the situation seems to have eased. The authority of the Freiburg council had not been seriously threatened. The only Bundschuh participants in the town on whom the council could lay it hands were a night-watchman, Heinrich Spies, and Martin Tüfel from the suburb of Adelhausen, but they were sympathisers rather than active members.[50] The calm behaviour of the guilds after the arson incident in the tavern 'zum Kiel' speaks for itself. But we are entitled to ask why Joß Fritz neglected to target the winegrowers' guild, with a substantial membership, which had the closest links to the surrounding peasantry. Yet the winegrowers would have proved poor allies, since the council deliberately used the guild as a reservoir of day-labourers, servants, and beggars, keeping it under strict surveillance and well separated from the other craft guilds. Moreover, the winegrowers were the only one of the town's twelve guilds who were not allowed to carry their own weapons. How far the winegrowers had been marginalized from the remainder of the population was to be fully confirmed during the Peasants'

[48] Tom Scott, 'Der "Butzenkrieg". Der Aufstand zu Rufach 1514', in Heinrich R. Schmidt, André Holenstein, and Andreas Würgler (eds), *Gemeinde, Reformation und Widerstand. Festschrift für Peter Blickle zum 60. Geburtstag* (Tübingen, 1997), pp. 355–69. [Engl. version in this volume.]

[49] Rosenkranz, *Bundschuh*, 1, pp. 405 f. On the Poor Conrad in Württemberg see now Andreas Schmauder, *Württemberg im Aufstand. Der Arme Konrad 1514. Ein Beitrag zum bäuerlichen und städtischen Widerstand im Alten Reich und zum Territorialisierungsprozeß im Herzogtum Württemberg an der Wende zur frühen Neuzeit* (Schriften zur südwestdeutschen Landeskunde, 21) (Leinfelden-Echterdingen, 1998).

[50] Scott, *Freiburg and the Breisgau*, p. 182; Rosenkranz, *Bundschuh*, 2, pp. 172–3.

War. After the town's surrender, a demonstration in the guild took place against the council's efforts to impose its will by curtailing the guild's liberties, but neither the remaining guilds nor the surrounding peasantry offered any gesture of solidarity, let alone active support for the winegrowers.[51]

It is also significant that Joß Fritz had no list of demands to offer—apart from deliberately general slogans—that would have echoed the practical interests of the urban craftsmen. Any alliance of solidarity between town and country had the rug pulled from under it from the outset. All that Fritz could hope for was a tactical alliance, as the Sélestat Bundschuh had demonstrated up to a point. Had the Lehen Bundschuh coincided with the machinations of Konrad Walzenmüller, then it would possibly have gained a fifth column in the town. In that case, a quite different set of circumstances would have determined the spread and outcome of the conspiracy.

In hunting down the participants the Freiburg council characteristically took the leading role. A week before the Biengen churchale it had already sent spies into the countryside, and on the eve of the festival had ordered an armed mounted patrol into the Breisgau villages. By that time the ringleaders had long fled. A councillor, Ulrich Wirtner, was instructed to discuss reprisals with the Outer Austrian government. The council insisted that the rebels had no cause whatever to rise up—an astonishing attitude when one recalls the tough struggle to protect its peasant outburghers from the village lords' chicanery in the course of the fifteenth century.

The Bundschuh acquired considerable resonance in contemporary propaganda. An anonymous account of the events, 'The Bundschuh. This Booklet tells of the Evil Venture of the Bundschuhers, How It Began, Ended and Concluded' (*Der Bundtschu. Disz Biechlein sagt von dem bösen Fürnemen der Bundtschuher, wye es sich angefengt, geendet und auskumen ist*) appeared around the turn of the century from the publishing house of the Basel printer Pamphilus Gengenbach, with a rhymed introduction by Gengenbach himself, warning of illegitimate rebellion (see Fig. 4.1). Later editions of the pamphlet, which was rapidly disseminated, were illustrated with woodcuts showing the Bundschuh flag, but the motto invoking godly justice was not included.

---

[51] Scott, *Freiburg and the Breisgau*, pp. 217–19.

Fig. 4.1. *Der Bundtschu.* Basel: Pamphilus Gengenbach, 1514. Title-page.

Fig. 4.2. *Narrenschiff vom Bundtschuh*. Basel, 1514. Title-page.
The rebels, with Joß Fritz at their head and their ensign Jacob Huser, whose flag displays a poisonous scorpion, wear fool's caps, but with laced boots in place of bells.

Also around 1500 an anonymous 'Song of the Bundschuh' (*Lied von dem Bundtschuch*) was printed, which may have originated in the Freiburg Meistersinger School. Further redactions of Gengenbach's pamphlet appeared, above all the 'Ship of Fools of the Bundschuh' (*Narrenschiff vom Bundtschuh*), decorated with woodcuts by the famous Swiss draughtsman Urs Graf (see Fig. 4.2).[52] But before the Bundschuh became the stuff of legend, Joß Fritz tried a third time to instigate a radical uprising of town and country throughout the Upper Rhine as a whole.

V *The Upper Rhine Bundschuh of 1517*

From the failure of his plans Joß Fritz concluded that a new Bundschuh could only hope to succeed if it proceeded differently and embraced different goals. Strategically, it made no sense to begin from a single village; rather, recruitment should take place simultaneously in many localities and communes on both banks of the Rhine. A regional conspiracy also required agile and resourceful agitators. Accordingly, Fritz increasingly dismissed the peasants, who were tied to their fields and to their villages. Instead, he came to rely on the crowds of vagabonds who thronged the highways of the Upper Rhine. Strolling players, beggars, discharged mercenaries, quacks, and gamblers, who together made up a hive of intelligence, clandestinely gained adherents for the Bundschuh in taverns and at fairs. One of them, who emerged as a leader alongside Joß Fritz, was a certain Stoffel (or Veltin) from Freiburg, a shadowy figure about whom nothing is known.

Fritz set about his task of subverting the population in territorial towns and imperial cities in earnest. Cells of rebels were subsequently uncovered in the Alsatian towns of Molsheim, Rouffach, and Soultz, all belonging to the bishopric of Strasbourg, in Barr, and in the smaller imperial cities of Rosheim and Obernai. Whether the conspiracy was as widespread in the Breisgau towns does not emerge from the interrogation minutes. In the countryside, participants from

---

[52] Peter Seibert, *Aufstandsbewegungen in Deutschland 1476–1517 in der zeitgenössischen Reimliteratur* (Reihe Siegen. Beiträge zur Literatur- und Sprachwissenschaft, 11) (Heidelberg, 1978), pp. 160–247.

over a hundred villages are attested, subjects of a wide range of feudal lordships, ecclesiastical and secular. These included the bishopric and the cathedral chapter of Strasbourg, the margraves of Baden, and the counts of Fürstenberg, Bitche-Zweibrücken, and Hanau-Lichtenberg.[53] Rural subjects of the city of Strasbourg were also involved.

This thorough and extensive preparation would hardly have been conceivable without a change of goals. A general rising embracing town and country from the outset could no longer take account of locally conditioned grievances on the part of peasants and townsfolk living under such a diversity of lordships. Therefore the Bundschuh made do with two overarching guiding principles: the demand for the cancellation of all debt- and interest-payments and the abolition of all feudal burdens.

Traces of religious inspiration became altogether more muted. The maxim of divine justice was simply dropped, and the participants were to rally under the slogan of 'St George!'[54] There is no mention of a flag showing religious symbols in any of the subsequent confessions, but that may be the fault of sparse sources. There was also to be no oath. The conspirators were to recognize each other by placing their thumb under their two forefingers and murmuring 'It is good'. Anticlerical overtones seem to have receded entirely into the background. If the confession of Klaus Fleckenstein from Riedseltz can be believed, the aim was henceforth 'to recognize or obey no authority' except 'the Roman Emperor and the Church'.[55] In this context, for 'Church' read 'pope', just as the aims of the 1513 Bundschuh had indicated: it is quite impermissible to read this passage as deliberately shielding the ecclesiastical feudal seigneurs.[56] What had not changed was the intention to seek military aid from the Confederates. But this time around the campaign of liberation was to begin on both banks of the Rhine separately, before the two troops joined forces in late September to march as a united army to the Swiss. Earlier, the rebels planned to subdue Rosheim, to attack Mittelbergheim, where they were counting upon considerable sup-

---

[53] Rosenkranz, *Bundschuh*, 1, pp. 453–5.

[54] Ibid., 2, p. 309.

[55] Ibid., 2, p. 308: *keiner oberkeit gewertig und gehorsam sein* . . . [außer] *einem römischen keiser und der kirchen.*

[56] For a dissenting view see Zimmermann, 'Grundgedanken', pp. 148–9.

port, and then with urban reinforcements to lay siege to Wissembourg and in the north to Haguenau, the capital of the imperial bailiwick of Alsace. On the right bank of the Rhine Kenzingen was to be captured under cover of arson, while in Teningen and Denzlingen an old beggar was to set fire to the home of the village priest, before the troops of the Breisgauers and Black Foresters went on to meet at Freudenstadt.[57]

It would only have been a question of time before the rebels laid siege to Freiburg. Here, too, the attack resorted to the methods of guerrilla warfare. But the peasant who had been charged with instigating a further attack of arson in the town revealed the plan to his priest in the confessional in mid-August. The priest immediately informed the council (disregarding the secrecy of the confessional!), but in fact rumours of a new uprising were already circulating by May.[58] Only when two participants fell into the hands of the margravial bailiff of Rötteln at the beginning of September, however, was the Bundschuh revealed in its entirety. One of the captives, Michael from Dinkelsbühl, who had already taken part in the Poor Conrad revolt in Württemberg in 1514, turned out to be a ringleader, and in the course of an exhaustive confession extracted without torture he revealed the names of over one hundred conspirators.[59]

An accurate verdict on the Upper Rhine Bundschuh's chances of success, if it had not been betrayed, is hard to reach in view of the paucity of sources. It must remain questionable whether Fritz could have won over the strategically indispensable larger towns to his cause. In Wissembourg and Haguenau, for example, no group of adherents can be discerned beyond the ranks of the peasant burghers, just as in the Peasants' War itself.[60] For Freiburg the conclusion is

---

[57] Rosenkranz, *Bundschuh*, 2, pp. 268, 283–4; Scott, *Freiburg and the Breisgau*, p. 187.

[58] AMS, Archives du Grand Chapitre, III (I), fo. 65v; Jean Rott (ed.), 'Documents inédits sur le "Bundschuh" et la Guerre des Paysans en Alsace', *Revue d'Alsace*, 105 (1979), pp. 59–65, here at p. 64.

[59] Rosenkranz, *Bundschuh*, 2, pp. 269–89.

[60] See Jean-Laurent Vonau, 'La Guerre des Paysans dans l'Outre-Forêt', in Alphonse Wollbrett (ed.), *La Guerre des Paysans 1525* (Société d'Histoire et d'Archéologie de Saverne et Environs: Études Alsatiques, supplément 93) (Saverne, 1975), p. 41; André-Marcel Burg, 'La Guerre des Paysans dans la région de Haguenau', ibid., p. 50. See now also Tom Scott, 'Südwestdeutsche Städte im Bauernkrieg. Bündnisse zwischen Opportunismus und Solidarität', in Bernhard Kirchgässner and Hans-Peter Becht (eds), *Stadt und Revolution* (Stadt in der Geschichte. Veröffentlichungen des

just as sobering. But Joß Fritz had by no means abandoned all hope. A third time he made good his escape. And although his track entirely vanished, he continued his agitation underground, for at the onset of the Peasants' War in the Hegau a final mention of him occurs: 'Among these peasants there was also Fritz from Grombach in the bishopric of Speyer, with an old grey beard, who continued to proclaim he could or would not die until the Bundschuh had run its course.'[61] It was no accident that the scene of his last hurrah lay directly on the frontier of the Swiss Confederation.

VI *From Bundschuh to Peasants' War*

The attraction of the Bundschuh as a symbol of popular resistance diminished somewhat after the collapse of the third Bundschuh under the leadership of Joß Fritz, but lived on in popular consciousness. In 1518 in the Breisgau there was a significant sequel during a dispute among the miners at Todtnau in the Black Forest. When one mineworker in the drinking-parlour uttered the threat that 'he would bring the Swiss over the mountains any time they [the miners] chose' to help enforce the miners' demands, a brawl ensued during which the mining shareholders feared that matters would take such a turn 'that great contempt and conspiracy might result (from which a Bundschuh might arise)'.[62] The connection between the Bundschuh and Swiss freedom is once again clear for all to see.

The efforts of duke Ulrich (expelled from his duchy of Württemberg which was subsequently occupied by Austria) to regain his principality in 1522 by hiring mercenaries in Switzerland and around Lake Constance under the banner of the Bundschuh can also be seen as

---

Südwestdeutschen Arbeitskreises für Stadtgeschichtsforschung, 27) (Stuttgart, 2001), pp. 9–36, esp. 21, 24, 34. [Engl. version in this volume.]

[61] GLA 65/112, fo. 1v: *Under solichen bauwern ist auch Fritz von Grumbach vß dem Stiefft Speÿer mit einem alten grauwen Barts gewesen, der sich alwegen hat horen lassen, er konne oder moge nit ersterben, der Bunthschuch hab dan zuvor sein furgangkh erlanngt.* Printed in Franz Joseph Mone (ed.), *Quellensammlung der badischen Landesgeschichte*, 2 (Karlsruhe, 1854), p. 17.

[62] Rosenkranz, *Bundschuh*, 2, p. 309: *so hat doch daruber ain underthaner zw Tottnaw mit namen Conrat Ogkers sich daselbst auf der trinkhstuben merkhen lassen, si sollen sich nicht trugkhen lassen, er wölle die Sweitzer uber die gepirg bringen, wan si wöllen ... das dan zw großer verachtung und conspiracion (daraus ain puntschuech entspringen möcht) dienen ist.* Zimmermann, 'Grundgedanken', p. 155.

a form of popular resistance against the illegitimate exercise of authority.[63] Although these plans came to naught, duke Ulrich continued to intrigue. In the autumn of 1524 from his fortress of Hohentwiel by Singen he again sought to incite the peasants of the Hegau to rise up, a venture which led them in January 1525 to begin a march northwards into Württemberg territory, accompanied by discharged Swiss mercenaries.[64] When the campaign petered out in the spring, the recruits simply went over to the rebels at the outbreak of the Peasants' War. But the result was that the Bundschuh as a symbol and a programme was overlaid and overtaken by the Reforming doctrines that informed the peasants' articles of grievance.[65]

Moreover, in the initial stages of the Peasants' War the theatre of action switched from the Upper Rhine to Lake Constance and into Swabia, even though the situation in the Breisgau remained tense. The anticlericalism which had once stamped the Bundschuh movement soon turned into a clamour for Reforming doctrines. Evangelical preachers found refuge for a time in a series of Breisgau towns—Jakob Otter in Kenzingen,[66] Otto Brunfels in Neuenburg—but the countryside was, if anything, even more restive. Alongside village priests sympathetic to Reform hedge-priests were at work, preaching a more radical message. The most active among them was Hans Murer from Horb, a self-styled graduate and medical doctor, who during 1522/23 roamed the Breisgau countryside with twenty-four 'disciples', stirring up discontent. He styled himself Karsthans (Jack with the Hoe), the evangelical peasant who had been portrayed in the squib of the same name in 1521 as the symbol of the simple, uncorrupted Christian. A mason's apprentice brought before the Outer Austrian government in Ensisheim claimed to have been about to hoist a Bundschuh flag in order to rally the common man to the Gospel.[67]

---

[63] Scott, *Freiburg and the Breisgau*, p. 190 and n. 4.

[64] Johann Heinrich Schreiber (ed.), *Der deutsche Bauernkrieg. Gleichzeitige Urkunden*, 3 vols (Freiburg im Breisgau, 1863–66), 1, pp. 82–3, 105; 2, pp. 15, 16–17, 27; Franz Ludwig Baumann (ed.), *Akten zur Geschichte des deutschen Bauernkrieges aus Oberschwaben* (Freiburg im Breisgau, 1877), pp. 92–3, 256.

[65] Zimmermann sees here no concatenation or gradual transition but an 'epochal caesura'. Idem, 'Grundgedanken', p. 161.

[66] See Ralf Lusiardi, 'Ackerbürgerstadt und Evangelium. Die evangelische Bewegung in der vorderösterreichischen Landstadt Kenzingen', *Zeitschrift für die Geschichte des Oberrheins*, 141 (1993), pp. 185–211; Scott, *Freiburg and the Breisgau*, pp. 199–202.

[67] StAFr, C 1 Kirchensachen 143; Scott, *Freiburg and the Breisgau*, p. 192.

Amidst this turmoil Freiburg at first appeared as an island of calm, notwithstanding Murer's intrigues during his occasional sojourns in the town. Since the council was bent upon punishing any sign of Reforming sympathies, it is no surprise that Murer intended to expel the leading council members at the next opportunity. In cementing its loyalty to the Catholic faith both internal considerations and diplomatic calculations played a role in Freiburg. After decades of turbulence the council had finally achieved economic and demographic stability as a result of a new consensus between itself and the commons on the basis of the 'reformation of the guilds' in 1495. This fragile balance the council had no intention of upsetting by allowing Reforming doctrines with their explosive potential to intrude. In terms of foreign policy, as we have seen, the town's pre-eminence depended essentially upon the goodwill and patronage of the Habsburgs, especially during Maximilian's reign. Subsequently, archduke Ferdinand's resolute commitment to the old faith robbed the town of any room for manoeuvre since its stake in political power was henceforth indissolubly linked to Catholicism. Even though stirrings of unrest occurred from time to time the consensus between council and commons in the end withstood the upheavals of the years of Reformation and Peasants' War—a remarkable achievement, if one compares Freiburg with so many other urban communes on the Upper Rhine.[68]

[68] Ibid., pp. 194–99.

CHAPTER FIVE

FROM THE BUNDSCHUH TO THE PEASANTS' WAR: FROM REVOLUTIONARY CONSPIRACY TO THE REVOLUTION OF THE COMMON MAN

I

At the beginning of 1525 the master of the bishop of Strasbourg's household, Jacob von Oberkirch, received the following instructions for the forthcoming negotiations at the territorial Diet in Haguenau, whose wording forms a bridge between the Bundschuh and the Peasants' War.* In contrast to the earlier Bundschuh revolts in the bishopric of Speyer and elsewhere

> The present Bundschuh has been launched for far more insidious reasons (and which exercise the common man a great deal more), not without especial deviousness, under the cloak of true piety, as if they were seeking nothing other than God's honour, and as if the truth of the Gospel had previously been concealed, whereby the common man has been misled and in the highest aggrieved.[1]

A new Bundschuh under the sign of the Gospel implies a direct path from the revolutionary conspiracies on the Upper Rhine to the open

---

* Archives are cited by the following abbreviations:

ADHR: Archives Départementales du Haut-Rhin, Colmar
AMS: Archives Municipales de Strasbourg
FWWA: Fürstlich Waldburg-Wolfegg'sches Gesamtarchiv, Schloß Wolfegg
GLA: Badisches Generallandesarchiv, Karlsruhe
SAZh: Staatsarchiv des Kantons Zürich
StAA: Stadtarchiv Augsburg
StAFr: Stadtarchiv Freiburg im Breisgau
TLA: Tiroler Landesarchiv, Innsbruck.

[1] Günther Franz (ed.), *Der deutsche Bauernkrieg. Aktenband*, 2nd edn (Darmstadt, 1968), p. 190: *So sey aber der ytzig bundschuch gar vil mit andern subtilern ursachen und die den gemeinen man gar vil hoher bewegen, nit one sunder schwindlistigkeyt angriffen, under dem scheyn rechter andacht, als ob man allein gottes eer suche, die warheyt des ewangeliums bishere verhalten bliben, dadurch der gemeyne man verfurt und zum hochsten beschwert sey* [. . .]. Cf. Paul Böckmann, 'Der gemeine Mann in den Flugschriften der Reformation', *Deutsche Vierteljahrsschrift für Literaturwissenschaft und Geistesgeschichte*, 22 (1944), pp. 186–230, esp. 222.

rebellion which seized the whole of south-west Germany in 1525.

But it is quite improper to speak of a gradual transition or, in Marxist parlance, 'an ascending line of class struggle'. Between the discovery of Joß Fritz's last conspiracy in 1517 and the public protests of the Stühlingen peasants, together with the attack on the charterhouse of Ittingen near Frauenfeld by evangelicals from Zürich's territory and some Thurgau peasants at midsummer 1524, seven years had elapsed, which are generally regarded as the calm before the storm. In the meantime, the theatre of revolt had switched from the Upper Rhine to Lake Constance and Upper Swabia. The onset of the Peasants' War in Upper Swabia—at the beginning of 1525 there was trouble brewing among the subjects of the imperial free city of Ulm in Baltringen—displays no trace of any influence by the previous unrest in the Hegau and Klettgau.

These disjunctions cannot be dismissed as trivial since we know that Joß Fritz continued his clandestine agitation into the early months of the Peasants' War. According to reports from the Hegau among the rebels there was

> also Fritz from Grombach in the bishopric of Speyer, with an old grey beard, who continued to proclaim he could or would not die until the Bundschuh had run its course.[2]

The connection between the Bundschuh and the Peasants' War on the Upper Rhine and *Hochrhein* (the Rhine above Basel) may in my view be pursued by investigating two themes: the evangelical peasant Karsthans (Jack with the Hoe) as a literary figure and a living alias; and the example of the Swiss, who were invoked for support and legitimation. These two motifs finally intermeshed, so that in certain circumstances it is possible to regard evangelical and republican freedom as two sides of the same coin.[3]

---

[2] GLA 65/112, fo. 1v: *auch Fritz von Grumbach vß dem Stiefft Speÿer mit einem alten grauwen Barts gewesen, der sich alwegen hat horen lassen, er konne oder moge nit ersterben, der Bunthschuch hab dan zuvor sein furgangkh erlanngt.* Printed in Franz Joseph Mone (ed.), *Quellensammlung der badischen Landesgeschichte,* 3 vols (Karlsruhe, 1854), 2, p. 17. According to a member of the audience, this passage is corrupt: in 1525 Joß Fritz was in the Sundgau. A source for this assertion, however, was not forthcoming.

[3] See Peter Blickle, '"Es sol der Schwanberg noch mitten in Schweitz ligen." Schweizer Einflüsse auf den deutschen Bauernkrieg', *Jahrbuch für fränkische Landesforschung,* 60 (2000), pp. 113–25.

II

In 1521 the pamphlet 'Karsthans, with Four Persons who are Conducting a Conversation among Themselves' (*Karsthans mit vier Personen, so vnder inen selbs ain gesprech vnd red halten*) (see Fig. 5.1) appeared, which was intended as a reply to Thomas Murner's anonymous and biting satire on Luther's teachings. At the outset, Karsthans steps forth as an ignorant peasant, who vents his hatred above all against monks, but who still wishes to remain pious. In the second part of the dialogue, however, Karsthans, enlightened by Luther's teachings, turns out to be capable of understanding theological arguments, since the Reformers take him seriously as a layman and a rational person. The stereotype of the peasant has therefore undergone a transformation from negative to positive, which derives from its literary function.[4] The figure of Karsthans in the dialogue, in the judgement of Thomas Kaufmann, is the literary counterpoint to Murner's claim to general representativeness, grounded in his anonymity.[5]

The figure is remarkable in two respects. It crops up suddenly and abruptly, seemingly without precedent; moreover, it represents a stark contrast to the figure of the late mediaeval peasant as a dolt or a boor. Within the space of a year the 'peasant with the hoe' had nevertheless become the epitome of the evangelical layman, and a natural reference-point for his anticlericalism.[6] In all, ten printings of the pamphlet are recorded from presses in Strasbourg, Basel, and Augsburg,[7] whose authorship has still not firmly been established to the present day. If it is not, as used to be believed, from the pen of Vadian in St Gallen, then at least a Swiss author is suggested by references to Karsthans as 'valiant' (*wehrhaft*); that is, he is linked to the tradition of heroic resistance by Helvetic peasants.[8] In the

[4] Ninna Jørgensen, *Bauer, Narr und Pfaffe. Prototypische Figuren und ihre Funktion in der Reformationsliteratur* (Acta Theologica Danica, 23) (Leiden/New York/Copenhagen/Cologne, 1988), pp. 7–8, 42–4. See also Werner Wunderlich, *Die Spur des Bundschuhs. Der deutsche Bauernkrieg in der Literatur 1476–1976* (Literaturwissenschaft—Gesellschaftswissenschaft, 35) (Stuttgart, 1978), pp. 26–8.

[5] Thomas Kaufmann, 'Anonyme Flugschriften der frühen Reformation', in Bernd Moeller (ed.), *Die frühe Reformation in Deutschland als Umbruch* (Schriften des Vereins für Reformationsgeschichte, 199) (Heidelberg, 1998), pp. 191–267, esp. 229.

[6] Jørgensen, *Bauer, Narr und Pfaffe*, p. 1.

[7] Böckmann, 'Der gemeine Mann', p. 195.

[8] On Swiss peasants' valiantness see Paul Freedman, *Images of the Medieval Peasant* (Stanford, CA, 1999), pp. 190–99.

Fig. 5.1. *Karsthans, the peasant with the Hoe.* Title-page woodcut of the Augsburg edition, 1521.
Karsthans is engaging his friend Mercurius, a young student, and Murner (with a cat's head, indicating a dreadful animal) in conversation.

Fig. 5.2. *This Two Swiss Peasants Have Done.* Augsburg: Melchior Ramminger, 1521.

Eyn Gemeyner Dorffryde

der Bawren/den sie in diesem Jar auff-
gericht vnd zůsamen geschwo-
ren haben ꝛc.

☞ Fritzen Lauwel/kům hör mir zů/
Ferch schweyß/was will sich machen nů.
Wir hon eyn Dorffrid auffgericht.
Ich bitt/merck eben diß gedicht/
Wie wirs halten/vnd vnnß soll gan/
Wir werden Gleydt/fryd/vnd schirm han/
Alß wir die spieß tragen/zů rück/
Das schaffen der welt üppig dück.
Drumb laß vnnß dem auch dencken nach/
Das wir nit werden matt vnd schach.

Fig. 5.3. *A Common Village Peace of the Peasants.* Strasbourg: Johann Knobloch the Elder, 1526.

subsequent pamphlet 'New Karsthans', possibly composed by the Strasbourg Reformer Martin Bucer, the right of peasants to bear arms is transferred to the nobility. 'A peasant who set himself up as Luther's valiant protector', Ninna Jørgensen concludes, 'would have been taken directly as a Bundschuh conspirator.'[9]

How is this figure to be interpreted? Is the hoe merely a sign of the peasant as husbandman or is it a weapon? Sometimes the hoe is replaced by the flail, as in the title-page of the contemporary pamphlet 'This Two Swiss Peasants have Done' (see Fig. 5.2). In the well-known evangelical image of the godly mill there appears in the background just behind Luther and Erasmus the figure of Karsthans with a sword and a flail, which he wields in threatening fashion.[10] In its appearance, of course, the threshing-flail strongly resembled the chain morning-stars violently swung by mercenaries in battle. Such images, therefore, can at all events be regarded as inflammatory and aggressive.[11]

After the Peasants' War Karsthans appears one last time as Cousin Nick begging his counterpart Frige Lauwel to join a village association for the maintenance of peace (see Fig. 5.3). The maxims by then had become safe-conduct, peace, and protection, 'as we carry the pikes back home'. A true Christian peace after the failure of the Peasants' War can no longer be achieved; nevertheless, the peasant retains his dignity and creative capacity.[12]

This more positive evaluation of the figure of the peasant should not be restricted to the image of an evangelical Karsthans alone. In the relevant scholarship the contrast between positive and negative

---

[9] Jørgensen, *Bauer, Narr und Pfaffe*, p. 99.

[10] On this image see Robert W. Scribner, *For the Sake of Simple Folk. Popular Propaganda for the German Reformation* (Cambridge, 1981), pp. 104–5; idem, 'Images of the Peasant, 1514–1525', in János M. Bak (ed.), *The German Peasant War of 1525* (London, 1976), pp. 29–46, esp. 32–3. Cf. Wunderlich, *Spur des Bundschuhs*, p. 28.

[11] Sometimes the signs were reversed. The 'peasant of Wöhrd', a runaway Franciscan friar by the name of Diepold Peringer, preached Luther's doctrines around Nuremberg. In a woodcut by Erhard Schön he appears in a Nuremberg pamphlet of 1524 with a threshing-flail, but in an Erfurt imprint of the same year as a preaching peasant with a hoe. Franz-Heinrich Beyer, *Eigenart und Wirkung des reformatorisch-polemischen Flugblatts im Zusammenhang der Publizistik der Reformationszeit* (Frankfurt am Main, 1994), pp. 48–9, 224, 273.

[12] See Hans-Joachim Köhler, '"Der Bauer wird witzig." Der Bauer in den Flugschriften der Reformationszeit', in Peter Blickle (ed.), *Zugänge zur bäuerlichen Reformation* (Bauer und Reformation, 1) (Zürich, 1987), pp. 187–218, esp. 203–4, 212.

images of the peasant has all too often been linked to changes which the Reformation occasioned. The late mediaeval image of Karsthans derives ultimately from a passage in Geiler von Kaysersberg's writings which is invariably torn from its context, doubtless because it is an entry in Grimms' Dictionary.[13] The minster preacher of Strasbourg, it is alleged, used Karsthans as a term of denigration to characterize the coarse and backward peasant dolt.[14] As the leading critic of Estates of his day, however, Geiler was not appropriating this verdict to himself, but rather placing it in the mouth of the nobleman (in chapter 52 'On Marriage' of his German version of Sebastian Brant's 'Ship of Fools'):

> The townsman says he has a noblewoman, who is definitely of that Estate, but poor as a church mouse; therefore, I would rather be a rich peasant than a poor nobleman. The nobleman says for his part, why should I have any truck with Karsthans or a peasant dolt: he knows neither honour or disgrace, neither breeding nor manners; when he rides, he sits bolt upright, as if swept into the saddle on a wave, and much more in the same vein.[15]

To interpret Geiler's view of the peasantry on the evidence of this passage as negative is entirely impermissible. Yet a gradual shift in attitudes towards the peasantry, and to the value of peasant labour, is visible in other fifteenth-century authors—notably in the Nuremberg writer Hans Rosenplüt's poem 'In Praise of the Peasant'[16]—but these

[13] Jacob Grimm and Wilhelm Grimm (eds), *Deutsches Wörterbuch*, 5 (Leipzig, 1873), p. 232: *was sol ich mit dem karsthansen oder bawernklotz zu schaffen haben.*

[14] Böckmann, 'Der gemeine Mann', p. 194; Werner Besch, 'Der *gemeine Mann* in Luthers Schriften', in Gunther Hirschfelder (ed.), *Kulturen—Sprachen—Übergänge. Festschrift für H. L. Cox zum 65. Geburtstag* (Cologne/Weimar/Vienna, 2000), pp. 113–33, esp. 116.

[15] Nikolaus Höniger, *Weltspiegel oder Narrenschif ('Alles auff Sebastian Brandts Reimen gerichtet, Durch* [. . .] *Johan. Geyler* [. . .] *jetzt aus dem Latein inn das recht hoch Teutsch gebracht* [. . .] *durch Nicolaum Höniger')* (Basel, 1574), p. 193: *Der Bürger spricht er hat eine Edelfrau, die gut von Adel, aber blut arm, darumb wil ich lieber ein reicher Bawer sein, weder ein armer Edelmann. Deßgleichen sagt der Edelmann, was sol ich mit dem Karsthans oder Bawrenklotz zu schaffen haben, er kan doch weder schimpff noch glimpff, weder zucht noch mores, wenn er reitet, sitzt er gleich auf dem Pferdt, als het in dz wasser darauff gefüret, und deren dingen vil mehr.* For checking this exceedingly obscure reference I am indebted to Hans-Joachim Hecker (Munich).

[16] Freedman, *Images of the Medieval Peasant*, pp. 213–14; Günther Franz (ed.), *Quellen zur Geschichte des deutschen Bauernstandes im Mittelalter* (Darmstadt, 1974), pp. 549–52.

all express literary tropes and are by no means indications of any serious engagement with the fate of the peasant.

The figure of Karsthans was deployed in literary terms alongside the pamphlet 'New Karsthans' by Ulrich Boßler from Haßfurt and Johann Eberlin von Günzburg for propaganda purposes.[17] Indeed, even Luther was writing from his seclusion in the Wartburg to Melanchthon at the end of May 1521 that in Germany there were many Karsthanses.[18] But in the run-up to the Peasants' War in south-west Germany of far more interest are the intrigues of a veritable Karsthans, who was agitating clandestinely for the cause of the Gospel from the spring of 1522 onwards on the Upper Rhine, in Württemberg, and also in Switzerland (a point hitherto essentially overlooked). The person in question was Hans Murer, by his own account a graduate and physician, who was supposed to have spent a considerable time in Turkey and Bohemia![19] The authorities were quickly onto his track but could not get their hands on him, since he resorted to the same tactics as had Joß Fritz earlier. That is to say, Murer never spent long in one place, was constantly on the move, on occasion accompanied by up to twenty-four 'disciples'. By means of secret conversations in inns and in people's homes he sought to win a following in both town and country: Wissembourg and Sélestat in Alsace, in the territory of Strasbourg, in the Kaiserstuhl and elsewhere in the Breisgau, and in the Black Forest. In Horb, he is said to have lodged in Henslin from Nagold's tavern.[20] The Freiburg council could even give a 'wanted person' description of him:

> He is a fat, short person, whose father-in-law once resided here in Freiburg, and is now dead, Hans Zunduff by name [. . .]; wears a grey jacket without sleeves, black hose, and sports a broad grey hat.

The council was in no doubt that 'beyond peradventure he is one of the true instigators who are peddling treasonable Bundschuh notions'.[21]

---

[17] Böckmann, 'Der gemeine Mann', p. 197; Jørgensen, *Bauer, Narr und Pfaffe*, p. 112.

[18] *D. Martin Luthers Werke, Briefwechsel*, Weimarer Ausgabe, 2 (Leipzig, 1931), p. 348: *Si Papa omnes aggredietur, qui mecum sentiunt, sine tumultu non erit Germania* [. . .] *Deus suscitat spiritus multorum atque adeo et vulgi corda* [. . .] *Habet Germania valde multos Karsthansen.*

[19] StAFr, B 5 XI, 12, fo. 88r.

[20] Ibid., fo. 67r, 74v–75r, 75v, 87r–v, 87v–89r; GLA 46/4546; AMS, AA 374, fo. 31r–v.

[21] StAFr, B 5 XI, 12, fo. 74v–75r: *Ist eine dicke, kurtze person, des stieff vatter by uns*

It is self-evident that the Catholic authorities would see the spread of evangelical doctrines as heralding rebellion and a new Bundschuh; Hans Murer's activities as Karsthans, however, make it likely that he and his followers were consciously imitating Joß Fritz's method of operation, and that they regarded evangelical freedom as the summation of the goals which Fritz is supposed to have proclaimed, namely divine justice and the cancellation of all feudal burdens. The statements of witnesses forwarded by the Freiburg council to the Austrian government of occupation in Stuttgart leave no doubt that Murer was exploiting anticlerical feelings in his recruitment, just as Joß Fritz had done, alongside his theological rejection of the Catholic Church—denial of purgatory, the demand for communion under both kinds, and the uselessness of confession. Hans Murer, in addition, did not hesitate to embrace violence. According to one Freiburg witness, he intended to drive out the sitting Catholic council at the next opportunity,[22] clearly echoing the programme of the Lehen Bundschuh of 1513 and the Bundschuh conspiracy throughout the Upper Rhine in 1517.

We might be tempted to think that Hans Murer had only the Catholic authorities in his sights and had no intention of unleashing a general uprising. But his agitation in Switzerland casts severe doubt on this assumption. From his own mouth, as one Freiburg witness reported, Murer as Karsthans had spent time in Bern and elsewhere in the Confederation. An apprentice stonemason apprehended by the Outer Austrian government in Ensisheim in January 1523 confessed before his execution that in his house near Basel on Palm Sunday 1522 Karsthans had joined in the eating of a sucking-pig in defiance of the Lenten provisions on fasting.[23] In reality, what had taken place was a communal meal in Schloß Klybeck by

hie zu fryburg gesessen vnd gestorben mit namen hanns zunduff [. . .]; *hat ein grawen rock an, on ermell, swartz hossen vnd ein breitten grawen hut vff. . . . dann on zwiuel er ist der rechten houptsecher einer, die yetzt mit den verrätterischen pundtschuchischer sachen vmb gendt.*

[22] Ibid., fo. 88v: [. . .] *in kurtzen tagen so wirdt man die obristen im rat zu fryburg in der statt vmb jagen.*

[23] Ibid., fo. 89r. Cf. the entry in an Ensisheim chronicle, which describes the stonemason as a citizen of Sélestat, who also held burgher's rights in Basel. It is cited in Hans-Christoph Rublack, 'Reformation in Vorderösterreich und Konstanz', in *Luther und die Reformation am Oberrhein. Ausstellung der Badischen Landesbibliothek und der Evangelischen Landeskirche in Baden* (Karlsruhe, 1983) (Exhibition catalogue), pp. 103–27, here at p. 103.

Basel, which belonged to the Basel surgeon and paper-maker Sigmund. Several Basel clergy and chaplains took part, along with the Cologne humanist Herman von dem Busche. The company, therefore, was far from being a clique of clandestine agitators.[24] But some priests (Catholic, of course) also informed the Freiburg council 'that Karsthans has agitated and preached on Zürich's territory to such a degree that he has been expelled from it'.[25] Even for the Zürich council, protector of Zwingli and supporter of his cause, Karsthans, it seems, was a dubious character. That evangelical convictions were entirely compatible with seditious intentions emerges in any case from the confession of the stonemason in Ensisheim, according to whom it was planned to hoist a Bundschuh flag.[26]

III

If Hans Murer as Karsthans represents a bridging figure on the Upper Rhine between the Bundschuh and a revolt in the name of the Gospel, then the tradition of the Bundschuh as a political revolution was mobilized in these years under quite a different sign at the western end of Lake Constance, thereby establishing a link between the Upper Rhine and the first scenes of action in the Peasants' War. This came about through the undercover attempts by duke Ulrich of Württemberg to regain the principality, from which he had been driven out in 1519, by raising an army of hired mercenaries and peasants on both banks of the Rhine. According to the surviving sources, in 1522 Ulrich had begun to recruit a troop of mercenaries from his stronghold of the Hohentwiel near Singen in the Hegau, which was to rally under a white damask flag with a

[24] Rudolf Wackernagel, *Geschichte der Stadt Basel*, 3 vols (Basel, 1907–24), 3, p. 327. I am grateful to Kaspar von Greyerz for tracking down this reference. The fact that the host was a surgeon and Hans Murer allegedly a medico should not give rise to vacuous speculation. However, Sigmund had made himself so objectionable to the authorities that he was forced to leave, whereupon the council bought Schloß Klybeck in July 1522, only to sell it on nine months later to a doctor, Berthold Barter. Ibid., p. 55.

[25] StAFr, B 5 XI, 12, fo. 89r: *das Karsthanns in zuricher gebiett der massen gehandelt vnd gepredigt, das man inne dar*[v]*s verpotten hab.*

[26] StAFr, C 1 Kirchensachen 143, no. 23.

golden Bundschuh under a sun. On the flag was to appear the motto, 'Whoever will be free let him step forth under this sun's rays.'[27]

It is hard to be sure what veracity to attribute to these reports. The original rumours seen to have emanated from the imperial free city of Überlingen, which reported them to the deputy governor of the Stuttgart administration, Wilhelm Truchseß von Waldburg, in answer to his enquiry. But it added the proviso, 'so far we have not credited these reports'. Yet the rumours had not been plucked out of thin air, for in the summer of 1522 the Zürich bailiff of Oberberg and Gossau admitted in a letter to the council to having been caught up in duke Ulrich's intrigues at the beginning of the year, for which he had been arrested. During his imprisonment he could not therefore (as the council had accused him) have received money from duke Ulrich or have recruited soldiers to his cause.[28] Towards the end of the year, however, new reports were coming in which appeared to confirm the rumours. The mercenaries were to gather at Frauenfeld, unfurl the flag, and then march to the Hohentwiel. As Überlingen indicated, support was less likely to come from the Swiss towns than from the countryfolk. Peasants from Luzern, Solothurn, Basel, Fribourg, and Zug were supposed to have struck a deal with duke Ulrich.[29]

When the Upper Austrian government in Innsbruck made enquiries of the man on the spot, the Austrian bailiff of Nellenburg, Hans Jacob von Landau—whose remit was the Hegau—the latter had heard neither of a flag, nor of any Bundschuh.[30]

The Stuttgart administration nevertheless felt bound to send a missive to the Confederates, warning them of a general uprising:

> For it is unfortunately anyway the case that the common man everywhere and for the most part is eager to find ways and means of casting off all debts and to share and hold in common [goods] with the

[27] StAA, Literaliensammlung 1522: 5 Dec. 1522; SAZh, A 195/1, no. 157; cf. Anna Feyler, 'Die Beziehungen des Hauses Württemberg zur schweizerischen Eidgenossenschaft in der ersten Hälfte des XVI. Jahrhunderts' (Diss. phil. Zürich, 1905), pp. 240–1.

[28] Emil Egli (ed.), *Aktensammlung zur Geschichte der Zürcher Reformation in den Jahren 1519–1533* (Zürich, 1879; repr. Aalen, 1973), p. 87.

[29] StAA, Literaliensammlung 1522: 5 Dec. 1522.

[30] TLA, Oberösterreichische Hofregistratur, Reihe A, laufender Faszikel 12 (Abteilung IV, Position 33), 1 Dec. 1522; cf. StAFr, K 1/27, 35: The Upper Austrian government to [Hans Jacob von Landau], 4 Nov. 1522.

> wealthier folk; moreover, it will not have remained hidden from you, given your intelligencers, that the Bundschuh by its nature is far-flung and entirely unpredictable . . .[31]

That this missive was intended to browbeat the Swiss emerges from the next few lines, in which the administration recalled the fact that many Swiss had property and *rentes* in Württemberg, which would be put at risk in any military campaign. Thereupon Dr Johann Raming, later the bishop of Konstanz's vicar-general, was sent as a negotiator to the Confederate Diet, whose credentials drew explicit attention 'to plans to initiate and instigate a Bundschuh which from the outset would be directed against us and the principality'.[32]

What is striking about this missive is less the crass attempt to intimidate the Swiss than the reference to demands by the common man that went well beyond duke Ulrich's territorial ambitions. They mark the first meshing of Bundschuh slogans with notions that encompassed evangelical equality and brotherhood. In 1517, after all, in his last conspiracy Joß Fritz had abandoned locally specific articles of grievance in favour of two overarching maxims—the cancellation of all debt- and interest-payments, together with the abolition of all feudal dues.[33] Among Zwingli's radical followers, especially in the countryside, notions of radical congregationalism (in James Stayer's words) were gaining currency, which became concentrated in the issue of tithing.[34] Whether that amounts to a commitment to brotherliness and the community of goods remains an open question. At all events, Zwingli had uttered the slogan of *omnia communia* in

---

[31] SAZh, A 195/1, no. 158. 10 Dec. 1522: *dann laider so ist, one das der gemain man allenthalb vnnd zum mererteil begirig, weg vnnd fugen zusuchen, das all schulden ab vnnd sie mit den vermögenlichenn tailen vnnd gemain haben söllten; zu dem euch alls den erfarnen vnuerborgen, das des pundtschuchs aigenschafft weitlöifig vnnd ganntz vngewiß* [. . .].

[32] Ibid., no. 161. 11 Dec. 1522: *ain pundtschuch vffzuwerffen vnnd zuerwecken, wellicher anfangs wider vnns vnnd dis furstennthumb komen vnnd dienen sölte.*

[33] StAFr, B 5 XI, 10, fo. 62r; Albert Rosenkranz (ed.), *Der Bundschuh. Die Erhebungen des südwestdeutschen Bauernstandes in den Jahren 1493–1517*, 2: *Quellen* (Schriften des Wissenschaftlichen Instituts der Elsaß-Lothringer im Reich, 12, 2) (Heidelberg, 1927), pp. 266, 290; AMS, AA 365, fo. 30r. See Tom Scott, 'Freiburg und der Bundschuh', in Hans Schadek (ed.), *Der Kaiser in seiner Stadt. Maximilian I. und der Reichstag zu Freiburg 1498* (Freiburg im Breisgau, 1998), pp. 333–53, esp. 346. [Engl. version in this volume.]

[34] James M. Stayer, 'Die Anfänge des schweizerischen Täufertums im reformierten Kongregationalismus', in Hans-Jürgen Goertz (ed.), *Umstrittenes Täufertum 1525–1975. Neue Forschungen* (Göttingen/Zürich, 1975), pp. 19–49, esp. 29–31.

his reply to the bishop of Konstanz's 'Admonition' (*Ermahnung*) in his tract of August 1522, *Apologeticus Archeteles*.[35]

Initially, duke Ulrich's plans came to naught, but in 1524 he revived them as peasant unrest in the southern Black Forest began to destabilize the Klettgau and Hegau, thereby creating a favourable environment for the intervention of third parties with their own agenda.

IV

The uprising of peasants in the landgraviate of Stühlingen in the southern foothills of the Black Forest on midsummer's eve 1524 normally marks the beginning of the Peasants' War. Immediately thereupon subjects of the Benedictine abbey of St Blasien in the neighbouring villages of Ewattingen and Bettmaringen rose in revolt. As it turned out, preliminary contact between the Stühlingers and the Forest peasants had already been established, so that thoughts of a revolt which transcended existing lordships were immanent from the outset. Around this time subjects of the city of Schaffhausen also rallied in Hallau, a village which had been at odds with the cathedral chapter of Konstanz over tithing from 1521.[36] The Stühlingen rising is commonly regarded as moderate, since the peasants wished to negotiate with their lords, the counts of Lupfen and Stühlingen, according to ancient custom over infringements of their communal rights. The Schaffhausen peasants, by contrast, presented a veritable catalogue of demands, which took the Word of God as its general legitimating principle—a foretaste of the Twelve Articles of the Upper Swabian peasants in the spring of 1525.[37]

---

[35] *Huldreich Zwinglis Sämtliche Werke*, 1, ed. Emil Egli (Berlin, 1905), p. 309: *substantiam nullam quisquam suam dicit, omnia communia censentur, cupit quisque alium beneficiis anteventere, mansuetudine demereri, laborem alterius partiri, aegestatem levare* [. . .]. See James M. Stayer, *The German Peasants' War and Anabaptist Community of Goods* (Montreal/Kingston, Ont./London, Ont./Buffalo, NY, 1991), p. 97. Similar utterances can be found in Erasmus and Hubmaier, as James Stayer was kind enough to inform me.

[36] Paul Herzog, *Die Bauernunruhen im Schaffhauser Gebiet 1524/25* (Aarau, 1965), pp. 14–15.

[37] TLA, Oberösterreichische Hofregistratur, Reihe A, laufender Faszikel 12 (Abteilung IV, Position 30), 14 July 1524: *So dann haben sich deren von Schaffhusen vnderthon vff dem Land zusamen gerottet vnd entschlossen, hinfur keinen herren dann allein got zuhaben.* See Tom Scott, 'Reformation and Peasants' War in Waldshut and Environs. A Structural Analysis', part 1, *Archiv für Reformationsgeschichte*, 69 (1978), p. 94 and n. 51 [repr. in this volume].

That a revolution under the sign of the Gospel nevertheless began in Stühlingen and not on Schaffhausen territory can be explained by the fact (apart from the Confederates' attempts at mediation) that the Stühlingen rising threw up a peasant leader who from the outset was bent upon a general campaign of liberation. He was Hans Müller, a serf of St Blasien from Bulgenbach, who combined in his person strands of conspiratorial agitation, appeals to the Swiss, alliances of convenience with duke Ulrich, and, finally, radical evangelical conviction. Andreas Lettsch, St Blasien's notary, whose chronicle yields essential information about the initial stages of revolt, knew Hans Müller at first hand:

> He was a fine figure of a man, tall of stature, who previously had fought in France, and who for a layman had a real gift of speech.[38]

While the communal representatives of the Stühlingers embarked upon protracted negotiations, which were brought to a provisional conclusion in mid-September thanks to mediation by the Schaffhausen council, a group of activists led by Hans Müller adopted entirely different tactics. Already at the end of July a contingent of six hundred Stühlingers had marched to the small Austrian town of Waldshut on the *Hochrhein*, where it encamped for three days. From 1521 onwards Waldshut had been home to the radical Reformer Balthasar Hubmaier as pastor, who began preaching Zwinglian doctrines, but later turned to Anabaptism.[39]

Waldshut therefore became a beacon of evangelical resistance to the Catholic authorities. For that reason, older research regarded Müller's march as a declaration of solidarity on the part of the Stühlingers with the exposed Austrian territorial town.[40] There is much truth in that verdict. From his activities in the weeks that followed it is clear that Müller was hoping to unleash a general revolt, for he had a black, white and red flag hoisted (whether it contained figures or slogans is not recorded), with which his followers scoured the districts along the Rhine drumming up support.

---

[38] Günther Franz (ed.), *Quellen zur Geschichte des Bauernkrieges* (Darmstadt, 1963), p. 87.

[39] Scott, 'Reformation and Peasants' War', part 1, pp. 83 ff.; Torsten Bergsten, *Balthasar Hubmaier. Seine Stellung zu Reformation und Täufertum 1521–1528* (Kassel, 1961).

[40] Wilhelm Stolze, 'Die Stühlinger Erhebung des Jahres 1524 und ihre Gründe', *Historische Zeitschrift*, 139 (1929), p. 298.

The march of the Stühlingers to Waldshut fits seamlessly into this pattern of agitation: these were demonstration marches,[41] without implying that the radical Stühlingers were necessarily seeking to form an evangelical alliance. This proviso applies to the Stühlingers' second march to Waldshut in the early days of September as well. On that occasion eight hundred men under their banner entered the town, from which Hubmaier had already fled.[42] In the light of a looming danger of attack by the Austrian authorities against the Stühlingers and Waldshut, the march could be seen in the first instance as a prophylactic move, an alliance from defensive motives. But closer inspection reveals it to be a deliberate attempt by the radicals under Hans Müller to push the majority of Stühlingen peasants to one side and, by means of an active alliance with an urban commune, to broaden the basis of resistance, and thus transform the revolt into a territorial war of liberation. That was, after all, the tactic which fired the Bundschuh conspiracies of Joß Fritz. What fuelled the march, therefore, was less ideological solidarity than strategic calculation. If the purpose of the alliance had indeed been to form an evangelical brotherhood (as is often argued),[43] it would be impossible to explain why the Stühlingers withdrew from Waldshut after so short a time. The territorial town's predicament was only resolved with the arrival at the beginning of October of a detachment of volunteers from Zürich. In the months that followed Waldshut became increasingly peripheral to Müller's plans.

V

In the meantime, duke Ulrich had resumed his plan of conquest that in 1522 had run into the buffers. According to a report reach-

---

[41] See Hans-Martin Maurer, 'Der Bauernkrieg als Massenerhebung. Dynamik einer revolutionären Bewegung', in Kommission für geschichtliche Landeskunde in Baden-Württemberg (ed.), *Bausteine zur geschichtlichen Landeskunde von Baden-Württemberg* (Stuttgart, 1979), pp. 255–95.

[42] Bergsten, *Hubmaier*, p. 147 n. 18.

[43] See M. M. Smirin, *Die Volksreformation des Thomas Münzer und der grosse Bauernkrieg*, transl. from Russian by Hans Nichtweiss (Berlin, 1952), pp. 401–2, 405. The term 'evangelical brotherhood' is mentioned in Heinrich Hug's Villingen Chronicle, but unambiguously as a subsequent gloss. See Arnold Elben, *Vorderösterreich und seine Schutzgebiete im Jahre 1524. Ein Beitrag zur Geschichte des Bauernkriegs* (Stuttgart, 1899), p. 155 n. 3.

ing the Austrian commissioners at Engen in the Hegau, he had taken up quarters once again in his fortress of Hohentwiel with a retinue, artillery, and provisions.

> What his plans are with the soldiers he has up at Twiel we cannot at this moment determine. But we suppose and consider, since we have received reports that the peasants everywhere in the Hegau have entered upon a secret conspiracy and understanding among themselves, that they are intending to commit disobedience by withholding rents and services from their lords. And they intend on 2nd October in a village called Hilzingen, which lies near Twiel, on the day of the church-ale there, to assemble, come to an agreement, and thereby make an alliance, since he [duke Ulrich] has gained the peasants' allegiance and support, so that on this very day he is purposing to invade the land of Württemberg and planning to start a war.[44]

In such an event, the authorities feared, the Stühlingers, Fürstenbergers, and other peasants would join his campaign. And that is indeed what came to pass. At the Hilzingen church-ale, the Hegau peasants rallied in droves.[45] Shortly thereafter Freiburg could report that Basel had lent duke Ulrich 10,000 fl. against his county of Montbéliard as a security[46]—as an exile, duke Ulrich was permanently strapped for cash. But Ulrich's agitation in the first instance did not succeed, since Überlingen's mediation persuaded the Hegau peasants to submit their grievances to the district court in Stockach.

At that, Hans Müller made it abundantly plain that he and his followers dismissed any legal arbitration out-of-hand, for within days he had launched a bold and extensive campaign northwards towards the Baar and the county of Hohenberg, accompanied by a detachment of Stühlingers, Fürstenbergers, and Black Foresters, in order to gain

---

[44] Johann Heinrich Schreiber (ed.), *Der deutsche Bauernkrieg. Gleichzeitige Urkunden*, 3 vols (Freiburg im Breisgau, 1863–66), 1, p. 83: *Was Fürnemens er aber mit solchem Volk so er uf Twiel hat, können wir noch diser Zit nit wissen. Wir vermuten und gedenken aber, diewil wir bericht sein, dass die Bauern allenthalben hieumb im Hegew, auch ein heimliche Conspiration und Verständnüß mit einander haben, dass sie sich auch untersten wollen, in die Ungehorsam zu treten, und ihren Herren kein Zins und Dienstberkeit mer zu thun; und sich solchs auf den andern Tag Octobris in einem Dorf, genannt Hülzingen, so zunächst unter Twiel liegt, auf denselben Tag daselbst Kirchtag seyn wirdet, da sie dann alle dahin kommen, vergleichen und deßhalben ein Bundnuß machen sollen, dann er diselben Bauern an sich hangen und ziehen, damit er dann auf heutigen Tag schon in Handlung ist, und sich* [. . .] *in das Land Wirtemberg zu fallen und ein Krieg anzufahen untersten werde.*

[45] Franz, *Quellen zur Geschichte des Bauernkrieges*, p. 90.

[46] Schreiber, *Bauernkrieg*, 1, p. 105.

further adherents, in the course of which he had no compunction in threatening violence. The subjects of the county of Klettgau, whom he sought to win over to his troop, were only able to escape his coercion by invoking the treaty of protection (*Burgrechtsvertrag*) which their overlord, count Rudolf von Sulz, had concluded with Zürich.[47]

Although at first the Klettgauers remained at peace, a detachment under Clewi Maier split off at the end of December to take part in Hans Müller's second campaign over the Black Forest.[48] Müller had succeeded once again, as he had done in Stühlingen, in dividing the peasantry. How far it was possible to turn a radical minority of activists into a majority—or, put more pointedly, whether the minority could convert or coerce the majority—remained to be seen. None the less, it is striking that at the turn of the year peasants from Stühlingen, the Hegau, the Klettgau, and the Baar all brushed aside any attempt at mediation. The readiness to negotiate previously evinced by substantial sections of the peasantry had visibly evaporated. On a tactical level, Müller's demonstration marches created a sense of constant unrest and put peace-loving peasants under pressure. For their part, the authorities were incapable of mounting any credible counter-offensive.[49] At the same time, however, the commissioners at the drawn-out negotiations in Stockach pointed out that the peasants had appealed to Zürich, Basel, and Schaffhausen for assistance.[50]

It is no secret that the concept of Swiss freedom has been the subject of considerable debate among historians. But it is hardly a matter of dispute that the south-west German peasants in invoking Helvetic rural liberty were by and large the victims of a delusion.[51]

---

[47] Tom Scott, 'Reformation and Peasants' War in Waldshut and Environs. A Structural Analysis', part 2, *Archiv für Reformationsgeschichte*, 70 (1979), pp. 140–1 [repr. in this volume]. Further references are included there.

[48] Ibid., p. 142; Franz Ludwig Baumann, 'Die Eidgenossen und der deutsche Bauernkrieg bis März 1525', *Sitzungsberichte der philosophisch-philologischen und der historischen Classe der königlich bayerischen Akademie der Wissenschaften zu München*, 1896, pp. 113–41, esp. 130.

[49] Despite intensive research the impact on the peasants of Thomas Müntzer, who spent six weeks in the Klettgau, remains entirely obscure. Scott, 'Reformation and Peasants' War', part 2, pp. 146–8.

[50] Ibid., p. 149.

[51] Idem, 'Liberty and Community in Medieval Switzerland', *German History*, 13 (1995), pp. 98–113 [repr. in this volume]; Guy P. Marchal, 'Die "alten Eidgenossen" im Wandel der Zeiten. Das Bild der frühen Eidgenossen im Traditionsbewußtsein

Moreover, in the conflicts between the Swiss and the House of Austria along the Rhine that culminated in the so-called Swabian or Swiss War of 1499, it was chiefly the rural population who suffered from Swiss incursions.[52] In the following years there were repeated raids for booty, which prompted subjects of the Outer Austrian county of Ferrette in Upper Alsace to complain in 1513

> that the Baselers and other Swiss have plundered us severely, and even the Solothurners, our neighbours; [. . .] so that we cannot raise our heads without risk, and sit here as if trussed up in a sack.[53]

Georges Bischoff has accordingly spoken of *une antipathie des habitants du baillage pour les dangereux voisins*.[54] Even if the peasants of south-west Germany were not concerned to proclaim any solidarity with the Swiss, but were merely seeking military support for tactical reasons, it must have been obvious from the outset that the Confederates after the conclusion of the Compact of Stans in 1481 never contemplated for a moment a territorial incursion into the districts north of the Rhine.[55] Nevertheless, the *belief* in the availability of Swiss military aid died hard, and that, too, is a fact which in itself cannot be ignored.

Let us return briefly to the Bundschuh. Recently Gunter Zimmermann has declared that the maxim of divine justice in Joß Fritz's

und in der Identitätsvorstellung der Schweizer vom 15. bis ins 20. Jahrhundert', in Historischer Verein der Fünf Orte (ed.), *Innerschweiz und frühe Eidgenossenschaft. Jubiläumsschrift 700 Jahre Eidgenossenschaft*, 2 vols (Olten, 1990), 2, pp. 309–26.

[52] See Werner Meyer, 'Krisen, Korruption und Kampfbegierde—Der politische, ideologische und emotionale Konfliktrahmen des Schwabenkrieges von 1499', in Regierungsrat des Kantons Solothurn (ed.), '*an sant maria magtalena tag geschach ein grose schlacht.' Gedenkschrift 500 Jahre Schlacht bei Dornach 1499–1999* (Solothurn, 1999), pp. 9–52, esp. 41–2, 48 [also *Jahrbuch für solothurnische Geschichte*, 72 (1999)]; Peter Niederhäuser, '"Uns aus Notdurft in die Gegenwehr schicken"—Winterthur, das Weinland und die angrenzenden Gebiete im Schwabenkrieg von 1499', *Zürcher Taschenbuch auf das Jahr 2001*, pp. 119–70, esp. 130–2, 138 f.

[53] Franz, *Aktenband*, p. 40.

[54] Georges Bischoff, 'Les grèves anti-seigneuriales de Ferrette. Les habitants d'un baillage du Sundgau et leur seigneur au début du XVIe siècle', *Revue d'Alsace*, 105 (1979), pp. 35–52, here at p. 42.

[55] Franz Ludwig Baumann, 'Die Eidgenossen und der deutsche Bauernkrieg seit dem Märze 1525', *Sitzungsberichte der philosophisch-philologischen und der historischen Classe der königlich bayerischen Akademie der Wissenschaften zu München*, 1899, 1, pp. 37–71, esp. 44. That does not exclude the possibility, though, that individual Swiss cantons harboured thoughts of territorial expansion, for instance Zürich in regard to the Klettgau. Niederhäuser, '"Uns aus Notdurft in die Gegenwehr schicken"', pp. 120–1.

Bundschuh conspiracies finds no confirmation in the sources. Only the Peasants' War has a claim to the maxim, thanks to the impact of evangelical doctrines. What inspired the Bundschuh, rather, was the republican freedom of the Swiss.[56] This argument, in my view, considerably overshoots the mark. Furthermore, Zimmermann's desire to attribute revolutionary quality to the Peasants' War alone is not convincing. All the same, the intention of seeking military support from the Swiss does lie at the heart of Fritz's *strategic* thinking. After the failure of the Upper Rhine Bundschuh in 1517 there was a telling sequel among the miners at Todtnau on the Schauinsland. During a quarrel in the tavern, one wage-worker had threatened that 'he would bring the Swiss over the mountains any time they chose'. At that, several mining shareholders expressed the fear that the affair would spread to a point 'that great contempt and conspiracy might result (from which a Bundschuh might arise)'.[57]

To assess the hopes that the peasants may have vested in the Swiss after 1520 is complicated by the Reforming doctrines radiating from Zürich. The Klettgauers for the most part certainly adopted Zwingli's cause, even if their defiant stance at the end of December 1524 did not necessarily spring from a principled commitment to the Gospel.[58] A salient characteristic of the radical Stühlinger, Klettgau, Hegau, and Forest peasants, however, is that until the spring of 1525 they deployed the slogans of godly justice or evangelical freedom neither as legitimation nor as encouragement. Instead, they were banking on duke Ulrich. At the end of January the captain of the radical Klettgauers, Clewi Maier, was to pitch camp at Schaffhausen and wait there with other commanders for the start of duke Ulrich's campaign of conquest.[59] It is true that on 29th January the Klettgauers first marched to Waldshut, which embraced them warmly.[60] But the

[56] Gunter Zimmermann, 'Die Grundgedanken der Bundschuhverschwörungen des Joß Fritz', *Zeitschrift für die Geschichte des Oberrheins*, 142 (1994), pp. 141–64, esp. 142, 149, 154–5.

[57] Rosenkranz, *Bundschuh*, 2, p. 309.

[58] Scott, 'Reformation and Peasants' War, part 2, p. 141. For a dissenting view see Peter Blickle and a Berner Arbeitsgruppe, 'Zürichs Anteil am deutschen Bauernkrieg. Die Vorstellung des göttlichen Rechts im Klettgau', *Zeitschrift für die Geschichte des Oberrheins*, 133 (1985), pp. 81–101.

[59] FWWA, WoWo 9890; Franz Ludwig Baumann (ed.), *Akten zur Geschichte des deutschen Bauernkrieges aus Oberschwaben* (Freiburg im Breisgau, 1877), pp. 92–3, no. 75.

[60] Scott, 'Reformation and Peasants' War, part 2, pp. 150–3.

immediate trigger for this detour was the withdrawal of the band of Zürich volunteers, which exposed the town once again to the threat of an Austrian attack. It did nothing to alter the longer-term aims of the radicals, for on 9th February duke Ulrich had his artillery brought from Hohentwiel to Hilzingen, where the Hegau peasants were at the ready.[61] On 23rd February he set off northwards with twenty-two companies and a hundred horse, including eight bands of Swiss and Hans Müller's Black Forest peasants. As the town of Villingen dismissively reported:

> We have reliable intelligence that he has no more than a hundred horse, and around 10,000 Confederates, not more, debauched folk, no armour, few riflemen, and many among them who [have] no weapons at all.[62]

Duke Ulrich's campaign in Württemberg was *au fond* a fiasco. Although he quickly took Stuttgart, his capital, he fell victim to the change in the international diplomatic climate that followed the crushing defeat of the French king (who was Ulrich's protector) at the hands of imperial troops at the battle of Pavia on 24th February. Many Swiss mercenaries in French service fell in the battle, with the upshot that the Confederate Diet was prompted to recall its citizens forthwith from Ulrich's army. On 17th March Ulrich with a mere ten men at his side crept back to his fortress of Hohentwiel. In point of fact, his failure was already predictable before news of the battle of Pavia had arrived. Hardly had he set off than his following began to crumble. The Swiss mercenaries started to head for home in dribs and drabs after only three days; a day later Hans Müller with 150 Foresters did likewise 'saying, duke Ulrich promised them much, but has given them no pay, in any case has no money'.[63]

That was the true reason for the inglorious finale to his campaign. What enticement the duke could ever plausibly have offered the peasants—against the background of his behaviour in the Poor Conrad revolt!—is hard to judge. It is equally difficult to see how an experienced mercenary and canny tactician such as Hans Müller could have been taken in by so unscrupulous a character as Ulrich. The

[61] Schreiber, *Bauernkrieg*, 2, p. 9.
[62] *Ibid.*, p. 15.
[63] *Ibid.*, p. 16.

abrupt halt to Müller's participation does at least suggest that he had at best signed up for an alliance of convenience, not of solidarity.

Yet Müller did not allow himself to be thrown off course by his bitter disappointment. He immediately drew off his troops westwards towards the Black Forest, where he was confident of the greatest following. From there he planned a new campaign of liberation, which at long last came to stand under an evangelical banner. Echoing the Christian Union of Upper Swabia he rechristened his army the Christian Union of the Black Forest. At the beginning of April he marched over the Black Forest in two broad sweeps, albeit with puzzling about-turns and sidetracks, until his troops, together with the united Breisgau and Markgräfler bands, forced the town of Freiburg to capitulate on 23rd May—the climax of the Peasants' War on the Upper Rhine.

VI

For Hans Müller and his followers the slogan of evangelical freedom constituted the ideological reinforcement of a deliberate revolutionary consciousness which had accompanied his agitation from the outset: it did not first make him into a revolutionary. His Christian Union of the Black Forest committed itself to the Twelve Articles and the Federal Ordinance of Upper Swabia, and it is possible that Müller himself may have been influenced by the radical religious teachings of Balthasar Hubmaier.[64] Several clues suggest, however, that the core of his revolutionary conviction lay elsewhere. It is, in this respect, beyond dispute that he pursued his strategy without reference to the Christian Union of Upper Swabia. For when the latter sought military assistance from Müller at the beginning of April and called on him to occupy Tiengen and Waldshut as the prelude to conquering the Black Forest,[65] he ignored its request altogether.

[64] Scott, 'Reformation and Peasants' War', part 2, pp. 146–8.

[65] Johann Heinrich Schreiber, 'Balthasar Hubmaier. Stifter der Wiedertäufer auf dem Schwarzwalde', *Taschenbuch für Geschichte und Altertum in Süddeutschland*, 2 (1840), pp. 204–5 n. 1: *Die Buren haben Rabensburg ingenommen und besetzt, dessglichen Tettnang, Mörsburg und Markdorf, und liegen jetzund vor Ueberlingen; haben auch Hans Müller von Bulgenbach, so jetzt zu Bonndorf sitzt, zugeschrieben, er sölle mit sinen Buren uf syn, so wöllen sie Thiengen und Waldshut innemen und besetzten, dessglichen den Schwarzwald auch innemen.* Cf. StAFr, C 1 Militaria 100: Laufenburg to Freiburg, 7 April 1525.

Instead, he undertook the aforementioned campaign across the Black Forest into the valley of the Upper Rhine. At no point did he enter into alliance with the peasants of Upper Swabia.

What vision drove him on? There can be no doubt that Müller, like Joß Fritz before him, sought an alliance with the Swiss. Whether that was pure tactics or had its roots in a deeper identification with republican freedom our sources do not tell us. After his arrest he confessed under torture that, if the siege of Radolfzell had succeeded, the Hegauers would straight away have allied themselves with the Swiss peasantry.[66] The words may, of course, have been put into his mouth. A hitherto overlooked source, however, strengthens the suspicion that Müller planned to recruit an army of mercenaries in order to launch a general war of liberation in league with the Swiss. A captured peasant, Thoman Moser from Kuppenheim near Herrenberg, confessed in late June that according to hearsay Hans Müller intended to lead a party of soldiers to Milan. But when Moser travelled to the Hegau, he received no instructions to head for Milan. Instead, the captains encamped at Schaffhausen and Baden in the Aargau were being commanded to recruit mercenaries in Milan.[67] It would be unwise to overinterpret this somewhat confused testimony, but it does indicate that Müller, like Joß Fritz before him, saw himself as a revolutionary by profession and a perpetual activist, for whom sedition and conspiracy had become almost ends in themselves.

If one is searching for a genuine conflation of republican freedom and Christian brotherliness in the Peasants' War, then it is less to be found among the peasants than in the discourse of the learned Reformers themselves—in Zwingli, or above all in Christoph Schappeler, the preacher of Memmingen, who had given the Twelve Articles their religious cladding. In the pamphlet To the Assembly of the Common Peasantry (now confidently ascribed to Schappeler)[68] a

[66] *Amtliche Sammlung der älteren Eidgenössischen Abschiede*, 4, 1a, ed. Johannes Strickler (Brugg, 1873), p. 763. After the siege was abandoned many Hegauers fled into Switzerland, where they hoped for support from Schaffhausen's villages. But the rural unrest discharged itself in a revolt in Schaffhausen itself in which the peasants made common cause with the city's wine-growers against the council. Herzog, *Bauernunruhen*, pp. 49–50, 129–31.

[67] ADHR, 17 J 19, 30 June 1525.

[68] Peter Blickle, 'Republiktheorie aus revolutionärer Erfahrung (1525)', in idem (ed.), *Verborgene republikanische Traditionen in Oberschwaben* (Oberschwaben. Geschichte und Kultur, 4) (Tübingen, 1998), pp. 195–210.

revolutionary programme is set out, which in Peter Blickle's words 'reconciles the political self-perception of the Swiss, the theology and ethics of Huldrich Zwingli, and the central demands of the Upper Swabian peasants into a political theory that in the concrete situation was intended to justify peasant resistance and therewith the revolution [of the common man]'.[69]

---

[69] Idem, '"Es sol der Schwanberg noch mitten in Schweitz ligen"', p. 122. For comparative purposes, it is instructive to look at the activities of Michael Gaismair in Tirol during the Peasants' War, the drafting and interpretation of his so-called Territorial Constitution for Tirol, with its combination of practical proposals and theological notions derived from Zwingli, and his subsequent anti-Habsburg agitation from Venetian soil during his outlawry. See most recently Tom Scott, 'The Reformation and Modern Political Economy: Luther and Gaismair Compared', in Thomas A. Brady, Jr, *Die deutsche Reformation zwischen Spätmittelalter und Früher Neuzeit* (Schriften des Historischen Kollegs: Kolloquien 50) (Munich, 2001), pp. 173–202 (with further bibliographical references).

CHAPTER SIX

SOUTH-WEST GERMAN TOWNS IN THE PEASANTS' WAR: ALLIANCES BETWEEN OPPORTUNISM AND SOLIDARITY*

I

On 22nd April 1525, the Strasbourg magistrate and emissary, Jakob Sturm, who on the instructions of the imperial regency council had ridden to the Neckar Valley–Odenwald troop at Heilbronn, sent a report on the situation in the imperial free city to his colleagues back home.

> [After the Weinsberg Massacre the troop] marched to Heilbronn, and by threatening to cut down the vines brought matters to a point where the honourable council of the city, under pressure from the common man and especially the women, was obliged to open the gates on Easter Tuesday [18th April], and up to this day their captain, Jörg Metzger from Ballenberg by name, along with other commanders are here in the city in large numbers; they have a parlour to themselves in the city hall, where they deliberate. They have posted their own men from the troop at the city gates . . .; have taken possession of all convents and residences of the clergy and are plundering them; they have found an exorbitant amount of cash in the residence of the Teutonic Order—a whole chest stuffed with money, as their field-clerk told me himself, who was present. The Heilbronners have to agree to all this . . .

The city council was unable to prevent an alliance with the peasant troop:

* Archives are cited by the following abbreviations:
ADHR: Archives Départementales du Haut-Rhin, Colmar
AMKy: Archives Municipales de Kaysersberg
AMS: Archives Municipales de Strasbourg
FWWA: Fürstlich Waldburg-Wolfegg'sches Gesamtarchiv, Schloß Wolfegg
HSA: Württembergisches Hauptstaatsarchiv, Stuttgart
StAFr: Stadtarchiv Freiburg im Breisgau
StAVl: Stadtarchiv Villingen

> It has now been publicly announced, as I write this letter, that in Heilbronn any citizen or apprentice who desires to join the troop should appear at the city gate; the council has to permit anyone who wishes to go to do so.[1]

This contemporary account of the events at Heilbronn can be applied *pari passu* to the assessment of south-west German towns in the Peasants' War advanced by the bulk of recent scholarship. The decisive features can be summed up as follows:

1. Latent or overt tensions between council and commons;
2. Deep-seated anticlericalism, negatively interpreted as a desire to seize clerical property, positively cast as the demand that the clergy should be incorporated into the commune as a civic legal entity;
3. Open partisanship for the peasants among a broad cross-section of the population, with the spread of Reforming doctrines acting as a clasp between town and country.

All these elements were present in Heilbronn, where the Reformer Johann Lachmann had gained a strong following even amongst members of the council. Consequently, Peter Blickle regards Heilbronn as a paradigm of the stance adopted by imperial cities, not only in the south-west of the empire, but also in Franconia and Swabia. This verdict presupposes that one concentrates on the main outline of events as they unfolded rather than being distracted by local deviations.[2] In the case of territorial towns, whose social and economic profile hardly exceeded that of the peasants in the countryside (and that was especially true of the peasant burgher towns), cooperation

---

[1] Hans Virck (ed.), *Politische Correspondenz der Stadt Strassburg im Zeitalter der Reformation*, 1 (Strasbourg, 1882), p. 197 (no. 344): *darnoch fur Heylpronnen geruckt, vnd durch trowung die reben abzuhowen, die sach dohin brocht das usz betrang des gemeinen mans vnd namlich der weyber jnen ein Ersammer rott die Statt hat offnen müssen uff den osterdinstag, vnd sind also uff heutigen tag jr oberster mitt nammen Jerg metzger von Ballenberg sampt andern hauptleut in grosser anzall hie in der Statt, haben ein sonder stuben uff dem Rotthusz, dorin sy zu ratt gonde, haben die thor mit jeren leuten besetzt lossen vom hauffen usz* [. . .], *haben alle closter und hoffe der geistlichen ingenommen, vnd blündern sy, haben gross uberschwencklich barschafft in des teutschen meisters hoff funden ein gantze kisten voll gelts als mir jr veldtschryber selbs gesagt so do bey gewesen, müssen die von Haylpron alles gestatten* [. . .]. *Man hatt yetz alsz ich den brieue schreyb zu Heyltprun umbgeschlagen, das alle burger und dinstgesellen so mytt dem huffen ziehen wollen sollen vor dem thor erscheinen, hatt der Rot iederman erlauben müssen so ziehen will* [. . .].

[2] Peter Blickle, *Die Revolution von 1525*, 3rd edn (Munich, 1993), pp. 180 f.

between peasants and townspeople, according to Blickle, could be achieved effortlessly.[3]

The following remarks are less designed to retouch this picture, let alone expose it as a forgery, than to point out pentimenti that have hitherto been overlooked. These lay bare certain contradictions which suggest that the towns' participation in the Peasants' War was conditioned more by opportunism than by solidarity. In view of the very patchy sources and a lack of earlier investigations (especially for Württemberg) it is impossible to deal in detail with all the towns of south-west Germany. Instead, we shall concentrate on the Upper Rhine, which has been reasonably well covered since the researches of Karl Hartfelder.[4] For ease of reference, the results of analysis of the printed and unprinted sources are presented in tabular form. In order to keep the footnotes to a reasonable size, source references and a commentary on the tables are contained in a separate appendix. The three tables which follow do, however, require some preliminary elucidation.

Table 6.1. Voluntary alliances with the peasant troops.

1. Alsace-Lorraine	**2. Baden/Breisgau**	**3. Kraichgau/Palatinate**	**4. Black Forest/Baar**	**5. Württemberg/Swabia**
Montreux	Staufen	Gochsheim	Waldshut	Großbottwar
Landser	Lichtenau	Bruchsal	Stühlingen	Besigheim
Wattwiller [?]	Steinbach [?]	Eppingen	Fürstenberg	Beilstein
Soultz (Upper Mundat)	Durlach	Sinsheim	Hüfingen	Bönnigheim
Barr			Bräunlingen	Güglingen
Bernhardswiller			Geisingen	Lauffen
Boersch			Rottweil	Brackenheim
Molsheim			Dornhan [?]	Weinsberg
Wasselonne			Dornstetten	
Marmoutier				
Pfaffenhoffen [?]				
Lauterbourg				

[3] Ibid., p. 181. For Alsace see more cautiously Francis Rapp, 'La Guerre des Paysans dans la vallée du Rhin supérieur. Quelques problèmes d'interprétation', in *Charles-Quint, le Rhin et la France. Droit savant et droit pénal à l'époque de Charles-Quint* (Publications de la Société Savante d'Alsace et des Régions de l'Est, recherches et documents 17) (Strasbourg, 1973), p. 144.

[4] Karl Hartfelder, *Zur Geschichte des Bauernkriegs in Südwestdeutschland* (Stuttgart, 1884).

Table 6.2. Involuntary alliances with the peasant troops.

[A = Pressure from within the town; B = External pressure]

1. Alsace-Lorraine	2. Baden/Breisgau	3. Kraichgau/Palatinate	4. Black Forest/Baar	5. Württemberg/Swabia
Altkirch [B]	Neuenburg [B]	Philippsburg [Udenheim] [B]	Aach [B]	Stuttgart [B]
Belfort [B]	Freiburg [B]	Neustadt an der Weinstraße [B]	Engen [B]	Heilbronn [A+B]
Masevaux [B]	Breisach [A+B]		Triberg [B]	Wimpfen [A?+B]
Thann [A]	Waldkirch [B]		Wolfach [B]	
Cernay [B]	Burkheim [B]		Sulz am Neckar [B]	
St Amarin [B]	Endingen [A+B]		Horb [B]	
Guebwiller [A]	Kenzingen [B]			
Ammerschwihr [A+B]	Ettenheim [B]			
Kaysersberg [A+B]	Lahr [B]			
Kientzheim [A]	Oberkirch [A+B]			
Riquewihr [A+B]	Stollhofen [A]			
Ribeauvillé [A+B]				
Guémar [A]				
Bergheim [B]				
Bouxwiller [B]				
Seltz [B]				

Table 6.3. Towns which did not ally with the peasant troops.

[1 = Strong fortifications; successful resistance; warnings from the authorities. 2 = Ignored by the peasants. 3 = Role as intermediary. 4 = Preventative measures by the council. *Italics* = territorial towns]

1. Alsace-Lorraine	2. Baden/Breisgau	3. Kraichgau/Palatinate	4. Black Forest/Baar	5. Württemberg/Swabia
Delle [1]	Gengenbach [2]	*Bretten* [2]	*Säckingen* [1]	Konstanz [2+3]
Mulhouse [4]	Offenburg [2+3]	Speyer [4]	*Laufenburg* [1]	*Radolfzell* [1]
Ensisheim [1]	*Pforzheim* [2]		*Blumberg* [2]	*Tübingen* [1]
Rouffach [2]			*Villingen* [1+2]	
Colmar [4]				
Sélestat [4]				
Benfeld [1]				
Andlau [1]				
Obernai [1]				
Rosheim [1]				
Mutzig [1]				
Strasbourg [3]				
Haguenau [1]				
Lichtenberg [1]				
Wissembourg [4]				
Sarreguemines [1]				

1. The boundaries between the three groups of towns, which either voluntarily or involuntarily allied with the peasants or else kept their distance from the revolt, are naturally fluid. How to distinguish between deliberate and enthusiastic alliances born of principled solidarity on the one hand and hesitant communities of action deriving from a recognition of the futility of prolonged resistance on the other is often not at all easy.

2. The number of towns which voluntarily allied with the peasants is certainly pitched too low. A glance at the map suffices to indicate about how many—mostly smaller—towns we have no reliable information. For the many winegrowing small towns in the Neckar valley in northern Württemberg, for example, we are reliant upon the fortuitous survival of Jakob Sturm's report from Heilbronn; more detailed chronicle accounts are entirely lacking. In an urbanized landscape such as south-west Germany this is all more so since the larger villages hardly differed from the circumvallated small towns in population and economy.

3. Where alliances with the peasant troops came about forcibly, internal and external pressures often mutually reinforced each other. Partisans of the peasants among the commons openly urged joining the troop, acted as messengers between the town and the peasants' camp, supplied the peasants with provisions and ammunition on the quiet, and kept their captains informed about the mood within the walls. For their part the peasant leaders assured the opposition forces in the town of their support in the seizure of church property or in their struggle against an oligarchical council. The many references to irresistible pressure from outside are of course often subsequent glosses by the magistrates, eager to conceal the degree of sympathy among the population in attempting to justify their actions before imperial or territorial tribunals of enquiry.

4. The towns which did not take part in the Peasants' War in south-west Germany are more numerous—and also less of a piece—than has hitherto been supposed. Among the more than twenty identifiable towns in this category are naturally several which sheltered peasant sympathizers, and indeed some which may well have been on the brink of allying with the peasants. Nevertheless, the council in many instances understood how to avert the danger through timely concessions or preventative measures.

That the more powerful and economically more advanced towns were inclined to rebuff the peasants—the larger towns of the Alsatian

Decapolis are particularly striking in this regard—is sufficiently well known.[5] That this was also the case with certain territorial towns is even more remarkable. Some, it is true, functioned as residences or were important strongholds of the princes. But that can hardly explain the reserved attitude of dwarf towns such as Delle in the Sundgau. A preliminary conclusion, therefore, might be that the customary constitutional distinction between imperial cities and territorial towns is no reliable indicator of their stance in the Peasants' War.

II

Before we look at the attitude of the towns in more detail, it makes sense to enquire what expectations the peasants themselves vested in the towns: these were essentially practical and strategic in character. To maintain sizeable peasant troops in the field required substantial and continuous provisioning, which could not be provided by villages in the countryside alone. The troops therefore took advantage of the granaries and cellars of the convents, but the urban residences or palaces of the convents and foundations, not least the Teutonic Order and the Knights Hospitaller, also held substantial stocks, so that the rebels often announced that they were seeking entry to the towns simply in order to take revenge on the clergy. Put in concrete terms, that meant demanding the handing over of all the clergy's reserves of produce, which the rebels then either consumed themselves or else offered for sale. Frequently this request was coupled with assurances that they intended no harm to either council or commons.

The towns, moreover, had an indispensable reservoir of troops and arms at their disposal. The captain of the Sundgau troop, Henni Wetzel, consciously set his sights on the winegrowing communities along the Vosges foothills for that very reason, for he could not rely on sufficient ordnance from the thinly settled plain of the Upper

---

[5] Philippe Dollinger, 'Un aspect de la Guerre des Paysans en Alsace: l'organisation du soulèvement', in idem, *Pages d'Histoire. France et Allemagne médiévales, Alsace* (Collection de l'Institut des Hautes Études Alsaciennes, 25) (Paris, 1977), p. 139; idem, 'La Guerre des Paysans en Alsace. Aperçu général et caractères', in Alphonse Wollbrett (ed.), *La Guerre des Paysans 1525* (Société d'Histoire et d'Archéologie de Saverne et Environs. Études Alsatiques, supplément 93) (Saverne, 1975), p. 6.

Rhine valley.[6] Even the capture of smaller towns offered some security against a seigneurial counteroffensive on account of their walls. When the Outer Austrian government together with numerous Alsatian and Breisgau nobles entrenched themselves behind the walls of Ensisheim—the peasants understandably refrained from besieging the well-fortified town which had a double moat[7]—they were pursuing a tactic which the rebels themselves could equally well have embraced.

Whether the peasant troops from the outset pursued a deliberate strategy of forcing the larger urban strongholds to capitulate is, however, a moot point. Unlike the Bundschuh conspiracies on the Upper Rhine under Joß Fritz, which followed a clear military logic, whereby the smaller towns were to be taken first, in order to gain *points d'appui* and to seize artillery, before proceeding to besiege well-fortified regional centres such as Freiburg and Breisach,[8] the prolonged marches of the peasants in the winter of 1524 and the spring of 1525 were more in the nature of demonstration marches, as Hans-Martin Maurer has styled them.[9] The most striking example is afforded by the links between the Stühlingen peasants and the town of Waldshut, which had been deeply influenced by the teachings of the radical Reformer Balthasar Hubmaier. After the initial arbitration between the counts of Lupfen and their subjects in the landgraviate of Stühlingen on 24th July, six hundred ostensibly armed Stühlingers defied the truce by marching openly to Waldshut, where they encamped for three days.[10] On 1st September another eight hundred Stühlingers, led by

[6] Georges Bischoff, 'La Haute-Alsace et la Guerre des Paysans', in Wollbrett, *Guerre des Paysans*, p. 114.

[7] Hartfelder, *Zur Geschichte des Bauernkriegs*, pp. 36 f.

[8] Tom Scott, *Freiburg and the Breisgau. Town-Country Relations in the Age of Reformation and Peasants' War* (Oxford, 1986), pp. 180, 187, revising the older views of Albert Rosenkranz, *Der Bundschuh. Die Erhebungen des südwestdeutschen Bauernstandes in den Jahren 1493–1517*, 2 vols (Schriften des Wissenschaftlichen Instituts der Elsaß-Lothringer im Reich, 12) (Heidelberg, 1927), 1, pp. 321 ff. See also Tom Scott, 'Joß Fritz und der Bundschuh', in Horst Buszello, Dieter Mertens, and Tom Scott, '"Lutherey, Ketzerey, Uffrur". Die Stadt zwischen Reformation, Bauernkrieg und katholischer Reform', in Heiko Haumann and Hans Schadek (eds), *Geschichte der Stadt Freiburg im Breisgau*, 2 (Stuttgart, 1994), p. 32.

[9] Hans-Martin Maurer, 'Der Bauernkrieg als Massenerhebung. Dynamik einer revolutionären Bewegung', in Kommission für geschichtliche Landeskunde in Baden-Württemberg (ed.), *Bausteine zur geschichtlichen Landeskunde von Baden-Württemberg* (Stuttgart, 1979), pp. 268 ff.

[10] Tom Scott, 'Reformation and Peasants' War in Waldshut and Environs. A Structural Analysis', part 1, *Archiv für Reformationsgeschichte*, 69 (1978), p. 95 [repr. in

Hans Müller from Bulgenbach, marched again in full array to Waldshut in order to conclude a public treaty of protection with the town.[11] There is a consensus of research that both marches were intended in the first instance as demonstrations of solidarity and intentional provocations; they certainly contributed little to Waldshut's need for military reinforcements, as in the following months the troop led by Hans Müller turned its back on the town, to which it clearly ascribed no strategic importance. As a result, Waldshut opened its gates at the beginning of October to a company of volunteers from Zürich.[12]

During December 1524 Müller's army forayed far northwards into the Black Forest and the Baar with the aim of intimidating the feudal lords and of attracting further adherents. Not until the spring of 1525 did he set forth anew as captain of the Christian Assembly of the Black Forest, but by then on a route whose ultimate destination is beyond dispute: the surrender of the strategically vital town of Freiburg im Breisgau.[13] Freiburg is the only town, indeed, among the larger communes of south-west Germany that the peasants were able to capture. Stuttgart surrendered voluntarily, once the Austrian government of occupation had fled to Tübingen;[14] Heilbronn also capitulated without being bombarded. The siege of Radolfzell was abandoned.

If the military advantage of alliances with the south-west German towns is immediately apparent, what ideological support did the peasants expect from the urban population? Did the rebels regard the towns as natural allies, or were they rather obstacles to be overcome, or even enemies to be defeated? Peter Blickle's verdict is unequivocal: 'The clasp for common action on the part of peasants and townsfolk was undoubtedly the Gospel, or, more precisely, the conversion of Reforming theology into a political theology.'[15]

---

this volume]. See most recently Hiroto Oka, *Der Bauernkrieg in der Landgrafschaft Stühlingen und seine Vorgeschichte seit der Mitte des 15. Jahrhunderts* (Konstanz, 1998), p. 8. His statement that this march has been ignored by historians, apart from Wilhelm Stolze, is incorrect in the light of my remarks.

[11] Scott, 'Reformation and Peasants' War', part 1, pp. 98–101.

[12] Ibid., p. 101; Oka, *Bauernkrieg*, p. 17.

[13] Scott, 'Reformation and Peasants' War', part 1, pp. 101 f.; idem, 'Reformation and Peasants' War in Waldshut and Environs. A Structural Analysis', part 2, *Archiv für Reformationsgeschichte*, 70 (1979), pp. 154 f. [repr. in this volume].

[14] Maurer, 'Bauernkrieg als Massenerhebung', p. 269.

[15] Blickle, *Revolution von 1525*, p. 182.

A gulf did indeed exist between the expectations which the Altorf troop under Erasmus Gerber vested in the city of Strasbourg as protector of the Gospel and the hatred towards the Catholic stronghold of Freiburg manifested by the combined Breisgau and Black Forest troop besieging it. The origins of the Peasants' War in Alsace are inconceivable without the ideological *rayonnement* of Strasbourg. Jean Rott has pointed to the lively traffic in Reforming propaganda between Strasbourg and its environs as early as 1523.[16] Long before the famous sermons of the gardener and pamphleteer Clemens Ziegler around Mont Sainte-Odile in the spring of 1525 Strasbourg craftsmen were active as lay preachers in villages belonging to the city and its cathedral chapter. In February 1524 a Strasbourg tailor preached to peasants at Ingwiller; at the end of that year coopers, tailors, and gardeners were spreading Reforming doctrines in Brumath, Lampertheim, Vendenheim, and Weyersheim.[17] It is no surprise therefore that evangelical demands were voiced in several Strasbourg small towns and villages—Wasselonne, Dorlisheim, Ittenheim, Handschuheim, Illkirch, Grafenstaden, Marlenheim. A commitment to the new doctrines as a clasp between town and country found concrete expression over the issue of tithing, at least in the case of the peasant burghers, who were liable to render the tithe from their fields and plots.[18] The rural parishes demanded a reduction of the tithe or else its deployment in maintaining evangelical preachers. These demands can all be found in the Twelve Articles of the Swabian peasants, which did not reach Alsace until April 1525.

Strasbourg's ideological *rayonnement* must be regarded as unique. Elsewhere urban Reformers were active among the rural population: the Mulhouse chaplain Ulrich Clareti gained adherents for Lutheran doctrines among the miners in the Val de Rosemont,[19] while the Wissembourg Reformer Hans Schwebel and his associates converted the bailiwicks of Cleebourg and Gutenberg, which later became the

---

[16] Jean Rott, 'Artisanat et mouvements sociaux à Strasbourg autour de 1525', in *Artisans et Ouvriers d'Alsace* (Publications de la Société Savante d'Alsace et des Régions de l'Est, grandes publications, 9) (Strasbourg, 1965), p. 144; idem, 'La Guerre des Paysans et la Ville de Strasbourg', in Wollbrett, *Guerre des Paysans*, pp. 23 f.

[17] Ibid., p. 24; Rott, 'Artisanat', p. 144.

[18] See Gunter Zimmermann, *Die Antwort der Reformatoren auf die Zehntenfrage. Eine Analyse der Zusammenhänge von Reformation und Bauernkrieg* (Europäische Hochschulschriften, 3rd series, 164) (Frankfurt am Main/Bern, 1982), pp. 51 ff.

[19] Bischoff, 'Haute-Alsace', p. 119 n. 14.

main areas of recruitment for the Cleebourg troop.[20] But in Strasbourg it was principally craftsmen—in other words, layfolk—whose occupation brought them into close contact with the rural population; wine-growers, gardeners, coopers, and carters, who proclaimed an 'applied', that is, a politicized theology.[21]

We will return to the reasons why the Alsatian rural population never forged an alliance with the imperial city of Strasbourg. But first we must ask what Strasbourg's ideological influence actually effected among the peasantry. Did the rebels pledge themselves to the achievement of a Reforming programme (which need not have excluded the simultaneous pursuit of secular goals)? In short, did the Reformation movement in Strasbourg under communal-congregational inspiration set its stamp upon the course of the Peasants' War in Middle Alsace?

Recently, Gunter Zimmermann has given a decisively affirmative answer to this question. He stresses that the outbreak of rebellion around Strasbourg was a direct result of commitment to the Gospel, pointing not only to Clemens Ziegler's activities[22] but also to the impact of the evangelical theologian Andreas Preunlin, who had been sent by the Strasbourg magistracy itself to the village of Dorlisheim, where on Easter Sunday, 16th April, he preached to the entire army of the Altorf troop. Before that, however, Preunlin and all the male inhabitants of Dorlisheim had resolved to meet on Palm Sunday, 9th April, at Ottrott, in order with the assembled countryfolk 'to form a committee in order to bring the preachers together in a colloquy'.[23]

That the peasants were demanding a religious disputation between Catholic and evangelical theologians is for Zimmermann proof that they were not bent upon a violent revolt, but sought rather the breakthrough of evangelical truth. It is inadmissible, therefore, to deny the Peasants' War in Alsace any theological dimension.[24] The

[20] Jean-Laurent Vonau, 'La Guerre des Paysans dans l'Outre-Fôret', in Wollbrett, *Guerre des Paysans*, p. 39.

[21] Rott, 'Guerre des Paysans', p. 23.

[22] On Ziegler see Jean-Michel Boehler, 'Clément Ziegler, un prédicateur populaire au pied du Mont Ste-Odile', in Wollbrett, *Guerre des Paysans*, pp. 15–19.

[23] Gunter Zimmermann, 'Die ersten Tage des Bauernkriegs im Elsaß', *Zeitschrift für die Geschichte des Oberrheins*, 135 (1987), pp. 122 f.: *einen usschüz zu machen, domit man die bredicanten zusammenbring zu dispütieren.*

[24] Ibid., p. 125.

Dorlisheimer Veit Kaufmann who divulged this information went on to claim 'that they had assembled solely to support the Gospel and the Word of God'. Zimmermann, nevertheless, overlooks the overt attempt at exculpation by a participant in the revolt towards his overlord, namely the council of one of the leading evangelical imperial cities, whose emissary Martin Betscholt had ridden out to Dorlisheim precisely in order to admonish the peasants to keep the peace.[25]

To regard the Peasants' War in Middle Alsace primarily as a theological movement goes in my view much too far, even if one takes into account the undeniable influence of evangelically-minded craftsmen in Strasbourg. That is not to deny that the peasants had taken the precept of the freedom of a Christian to heart. Rather, it is to ponder how far evangelical beliefs were sufficient in themselves to bring about effortlessly alliances between town and country.

In research on the Peasants' War over the last generation this issue has provoked considerable controversy. This is not the place to describe the differing positions;[26] instead, let us investigate more closely several oddities in the three tables. 1. Even those towns which allied voluntarily with the peasants did not always reach this decision without further ado. At the beginning of December 1524, during the first skirmish of the Peasants' War between the Black Foresters under Hans Müller and the lords of Schellenberg, the small Schellenberg town of Hüfingen closed its gates to the peasants, claiming that its overlords were not present [to sanction opening them]. Not until 13th April did Hüfingen throw open its gates to the Christian Union of the Black Forest without resistance; the citizens, according to Heinrich Hug's Villingen Chronicle, 'freely let them in; that was a bad affair'.[27] Many towns in which groups of citizens were advocating and agitating for an alliance with the peasants still took a long time to join the revolt. The little winegrowing village of Thann in the Sundgau, which the peasants had at first shunned on account of its strong fortifications, only capitulated a week later as a result

[25] Ibid., pp. 128 f.

[26] See Tom Scott, 'The Peasants' War. A Historiographical Review', *Historical Journal*, 22 (1979), pp. 693–720, 953–74.

[27] Christian Roder (ed.), *Heinrich Hugs Villinger Chronik* (Bibliothek des Litterarischen Vereins in Stuttgart, 164) (Tübingen, 1883), pp. 105, 112: *ließens frig hineinziehen; das war ubel gehandlet.*

of internal unrest.[28] Further to the north the Ebersmunster troop pitched camp at Ribeauvillé on 8th May, but was refused entry to the town, even though large sections of the commons sympathized with the peasants. Six days later it did at last surrender, but not before the troop had marched off to take Bergheim.[29] The neighbouring Württemberg commune of Riquewihr's predicament lasted even longer. The first call to swear brotherhood was sent out on 25th April by the troop, which remained encamped before the town until 3rd May. Although several citizens, including a councillor, were seized as hostages, the decision to ally with the troop and swear loyalty was not finally taken until five days later, a span of three weeks in total.[30]

2. It was not always the case, as is commonly supposed, that internal opposition groups necessarily pressed for an alliance against the wishes of the civic authorities. The fault-line by no means ran cleanly between council and commons; the latter at times turned out to be irresolute and divided against themselves. In Guebwiller three guilds spoke up in favour of the peasants—the middle and lower wine-growers' guilds and the bakers'—while the remaining four guilds would have preferred to keep the peasants at bay. But these four guilds included the upper wine-growers! In Guebwiller, therefore, no overarching solidarity was achieved even among the wine-growers, who after all were the peasants' closest associates.[31]

In Mulhouse it was the smiths who off their own bat planned to attack the residence of the abbey of Lucelle. When the council warned them to remain calm and promised to consult the guilds as a whole, the smiths defiantly demanded that the commons be summoned to assemble in the market-place. After this request was turned down, the guilds assembled individually and condemned the smiths' independent initiative, but pleaded that they should be shown leniency.[32]

---

[28] Bischoff, 'Haute-Alsace', p. 114; Hartfelder, *Zur Geschichte des Bauernkriegs*, p. 27; Manfred Krebs, 'Die Rechtfertigungsschriften der vorderösterreichischen Städte vom Jahre 1526. Dokumente zur Geschichte des Bauernkriegs am Oberrhein', *Zeitschrift für die Geschichte des Oberrheins*, 93 (1941), pp. 16–17, 19–29.

[29] Hartfelder, *Zur Geschichte des Bauernkriegs*, pp. 75–87.

[30] Ibid., pp. 93–6.

[31] Ibid., pp. 25 f.; Bischoff, 'Haute-Alsace', p. 114.

[32] Hartfelder, *Zur Geschichte des Bauernkriegs*, pp. 59–61; Philippe Mieg, 'Mulhouse et la Révolte des Paysans de 1525', *Revue d'Alsace*, 89 (1949), pp. 177–96; Bischoff, 'Haute-Alsace', p. 114.

In the imperial city of Obernai the commons were likewise split; as the council informed Strasbourg, some citizens from the suburbs had joined the peasants, but still the city managed to withstand an attack by the peasants troop on 19th May, without being further destabilized from within.[33]

In the larger towns it is quite possible to detect varying motives and programmes on the part of the commons, even if by and large they favoured the peasants' cause. Karl-Heinz Mistele's researches on Heilbronn have revealed two groups at work: one circle around the relatively prosperous wine-grower Hans Spet, which was demanding the recasting of the council and the appointment of new members, whereby Spet himself hoped to become mayor; the other circle around the baker and inn-keeper Wolf Leip, who was on close terms with the radical peasant leader Jecklin Rorbach. Leip, too, wished to get rid of the council oligarchy, but he seems also to have taken on board the slogans of Christian equality and brotherly love, which clearly originated in the peasants' camp.[34]

In this context it does not need to be stressed that under cover of a general revolt in the countryside urban opposition groups could pursue a purely internal agenda, with recourse to the overarching legitimation provided by Reforming doctrines being in no sense detrimental to their cause.

3. It is nevertheless striking how many council regimes in the larger towns succeeded in preventing their citizens from allying with the peasants by calculated measures, above all the members of the Alsatian Decapolis and the imperial city of Speyer. There were extraordinary similarities in the way the pattern of internal conflict in these towns unfolded. For one thing, their magistracies understood how to come to terms with the commons, whether by polling the guilds or wards, or by integrating any commons' committees into the conduct of council business. For another, they took measures in good time against the clergy, by inventorying church property, suspending the ecclesiastical courts, cancelling interest-payments and annuities, and requiring the clergy to pay taxes and to perform

---

[33] Hartfelder, *Zur Geschichte des Bauernkriegs*, pp. 65–8, 70–2.

[34] Karl-Heinz Mistele, *Die Bevölkerung der Reichsstadt Heilbronn im Spätmittelalter (eine sozialgeschichtliche Untersuchung anhand der Steuerbücher des 15. und 16. Jahrhunderts)* (Veröffentlichungen des Archivs der Stadt Heilbronn, 8) (Heilbronn, 1962), pp. 104 f., 107 f.

guard-duties. In a word, the clergy, and in particular the regular clergy, were stripped of their immunities.

In Mulhouse the first steps in that direction had already been taken in 1523, so that two years later all the council had to consider was the issue of priests performing guard-duty. In the meantime, moreover, the city's six guildmasters had been invited to attend council meetings.[35] In Colmar the first signs of unrest manifested themselves in the winter of 1524, when the commons submitted a list of Thirteen Articles. At the beginning of January 1525 the committee of twelve who had drawn up the articles in the first place, together with the four captains, was called to account by the magistrates,[36] who had already consulted the so-called council of dempsters, a body inserted between council and commons apparently as a safety-valve, for it met only when instructed by the council. Having thus successfully sidelined the committee of twelve,[37] the council was nevertheless faced with renewed difficulties in the spring, as peasant unrest loomed. In Holy Week a rumour was circulating that six hundred wine-growers and gardeners planned to attack the Franciscan friary, whereupon the guild captain suggested forming a commons' committee to defuse the situation! As a result, the council agreed and thenceforth involved the new committee (which tellingly did not include any of the trouble-makers from the previous December) in its important decisions, especially in the resolution to inventory the convents' property and to demand that the clergy swear an oath of loyalty to the commune.[38] In Sélestat, by contrast, where the council was confronted by a powerful citizens' movement, the committee which in the autumn of 1524 had likewise submitted its grievances in a list of Eight Articles was thereafter repeatedly reorganized in order to exert increased pressure on the council. The initial concessions which the Catholic council had wrung without great enthu-

[35] Mieg, 'Mulhouse et la Révolte', pp. 178 f., 185.

[36] Kaspar von Greyerz, '"Liber ortę seditionis inter nonnullos contra senatum . . ." Die Colmarer Unruhen vom Dezember 1524/Januar 1525 aus der Sicht des Stadtschreibers Johannes Hummel', in Heinrich R. Schmidt, André Holenstein, and Andreas Würgler (eds), *Gemeinde, Reformation und Widerstand. Festschrift für Peter Blickle zum 60. Geburtstag* (Tübingen, 1998), pp. 371–89.

[37] Ibid., pp. 375 n. 18, 379.

[38] Hartfelder, *Zur Geschichte des Bauernkriegs*, pp. 105–10; Lina Baillet, 'Deux villes de la Moyenne Alsace. Sélestat et Colmar, face aux conflits religieux et sociaux', in Wollbrett, *Guerre des Paysans*, p. 100.

siasm from the convents in April 1525 failed to satisfy the committee. In mid-May the latter proposed to introduce the Gospel and the Word of God to Sélestat. But even then the council was able to spin matters out long enough for news of the massacre of the peasants at Saverne to create an entirely new constellation of power in Alsace.[39]

In Wissembourg, where the council's room for manoeuvre was restricted by its proximity to the Palatinate, it was still able—with the agreement of the citizens' committee which had been formed at the end of April—to bring the ransacking of the convents and foundations under its supervision. Though the burning of deeds and rent-rolls by no means ceased, it served in the longer term as a pretext for the council to impose Fourteen Articles on the canons that would have led to the introduction of Reforming doctrines and the reduction of all clerical privileges. But the approach of a Palatine army before Wissembourg put an abrupt end to these designs.[40]

In Speyer, finally, the cathedral chapter and three other foundations in a pre-emptive move had already offered the council in late February money and produce to sustain the population in their hour of need. The gesture proved insufficient for adherents of the Gospel in the city, who formed a committee to press their demands. When the Bruhrain troop threatened the city at the end of April, the magistrates conducted a poll of the guilds about how to deal with the clergy, after the mayor had enjoined the foundations to accept Eight Articles of Reforming inclination. But there was already such an uproar among the commons that on 8th May the heads of all the ecclesiastical houses were required to swear a citizen's oath and to

[39] Hartfelder, *Zur Geschichte des Bauernkriegs*, pp. 112–17. His wayward and incomplete account should be complemented and corrected by Joseph Gény, *Die Reichsstadt Schlettstadt und ihr Antheil an den socialpolitischen und religiösen Bewegungen der Jahre 1490–1536* (Erläuterungen und Ergänzungen zur Janssens Geschichte des deutschen Volkes, 1, 5/6) (Freiburg im Breisgau, 1900), pp. 144 f., 163–71, 176 f. The committee appeared for the first time in June 1524, after the Reform-inclined teacher at the grammar school, Johann Sapidus, gave an address in the parlour of the upper wine-growers before 200 citizens. Thereupon a committee demanded that Sapidus present their grievances to the council. Ibid., p. 129.

[40] Hartfelder, *Zur Geschichte des Bauernkriegs*, pp. 155 f., 160–5. An improved chronology of events is offered by Hans-Georg [i.e. Jean] Rott, 'Der Bauernkrieg und die Stadt Weißenburg im Elsaß. Bemerkungen zur Quellenlage und Versuch einer genaueren Chronologie', in Peter Blickle (ed.), *Bauer, Reich und Reformation. Festschrift für Günther Franz zum 80. Geburtstag am 23. Mai 1982* (Stuttgart, 1982), pp. 264–6.

join the civic militia. The exchange of correspondence between the Bruhrain troop and certain unnamed guilds nevertheless persisted, though in the weeks that followed Speyer remained calm, until elector Palatine Ludwig dealt the peasants a summary defeat at Pfeddersheim. Although the privileges of the ecclesiastical houses were restored, the council continued to try to wrest fiscal and jurisdictional authority over the foundations into its own hands. In the treaty of Heidelberg of 14th August 1525, however, it had to be content with an annual composition fee of a mere 200 fl.[41]

These examples make plain that those council regimes which inclined in any case to the new doctrines found it easier to keep their commons under control than a Catholic magistracy such as Sélestat. But in the end what counted in all these towns was not the council's religious stance, but its political shrewdness and adroitness.

4. This applies especially to Strasbourg, whose magistracy was concerned from the outset to play an intermediary role. At the end of April the Neubourg troop called upon the butchers' and gardeners' guilds to hand over weapons and artillery. Two weeks later the combined Alsatian troops threatened to enter the city in order to seize the property of monks and nuns who had sought refuge there.[42] For Strasbourg's senate the situation was all the more precarious because a number of convents acquired outburgher's right and accordingly placed themselves under the city's protection.[43] The peasants were only prepared to give an undertaking to leave those clerics unharmed who had previously acquired rights of outburghership. With the agreement of the dempsters the Senate carried out a poll of all the guilds on 14th May, which posed a single question: should those clerics be

[41] Hartfelder, *Zur Geschichte des Bauernkriegs*, pp. 246–55; Willi Alter, *Der Aufstand der Bauern und Bürger im Jahre 1525 in der Pfalz* (Veröffentlichungen der Pfälzischen Gesellschaft zur Förderung der Wissenschaften, 93) (Speyer, 1998), pp. 144–76; *Geschichte der Stadt Speyer*, 1, 2nd edn (Stuttgart/Berlin/Cologne/Mainz, 1983), pp. 487–95.

[42] Rott, 'Guerre des Paysans', p. 26.

[43] According to a communication by the senate, the leader of the combined Alsatian troops Erasmus Gerber believed that only the abbey of Andlau (transformed into a foundation for noblewomen in 1499), the nunnery of Biblisheim, and the Carthusian priory outside the city walls were affected. Virck, *Politische Correspondenz*, 1, pp. 124 f. (no. 221). But in its correspondence with Obernai the senate claimed that the abbeys of Hohenburg and Niedermunster below Mont Sainte-Odile with property there were likewise Strasbourg outburghers, who accordingly should be protected. Hartfelder, *Zur Geschichte des Bauernkriegs*, p. 71.

protected who had accepted the burdens of citizenship? This was a shrewd linkage indeed, since among the very first demands of the Strasbourg commons' movement was that the clerics be integrated into the community of citizens. The question therefore elicited an altogether positive response, except for the gardeners in the Krutenau, a few smiths, and a narrow majority of gardeners in the suburb of Saint-Pierre.[44] But in the course of further negotiations, during which the hardliners were reminded of their inviolable right of freedom of movement—a right which they as citizens enjoyed without restriction, in contrast to the rural population—all remaining burghers toed the senate's line, apart from four gardeners.[45]

It is true that around twenty members of the boatmen's, butchers', and clothmakers' guilds were absent during the poll.[46] Given a total membership of the three guilds of between 350 and 400 persons, that represents a not insignificant average of 15 per cent, or in the case of the butchers over 20 per cent. Peter Blickle regards it as an open question, therefore, 'whether these men were not in fact partisans of the peasants'.[47] The sources, however, allow us to pin down the reasons for the guildsmen's absence. Out of twenty-five butchers, eleven were described as 'in armour' (*im Harnsch*), that is, serving in the civic militia; another butcher was on gate-duty. Two craftsmen were entered as sick, and another two abroad. Only eight names are marked as being not in the city, which may be connected with the exercise of their profession. Of the clothmakers a total of eighteen were described as absent; four were on messenger service, one was on guard-duty at the gates, several were sick or otherwise absent, and only one was described *expressis verbis* as being in the peasants' camp (*bÿ dem huffen*). Finally, in the guild 'zum Anker' (at the sign of the anchor), twenty-five boatmen did not take part in the poll. Apart from those involved in levying tolls, or performing watch- and guard-duties, eight were entered as not being in the city, two were *zu Kule* (across the Rhine at Kehl), while in only four cases does the entry 'are in the war' (*sint inen krieg*) indicate that they had joined the peasant rebels.[48]

---

[44] Rott, 'Artisanat', pp. 146–7; Virck, *Politische Correspondenz,* 1, pp. 154 f. (no. 274); Blickle, *Revolution von 1525,* pp. 175 f.

[45] Rott, 'Artisanat', p. 147; idem, 'Guerre des Paysans', p. 27.

[46] Idem, 'Artisanat', p. 168 n. 126.

[47] Blickle, *Revolution von 1525,* p. 176.

[48] AMS, AA 386, fo. 42v–43r, 46r, 47v.

Jean Rott has investigated the circumstances surrounding the failure of the Strasbourg population to make common cause with the peasants. His reflections allow us in conclusion to venture comparisons with other cities and thereby to build up a provisional typology of their stance in the Peasants' War. Rott refers to the concrete measures taken by the senate to ease the suffering of the population by distributing flour to the needy, and by reducing or even suspending tolls and excises. He also stresses how anticlericalism was defused by restricting clerical immunities and by buying back—that is, redeeming,—perpetual *rentes*.[49] More broadly he points to certain structural factors: *le compartimentage extrêmement poussé du monde arrisanal*, whose conjunctural peaks and troughs did not coincide in the various artisanal occupations.[50] Here his findings chime with those of Jürgen Bücking, who somewhat earlier had remarked of Konstanz, Salzburg, and Freiburg, 'the more socially differentiated and technically advanced the larger cities were, the more dismissive and aggressive was their attitude towards the peasants'.[51] Although Strasbourg was governed by a patriciate, some of whose members had very close ties to the feudal world beyond its walls, oligarchic tendencies were kept in check, once the constitutional amendment of 1482 had conceded the craftsmen a genuine say in the city's affairs.[52]

A comparison with Freiburg is unavoidable. After the troubles of the fifteenth century council and commons had come to an understanding which culminated in the so-called 'guild reformation' of 1495. In it, the guilds' desire to embrace an economic policy hostile to entrepreneurialism and protectionist in spirit was largely recognized.[53] Neither in Strasbourg nor in Freiburg had an early capitalist division of labour led to the growth of a proletariat. In Freiburg, moreover, the sharp conflicts with the convents before the turn of

---

[49] Rott, 'Artisanat', p. 150; Virck, *Politische Correspondenz*, 1, pp. 152 f. (no. 274).

[50] Rott, 'Artisanat', pp. 148 f.

[51] Jürgen Bücking, 'Der "Bauernkrieg" in den habsburgischen Ländern als sozialer Systemkonflikt, 1524–1526', in Hans-Ulrich Wehler (ed.), *Der Deutsche Bauernkrieg, 1524–1526* (*Geschichte und Gesellschaft*, Sonderheft 1) (Göttingen, 1975), p. 173.

[52] Rott, 'Artisanat', p. 149.

[53] Scott, *Freiburg and the Breisgau*, pp. 128–41; idem, 'Reformen in Haushalt und Verwaltung', in Dieter Mertens, Frank Rexroth, and Tom Scott, 'Vom Beginn der habsburgischen Herrschaft bis zum "Neuen Stadtrecht" von 1520', in Heiko Haumann and Hans Schadek (eds), *Geschichte der Stadt Freiburg im Breisgau*, 1 (Stuttgart, 1996), pp. 253–64.

the century over their rights as outburghers paying a composition fee had been defused, if not entirely resolved, by Maximilian's intervention. As a result, there were very few signs of deep-rooted anticlericalism in Freiburg on the eve of the Reformation and Peasants' War.[54] The rigidly Catholic stance adopted by the town earned it the hatred of the peasants, to be sure, but there is no evidence that a communal movement, whether evangelically minded or not, was agitating for an alliance with the peasants.[55]

The larger cities of the Alsatian Decapolis alongside Strasbourg and Freiburg understood—albeit under differing confessional signs—how to channel the mood within their walls against such an alliance. That Freiburg was in the end forced to surrender is a different issue altogether: even the best manipulation of opinion was helpless in the face of the town's water supply being cut off.

Against this background the events in Heilbronn take on a different hue. In the fourteenth century the guilds had been stripped of their political power, and survived only as craft associations. The top-heavy council behaved increasingly as a closed oligarchy.[56] It is therefore no surprise in the Peasants' War that the wine-grower Hans Nuener, speaking for many, exclaimed: 'That's a council of cronies, and there are too many of them.'[57] Moreover, the council proceeded most reluctantly against clerical privileges, especially those of the Teutonic Order, allegedly on account of Heilbronn's situation as an imperial city, but in any event a great deal less resolutely than the other cities we have been discussing.[58] Within a typology of other larger imperial and territorial towns in south-west Germany Heilbronn appears more as the exception than the rule. The majority of such towns either distanced themselves from the peasants' rising, or else concluded alliances at best out of necessity or opportunism.

---

[54] Scott, *Freiburg and the Breisgau*, pp. 133 f.; idem, 'Reformen in Haushalt und Verwaltung', p. 256. Cf. Petra Rohde, 'Die Freiburger Klöster zwischen Reformation und Auflösung', in Haumann and Schadek , *Geschichte der Stadt Freiburg*, 2, pp. 427–32.

[55] Scott, *Freiburg and the Breisgau*, pp. 190–9; idem, '"Lutherische Opinionen" wider den "waren cristenlichen Glauben". Freiburg und die Reformation', in Buszello, Mertens, and Scott, '"Lutherey, Ketzerey, Uffrur"', pp. 35–41.

[56] Mistele, *Bevölkerung der Reichsstadt Heilbronn*, pp. 93 f.

[57] Moritz von Rauch (ed.), *Urkundenbuch der Stadt Heilbronn*, 4 (Württembergische Geschichtsquellen, 20) (Stuttgart, 1922), p. 158 (no. 2926); cf. Mistele, *Bevölkerung der Reichsstadt Heilbronn*, pp. 93, 106.

[58] von Rauch, *Urkundenbuch*, 4, pp. 34 f. (no. 2794), 46 f. (no. 2808).

III

Recent research has largely ignored the role of south-west German towns in the Peasants' War, with the exception of Franziska Conrad's important study of the Reformation in the Lower Alsatian countryside.[59] Her findings chime with the arguments put forward here. She detects a general readiness on the part of the imperial cities in Alsace to intervene as mediators (or for their own defensive purposes) in the revolt, but rarely a willingness to assist the peasants by swearing an oath of allegiance or by providing volunteers. The reason, she argues, lies in their divergent understanding of the Reforming message:

> The inhabitants of an imperial city were unlikely to share the peasants' interpretation of biblical norms and Christian love of one's neighbour, since their concept of a Christian society implied a restructuring of the civic regime; the oath of loyalty to the civic commune, moreover, precluded burghers from pledging allegiance to the peasants' aims.[60]

Cloaked in the mantle of evangelical enthusiasm, however, opposition groups elsewhere—Heilbronn, for example—sought to recast the council's rule, or else to underpin and intensify existing efforts to that end. In such cases, timely accommodation by the council was usually enough to secure the commons' loyalty; where that did not occur, the blame lay with its dithering attitude towards the new doctrines. The situation in Sélestat has already been discussed. In Obernai, things looked much blacker (as Conrad describes): many citizens were already fighting on the peasants' side; and the council could not decide whether to tolerate evangelical preaching. The imperial bailiff of Alsace had already given his consent to the city's surrender when the peasants' defeat at Saverne averted that danger.[61]

Conrad contrasts the situation of the Alsatian imperial cities with the stance of the territorial towns. The latter, she claims, were the victims of the intensification of territorial lordship; their magistrates, moreover, saw themselves as representatives of seigneurial interests

---

[59] Franziska Conrad, *Reformation in der bäuerlichen Gesellschaft. Zur Rezeption reformatorischer Theologie im Elsaß* (Veröffentlichungen des Instituts für europäische Geschichte, Mainz, Abteilung für abendländische Religionsgeschichte, 116) (Stuttgart, 1984), pp. 139–55.

[60] Ibid., p. 154.

[61] Ibid., pp. 145 f.

rather than as guardians of the commonweal. This may well have been so in Boersch and Saverne; in Wolf Gerstenwell from Saverne's confession, for example, hatred of the council's arrogant posturing is graphically expressed.[62] By contrast, in Ribeauvillé and Riquewihr the mood was by no means unequivocal (despite what Conrad claims), but altogether confused and unstable, as we have already outlined. The dividing-line in attitudes towards the peasants did not, in any case, run neatly between council and commons. Several territorial towns showed themselves hostile to the peasants. It is correct to say, though, that such towns were more likely to be found on the right bank of the Rhine than in Alsace. One reason may be that the Breisgau and Ortenau were much less of a 'parsons' lane' (*Pfaffengasse*) of the empire than the Sundgau or Lower Alsace. Another may lie in the distinction between territorial towns that were represented in the territorial Estates, and simple country towns under seigneurial control. The stance of Freiburg and up to a point Breisach clearly differs from that of Staufen under its eponymous barons in the Outer Austrian Breisgau. Such a distinction also holds good, in another context, for the imperial cities. It makes little sense to lump together the Alsatian imperial cities by virtue of their parity of constitutional status. What had peasant burgher towns such as Kaysersberg, Munster, or Turckheim in common with the economically more powerful and specialized artisan and commercial centres such as Colmar or Sélestat—barring their privileged status as imperial cities?

Even in the case of the small winegrowing communes (whether imperial cities or territorial towns) an inclination towards the peasants in principle cannot always be assumed. The threat frequently uttered by the peasants to cut down the vines can hardly have been conducive to a feeling of solidarity; its effect must rather have been destabilizing and intended to intimidate the population, so that alliances of action could be forged, but seldom genuine communities of interest.[63]

---

[62] Johann Heinrich Schreiber (ed.), *Der deutsche Bauernkrieg. Gleichzeitige Urkunden* (*Urkundenbuch der Stadt Freiburg im Breisgau*, new series), 3 vols (Freiburg im Breisgau, 1863–66), 2, pp. 195 f. (no. CCCXXIII); Conrad, *Reformation*, pp. 149 f.

[63] For remarks on this distinction see Tom Scott, 'Bemerkungen zum Begriff "Gemeiner Mann". Das Stadt-Land-Verhältnis zur Zeit des Bauernkrieges', in Fridolin Dörrer (ed.), *Die Bauernkriege und Michael Gaismair. Protokoll des internationalen Symposions vom 15. bis 19. November 1976 in Innsbruck-Vill* (Veröffentlichungen des Tiroler Landesarchivs, 2) (Innsbruck, 1982), pp. 289–92.

Furthermore, it needs to be borne in mind that it is impossible to pinpoint the attitude of towns to the rebellious peasantry without taking into account the highly varying pattern of town-country relations. I have referred elsewhere to conflicts between artisanal towns and burgeoning rural crafts, as well as to the competition from village markets on the Upper Rhine.[64] Rolf Kießling has subsequently applied these reflections with greater depth to the situation in eastern Swabia.[65] Similar reservations have recently been entered by Sven Tode in his comparative study of four Thuringian towns, Erfurt, Mühlhausen, Langensalza, and Thamsbrück. His conclusion is that a simple gradient between larger (imperial) cities and smaller (administrative) towns in respect of their involvement in the Peasants' War did not exist. A long-distance trading commune such as Erfurt was much less exposed to rural competition than a small administrative town such as Thamsbrück, so that the former could adopt a much more relaxed (or indifferent) attitude towards the peasants than the latter, which was reliant upon the support of its territorial lords in order 'to profit from the peasants' surplus and to secure sales of its craft goods'.[66]

Although the close ties between town and country did encourage many Thuringian small towns to take part in the Peasants' War, in the case of Thamsbrück, economically exposed and insecure, the most that was achieved was an alliance of action in storming the convent of Homburg. Even if one is reluctant to accept Tode's pattern of explanation, with its many stages, for the behaviour of Thuringian towns in the Peasants' War in every respect, his general conclusion deserves to be quoted:

> The clasp offered by a political theology, existing alongside an allegedly identical set of economic interests between villages and small (or dwarf)

[64] Scott, *Freiburg and the Breisgau*, pp. 116–20; idem, 'Economic Conflict and Co-Operation on the Upper Rhine, 1450–1600', in E. I. Kouri and Tom Scott (eds), *Politics and Society in Reformation Europe. Essays for Sir Geoffrey Elton on His Sixty-Fifth Birthday* (Houndmills, Hants/London, 1987), pp. 201–31; Tom Scott, *Regional Identity and Economic Change. The Upper Rhine, 1450–1600* (Oxford, 1997), pp. 102–21.

[65] Rolf Kießling, *Die Stadt und ihr Land. Umlandpolitik, Bürgerbesitz und Wirtschaftsgefüge in Ostschwaben vom 14. bis ins 16. Jahrhundert* (Städteforschung. Veröffentlichungen des Instituts für vergleichende Städtegeschichte in Münster, A 29) (Cologne/Vienna, 1989).

[66] Sven Tode, *Stadt im Bauernkrieg 1525. Strukturanalytische Untersuchungen zur Stadt im Raum anhand der Beispiele Erfurt, Mühlhausen/Thür., Langensalza und Thamsbrück* (Frankfurt am Main/Berlin/Bern/New York/Paris/Vienna, 1994), p. 312.

> towns, seems to have been limited to direct common action based on shared anticlericalism. The opposition between town and country was not in the end overcome, not even, or particularly not, by a common desire for autonomy on the part of town and country.[67]

This verdict on a region almost as densely urbanized as the Upper Rhine can be applied, albeit with some modifications, in principle to our own region as well.

[67] Ibid., pp. 304–7, 315 f.; quotation at p. 320.

APPENDIX: SOURCE REFERENCES AND COMMENTARY

A. *Table 6.1. Voluntary Alliances with the Peasant Troops*

1. *Alsace-Lorraine*

Montreux: Peasants from Montreux and the surrounding district made up the bulk of the 'foreign' (*welsch*) [i.e. francophone] troop of Grosnes, which threatened Delle. See Delle's justification in Krebs, 'Rechtfertigungsschriften', pp. 37 f.

Landser: The role of the magistrate of Landser, Hans Pflümlin, as secretary of the Sundgau troop suggests that the small administrative town as a whole took part in the uprising. See ibid., pp. 23, 38, 39; Hartfelder, *Zur Geschichte des Bauernkriegs*, p. 43.

Wattwiller: According to Altkirch's justification, Wattwiller along with Soultz and Guebwiller surrendered at the end of April. Krebs, 'Rechtfertigungsschriften', p. 44. How voluntary this submission was is hard to gauge. During the autumn campaign of the Sundgau troop Thann, Guebwiller, and the abbot of Murbach sent reinforcements to Wattwiller, which belonged to the abbey. The troop was refused entry, and an attack was successfully repulsed. A second assault also failed. Hartfelder, *Zur Geschichte des Bauernkriegs*, pp. 48–50.

Soultz (Upper Mundat): Ibid., p. 25. After the battles of Saverne and Scherwiller the Sundgau troop under Henni Wetzel continued its campaign of resistance into the autumn. At the beginning of September the troop reappeared before Soultz, but this time it was refused entry, since the little town had in the meantime reached an accommodation with its overlord, the bishop of Strasbourg. Ibid., pp. 47–8.

Barr: On 16th April a troop was formed at Barr which then plundered the convent of Truttenhausen. Ibid., p. 68.

Bernhardswiller: Ibid., pp. 66 f.

Boersch: Ibid., p. 66; fundamental is Conrad, *Reformation*, pp. 150–2.

Molsheim: Erasmus Gerber's birthplace and *point d'appui* of the combined

Alsatian troops. Marcel Thomann, 'Mentalités et révolution dans une petite ville d'Alsace. "Pauvres gens" et seigneurs à Marmoutier', in Wollbrett, *Guerre des Paysans*, p. 76.

Wasselonne: From the list of fines it appears that the majority of the town took part in the War. The Strasbourg officials in collecting the fines were at pains to distinguish between those who had participated and those who had not. Virck, *Politische Correspondenz*, 1, p. 193 (no. 341).

Marmoutier: From a very early stage citizens of Marmoutier and inhabitants of the surrounding March joined the Altorf troop. The town opened its gates to the peasants immediately, whereupon the abbot and the monks fled to Strasbourg. Thomann, 'Mentalités', pp. 75 f.

Saverne: Alphonse Wollbrett, 'Saverne-Lupstein dans la tourmente', in idem, *Guerre des Paysans*, pp. 56, 58; Conrad, *Reformation*, pp. 149 f.

Pfaffenhoffen: It is not clear whether Pfaffenhoffen did ally voluntarily, but the machinations of Reinfrit Metziger, one of the captains of the Neubourg troop, make it probable. Fritz Eyer, 'La Guerre des Paysans dans la comté de Hanau-Lichtenberg et les seigneuries voisines', in Wollbrett, *Guerre des Paysans*, pp. 43 f. Metziger's confession is in Günther Franz (ed.), *Der deutsche Bauernkrieg. Aktenband*, 2nd edn (Darmstadt, 1968), pp. 237 f. (no. 80).

Lauterbourg: The troop of the same name gathered around the town, and was led by the mayor Niklaus Winstall. The troop was particularly active on the right bank of the Rhine in the Bruhrain. Hartfelder, *Zur Geschichte des Bauernkriegs*, pp. 200 f.

2. *Baden/Breisgau*

Staufen: The town sheltered several eager partisans of the peasants, above all the town clerk Gregorius Müller, who was chosen as captain of the combined Breisgau troops. Ibid., pp. 294–7.

Lichtenau: Count Ludwig of Hanau-Lichtenberg is said to have let the peasants have supplies of lead, gunpowder, and provisions. This behaviour, born of opportunism, reaped its own reward after the battle of Saverne. Eyer, 'Guerre des Paysans', p. 44; Virck, *Politische Correspondenz*, 1, p. 213 (no. 368); cf. p. 214 (no. 372).

Steinbach: The small town, under the overlordship of the margraves of Baden-Baden, handed over provisions to the Schwarzach troop at the end of April. Whether it subsequently formally allied with the peasants is not clear from the sources. Ibid., p. 204 (no. 352); Hartfelder, *Zur Geschichte des Bauernkriegs*, p. 381.

Durlach: Ibid., pp. 209, 216.

3. *Kraichgau/Palatinate*

Gochsheim, Eppingen, Sinsheim: Günther Franz (ed.), *Peter Harers Wahrhafte und gründliche Beschreibung des Bauernkriegs* (Schriften der Pfälzischen Gesellschaft zur Förderung der Wissenschaften, 25) (Kaiserslautern, 1936), pp. 54 f.; Hartfelder, *Zur Geschichte des Bauernkriegs*, p. 381.

Bruchsal: Franz, *Peter Harers Beschreibung*, pp. 38 f.; Hartfelder, *Zur Geschichte des Bauernkriegs*, pp. 212 f.

4. *Black Forest/Baar*

Waldshut: Scott, 'Reformation and Peasants' War', part 1, pp. 82–102; idem, 'Reformation and Peasants' War', part 2, pp. 140–70; Oka, *Bauernkrieg*, pp. 7–11, 17, 47 f., 55.

Stühlingen: It is not clear whether the small town participated in the outbreak of the Peasants' War. No representative of the town was present at the negotiations in September 1524 in Schaffhausen, which led to a provisional treaty with the counts of Lupfen. Not until the 62 Articles presented on 6th April 1525 was the *stetlin Stulingen sampt dem dorf* mentioned. Ibid., p. 53.

Fürstenberg: Roder, *Villinger Chronik*, p. 113.

Hüfingen: Ibid., pp. 105, 112.

Bräunlingen: The town was occupied 'without resistance' (*nach irm willen*). Ibid., p. 112.

Geisingen: The town seems to have fallen to the peasants without opposition. Ibid., p. 113.

Rottweil: The imperial city which had been an associate member (*zugewandter Ort*) of the Swiss Confederation since 1462 played an opaque role in the Peasants' War. When duke Ulrich of Württemberg sought to reconquer his duchy in the spring of 1525 with hired Swiss mercenaries and the Black Forest troop under Hans Müller, Rottweil acquired considerable strategic importance. In mid-March the duke set up temporary headquarters in the city; at the end of April he had two flags emblazoned with the Württemberg hart's horn made there. But the commons are said to have congratulated themselves on coming to an understanding with the peasants whereby they were left in peace. Schreiber, *Bauernkrieg*, 2, p. 27 (no. CLXIII); FWWA, WoWo 9890, fasc. 6/22 (excerpts in Franz Ludwig Baumann (ed.), *Akten zur Geschichte des Bauernkrieges aus Oberschwaben* (Freiburg im Breisgau, 1877), p. 256 (no. 250)). According to the Villingen Chronicle, 6000 peasants rallied on 4th May in the old town of Rottweil, on the same day as duke Ulrich and his army turned up. Whether or not this was chance, the meeting came to nothing, for Hans Müller and his Christian Union of the Black Forest set off westwards for Deißlingen on 4th May nevertheless, while duke Ulrich in the few days remaining before the decisive defeat of the Württemberg peasants at Böblingen on 12th May seems to have pursued no clear strategic plan. Roder, *Villinger Chronik*, p. 114.

Dornhan: The town was captured by the North Black Forest troop, presumably without resistance. Baumann, *Akten*, p. 256 (no. 250).

Dornstetten: At the outset Dornstetten refused to join the North Black Forest troop, but it surrendered under threats. Thereupon a Dornstetten letter of articles was composed with a strongly anticlerical slant. Johann Ottmar, 'Der Bauernaufstand von 1525 zwischen Nordschwarzwald und oberem Neckar', in Franz Quarthal (ed.), *Zwischen Schwarzwald und Schwäbischer Alb. Das Land am oberen Neckar* (Veröffentlichungen des Alemannischen Instituts, 52) (Sigmaringen, 1984), pp. 184–6.

5. *Württemberg/Swabia*

Großbottwar, Besigheim, Beilstein, Bönnigheim, Güglingen, Lauffen, Brackenheim: Virck, *Politische Correspondenz*, 1, p. 197 (no. 344); see also for *Lauffen, Bottwar*: Baumann, *Akten*, pp. 278 f. (no. 290), 279 f. (no. 291).

Weinsberg: Virck, *Politische Correspondenz*, 1, p. 197 (no. 344); Günther Franz (ed.), *Quellen zur Geschichte des deutschen Bauernkrieges* (Darmstadt, 1963), pp. 335 f. (no. 104).

B. *Table 6.2. Involuntary Alliances with the Peasant Troops*

1. *Alsace-Lorraine*

Altkirch: Bischoff, 'Haute-Alsace', p. 114; Krebs, 'Rechtfertigungsschriften', pp. 41–8.

Belfort: Although Belfort was forced to surrender, it was not occupied by the 'francophone troop' (the *welscher Haufen* under Henni Wetzel). Bischoff, 'La Guerre des Paysans et l'Alsace', in Dörrer, *Die Bauernkriege und Michael Gaismair*, pp. 266 f.; Jean-Marc Debard, 'La Guerre des Paysans dans les marges occidentals du monde germanique. 1525 dans la Porte de Bourgogne, le Comté de Montbéliard et le Baillage d'Amont de Franche-Comté', *Pays d'Alsace*, 1976, nos 3, 4; pp. 6 f.; Krebs, 'Rechtfertigungsschriften', pp. 35 f.; cf. p. 37.

Masevaux: Bischoff, 'Haute-Alsace', p. 114; Krebs, 'Rechtfertigungsschriften', pp. 29–34.

Thann: Hartfelder, *Zur Geschichte des Bauernkriegs*, p. 27; Bischoff, 'Haute-Alsace', p. 114; Krebs, 'Rechtfertigungsschriften', pp. 20–9.

Cernay: Hartfelder, *Zur Geschichte des Bauernkriegs*, p. 27; Bischoff, 'Haute-Alsace', p. 114; Krebs, 'Rechtfertigungsschriften', pp. 17–20.

St Amarin: Bischoff, 'Haute-Alsace', p. 114.

Guebwiller: Hartfelder, *Zur Geschichte des Bauernkriegs*, pp. 25 f.; Krebs, 'Rechtfertigungsschriften', p. 14 n. 1.

Ammerschwihr: The council attempted to keep the peasants at arm's length. When the siege began, a wine-grower and former mercenary Battmann Reinhart proclaimed in the market-place: 'Rather let us die at the hands of the Germans [i.e. the peasants] than the foreigners, who violated our women and children when they fell upon Alsace' (*Lieber unter den Deutschen sterben als unter den Welschen, die beim Einfall ins Elsaß unsere Frauen und Kinder geschändet haben*). He was referring to the irruptions of the Armagnacs and Burgundians in the 15th century. A group of dissidents among the citizenry is also said to have pressed for an alliance with the peasants. Hartfelder, *Zur Geschichte des Bauernkriegs*, pp. 97 f.; Bischoff, 'Haute-Alsace', p. 115.

Kaysersberg: The town was fired upon from above the castle. Hartfelder, *Zur Geschichte des Bauernkriegs*, p. 90 believes that neither the council nor the commons were convinced adherents of the peasants. The council minute-books, however, reveal clear tensions between council and commons, as well as open partisanship for the peasants. AMKy, BB 10, fo. 121r, 122v, 126r, 128r, 129r, 138r; Conrad, *Reformation*, p. 148 takes a slightly different view.

Kientzheim: Hartfelder, *Zur Geschichte des Bauernkriegs*, p. 57; Bischoff, 'Haute-Alsace', p. 115.

Riquewihr: According to the contemporary chronicler Eckhard Wiegersheim many inhabitants of the Württemberg territorial town sympathized with the peasants. Indeed, two citizens led the storm on the abbey of Pairis's manor at Buxhof as captains of the Buxhof troop. Despite numerous efforts to persuade the troop to withdraw and the taking hostage of a councillor, Riquewihr finally had to surrender and provide the troop with a contingent, including Wiegersheim himself. Christian Pfister, 'La Guerre des Paysans dans les seigneuries de Riquewihr et Ribaupierre', *Bulletin de la Société d'Archéologie de Riquewihr*, 9 (1924), pp. 5–27; Bischoff, 'Haute-Alsace', p. 115; Conrad, *Revolution*, pp. 153 f.

Ribeauvillé: We are particularly well informed about events in Ribeauvillé because Ulrich von Rappoltstein, son of the Outer Austrian bailiff Wilhelm von Rappoltstein, who inclined towards the new doctrines, kept a detailed and relatively unbiased diary. Lina Baillet, 'La Guerre des Paysans. Un cas de conscience dans la famille de Ribeaupierre', *Bulletin philogique et historique*, 1967, pp. 357–437. See in addition: ADHR, E 659, 30 Aug. 1525: confession of the tailor Hans Schott. In general see Hartfelder, *Zur Geschichte des Bauernkriegs*, pp. 75–95; Conrad, *Reformation*, pp. 152 f.

Guémar: Bischoff, 'Haute-Alsace', p. 115.

Bergheim: The Ebersmunster troop took Bergheim on 12th May, and proceeded to destroy the books and tablets of the Jewish community, plunder the synagogue, and herd its members together in a house, where it was only prepared to release them for a ransom. Hartfelder, *Zur Geschichte des Bauernkriegs*, pp. 83 f., 95 f.

Bouxwiller: Although the small Hanau-Lichtenberg town was not attacked by rural subjects of the counts, it fell victim to a detachment of the Cleebourg troop, which stormed several citizens' houses and ransacked the castle together with its muniments. In mid-May the three north Alsatian troops joined forces at Bouxwiller. Eyer, 'Guerre des Paysans', pp. 44, 46.

Seltz: The Palatine town of Seltz was taken by a troop which numbered Wissembourg citizens in its ranks, but it was soon liberated. Hartfelder, *Zur Geschichte des Bauernkriegs*, pp. 163, 168.

2. Baden/Breisgau

Neuenburg: Because of its situation as an important crossing-point on the Rhine, Neuenburg had too much strategic significance to be ignored by the Breisgau peasants, who were hoping to link up with the Sundgau troop. After a short siege the town capitulated on 9th May. Ibid., pp. 297 f.; Karl Seith, *Das Markgräflerland und die Markgräfler im Bauernkrieg des Jahres 1525* (Vom Bodensee zum Main, 28) (Karlsruhe, 1926), pp. 49 f.

Freiburg: Scott, *Freiburg and the Breisgau*, pp. 190–235; idem, 'Brüderliche Liebe und göttliches Recht. Die Stadt und der Bauernkrieg', in Buszello, Mertens, and Scott, '"Lutherey, Ketzerey, Uffrur"', pp. 41–52. The town's treaty with the peasants is printed in Schreiber, *Bauernkrieg*, 2, pp. 131–3 (no. CCLX); its justification, ibid., 3, pp. 148–54 (no. CCCCLXV) (with emendations and additions in Krebs, 'Rechtfertigungsschriften', pp. 67 f.). For the situation in the town during the siege see the petition for safe-conduct by Peter Beck zur Muschel. StAFr, 1 VI a (37), 1520–27: 14 Oct. 1525.

Breisach: Already in November 1524 considerable tensions had arisen between council and commons, doubtless stemming from the spread of Lutheran doctrines in an Outer Austrian territorial town. StAFr, B 5 XI, 12/1, fo. 244r–v. In May 1525 there was renewed conflict between council and commons, with Strasbourg being asked to act as mediator. Virck, *Politische Correspondenz*, 1, p. 156 (no. 277). In the Peasants' War itself the council ordered the Marienau convent to be razed and its community of nuns dissolved without seeking permission from its territorial ruler, and without considering the alternative of relocating the community within the town walls. This was presumably intended to pacify the commons. Berent Schwineköper, 'Klosteraufhebungen als Folge von Reformation und Bauernkrieg im habsburgischen Vorderösterreich (Zisterzienserinnenkloster Marienau, Augustiner- und Franziskanerklöster zu Breisach 1525/26 ff.)', *Zeitschrift des Breisgau-Geschichtsvereins ('Schau-ins-Land')*, 97 (1978), pp. 65 f., 72. On 26th May the town joined an alliance with the combined Breisgau troops. Treaty in Schreiber, *Bauernkrieg*, 2, pp. 145–7 (no. CCLXXIII); a document of justification has not survived. See in general Hartfelder, *Zur Geschichte des Bauernkriegs*, pp. 330–3.

Waldkirch: Treaty of surrender in Schreiber, *Bauernkrieg*, 2, pp. 133–5 (no. CCLXI); justification in Krebs, 'Rechtfertigungsschriften', pp. 68–72.

Burkheim: Justification, ibid., p. 50 f.

Endingen: Despite the threats of the Kiechlinsbergen troop under Hans Ziler from Amoltern, Endingen resisted the peasants for a fortnight, before having to swear loyalty. Dieter Speck, 'Endingen als vorderösterreichische Stadt', in Bernhard Oeschger (ed.), *Endingen am Kaiserstuhl. Die Geschichte der Stadt* (Endingen, 1988), p. 102; Krebs, 'Rechtfertigungsschriften', pp. 14 and n. 2, 48–50.

Kenzingen: After the turmoil surrounding the Lutheran preacher Jakob Otter the previous year, Kenzingen at first remained calm in the Peasants' War. But when the peasants demanded the handing over of all monastic property, the town had to surrender. The hatred of the surrounding villages, especially Herbolzheim, towards a town perceived as arrogant, which had a long history to it, was a contributory factor. Hartfelder, *Zur Geschichte des Bauernkriegs*, p. 411; Hans Schadek, 'Das Kloster Ettenheimmünster im Bauernkrieg', in Dieter Weis (ed.), *St. Bartolomäus Ettenheim* (Munich/Zürich, 1982), pp. 222 f.; Ralf Lusiardi, 'Ackerbürgerstadt und Evangelium. Die evangelische Bewegung in der vorderösterreichischen Landstadt Kenzingen', *Zeitschrift für die Geschichte des Oberrheins*, 141 (1993), pp. 185–211, esp. 208; StAFr, K 1/27 [Nachlaß Schreiber], 38, pp. 1–11 (justification of the village of Herbolzheim). Kenzingen's justification in Krebs, 'Rechtfertigungsschriften', pp. 51–67.

Ettenheim: The little Strasbourg administrative town came under threat particularly because it had taken safe-keeping of the abbey of Ettenheim's property, which the peasants demanded be handed over. Its appeal to Strasbourg for permission to do so was overtaken by the approach of the Ettenheimmünster troop. Hartfelder, *Zur Geschichte des Bauernkriegs*, pp. 405 f., 408, 417 f.; Schadek, 'Kloster Ettenheimmünster', pp. 220 f.

Lahr: The administrative town of the lordship of Lahr, which was shared between the counts of Moers-Saarwerden and the margraves of Baden, notwithstanding initial threats to attack the abbey of Schuttern, clung to the provisions of the treaty of the Ortenau, but was still obliged to open its gates to the peasants on 5th June. Virck, *Politische Correspondenz*, 1, pp. 212–13 (no. 367); 217–18 (no. 383); 218–19 (no. 386); 219–20 (no. 387); Hartfelder, *Zur Geschichte des Bauernkriegs*, p. 402.

Oberkirch: Although at first calm reigned in mid-April, unrest broke out among the commons on 27th April. Once the Oberkirch troop had been formed, it took the town at the beginning of May. Ibid., pp. 377, 383–4; Virck, *Politische Correspondenz*, 1, p. 199 (no. 347).

Stollhofen: In imitation of the events at Oberkirch the commons of Stollhofen rose on 28th April. The Strasbourg emissaries and the Baden chancellor Dr Hieronymus Vehus, who were in the town at the time, had considerable difficulty in restoring calm. Nevertheless, on 1st May Stollhofen capitulated, and it was reported that the peasants were riding in and out at will. Ibid., 1, pp. 200 (no. 349); 206 (no. 355); Hartfelder, *Zur Geschichte des Bauernkriegs*, p. 379.

3. *Kraichgau/Palatinate*

Philippsburg (*Udenheim*): On 3rd May representatives of the imperial city of Speyer and of the cathedral chapter concluded a treaty with the peasants at Udenheim, which provided for a palpable reduction in clerical privileges, including stripping the chapter of all its authority and installing the bishop as sole ruler. Whether the town joined the Bruhrain troop at this point is unclear, for on 8th May the Lauterbourg troop appeared before Udenheim claiming that the Bruhrainers had summoned them. Ibid., pp. 220–222.

Neustadt an der Weinstraße: Although on 30th April its capitulation had been demanded by the Geilweiler troop, the town only surrendered a week later on 7th May. Ibid., p. 204; Alter, *Aufstand*, pp. 225–37.

4. *Black Forest/Baar*

Aach, *Engen*: The little towns came under fire, which makes a voluntary alliance with the peasants unlikely. Roder, *Villinger Chronik*, p. 113.

Triberg: Ibid., p. 119; Kurt Klein, 'Der Bauernkrieg in der Ortenau und das Elsaß', in Wollbrett, *Guerre des Paysans*, p. 131.

Wolfach: According to Hartfelder, *Zur Geschichte des Bauernkriegs*, p. 399, the peasants took Wolfach, Rippoldsau, and Schappach one after the other. He refers to Baumann, *Akten*, p. 403 (no. 427), but there it simply says that the peasants had demanded Wolfach's allegiance. Klein, 'Bauernkrieg', p. 131, however, argues that the Alpirsbacher troop abandoned its attack on Wolfach on account of its strong fortifications, after two of its leaders had been captured there.

Sulz am Neckar: The town withstood a siege by the North Black Forest troop until a fireball was thrown into the town. After its capitulation the troop demanded a contingent of 150 men, but was beaten down to a mere 25. Ottmar, 'Bauernaufstand', pp. 192 f.; Baumann, *Akten*, p. 259 (no. 257).

Horb: Ibid., pp. 258 (no. 253), 259 (no. 257).

5. *Württemberg/Swabia*

Stuttgart: Maurer, 'Bauernkrieg als Massenerhebung', p. 269.

Heilbronn: Mistele, *Bevölkerung der Reichsstadt Heilbronn*, pp. 98–110; von Rauch, *Urkundenbuch*, 4.

Wimpfen: Wimpfen was hardly affected by the Peasants' War directly. The reason lies in the fact that the Neckar Valley-Odenwald troop took possession of the much more important city of Heilbronn, where it established its headquarters. Emissaries of the Wimpfen council negotiated a peace agreement with the peasants there, whereby the town joined the Christian Union and undertook to pay a subscription of 1200 fl. After that, the peasants left Wimpfen unscathed. But resentment of the chapter of canons in Wimpfen in the valley permits the hypothesis that peasant sympathizers were to be found among the population. At all events, 40 Wimpfeners allegedly joined the troop of their own free will. Moreover, property belonging to the Teutonic Order also found its way illegally into Wimpfeners' hands. Andreas Hafer, 'Wimpfen. Stadt-Raum-Beziehungen im späten Mittelalter' (Diss. phil. Darmstadt, 1991), pp. 493–510. This material is not included in the published version of Hafer's dissertation: Andreas Hafer, *Wimpfen. Stadt-Raum-Beziehungen im späten Mittelalter*

(Veröffentlichungen der Kommission für geschichtliche Landeskunde in Baden-Württemberg, B 130) (Stuttgart, 1993). For this information I am most grateful to Horst Görlich of the town archives of Bad Friedrichshall.

C. *Table 6.3. Towns which did not Ally with the Peasant Troops*

1. *Alsace-Lorraine*

Delle: Despite being threatened by the 'foreign troop' of Grosnes, and later by the Sundgau troop, the council, ostensibly with the support of the commons, contrived to spin out the negotiations in Habsheim until Basel brought about a truce. Bischoff, 'Haute-Alsace', p. 115; justification in Krebs, 'Rechtfertigungsschriften', pp. 36–41.

Mulhouse: Mieg, 'Mulhouse et la Révolte des Paysans', pp. 177–96; Hartfelder, *Zur Geschichte des Bauernkriegs*, pp. 59–61; with inaccuracies Conrad, *Reformation*, p. 148.

Ensisheim: Hartfelder, *Zur Geschichte des Bauernkriegs*, pp. 35–7.

Rouffach: In contrast to the unrest in 1514 in the Upper Mundat the town remained quiet in 1525. Tom Scott, 'Der "Butzenkrieg". Der Aufstand zu Rufach 1514', in Schmidt, Holenstein, and Würgler, *Gemeinde, Reformation und Widerstand*, pp. 367–69 [Engl. version in this volume]; Theobald Walter, *Abrégé de l'histoire de la ville de Rouffach* (Colmar, 1920), p. 19.

Colmar: Hartfelder, *Zur Geschichte des Bauernkriegs*, pp. 27, 102–11; von Greyerz, '"Liber ortę seditionis"', pp. 371–89; Baillet, 'Deux villes de la Moyenne Alsace'; Georges Bischoff, 'Colmar et la crise révolutionnaire de 1524–25', *Annuaire de Colmar*, 1975/76, pp. 43–54; Kaspar von Greyerz, *The Late City Reformation in Germany. The Case of Colmar, 1522–1628* (Veröffentlichungen des Instituts für europäische Geschichte, Abteilung für abendländische Religionsgeschichte, 98) (Wiesbaden, 1980); Conrad, *Reformation*, pp. 147 f.

Sélestat: Hartfelder, *Zur Geschichte des Bauernkriegs*, pp. 112–17; Gény, *Reichsstadt Schlettstadt*, pp. 114–82; Conrad, *Reformation*, pp. 140–2.

Benfeld: To counter the threat to the Strasbourg territorial town posed by the Ittenwiller and Truttenhausen troops the Strasbourg senate sent 50 infantry as reinforcements. Virck, *Politische Correspondenz*, 1, pp. 133 (no. 241), 146 (no. 263), 147 f. (no. 265), 150 (no. 272), 170 f. (no. 298).

Andlau: Although the Ebersmunster troop threatened to enter the town to seize the property of the abbey, the Strasbourg magistracy severely warned the troop to desist since the abbey had outburgher's rights in the city. This warning apparently succeeded. Ibid., 1, pp. 144 f. (nos 256 f.).

Obernai: Hartfelder, *Zur Geschichte des Bauernkriegs*, pp. 65–8, 70–2; corrected by Conrad, *Reformation*, pp. 145 f.

Rosheim: The council of the imperial city offered assurances that it had not sworn allegiance to the peasant troop. The magistrate Georg Ittel turned out to be a partisan of the peasants, but he was unable to persuade his fellow-citizens to follow him. From the immediate environs (and the city itself?) many partisans had gone over to the peasants. Hartfelder, *Zur Geschichte des Bauernkriegs*, p. 65; Virck, *Politische Correspondenz*, 1, p. 175 (no. 308); cf. p. 110 (no. 195); Dollinger, 'Un aspect de la Guerre des Paysans', p. 140.

Mutzig: On 11th May Erasmus Gerber demanded that the town immediately join his troop, but the approach of a Lorraine army made this threat redundant. Virck, *Politische Correspondenz*, 1, p. 149 (no. 270).

Strasbourg: Rott, 'Guerre des Paysans, pp. 23–32; idem, 'Artisanat', pp. 137–70; Conrad, *Reformation*, pp. 142–5. Karl Hartfelder, 'Straßburg während des Bauernkriegs 1525', *Forschungen zur deutschen Geschichte*, 23 (1883), pp. 211–85 is now very dated.

Haguenau: The Neubourg troop demanded that the two largest guilds, the gardeners and the poor Konstoffler, should render assistance, and threatened to besiege the town if they refused. An answer was not forthcoming; nevertheless, the capital of the imperial bailiwick of Alsace, in which the bailiff Hans Jakob von Mörsberg was resident, remained calm. Franz, *Der deutsche Bauernkrieg. Aktenband*, p. 238 (no. 80); André-Marcel Burg, 'La Guerre des Paysans dans la région de Haguenau', in Wollbrett, *Guerre des Paysans*, p. 50.

Lichtenberg: Because count Philipp of Hanau-Lichtenberg had already introduced some Reforming measures, including the abolition of the small tithe, the Neubourg troop sought his advice. Moreover, he allowed 200 of his subjects to take part in the plundering of the abbey of Neuwiller-lès-Saverne. Thereupon the troop desisted from attacking the castle and town of Lichtenberg. Eyer, 'Guerre des Paysans', pp. 43 f.

Wissembourg: Hartfelder, *Zur Geschichte des Bauernkriegs*, pp. 151–71; Rott, 'Bauernkrieg und Weißenburg', pp. 252–67; Vonau, 'Guerre des Paysans dans l'Outre-Fôret', pp. 39–42; Conrad, *Reformation*, pp. 140–2; Alter, *Aufstand*, pp. 62–110.

Saarguemines: Eyer, 'Guerre des Paysans, p. 44.

2. *Baden/Breisgau*

Gengenbach: In the spring of 1525 the bailiff of the Ortenau, count Wilhelm von Fürstenberg, and evangelically-minded town councillors sought to have the abbey of Gengenbach dissolved, and for a time took the abbot and the monks into custody. But the plan came to nothing. Hartfelder, *Zur Geschichte des Bauernkriegs*, pp. 397 f.

Offenburg: It seems that the imperial cities of the Ortenau were largely ignored by the peasants. Instead, Offenburg, as the venue for negotiations which led to the Offenburg treaties, played the role of (*quasi* passive) intermediary. Klein, 'Bauernkrieg in der Ortenau', p. 50.

Pforzheim: The destruction of the town archives in World War II makes it difficult to reconstruct the attitude of the town. From the fact that the bailiff of Böblingen Leonhard Breitschwert sought refuge (after the battle there) in Pforzheim it might be concluded that the Baden-Durlach administrative town was overlooked by the rebels. See J. G. F. Pflüger, *Geschichte der Stadt Pforzheim* (Pforzheim, 1862; repr. 1989, ed. Hans-Peter Becht), p. 267. I am most grateful to Dr Becht for his information.

3. *Kraichgau/Palatinate*

Bretten: The council of the Palatine territorial town succeeded in keeping the commons at peace by means of shrewd pre-emptive measures, including the timely distribution of bread and wine, even though a civic servant, Wendel Arnolt, putatively acting in the council's name, was working for the surrender of the town to the

Württemberg troop under Jecklin Rorbach. The despatch of a Palatine contingent to Bretten was averted, but the danger of a capitulation nevertheless passed, as the troop headed off in another direction towards Stuttgart. Hartfelder, *Zur Geschichte des Bauernkriegs*, pp. 231–40.

Speyer: Ibid., pp. 241–55; Alter, *Aufstand*, pp. 144–76; *Geschichte der Stadt Speyer*, 1, pp. 487–95.

4. *Black Forest/Baar*

Säckingen: Schreiber, *Bauernkrieg*, 2, pp. 161 f. (no. CCXCII); 3, p. 149 (no. CCCCLXV); ADHR, E 659, 23 April 1525: The Outer Austrian deputy governor Hans Imer von Gilgenberg and the Ensisheim government to the governor Wilhelm von Rappoltstein.

Laufenburg: Schreiber, *Bauernkrieg*, 2, pp. 14 f. (no. CLV), 29 (no. CLXV), 32 f. (no. CLXVIII); ADHR, E 659, 23 April 1525 (as Säckingen).

Blumberg: The little town did not lie on the march route of the Christian Union of the Black Forest. See Roder, *Villinger Chronik*, p. 113.

Villingen: On its march westwards at the end of April and beginning of May the Christian Union of the Black Forest sent the town from its camp at Vöhrenbach the so-called Letter of Articles. The town itself, however, was not besieged and did not respond to the Letter of Articles. Rather, the messenger was captured, as was a second on 10th May, who demanded the handing over of the notary of the monastery of St Georgen. When the peasants of the Baar rallied for a second time on the retreat of the Christian Union at the end of May, an imminent attack on Villingen looked likely. Accordingly, the council took defensive measures, and also sanctioned the formation of a commons' committee, to which 12 guildsmen and 10 councillors belonged. Although Hans Müller encamped with the troop for several days at Hüfingen, Bräunlingen, and Donaueschingen, he finally drew off southeastwards in order to reinforce the siege of Radolfzell. Ibid., pp. 116–30; Scott, 'Reformation and Peasants' War', part 2, pp. 146 f., 156 (where it is erroneously stated that Villingen was besieged). An inaccurate and rapid survey is given by Paul Revellio, *Beiträge zur Stadt Villingen. Gesammelte Arbeiten* (Villingen, 1964), pp. 263–78. In different circumstances Villingen would probably have been attacked in revenge for the punishment of its rebellious peasants in the Brigach valley. See StAVl, JJ 212 (no. 1109), Y 2 (no. 1997), Y 1 (no. 1107). On the Letter of Articles see Gottfried Seebaß, *Artikelbrief, Bundesordnung und Verfassungsentwurf. Studien zu drei zentralen Dokumenten des südwestdeutschen Bauernkrieges* (Abhandlungen der Heidelberger Akademie der Wissenschaften, philosophisch-historische Klasse, 1988, no. 1) (Heidelberg, 1988).

5. *Württemberg/Swabia*

Konstanz: When a peasant contingent appeared before the walls demanding that the suburb and convent of Peterhausen should swear allegiance, the council had the entire clergy, with the exception of the bishop and the cathedral chapter, take a civic oath. This 'domesticating of the clergy' pulled the rug from under the feet of peasant partisans within the imperial city. Wolfgang Dobras, 'Konstanz zur Zeit der Reformation', in Martin Burkhardt, Wolfgang Dobras, and Wolfgang Zimmermann, *Konstanz in der frühen Neuzeit* (*Geschichte der Stadt Konstanz*, 3) (Konstanz, 1991), p. 54. Since Konstanz was not a member of the Swabian League, it could adopt a neutral position. The council allowed both the surrounding nobility and the Meersburg troop access to its market in order to buy provisions. Already in the spring of 1525 Konstanz had taken on certain intermediary responsibilities. Hans-Christoph Rublack, *Die Einführung der Reformation in Konstanz von den Anfängen bis zum Abschluß 1531* (Quellen und Forschungen zur Reformationsgeschichte, 40 [also: Veröffentlichungen des Vereins für Kirchengeschichte in der evangelischen Landeskirche Baden, 27]) (Heidelberg/Karlsruhe, 1971), pp. 142–4.

Radolfzell: Roder, *Villinger Chronik*, p. 113.

Tübingen: Maurer, 'Bauernkrieg als Massenerhebung', p. 269.

Map 6.1.(a). South-West German Towns in the Peasants' War.

Map 6.1(b): South-West German Towns in the Peasants' War.

PART II

ECONOMIC LANDSCAPES

CHAPTER SEVEN

ECONOMIC LANDSCAPES

I

From earliest times certain natural regions can be discerned in Germany, loosely defined by geology, geography, or climate. These included the main river valleys of the Rhine and Main, the east Frisian marshlands, the vast north German plain, the belt of forest stretching across central Germany from Thuringia to the Palatinate, or the Swabian Alb. Upon these were later superimposed the divisions of colonization and settlement: the frontier of the Roman *limes*, the ethnic boundary between German and Slav, and the linguistic distribution of High and Low German dialects. By the later Middle Ages, however, regional identities became increasingly shaped by political and economic factors. Just as local princes began to forge their scattered possessions and miscellaneous jurisdictions into coherent and consolidated territories, so too the shifting balance of land and people, resources and demand, encouraged the emergence throughout Germany of distinctive economic landscapes.

These landscapes fall broadly into three types: those which remained predominantly agrarian; those which displayed a mixture of agriculture and manufacturing based on specialized rural crops, including wool; and those which were given over to mining and industrial production dependent upon natural and mineral resources. Common to all three types, however, was the fact that their character as *economic* landscapes derived neither from endogenous conditions (soil, climate, altitude, natural resources) nor from exogenous circumstances (location and transport, organization of production, consumer demand) alone, but above all from the interplay, often highly complex, of these various factors.

To illustrate this point, let us look briefly at each type of landscape. Up to 1600 Germany remained a predominantly agrarian society, with perhaps 80 per cent of the population living and working on the land. But this bald statement conceals significant variations between regions. In many parts of Germany mixed agriculture and the traditional three-field system of the high Middle Ages continued unaltered, but elsewhere increasing diversity can be observed, with certain areas devoted exclusively to tillage, or to stock-rearing and dairying. Yet even in such instances, arable and pastoral husbandry cannot be entirely separated. Stock-rearing and grain-growing, as Heide Wunder has observed, were closely interlinked, since apart from supplying meat and milk pastoralism provided essential energy to the cerealist in the form of draught animals for ploughing and carting, as well as dung to manure the soil.[1] It was precisely the existence of large-scale cattle-grazing on the marshes of Frisia and Emsland, or in parts of Mecklenburg between the Elbe and the Oder, which made possible intensive forms of cereal agriculture. The annual turning of the topsoil humus admixed with stable dung (*Plaggendüngung*) permitted what became known as the 'perpetual cultivation of rye', by means of a one-field system which was able to dispense with traditional crop rotation.[2] Even in areas of virtual monoculture, moreover, the argument still applies. Beyond the grain-producing estates east of the Elbe, for instance, which developed partly in response to overseas demand from western European markets, lay a belt of pastureland in eastern Poland, Moldavia, and the Hungarian plain whose livestock likewise came to dominate western markets in the sixteenth century.[3] Regional interdependence in such cases is merely writ much larger.

Though soil and climate clearly influenced the distribution of farming types, wider economic considerations also played a part. Since the days of von Thünen in the nineteenth century, distance from the market has above all been advanced to explain the differences in arable cultivation between, say, the multi-course rotation of the Netherlands, the regulated convertible husbandry found in Holstein, or the three-course rotation prevalent in the corn-belt of eastern Europe. These field systems, plotted in a series of 'circles', represented the 'relatively best' agrarian system for each particular region

[1] Heide Wunder, 'European Agriculture', in *New Cambridge Modern History*, 2: *The Reformation*, 2nd edn, ed. G. R. Elton (Cambridge, 1990), p. 33.

[2] Wilhelm Abel, *Geschichte der deutschen Landwirtschaft vom frühen Mittelalter bis zum 19. Jahrhundert* (*Deutsche Agrargeschichte*, 2), 2nd edn (Stuttgart, 1967), pp. 85–6.

[3] Othmar Pickl, 'Routen, Umfang und Organisation des innereuropäischen Handels mit Schlachtvieh im 16. Jahrhundert', in Alexander Novotny and Othmar Pickl (eds), *Festschrift Hermann Wiesflecker zum sechzigsten Geburtstag* (Graz, 1973), p. 145.

in the light of both natural conditions and consumer demand. The merit of such a categorization is that it points away from purely structural and seemingly unchanging determinants in agricultural production towards the variable dynamics of transport costs and market-led demand.[4] Even here, though, the suggested interaction may be couched too simply. Markets, as Robert Dodgshon has reminded us, were privileged foundations rather than spontaneous creations. Their artificial character was a function of political as much as of economic interests, so that the pull of urban demand expressed through the market exerted a 'stilted' influence upon agricultural production.[5]

When we turn to the second type of economic landscape, the interconnectedness of agriculture and textile manufacturing is readily apparent. The linen industry on the northern littoral of Lake Constance provides an instructive example. The cultivation of flax and its manufacture into linen throughout Upper Swabia and into the Allgäu can be traced back to the thirteenth century. The low-lying marshy tracts along the rivers Iller and Lech, together with a high rainfall on the northern edge of the Alps, clearly created suitable conditions for flax-growing,[6] but after spinning and weaving the cloth still had to be bleached. Although various processes were employed, they all used milk at one stage or another, either for bucking (that is, steeping in an alkaline lye) or for soaking in vats of buttermilk, before the cloths were finally crofted (spread out and kept moist on bleaching-grounds for several months). The co-existence of dairying and linen manufacture in the region, therefore, was far from coincidental; the one functionally determined the other. When linen-weaving spread to other areas in the sixteenth century with dairying traditions, such as parts of Westphalia and Flanders, the rapid growth of the industry led to periodic shortages of milk for bleaching.[7]

[4] Wilhelm Abel, *Agricultural Fluctuations in Europe. From the Thirteenth to the Twentieth Centuries*, transl. Olive Ordish (London, 1980), pp. 113–14; Peter Kriedte, *Peasants, Landlords and Merchant Capitalists. Europe and the World Economy 1500–1800* (Leamington Spa, 1983), p. 27.

[5] Robert A. Dodgshon, *The European Past. Social Evolution and Spatial Order* (Houndmills, Hants/London, 1987), pp. 238–9.

[6] Rolf Kießling, *Die Stadt und ihr Land. Umlandpolitik, Bürgerbesitz und Wirtschaftsgefüge in Ostschwaben vom 14. bis ins 16. Jahrhundert* (Städteforschung. Veröffentlichungen des Instituts für vergleichende Städtegeschichte in Munster, A 29) (Cologne/Vienna, 1989), p. 448.

[7] Raymond van Uytven, 'Die ländliche Industrie während des Spätmittelalters in

Yet these connections by themselves are still inadequate to account for the rise of a linen industry around Lake Constance in the later Middle Ages. The advantages of location, while genuine enough in the Allgäu, were much less obvious at the western end of the lake, with an altogether warmer climate and less emphasis on dairying. Moreover, despite the growth of trade between Italy and southern Germany after the opening up of major Alpine passes, it is not even clear that a good location in terms of transport and trade routes was particularly decisive, for the linen industry was firmly established well before the rise of the great Swiss or Swabian merchant enterprises such as the Diesbach-Watt company of St Gallen or the Great Ravensburg Trading Company.[8] The development of Upper German linen (and later fustian) manufacturing seems to have depended just as much upon population growth, which created pressure within the primary sector for rural by-employment, along with a matching consumer demand from townsfolk in an area of relatively dense urbanization. The subsequent consolidation and continuing prosperity of the industry owed a great deal in their own turn both to shifts in the division of labour between town and country, notably in the emergence of the early capitalist putting-out system (*Verlagssystem*), and to the enforcement of strict quality controls (and, not least, to responsiveness to changes in fashion).[9]

In the third type of landscape, that of mining and industrial production, the links between available resources, whether natural or mineral, and the rise of certain forms of manufacturing are the most complex of all. Without the belt of forest stretching across central

den südlichen Niederlanden', in Hermann Kellenbenz (ed.), *Agrarisches Nebengewerbe und Formen der Reagrarisierung im Spätmittelalter und 19./20. Jahrhundert* (Forschungen zur Sozial- und Wirtschaftsgeschichte, 21) (Stuttgart, 1975), p. 74.

[8] Wolfgang von Stromer, 'Gewerbereviere und Protoindustrien in Spätmittelalter und Frühneuzeit', in Hans Pohl (ed.), *Gewerbe- und Industrielandschaften vom Spätmittelalter bis ins 20. Jahrhundert* (*Vierteljahrschrift für Sozial- und Wirtschaftsgeschichte*, Beiheft 78) (Stuttgart, 1986), pp. 47, 57.

[9] Bernhard Kirchgässner, 'Der Verlag im Spannungsfeld von Stadt und Umland', in Erich Maschke and Jürgen Sydow (eds), *Stadt und Umland. Protokoll der X. Arbeitstagung des Arbeitskreises für südwestdeutsche Stadtgeschichtsforschung, Calw. 12.–14. November 1971* (Veröffentlichungen der Kommission für geschichtliche Landeskunde in Baden-Württemberg, B 82) (Stuttgart, 1974), p. 86; von Stromer, 'Gewerberievere', pp. 76, 78. See idem, 'Der Verlag als strategisches System einer an gutem Geld armen Wirtschaft, am Beispiel Oberdeutschlands in Mittelalter und Früher Neuzeit', *Vierteljahrschrift für Sozial- und Wirtschaftsgeschichte*, 78 (1991), pp. 153–71.

Germany, for instance, much of the extractive and metal-working industry of Franconia and Hessen would have been unable to flourish. But the forests were often in themselves less important than the by-products derived from timber. Even for fuel, the iron industry relied not upon raw timber but on charcoal. Many upland areas of the Sauerland were given over to charcoal-burning, with entire villages specializing in supplying the local iron-foundries. Indeed, the organization of production began to display rudimentary forms of vertical integration, as miners, charcoalers, ironsmiths, and iron-founders combined in a single craft guild.[10] Other craft industries in the same region, however, required timber derivatives not for fuel, but in the treatment or manufacturing process itself. The spread of leather-working in the Siegerland presumed a particular form of deciduous arboriculture, namely coppicing (*Haubergwirtschaft*), whereby bark from young oaks was stripped, dried, and used to make tanbark.[11] For its part, the extensive glass industry in eastern Westphalia and northern Hessen relied upon plentiful supplies of potash, made by leaching wood-ash which was then evaporated in pots.[12]

The most intricate equation between natural resources and the location of industry, however, occurred in the mining and refining of base and precious metals. All forms of extraction and smelting required limitless supplies of wood and water, but these were not always to be found in the vicinity of the ores themselves. The rise of the Thuringian copper-mining industry in the fifteenth century may illustrate the point. The ore was found and mined in northern Thuringia, around Mansfeld, Eisleben, and Sangerhausen, but the smelteries were, with one exception, located much further south, above Erfurt and Weimar, where the countryside was thickly forested, and watered by the rivers Gera, Ilm, and Saale.[13] But these natural features alone do not suffice to explain the location of smelteries.

[10] Hermann Kellenbenz, 'Rural Industries in the West from the End of the Middle Ages to the Eighteenth Century', in Peter Earle (ed.), *Essays in European Economic History* (Oxford, 1974), p. 62.

[11] Abel, *Geschichte der deutschen Landwirtschaft*, p. 83.

[12] William John Wright, *Capitalism, the State and the Lutheran Reformation. Sixteenth-Century Hesse* (Athens, OH, 1988), p. 124.

[13] Ekkehard Westermann, *Das Eislebener Garkupfer und seine Bedeutung für den europäischen Kupfermarkt 1460–1560* (Cologne/Vienna, 1971), p. 80; see in general Hermann Kellenbenz, *The Rise of the European Economy. An Economic History of Continental Europe 1500–1750* (London, 1976), p. 105.

The new technology of liquation, upon which the fortunes of the Thuringian mining industry were built, required extensive plant, with six to eight furnaces in a row covering a considerable area. The capital cost of such investment ensured that the liquation works must be located with good access to perceived markets, as in the case of the Augsburg merchant house of Fugger's smeltery at Hohenkirchen in the Thuringian Forest, which was conveniently placed at the point of intersection of trade routes to Nuremberg, Frankfurt, and Leipzig.[14] By itself, however, the development of new technical processes of extraction, refining, and manufacturing—the invention of the wet-stamping-mill, the switch from bloomery to blast-furnace, as well as the discovery of liquation itself—cannot fully account for the mining boom of the fifteenth and sixteenth centuries in certain parts of Germany. Some technological processes were already well known—the hydraulic pump, for instance, had been perfected in the early fifteenth century[15]—but without the finance to deploy them these inventions lay idle. That only serves to underscore the point that the more advanced the industry the more complex was the interplay between the various factors of production.

In the genesis of economic landscapes, therefore, we may discern a hierarchy of complexity from the traditional forms of mixed agriculture up to the technically most advanced areas of specialized industrial production. Of course, the three types of economic landscape were not necessarily distinct; indeed, where they overlapped, the stimulus to economic activity was likely to be all the greater. The classic example is provided by Alsace. In the fertile valley of the Upper Rhine, agricultural diversity held the key to wider economic prosperity. On the temperate plains of the valley floor cereals throve: wheat and rye for bread; oats for bran; barley for brewing. On the slightly higher ground large flocks of sheep were pastured, which provided wool for the local textile industry. Then, on the sheltered eastern slopes of the Vosges, vineyards were strung out from Thann to Marlenheim, whose wine was the most prized in Germany. Behind them lay the moister valleys cutting into the mountains, which

---

[14] Westermann, *Eislebener Garkupfer*, p. 78.

[15] Wolfgang von Stromer, 'Verflechtungen oberdeutscher Wirtschaftszentren am Beginn der Neuzeit', in Wilhelm Rausch (ed.), *Die Stadt an der Schwelle zur Neuzeit* (*Beiträge zur Geschichte der Städte Mitteleuropas*, 4) (Linz, 1980), p. 24.

were largely given over to dairying and cheese-making. On the heights, alpine meadows provided pasture for fattening cattle by transhumance in the summer months. Finally, for good measure, in the higher mountain valleys such as the Val de Lièpvre and the Val du Villé, silver mines provided a lucrative source of income for urban merchants and entrepreneurs.[16] For Alsace was not only fertile: its economy was urbanized and commercialized. Wool-weaving was concentrated in Strasbourg, one of the largest cities of the empire, with a population of around 25,000 at the turn of the fifteenth century, but there were further centres of production in Colmar, and in a cluster of Lower Alsatian cities between Wissembourg and Haguenau. In the same stretch of countryside, moreover, madder was cultivated as an industrial crop for dyeing cloth. Even in the remoter valleys textiles were woven; in Masevaux on the Doller, linen ticking was manufactured to be traded at the Frankfurt fairs. Ease of transport down the rivers Ill and Rhine ensured that Alsace's produce and manufactures reached international markets; its wine, for instance, was exported as far afield as England, Scandinavia, and the Baltic.[17] What determined Alsace's economic vigour, it appears, was neither its agriculture nor its industry in isolation, but rather the interdependence of its rural and urban economies. In defining economic landscapes, therefore, the example of Alsace should caution us against ascribing a dominant role to either town or country: cities and their hinterlands should be seen as complementary dimensions of an integrated regional economy.[18] They constituted, in Hektor Ammann's words, an economic unit (*Wirtschaftseinheit*).[19]

---

[16] Hektor Ammann, 'La place de l'Alsace dans l'industrie textile du Moyen Âge', in *La Bourgeoisie alsacienne. Études d'histoire sociale* (Publications de la Société Savante d'Alsace et des Régions de l'Est, grandes publications, 5), 2nd edn (Strasbourg, 1967), pp. 76–7.

[17] Idem, 'Von der Wirtschaftsgeltung des Elsaß im Mittelalter', *Alemannisches Jahrbuch*, 1955, p. 56.

[18] John Langton and Göran Hoppe, *Town and Country in the Development of Early Modern Western Europe* (Historical Geography Research Series, 11) (Norwich, 1983), p. 40 *et passim.*

[19] Hektor Ammann, *Die wirtschaftliche Stellung der Reichsstadt Nürnberg im Spätmittelalter* (Nürnberger Forschungen, 13) (Nuremberg, 1970), pp. 194 ff., 223.

II

These preliminary reflections should be borne in mind as we turn to examine the three types of economic landscape in greater detail. Within the agricultural sector patterns of inheritance, field systems and crop rotation, tenure and landlordship may all have influenced farming practices, but what was cause and what effect remains notoriously difficult to decide. Throughout most of Germany (and Scandinavia) impartible inheritance was the rule; only in south-west Germany, the Middle Rhine, much of Hessen, and pockets of Silesia can partible inheritance be found, even though it was the custom throughout most of western Europe, especially the Mediterranean lands, and much of the Slavic east. Although partible inheritance appears to have spread first along the fruitful valley and river basin landscapes in the southern, warmer latitudes, any inference that soil, topography, and climate were its chief determinants is rapidly refuted by its establishment in the less fertile upland areas to the west and east—the Hunsrück and Eifel ranges, the Westerwald, and the Bergisches Land.[20] An earlier generation of scholars, struck by the geographical peculiarity of impartibility, sought instead an explanation in ethnic or racial differences. The integrity of the Germanic kinship group, it was argued, demanded the indivisibility of landholdings, a practice which the migrant tribes carried southwards and westwards into Roman territories. By that token, the partible inheritance of the south-west must have represented a subsequent retreat from the advance of Germanic custom.[21] When that might have occurred, however, is altogether unclear: during the era of internal colonization in the twelfth and thirteenth centuries impartible inheritance had become the norm in the newly settled upland areas of Swabia and Franconia.[22] Renewed pressure on land after 1500 in parts of southern Germany, moreover, impelled both landlords and tenant farmers to resist attempts to subdivide holdings and to make impartibility legally binding.[23] In general, however, what stands out is the remarkable continuity in

---

[20] Barthel Huppertz, *Räume und Schichten bäuerlicher Kulturformen in Deutschland. Ein Beitrag zur Deutschen Bauerngeschichte* (Bonn, 1939), p. 28; Abel, *Geschichte der deutschen Landwirtschaft*, pp. 71–2.

[21] Huppertz, *Räume und Schichten*, pp. 53–4.

[22] Kellenbenz, *Rise of the European Economy*, p. 60.

[23] For Upper Swabia see David Sabean, *Landbesitz und Gesellschaft am Vorabend des*

the distribution of inheritance patterns throughout Germany from the ninth to the twentieth century; that should discourage us from seeking too close a causal connection between specific inheritance customs and certain forms of agriculture. It is true that areas of partible inheritance, especially in the Rhineland, display an abundance of viticulture and industrial crops, together with extensive rural crafts and manufacturing. Equally, such areas coincide with the greatest concentration of towns in late medieval Germany, which may have stimulated the market integration of the rural economy and therewith the commercialization of production and the creation of a land market.[24] But the rise of landscapes bearing the imprint of rural industries was by no means confined to the south-west; they arose in areas of thoroughgoing impartibility as well, such as eastern Swabia and Westphalia. Partible inheritance should therefore not be adduced as a catch-all explanation for the economic transformation of early modern Germany towards proto-industrialization.[25]

As prevalent as, and largely coterminous with, impartible inheritance was the traditional system of open fields in Germany. On them winter cereals (wheat and rye, or in parts of the south-west, principally Württemberg, spelt) were followed by summer grains (oats and barley) and then fallow in a regulated rotation. Together with the three-field system of tillage, beasts were grazed on the common land or forest, though often the fallow year was itself used for pasturing, rather than repeatedly ploughing to aerate and improve the soil (*Schwarzbrache*).[26] In certain circumstances, however, this classic system of mixed agriculture could be sufficiently intensified in stretches of the north German plain, as we have seen, to enable a one-field system with continuous rye cultivation to develop. The origins of the two-field system in many parts of the Rhineland and its fringes are, by contrast, much harder to pin down. On the one hand, it was

Bauernkriegs. Eine Studie der sozialen Verhältnisse im südlichen Oberschwaben in den Jahren vor 1525 (Quellen und Forschungen zur Agrargeschichte, 26) (Stuttgart, 1972), pp. 40 ff.; for Hohenlohe see Thomas Robisheaux, *Rural Society and the Search for Order in Early Modern Germany* (Cambridge, 1989), p. 81.

[24] Huppertz, *Räume und Schichten*, p. 55.

[25] See Peter Kriedte, Hans Medick, and Jürgen Schlumbohm, *Industrialisation before Industrialisation. Rural Industry in the Genesis of Capitalism* (Cambridge, 1981), p. 214, n. 14.

[26] Friedrich-Wilhelm Henning, *Landwirtschaft und ländliche Gesellschaft in Deutschland: 800–1750*, 2nd edn (Paderborn/Munich/Vienna/Zürich, 1985), p. 78.

the ancient and primitive method of cultivation which typified Roman agriculture beyond the Mediterranean up to the ninth century.[27] This system survived in certain areas of what had once been the eastern border of Gaul, notably in the upland regions of the Palatinate. Here the prevalence of loess soils, liable to erosion, hindered the cultivation of meadow, pasture, and forest, so that the fallow had to be extended over both time and space in order to provide enough manure. In such instances, three-year rotation was practised on an infield, while on the outfield fallow succeeded oats in a system of alternate husbandry (*Feldgraswirtschaft*). Two-field systems, however, were also widespread on the lower-lying riverine lands along the Moselle and the Middle Rhine, downstream of Koblenz, where even the infield might be given over to a simple alternation between rye and fallow.[28] On the other hand, it has been argued that the spread of the two-field system in the later Middle Ages was attributable to the growth of specialized and commercial agriculture. Along the Rhine and Moselle, for instance, a special type of alternate husbandry developed, whereby tillage was succeeded by coppicing in order to provide tanbark and vine-props (*Lohheckenwirtschaft*).[29] By the beginning of the sixteenth century, indeed, the two-field system had apparently penetrated Alsace, in response to intensified cereal cultivation, a thriving viticulture, and the planting of industrial crops such as hemp and madder (and later tobacco).[30] Correlations of this kind clearly existed, but they must not be pressed too far. It is obvious that not all areas of loess soil had two-field systems; equally, the changes in land management contingent upon a heightened demand for grain in Alsace do not seem to have taken place in other regions of similarly dense urbanization and market demand such as Swabia.[31] To ascribe the spread of two-field cultivation in wine-growing areas to an economic conjuncture in any case presents problems. The structural requirements of viticulture in Alsace, for example, namely

[27] Ibid., p. 79.

[28] Gertrud Schröder-Lembke, 'Wesen und Verbreitung der Zweifelderwirtschaft im Rheingebiet', *Zeitschrift für Agrargeschichte und Agrarsoziologie*, 7 (1959), pp. 14–31.

[29] Abel, *Geschichte der deutschen Landwirtschaft*, p. 83.

[30] Étienne Juillard, 'L'assolement biennal dans l'agriculture septentrionale', *Annales de géographie*, 1952, pp. 34–49.

[31] Hugo Ott, *Studien zur spätmittelalterlichen Agrarverfassung im Oberrheingebiet* (Quellen und Forschungen zur Agrargeschichte, 23) (Stuttgart, 1970), pp. 94–6.

copious labour and plentiful manure, rather than the functional stimulus of the export market, may have promoted the two-field system by restricting the scope for traditional mixed agriculture: necessity, not opportunity, in other words, may have encouraged its spread.[32] Moreover, the two-field system in Alsace was neither new nor ubiquitous at the close of the Middle Ages; it can be found centuries earlier in patches on both banks of the Upper Rhine, sometimes interchangeably with a three-field system where crop rotation was not subject to regulation by course (*Verzelgung*).[33]

In certain parts of Germany mixed agriculture was beginning to give way at the end of the Middle Ages either to multi-course rotation, or else to an exclusive concentration on stock-rearing and dairying. In both cases, the traditional open-field system became subject to partial enclosure. In the rich pasture lands of Schleswig-Holstein and along the Frisian coast to the Dutch border a form of regulated convertible (or 'up-and-down') husbandry (*Koppelwirtschaft*) developed, whereby a series of corn years could be followed by anything from three to six years' grazing. This rotation could even dispense with a fallow year, provided that fodder crops (such as nitrogenous legumes and vetches) were planted as catch-crops in the intervening period. This pattern foreshadows the 'improved' agriculture of the eighteenth century (*Fruchtwechselbau*; in French, *assolement*).[34] Cattle-pastures (*Koppeln*) were created by intakes from both forest and waste, and from the existing common. Such pastures, however, usually involved only hurdling or folding (temporary fencing, rather than permanent enclosures, while the stint of beasts to be grazed was limited by cattle-gates). There was no widespread enclosure movement in northern Germany in the sixteenth century as supposedly occurred in England.[35] In the mountainous regions of Switzerland, by contrast, where good pasture was at a premium, much more common land in the Alps, as a study of Fribourg (Freiburg im Üchtland) has shown, was bought up by nobles and peasants to be turned into private hay meadows for summer grazing, in order to release low-lying fields for winter

32 Abel, *Geschichte der deutschen Landwirtschaft*, p. 87.

33 Ott, *Studien zur Agrarverfassung*, p. 107.

34 Abel, *Geschichte der deutschen Landwirtschaft*, p. 176.

35 Idem, *Agricultural Fluctuations*, p. 140. Although this point is recognized by the author, his translator on p. 108 of the English edn erroneously translates *Koppelwirtschaft* as 'enclosure system'.

fodder.[36] In general, pastoralism in northern Germany tended to serve the market for both meat and dairy produce, whereas in the Alps there was a greater concentration upon dairying. The sharply increased demand for meat from the urban centres of southern and western Germany could no longer be covered by purely regional supplies; instead, the cities came to rely upon livestock imports driven on the hoof, often over immense distances, from Burgundy, Hungary, Poland, and Scania.[37]

The pattern of landlordship had likewise undergone significant changes by 1500. The manorial system of the high Middle Ages had largely disappeared, or else survived in a 'petrified' form. Most secular lords had long since divested themselves of their demesne, which was parcelled out to tenants, often on short leases, and instead derived their feudal revenues purely from rents. Even monastic lords such as the Cistercians, who had pioneered direct exploitation of their estates on a commercial basis (granges; *Grangienwirtschaft*), had in most cases abandoned the practice by the sixteenth century.[38] Hereditary tenure became the rule, though there were considerable variations throughout western Germany. The strongest tenure was to be found where peasant holdings were largest, on the hereditable leaseholds of Bavaria (*Erbpacht*) or the copyhold (*Meierrecht*) prevalent in northwestern Germany.[39] Revocable leases for fixed terms (*Zeitpacht*) were only common where agriculture had become commercialized, and organized on capitalist lines: on the Middle and Lower Rhine stretching into the Low Countries, and on the coastal strip of Frisia and western Holstein (Eiderstedt, Dithmarschen). Here the real (that is, tenurial) dependence of the peasantry was superseded by a purely contractual obligation.[40] Nevertheless, feudal landlordship (*Grundherrschaft*)

---

[36] Hans Conrad Peyer, 'Wollgewerbe, Viehzucht, Solddienst und Bevölkerungsentwicklung in Stadt und Landschaft Freiburg i. Ue. vom 14. bis 16. Jahrhundert', in Kellenbenz, *Agrarisches Nebengewerbe*, p. 83.

[37] Abel, *Geschichte der deutschen Landwirtschaft*, pp. 92–3.

[38] Friedrich Lütge, *Geschichte der deutschen Agrarverfassung vom frühen Mittelalter bis zum 19. Jahrhundert* (*Deutsche Agrargeschichte*, 3), 2nd edn (Stuttgart, 1967), pp. 89–90. He cites as a typical instance the abbey of Bebenhausen by Tübingen. For an exceptional instance of continuity in Cistercian land-management see Winfried Schenk, *Mainfränkische Kulturlandschaft unter klösterlicher Herrschaft. Die Zisterzienserabtei Ebrach als raumwirkende Institution vom 16. Jahrhundert bis 1803* (Würzburger Geographische Arbeiten, 71) (Würzburg, 1988).

[39] Kellenbenz, *Rise of the European Economy*, p. 60.

[40] Henning, *Landwirtschaft*, p. 206; Lütge, *Agrarverfassung*, p. 191.

survived as the framework for the socio-legal subjection of the peasantry, even if in some areas the economic relations between lord and tenant had been transformed.

In eastern Germany, that is, the lands east of the Elbe as far as east Prussia, *Grundherrschaft* underwent a complex and protracted transformation into a new type of large feudal seigneurie (*Gutsherrschaft*), whose peasants were progressively stripped of their land and reduced to the status of a servile labour force, in what is known as the 'second serfdom'. This concentration of seigneurial power enabled a distinctive entrepreneurial domanial economy (*Gutswirtschaft*) to develop, in which the peasantry was subordinated by feudal ties ('extra-economic coercion') to a supposedly capitalist mode of production supplying overseas markets—a system reminiscent of the plantation economies of the New World. The links between domain lordship and the domanial economy, however, are by no means straightforward. It used to be thought that the demand for grain from western Europe encouraged the growth of large-scale arable estates that, given the relative sparsity of population in the east-Elbian territories, were obliged to resuscitate forms of feudal compulsion in order to secure an adequate work force. This argument is untenable on three counts. First, the rise of *Gutsherrschaften* preceded—by as much as two centuries in some cases—the emergence of *Gutswirtschaften*. Second, intensified feudal lordship was sometimes harnessed to forms of production quite distinct from labour-intensive cereal agriculture. Third, the development of large estates using direct labour was not confined to eastern Germany. Let us examine these points more closely.

The system of *Gutsherrschaften* was essentially in place by the beginning of the sixteenth century, but its origins lie in the fourteenth, in the aftermath of plague and epidemic. Deserted peasant holdings reverted to their seigneurs, who at that time had no incentive whatever to invest in cereal agriculture, given the slump in grain prices and the reduction in the labour force. That argument effectively disposes of any theory that *Gutsherrschaft* was predicated upon an overseas demand for cereals.[41] Lords had a unique opportunity to consolidate

[41] Holm Sundhaußen, 'Zur Wechselbeziehung zwischen frühneuzeitlichem Außenhandel und ökonomischer Rückständigkeit in Osteuropa. Eine Auseinandersetzung mit der "Kolonialthese"', *Geschichte und Gesellschaft*, 9 (1983), pp. 544–63.

their scattered estates by gathering rights of landlordship and feudal jurisdiction into one hand, and by attempting to stem landflight to the towns. Only with the population recovery at the end of the fifteenth century did any clear economic motive arise to develop commercial agriculture; the real demand from western Europe for grain only dates from this period, even if a trickle of exports from the Vistula estuary can be traced back to the late thirteenth century. That does not, of course, explain why lords chose direct exploitation in preference to creaming off the profits through higher peasant rents. The answer seems to be that, on terrain uniquely suitable for intensive cereal agriculture, as much as three-quarters of the crop was marketed, a proportion so high that it made direct labour not only the most efficient way to organize production, but also far more lucrative than the revenue from rents and feudal renders.[42]

The most striking exception to this pattern is to be found in Silesia and Upper Lusatia. There, as much as four-fifths of the land was held by peasants with good title and hereditary tenure, who were personally free.[43] Many of their holdings, however, were very small, ten hectares or less, and partible inheritance was widespread. Rural by-employment and specialized crops were common, with extensive linen production, and the cultivation of madder in the district around Wrocław. At the same time, western Silesia had become an urbanized landscape by 1500, as a string of towns was founded along the mountain ranges on the left bank of the Oder, where minerals, principally iron but also gold and silver, had been discovered in the later Middle Ages.[44] Against this background a domanial economy was most unlikely to develop, yet by the mid-sixteenth century *Gutsherrschaft* was on the advance. Here the feudal lords used their concerted seigneurial power to promote crafts and textile production. Rather

---

[42] Henning, *Landwirtschaft*, pp. 166–70. Those who argue that *Gutswirtschaft* preceded *Gutsherrschaft* can at least point to the fact that the structure of east-Elbian society and population made increasing labour services much easier than increasing rents. See Lütge, *Agrarverfassung*, p. 139. On this issue (though with a terminological confusion between *Gutsherrschaft* and *Gutswirtschaft*) see fundamentally the historiographical account in Heinrich Kaak, *Die Gutsherrschaft. Theoriegeschichtliche Untersuchungen zum Agrarwesen im ostelbischen Raum* (Veröffentlichungen der Historischen Kommission zu Berlin, 79) (Berlin/New York, 1991).

[43] Lütge, *Agrarverfassung*, pp. 126–7.

[44] Ludwig Petry, 'Breslau in der schlesischen Städtelandschaft des 16. Jahrhunderts', in Rausch, *Die Stadt an der Schwelle zur Neuzeit*, pp. 259–61.

than expropriating tenants, they released demesne and common land for new settlement by cottagers, and encouraged the transfer of linen manufacturing away from the towns to their own estates, where it was integrated into the system of feudal rents. Nevertheless, a good share of the peasantry escaped the clutches of hereditary serfdom, so that Silesia and Lusatia remained regions with a highly variegated structure of social and economic relationships.[45]

By contrast, forms of direct exploitation need not exclusively be associated with *Gutsherrschaft*. In the swathe of territories stretching from eastern Lower Saxony and Anhalt through Thuringia and Saxony itself, as well as in parts of Bavaria and Upper Austria, we encounter an interval type of landlordship, using both wage-labour from free peasants and the labour-services of serfs to manage sizeable estates, which Alfred Hoffmann has termed 'economic lordship' (*Wirtschaftsherrschaft*).[46] In one such area, the district round Magdeburg, commercial leases on the larger peasant farms co-existed with a landless servile workforce within one estate. Such domains certainly developed in response to the market, but that demand was as much local as international, and was geared towards the main crop, barley, which supplied regional brewing centres like Braunschweig, rather than the lesser crops of wheat and rye. As long as the chief means of production, namely land, remained in peasant hands, this type of domain should be regarded as a special form of *Grundherrschaft*, rather than a weakened version of *Gutswirtschaft*,[47] not least since in Bavaria serfdom in the east-European sense had all but disappeared. Still, genuine *Gutswirtschaften* can also be found outside eastern Germany alongside instances of pure *Grundherrschaft*. In Schleswig-Holstein the large estates of eastern Holstein practised a domain economy which

[45] Abel, *Geschichte der deutschen Landwirtschaft*, p. 161; Kriedte, Medick, and Schlumbohm, *Industrialisation*, pp. 18, 20; Richard C. Hoffmann, *Land, Liberties, and Lordship in a Late Medieval Countryside. Agrarian Structures and Change in the Duchy of Wrocław* (Philadelphia, 1989), pp. 353–5, 365–7.

[46] Alfred Hoffmann, 'Die Grundherrschaft als Unternehmen', *Zeitschrift für Agrargeschichte und Agrarsoziologie*, 6 (1958), pp. 123–31; Lütge, *Agrarverfassung*, pp. 162–3, 170–1.

[47] Hartmut Harnisch, *Bauern – Feudaladel – Städtebürgertum. Untersuchungen über die Zusammenhänge zwischen Feudalrente, bäuerlicher und gutsherrlicher Warenproduktion und den Ware-Geld-Beziehungen in der Magdeburger Börde und dem nordöstlichen Harzvorland von der frühbürgerlichen Revolution bis zum Dreißigjährigen Krieg* (Abhandlungen zur Handels- und Sozialgeschichte, 20) (Weimar, 1980), pp. 190, 199–202.

relied heavily upon serf labour, whereas central and western Holstein are (to this day) classic landscapes of large peasant farms, hereditary and free, just as in the rest of north-west Germany.[48]

Having discussed varieties of landholding and land management, we may conclude our review of the first type of economic landscape with an examination of the non-industrial specialized crops grown in Germany, namely vines and hops. Apart from the northernmost latitudes and the Alpine slopes, there was hardly a region of Germany that had no viticulture at the end of the Middle Ages. Yet by 1600 the area planted with vines had begun to contract dramatically. To explain such a rapid reversal, two points need to be borne in mind. On the one hand, in the main growing regions viticulture became restricted to the most favoured sites, that is, those whose wines were in demand beyond the immediate locality, as land was taken back into cereal cultivation to feed the swelling sixteenth-century population. On the other hand, the high price of wine, determined above all by the labour-intensive nature of viticulture, made it vulnerable to competition from other beverages, principally beer.

Vineyards required seasonally eight times the manpower of cereal agriculture, quite apart from an assured provision of manure, vine-props, barrels, and staves.[49] It is no surprise, therefore, that they should chiefly have flourished in the areas of densest population and greatest commercial demand, in short, the urbanized regions of the south and west. By the same token, however, vineyards were planted wherever the hunger for land, the subdivision of holdings, and the prospects of a ready cash return at market were greatest—that is to say, not always in places where quality was best assured.[50] Towards the end of the sixteenth century as many as 350,000 hectares were

---

[48] See Edgar Melton, '*Gutsherrschaft* in East Elbian Germany and Livonia, 1500–1800: A Critique of the Model', *Central European History*, 21 (1988), pp. 315–49. See also Michael North, 'Die frühneuzeitliche Gutswirtschaft in Schleswig-Holstein. Forschungsüberblick und Entwicklungsfaktoren', *Blätter für Deutsche Landesgeschichte*, 126 (1990), pp. 223–42.

[49] Roy L. Vice, 'Vineyards, Vinedressers and the Peasants' War in Franconia', *Archiv für Reformationsgeschichte*, 79 (1988), p. 139. See now fundamentally Tom Scott, 'Medieval Viticulture in the German-speaking Lands', *German History*, 20 (2002), pp. 95–105.

[50] Helmut Hahn, *Die deutschen Weinbaugebiete. Ihre historisch-geographische Entwicklung und wirtschafts- und sozialgeographische Struktur* (Bonner Geographische Abhandlungen, 18) (Bonn, 1956), p. 22.

under vines, that is, at least four times the extent of viticulture today.[51] On the fringes of the main growing areas, vines crept into the narrower, shadier valleys and up the cooler slopes: in the Rhineland, into the foothills of the Eifel around Mechernich; from Siegburg past Cologne down the Lower Rhine to Xanten; up the valleys of the Upper Ahr, the Lahn as far as Wetzlar and the Saar to Saarbrücken; in the Palatinate, onto the higher reaches of the Haardt plateau, the Donnersberg hills, and down into Lorraine; in Württemberg, onto the foothills of the Swabian Alb and into Upper Swabia; in Franconia, over the whole of the Main plain and into Lower Bavaria and the Danube valley as far as Lower Austria and Burgenland.[52] Vines were even planted on the north German plain, in Mecklenburg, Holstein, Brandenburg, and east Prussia.[53] These marginal areas were naturally the first to contract after 1500, but there were other growing regions of considerable importance in the sixteenth century which have now also disappeared. In Lusatia there were extensive vineyards south of Frankfurt an der Oder, and in Saxony on the Elbe around Meißen. But there was also viticulture in Thuringia: in the Saale valley around Jena; on the Unstrut from Naumburg to Freyburg; and on the Gera between Arnstadt and Erfurt. These wines were not all consumed locally; rather, they supplied the needs of most of Saxony to the north and east.[54]

The main areas of good-quality wines have, by contrast, remained remarkably unchanged from the Middle Ages to the present day: Alsace, the Neckar valley in Württemberg, the Lower Main in Franconia, the Moselle and its tributaries, and the Rhine from Speyer down to Koblenz. It is striking that all Germany's principal viticultural regions—as in France, but unlike Italy or Spain—were situated on or close to rivers; indeed, the Rhine provided the vital artery of transport which enabled German wines to be sold outside their region of origin. Of the areas along its valley Alsace, as we have

---

[51] Vice, 'Vineyards', p. 138.

[52] Hahn, *Die deutschen Weinbaugebiete*, p. 19. For Austria see most recently Helmut Feigl and Willibald Rosner (eds), *Probleme des niederösterreichischen Weinbaus in Vergangenheit und Gegenwart. Die Vorträge des neunten Symposions des Niederösterreichischen Instituts für Landeskunde Retz. 4.–6. Juli 1988* (Studien und Forschungen aus dem Niederösterreichischen Institut für Landeskunde, 13) (Vienna, 1990).

[53] Kellenbenz, *Rise of the European Economy*, p. 94.

[54] Wieland Held, *Zwischen Marktplatz und Anger. Stadt-Land-Beziehungen im 16. Jahrhundert in Thüringen* (Weimar, 1988), pp. 111–13.

noted, enjoyed the highest reputation: its wines supplied the German south-west and Switzerland, but they were also bought up by merchants from Frankfurt and, to a lesser extent, Cologne for shipment to much of northern Europe.[55] Wine made Strasbourg's fortune in the fourteenth and fifteenth centuries, and severe penalties were imposed to prevent Alsatian wine being adulterated with other wines from the Breisgau on the adjoining right bank, or from further afield.[56] The reputation of Alsatian and Rhenish wines lay essentially in the white varieties, but it is well-nigh impossible to gain an accurate impression of what was grown before 1700. In Alsace the best wines were made from Muscat and Traminer grapes, with Riesling the only varietal of true quality on the Rhine and Moselle.[57] It is unlikely, however, that these wines constituted more than a fraction of production; the bulk of the harvest was made up by lesser varieties such as Sylvaner and Elbling. Surprisingly, perhaps, red-wine grapes were widely planted in Alsace and Baden (principally the Burgundian Pinot Noir),[58] and much of the harvest in Württemberg, then as now, may well have been of light red wine.

Only in the sixteenth century did beer begin its triumphant march into the front rank of German beverages. Until then, the cultivation of hops and the malting of barley had been largely confined to northern Germany, where wine was less readily available and comparatively expensive. Several of the Hanseatic cities were major brewing centres—the ports of Hamburg, Lübeck, Wismar, Rostock, and Danzig along the Baltic coast, and the inland cities of Hannover, Einbeck, Goslar, and Braunschweig in Lower Saxony.[59] But there was also a famous brewing tradition in eastern Franconia (Kulmbach, Bamberg,

---

[55] François-Joseph Fuchs, 'L'espace économique rhénan et les relations commerciales de Strasbourg avec le sud-ouest de l'Allemagne au XVIe siècle', in Alfons Schäfer (ed.), *Festschrift für Günther Haselier aus Anlaß seines 60. Geburtstages am 19. April 1974* (Oberrheinische Studien, 3) (Karlsruhe, 1975), pp. 301–3; Wolfgang Herborn and Klaus Militzer, *Der Kölner Weinhandel. Seine sozialen und politischen Auswirkungen im ausgehenden 14. Jahrhundert* (Vorträge und Forschungen, 25) (Sigmaringen, 1980), pp. 38–40.

[56] Philippe Dollinger, 'La Ville libre à la fin du Moyen Âge (1350–1482)', in Georges Livet and Francis Rapp (eds), *Histoire de Strasbourg des origines à nos jours*, 2: *Strasbourg des grandes invasions au XVIe siècle* (Strasbourg, 1981), p. 153.

[57] Médard Barth, *Der Rebbau des Elsaß und die Absatzgebiete seiner Weine. Ein geschichtlicher Durchblick*, 1 (Strasbourg/Paris, 1958), p. 88.

[58] Ibid., pp. 81–4.

[59] Kellenbenz, *Rise of the European Economy*, p. 94; Abel, *Geschichte der deutschen Landwirtschaft*, p. 181.

Nuremberg), and hops began to be grown in Bavaria as well, which until 1500 had been more a wine-growing region, though not until the late seventeenth century did Bavarian beer come to be highly prized.[60]

III

Diversification and specialization within the primary sector could reach the stage where we may identify a new type of economic landscape, in which manufacturing was based upon the cultivation of industrial crops to make cloths or dyestuffs, or on pastoralism to supply the raw material, wool. The growth of the textile industry in late medieval Germany was to have a profound influence on modes of production and the nature of town-country relations. We have already referred to the rise of linen-manufacturing around Lake Constance and throughout much of Upper Swabia. Initially, production was located in the larger towns and cities, notably Konstanz, St Gallen, Lindau, and Kempten, which drew unprocessed flax from the surrounding countryside. But in the course of the fifteenth century production began to move out to the smaller towns and villages; rural weavers made and marketed their own (often lesser) types of cloth, upheld a separate quality control, and shunned the civic cloth exchanges. That suggests that rural manufacturing in such circumstances—especially to the south and at the western end of Lake Constance—was not always or necessarily the outflow of a widespread putting-out system which brought country weavers into dependence upon urban capitalists.[61] Further afield in eastern Swabia, however, putting out work to country weavers occurred from the outset: in Memmingen, the urban weavers tried to counteract this threat to their livelihood by entering into collective guild contracts with merchants to supply cloth at an agreed price (*Zunftkauf*).[62] To what extent rural put-out weavers should be seen as the victims of

[60] Henning, *Landwirtschaft*, p. 130; Abel, *Geschichte der deutschen Landwirtschaft*, p. 127.
[61] Hektor Ammann, 'Die Anfänge der Leinenindustrie des Bodenseegebiets', *Alemannisches Jahrbuch*, 1953, pp. 251–313, and map, p. 253; Kirchgässner, 'Verlag', p. 86.
[62] Kießling, *Die Stadt und ihr Land*, p. 482.

early-capitalist exploitation remains an open question. In Kempten, for instance, the centre of the Allgäu linen industry, 400 urban weavers with 300 apprentices were matched by 600 outburghers, country-dwellers in benefit of civic liberties, who were almost certainly linen-weavers.[63] Kempten may well have extended burgher's rights to this segment of the rural population in order to discourage emigration to an already populous city (on the pattern of cities such as Ghent and Bruges in fourteenth-century Flanders), but, whatever the reason, the result was an escape from serfdom and the acquisition of a certain degree of economic independence.[64]

By the sixteenth century other areas of linen production had come to the fore. In Westphalia, as woollen manufacturing declined linen-weaving prospered, particularly in the rolling countryside between Osnabrück, Ravensberg, and Minden, and down into the plains between Diepholz and Hoya, in effect the catchment area of the rivers Ems and Weser.[65] Flax was also grown around Münster and to the south, in the Bergisches Land. Further east, flax was widely cultivated between the Erzgebirge in southeastern Saxony and Upper Lusatia. Chemnitz was the focal point of Saxon production, whilst Lusatian cities such as Görlitz, Bautzen, Löbau, and Kamenz were not only centres of linen-weaving but also entrepôts for the trade in woollen cloth and woad.[66] Silesia's linen industry, as we have seen, was able to flourish even when integrated into feudal domain lordship. In all these northern regions *Verlag* was the standard mode of production, partly because linen production had spread in response to a growing international market, and partly because the need for rural by-employment in these areas, which, apart from Silesia, were ones of impartible inheritance, combined with a relatively weak guild tradition in the towns to leave the field open to capitalist entrepreneurs, some of whom held thousands of cottage weavers under

---

[63] Tom Scott (ed.), *Die Freiburger Enquete von 1476. Quellen zur Wirtschafts- und Verwaltungsgeschichte der Stadt Freiburg im Breisgau im fünfzehnten Jahrhundert* (Veröffentlichungen aus dem Archiv der Stadt Freiburg im Breisgau, 20) (Freiburg im Breisgau, 1986), pp. 15–16.

[64] David Nicholas, *Town and Countryside. Social, Economic, and Political Tensions in Fourteenth-Century Flanders* (Rijksuniversiteit te Gent: Werken uitgegeven door de Faculteit van de Letteren en Wijsbegeerte, 152) (Bruges, 1971), pp. 220–1, 242.

[65] Kellenbenz, 'Rural Industries', p. 61.

[66] Richard Dietrich, 'Das Städtewesen Sachsens an der Wende vom Mittelalter zur Neuzeit', in Rausch, *Die Stadt an der Schwelle zur Neuzeit*, p. 208.

contract.[67] From the 1560s linen exports from these areas were penetrating southern Germany, where they competed with the local cloths.[68]

The significance of linen in the definition of an economic landscape was heightened by the demand for paper after the invention of moveable type in the mid-fifteenth century. Flax provided the raw material for the production of rag-paper, which was already flourishing in several south-west German and Swiss cities before the advent of printing. There were concentrations of paper mills around Ravensburg, Basel, Fribourg, and Épinal in the Vosges, though the technique of paper-making was quickly transferred to other centres of printing throughout Germany.[69] The natural conditions which favoured the cultivation of flax also applied to hemp, from which rough canvas and ropes were made, as well as a coarse cloth known confusingly in German as hempen linen (*Hanfleinwand*). But hemp never dominated the production of any one region so as to stamp it as an economic landscape in its own right, with the possible exception of some areas in the north, such as the Münsterland around Tecklenburg, which was heavily engaged in manufacturing canvas for the shipping industry in the Hanseatic ports.[70]

It was with the spread of fustian-manufacturing from the late fourteenth century onwards that early capitalism came to dominate the heartlands of the textile industry in Upper Swabia. Fustian, cloth woven from a linen warp and a cotton weft,[71] required the import of raw cotton from the Mediterranean, which was brought in by long-distance merchants who supplied the local spinners and weavers. While putting-out was confined initially to the larger towns, such as Nördlingen, where the merchants had their headquarters,[72] it quickly

---

[67] Ingomar Bog, 'Wachstumsprobleme der oberdeutschen Wirtschaft 1540–1618', in Friedrich Lütge (ed.), *Wirtschaftliche und soziale Probleme der gewerblichen Entwicklung im 15.–16. und 19. Jahrhundert. Bericht über die zweite Arbeitstagung der Gesellschaft für Sozial- und Wirtschaftsgeschichte in Würzburg 8.–10. März 1965* (Forschungen zur Sozial- und Wirtschaftsgeschichte, 10) (Stuttgart, 1968), p. 53; Kellenbenz, *Rise of the European Economy*, p. 76.

[68] Kießling, *Die Stadt und ihr Land*, pp. 501–2.

[69] von Stromer, 'Gewerbereviere', pp. 104–6, and map, p. 105.

[70] Kellenbenz, 'Rural Industries', p. 61.

[71] Not a cotton warp and a linen weft, as erroneously stated in Friedrich-Wilhelm Henning, *Wirtschafts- und Sozialgeschichte*, 1: *Das vorindustrielle Deutschland 800 bis 1800*, 4th edn (Paderborn/Munich/Vienna/Zürich, 1985), p. 146.

[72] Kießling, *Die Stadt und ihr Land*, p. 219.

spread to the countryside, as entrepreneurs sought to circumvent guild restrictions and production limits, and to find cheaper sources of labour. In striking contrast, where fustian-manufacturing did not supplant linen-weaving—St Gallen is an obvious example—the system of *Verlag* was hardly deployed before the sixteenth century.[73] Competition between country weavers (*Gäuweber*), who supplied their capitalist employers directly, and the Swabian cities intensified during the fifteenth century. The latter tried to prohibit putting-out within a radius of ten to fifteen miles, but such edicts were mostly unsuccessful against powerful merchant companies such as the Fuggers (whose founder, Hans Fugger, had himself been a peasant and part-time weaver who emigrated to Augsburg from the Lech valley in the mid-fourteenth century), which grouped their rural weavers around rival centres of production—Weißenhorn and Pfaffenhofen, for instance, against Ulm. The latter, though, tried to hit back by enforcing more stringent quality controls and higher inspection fees, which elicited protests from its competing neighbours.[74] Similarly, Biberach saw its trade slip away to rural weavers in the pay of the Haug merchant company of Augsburg and the Zangmeisters of Memmingen.[75] Another bone of contention arose in the early 1400s as rural spinners began to prepare linen-yarn ready for the loom by threading it onto warps (*Wepfen*), thereby encroaching on a more advanced state of production. The cities vacillated in their response: some, in the Allgäu, strove to confine production to the countryside; others, in Swabia, were ready to admit both urban and rural production, provided that they could prevent its organization by *Verlag*.[76] In general, however, the division of labour which marked fustian production could bring certain advantages to urban weavers, who were thereby encouraged to concentrate on the more complex finishing processes with greater added value and hence greater rewards.

---

[73] Kirchgässner, 'Verlag', pp. 96–7.

[74] Hermann Kellenbenz, 'The Fustian Industry of the Ulm Region in the Fifteenth and Early Sixteenth Centuries', in Negley B. Harte and Kenneth G. Ponting (eds), *Cloth and Clothing in Medieval Europe. Essays in Memory of Professor E. M. Carus Wilson* (Pasold Studies in Textile History, 2) (London, 1983), p. 262.

[75] Kellenbenz, *Rise of the European Economy*, pp. 81–2.

[76] Rolf Kießling, 'Stadt und Land im Textilgewerbe Oberschwabens vom 14. bis zur Mitte des 16. Jahrhunderts', in Neithard Bulst, Jochen Hoock, and Franz Irsigler (eds), *Bevölkerung, Wirtschaft und Gesellschaft. Stadt-Land-Beziehungen in Deutschland und Frankreich 14. bis 19. Jahrhundert* (Trier, 1983), pp. 124–6.

By far the most extensive textile production in late medieval and early modern Germany, however, remained wool. The areas of manufacture ranged from northern Swabia, Franconia, and Bavaria, through central Württemberg, much of Lower Alsace and the Middle Rhine, to the district west of Cologne, and on eastwards through Hessen into Thuringia, Bohemia, and Moravia. Woollen manufacturing, although fully commercialized, was somewhat less exposed to the characteristic early-capitalist practice of putting-out, for production was concentrated largely in towns, with only spinning as a part-time, and above all female, occupation in the countryside. But where manufacturing rapidly expanded in the sixteenth century in response to export demand—southern Thuringia is a case in point—urban weavers were obliged to accept piecework contracts by *Verlag*.[77] Cologne, as a major metropolis both of production and distribution, also used *Verlag* to extend the manufacturing region of cloth bearing its seal of quality as far afield as Aachen.[78] These were exceptional instances, however, not the rule. Neither Strasbourg, as the mercantile capital of the Upper Rhine, nor Braunschweig, the most export-oriented of the Hanseatic cities, resorted to any degree of putting-out in order to increase their share of the market, perhaps because, in the former, workshops were geared to the production of cheaper cloths for lining rather than quality export woollens,[79] while, in the latter, the clothmakers' guild which controlled all stages of production did not display the common early-capitalist division between merchant drapers and master wool-weavers.[80] Cloth production created in turn a lively market for dyestuffs and dyeing agents, notably madder, woad, and alum. The blue dye obtained from woad remained in greatest demand until it was overtaken in the sixteenth century by indigo

[77] Held, *Zwischen Marktplatz und Anger*, pp. 174–5.

[78] Franz Irsigler, 'Stadt und Umland im Spätmittelalter. Zur zentralitätsfördernden Kraft von Fernhandel und Exportgewerbe', in Emil Meynen (ed.), *Zentralität als Problem der mittelalterlichen Stadtgeschichtsforschung* (Städteforschung. Veröffentlichungen des Instituts für vergleichende Städtegeschichte in Münster, A 8) (Cologne/Vienna, 1979), pp. 4–5; on Cologne's cloth production in general see Franz Irsigler, 'Kölner Wirtschaft im Spätmittelalter', in Hermann Kellenbenz (ed.), *Zwei Jahrtausende Kölner Wirtschaft*, 2 vols (Cologne, 1975), 1, pp. 218–319.

[79] Ammann, 'Wirtschaftsgeltung des Elsaß', p. 81.

[80] Ernst Pitz, 'Wirtschaftliche und soziale Probleme der gewerblichen Entwicklung im 15./16. Jahrhundert nach hansisch-niederdeutschen Quellen', in Lütge, *Probleme der gewerblichen Entwicklung*, pp. 39–40.

from the Orient. Until then, Erfurt and its hinterland in Thuringia was the principal area of production, which throve in part by supplying local manufacturers but chiefly by exporting woad to the many centres of cloth production in neighbouring Hessen.[81] A symbiosis or complementarity between adjacent regions of specialized production can therefore be observed in the central German woollen industry, though elsewhere—in Alsace and on the Lower Rhine—dyestuffs were cultivated within the areas of cloth manufacture itself.

The growing demand for woollen cloth in certain instances encouraged a switch from other textiles, particularly in northern Swabia, where Nördlingen progressed from linen- through fustian-weaving to the manufacture of loden, the heavy, felted, short-pile cloth used for blankets and coats.[82] By the end of the sixteenth century, indeed, loden production had spread southeastwards into many Bavarian towns as far as Munich. The popularity of wool over coarser, mixed cloths such as fustian was further enhanced by the development of lighter, softer woollens in the sixteenth century, known collectively as the 'new draperies'. In fact, the 'new draperies' proper were short-staple woollen cloths, pioneered in Flanders as a cheaper alternative to traditional luxury woollens, whereas the new cloths widely made in both Germany and England were either worsted (that is, long-staple) cloths, or else blends with a worsted warp and a woollen (short-staple) weft.[83] These light, unsheared cloths—says and serges, as they were called—had already been promoted on a territorial level in Baden and Württemberg around 1500,[84] and by the mid-sixteenth century the leading textile cities of southern Germany—Strasbourg, Ulm, Augsburg—were likewise making says in the form of barracans and grosgrams.[85] Apart from the 'new draperies' a few

---

[81] Hektor Ammann, 'Die Friedberger Messen', *Rheinische Vierteljahrsblätter*, 15/16 (1950/51), pp. 192–225; *Hessen und Thüringen. Von den Anfängen bis zur Reformation* (Exhibition Catalogue, Marburg and Eisenach, 1992), pp. 230–4 and map, p. 232.

[82] Kießling, *Die Stadt und ihr Land*, pp. 214–15.

[83] John H. Munro, 'Monetary Contraction and Industrial Change in the Late-Medieval Low Countries, 1335–1500', in Nicholas J. Mayhew (ed.), *Coinage. The Low Countries 800–1500* (British Archaeological Reports, 54) (Oxford, 1979), pp. 118–19. See now fundamentally Robert S. DuPlessis, 'One Theory, Two Draperies, Three Provinces, and a Multitude of Fabrics: The New Drapery of French Flanders, Hainault, and the Tournaisis, *c.* 1500–*c.* 1800', in Negley B. Harte (ed.), *The New Draperies in the Low Countries and England, 1300–1800* (London, 1997), pp. 129–72.

[84] Kirchgässner, 'Verlag', pp. 100–2.

[85] Donald C. Coleman, 'An Innovation and Its Diffusion. The "New Draperies"', *Economic History Review*, 2nd series, 22 (1969), p. 426.

centres began to specialize in cotton and silk, notably in Switzerland, where Basel had already developed a cotton industry based on putting out work to weavers in Alsace and the Breisgau in the fifteenth century. In north Germany the only important centre of silk-weaving in the fifteenth century was Cologne, but by the mid-sixteenth century refugees from Tridentine Italy had brought their expertise in silk-weaving to Zürich and other Protestant cities.[86]

IV

The third type of economic landscape, that of mining and the metal-working industries, has sometimes been seen as the pacemaker in a decisive transformation towards a fully industrial economy based on capitalism. Yet quite apart from the restricted geographical dispersion of such areas up to the end of the sixteenth century, we should remember that the twin hallmarks of industrial production—the factory system and the replacement of manual labour by machines—only existed in rudimentary form; 'proto-factories' could survive for centuries without giving rise to any widespread industrialization.[87] In one particular branch of the extractive industry, moreover, namely salt-mining, the nature of production might in fact inhibit the development of a factory system. Where salt was extracted by evaporation from brine, as in the salt-springs of Frankenhausen in Thuringia, or Allendorf-Sooden in Hessen, the work was neither capital-intensive nor technologically complex. In Thuringia individual salt-miners were engaged in extended commodity production rather than in early-capitalist entrepreneurialism.[88] No shareholding companies developed to exploit the salt-works, as happened in the silver and copper mines of southern Saxony, though in Hessen the Allendorf salt-springs were run as a state monopoly on a capitalist footing.[89] Where salt had to be hewn from saliferous rock, however, as in the mines of Bavaria, Tirol, and Salzburg, the techniques of extraction

[86] Rudolf Holbach, 'Formen des Verlagswesens im Hanseraum vom 13. bis zum 16. Jahrhundert', *Hansische Geschichtsblätter*, 103 (1985), p. 48; Kirchgässner, 'Verlag', pp. 98–9.
[87] von Stromer, 'Gewerbereviere', pp. 42 ff.
[88] Held, *Zwischen Marktplatz und Anger*, pp. 170–1.
[89] Wright, *Capitalism, the State and the Lutheran Reformation*, p. 125.

were more costly: winches and pulleys were needed to bring the salt to the surface, while the salt-pans installed in Hall, for example, were on an industrial scale. Salt-mining in the Alps was under princely control from the thirteenth century, and considerable sums were invested to improve roads over the Alps to compete in northern Italy against sea salt marketed by Venice.[90]

The other extractive industry which did not necessarily require new techniques of production was glass-making. Glassworks, as we have seen in the case of Hessen, were less dependent on the location of raw materials—silicates—than on the availability of the derivatives used in the manufacturing process itself. Both sand and clay (for the firing ovens) were plentiful in the forests of northern and southern Hessen, the Reinhard, Kaufungen, and Spessart districts. But glassworks also flourished in areas where timber (and hence potash) abounded but the soils were not especially siliceous, notably in the Black Forest, where quartz sand was hauled up from the Rhine valley. Glass foundries might be grouped into a federation of producers, as in Hessen, but it was just as common for glassmakers to remain journeymen who staked out a plot of forest which they felled until exhausted, before moving on.[91] For that reason, along with the relatively straightforward technology, glass-making remained an industry without any significant capitalist penetration of production and distribution, and, by the same token, one which rarely dominated a particular region for long enough to constitute an economic landscape. Even in Hessen, the extensive glass industry, which had already moved northwards in the course of the sixteenth century, was in decline by 1600, as woodland resources were used up.[92]

The extraction and processing of precious and base metal ores, by contrast, could only expand with sufficient capital backing and the stimulus of new technology. Where copper, silver, lead, and iron abounded—in southern Westphalia, Saxony, Bohemia, the Upper Palatinate, Tirol, and Styria—the first genuinely industrial landscapes

---

[90] Rudolf Palme, 'Alpine Salt-Mining in the Middle Ages', *Journal of European Economic History*, 19 (1990), pp. 117–36; Josef Riedmann, 'Mittelalter', in Josef Fontana *et al.* (eds), *Geschichte des Landes Tirol*, 1 (Bolzano/Innsbruck/Vienna, 1985), pp. 510–11.

[91] Eberhard Gothein, *Wirtschaftsgeschichte des Schwarzwaldes und der angrenzenden Landschaften*, 1: *Städte- und Gewerbegeschichte* (Strasbourg, 1892), p. 807.

[92] Wright, *Capitalism, the State and the Lutheran Reformation*, pp. 124–5.

of late medieval and early modern Germany emerged. In many of these areas subsidiary deposits of other minerals were discovered: gold in parts of Bohemia and Lusatia; bismuth, cobalt, and tin (which, in the form of tinplate, was used to coat iron to prevent rusting) in southern Saxony. Indeed, Saxony became a region of economic diversification almost on a par with Alsace, where commercialized pastoral agriculture, the cultivation of industrial crops such as woad, and a woollen and linen industry interacted with the boom in mining and metallurgy to create a dynamic push-pull of supply and demand. Other areas, though, might acquire their distinctive economic contours from the mining of a single mineral: calamine (*Galmei*, zinc carbonate; in the USA smithsonite), which was alloyed with copper to produce brass, was discovered west of Cologne; mercury was found in the Rhineland Palatinate, while the pit-coal deposits of the Ruhr (and southern Saxony) were being mined as early as the fifteenth century.

The major technical innovation of the later Middle Ages in metallurgy was the invention of liquation (*Saiger-, Abdarrverfahren*), whereby silver could be extracted from argentiferous raw copper through the admixture of lead. Hitherto, the mining of silver had largely been confined to areas of argentiferous lead ores in the Carpathian and Harz Mountains, and the Austrian Alps from Tirol through to Carinthia, with smaller reserves in the Vosges and the Black Forest. The silver was separated from the lead by cupellation, a technique known to antiquity, whereby the lead was melted in a marl-lined hearth and then oxidized, so that the silver was left as a metal 'bun' on the hearth.[93] Liquation, on the other hand, was a much more costly and time-consuming process, which required copious supplies of lead. In the copper-shale district of Thuringia, on whose southern fringes the greatest concentration of liquation works was to be found, lead, despite its weight, had to be imported from as far afield as the Eifel and Westphalia. In the liquation process itself, the lead was burnt up, which produced white lead (lead oxide); that could then be returned to lead by reduction through charcoal: nevertheless, the wastage was high.[94] The discovery of liquation transformed

[93] For technical information on cupellation and liquation I am deeply grateful to Dr J. W. Barnes of the University of Swansea.

[94] von Stromer, 'Gewerbereviere', p. 98. Westermann's statement in *Eislebener Garkupfer*, p. 188, that most of the lead was used up is incorrect.

the mining industry of central Germany and, subsequently, the Alps, where new argentiferous copper deposits were discovered near the lead ores. By the end of the fifteenth century, on one estimate, Schwaz in Tirol was alone producing 80 per cent of the silver and 40 per cent of the copper of central Europe.[95] Despite the opening-up of new mines, such as Kitzbühel, in the early decades of the sixteenth century, however, the silver boom finally collapsed in the face of cheaper imports from the Americas. But the advantage of liquation was that it permitted a new phase of metallurgical enterprise to flourish through a shift in emphasis to copper production which, in its alloy of brass, supplied the growing armaments industry of the 'iron century' of warfare in early modern Europe. By the mid-sixteenth century, for instance, the bulk of Thuringian mining output was copper rather than silver, though after 1550 there appears to have been a gradual decline in the use of copper for household goods.[96]

In the mining industry the putting-out system was very widespread, not only on account of the high capital cost of extracting and refining, or the expense of transport between the mines and the smelteries, but also because its production as bullion or as metal was traded internationally. The leading merchants of Nuremberg and Augsburg were deeply involved in all the mining regions of central Europe. The Fuggers, to take the prime example, owned smelteries or maintained trading depots from Thuringia through Slovakia (at Banská Bystřica/Neusohl) to Carinthia (Fuggerau by Villach) as well as in Tirol itself, whose economy they effectively controlled. Yet the risks were great in an industry so vulnerable to the external hazards of warfare or the loss of mining licences and monopolies, and to the internal dislocations caused by the flooding of mines, explosions, and collapse of shafts, or else incautious overproduction, let alone the perpetual threat of labour unrest. Many entrepreneurs went bankrupt, or withdrew and cut their losses, so that it comes as no sur-

[95] Riedmann, 'Mittelalter', p. 515; Reinhard Hildebrandt, 'Augsburger und Nürnberger Kupferhandel 1500–1619. Produktion, Marktanteile und Finanzierung im Vergleich zweier Städte und ihrer wirtschaftlichen Führungsschicht', in Hermann Kellenbenz (ed.), *Schwerpunkte der Kupferproduktion und des Kupferhandels in Europa 1500–1650* (Kölner Kolloquien zur internationalen Sozial- und Wirtschaftsgeschichte, 3) (Cologne/Vienna, 1977), pp. 194–5.

[96] Westermann, *Eislebener Garkupfer*, pp. 25, 42–3.

prise to find that the mining industry in Thuringia, the area which had prospered most from the invention of liquation, was by the 1540s no longer controlled by distant merchants but by its territorial princes, the counts of Mansfeld. A similar story can be told of the Fuggers' involvement at Banská Bystřica.[97]

These observations should make us cautious about ascribing an intrinsic dynamic to the spread of early capitalism in Germany; indeed, its most characteristic form, the putting-out system, was far from being a peculiarly late medieval development.[98] Yet in areas of iron production the entire economy might be invigorated by the manufacture of high-value metalwares—precision tools, clocks, and scientific instruments—provided that sufficient capital and technology were available. Iron-ore deposits were found in many parts of the empire in the Middle Ages—the Eifel and Hunsrück, Siegerland and Sauerland, parts of the Black Forest and eastern Swabia, the Upper Palatinate, much of Bohemia into Moravia and Lusatia, and in Styria and Carinthia—but the only two areas which by the sixteenth century had made the successful transition from isolated forges employing primitive technology and supplying local needs to fully industrialized landscapes with specialized factory production were the Süderland (the county of Mark in the western Sauerland) and the Upper Palatinate. It is no accident that these two districts lay near the major international trading cities of Cologne and Nuremberg and enjoyed good communications and a strategic market position. In the Süderland, the towns of Solingen, Altena, Iserlohn, and Lüdenscheid were already famous in the fifteenth century for the manufacture of wire (by drawing, not smithying), tools, and household metal goods such as cutlery which required the use of moulds and presses as well as forges and furnaces. So advanced was production that the Süderland came to concentrate on finished articles, and was content to import pig-iron from further south in the Siegerland.[99] This latter district had undergone considerable economic

[97] Ibid., pp. 55–6.

[98] Franz Mathis, *Die deutsche Wirtschaft im 16. Jahrhundert* (*Enzyklopädie Deutscher Geschichte*, 11) (Munich, 1992), pp. 60–5, 86–97.

[99] Franz Kirns, 'Das Eisengewerbe im Süderland von 1500 bis 1650', in Hermann Kellenbenz (ed.), *Schwerpunkte der Eisengewinnung und Eisenverarbeitung in Europa 1500–1650* (Kölner Kolloquien zur internationalen Sozial- und Wirtschaftsgeschichte, 2) (Cologne/Vienna, 1974), p. 180.

development in the later Middle Ages; in its flourishing iron industry blast-furnaces had replaced bloomery by 1500, and the putting-out system was prevalent.[100] Yet, unlike the Süderland, the Siegerland never became a fully industrialized region, largely because of its remoteness and the lack of entrepreneurial initiative: ironworking remained under the control of local lords or the landgraves of Hessen, who were more concerned with domestic needs than distant export markets.

The most advanced industrial area of all was undoubtedly the district around Nuremberg, which drew on iron supplies from the Upper Palatinate with its twin metallurgical centres of Sulzbach and Amberg. By the early fourteenth century the technique of tinplating iron had been pioneered, which for long remained confined to Nuremberg and Wunsiedel in the Fichtelgebirge.[101] Likewise, the technology of wire-drawing was in use from the early fifteenth century, though not fully automated until the late sixteenth.[102] Wire mills were established all around the city on the rivers Rednitz and Pegnitz. Just as in the Süderland, Nuremberg, as the region's economic powerhouse, sought less to dominate the metallurgical processes itself than, by deploying *Verlag*, to secure supplies of semi-finished ironware which it could then manufacture into specialized finished goods. A list of crafts in the city in which the putting-out system operated records in 1535 hook-, blade-, compass-, knife-, needle- and wire-making, as well as armourers and tinsmiths, alongside certain clothing trades (fustian-weaving, glove-making) and printing. The city and its entrepreneurs used the putting-out system less to organize the surrounding countryside into an industrial zone for mass production—unlike the Upper Swabian cities with their rural linen and fustian industries—than to reserve the latter stages of production to urban craftsmen in their employ, and to export their wares to foreign markets.[103] The concept of the *Wirtschaftseinheit*, the economic unit embracing town and

[100] Fritz Geisthardt, 'Frühes Eisengewerbe an Sieg, Dill und Lahn', ibid., p. 192.

[101] Hermann Aubin, 'Formen und Verbreitung des Verlagswesens in der Altnürnberger Wirtschaft', in Stadtarchiv Nürnberg (ed.), *Beiträge zur Wirtschaftsgeschichte Nürnbergs*, 2 (Beiträge zur Geschichte und Kultur der Stadt Nürnberg, 11, 2) (Nuremberg, 1967), p. 629.

[102] von Stromer, 'Gewerbereviere', pp. 87, 89.

[103] Aubin, 'Formen und Verbreitung', pp. 635, 641.

country, implied not so much dominance by the city of its hinterland as the fulfilment of mutual needs: the smaller surrounding towns were as eager to grab a share of Nuremberg's industrial prosperity as the city's merchants were to control local production.[104]

The intensification of town-country relations within a given region is the most obvious hallmark of the development of economic landscapes in Germany from the later Middle Ages. It would be wrong to conclude this review, however, without making three qualifications. In the first place, the growth of economic regionalism was only possible where town and country made up an economic unit. Where cities earned their livelihood as entrepôts and their merchants as middlemen and carriers, there was no reason why such economic activity should impinge upon the hinterland at all. That is most noticeably the case in the coastal cities of the Hanseatic League, whose trade derived much less from importing and exporting to and from northern Germany than from long-distance cargo-carrying between Russia, the Baltic, and western Europe. In cities such as Lübeck and Hamburg the urban economy of small commodity-producers remained largely intact; the division of labour, capital-intensive production, and the putting-out system were underdeveloped until the sixteenth century; and there was little attempt to extend commercial influence to the countryside, where the territorial lords were in any case at pains to protect their local crafts and industry from urban encroachment. Indeed, the coastal Hanseatic cities—fish out of water, rather than the natural foci of their regions—faced growing artisanal competition from their hinterlands in the course of the sixteenth century, though by then centres such as Lübeck had begun to employ put-out rural workers in the copper industry and in cooperage.[105]

Secondly, the growth of economic regions did not preclude the rise of international commerce over long distances between the empire as a whole and its neighbours: the one, in fact, was predicated upon the other. The more the economic specialization in a particular area, the greater was the need to import goods from elsewhere. The prime example in the sixteenth century, as has already been suggested, was

[104] Ammann, *Wirtschaftliche Stellung Nürnbergs*, p. 204.

[105] Pitz, 'Probleme der gewerblichen Entwicklung', pp. 34, 37; Holbach, 'Formen des Verlags', pp. 53–4, 61–2.

the development of an international trade in cattle. Population pressure and the demand for grain in the west squeezed the amount of land available for stock-rearing. Instead of the smaller, leaner cattle raised in the west, merchants began to bring in the larger grey cattle from Hungary and Poland which had been fattened, significantly enough, not on the domain estates of lords or on peasant smallholdings but on the vast tracts of semi-wild steppe.[106] A cluster of cattle markets grew up on the frontiers of the empire around Wrocław and east of Vienna, with further staging-posts in Germany itself, notably at Buttstädt in Thuringia. By the sixteenth century, however, the eastern European cattle trade was itself in turn being challenged by imports from Denmark and Scania. Lean steers were brought via the north German cities for fattening on the lush pasturelands of the Elbe and Weser marshes, before being driven further south for sale. As pastoralism retreated before the expansion of cereal agriculture in the west, the new international system of livestock marketing became, in Ian Blanchard's words, the mainstay of metropolitan meat-provisioning throughout the whole of western Europe.[107] Yet the market exchange between areas of pastoral and cereal agriculture could also serve to intensify economic activity within a smaller compass. Alsace, as the bread-basket for much of southwest Germany and Switzerland, was dependent upon meat imports from the rich grazing lands of Burgundy and the Franche-Comté, so that the cattle-market at Cernay (Sennheim) became the hub of commercial activity between two immediately adjacent regions.[108]

The final consideration is perhaps the most important of all. Economic regions did not thrive (or decline) in a vacuum: they were vulnerable to political disruption and military depredation. The Cities'

---

[106] Jan Baszanowski, 'Ochsenzuchtgebiete und Ochsenausfuhr aus Polen vom 16. bis 18. Jahrhundert', in Ekkehard Westermann (ed.), *Internationaler Ochsenhandel (1350–1750). Akten des 7th International Economic History Congress Edinburgh 1978* (Beiträge zur Wirtschaftsgeschichte, 9) (Stuttgart, 1979), p. 128.

[107] Ian Blanchard, 'The Continental European Cattle Trade 1400–1600', *Economic History Review*, 2nd series, 39 (1986), pp. 433, 441. See also Franz Lerner, 'Die Bedeutung des internationalen Ochsenhandels für die Fleischversorgung deutscher Städte im Spätmittelalter und in der frühen Neuzeit', in Westermann, *Internationaler Ochsenhandel*, pp. 197–217.

[108] Jean Vogt, 'Grandeur et décadence du marché de bétail de Cernay (Deuxième moitié du XVIe et début du XVIIe siècle)', *Annuaire de la Société d'Histoire des Régions de Thann-Guebwiller*, 1970–72, pp. 131–8.

War of 1449–52, for instance, severely disrupted Nuremberg's economy and commerce and provided an opening for its rival Augsburg, of which the latter was quick to take advantage.[109] Augsburg's merchants, especially the Fuggers and Welsers, built upon that opportunity in the succeeding decades, as they forged a financial alliance with the Habsburgs in return for access to the lucrative silver and copper mines of Tirol. Likewise, the periodic campaigns against the Turks from the 1470s brought economic dislocation to Nuremberg and many of the Swabian manufacturing cities. The *coup de grâce* for Nuremberg finally came in the mid-sixteenth century, when the Margrave's War against Albrecht Alcibiades of Brandenburg-Ansbach cost the city four and a half million fl. and ruined its finances.[110] In an age of transition, poised between medieval merchant-venturer capitalism and the industrial capitalism of early modern Europe, the development of economic landscapes in Germany was uneven and uncertain, constantly exposed to setbacks from without and within, that is, to political as well as economic constraints.

[109] von Stromer, 'Verflechtungen', pp. 22–3.

[110] Bog, 'Wachstumsprobleme der oberdeutschen Wirtschaft', pp. 71, 75.

CHAPTER EIGHT

TOWN AND COUNTRY IN THE GERMAN-SPEAKING LANDS, 1350–1600

Introduction

The pattern of town-country-relations in the German-speaking lands from the Alps to the North Sea from the fourteenth to the seventeenth centuries displayed a greater variety than in any other part of Europe. It ranged from fully-fledged city-states in the Swiss Confederation, sovereign principalities in their own right, to spheres of regional economic influence in the southern Low Countries, where the leading cities dominated the economy of their hinterlands without achieving exclusive jurisdiction. Yet the extremes of this spectrum should not be taken to reflect a conscious alternative on the part of the cities, either in their subjective intentions or in their objective possibilities. The leading Flemish cities—Ghent, Bruges, and Ypres—did indeed try to carve out city-states, but failed; while the powerful Swiss cities—Bern, Luzern, Zürich, and Basel—though ruling their hinterlands essentially as feudal overlords were not blind to the economic and financial opportunities which their territories afforded. None the less, in the light of their actual historical development, the cities of Flanders and Switzerland were indeed at the opposite ends of a spectrum, across which the cities of Germany were located at intermediate points. Some, such as Nuremberg, attempted to acquire land that would directly serve their commercial interests as a source of labour or raw materials; others, such as Augsburg or Cologne, came to dominate the economies of their hinterlands in the organization of production and distribution without ever amassing a landed territory of any size. Nuremberg was a city-state in all but name; Augsburg and Cologne echoed the regional economic sway exercised by the Flemish cities.

In either dimension, cities were concerned to extend their centrality—whether jurisdictional, political, economic, or social—over their surrounding countryside; in other words to establish a hierarchy of influence or dependence. But it should not be forgotten that relations between town and country were shaped by horizontal as well as vertical ties, that is, by cooperation between cities as well as by competition. This, too, was a particular feature of the German-speaking lands, reflected in both political and commercial alliances. The fourteenth and fifteenth centuries were the heyday of urban leagues of mutual defence and protection against the pretensions of both emperor and princes. Some were no more than temporary, such as the Swabian town league of the 1370s and 1380s; others, such as the Alsatian Decapolis after 1354, were put on a permanent footing; but all saw their function as essentially regional. Commercial alliances, by contrast, were less circumscribed: Germany gave rise to the largest association of merchant venturers in European history, the Hanseatic League, numbering over eighty cities at its peak, strewn across the map of northern Germany. The Hansa might have developed as an integrated commercial network, with members linked horizontally as relay-points along defined arteries of trade, especially once its character had evolved from a looser 'merchant' to a tighter 'city' Hansa by the fifteenth century, but regional tensions bedevilled Hanseatic history: its members found themselves pulled either towards its capital city, Lübeck, and therewith to commercial engagement in the Baltic, or else towards its rival Cologne, which dominated the export trade of the west German interior down the river Rhine. Those Hanseatic cities which saw themselves primarily as entrepôts in the carrying trade, rather than as outlets for the economy of their hinterlands, developed a different pattern of town-country relations from other members who were partly engaged in local industry and in putting-out.

The following analysis begins by tracing the varieties of urban territorial expansion, before turning to the rise of regional economic systems in which a metropolis and its hinterland of lesser towns and villages were integrated in a complementary network of economic functions, in what Hektor Ammann has termed an 'economic unit' (*Wirtschaftseinheit*).[1] Though this distinction is in some respects artificial, it offers a reasonable way of uncovering underlying patterns in the otherwise irreducible complexity of town-country relations in pre-modern Germany.

---

[1] Hektor Ammann, *Die wirtschaftliche Stellung der Reichsstadt Nürnberg im Spätmittelalter* (Nürnberger Forschungen, 13) (Nuremberg, 1970), pp. 194 ff.

Institutional Patterns

Stages of Expansion

Urban territorial expansion has traditionally been seen as unfolding through three distinct stages: 1. the acquisition by individual citizens of property rights and revenues (which might include jurisdictions or markets) in the countryside; 2. the development of personal or corporate ties between country dwellers and cities in the form either of outburghership, that is, the extension of the legal privileges of citizenship to nobles, ecclesiastical foundations, or even peasants, without requiring them to take up urban residence, or else of protective agreements which afforded the cities access to strategic strongholds in times of military emergency or more continuous supervision of turnpikes and bridges in peacetime (*Öffnungs-, Burgrecht*); 3. the acquisition of lands and subjects by the city as a corporation, either as a mortgage which might later be redeemed, or as the launching-pad for consolidation into a dependent territory, over which the magistracy possessed exclusive jurisdiction. It must be stressed that these stages are not always clearly distinguishable, let along chronologically successive, and that in certain circumstances an informal *Umlandpolitik* (as it would be termed in German) might go much further towards securing a city's domination of its surrounding countryside than the formal construction of a rural territory. Indeed, some historians have argued that it is quite misleading to talk of a *Territorialpolitik* at all; they would prefer the more neutral term *Landgebietspolitik* (that is, the acquisition of rural estates), since a deliberate territorial policy with anti-feudal overtones can rarely be ascribed to the ruling elites of German cities.[2]

[2] See Hans-Joachim Behr, 'Die Landgebietspolitik nordwestdeutscher Hansestädte', *Hansische Geschichtsblätter*, 94 (1976), p. 18; Werner Rösener, 'Aspekte der Stadt-Land-Beziehungen im spätmittelalterlichen Deutschland', in Jean-Marie Duvosquel and Erik Thoen (eds), *Peasants and Townsmen in Medieval Europe. Studia in honorem Adriaan Verhulst* (Belgisch Centrum voor landelijke Geschiedenis, 114) (Ghent, 1995), pp. 668–9. For Braunschweig see Heinz Germer, *Die Landgebietspolitik der Stadt Braunschweig bis zum Ausgang des 15. Jahrhunderts* (Studien und Vorarbeiten zum historischen Atlas Niedersachsens, 16) (Göttingen, 1937). For tacit cooperation between city, ecclesiastical prince, and cathedral chapter, see for Bremen Manfred Wilmanns, *Die Landgebietspolitik der Stadt Bremen um 1400 unter besonderer Berücksichtigung der Burgenpolitik des Rates im Erzstift und in Friesland* (Veröffentlichungen des Instituts für historische Landesforschung der Universität Göttingen, 6) (Hildesheim, 1973), pp. 11, 265.

A closer examination of these various stages will help to reveal the mixture of motives which informed the cities' actions. For a string of south German imperial cities in Swabia Rolf Kießling has shown that the acquisition of rural property by individual burghers was the necessary—though not always the sufficient—precondition of any subsequent territorial consolidation. The range of such acquisitions corresponded closely to the size of the city itself. For Augsburg, the regional metropolis, the radius of bourgeois property extended for as much as 40 or even 60 kms; for sub-regional centres such as Memmingen, Nördlingen, or Kaufbeuren it was no more than 20 kms; but for local market towns such as Kempten, Donauwörth, or Lauingen a mere 10 to 15 kms.[3] In the case of Augsburg (which was too hemmed in by its bishopric and by the duchy of Bavaria to convert these extensive individual rights into a fully-fledged territory) citizens invested in land for a variety of reasons:—status and privilege, assembling over time a congeries of estates as the nucleus of a dynastic lordship upon which a patent of nobility might be conferred:—financial insurance, using estates as a security or cash reserve to offset risks incurred in long-distance trade:—commercial exploitation, viewing land as the vehicle for agricultural improvement (as the famous merchant house of Fugger did with its lordship of Mickhausen, where it ruthlessly enclosed land, evicting sitting tenants and replacing them with cottars, in order to reap the profits from intensive sheep-farming).[4] Konrad Fritze has confirmed this differentiated picture in his studies of the Wendish cities of the

[3] Rolf Kießling, 'Bürgerlicher Besitz auf dem Land—ein Schlüssel zu den Stadt-Land-Beziehungen im Spätmittelalter, aufgezeigt am Beispiel Augsburgs und anderer ostschwäbischer Städte', in Pankraz Fried (ed.), *Bayerisch-schwäbische Landesgeschichte an der Universität Augsburg 1975–1977. Vorträge, Aufsätze, Berichte* (Augsburger Beiträge zur Landesgeschichte Bayerisch-Schwabens, 1) (Sigmaringen, 1979), pp. 130–2. His sample embraces Augsburg, Nördlingen, Donauwörth, Lauingen, Memmingen, Kempten, Kaufbeuren, Mindelheim, and (in part) Ulm.

[4] Rolf Kießling, 'Herrschaft—Markt—Landbesitz. Aspekte der Zentralität und der Stadt-Land-Beziehungen spätmittelalterlicher Städte an ostschwäbischen Beispielen', in Emil Meynen (ed.), *Zentralität als Problem der mittelalterlichen Stadtgeschichtsforschung* (Städteforschung. Veröffentlichungen des Instituts für vergleichende Städtegeschichte in Münster, A 8) (Cologne/Vienna, 1979), pp. 211–12. Augsburg, by its size, was perhaps exceptional, but even in the smaller Swabian cities the spectrum of motives for bourgeois land purchases was considerable. For Memmingen see Rolf Kießling, *Die Stadt und ihr Land. Umlandpolitik, Bürgerbesitz und Wirtschaftsgefüge in Ostschwaben vom 14. bis ins 16. Jahrhundert* (Städteforschung. Veröffentlichungen des Instituts für vergleichende Städtegeschichte in Münster, A 29) (Cologne/Vienna, 1989), pp. 353–4.

Hanseatic League along the Baltic coast. Here, too, he can identify burghers who bought up estates as a capital reserve or substitute bank: not surprisingly, the turnover of such estates could be very rapid. This somewhat conservative stance he contrasts with the aggressive intervention of certain Stralsund merchants in the grain and wool production of the island of Rügen in the early fifteenth century, where they established a purchasing monopoly and made substantial profits.[5] Even so, Fritze posits an annual return on landed property as high as 8–9 per cent, a rate which seems out of line with figures calculated from other German cities; Nuremberg's citizens, for instance, expected no more than a 3–5 per cent return on what was chiefly regarded as a defensive investment.[6]

Elsewhere, however, agricultural investment by burghers could invigorate the rural economy. In Thuringia, another region where pastureland was being bought up to create sheep-farms, burghers of Erfurt were acquiring land for the cultivation of woad as an industrial crop, whose production and distribution were channelled through the city's market;[7] a similar development can be traced in Cologne's hinterland around Düren and Jülich. As early as the fourteenth century Cologne's bourgeois investors were sowing vetches and clover

---

[5] Konrad Fritze, *Am Wendepunkt der Hanse. Untersuchungen zur Wirtschafts- und Sozialgeschichte wendischer Hansestädte in der ersten Hälfte des 15. Jahrhunderts* (Veröffentlichungen des Historischen Instituts der Ernst-Moritz-Arndt-Universität Greifswald, 3) (Berlin, 1967), pp. 109–11; idem, *Bürger und Bauern zur Hansezeit. Studien zu den Stadt-Land-Beziehungen an der südwestlichen Ostseeküste vom 13. bis zum 16. Jahrhundert* (Abhandlungen zur Handels- und Sozialgeschichte, 16) (Weimar, 1976), pp. 91–2; idem, 'Soziale Aspekte der Stadt-Land-Beziehungen im Bereich der wendischen Hansestädte (13. bis 16. Jahrhundert)', in Hans K. Schulze (ed.), *Städtisches Um- und Hinterland in vorindustrieller Zeit* (Städteforschung. Veröffentlichungen des Instituts für vergleichende Städtegeschichte in Münster, A 22) (Cologne/Vienna, 1985), p. 29; Konrad Fritze, 'Stadt-Land-Beziehungen im hansischen Bereich im Mittelalter', in idem, Eckhard Müller-Mertens, and Johannes Schildhauer (eds), *Gewerbliche Produktion und Stadt-Land-Beziehungen* (Abhandlungen zur Handels- und Sozialgeschichte, 18: Hansische Studien, 4) (Weimar, 1979), pp. 111–14.

[6] Fritze, *Am Wendepunkt der Hanse*, p. 105 (figures principally for Stralsund and Rostock). For Nuremberg see Karl-Friedrich Krieger, 'Bürgerlicher Landbesitz im Spätmittelalter: Das Beispiel der Reichsstadt Nürnberg', in Schulze, *Städtisches Um- und Hinterland*, p. 92. In any case, Fritze does not regard citizens' capital investment in rural property as a true commercial investment; following Marx's arguments in vol. 3 of *Das Kapital*, he argues that the yield did *not* represent a rate of return on capital invested in land, but on capital surrendered simply in order to acquire the land. Fritze, *Bürger und Bauern*, p. 97.

[7] Wieland Held, *Zwischen Marktplatz und Anger. Stadt-Land-Beziehungen im 16. Jahrhundert in Thüringen* (Weimar, 1988), pp. 86–7, 108–9.

as catch-crops to improve the nitrogen content of the soil on their rural estates,[8] while in the same period in the environs of Nuremberg pine trees were being planted on sandy soil ill-suited to tillage, until in the sixteenth century council and citizens combined to promote irrigation by means of bucket-wheels which could turn dry land into lush meadows.[9]

Where urban ecclesiastical and charitable foundations, rather than individual citizens, acquired rural property, the opportunities accruing to city magistracies were all the greater, since they frequently held the stewardships of such corporations.[10] Smaller and less powerful cities in Swabia, for instance, faced with hostility from the surrounding nobility, were particularly adept at gaining control of their hinterlands by stealthily appropriating their hospitals' rural holdings.[11] This could occur in the larger cities as well: Memmingen's Lower Hospital (effectively under civic control by the fifteenth century) played a crucial role in enabling the city to carve out a rural territory,[12] while even Augsburg initially acquired indirect domination over its hinterland through stewardship of the city's hospitals, parish funds, and friaries. In this manner, not only their lands and subjects but the jurisdictional authority over them as well passed into civic hands.[13]

---

[8] Franz Irsigler, 'Kölner Wirtschaft im Spätmittelalter', in Hermann Kellenbenz (ed.), *Zwei Jahrtausende Kölner Wirtschaft*, 1 (Cologne, 1975), pp. 237–8; Franz Irsigler, 'Stadt und Umland im Spätmittelalter. Zur zentralitätsfördernden Kraft von Fernhandel und Exportgewerbe', in Meynen, *Zentralität*, p. 5.

[9] Fritz Schnelbögl, 'Die wirtschaftliche Bedeutung ihres Landgebiets für die Reichsstadt Nürnberg', in Stadtarchiv Nürnberg (ed.), *Beiträge zur Wirtschaftsgeschichte Nürnbergs*, 1 (Beiträge zur Geschichte und Kultur der Stadt Nürnberg, 11, 1) (Nuremberg, 1967), pp. 62–3, 67–8.

[10] Rolf Kießling, 'Das Umlandgefüge ostschwäbischer Städte vom 14. bis zur Mitte des 16. Jahrhunderts', in Schulze, *Städtisches Um- und Hinterland*, pp. 36–7.

[11] Wolfgang Leiser, 'Territorien süddeutscher Reichsstädte', *Zeitschrift für bayerische Landesgeschichte*, 38 (1975), p. 971; Peter Blickle, 'Zur Territorialpolitik der oberschwäbischen Reichsstädte', in Erich Maschke and Jürgen Sydow (eds), *Stadt und Umland. Protokoll der X. Arbeitstagung für südwestdeutsche Stadtgeschichtsforschung Calw 12.–14. November 1971* (Veröffentlichungen der Kommission für geschichtliche Landeskunde in Baden-Württemberg, B 82) (Stuttgart, 1974), pp. 54–71.

[12] Kießling, *Die Stadt und ihr Land*, pp. 278 ff.

[13] Idem, 'Herrschaft—Markt—Landbesitz', p. 189. See fundamentally idem, *Bürgerliche Gesellschaft und Kirche in Augsburg im Spätmittelalter. Ein Beitrag zur Strukturanalyse der oberdeutschen Reichsstadt* (Abhandlungen zur Geschichte der Stadt Augsburg, 19) (Augsburg, 1971).

Outburghership

Such a conflation of landlordship and jurisdictional lordship encouraged cities to extend rights of citizenship to their allies and dependents in the countryside. Outburghership (as it may conveniently be termed in English) was a pervasive institution in the German-speaking lands, though its significance has been overshadowed by the cities' areal expansion. Only in the Swiss Confederation and in the southern Low Countries has outburghership been accorded its due weight, but a comparison between these two areas once again highlights the very contrasting purposes that it might serve. There is now broad agreement that the constitution of the Swiss Confederation owed much less to the oath sworn on the Rütli meadow by the men of the inner cantons in 1291 than to a cumulative process over the next century, whereby the rural cantons entered into a series of protective alliances with the leading cities of northern Switzerland.[14] What undergirded this remarkable development was the large-scale manumission of serfs, who then acquired burgher's rights, in some cases by the thousands, in such cities as Luzern, Bern, and Zürich. Outburghership, moreover, lay as much in the cities' as in the peasants' interests: it was the principal means whereby Bern contrived to undermine the power of the local nobility and so construct a vast rural territory which became the largest city-state north of the Alps.[15]

---

[14] See Tom Scott, 'Liberty and Community in Medieval Switzerland', *German History*, 13 (1995), pp. 98–113, esp. 110 [repr. in this volume]. On this point see fundamentally Hans Conrad Peyer, *Verfassungsgeschichte der alten Schweiz* (Zürich, 1978).

[15] Scott, 'Liberty and Community', pp. 110–11, with detailed references. For Zürich see also Anton Largiadèr, 'Die Anfänge des Zürcherischen Stadtstaates', in *Festgabe Paul Schweizer* (Zürich, 1922), pp. 1–92, esp. 20 ff. The view, recently advanced by David Nicholas, *The Later Medieval City 1300–1500* (London/New York, 1997), pp. 93–4, that Metz in Lorraine had the largest territory is quite erroneous. In the 14th century, it is true, Metz had acquired extensive judicial, protective, and fiscal rights over a large tract of its hinterland, which was styled *'le Pays et Jurisdiction de Metz'*. But as Jean Schneider (upon whose researches Nicholas claims to rest his assertion) pointed out, *[l]e territoire urban s'est d'abord défini comme 'le pays appartenant aux seigneurs tant ecclésiastiques que séculiers habitant la ville de Metz'*. Jean Schneider, 'La ville de Metz aux XIIIe et XIVe siècles' (Doctorat ès Lettres, University of Paris, 1950) (Nancy, 1950), p. 424. And he concluded that *[v]ers 1400, le pays de Metz ne représente pas encore une formation territoriale achevée*. Ibid., p. 448. Thereafter, in the 15th century, the city lost much of its centrality to the duchy of Lorraine. Cf. idem (ed.), *Recherches sur la vie économique de Metz au XVe siècle. Le livre de comptes des merciers messins Jean Le Clerc et Jacquemin de Moyeuvre (1460–1461)* (Metz, 1951), pp. 12–13. Schneider may inadvertently have given rise to this misconception by his insistence that Metz's ability to mobilize its *pays* militarily and to impose taxes outstripped that of the

In the southern Low Countries, by contrast, outburghership never became the instrument of state-building. Although the dominant cities of Flanders—the *drie steden* of Ghent, Bruges, and (with some reluctance) Ypres—all held outburghers (including members of the local nobility), it was the lesser towns who most assiduously granted citizen's rights to the rural population, not least as a demographic and economic insurance policy against being outvoted or swallowed up by the *drie steden*, which by the early fourteenth century had succeeded in dividing Flanders among themselves into separate spheres of influence known as 'quarters'.[16] Indeed, there is some evidence that the counts of Flanders themselves encouraged the lesser towns to acquire *buitenpoorters* as a political counterweight to their arch-rivals, the *drie steden*.[17] Whereas the latter sought to regulate outburghership strictly, for instance by attempting to enforce a residence requirement for part of the year *intra muros*, the former often found themselves faced with the problem of double citizenship, as their *buitenpoorters* took out burgher's rights in other small towns or in the larger cities.[18] This underscores the primarily commercial benefits which *buitenpoorterij* was perceived as offering those whose economic activity required ready access to urban markets: politically, it worked to thwart, not to abet, any territorial consolidation in the form of city-states. However, it would be wrong to deduce that outburghership bestowed any automatic economic advantage on the lesser towns and cities of Flanders collectively. In the southern part of Ghent's quarter (to take a telling example), both Aalst (Alost) and Geraardsbergen (Grammont) possessed large numbers of outburghers, but in the later Middle Ages the former was thriving, whereas the decline in the latter's textile industry prompted a commercial reorientation towards servicing its immediate hinterland, with outburghership intended to underpin the new relationship (albeit without much success).[19]

---

largest German city-state, namely Nuremberg. Idem, 'La ville de Metz', p. 448. But that comparison only holds good for the 15th century, before Nuremberg had acquired the *Neue Landschaft* in 1504.

[16] David Nicholas, *Town and Countryside. Social, Economic, and Political Tensions in Fourteenth-Century Flanders* (Rijksuniversiteit te Gent: Werken uitgegeven door de Faculteit van de Letteren en Wijsbegeerte, 152) (Bruges, 1971), pp. 235–49 *et passim*. But see now Peter Stabel, *Dwarfs among Giants. The Flemish Urban Network in the Late Middle Ages* (Studies in Urban Social, Economic and Political History of the Medieval and Modern Low Countries, 8) (Leuven/Apeldoorn, 1997), pp. 94–106.

[17] Ibid., p. 95.

[18] Ibid., p. 99.

[19] Ibid., pp. 96–7, 103.

The function of outburghers for the German cities fell variously between the two poles of Switzerland and Flanders. Up to the mid-fourteenth century, many free and imperial cities, particularly in southern Germany, had acquired outburghers under several headings: individual noblemen, convents as corporate citizens, even peasants (the latter usually called paleburghers). Once emperor Charles IV's Golden Bull of 1356 had outlawed the acceptance of paleburghers by cities, however, the number of peasant outburghers generally declined, though they rarely disappeared altogether. Only Nuremberg, with its strong imperial connections, seems to have observed the ban on paleburghers rigorously—at least in the sense that any such country-dwellers had to emigrate to the city within a given time limit.[20] In the case of Frankfurt, another city with close imperial ties, the institution of paleburghership was superseded by the assertion of judicial authority over all its rural dependents (which amounted to much the same thing), while noble outburghership was replaced in the later fifteenth century by a series of service and protective alliances, including access to castles (*Öffnungsrecht*).[21] But a string of Swabian cities—Nördlingen, Memmingen, and Lauingen, as well as Augsburg—managed to retain both noble and peasant outburghers,[22] while in Alsace the number of Strasbourg's peasant outburghers may even have increased. Many more towns and cities than is commonly believed possessed outburghers, and they included territorial towns, whose subordination to princely overlordship should have rendered such a policy virtually impossible to sustain. That, in turn, helps to throw light upon the reasons for acquiring and retaining outburghers. For a city such as Cologne, caught between powerful ecclesiastical and secular princes (just as Augsburg was), the many treaties of outburghership concluded with leading noble families in its environs may be regarded

[20] Wolfgang Leiser, 'Das Landgebiet der Reichsstadt Nürnberg', in Rudolf Endres (ed.), *Nürnberg und Bern. Zwei Reichsstädte und ihre Landgebiete* (Erlanger Forschungen, A 46) (Erlangen, 1990), p. 246.

[21] Elsbet Orth, 'Stadtherrschaft und auswärtiger Bürgerbesitz. Die territorialpolitischen Konzeptionen der Reichsstadt Frankfurt im späten Mittelalter', in Schulze, *Städtisches Um- und Hinterland*, pp. 149–50; Bernd Schneidmüller, 'Städtische Territorialpolitik und spätmittelalterliche Feudalgesellschaft am Beispiel von Frankfurt am Main', *Blätter für deutsche Landesgeschichte*, 118 (1982), p. 131.

[22] Kießling, *Die Stadt und ihr Land*, pp. 36, 300, 553, 695; idem, 'Herrschaft—Markt—Landbesitz', p. 192. Even before the Golden Bull, a group of Swabian cities (Memmingen, Kempten, Isny, and Leutkirch) had reached a compact in 1298 not to accept further paleburghers. Idem, *Die Stadt und ihr Land*, p. 300.

as the specific substitute for the city's inability to construct a rural territory.[23] Elsewhere, binding wealthy rural convents to civic interests by obliging them to take out corporate citizenship, as practised by Augsburg, was a useful means of harnessing and channelling their economic clout.[24]

In general, no doubt, outburghership satisfied essentially defensive purposes: to secure a demographic and fiscal reservoir that would buttress the oppidan population and finances, and reinforce the civic militia in time of war. In Freiburg im Breisgau, for instance, an Outer Austrian territorial town on the Upper Rhine that clung tenaciously to its peasant outburghers until the sixteenth century, despite concerted opposition from its princely neighbours, the margraves of Baden (and indeed from its own noble outburghers as well), its rural citizens may have added another 10 per cent to the population of a commune which was undergoing a severe demographic and economic crisis.[25] But hitherto overlooked sources for Swabia provide a hint that outburghership may on occasion have operated in tandem with the cities' efforts to control the manufacturing output of their hinterlands. Towards the end of the fifteenth century in Kempten, the centre of the Allgäu linen industry, 400 urban weavers with 300 apprentices were matched by 600 outburghers who, the context implies, were almost certainly linen-weavers, too, employed as outworkers.[26] Its close neighbour Isny, moreover, which sheltered 150 linen-weavers within its walls, also recorded an unspecified number of outburghers accountable to the city but residing in the surrounding villages under feudal lords.[27] This evidence must not be pressed too far, but it does suggest an echo of the experience of the lesser Flemish cities.

---

[23] Hans J. Domsta, *Die Kölner Außenbürger. Untersuchungen zur Politik und Verfassung der Stadt Köln von der Mitte des 13. bis zur Mitte des 16. Jahrhunderts* (Rheinisches Archiv, 84) (Bonn, 1973).

[24] Kießling, 'Herrschaft—Markt—Landbesitz', p. 190.

[25] Tom Scott, *Freiburg and the Breisgau. Town-country Relations in the Age of Reformation and Peasants' War* (Oxford, 1986), pp. 78–98.

[26] Idem, 'Economic Landscapes', in Bob Scribner (ed.), *Germany: A New Social and Economic History*, 1: *1450–1630* (London/New York/Sydney/Auckland, 1995), p. 15 [repr. in this volume]; Tom Scott (ed.), *Die Freiburger Enquete von 1476. Quellen zur Wirtschafts- und Verwaltungsgeschichte der Stadt Freiburg im Breisgau im fünfzehnten Jahrhundert* (Veröffentlichungen aus dem Archiv der Stadt Freiburg im Breisgau, 20) (Freiburg im Breisgau, 1986), p. 13. See Rolf Kießling, 'Handel und Gewerbe, Stadt-Land-Beziehungen', in Volker Dotterweich *et al.*, (eds), *Geschichte der Stadt Kempten* (Kempten, 1989), p. 131.

[27] Scott, *Enquete*, p. 11.

The Construction of Landed Territories

When we turn to the construction of landed territories as such, an immediate difference between north and south Germany becomes apparent. While many south German imperial cities, including quite small ones, and even some territorial towns, were able to transform a miscellany of estates, jurisdictions, and protective agreements into consolidated dependencies, in the north only a handful of larger cities succeeded, and even then mainly by means of mortgages rather than outright purchases (with Erfurt as a prominent exception). That was particularly true of the leading Hanseatic cities: Braunschweig and Lüneburg as inland members almost exclusively, and the major ports of Bremen, Hamburg, and Lübeck to a large degree, relied upon acquisitions by mortgage.[28] Despite the political constraints which stood in the way of a concerted territorial policy in northern Germany, the recourse to mortgages was determined in the end by commercial considerations. For the Hanseatic cities peace, the protection of trade routes, and the maintenance of commercial privileges were much more important than the acquisition of rural territories for their own sake.[29] Mortgages were a convenient means of reaching an accommodation with neighbouring princes who might otherwise prey upon the cities' merchants.

This can readily be illustrated by Lüneburg's behaviour in 1392, when it handed back a string of mortgaged lordships to the dukes of Braunschweig in return for the proclamation of a regional public peace (*Landfriede*), enshrined in a treaty known as the *Sate*.[30] Commercial interests also help to explain the location of mortgaged territories. Rather than being grouped around the cities, as would have been the case if they had been the hinterlands of cities acting as central places in a market network, the mortgages were distributed, not radially, but axially, that is, along strategic trade routes, overland or by sea. That is clearly visible in the case of the Hanseatic capital Lübeck,

---

[28] Behr, 'Landgebietspolitik', pp. 26–8. This applies also to Bremen as a territorial town; its active mortgage policy coincided with its membership of the Hanseatic League from 1358 (Bremen only became an imperial city in 1646). Wilmanns, *Landgebietspolitik*, pp. 13, 15, 36 *et passim*.

[29] Elisabeth Raiser, *Städtische Territorialpolitik im Mittelalter. Eine vergleichende Untersuchung über verschiedene Formen am Beispiel Lübecks und Zürichs* (Historische Studien, 406) (Lübeck/Hamburg, 1969), p. 27.

[30] Ibid., p. 28.

which acquired the town and bailiwick of Mölln from the dukes of Saxony-Lauenburg in 1359, and held them in mortgage until 1683. Mölln was a vantage-point southwards on the river Stecknitz, the main link to the lucrative brine-pits of Lüneburg, a vital artery which the city canalized at the end of the fourteenth century.[31] In the following two centuries similar considerations prompted Lübeck to purchase as mortgages the island of Fehmarn (1437–91), overlooking shipping routes in the western Baltic, from the dukes of Schleswig, and then the island of Bornholm (1525–76) off the southern coast of Sweden after its capture by the Hanseatic League from the Danish crown.[32] Any financial benefit from these mortgages was entirely secondary. Lübeck's expenditure on Mölln at one point greatly exceeded its income, yet up to the seventeenth century the city never increased taxes or renders from the town and bailiwick.[33] Fehmarn, for its part, had cost Lübeck 18,000 marks in 1437, but in the fifty-three years of the mortgage the city made a net profit of no more than 24,000 marks, the equivalent of an annual rate of return of a mere 2.5 per cent.[34]

The drawback to mortgages was that they could so easily be redeemed (Mölln's three centuries in Lübeck's hands were quite exceptional). Lübeck's one attempt to construct a territorial buffer (as opposed to a commercial vantage-point) by acquiring in mortgage the sizeable bailiwick of Segeberg to the west from the counts of Holstein in the mid-fourteenth century lasted no more than a generation.[35] All told, many Hanseatic and north German cities lost territory over time from their heyday in the fourteenth century—Lübeck (despite its subsequent mortgages), Braunschweig, Lüneburg, Soest, and Goslar,[36] and that was also true of the one imperial city in central Germany which had resorted to a mortgage policy, namely Frankfurt am Main. Of its nineteen acquisitions by mortgage during the fourteenth and fifteenth centuries, mostly concentrated along

---

[31] Georg Fink, 'Lübecks Stadtgebiet (Geschichte und Rechtsverhältnisse im Überblick)', in Ahasver von Brandt and Wilhelm Koppe (eds), *Städtewesen und Bürgertum als geschichtliche Kräfte. Gedächtnisschrift für Fritz Rörig* (Lübeck, 1953), pp. 263–7. Fink disputes that Mölln in strictly legal terms was held in mortgage.

[32] Ibid., pp. 277–8.

[33] Raiser, *Städtische Territorialpolitik*, pp. 89–90.

[34] Fritze, *Bürger und Bauern*, pp. 62, 72.

[35] Fink, 'Lübecks Stadtgebiet', pp. 274–5.

[36] Raiser, *Städtische Territorialpolitik*, p. 18; Behr, 'Landgebietspolitik', p. 35.

commercial arteries to the north and north-west of the city, only thirteen remained by 1500; redemption had claimed the remainder.[37]

It would be quite wrong to leave the impression, however, that north German cities only acquired territories by mortgage, or that their motives were exclusively commercial. Of the Wendish cities of the Hanseatic League, Rostock, Greifswald, and Stralsund all built up modest territories in the fifteenth century, with around a score of villages each, which they controlled outright; only Wismar had almost none.[38] Stralsund's expansion, admittedly, was the outflow of a deliberate policy of protecting its trade routes on both land and sea; to that end it constructed a *Landwehr*, a rampart-and-ditch, surmounted by a thorn hedge, with the roads traversing it guarded by gates and watchtowers.[39] Other Hanseatic cities had *Landwehren*, too—Lübeck (which owned a good deal of land close to the city, aside from its mortgages further afield), Hamburg, and Braunschweig[40]—though the best-known *Landwehren* were those of Rothenburg ob der Tauber and Schwäbisch Hall in the south. The few imperial cities in northern Germany all managed to acquire dependent territories—Dortmund, Soest, Goslar, and Mühlhausen.[41] But the most remarkable instance was that of Erfurt which, despite being effectively shorn of its imperial status by the predations of the archbishops of Mainz during the fifteenth century (which obliged the city to enter into protective agreements with the dukes of Saxony), could boast in 1500 a territory of at least 610 square kms, comprising over sixty villages and the small town of Sömmerda.[42] This achievement is not solely intelligible against the background of Erfurt's considerable capital

---

[37] Orth, 'Stadtherrschaft', pp. 115–16. Mortgages were by no means unknown in south German cities, too. Nördlingen pursued an active territorial policy in the 15th century, buying up lordships from the counts of Oettingen—but always with the latter reserving the right of redemption. Kießling, *Die Stadt und ihr Land*, pp. 56–7.

[38] Fritze, *Bürger und Bauern*, pp. 65–6.

[39] Ibid., pp. 67–8.

[40] Behr, 'Landgebietspolitik', p. 19.

[41] Rösener, 'Aspekte der Stadt-Land-Beziehungen', p. 668; Held, *Zwischen Marktplatz und Anger*, p. 92.

[42] Ibid., p. 92. Held gives a figure of 83 villages and 610 km^2. Sven Tode, *Stadt im Bauernkrieg 1525. Strukturgeschichtliche Untersuchungen zur Stadt im Raum anhand der Beispiele Erfurt, Mühlhausen/Thür., Langensalza und Thamsbrück* (Frankfurt am Main/Berlin/Bern/New York/Paris/Vienna, 1994), pp. 77, 80 gives a more cautious figure of around 60 villages, but reckons the territory at 900 km^2, surely much too large.

investment in Thuringian woad production; it also stemmed from the city's position at the intersection of major trade routes, the *Hellweg* from east to west, and Hanseatic highways running from north to south. In addition, it benefited from a reciprocal relationship with the cloth towns of Lusatia and Silesia, above all Görlitz. Both market centrality and the city's place in an urban network, in other words, contributed to Erfurt's economic *rayonnement* as the precondition of its territorial expansion.[43]

Table 8.1. Territories of German and Swiss Cities in the early sixteenth century (km^2).

Rank	German cities	Size	Rank	Swiss cities	Size
1	Nuremberg*	1,200	1	Bern**	9,000
2	Ulm	850	2	Zürich	1,700
3	Erfurt***	610	3	Luzern	1,485
4	Rothenburg ob der Tauber	400	4	Solothurn	780
5	Schwäbisch Hall	330	5	Basel	460
6	Strasbourg Rottweil	220	6	Schaffhausen	295
			7	Zug	240

* Includes the *Neue Landschaft* (1504)
** Includes the Vaud (acquired 1536)
*** See note 42

It remains true, none the less, that the greatest concentration of civic territories was to be found among the ranks of the south German imperial cities (see Table 8.1). Leading the way, and half as large again as its nearest rival, was Nuremberg, once it had acquired the *Neue Landschaft* from the Palatinate in 1504.[44] Then came Ulm, which

[43] Tom Scott and Bob Scribner, 'Urban Networks', in Scribner, *Germany*, pp. 137–9.

[44] Leiser, 'Landgebiet', pp. 227, 232, 235, revising downwards the area of 1,500 km^2 given by Gerd Wunder, 'Reichsstädte als Landesherrn [sic]', in Meynen, *Zentralität*, p. 79 for the beginning of the 19th century. The view propounded by several modern English-language scholars that Nuremberg's territory amounted to no more than 80 km^2 (25 sq. miles) is nonsensical. See Nicholas, *Later Medieval City*, p. 98; Rhiman A. Rotz, '"Social Struggles" or the Price of Power? German Urban Uprisings in the Late Middle Ages', *Archiv für Reformationsgeschichte*, 76 (1985), p. 77; Gerald Strauss, *Nuremberg in the Sixteenth Century. City Politics and Life between Middle Ages and Modern Times*, revised edn (Bloomington, IN/London, 1976), p. 7. It appears

began buying up lordships in western Swabia from its surrounding secular and ecclesiastical nobility in the late fourteenth century. By the sixteenth, its territory encompassed three towns, fifty-five villages, and twenty-two other dependencies.[45] After Erfurt, in third place, came the Franconian city of Rothenburg (whose territory derived largely from the estates of one bourgeois proprietor amassed around 1400),[46] Schwäbisch Hall in northern Württemberg, Rottweil on the eastern fringes of the Black Forest, and Strasbourg, the metropolis of Alsace.[47] Apart from their imperial or free status, these cities had no common denominator. They were, however, only the tip of the iceberg. In Upper Swabia alone, apart from Ulm, and Biberach's very scattered possessions, two further groups of cities can be distinguished: those with medium-sized territories of some influence, among them Memmingen and Lindau, and others whose territory barely extended beyond the immediate urban precinct, such as Kempten (confined by its powerful abbey) and Isny.[48]

But size, of itself, is not an adequate criterion for measuring the economic and demographic significance of these territories. For the largest city territories, those of Nuremberg and Ulm, the rural population added another 40 per cent and 60 per cent respectively to the urban total; in Rothenburg and Schwäbisch Hall, by contrast, each with a population of 5,000 or just over, their territories added as much as 150 per cent or 220 per cent respectively to the oppidan figures.[49] Beyond Swabia, the population of Strasbourg's direct territory came to 10,000, that is, just under half the number living within the city walls, but if the lands indirectly under civic control (bourgeois estates and the properties of convents and foundations)

---

to be based on a confusion between German miles and English statute miles (1 German mile = 4.6 statute miles), though in Strauss's case he is apparently referring to Nuremberg's *Stadtmark*, not its landed territory.

[45] Helmut Schmolz, 'Herrschaft und Dorf im Gebiet der Reichsstadt Ulm', in Maschke and Sydow, *Stadt und Umland*, p. 168. The acquisitions were principally from the counts of Helfenstein and Werdenberg-Sargans, the lords of Rechberg, and the abbey of Ochsenhausen.

[46] Ludwig Schnurrer, 'Der Bürger als Grundherr: Die Grundherrschaft Heinrich Topplers aus Rothenburg (1408)', in Schulze, *Städtisches Um- und Hinterland*, p. 62.

[47] Gerhard Wunder, *Das Straßburger Gebiet. Ein Beitrag zur rechtlichen und politischen Geschichte des gesamten städtischen Territoriums vom 10. bis zum 20. Jahrhundert* (Schriften zur Verfassungsgeschichte, 13) (Berlin, 1965), p. 105.

[48] Blickle, 'Territorialpolitik', p. 56.

[49] Gerd Wunder, 'Reichsstädte als Landesherrn', p. 79.

are taken into account, they add another 13,000 persons (and 500 square kms!) to the previous total.[50] And even Frankfurt's territory, though diminutive (a mere 110 square kms), was densely populated, with 5,000 subjects at the end of the *ancien régime*.[51]

However impressive these figures may be, the fact remains that German city territories rarely rivalled their Swiss counterparts (see Table 8.1). Even a relatively insignificant canton such as Solothurn was larger than any German city-state except Nuremberg and Ulm. And indeed the comparison shows how poorly size correlates with economic clout. In the course of the sixteenth century, Basel became the financial nerve-centre of the Confederation, with almost 59 per cent of finance for public loans being raised on the city's capital market,[52] yet its territory, hemmed in by topography (the Jura alps to the south) and by political geography (the block of Outer Austrian lands in Upper Alsace) remained relatively modest in size. In terms of manufacturing and commerce, moreover, it is arguable that Zürich was much more important than the essentially agricultural Bern, more than five times its extent. Much the same applies to Germany, where only the first three cities had territories commensurate with (and contributing to) their economic ranking. Rothenburg, Schwäbisch Hall, and Rottweil, by contrast, had an economic sphere of influence decidedly inferior to, say, Nördlingen, Konstanz, or Memmingen. And spanning the emerging political frontier on the Upper Rhine in the sixteenth century, Basel (Swiss from 1501), despite the constraints already mentioned, controlled a territory still twice the size of the regional metropolis, Strasbourg, a linchpin of Germany's international commerce.

The Purposes of Territorial Expansion

Such discrepancies should counsel us against assuming too uniform or consistent a purpose in the territorial policy of the south German

[50] Gerhard Wunder, *Straßburger Gebiet*, p. 105. In the 17th century, Strasbourg's indirect territory shrank appreciably, but its direct territory remained unaltered.

[51] Orth, 'Stadtherrschaft', p. 117.

[52] Martin H. Körner, *Solidarités financières suisses au XVIe siècle. Contribution à l'histoire monetaire, bancaire et financière des Cantons suisses et des États voisins* (Bibliothèque Historique Vaudoise, 66) (Lausanne, 1980), p. 440.

cities. As often as not, territorial expansion was opportunist and piecemeal, beset by hesitations and reversals;[53] even single-mindedness and success might have their price—as Nuremberg discovered after its conquest of the *Neue Landschaft* unleashed a string of suits before the imperial court of chancery which continued unabated up to 1806![54] Both Nuremberg and Ulm on occasion spurned the chance of acquiring yet more territory, reckoning that it would bring more trouble than it was worth.[55] And yet the fact that so many cities chose to pursue a territorial policy at all suggests (apart from the objective possibility of doing so) some underlying common strands.

At the outset we may posit the cities' need to secure their own subsistence: protecting supplies of essential foodstuffs, above all grain, was a constant preoccupation.[56] Beyond that, the southern cities regarded their rural dependencies as a useful source of income, unlike the Hanseatic cities, which were less concerned with the economic potential of their hinterlands. Rothenburg ob der Tauber, for instance, derived just under 5 per cent of its annual civic revenues from its territory,[57] a rate of return that may be regarded as broadly typical. But in some instances the figure could be much higher: around 10 per cent of Frankfurt's civic taxes came from just ten of its villages,[58] while in years of good harvest a startling 22 per cent of Ulm's income derived from its extensive rural territory.[59] The desire to exploit the economic and fiscal potential of their dependencies went hand-in-hand with the need to safeguard the cities' market area and especially their market precincts (*Bannmeilen*), a point to be pursued below.

The cities undoubtedly saw their territories as demographic reservoirs, compensating for the notorious inability of pre-industrial towns to reproduce their populations without immigration. But that in no sense betokened a willingness on the part of the south German cities to confer upon their rural subjects any preferential status, let alone citizenship. Almost without exception, the latter were, and remained, serfs,[60] though the inhabitants of dependent towns, as with Geislingen,

[53] Schneidmüller, 'Städtische Territorialpolitik', p. 117.
[54] Leiser, 'Landgebiet', pp. 235–6.
[55] Gerd Wunder, 'Reichsstädte als Landesherrn', p. 82.
[56] Leiser, 'Territorien', p. 967.
[57] Gerd Wunder, 'Reichsstädte als Landesherrn', p. 87.
[58] Schneidmüller, 'Städtische Territorialpolitik', p. 134.
[59] Gerd Wunder, 'Reichsstädte als Landesherrn', p. 87.
[60] Ibid., p. 88 (Ulm, Schwäbisch Hall, Heilbronn, Rothenburg); Schneidmüller, 'Städtische Territorialpolitik', pp. 133, 135 (Frankfurt am Main).

Albeck, and Leipheim under Ulm's sovereignty, lived under a lighter form of residential serfdom, whereas its villagers were bound by a heavier personal serfdom.[61] *Per contram*, where cities and towns already held peasant outburghers, it is not at all clear (if Freiburg im Breisgau is anything to go by) that in the constant friction with local feudal lords they were able to prevent them being treated functionally as serfs.[62]

Can these findings, in conclusion, yield a typology of cities and their motives for pursuing a territorial policy? A tentative scheme has been put forward by Elisabeth Raiser, who distinguishes between policies embraced by: 1. the *Aristokratenstadt*, the city dominated by a patriciate deriving much of its prestige and wealth from feudal landholding; 2. the *Fernhandelsstadt*, the long-distance trading town; 3. the *Gewerbestadt*, or artisanal town, engaged in crafts and manufactures. From the outset, she emphasizes that these three categories frequently overlap. The pre-eminent example of a feudal-patrician city north of the Alps is Bern, whose magistrates, the *Twingherren*, were primarily concerned to buttress their rural power, rather than to invest in trade, with the result that the pursuit of territorial aggrandizement became the city's *raison d'être*, in which endeavour it was extraordinarily successful, yet left the agricultural economy of its hinterland largely untouched.[63] It has to be said, though, that Bern was highly unusual, even among Swiss cities. Its rival Zürich, whose magistracy most certainly included feudal magnates and pensionaries profiting from the trade in mercenary service, was also a city of textile manufacturers and merchants, who were likewise represented on the council.[64] Zürich's territorial policy, therefore, was driven not

---

[61] Schmolz, 'Herrschaft und Dorf', p. 173.

[62] Scott, *Freiburg and the Breisgau*, pp. 78 ff.

[63] Raiser, *Städtische Territorialpolitik*, pp. 23–4. In the 14th century Bern was famously described as *in gewissem Sinn die Zentralburg einer Korporation adliger Herrschaftsinhaber.* Adolf Gasser, *Entstehung und Ausbildung der Landeshoheit im Gebiete der Schweizerischen Eidgenossenschaft. Ein Beitrag zur Verfassungsgeschichte des deutschen Mittelalters* (Aarau/Leipzig, 1930), p. 394, but that was less true by the later 15th century, especially after the *Twingherrenstreit* of 1470, as patricians began to withdraw from civic office, acquire patents of nobility, and retire to stewardships of rural bailiwicks. See François de Capitani, 'Sozialstruktur und Mechanismen der Herrschaft in der spätmittelalterlichen Stadt Bern', in Endres, *Nürnberg und Bern*, pp. 3–4.

[64] Norman Birnbaum, 'The Zwinglian Reformation in Zurich', *Past and Present*, 15 (1959), pp. 28–32.

only by the need to protect its patricians' landed interests but also by commercial imperatives, above all control of the rivers which bore Zürich's trade northwards to the Rhine and southwards on the upland routes over the alpine passes to Italy. Perhaps the only true comparison is with Metz, which over the centuries did everything in its power to entrench the rural lordships of its patricians, to the point where, in 1550, five Messin families owned two-thirds of all the city's rural property.[65] The difficulty here, however, is that, strictly speaking, *'le pays de Metz'* never became a *territorium clausum*; indeed, by the sixteenth century Metz was fast losing lands and judicial rights to the ascendant dukes of Lorraine.[66]

About Raiser's second category there is general agreement. Long-distance trading cities, as we have seen, were more concerned with safeguarding trade routes and commercial privileges than in acquiring territory for its own sake. Hence, where lands were acquired (often by mortgage), they lay axially along arteries of trade, rather than radially as the market area of a central place.[67] This is primarily the case with the cities of the Hansa,[68] but it might apply elsewhere, as with Frankfurt am Main. Yet there were many more cities throughout Germany which *combined* the roles of entrepôt and central place. Erfurt is a classic example, while Ulm, the centre of the west Swabian textile industry, bought the county of Helfenstein largely because its territory controlled the principal highway over the Swabian Alb. It is precisely at this point that we should recall that two of Germany's foremost centres of manufacturing and commerce—Augsburg and Cologne—prospered without recourse to any rural territory at all![69]

For Raiser's third category, the artisanal town, a rural territory fulfilled an essential function as a supplier of produce and raw materials, and as a consumer of urban goods and services. Hence, these towns were particularly keen to enforce exclusive buying and selling at the town's market (*Marktzwang*) and, as a corollary, to suppress

---

[65] Raiser, *Städtische Territorialpolitik*, p. 26; Schneider, 'La ville de Metz', pp. 406–7, 412.

[66] See above, note 15.

[67] Raiser, *Städtische Territorialpolitik*, pp. 27–8; Nicholas, *Later Medieval City*, p. 98.

[68] Behr, 'Landgebietspolitik', pp. 23, 25; Fritze, 'Stadt-Land-Beziehungen', p. 110.

[69] Augsburg did possess a very small territory to the north of the city, the Lower Bailiwick. Kießling, 'Herrschaft—Markt—Landbesitz', p. 187.

any marketing or forestalling within their own territory, or at least within their market franchise (*Bannmeile*).[70] The merit of this category is that it can encompass a span from large cities to small towns (she herself instances Zürich, Ulm, and Soest, though the first two could well be accommodated in her previous categories). It certainly helps to account for the territorial policy of the many medium to small Upper Swabian cities, without implying that such lesser communities were the only ones to feel the need to control their immediate hinterlands. The problems with this category, however, are twofold. In the first place, it fails to recognize that some towns and cities secured control of their market area, not by acquiring a dependent territory, but by extending their urban precinct (*Stadtmark*) into the countryside. The most striking example is the small imperial city of Wimpfen on the river Neckar,[71] which extended its so-called *Markung* to embrace an area to the south and west of around 30 square kms, taking in orchards, vineyards, and meadows, which it equated with the ambit of its *Bannmeile*. This area was quite distinct from Wimpfen's rural territory (very modest in size), which was centred upon the Forest of Wimpfen (an old royal chase), 11 kms to the north-west, together with a few odd villages elsewhere.[72] Wimpfen could be dismissed as a curiosity, were it not that several north German cities—Hildesheim, Einbeck, Göttingen—pursued a similar strategy of extending their *Stadtmark* and protecting it by a series of *Landwehren*[73] (which did not preclude a separate territorial policy, quite vigorous in the case of Göttingen).[74]

---

[70] Raiser, *Städtische Territorialpolitik*, pp. 30–1.

[71] In fact, a double town, comprising a settlement by the river (Wimpfen im Tal) and a townlet on the hill above (Wimpfen am Berg), clustered round a castle. Wimpfen, despite its status as an imperial city, may be classed as a dwarf town, whose economic activity was intensely local. Scott and Scribner, 'Urban Networks', pp. 117–18.

[72] Andreas Hafer, *Wimpfen: Stadt-Raum-Beziehungen im späten Mittelalter* (Veröffentlichungen der Kommission für geschichtliche Landeskunde in Baden-Württemberg, B 130) (Stuttgart, 1993), pp. 132–5, 174 (map), 268 ff. Wimpfen is also curious, inasmuch as the acquisition of estates and rights in the countryside by individual burghers followed, rather than preceded, the development of its territory. Ibid., p. 338.

[73] Jürgen Köppke, *Hildesheim, Einbeck, Göttingen und ihre Stadtmark im Mittelalter. Untersuchungen zum Problem von Stadt und Umland* (Schriftenreihe des Stadtarchivs und der Stadtbibliothek Hildesheim, 2) (Hildesheim, 1967), pp. 103–6, 140–2, 145–6 *et passim*.

[74] Rösener, 'Aspekte der Stadt-Land-Beziehungen', p. 670.

The second objection is more serious. The response of German and Swiss cities to those who defied their *Marktzwang* or who infringed their *Bannmeile* was far from uniform. Reactions to the rise of country crafts, rural guilds, and village markets ranged from suppression through supervision to integration—or even calm indifference. This variety of responses can hardly be explained by differences of territorial policy, predicated upon Raiser's threefold typology of towns and cities. Rather, it can only be understood in the light of the cities' wider relations with their surrounding countryside in terms of centrality within a regional economic system. To that we must now turn.

Economic Relations

Urban Hierarchies and Networks

In Germany, the work of historical geographers has been particularly influential in analyzing the economic relations between town and country. Taking the town's primary function to be a market, Hektor Ammann argued that around any town three zones of centrality might be discerned. At first there was the immediate marketing area—the smallest unit of an urban economy, in his definition—constituted by those who regularly visited the town's weekly market to exchange their produce and goods for urban supplies and manufactures. A second, wider marketing space extended beyond this narrower zone, comprising a sphere of economic influence in which the town's manufactures were sold and from which outside artisans and merchants were periodically attracted to the town. Depending on the goods offered for sale, this broader marketing area could be quite extensive, even encompassing the narrower market areas of smaller towns. Ammann regarded this area as roughly equivalent to the catchment area (*Einzugsgebiet*) of the town's annual market. The third area of economic *rayonnement* was determined by the intensity of long-distance trade, and roughly corresponded to the recruitment of a town's larger regional annual market or, in some cases, international fair.[75] Although Ammann's threefold typology in general holds good,

[75] Hektor Ammann, 'Vom Lebensraum der mittelalterlichen Stadt. Eine Untersuchung an schwäbischen Beispielen', *Berichte zur deutschen Landeskunde*, 31 (1963), pp. 290–3, summarizing the finding of his many local case-studies.

subsequent research has refined the radii of his circles to suggest that the immediate market area (*Umland*) may range from 10 to 30 kms, depending on the pull of the urban centre; the wider market area (*Hinterland*) may stretch up to 50 or 60 kms, but rarely further; while the outer sphere of influence (*Einflußbereich*), from which visitors to the annual fair might be drawn or migrants attracted to the city's labour market, could extend to 100 kms (in the case of true metropolises even further).[76]

Ammann's typology is clearly indebted to the pioneering work of Walter Christaller on central places in southern Germany.[77] But it is evident that Christaller's perfect-mesh rank-size dispersion of towns based on their centrality as markets quickly comes up against inconvenient anomalies, with some areas of Germany woefully underprovided with towns of any kind, and others where clusters of towns jostle for centrality, giving rise to overlapping and apparently competing hinterlands.[78] This dilemma can be resolved if we cease to think of centrality as purely radial. Instead, it may be shaped by a network system, which is axial, linking towns as 'nodes, junctions, outposts or relays' of a trading network.[79] This axial principle has already been detected in the territorial policies of many Hanseatic cities. But it has a much wider application throughout the German lands, where the arteries of trade so strongly followed the country's extensive river system.[80] On the Upper Rhine, for instance, the wine-exporting communes of Alsace were located along the river Ill at regular intervals 'like pearls on a string', with their market areas no longer circular but squeezed into ellipses, whose short axis was formed by the river, so that they resembled the sails of a schooner mirrored in the water, with the ellipses projecting both skywards and down-

---

[76] Peter Schöller, 'Der Markt als Zentralisationsphänomen. Das Grundprinzip und seine Wandlung in Zeit und Raum', *Westfälische Forschungen*, 15 (1962), pp. 85–92. For a recent critique see Dorothee Rippmann, *Bauern und Städter. Stadt-Land-Beziehungen im 15. Jahrhundert. Das Beispiel Basel, unter besonderer Berücksichtigung der Nahmarktbeziehungen und der sozialen Verhältnisse im Umland* (Basler Beiträge zur Geschichtswissenschaft, 159) (Basel/Frankfurt am Main, 1990), pp. 47–8.

[77] Walter Christaller, *Central Places in Southern Germany*, transl. Carlisle W. Baskin (Englewood Cliffs, NJ, 1966) (German original: Jena, 1933).

[78] Scott and Scribner, 'Urban Networks', pp. 125–9.

[79] Paul M. Hohenberg and Lynn Hollen Lees, *The Making of Urban Europe 1000–1950* (Cambridge, MA/London, 1985), p. 62.

[80] Scott and Scribner, 'Urban Networks', pp. 131–7.

wards.[81] Again, topography and natural endowment might ensure that centrality was dendritic, with a metropolis as the gateway of an elongated hinterland with branches emanating from it.[82] That was the case with many ports, channelling goods from a delta-like hinterland through a narrow outlet, or else of towns located where mountain valleys debouched into the plain. These varieties of centrality, moreover, were neither mutually exclusive nor immutable: they might complement each other and shift over time. By the mid-sixteenth century, for instance, Nördlingen in northern Swabia had lost much of its significance as a long-distance trading city, boasting an international fair, to become the market centre for its hinterland. Its economic centrality, in other words, was by then more radial than axial, as the city cautiously sought to dominate its immediate market area (*Umland*).[83]

Market Franchises

In this sense, *Umlandpolitik* denotes the totality of means at a city's disposal by which to exert influence over its surrounding countryside. For that reason, Rolf Kießling has argued, the term is preferable to the more narrowly defined concept of *Territorialpolitik*.[84] This is quite acceptable, provided that we recognize that control of the immediate market area alone was often only the launching-pad for a much more ambitious policy of regional economic hegemony. This is particularly evident where the cities' market franchises were concerned. Most German towns and cities sought to uphold a *Bannmeile* with a radius of at least 1 or 2 miles (4.6 or 9.2 statute miles: 7.4 or 14.7 kms), within which no other market might be held, any attempts to evade or pre-empt the urban market by forestalling or hawking were forbidden, and foreign lords were prohibited from levying tolls or turnpike charges.[85] In the period from 1350 to 1600 such franchises were proclaimed—to take Kießling's evidence from

[81] Christaller, *Central Places*, pp. 57–8; Tom Scott, *Regional Identity and Economic Change. The Upper Rhine, 1450–1600* (Oxford, 1997), p. 79.

[82] Carol A. Smith, 'Exchange Systems and the Spatial Distribution of Elites: The Organization of Stratification in Agrarian Society', in eadem (ed.), *Regional Analysis*, 2: *Social Systems* (New York/San Francisco/London, 1976), pp. 309–74.

[83] Kießling, *Die Stadt und ihr Land*, p. 259.

[84] Idem, 'Umlandgefüge', p. 38.

[85] Ibid., pp. 40–1; idem, *Die Stadt und ihr Land*, p. 91.

Swabia—by Nördlingen and Lauingen. What stands out, however, is that these ordinances often applied only to certain commodities—a one-mile prohibition on forestalling corn or timber in Nördlingen's case in 1510[86]—and that they were frequently extended. In the mid-sixteenth century Lauingen doubled its general franchise from 1 to 2 miles in an effort to ward off Augsburg's commercial penetration, but imposed a four-mile (19.5 kms) franchise for loden cloth subject to its quality control (*Schau*), since the town could not obtain sufficient supplies of wool in the locality.[87] Larger metropolises were noticeably more aggressive in extending their *Bannmeilen*. Augsburg began in the fifteenth century with a modest one-mile franchise, but by 1500 this had risen to 3 miles, and thereafter was extended to 6 or even 10 miles (73.6 kms) on occasion.[88] By this means Augsburg contrived to subordinate much of the textile production of eastern Swabia to its *Schau*, and thereby was able to dominate its marketing and distribution. By contrast, a small Swabian territorial town such as Mindelheim had no need to impose a market franchise or invoke *Marktzwang* at all, since its overlords, the lords of Frundsberg, while stripping the community of any political autonomy, ensured that at the same time it functioned as the principal central place for their territory as a whole, so that the latter's boundaries constituted the *Bannmeile*.[89] By the sixteenth century the franchise area for most medium-sized towns in Swabia had reached 2 or 3 miles, for the larger cities 6 to 8 miles.[90]

The Subordination of the Hinterland

The extension of market franchises went hand-in-hand with increasing efforts to subordinate the economy of their hinterlands to the cities' domestic needs, above all through shifts in production and in

---

[86] Ibid., p. 194.

[87] Ibid., p. 617.

[88] Idem, 'Umlandgefüge', pp. 40–1; idem, 'Herrschaft—Markt—Landbesitz', p. 195.

[89] Idem, *Die Stadt und ihr Land*, pp. 635–6, 670, 706; idem, 'Die "Nachbarschaft" und die "Regionalisierung" der Politik: Städte, Klöster und Adel in Ostschwaben um 1500', in Ferdinand Seibt and Winfried Eberhardt (eds), *Europa 1500. Integrationsprozesse im Widerstreit. Staaten, Regionen, Personenverbände, Christenheit* (Stuttgart, 1987), p. 271.

[90] Ibid., p. 265.

the division of labour. Several areas of late medieval Germany witnessed the rapid spread of rural crafts and manufacturing, whose output in many cases was organized along early capitalist lines through the putting-out system (*Verlagssystem*). But however much the transformation of the rural economy was ultimately the consequence of urban investment and labour recruitment, its preconditions lay within the countryside itself. Swabia once again may serve as an example.

Chronologically, the rise of linen manufacturing on the northern littoral of Lake Constance can be traced back to the thirteenth century, that is, well before the rise of the powerful Swiss and Swabian merchant houses such as the Diesbach-Watt company of St Gallen or the Great Ravensburg Trading Company, and even before the opening up of new trade routes over the Alpine passes to Italy had conferred upon the region any obvious locational advantage by straddling a major commercial artery.[91] Here population pressure, in an area largely of partible inheritance at the western end of the lake, created pressure within the agrarian economy for by-employment, whose output satisfied a brisk demand in an area of relatively dense urbanization. Yet the linen industry was firmly established from an equally early date in the much less populous eastern Swabia and Allgäu, areas of impartible inheritance, somewhat wetter and colder than along Lake Constance, which were largely given over to dairying.

This suggests that location, in terms of climate and topography, could be as important as population pressure. For the low-lying marshy tracts along the rivers Iller and Lech, together with high rainfall on the northern slopes of the Alps, clearly created ideal conditions for flax-growing,[92] but after spinning and weaving the cloth still had to be bleached. Although various processes were employed, they all at one stage or another used milk before the cloths were finally crofted on bleaching-grounds. The co-existence of dairying and linen manufacture in eastern Swabia, therefore, was not accidental: the former functionally determined the latter.[93] Self-evidently,

---

[91] Hektor Ammann, 'Die Anfänge der Leinenindustrie des Bodenseegebiets', *Alemmanisches Jahrbuch*, 1953, pp. 251–313; Wolfgang von Stromer, 'Gewerbereviere und Protoindustrien in Spätmittelalter und Frühneuzeit', in Hans Pohl (ed.), *Gewerbe- und Industrielandschaften vom Spätmittelalter bis ins 20. Jahrhundert* (*Vierteljahrschrift für Sozial- und Wirtschaftsgeschichte*, Beiheft 78) (Stuttgart, 1986), pp. 47, 57.

[92] Kießling, *Die Stadt und ihr Land*, p. 448.

[93] Scott, 'Economic Landscapes', pp. 2–3.

too, the availability of natural resources determined the spread and location of rural industries: whether it was a plentiful supply of water to full cloths or drive mills; forests to yield charcoal for foundries or potash for glass-works; or mineral resources of ore and precious metals to furnish the raw material for the metallurgical industries.

Yet the cities' attempts to harness their hinterlands as an economic and demographic resource, evident from the mid-fourteenth century onwards, were fraught with contradiction: for they sought at once to stimulate *and* to regulate rural production. Rural crafts and manufactures were encouraged—so long as they did not compete with the cities' domestic output. But this was easier said than done, especially if individual entrepreneurs deliberately disregarded civic ordinances to corner a particular market and to distribute its output to domestic and international customers directly, bypassing the urban exchanges and staples. Ideally, the countryside was to be restricted to working up raw materials or to the first stages of the manufacturing process itself. This can be illustrated by the development of the textile industry in Upper Germany.

As well as cultivating flax and spinning it into yarn, rural linen-weavers had originally produced lesser cloths of their own. But with the rise of fustian manufacture the social relations of production altered. Because cotton was not an indigenous crop, but had to be imported from the Mediterranean, fustian-weaving came to be organized by urban merchants with long-distance trading connections. These entrepreneurs preferred to restrict the manufacture of the more profitable fustian to the urban guilds, where quality control was easier to enforce, but after some initial resistance rural weavers were allowed to thread their linen yarn onto warps, ready for the loom, which would then be sold to urban weavers or merchants for weaving with a cotton weft.[94] This division of labour came to prevail throughout Middle Swabia (though it was frowned upon in the Allgäu and in the city of Konstanz), and even spread to the manufacture of purely linen cloths such as *Golschen*.[95] In this fashion, many smaller

---

[94] Rolf Kießling, 'Stadt und Land im Textilgewerbe Ostschwabens vom 14. bis zur Mitte des 16. Jahrhunderts', in Neithard Bulst, Jochen Hoock, and Franz Irsigler (eds), *Bevölkerung, Wirtschaft und Gesellschaft. Stadt-Land-Beziehungen in Deutschland und Frankreich 14. bis 19. Jahrhundert* (Trier, 1983), p. 124; Kießling 'Umlandgefüge', pp. 42–3; idem, 'Herrschaft—Markt—Landbesitz', pp. 200–1.

[95] Idem, 'Stadt und Land', pp. 125–6. *Golschen* is normally understood to be

towns and markets, together with their catchment areas, became contracted suppliers (*Zulieferer*) of warps to the larger mercantile cities.[96] The pattern which typically developed was for the cities to ban weaving in their immediate *Umland* or market franchise area, to regulate the production of warps in their hinterland, and, should further supplies be required from their wider sphere of influence, to enter into collective guild purchase agreements with brokers at a fixed price (*Zunftkäufe*).[97]

This division of labour was largely specific to the fustian industry. In northern Swabia, which by 1500 had become predominantly an area of wool production, its chief city, Nördlingen, underwent a reorientation from linen- through fustian-weaving to become the centre of loden manufacturing.[98] Loden production remained an essentially urban trade, with countryfolk reduced to spinning yarn rather than weaving the yarn on home looms.[99] Even in thoroughgoing fustian regions, moreover, the pattern of concentric circles of differential activity might be subverted by buccaneering merchant houses, such as the Fuggers, who lured rural spinners and weavers in Ulm's hinterland away from civic supervision and into their employ, setting up rival enterprises under their own control in the small towns of Weißenhorn and Pfaffenhofen.[100] Here the Fuggers were able to capitalize on the fact that Ulm had permitted many more full-time fustian-weavers (anywhere between 300 and 600) to ply their trade in its hinterland and to supply the city's market with finished cloths than its more restrictive east Swabian counterparts.[101]

---

coarse linen (idem, 'Umlandgefüge', p. 49; idem, *Die Stadt und ihr Land*, p. 484), but elsewhere Kießling takes it as high-quality linen (i.e. lawn): idem, 'Stadt und Land', p. 125.

[96] Ibid., p. 127.

[97] Idem, *Die Stadt und ihr Land*, p. 482; idem, 'Umlandgefüge', p. 41; idem, 'Entwicklungstendenzen im ostschwäbischen Textilrevier während der Frühen Neuzeit', in Joachim Jahn and Wolfgang Hartung (eds), *Gewerbe und Handel vor der Industrialisierung. Regionale und überregionale Verflechtungen im 17. und 18. Jahrhundert* (Regio Historica. Forschungen zur süddeutschen Regionalgeschichte, 1) (Sigmaringendorf, 1991), p. 30; see Rudolf Holbach, *Frühformen von Verlag und Großbetrieb in der gewerblichen Produktion (13.–16. Jahrhundert)* (*Vierteljahrschrift für Sozial- und Wirtschaftsgeschichte*, Beiheft 110) (Stuttgart, 1994), p. 165.

[98] Kießling, *Die Stadt und ihr Land*, pp. 214–15; idem, 'Umlandgefüge', pp. 48–9; idem, 'Stadt und Land', p. 119.

[99] Ibid., p. 127.

[100] Idem, 'Herrschaft—Markt—Landbesitz', pp. 202–3.

[101] Hermann Kellenbenz, 'The Fustian Industry of the Ulm Region in the Fifteenth and Early Sixteenth Centuries', in Negley B. Harte and Kenneth G. Ponting (eds),

Nevertheless, the characteristic rise of semi-finished products in the countryside, such as warps, albeit not universal in Swabia, was echoed in other branches of manufacturing, particularly the wood-working and iron industries, where rural craftsmen would make wooden wheels, barrel-staves, or bed-frames, ready to be finished by urban masters who clad them with iron.[102] This applied in other areas of Germany as well. In the course of the fifteenth century a wide range of semi-finished ironware was produced in Cologne's hinterland, which was delivered to urban craftsmen for polishing, trimming, embellishing, or undergoing the later and more skilled stages of production (such as attaching handles).[103]

Rural Putting-out

What impelled these developments was, above all, recourse to putting-out (*Verlag*). Evidence for supplying raw materials or the tools of trade, or else for advancing the necessary capital, to dependent pieceworkers can be traced in the textile industry of the cities of Upper Swabia, the Lake Constance area, and northern Switzerland for linen and fustian,[104] and in the Cologne region for woollen cloth, as far back as the late thirteenth century.[105] Less certain, however, is when merchants and richer craftmasters began to put out work to rural wage-labourers beyond the city walls. In some places, territorially organized *Verlag* did make its appearance very early—in the first half of the fourteenth century around Konstanz, Ulm, Augsburg, Memmingen, and in the Allgäu—but elsewhere, as in Nördlingen and northern

Cloth and Clothing in Medieval Europe. Essays in Memory of Professor E. M. Carus-Wilson (Pasold Studies in Textile History, 2) (London, 1983), pp. 261–4; Bernhard Kirchgässner, 'Der Verlag im Spannungsfeld von Stadt und Umland', in Maschke and Sydow, *Stadt und Umland*, p. 86; Kießling, 'Stadt und Land', p. 120; Holbach, *Frühformen*, p. 186.

[102] Kießling, 'Stadt und Land', p. 131; idem, 'Umlandgefüge', p. 43.

[103] Irsigler, 'Stadt und Umland', pp. 5–6.

[104] Rolf Kießling, 'Frühe Verlagsverträge im ostschwäbischen Textilrevier', in Hubert Mordek (ed.), *Aus Archiven und Bibliotheken. Festschrift für Raymund Kottje zum 65. Geburtstag* (Frankfurt am Main/Bern/New York/Paris, 1992), p. 443, following Ammann, 'Anfänge der Leinenindustrie', pp. 251–313.

[105] Franz Irsigler, 'Frühe Verlagsbeziehungen in der gewerblichen Produktion des westlichen Hanseraumes', in Konrad Fritze, Eckhart Müller-Mertens, and Johannes Schildhauer (eds), *Zins—Profit—ursprüngliche Akkumulation* (Abhandlungen zur Handels- und Sozialgeschichte, 21: Hansische Studien, 5) (Weimar, 1981), pp. 176, 181.

Swabia, there was no sign of outwork as late as 1400.[106] In the case of Cologne, weavers in the city's guilds were already complaining about competition from rural wool-workers before 1300, but on closer inspection it turns out that cloth was being manufactured in a string of smaller towns around Cologne, rather than in villages. Once such cloth had received the city's quality seal, it was sold on by Cologne's merchants as a 'domestic' product.[107]

The chief stimulus to the spread of *Verlag* to the countryside was the desire on the part of urban merchants to avoid irksome civic or guild restrictions on production and employment within the cities. But it was not long before feudal lords espied the economic advantage in promoting rural textiles themselves. In the countryside such lords stepped into the merchants' shoes by offering to buy up and distribute the output of their peasants' by-employment: in Swabia as early as 1410 the abbot of the powerful monastery of Ottobeuren was acting as an intermediary for the weavers of his territory, undertaking to deliver their linen cloth to merchants in the nearby city of Memmingen in conformity with the city's quality standard.[108] All the principal textile areas of Germany, from Thuringia[109] and Westphalia[110] in the north to the regions already discussed further south, were penetrated to some degree by the putting-out system, but its deployment varied according to the type of cloth produced. A comparison between linen and fustian manufacture will make this point clear. Where fustian-weaving came to predominate, the cost of importing raw cotton from abroad ensured that production required the injection of merchant capital; the first major *Verleger* around the city of Konstanz, for instance, was a financier and speculator, Ulrich Imholz, active in the early 1400s. But where fustian manufacturing

[106] Kießling, 'Frühe Verlagsverträge', pp. 444–5. This revises his more cautious dating to the early 15th century expressed in idem, 'Stadt und Land', pp. 117–19. For Memmingen, see also idem, *Die Stadt und ihr Land*, p. 482.

[107] Irsigler, 'Frühe Verlagsbeziehungen', pp. 181–2. He instances Herzogenbusch, Valkenburg, Erkelenz, Siegburg, Montabaur, and Hachenburg. See Holbach, *Frühformen*, pp. 97–8.

[108] Kießling, 'Frühe Verlagsverträge', p. 456.

[109] Held, *Zwischen Marktplatz und Anger*, p. 173; Holbach, *Frühformen*, p.114, who notes the case of Gera where, characteristically, the preparation of wool and its weaving were organized by outwork in *Verlag*, but dyeing and finishing were undertaken centrally in the town.

[110] Ibid., pp. 167–9 (Westphalia's linen industry).

failed to supplant linen-weaving—as with St Gallen, the tiny city-state which dominated the textile industry of eastern Switzerland—*Verlag* was hardly deployed until the early sixteenth century.[111]

The other branches of industry in which the putting-out system was commonplace were metal-, wood-, and leather-working, with an impact broadly similar to that in textile manufacturing. Just as with wool-weaving, though a century later, Cologne's merchants used *Verlag* to employ iron-workers in a vast swathe of countryside from the Eifel through Berg and Mark to the Sauerland to make semi-finished metalwares, not least for the city's weapons industry;[112] to that end the city established stamping- and grinding-mills in its subsidiary towns.[113] But the production of the main centres east of the Rhine—Solingen, Remscheid, Lüdenscheid, and Altena—was never monopolized by Cologne; indeed, Solingen enjoyed a flourishing independent trade with Antwerp and the Low Countries in the sixteenth century.[114] This somewhat looser network of town-country relations in metallurgical *Verlag* can also be observed in the area of greatest technological advance in late medieval Germany, Nuremberg with the district of the Upper Palatinate to the east. Nuremberg never organized its hinterland as an industrial zone for the mass production of metal goods in the way that the Upper Swabian cities did with linen- and fustian-weaving.[115] In 1534 the city's iron merchants were even prepared to cede all production by *Verlag* to a single merchant house, the Ambergers, in order to concentrate on distribution.[116] It was as long-distance traders and investors that they used putting-out to secure supplies of ore—copper, silver, lead—from the mines of Bohemia, the Erzgebirge, and Thuringia, rather than as *Verleger* controlling the production of Nuremberg's hinterland.[117]

[111] Kirchgässner, 'Verlag', pp. 93–7. Linen *Verlag* did occur in Swabia, however, before the 16th century, though it was never prevalent. Kießling, 'Frühe Verlagsverträge', pp. 451–2. On St Gallen's linen industry see fundamentally Hans Conrad Peyer, *Leinwandgewerbe und Fernhandel der Stadt St. Gallen von den Anfängen bis 1520*, 2 vols (St Gallen, 1959–60).

[112] Irsigler, 'Frühe Verlagsbeziehungen', pp. 181–2.

[113] Holbach, *Frühformen*, pp. 309–10.

[114] Ibid., p. 252.

[115] Hermann Aubin, 'Formen und Verbreitung des Verlagswesens in der Altnürnberger Wirtschaft', in Stadtarchiv Nürnberg (ed.), *Beiträge zur Wirtschaftsgeschichte Nürnbergs*, 2 (Beiträge zur Geschichte und Kultur der Stadt Nürnberg, 11, 2) (Nuremberg, 1967), p. 641.

[116] Ibid., p. 645.

[117] Ibid., pp. 649–53.

Along the trade routes to these mining regions villagers were employed on piecework to fashion wooden goods from the forests of the Fichtelgebirge and Thuringia. This axial *Verlag* was the origin of the city's fame as a producer of wooden toys, gewgaws, and carved objects, the so-called *Nürnberger Tand.*[118] Moreover, unlike textiles, in those cases where *Verlag* was used in metal production, especially in Nuremberg's pioneering wire-drawing sector (fully automated by 1590), it dominated the later, rather than the preliminary, stages of manufacture.[119]

The variations in the forms of *Verlag* which this brief survey has revealed should make us cautious about attributing to it a pivotal significance in the rise of early capitalism or the spread of proto-industralization. Hermann Aubin's researches on Nuremberg (the test-case, *par excellence*) led him firmly to the conclusion that early-capitalist business practices postdate the emergence of putting-out, whose origins he descries instead in the prevailing shortage of the means of production in the Middle Ages, though by the sixteenth century, with the vast expansion of Nuremberg's foreign trade and demand for its metal goods, that picture was rapidly changing.[120] With the exception of liquation plants in the mining industry, it is in fact very hard to point to capitalist investment (by putting-out or otherwise) which might have led to the establishment of factory production on an industrial scale. Where such proto-factories or industries did emerge before 1500—and Nuremberg's metallurgy is the prime example—they could survive for centuries without prompting any epochal shift to proto-industrialization.[121] That was true of textiles as well. In the district of Altenburg in the Siegerland south-east of Cologne, to take a particularly telling example, a large worsted

---

[118] Ibid., p. 646; Holbach, *Frühformen*, p. 533.

[119] von Stromer, 'Gewerbereviere', pp. 87–9.

[120] Aubin, 'Formen und Verbreitung', pp. 663, 666. *Verlag* hardly penetrated the overseas trading cities of the Hanseatic League; as entrepôts, small-scale commodity production was their hallmark. Ernst Pitz, 'Wirtschaftliche und soziale Probleme der gewerblichen Entwicklung im 15./16. Jahrhundert nach hansisch-niederdeutschen Quellen', in Friedrich Lütge (ed.), *Wirtschaftliche und soziale Probleme der gewerblichen Entwicklung im 15.–16. und 19. Jahrhundert. Bericht über die zweite Arbeitstagung der Gesellschaft für Sozial- und Wirtschaftsgeschichte in Würzburg 8.–10. März 1965* (Forschungen zur Sozial- und Wirtschaftsgeschichte, 10) (Stuttgart, 1968), p. 37. Ship-building provides a partial exception. Ibid., p. 39. For other scattered references see Holbach, *Frühformen*, pp. 370, 425.

[121] von Stromer, 'Gewerbereviere', pp. 42 ff.

textile enterprise (*Zeugwirkerei*) was founded in the sixteenth century by Heinrich Cramer, who employed Netherlandish cloth-workers equipped with the latest technology of yarn-spinning-wheels in 100 weaving sheds, complete with a fulling-mill and a dyeing plant. As well as production in this manufactory, piecework was put out to weavers in the surrounding villages, and Cramer also invested in extensive sheep farms to maintain the supply of raw wool.[122] Yet even this classic instance of vertical integration never gave any sign that Cramer's enterprise might be the prelude to full-scale industrialization of the region.

Rural Competition

The increasing economic domination of hinterlands by their cities in the period from 1350 to 1600, of which the putting-out system was the most striking manifestation, was not accepted without resistance; indeed, the activity of entrepreneurs who employed outworkers in the countryside in order to circumvent urban ceilings on production served to create competition for the cities' guilds and market. That was especially true of textiles, where complaints about rural weavers (*Gäuweber*), who wove to lesser standards, undercut urban price tariffs, and shunned the civic cloth exchanges were legion across the breadth of Upper Germany from Lake Constance to the Allgäu.[123] The problem of the *Gäuweber*, however, was certainly not caused by *Verlag* alone. Wherever the need for supplementary income arose, peasants might resort to weaving as a by-employment; indeed, the rise of an entire cottar class in Swabia has been attributed to the spread of rural weaving.[124] Memmingen's urban textile guilds fought a running battle around 1500 against the *Gäuweber*, many of them resident within the city's own territory,[125] while Nördlingen's

[122] Holbach, *Frühformen*, pp. 113–14.

[123] Kirchgässner, 'Verlag', p. 86; Kießling, 'Herrschaft—Markt—Landbesitz', pp. 202–3; idem, 'Stadt und Land', pp. 118–20.

[124] See Hermann Grees, *Ländliche Unterschichten und ländliche Siedlung in Ostschwaben* (Tübinger Geographische Studien, 58) (Tübingen, 1975).

[125] Kießling, *Die Stadt und ihr Land*, pp. 483–90; idem, 'Umlandpolitik, wirtschaftliche Verflechtung und innerstädtischer Konflikt in den schwäbischen Reichsstädten an der Wende vom Mittelalter zur Frühen Neuzeit', in Joachim Jahn, Wolfgang Hartung, and Immo Eberl (eds), *Oberdeutsche Städte im Vergleich: Mittelalter und Frühe Neuzeit* (Regio. Forschungen zur schwäbischen Regionalgeschichte, 2) (Sigmaringendorf, 1989), pp. 115, 120.

cloth industry was threatened by rural textiles deliberately promoted by the city's princely neighbours, the counts of Oettingen.[126]

Yet the textile cities of Upper Germany faced competition on a much broader front than that. Quite apart from the threat posed by rural industries, their artisans were exposed to competition from a wide variety of everyday craft goods produced in the countryside—Memmingen's cobblers and leatherworkers are just one example[127]—which owed nothing whatever to the impact of early capitalism or the use of the putting-out system. Moreover, notwithstanding the recourse to *Marktzwang*, their chartered markets were being challenged by rival foundations in their hinterlands—as Nördlingen, Memmingen, and Kempten all complained.[128] Even the territorial town of Mindelheim, despite being isolated from any immediate threat by the *cordon sanitaire* of Frundsberg lordship, found itself confronted with market competition from beyond its borders.[129]

The proliferation of country crafts and village markets was by no means confined to Swabia, or even to Germany: it was a pan-European phenomenon in this period,[130] whose aetiology can barely be explored here. Within Germany itself there is scarcely a region, from Mecklenburg or Saxony in the north to Bavaria, Swabia, and Switzerland in the south, where the threat of rural competition did not exercise urban magistrates (or territorial rulers, for that matter), though the coastal cities of the Hanseatic League seem to have remained relatively unscathed—or indifferent.[131] But it is generally agreed that the greatest concentration was in south-west Germany and Switzerland, areas of relatively dense population but with few

---

[126] Kießling, *Die Stadt und ihr Land*, p. 224.

[127] Ibid., pp. 508–9.

[128] Ibid., pp. 180–5, 443–7; Kießling, '"Nachbarschaft" und "Regionalisierung"', pp. 266, 270.

[129] Idem, *Die Stadt und ihr Land*, p. 690.

[130] Hermann Kellenbenz, 'Ländliches Gewerbe und bäuerliches Unternehmertum in Westeuropa vom Spätmittelalter bis ins XVIII. Jahrhundert', in *Deuxième Conférence Internationale d'Histoire Économique, Aix-en-Provence 1962* (École Pratique des Hautes Études—Sorbonne, Sixième Section: Sciences Économiques et Sociales, Congrès et Colloques, 8) (Paris/The Hague, 1965), pp. 377–427. Kellenbenz's main emphasis, however, is on crafts from the later 16th century onwards. See also idem, 'Rural Industries in the West from the End of the Middle Ages to the Eighteenth Century', in Peter Earle (ed.), *Essays in European Economic History* (Oxford, 1974), pp. 45–88.

[131] Fritze, *Am Wendepunkt der Hanse*, p. 108; idem, *Bürger und Bauern*, pp. 46–51; idem, 'Stadt-Land-Beziehungen', p. 111. The threat from rural crafts is put somewhat higher by Pitz, 'Wirtschaftliche und soziale Probleme', p. 34.

obvious signs (at least until the later sixteenth century) of rural immiseration (such as the rise of a cottar class).[132] On the Upper Rhine the middling territorial towns, rather than the larger independent imperial cities, seem to have been worst affected,[133] which might suggest that the pursuit of a *Territorialpolitik* offered some protection against economic competition from the countryside. That is exactly what some have argued for the Swabian imperial cities,[134] and, in northern Germany, for the city of Soest in Westphalia, which used its territorial sovereignty to enforce *Marktzwang* and to suppress artisan activity in the surrounding Börde.[135] As a general statement, however, this explanation does not hold water. It does not apply, as we have seen, to several important Swabian cities, and above all it ignores the experience of the powerful Swiss city-states, whose metropolises without exception were exposed to burgeoning crafts and informal marketing in their cantonal hinterlands.

By the sixteenth century, moreover, such craftsmen were banding together in rural guilds outwith civic control. Some cities might be able to suppress these guilds as formal associations; Zürich, Basel, and Schaffhausen succeeded, though Luzern was less successful.[136] But that did not make the underlying problem go away. Zürich, indeed, had earlier been forced to make sweeping concessions to craftsmen, petty traders, and middlemen in its hinterland in the wake of the so-called Waldmann affair in 1489.[137] Elsewhere, Bern and Luzern embraced a policy of partial toleration.[138] Perhaps the most interesting case, though, is that of Fribourg (Freiburg im Üchtland),

---

[132] See Wilfried Reininghaus, *Gewerbe in der Frühen Neuzeit* (*Enzyklopädie Deutscher Geschichte*, 3) (Munich, 1990), pp. 65 ff., 70.

[133] Scott, *Freiburg and the Breisgau*, pp. 116–18, 157–60; idem, *Regional Identity and Economic Change*, pp. 102–21, 122–72.

[134] Gerd Wunder, 'Reichsstädte als Landesherrn', p. 88.

[135] Klaus Diekmann, 'Die Herrschaft der Stadt Soest über ihre Börde' (Diss. jur. Münster, 1962), pp. 133–7; Raiser, *Städtische Territorialpolitik*, p. 31.

[136] Anne-Marie Dubler, *Handwerk, Gewerbe und Zunft in Stadt und Landschaft Luzern* (Luzerner Historische Veröffentlichungen, 14) (Luzern/Stuttgart, 1982), pp. 184–5, 198, 393.

[137] Christian Dietrich, *Die Stadt Zürich und ihre Landgemeinden während der Bauernunruhen von 1489 bis 1525* (Europäische Hochschulschriften, 3rd series, 229) (Frankfurt am Main/Bern/New York, 1985), pp. 22 ff., 44–5, 49–50, 53 ff., 90.

[138] Hans Conrad Peyer, 'Die Märkte in der Schweiz in Mittelalter und Neuzeit', in idem, *Gewässer, Grenzen und Märkte in der Schweizergeschichte* (Mitteilungen der Antiquarischen Gesellschaft in Zürich, 48, 3 [= Neujahrsblatt 143]) (Zürich, 1979), pp. 29–30.

where the council pursued a differential strategy according to the craft concerned. The weavers of quality woollen cloth were required to move to the town; the linen-weavers and other lesser textile workers were allowed to stay put; while the tanners—a significant trade in an area of commercial cattle-rearing—were permitted for occupational reasons to remain in the countryside, but had to submit to integration into (and therewith regulation by) the urban tanners' guild.[139] Whether any of these attempts to restrict rural crafts were crowned with much success is open to question. In the long run, for the territorial towns of Germany the issue was resolved by their princely rulers 'territorializing' crafts and manufacturing, that is to say, integrating rural crafts into a common structure embracing town and country, Bavaria being the classic example.[140] But that solution was only achieved at the price of eroding or destroying the traditional liberties and ancient market privileges of the territorial towns.[141] For their part, the imperial and free cities had to survive as best they could.

Patterns of Integration and Subordination

The pattern of town-country relations in the German-speaking lands between 1350 and 1600, therefore, admits of no easy generalizations. The size of a city's territory was no sure guide either to that city's economic clout,[142] or to its ability to absorb or suppress competition from its hinterland. More fundamentally, however, a city's economic *rayonnement* could lead to diametrically opposing patterns of town-country relations. To test this point, let us, in conclusion, survey the contrasting fortunes of three leading cities, Nuremberg, Cologne, and

[139] Idem, 'Wollgewerbe, Viehzucht, Solddienst und Bevölkerungsentwicklung in Stadt und Landschaft Freiburg i. Ue. vom 14. bis 16. Jahrhundert', in Hermann Kellenbenz (ed.), *Agrarisches Nebengewerbe und Formen der Reagrarisierung im Spätmittelalter und 19./20. Jahrhundert* (Forschungen zur Sozial- und Wirtschaftsgeschichte, 21) (Stuttgart, 1975), pp. 86–8.

[140] Kießling, *Die Stadt und ihr Land*, pp. 749–50.

[141] For the territorial ordinance of 1495 in the margraviate of Baden see Scott, *Regional Identity and Economic Change*, p. 108.

[142] See Christopher R. Friedrichs, 'The Swiss and German City-States', in Robert Griffeth and Carol G. Thomas (eds), *The City-State in Five Cultures* (Santa Barbara, CA/London, 1981), p. 124.

Augsburg. Nuremberg, with the largest territory of any German city, brought neighbouring towns and villages beyond its immediate *Umland* into the orbit of its cloth- and metal-working industries. This was more than an act of economic imperialism: the communities themselves were eager to grab a share of Nuremberg's industrial prosperity and marketing power. Beyond this hinterland lay an arc of cloth-producing towns to the south-west and another of metallurgical centres to the east, both possessing sufficient economic centrality to set bounds on Nuremberg's *rayonnement*. Within these arcs—in effect a circle—lay Nuremberg's 'economic unit', in which metropolis and subaltern central places combined in a mutually reinforcing integrated regional economic system.[143] Beyond that, of course, lay a wider sphere of influence, but once the levers of economic power were no longer direct but indirect, with the city reliant upon middlemen, then this outer third circle or *Einflußbereich* was clearly no longer part of the city's *Wirtschaftseinheit*.[144]

In the case of Cologne, a city without a landed territory, the economic unit was not only somewhat larger than Nuremberg's, with a maximum radius of around 70 kms, as opposed to the latter's 50 kms, it was, as we have seen, less thoroughly integrated, too. What stands out, above all, from Franz Irsigler's cartographic plotting of Cologne's *Wirtschaftseinheit* is the highly fluctuating size of its trade-specific areas of supply and putting-out. These range from a tightly-drawn ellipse for hops, through a somewhat larger oval for cloth, to a circle of steel suppliers lying entirely eccentric of the city east of the Rhine, with a yet larger and irregular circle of copper and iron suppliers concentric around the city, to the largest circle of all, that of suppliers of peltry.[145] It would be hazardous simply to equate Cologne's economic unit with the largest circle, not least because peltry was of much less importance to the city's economy than metal goods or cloth. Rather, we should conceive of the city's economic unit in terms of variable geometry, with different configurations and

143 Ammann, *Wirtschaftliche Stellung*, pp. 194–223.

144 See the general observations in Kießling, 'Umlandgefüge', p. 45.

145 Irsigler, 'Stadt und Umland', pp. 7, 14 (map). See now Herbert Eiden and Franz Irsigler, 'Environment and Hinterland: Cologne and Nuremberg in the Later Middle Ages', in James A. Galloway (ed.), *Trade, Urban Hinterlands and Market Integration c. 1300–1600* (Centre for Metropolitan History, Working Papers Series, 3) (London, 2000), pp. 43–57.

levels of intensity, provided that we avoid the twin errors of supposing that Cologne as the metropolis must necessarily always lie at the centre of its component hinterlands, or that the *Umland* closest to the city must constitute its essential regional core.

With Augsburg, by contrast, Cologne's direct counterpart as an overseas manufacturing and trading city without a dependent territory, an entirely different situation confronts us. Its economic unit, it is true, had a radius of around 60 to 70 kms; by 1550 its active textile hinterland, in terms of weavers under civic control or of migrants to the city, may even have been no more than 40 kms,[146] with the small and medium-sized towns therein fulfilling the role of sub-central collection-points or intermediate markets in a smoothly integrated system.[147] But on the fringes of its *Wirtschaftseinheit*, where its *rayonnement* should have been weakest, Augsburg began to act as a commercial predator with overt monopolistic tendencies. The city's fustian merchants and *Verleger* sought to throttle the textile industry of such centres as Lauingen (just within the 70-km. radius),[148] or Nördlingen[149] and Memmingen[150] (just outside), and even threatened the western Swabian metropolis of Ulm.[151] This in large measure accounts for Nördlingen's switch to loden production, and Lauingen's turn towards both wool and *Golschen*;[152] while, for its part, one of Memmingen's leading merchant dynasties, the Vöhlin, threw in the towel, upped sticks, and decamped to Augsburg early in the sixteenth century.[153] In the long run, the middling cities of eastern Swabia found their economic vitality stunted in the shade of Augsburg's commercial upas-tree—a contradictory result of market integration and the intensification of town-country relations which in the German context was exceptional, but which, as Maarten Prak has observed, seems to reflect a general pattern in the economy of early modern Europe as a whole.[154]

---

146 Kießling, 'Herrschaft—Markt—Landbesitz', p. 202.
147 Idem, *Die Stadt und ihr Land*, pp. 738–9.
148 Ibid., p. 617.
149 Ibid., p. 224.
150 Ibid., pp. 499, 525.
151 Idem, 'Umlandgefüge', pp. 48–9.
152 Ibid., pp. 48–9.
153 Idem, *Die Stadt und ihr Land*, p. 391.
154 Maarten Prak, 'Le regioni nella prima Europa moderna', in *Regioni, culture e ancora regioni nella storia economica e sociale dell'Europa moderna*, *Proposte e Ricerche: Economia e Società nella Storia dell'Italia Centrale*, 35 (1995), p. 21.

CHAPTER NINE

DEFINING AN ECONOMIC REGION: THE SOUTHERN UPPER RHINE, 1450–1600

I *The Region as Construct*

Although we live in Europe in an age of regionalism and the reassertion of regional identities, there is confusion about how regions should be defined. Some would argue that the region is somehow more 'natural' than the nation or the state, the classic instances of historical constructs. Yet what, if anything, distinguishes a region from a landscape? In English and French usage the terms are often interchangeable; in German they are not, although under the influence of research in the English-speaking world, *Landschaft* is being increasingly displaced by *Region*.[1] A historical landscape, in Ludwig Petry's words, is a 'landscape occupied and shaped by human beings'.[2] Settlement and land-use, therefore, are decisive; around these, human affinities and traditions develop. The German term *Kulturlandschaft* expresses this relationship precisely, for it points to the etymological and semantic link between cultivation and culture. A region, by contrast, implies something more than this. A region is not indeterminate: it is of a particular size, usually (though not invariably: here English and American usage differ) of middle rank, pitched between locality or district on the one hand and country or state on the other. Internally, the region is relatively homogenous; externally it is marked off from neighbouring regions by visible differences. But there is another feature that distinguishes the region from the mere landscape. Regions may be defined by function as well as homogeneity, that is, they serve purposes imposed upon them by man—economic, strategic,

[1] Hans Pohl, 'Einleitung', in idem (ed.), *Gewerbe- und Industrielandschaften vom Spätmittelalter bis ins 20. Jahrhundert* (*Vierteljahrschrift für Sozial- und Wirtschaftsgeschichte*, Beiheft 78) (Stuttgart, 1986), p. 11.

[2] Ludwig Petry, *In Grenzen unbegrenzt. Möglichkeiten und Wege der geschichtlichen Landeskunde* (Institut für geschichtliche Landeskunde an der Universität Mainz, Jahresausgabe 1961) (Mainz, 1961), p. 15.

political—which cannot necessarily be inferred solely in terms of their natural endowment or historical evolution. In the end, therefore, all attempts to define what regions are have to concede that they are both 'created' and 'given'. They exist both as reality and as idea, not only as fact but as fiction, shaped by human requirements and intrinsic potential as well as sustained by the accumulated weight of history and tradition.[3]

But do these general considerations apply when defining the specific character of an *economic* region? Modern historical geographers and regional planners have no difficulty in arguing that the city and its hinterland constitute the basis of an economic region; indeed, the absence of the advantages in communications and distribution which cities provide to their hinterland is taken as the hallmark of what are termed 'structurally weak' areas—rather than merely the insufficient endowment of the latter with natural resources.

Can this principle, therefore, be applied to economic regions in the past? Here there is no consensus at all among historians. Definitions can range from the local (a city and its hinterland) through the regional-territorial (northern Italy or the Rhône valley, for example) to the international, as in Fernand Braudel's classification of the Mediterranean as an *économie monde* in the sixteenth century. In American parlance the region is usually conceived on this latter extensive scale; in European usage it is the region as locality with which we are more familiar. These definitions can be systematized into a hierarchy of micro-, meso-, and macro-regions, but in terms of the historical sources it is usually only at the micro-level that we can test theory against practice.[4] But even then the region as an ideal-type can vary according to the size and economic clout of the city which constitutes its central place.

---

[3] Christopher Harvie, *The Rise of Regional Europe* (London/New York, 1994), p. 10; Klaus Graf, 'Das "Land" Schwaben im späten Mittelalter', in Peter Moraw (ed.), *Regionale Identität und soziale Gruppen im deutschen Mittelalter* (*Zeitschrift für historische Forschung*, Beiheft 14) (Berlin, 1992), p. 163.

[4] Maarten Prak, 'Le regioni nella prima Europa moderna', in *Regioni, culture e ancora regioni nella storia economica e sociale dell'Europa moderna, Proposte e Ricerche: Economia e Società nella Storia dell'Italia Centrale*, 35 (1995), pp. 12–14.

II *Economic Regions and Theories of Centrality*

Two models of economic regionality currently hold sway:

1. The self-sufficient or self-enclosed region, centred upon a regional capital or metropolis, and sustained by the interchange of goods and services between the lesser and greater central places;
2. The region as the hub or core of economic and commercial activity radiating beyond it, in which the leading central place need not occupy the middle point but may be located on the fringe of the region as a gateway or portal city.

The first of these models corresponds to the well-known pattern of centrality originally put forward in 1933 by Walter Christaller in his pioneering study of central places in southern Germany. It is essentially based on the marketing principle, though Christaller did concede that other organising principles—traffic/transport, or administrative—might obtain in certain circumstances.[5] How well it can reveal underlying patterns of settlement, location and the rank-order of central places (where we have the necessary sources to measure them) is demonstrated in Clé Lesger's study of the towns of North Holland in the early modern period.[6]

The alternative model describes, not radial, but axial centrality. It suggests that economic regionality may be discerned where cities are strung out along an axis of commerce, each contributing to the prosperity of the whole and interdependent of each other, but not necessarily tied so strongly into a rank-order hierarchy. The hinterlands of such cities may be diminutive, insignificant, and not subject to efforts to dominate their economies, characteristic of cities which function as market centres. This type of centrality operates according to the traffic or transport principle. Although Christaller returned briefly to the issue after World War II,[7] it has only recently been

[5] Walter Christaller, *Central Places in Southern Germany*, transl. Carlisle W. Baskin (Englewood Cliffs, NJ, 1966).

[6] Clemens Lesger, 'Regions, Urban Systems and Historical Central Place Analysis: Holland 1550–1800', in Peter Ainsworth and Tom Scott (eds), *Regions and Landscapes. Reality and Imagination in Late Medieval and Early Modern Europe* (Oxford/Bern/Berlin/Brussels/Frankfurt am Main/New York/Vienna, 2000), pp. 205–32.

[7] Walter Christaller, *Das Grundgerüst der räumlichen Ordnung in Europa. Die Systeme der*

advanced as a major explanation of European urbanization in the late medieval and early modern period.[8]

III *The Southern Upper Rhine as an Economic Region*

Although somewhat remote from the main geographical focus of the other papers in the volume *Regions and Landscapes*, which concentrate on northern France and the Low Countries, the southern Upper Rhine (see Map 9.1) nevertheless appears to offer itself as a prime candidate for an economic region based on both the market and on the traffic/transport principle:

1. It was bounded by natural frontiers and contained no obvious barriers to passage within it;
2. It disposed within its bounds of a variety of natural resources that allowed a diversified and hence resilient economy to develop;
3. It boasted cities which acted both as centres of exchange within the region and as distribution-points for the consignment of goods beyond the region;
4. It was located along a major artery of long-distance trade, which was water-borne and therefore relatively inexpensive.

These four points may be briefly elaborated:

Ad 1. We may note the Vosges and Black Forest mountains as natural barriers to the west and east, with the Swiss Jura representing a similar obstacle to the south (see Map 9.2);

Ad 2. The southern Upper Rhine was an area of economic diversity, the zones of activity differentiated by elevation. On the plain there was mixed agriculture (including industrial crops), pastoralism

europäischen Zentralen Orte (Frankfurter Geographische Hefte, 24, 1) (Frankfurt am Main, 1950).

[8] Paul M. Hohenberg and Lynn Hollen Lees, *The Making of Urban Europe 1000–1950* (Cambridge, MA/London, 1985). For a dendritic system of centrality, with the city as a 'gateway' at the apex of the tree trunk, see Carol A. Smith, 'Regional Economic Systems. Linking Geographical Models and Socio-economic Problems', in eadem (ed.), *Regional Analysis*, 1: *Economic Systems* (New York/San Francisco/London, 1976), pp. 3–63.

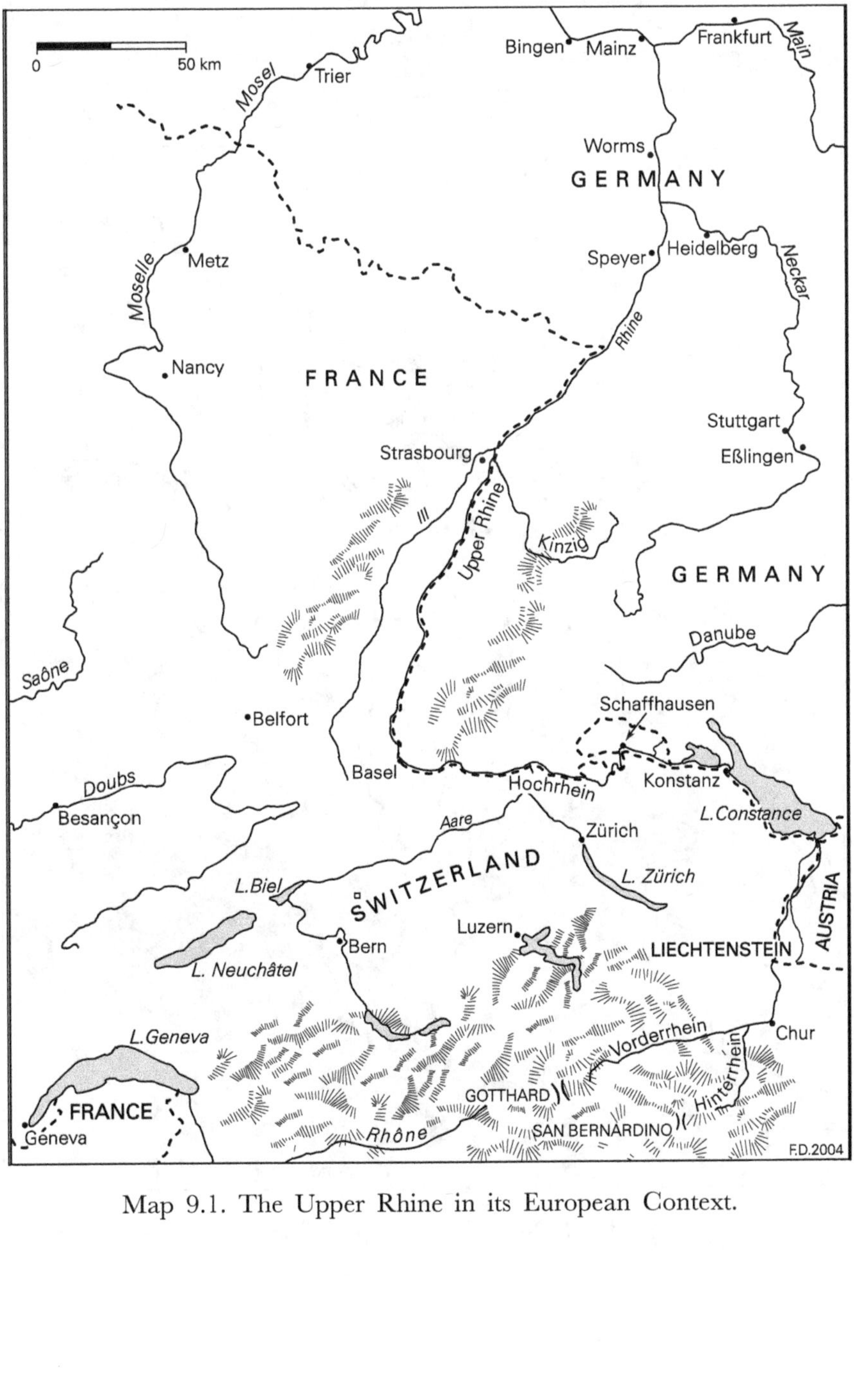

Map 9.1. The Upper Rhine in its European Context.

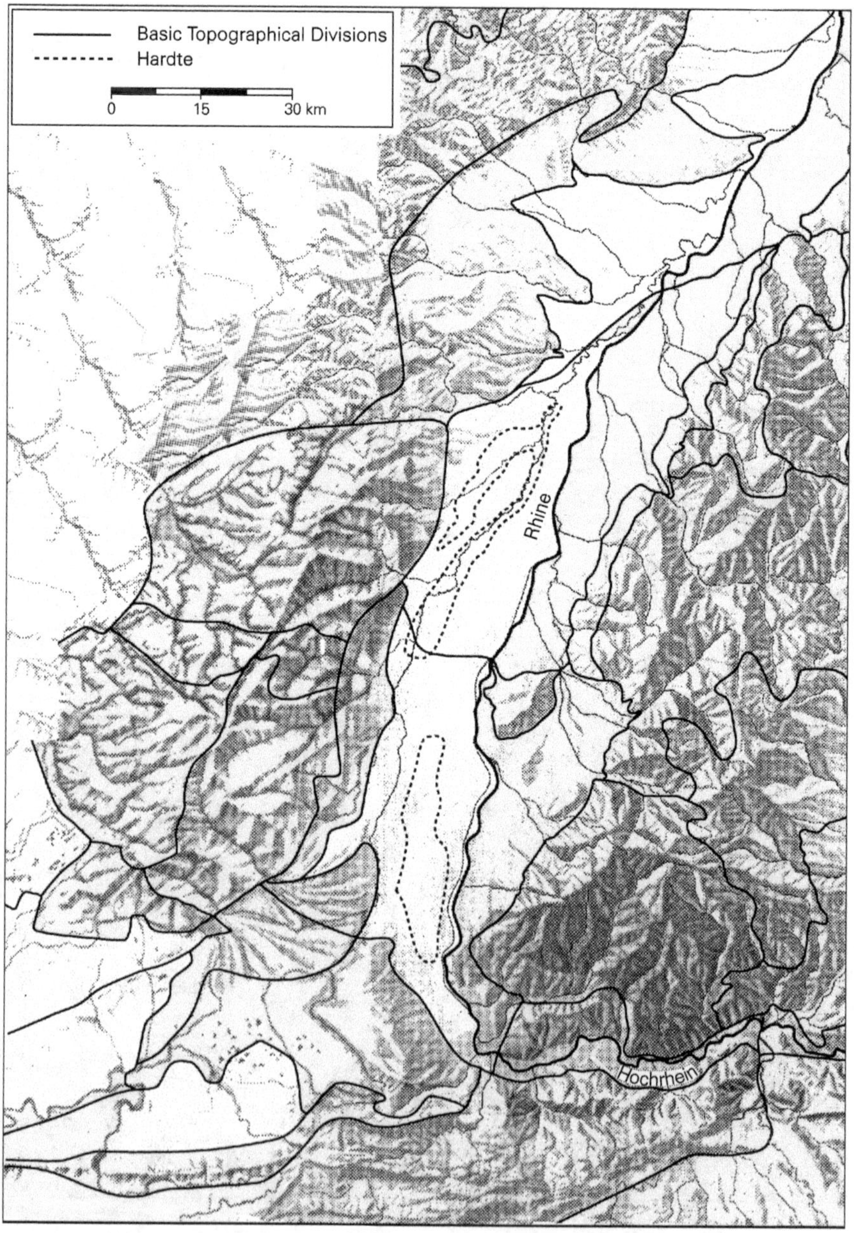

Map 9.2. Natural-topographical Divisions.

and wool textile manufacturing; on the foothills viticulture throve; the side valleys receding from the plain favoured dairying and transhumance and, lastly, in the mountains reserves of base and precious metals were discovered;

Ad 3. The region's metropolis, Strasbourg, functioned both as a centre of exchange and as an entrepôt for export; as a location for textile manufacturing; and, on the back of silver-mining, as a centre of credit and banking. Basel, too, as the regional sub-metropolis developed an extensive financial sector in the sixteenth century, when it came to service over 50 per cent of the Swiss cantons' credit requirement;

Ad 4. The Rhine was the principal artery of trade north of the Alps (see Map 9.3). It was fed by other major waterways, such as the Ill, which carried the region's premier export product of wine downriver to northern Germany and indeed overseas. Had the political constellation been otherwise, the Rhine might have developed as the heart of a European commercial empire, instead of succumbing to dynastic predators.

A *prima facie* case exists, therefore, for regarding the southern Upper Rhine before and after 1500 as fulfilling the requirements of an economic region. However, several reservations ought to be entered.

IV *A Critique of the Model*

Ad 1. However much mountain ranges constituted a barrier on three sides of the Upper Rhine basin, to the north the region was not only wide open, but linked umbilically by the artery of the Rhine to districts downriver.

None of the mountain ranges in fact presented insuperable barriers to passage. East-west commerce overland through the Vosges passes may have been as important in the economy of the Upper Rhine as the south-north axis of the river Rhine.[9] Basel's commercial links southwestwards through the Burgundian Gate to the Franche-Comté

[9] Odile Kammerer, 'Le carrefour alsacien-lorrain dans le grand commerce des XVe et XVIe siècles', in Jean-Marie Cauchies (ed.), *Aspects de la vie économique des pays bourguignons (1384–1559): Dépression ou prospérité?* (Publications du Centre Européen d'Études Bourguignonnes (XIVe–XVIe s.), 27: Recontres de Douai (25 au 28 septembre 1986)) (Basel, 1987), pp. 84–5.

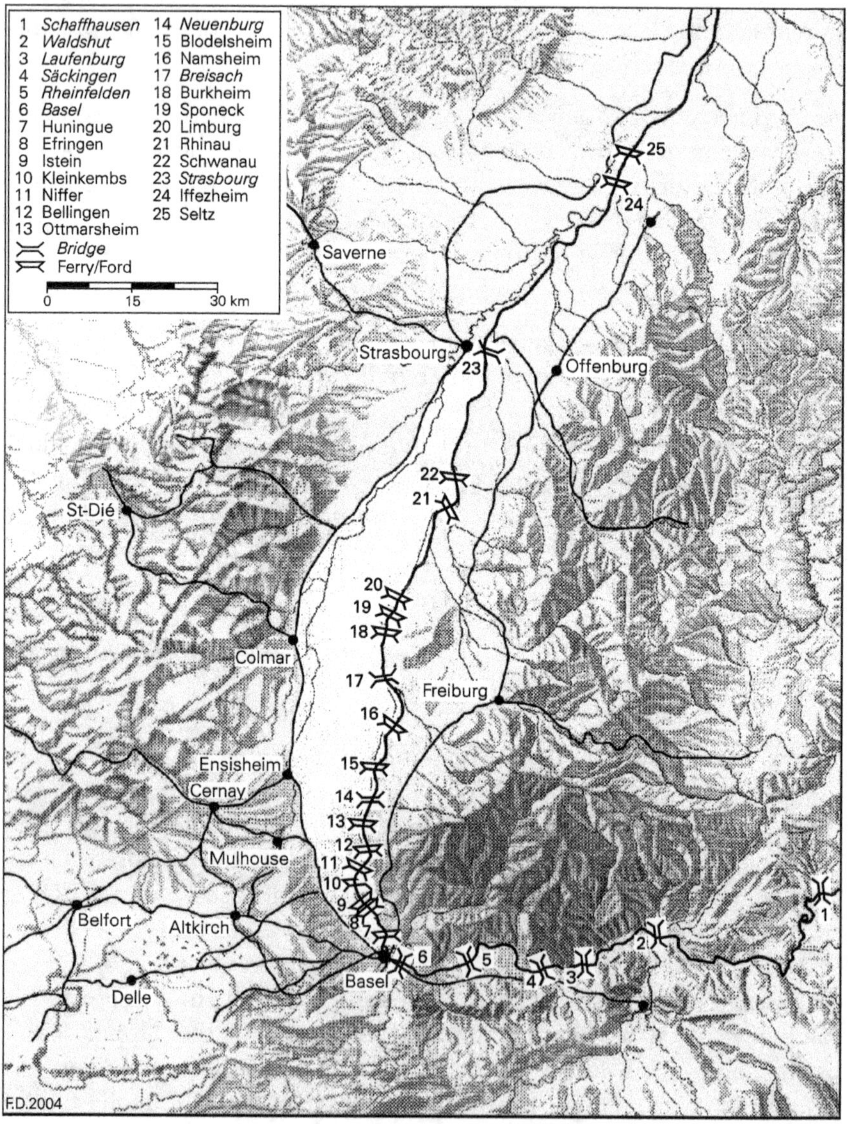

Map 9.3. Crossing-points and Mountain Passes on the Upper Rhine.

and Burgundy further qualify the notion of a naturally self-contained region.

Although the Rhine itself, despite an older school of French geographers and historians, never formed a dividing-line between Alsace and the Breisgau and Ortenau, the political fragmentation of the Upper Rhine presented institutional obstacles to economic integration and hence to the lowering of transaction costs.

Ad 2. Despite its distinct zones of economic activity, the southern Upper Rhine never became a region *either* of true economic specialization, in the manner suggested for the northern Netherlands by Jan de Vries,[10] or of true economic diversity, in which producers within one zone switched activity according to season—from flax to silk, to wine, and then to oil—as Stephan Epstein has described for late medieval Sicily.[11]

Ad 3. Far from subsisting in benign and mutually reinforcing reciprocity, as both the marketing and the traffic/transport patterns of centrality suggest, the metropolitan centres of the Upper Rhine were sworn commercial rivals, with Basel constantly seeking to wrest control of waterborne trade from Strasbourg. The effect of this mutually destructive competition was to drive trade off the water onto the more expensive land routes, thereby increasing transaction costs.[12]

At a much more modest level, the territorial towns on the right bank of the Upper Rhine faced stiffening competition from rural crafts and village markets which undermined their autonomy and livelihood. Here the claims of consolidating principalities had a particularly malign effect: political imperatives damaged economic interests.[13]

---

[10] Jan de Vries, *The Dutch Rural Economy in the Golden Age, 1500–1700* (New York/London, 1974).

[11] Stephan R. Epstein, *An Island for Itself. Economic Development and Social Change in Late Medieval Sicily* (Cambridge, 1989).

[12] Knut Schulz, 'Rheinschiffahrt und städtische Wirtschaftspolitik am Oberrhein im Spätmittelalter', in Erich Maschke and Jürgen Sydow (eds), *Die Stadt am Fluß. 14. Arbeitstagung in Kehl 14.–16. 11. 1975* (Stadt in der Geschichte. Veröffentlichungen des Südwestdeutschen Arbeitskreises für Stadtgeschichtsforschung, 4) (Sigmaringen, 1978), pp. 141–89.

[13] Tom Scott, *Freiburg and the Breisgau. Town-Country Relations in the Age of Reformation and Peasants' War* (Oxford, 1986), pp. 116–18; idem, *Regional Identity and Economic Change. The Upper Rhine, 1450–1600* (Oxford, 1997), pp. 122–52.

Ad 4. Internal institutional barriers to economic development also affected the Rhine as the principal artery of trade. Tolls offered themselves as a lucrative and easily administered source of revenue for princes, and the Rhine was notorious for the profusion of toll-stages; thirty-one alone between Strasbourg and the Dutch border, which survived until the Napoleonic era. Although it has been convincingly argued that tolls levied at a rate so high as to staunch the flow of goods must lead theoretically *ad absurdum*, and that the Rhine tolls were in practice often levied at a flat or compound rate much less onerous to merchants than the full tariff,[14] the sudden doubling of rates on the river Ill by the Austrian authorities after 1600, for example, undoubtedly hit Colmar's wine export trade hard.[15]

These critical observations serve to underscore two fundamental insights:

1. The definition and configuration of an economic region cannot be divorced from the institutional and political context within which economic activity took place. That was all the more true of pre-industrial Europe, where the modern market economy remained imperfectly developed and only partially free.
2. Despite the perfect-mesh dispersion of central places posited by all the patterns of centrality currently available (though the altogether looser and less geometric system described by Hohenberg and Lees does not assume a necessarily *regular* dispersion), the historical record instances competition rather than cooperation between central places at every turn. In the longer term, a truly dominant metropolis would contrive to subordinate its hinterland, drawing all important economic activity into its clutches and relegating the lesser towns to satellites. Although Strasbourg never succeeded in doing so on the Upper Rhine (Basel was too potent a counterweight), the economies of Tuscany under Florentine hegemony[16]

[14] Ulf Dirlmeier, 'Mittelalterliche Zoll- und Stapelrechte als Handelshemmnisse', in Hans Pohl (ed.), *Die Auswirkungen von Zöllen und anderen Handelshemmnissen auf Wirtschaft und Gesellschaft vom Mittelalter bis zur Gegenwart* (*Vierteljahrschrift für Sozial- und Wirtschaftsgeschichte*, Beiheft 80) (Stuttgart, 1987), pp. 19–39.

[15] Médard Barth, *Der Rebbau des Elsaß und die Absatzgebiete seiner Weine. Ein geschichtlicher Durchblick*, 2 vols (Strasbourg/Paris, 1958), 1, p. 429.

[16] Stephan R. Epstein, 'Cities, Regions, and the Late Medieval Crisis. Sicily and Tuscany Compared', *Past and Present*, 130 (1991), pp. 38, 42–3.

and eastern Swabia under Augsburg's commercial dominance[17] withered as if in the shade of a upas-tree. No longer was economic regionality understood as deriving from the mutually reinforcing interplay of a city and its complementary region; instead the region henceforth comprised a stunted torso with a hypertrophic head—a sure recipe for atrophy.

V *The Region between Economics and Politics*

Having stressed the institutional constraints upon the economic region as an ideal-type, and the reality of commercial rivalry overriding a notionally perfect dispersion of centrality, have we therefore consigned the concept of an economic region to historical irrelevance? For an economic region, if it is to serve as a category of historical analysis, must, as Sidney Pollard has observed, contain an operative as well as a purely descriptive element.[18]

I believe the concept of an economic region can be rescued, but only if we acknowledge the flexible interaction of institutional/political factors with commercial/economic ones. Over certain vital matters central places—from the level of the metropolis down to the local market town—had to cooperate, however much they may have competed in other areas. That was true, above all, of those issues which became of pressing concern during the sixteenth century, as populations recovered, pressure on scarce resources—land and its produce—grew, and inflation gathered pace. The provisioning of meat and grain—existential concerns *par excellence*—provides a classic case-study. For the authorities on the Upper Rhine, preoccupied with the question throughout the early modern period, such cooperation was always predicated upon a pre-existing *institutional* framework. In an area of advanced political fragmentation that could not be delimited by the early modern territorial principality and its boundaries;

---

[17] Prak, 'Regioni', p. 21; see Rolf Kießling, *Die Stadt und ihr Land. Umlandpolitik, Bürgerbesitz und Wirtschaftsgefüge in Ostschwaben vom 14. bis ins 16. Jahrhundert* (Städteforschung. Veröffentlichungen des Instituts für vergleichende Städtegeschichte in Münster, A 29) (Cologne/Vienna, 1989), pp. 714–41.

[18] Sidney Pollard, *Peaceful Conquest. The Industrialization of Europe 1760–1970* (Oxford, 1981), p. 32.

rather, it was provided by the quintessentially late medieval phenomenon of coinage leagues.

On the southern Upper Rhine two coinage areas existed in our period. One was controlled by the city of Strasbourg and extended throughout Lower Alsace and across the river into Ortenau (Middle Baden). The other, embracing Upper Alsace and the Breisgau, was regulated by a league of towns and princes, with no one power dominant. This league, the Rappen coinage association, underwent a remarkable reorientation from its inception in the late fourteenth century. Originally it had encompassed most of northern Switzerland as well as the southern Upper Rhine, its boundaries largely determined by jurisdictional and seigneurial interests. By the mid-fifteenth century, however, its area had contracted to the point where it corresponded to the geographic frontiers of the Upper Rhine, its remit essentially reflecting the economic and commercial interests of the region's leading cities and mints.[19] These members of the Rappen league, who took responsibility for the regulation and organization of meat and grain provisioning on the southern Upper Rhine, did not conceive of their sphere of action as narrowly circumscribed by the area of the Upper Rhine itself. Nor, indeed, was that how the Rappen league was perceived by its neighbours. For by the late sixteenth century, at the very time when the league was on the brink of extinction—having been brushed aside as rulers of Outer Austria by the Habsburgs, who were determined to impose the imperial coinage ordinance in place of regional monetary associations—the ruler of the county of Montbéliard in the Burgundian Gate earnestly deliberated whether to join the Rappen league. Although political considerations played their part—Montbéliard belonged to the dukes of Württemberg and was governed by a cadet branch of the dynasty—economic and commercial motives were decisive. Montbéliard lay at the intersection of two currency regions, that of the Rappen league and the circulation area of the Besançon pound, so that its rulers could just as readily have aligned themselves with a monetary association under the pull of Burgundy. But count Friedrich of Württemberg argued that Montbéliard's trade in wine and cloth was oriented much

[19] Julius Cahn, *Der Rappenmünzbund. Eine Studie zur Münz- und Geld-Geschichte des oberen Rheinthales* (Heidelberg, 1901); Scott, *Regional Identity and Economic Change*, pp. 175–200.

more towards Germany than to Burgundy: hence the southern Upper Rhine formed the indispensable bridge or conduit between the two.[20]

Provisioning with essential commodities provides an excellent test of the sense of the regional economic interests and solidarity which members of the Rappen league displayed throughout the sixteenth century. For what it reveals is that provisioning could not be handled within a purely political or monetary framework; in other words, neither membership of the league as such nor the circulation area of the Rappen coinage were adequate to define who should be brought into the negotiations over meat and grain provisioning or the geographical bounds to be embraced by the ensuing ordinances.

In terms of its agriculture the southern Upper Rhine, the area of the Rappen and Strasbourg coinages, was famously both a bread-basket and a wine-cellar, but by that token it was not self-sufficient in meat, which had to be imported from the upland pastures of the western Jura and the lush plains of Burgundy. As a result, the Rappen league's efforts centred upon ensuring regular supplies to the cattle mart at Cernay, strategically located on the main drove-road from Burgundy up through the Belfort Gap to Alsace (see Map 9.4). But the league members—and especially the government of Outer Austria, on whose territory Cernay lay—could never decide whether the mart at Cernay should serve only their own requirements or be promoted as an international (or at least inter-regional) mart in its own right. The tendency towards protectionism and price regulation repeatedly threatened to undermine the viability of the Cernay cattle mart, since traders either shunned it altogether in favour of more lucrative and less regulated markets elsewhere or else evaded the Rappen league's controls by buying up cattle for export beyond the league's borders. This dilemma manifests the inherent tension which could so easily arise between commitment to principles of economic centrality predicated upon the market (that is, local supply) and upon traffic and transport (that is, exports and commerce). Moreover, the league

---

[20] Jean-Marc Debard, *Les monnaies de la principauté de Montbéliard du XVIe au XVIIIe siècle. Essai du numismatique et d'histoire économique* (Annales Littéraires de l'Université de Besançon, 220: Cahiers d'Études Comtoises, 26) (Paris, 1980), pp. 22–36. See now also Tom Scott, 'Das Elsaß als wirtschaftliche Brückenlandschaft im 15. und 16. Jahrhundert', in Konrad Krimm and Rainer Brüning (eds), *Zwischen Habsburg und Burgund. Der Oberrhein als europäische Landschaft im 15. Jahrhundert* (Oberrheinische Studien, 21) (Ostfildern, 2003), pp. 215–28, esp. 226–7. [Engl. version in this volume.]

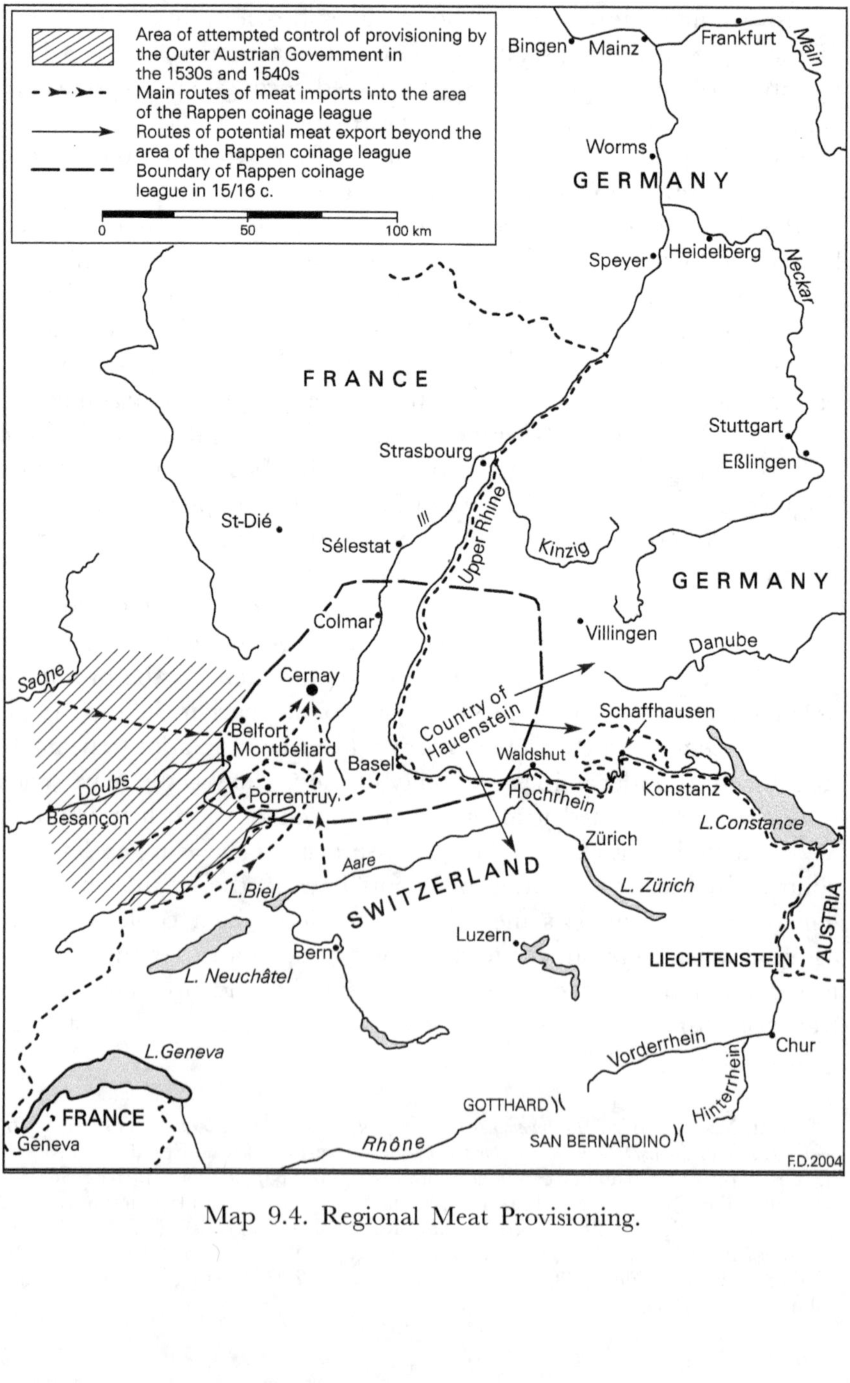

Map 9.4. Regional Meat Provisioning.

members found it increasingly difficult to confine the provisions (and therewith the potential benefits) of its Rappen meat ordinances and price tariffs to themselves alone. First the imperial city of Sélestat, situated just outside the area of the Rappen league to the north in the coinage area of Strasbourg, demanded access to the Cernay mart on the grounds that its commercial interests and links lay predominantly with its neighbours to the south within the Rappen league, above all Colmar, a claim that was finally conceded. And then, after mid-century, Strasbourg itself, on account of its overriding commercial clout and disproportionate demand for meat, was brought into the Rappen discussions, not least because its somewhat stronger coinage was encouraging butchers and merchants to descend upon the Rappen coinage area and sweep its market clean of meat.[21]

With grain provisioning the situation was almost entirely reversed. Until the later sixteenth century the southern Upper Rhine, and Alsace in particular, produced regular surpluses of grain, which were available for export. Stocks of corn were eagerly bought up by the Swiss cantons, whose agrarian economy was largely given over to pastoralism and dairying (see Map 9.5). Two immediate contrasts with the difficulties over meat provisioning became apparent. In the first place, faced with domestic abundance, members of the Rappen league could afford to take a much more relaxed view of the marketing and pricing of grain. As a consequence, deliberations between members were less frequent, and the sense of regional solidarity so evident in attempts to control the meat market was much less developed. The towns and cities within the Rappen area were happy to enter into bilateral deals with foreign purchasers and, except in times of dearth, paid much less heed to the interests of their neighbours. Secondly, the Rappen members' involvement in an export market encouraged them to perceive their regional identity in arterial or axial terms, following trade routes that led beyond the area of the southern Upper Rhine. Here the traffic or transport principle of centrality outweighed the market (local supply) principle, except when famine supervened.[22]

---

[21] Scott, *Regional Identity and Economic Change*, pp. 201–43.
[22] Ibid., pp. 244–72.

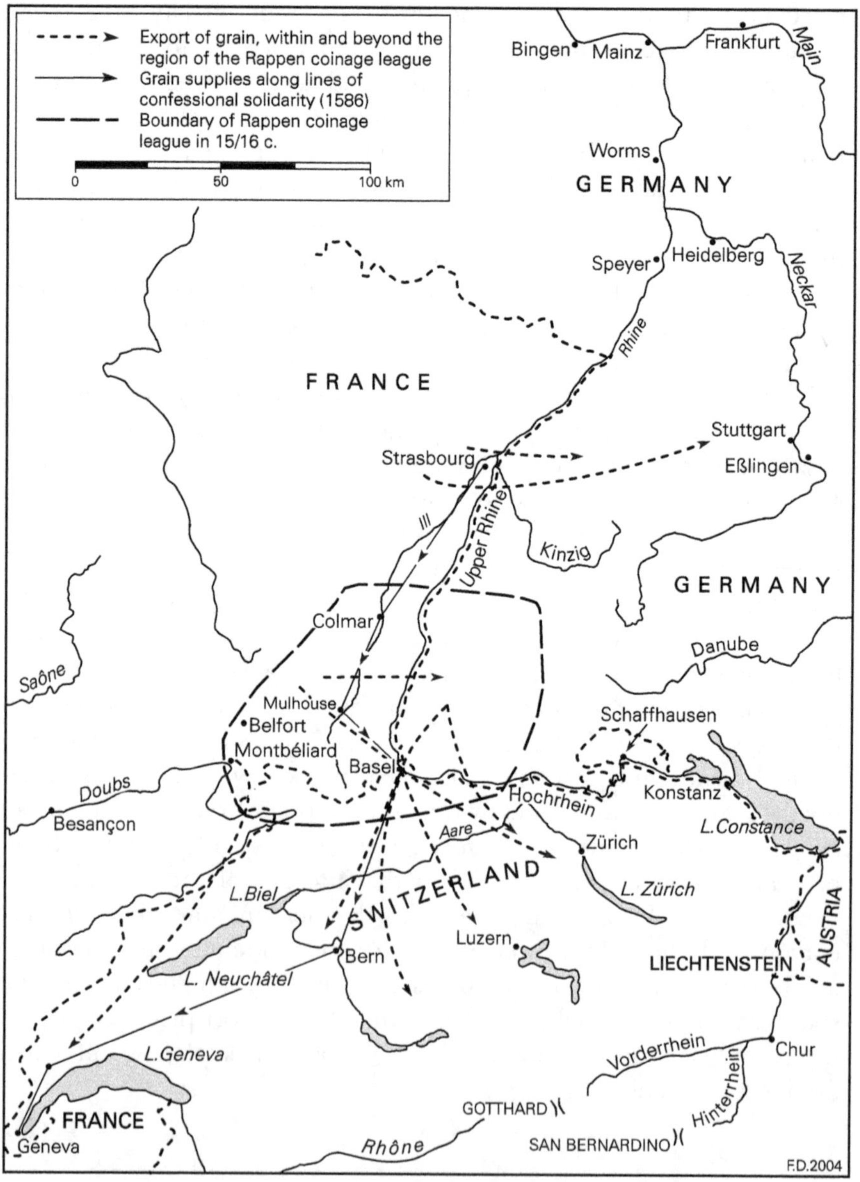

Map 9.5. Regional Grain Provisioning.

VI *The Region Redefined*

What emerges from a comparison of meat and grain provisioning, the former mostly a question of imports, the latter chiefly of exports, is the variable geometry which informed their view of regional economic interests. Where meat was concerned, the Rappen league sought to extend its influence southwestwards to the rich pasture lands of Burgundy and the Saône. This gravitational pull led them to ignore the eastern fringes of the Upper Rhine. When it came to grain provisioning, by contrast, the signs were reversed. The Upper Rhine's lucrative trade in grain exports to Switzerland caused the cities of the Rappen league to concentrate on regulating the grain market in the south and east, with the western flank of the Upper Rhine now marginalized.

The tension between radial and axial (or arterial) perceptions of regional identity and activity suggests that our definition of an economic region needs to be rethought. At the most obvious level, it transcends the stark alternative between the market and the transport principles of centrality. It is not simply that the southern Upper Rhine clearly embodied both principles of centrality at once, both as a richly endowed region living in large measure from the economic interchange between mountain and plain, and as a region straddling one of the major arteries of trade in northern Europe (and therewith an entrepôt or staging-post for goods passing through it as well as a major exporter of produce, chiefly wine, in its own right). Of these two, the dispersion of central places corresponds rather better to the transport than to the market principle, which need not surprise us. Yet even the recognition that the two principles of economic centrality conflate rather than conflict on the southern Upper Rhine leaves us with the image of a region whose boundaries can in some sense be spatially determined—if not as a hexagon then as a lozenge, to adopt Christaller's terminology. But that is precisely what the comparison of meat and grain provisioning calls into question. For here we are confronted with a sense of regional economic interests and cohesion which was in spatial terms not static but fluid. It derived from an amalgam of factors: geography, topography, market areas, commercial networks, as well as political (and, indeed, by the sixteenth century, confessional) allegiances. In that sense, economic cooperation on the southern Upper Rhine led not to the crystallization of a single regional identity, shaped by natural frontiers and political alliances (which is how the Rappen league as a purely coinage association had started out), but rather to the simultaneous coexistence of overlapping regional identities superimposed upon one another, predicated upon varying economic needs and opportunities and structured by principles of both centrality and arterial networks. Cartographically, these can be imagined as a succession of overhead-projector sheets laid on top of one another, all covering a core area, but each describing the varying outlines of a particular regional configuration stretching beyond it.

At first sight there are parallels to be drawn with findings from other areas. Following Hektor Ammann's researches on Nuremberg, in which he developed the concept of an 'economic unit' (*Wirtschaftseinheit*), a regional entity predicated upon the interaction of a city and its hinterland,[23] Franz Irsigler has traced Cologne's 'economic unit' in the fifteenth century in terms of the supply areas of its raw materials and semi-finished goods—cloth, hops, iron, copper, steel, and peltry. Far from yielding a series of concentric circles (as market areas and franchises might have done), the 'economic unit' of supplies takes on many strange shapes—some of them reminiscent of a Hans Arp sculpture—with many overlaps, with Cologne itself not necessarily forming the centre-point. Only in its totality, and then largely thanks to the very broad and regular dispersion of peltry supplies, does Cologne's 'economic unit' take on the appearance of a circle with the city firmly in the middle.[24] If that is true of a single city's hinterland, how much more complex the relations between cities within a given region are likely to be has been demonstrated by recent research on the development of Swabia as an economic region after the Thirty Years War. Here the historians concerned speak of the *Überlagerung unterschiedlich dimensionierter Regionen*, by which

---

[23] Hektor Ammann, *Die wirtschaftliche Stellung der Reichsstadt Nürnberg im Spätmittelalter* (Nürnberger Forschungen, 13) (Nuremberg, 1970), pp. 194–223.

[24] Franz Irsigler, 'Stadt und Umland im Spätmittelalter. Zur zentralitätsfördernden Kraft von Fernhandel und Exportgewerbe', in Emil Meynen (ed.), *Zentralität als Problem der mittelalterlichen Stadtgeschichtsforschung* (Städteforschung. Veröffentlichungen des Instituts für vergleichende Städtegeschichte in Münster, A 8) (Cologne/Vienna, 1979), pp. 1–14 (esp. map, p. 14). See now also Herbert Eiden and Franz Irsigler, 'Environment and Hinterland. Cologne and Nuremberg in the Later Middle Ages', in James A. Galloway (ed.), *Trade, Urban Hinterlands and Market Integration c. 1300–1600* (Centre for Metropolitan History, Working Paper Series, 3) (London, 2000), pp. 43–57 (map, p. 54).

they mean the overlaps between the varying market hinterlands of the Swabian cities.[25] But such cartographical and terminological resemblances are ultimately misleading. In the case of Swabia, the 'overlapping of regions of varying dimensions' occurred within the framework of a region whose identity came to be defined by its economic links with northern Switzerland, as its agriculture was increasingly geared towards supplying the largely pastoral Confederation with cereals.[26] This symbiosis rested upon a clear division of functions and markets, and in that sense allows the adjoining regions to be plotted cartographically, demarcated by economic boundaries.

The experience of the southern Upper Rhine, by contrast, points to a quite different conclusion. At an elementary level, the variability and mutability of regional economic interests and identity should caution us against envisaging an economic region primarily, let alone solely, in areal, spatial, or geographical terms (though the fact that geography and topography can play a role in shaping a sense of regional identity should not be dismissed). More importantly, however, any attempt to equate the economic region with a core area common to all the spatial configurations of economic activity is doomed to failure. For the core area, if it exists at all, does not correspond with any 'true' or 'natural' or 'essential' region: quite the opposite. In *economic* terms—that is the point of this paper—there was no such thing.

---

[25] Frank Göttmann, Horst Rabe, and Jörn Sieglerschmidt, 'Regionale Transformation von Wirtschaft und Gesellschaft. Forschungen und Berichte zum wirtschaftlichen und sozialen Wandel am Bodensee vornehmlich in der frühen Neuzeit, 1: Theoretische und methodische Grundprobleme', *Schriften des Vereins für Geschichte des Bodensees und seiner Umgebung*, 102 (1984), p. 128.

[26] Frank Göttmann, *Getreidemarkt am Bodensee. Raum—Wirtschaft—Politik—Gesellschaft (1650–1810)* (Beiträge zur südwestdeutschen Wirtschafts- und Sozialgeschichte, 13) (St Katharinen, 1991).

CHAPTER TEN

MEDIUM-SIZED AND SMALL TOWNS ON THE UPPER RHINE IN THE FIFTEENTH AND SIXTEENTH CENTURIES BETWEEN DOMINATION AND COMPETITION

I

'As two sides of an opened book'—in these words René Schickele eighty years ago apostrophized the land between the Vosges and the Black Forest. '. . . I saw clearly before me how the Rhine did not separate, but united, them, by holding them together in a firm embrace.'[1] A poet's love of his native land may be altogether understandable, given that the Upper Rhine has throughout history been a region repeatedly ravished and torn asunder, but Schickele's aphorism only partially corresponds to the natural-topographical divisions of the Upper Rhine and its evolution as a historical landscape. Commonplace assumptions which regard the Upper Rhine as a decidedly urbanized landscape should also be treated with some scepticism. At first sight, the Upper Rhine—here it is essentially the southern Upper Rhine which is meant—displays in the distribution and density of its urban settlements a unity unparalleled elsewhere in Germany. But appearances are deceptive (as Map 10.1 shows), for the towns are by no means evenly distributed: the map contains many blank patches. Moreover, despite the density of settlements, the population total remained relatively modest; it hardly reached the threshold that Jan de Vries in his study of European urbanization has posited for the 'urban quality' of a landscape.[2] A glance beyond the region to Württemberg helps to make the point. On the lower reaches of the Neckar little winegrowing towns proliferated;

[1] René Schickele, 'Rundreise des fröhlichen Christenmenschen', *Les Nouveaux Cahiers Alsaciens/Neue Elsässische Hefte*, 1, 7 (1922), p. 189; repr. in idem, *Terre d'Europe. Poèmes* (Paris, 1990), p. 44.

[2] Jan de Vries, *European Urbanization 1500–1800* (London, 1984).

Map 10.1[a]. Towns and Markets on the Upper Rhine and in South-West Germany, 1400–1600.

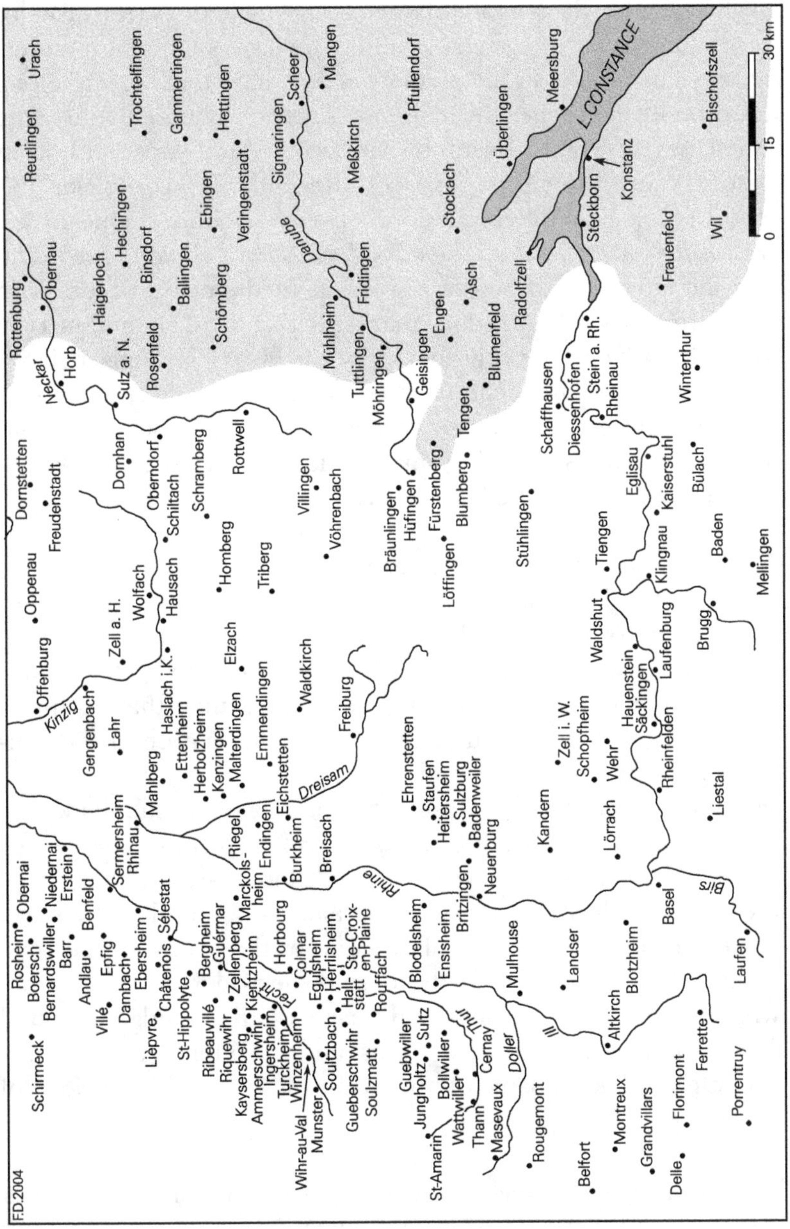

Map 10.1[b]. Towns and Markets on the Upper Rhine and in South-West Germany, 1400–1600.

between Eßlingen and Heilbronn fifteen dwarf towns can be counted, whose character barely differed from villages, and which taken together never achieved the degree of urbanization which de Vries takes as the precondition of the epochal shift to the age of modern industrialization. The many Franconian winegrowing small towns along the Main found themselves in a similar situation. Consequently, the question arises of what constitutes an urban landscape and what explanatory value the term possesses. Recently Franz Irsigler has proposed a typological differentiation between 'urbanized landscapes' (*Stadtlandschaften*) and 'urban landscapes' (*Städtelandschaften*), according to which the latter are to be understood as medium-sized areas with a varying degree of urbanization, marked either by a dominant type of town or by a clearly visible hierarchy of towns. 'Urbanized landscapes', by contrast, are characterized by an above-average provision of urban centres—more than 25 per cent of the population—and very intensive relations with their hinterlands, which cause the autonomy of the rural area tangibly to recede.[3] Only at a few points—along the edge of the Vosges on the left bank of the Rhine—can we identify values which would justify the description 'urbanized landscape', as Irsigler terms it. And even then it is doubtful whether a clear hierarchy of towns in this case can be discerned, since a profusion of small towns crowded together in a very restricted space, and they were more likely to compete with, rather than complement, each other. I will return to the problematic nature of the concept 'urban landscape' at the end.

If we attempt in the first instance empirically to subdivide the Upper Rhine as an urban landscape, a threefold picture emerges for the southern Upper Rhine, whose zones cannot always sharply be separated from each other. 1. The zone along the foothills of Alsace, which stretches into the Rhine valley as far as the course of the river Ill. 2. The valley floor between the Ill and the Rhine, almost devoid of towns, as well as the rolling landscape of the Sundgau, dotted with a few small administrative towns under Outer Austrian lordship.[4] 3. On the right bank of the Rhine a classical landscape of

---

[3] Franz Irsigler, 'Städtelandschaften und kleine Städte', in Helmut Flachenecker and Rolf Kießling (eds), *Städtelandschaften in Altbayern, Franken und Schwaben. Studien zum Phänomen der Kleinstädte während des Spätmittelalters und der Frühen Neuzeit* (*Zeitschrift für bayerische Landesgeschichte*, Beiheft 15, Reihe B) (Munich, 1999), p. 32.

[4] See Friedrich Metz, 'Die elsässischen Städte. Die Grundlagen ihrer Entstehung

older urban foundations, whose central-place function as markets for their hinterlands initially remained unchallenged. Only to the north, into the former Ufgau, where the margraves of Baden inherited several lordships which had promoted urban foundations, can a certain concentration of small towns be registered and hence an overlapping of their spheres of influence.[5]

Within the concept of an urban landscape, therefore, considerable variations can be observed, but all in all the southern Upper Rhine can be categorized as a region of medium-sized and small centres, with no strong influence from large cities. This conclusion seems to fly in the face of Strasbourg's exceptional position as the regional metropolis, or of Basel's function as a commercial junction between mountain and valley. Since the larger cities are not part of my present brief, suffice it to say that there were clear limits to Strasbourg's seigneurial penetration of its hinterland and its economic *rayonnement* within the Upper Rhine, despite the creation of its own currency area,[6] while Basel's intensive late mediaeval relations with its surrounding countryside—in a nutshell, through the putting-out system and investment in mining—yielded in the course of the sixteenth century to a key role in Confederate credit and financial politics, which was not dependent on its geographical location.[7] Neither Strasbourg nor Basel deliberately attempted to exploit (or, put more charitably, to harness) their hinterlands economically, unlike cities

und Entwicklung', in idem, *Land und Leute. Gesammelte Beiträge zur deutschen Landes- und Volksforschung* (Stuttgart, 1961), pp. 315–17.

[5] Rüdiger Stenzel, 'Die Städte der Markgrafen von Baden', in Jürgen Treffeisen and Kurt Andermann (eds), *Landesherrliche Städte in Südwestdeutschland* (Oberrheinische Studien, 12) (Sigmaringen, 1994), pp. 89–130, map p. 91.

[6] On Strasbourg's territory see Gerhard Wunder, *Das Straßburger Gebiet. Ein Beitrag zur rechtlichen und politischen Geschichte des gesamten städtischen Territoriums vom 10. bis zum 20. Jahrhundert* (Schriften zur Verfassungsgeschichte, 3) (Berlin, 1965); idem, *Das Straßburger Landgebiet. Territorialgeschichte der einzelnen Teile des städtischen Herrschaftsbereichs vom 13. bis zum 18. Jahrhundert* (Schriften zur Verfassungsgeschichte, 5) (Berlin, 1967). On Strasbourg's economic influence, emphasizing the role of long-distance trade, see François-Joseph Fuchs, 'Les foires et le rayonnement économique de la ville en Europe (XVIe siècle)', in Georges Livet and Francis Rapp (eds), *Histoire de Strasbourg des origines à nos jours*, 2: *Strasbourg des grandes invasions au XVIe siècle* (Strasbourg, 1981), pp. 259–361.

[7] Martin H. Körner, *Solidarités financières suisses au seizième siècle. Contribution à l'histoire monétaire, bancaire et financière des Cantons suisses et des États voisins* (Bibliothèque Historique Vaudoise, 66) (Lausanne, 1980); Franz Ehrensperger, 'Basels Stellung im internationalen Handelsverkehr des Spätmittelalters' (Diss. phil. Basel, 1972).

such as Augsburg, Nuremberg, Ulm, or Cologne, with or without landed territories.[8]

II

There is hardly an area of late medieval Germany that was not stamped by burgeoning rural crafts or by the establishment of new markets in villages or in places designated as markets (*Marktflecken*). The traditional autonomy and economic influence of the chartered urban markets was thereby fundamentally put at risk. The commercialization of the rural economy, as is well known, took many forms, and it is quite impermissible to equate rural craftsmanship by independent masters with put-out piecework by wage-dependent domestic labour (especially in textiles). Rural manufacturing, moreover, should only in certain circumstances be seen as the prelude to subsequent proto-industrialization. The Upper Rhine in this regard remained underdeveloped in comparison with Upper Swabia, as Rolf Kießling has demonstrated in his most recent essays;[9] it remained a

[8] Tom Scott, 'Town and Country in Germany, 1350–1600', in Stephan R. Epstein (ed.), *Town and Country in Europe, 1300–1800* (Themes in International Urban History, 5) (Cambridge, 2001), pp. 202–28, esp. 216–28 [expanded version repr. in this volume]; Rolf Kießling, *Die Stadt und ihr Land. Umlandpolitik, Bürgerbesitz und Wirtschaftsgefüge in Ostschwaben vom 14. bis ins 16. Jahrhundert* (Städteforschung. Veröffentlichungen des Instituts für vergleichende Städtegeschichte in Münster, A 29) (Cologne/Weimar/Vienna, 1989); Herbert Eiden and Franz Irsigler, 'Environs and Hinterland. Cologne and Nuremberg in the Later Middle Ages', in James A. Galloway (ed.), *Trade, Urban Hinterlands and Market Integration c. 1300–1600* (Centre for Metropolitan History, Working Paper Series, 3) (London, 2000), pp. 43–57.

[9] Rolf Kießling, 'Ländliches Gewerbe im Sog der "Proto-Industrialisierung". Ostschwaben als Textillandschaft zwischen Spätmittelalter und Moderne', *Jahrbuch für Wirtschaftsgeschichte*, 1998, 2, pp. 49–77; idem, 'Oberschwaben—eine offene Gewerbelandschaft. Wirtschaftliche Entwicklung und "Republikanismus"', in Peter Blickle (ed.), *Verborgene republikanische Traditionen in Oberschwaben* (Oberschwaben. Geschichte und Kultur, 4) (Tübingen, 1998), pp. 25–55; Rolf Kießling, 'Städtebünde und Städtelandschaften im oberdeutschen Raum. Ostschwaben und Altbayern im Vergleich', in Monika Escher, Alfred Haverkamp, and Frank G. Hirschmann (eds), *Städtelandschaft—Städtenetz—zentralörtliches Gefüge. Ansätze und Befunde zur Geschichte der Städte im hohen und späten Mittelalter* (Trierer Historische Forschungen, 43) (Mainz, 2000), pp. 79–116; Rolf Kießling, 'Die Zentralitätstheorie und andere Modelle zum Stadt-Land-Verhältnis', in Hans-Jörg Gilomen and Martina Stercken (eds), *Zentren. Ausstrahlung, Einzugsbereich und Anziehungskraft von Städten und Siedlungen zwischen Rhein und Alpen* (Zürich, 2000), pp. 17–40; Rolf Kießling, 'Der Wandel ökonomischer und

landscape with a diversified agrarian sector (including industrial crops) with little recourse to putting-out, which was essentially restricted to the so-called 'textile group' of towns and villages in Lower Alsace north of Strasbourg.[10] Nevertheless, there is a consensus of research that rural crafts and village markets were most prevalent in the south-west and in northern Switzerland.[11] What potential for conflict did they represent to the dominance of medium-sized and small towns over against their hinterlands?

The sources of friction fall under six headings:

1. Encroachment upon or disregard for the area of market franchise.
2. Disregard for other urban jurisdictional and regalian rights (through the establishment of toll-posts, salt-chests, or bath-houses).
3. Informal trade and distribution (peddling, forestalling).
4. Evasion of urban quality controls (*Schau*) in the case of textiles.
5. Competition from new market-places, and village markets.
6. Competition in manufacturing and artisan production in the countryside, which was not subject to any guild control.

The threshold of friction naturally varied from town to town.

Other things being equal, one might expect that the potential for conflict between a town and its surrounding countryside as the latter urbanized, that is to say, arrogated to itself the attributes and functions of towns, would have been most intense where the greatest density of settlement prevailed. But it is a hallmark of the southern Upper Rhine that circumstances there contradict our expectations. This is revealed if we compare the three zones already mentioned.

1. The foothills region of Alsace is marked by the multiplicity of smaller and greater lordships as rivals—among them Habsburg Outer Austria, the abbacy of Murbach, the bishopric of Strasbourg, sev-

---

politischer Beziehungen zwischen Dörfern und Städten vom Spätmittelalter bis zur Frühen Neuzeit', in Clemens Zimmermann (ed.), *Dorf und Stadt. Ihre Beziehungen vom Mittelalter bis zur Gegenwart* (Frankfurt am Main, 2001), pp. 67–84.

[10] Hektor Ammann, 'La place de l'Alsace dans l'industrie textile au Moyen Âge', in *La Bourgeoisie alsacienne. Études d'histoire sociale* (Publications de la Société Savante d'Alsace et des Régions de l'Est, grandes publications, 5) (Strasbourg, 1967), pp. 80–9.

[11] Wilfried Reininghaus, *Gewerbe in der frühen Neuzeit* (*Enzyklopädie Deutscher Geschichte*, 3) (Munich, 1990), pp. 65 ff.

eral imperial free cities, the fiefs of imperial knights, and the left-bank possessions of the house of Württemberg. From a seigneurial perspective, therefore, there was every reason to strengthen lordships economically and legally by rounding them off territorially and protecting them against foreign encroachment. In positive terms that would have entailed the foundation of privileged markets with central-place functions and the promotion of crafts within the territory. In negative terms it would have involved prohibitions on visiting foreign markets, embargoes on exports, and suchlike. Yet with barely an exception this path was never travelled, and the absence of isolationist or protectionist measures is all the stranger since some towns in the foothills of the Vosges lay so close together that they hardly had any hinterland to call their own. Here we may recall Sebastian Münster's famous quip in his *Cosmographei*: 'There the towns lie so close together that one may fire a rifle from one to the other, namely, Ammerschwihr, Kaysersberg, and Kientzheim.'[12]

This remark in itself helps to shed light on the reasons for urban solidarity on the narrowest of canvases. The small towns along the Vosges—in most cases merely walled winegrowing villages, as Hektor Ammann noted[13]—earned their livelihood from high-value viticulture chiefly destined for export. They really only competed with each other in export markets, although designations of origin in the late Middle Ages were extremely rare. Wine from Alsace was commonly referred to as 'wine from the upper land' (*oberländischer Wein*), in contrast to the 'lower land wines' (*niederländischer Wein*) from the Middle Rhine.[14] The winegrowing communes stood in close symbiosis with the embarkation-points and entrepôts on the Ill—Colmar, Sélestat, and Strasbourg, where it debouched into the Rhine. Here there are incipient signs of a hierarchy of central places according to economic function, whereby the dwarf towns as producers supplied the entrepôts,

---

[12] Sebastian Münster, *Cosmographei* (Basel, 1550), p. 526: *Vnd liegen daselbst die Stätte also nahe beyeinander, daß man mit einer Büchse von einer zu der andern schießen mag, nemblich Ammerswyler, Keysersberg und Konßheim.*

[13] Hektor Ammann, 'Das Städtewesen des Mittelalters', in Georg Wolfram and Werner Gley (eds), *Erläuterungsband zum Elsaß-Lothringischen Atlas. Landeskunde, Geschichte, Kultur und Wirtschaft Elsaß-Lothringens* (Schriften des Wissenschaftlichen Instituts der Elsaß-Lothringer im Reich an der Universität Frankfurt) (Frankfurt am Main, 1931), p. 125.

[14] Médard Barth, *Der Rebbau des Elsaß und die Absatzgebiete seiner Weine. Ein geschichtlicher Durchblick*, 2 vols (Strasbourg/Paris, 1958).

who in turn acted as collection-points and suppliers for the commercial metropolises—Strasbourg close by, Frankfurt and Cologne further afield—as Rolf Kießling has demonstrated in a different context for the Swabian textile industry increasingly oriented towards Ulm, Augsburg, and Memmingen.[15] What is striking is that the entrepôts along the Ill lay at regular intervals from each other, at around 30 kms; moreover, even the smaller towns on the Ill, Benfeld and Erstein, were situated equidistantly at an interval of 15 kms, and therefore fitted into a network of central places within a regular and comprehensive dispersion.

This provides an obvious explanation for the division of space within the foothills zone. The towns' relation to each other conformed not to the market principle of hinterland domination, but to the traffic or transport principle geared to exports, whereby the network of central places was divided not into hexagons but into lozenges.[16] Since these central places were only partially reliant upon dominating their immediate hinterland, the Alsatian towns as producers and distributors of wine could tolerate a much greater settlement density without acting as competitors for market share and market area in their immediate vicinity. Accordingly, their hinterlands were not shaped as honeycombs around the town, but rather as ellipses, whose long axes pointed to the commercial artery of the Ill. As a result, the tensions in relations between towns or between town and country largely receded into the background.

[15] Rolf Kießling, 'Kleinstädte und Märkte als regionalpolitische Instrumente. Ostschwaben vom 14. bis zum 16. Jahrhundert', in Flachenecker and Kießling, *Städtelandschaften*, pp. 243–88.

[16] On central-place theory and its application to Alsace see Tom Scott, *Regional Identity and Economic Change. The Upper Rhine, 1450–1600* (Oxford, 1997), pp. 73–99. The theory was originally elaborated by Walter Christaller, *Die zentralen Orte in Süddeutschland. Eine ökonomisch-geographische Untersuchung über die Gesetzmäßigkeit der Verbreitung und Entwicklung der Siedlungen mit städtischer Funktion* (Jena, 1933; repr. Darmstadt, 1968). (Engl. as *Central Places in Southern Germany*, transl. Carlisle W. Baskin (Englewood Cliffs, NJ, 1966).) In this work the traffic/transport principle is clearly subordinate to the market principle; only when Christaller returned to the subject after World War II did he devote more attention to the former. See idem, *Das Grundgerüst der räumlichen Ordnung in Europa. Die Systeme der europäischen Zentralen Orte* (Frankfurter Geographische Hefte, 24, 1) (Frankfurt am Main, 1950). On the traffic principle, but with less theoretical rigour, see Paul M. Hohenberg and Lynn Hollen Lees, *The Making of Urban Europe 1000–1500* (Cambridge, MA/London, 1985).

2. The zone of southern Alsace displays characteristics which differ markedly from the first zone. The floor of the Rhine valley and the rolling uplands stretching into the Burgundian Gate formed a closed territory (barring the enclave of the imperial free city of Mulhouse) which was the core of Habsburg Outer Austria, with its administrative capital in Ensisheim. In this area a largely uniform agrarian economy prevailed (it was, of course, famous as the breadbasket of Switzerland), albeit accompanied in the sixteenth century by a flourishing mining industry in the foothills of the southern Vosges.

Alsatian Outer Austria, moreover, was divided into districts, in a manner reminiscent of Württemberg or parts of Baden, though the Habsburgs were never able to replicate the system on the right bank of the Rhine. By virtue of this administrative structure the Sundgau was divided into administrative districts of approximately the same size, governed from relatively centrally located administrative towns (see Map 10.2). The administrative town and its hinterland were regarded as a unit, with only the various seigneurial fiefs interrupting its uniformity, especially since the nobility of Sundgau at the territorial Diets repeatedly sought to uphold its exemption from the Outer Austrian fiscal community.[17] But this truculence had its limits, since most of the noble families had resettled in the Sundgau in the course of the fifteenth century and had sought Habsburg protection there as political refugees from the republican Swiss.[18]

As seats of government the administrative towns clearly enjoyed a 'surplus of importance' (in Christaller's phrase) as central places, but any notion that this resulted in domination of their hinterlands in terms of economic advantage is wide of the mark. If anything, the outcome was a levelling of the differential between town and country, since the artisanal economy of the towns was reined in as craft production was territorialized, or else urban and rural crafts were comprehended in an all-embracing guild constitution. Only Belfort, the largest town of the Sundgau with perhaps 3,000 inhabitants, succeeded in corralling, though not suppressing, rural crafts

[17] Georges Bischoff, *Gouvernés et gouvernants en Haute-Alsace à l'époque autrichienne. Les États des pays antérieurs des origines au milieu du XVIe siècle* (Publications de la Société Savante d'Alsace et des Régions de l'Est, grandes publications 20) (Strasbourg, 1982), p. 118; idem, 'Die markanten Züge des österreichischen Elsaß', in Hans Maier and Volker Press (eds), *Vorderösterreich in der frühen Neuzeit* (Sigmaringen, 1989), p. 276.

[18] Bischoff, *Gouvernés*, p. 238.

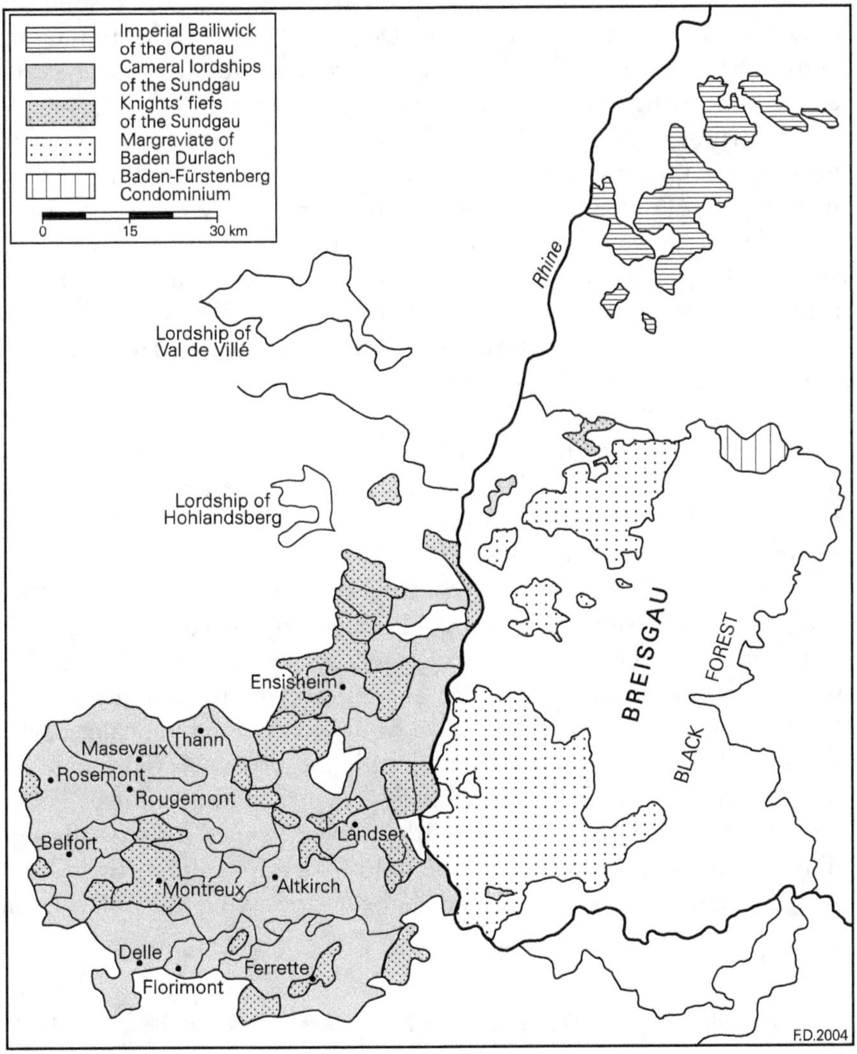

Map 10.2. The Outer Austrian Administrative Districts in the Sundgau.

by incorporating them into the civic guilds. Around 1500 a quarter of all Belfort's registered tanners and cobblers and just under half its butchers and cattle-dealers resided in the countryside in a radius of 20 kms.[19] The guild of ticking-weavers in Masevaux similarly embraced the entire valley of the Doller.[20] Whether the remaining administrative towns for their part were able to take rural crafts under their wing, as it were, is unclear.

That rural crafts posed a threat to the Outer Austrian towns in general emerges graphically from the grievances of the third Estate of towns and districts presented at the territorial Diets.[21] Whether the administrative towns of the Sundgau were thus affected is in view of the patchy sources hard to determine. But that a flourishing artisanal sector did exist on the left bank of the Rhine can be seen from the creation of territorial associations of journeymen, which in the fifteenth century almost became Alsace's trademark: potters, saddlers, tinsmiths, coppersmiths, ropemakers, cartwrights—the list could easily go on. A tilers' ordinance of 1443, which brought masters and journeymen together under one umbrella, expressly stated that it embraced all craftsmen in towns, villages, and in the countryside between Strasbourg and Basel.[22]

Although the administrative constitution of the Habsburg Sundgau probably put a stop to any establishment of village markets with lesser or no privileges, the threat posed by peddling and forestalling was by no means averted. For the interregional cattle-market at Cernay the evasion of its market-days by foreign cattle-dealers, who negotiated direct delivery contracts with the peasants, represented a serious problem (which need not be pursued in this context).[23] For the administrative towns, however, the danger loomed from an entirely different quarter. Already in the mid-fifteenth century the Outer Austrian government had issued a decree reserving the sale of salt

---

[19] Bruno de Villèle, 'Belfort à la fin du Moyen Âge' (Diss. phil. Besançon, 1971), pp. 96–7.

[20] Bischoff, *Gouvernés*, p. 212; Aimé Brun, 'Les corporations de la vallée de Masevaux', *Annuaire de la Société d'Histoire des Régions de Thann-Guebwiller*, 10 (1973/74), pp. 67–72.

[21] Scott, *Regional Identity and Economic Change*, pp. 105–7.

[22] Knut Schulz, *Handwerksgesellen und Lohnarbeiter. Untersuchungen zur oberrheinischen und oberdeutschen Stadtgeschichte des 14. bis 17. Jahrhunderts* (Sigmaringen, 1985), pp. 175–6.

[23] Scott, *Regional Identity and Economic Change*, pp. 201–43.

to towns and privileged market-places alone.[24] In this spirit, Belfort had its salt monopoly, which extended beyond the area under its jurisdictional control to take in the Val de Rougemont, confirmed by the emperor in 1450.[25] Yet complaints subsequently multiplied over salt-chests which had been set up in the countryside without the permission of the authorities, though only the better flow of sources in the sixteenth century allows us to get a handle on the situation. From urban grievances it emerges that competition stemmed not only from the countryside but was intensifying between the administrative towns themselves. Despite Belfort's efforts to cling to its salt monopoly, salt-dealers from the Val de Rougemont, for instance, were active in selling foreign salt direct to the localities, thereby evading Belfort's staple.[26] Even the Outer Austrian capital Ensisheim complained in 1568 about the establishment of salt-chests in five villages in its immediate environs, apparently without being able to take steps against it.[27]

Since salt was a regalian right, it is altogether surprising that the government did not immediately re-invoke its original mandate. After all, the existence of salt-chests in the countryside was far from a trivial matter, since they provided rural communes with a lucrative source of income. In the long-running conflicts between Zürich and its rural communes, for instance, culminating in 1489 in the so-called Waldmann affair, the trading monopolies which Zürich claimed were the main issue, with salt-provisioning taking pride of place. In the ensuing treaty of arbitration the peasant communes finally obtained the right to purchase their salt on the open market.[28]

It would be tempting to view the urban network of the Outer

---

[24] Hektor Ammann, *Wirtschaft und Lebensraum der mittelalterlichen Kleinstadt*, 1: *Rheinfelden* (n.p., n.d. [Aarau, 1947]), p. 22.

[25] Georges Bischoff, 'Belfort au XVe siècle—une duchesse et des comptes', in Yvette Baradel, Georges Bischoff, André Larger, Yves Pagnot, and Michel Rilliot, *Histoire de Belfort* (Roanne/Le Coteau, 1985), p. 91.

[26] StAFr, C 1 Landstände 7: *Beschwernus . . . der Statt Beffort*, n.d. (*c.* 1450); ibid.: *Beschwerden . . . der herrschafft Rosenfels*, 22 Jan. 1554. See Dieter Speck, *Die vorderösterreichischen Landstände im 15. und 16. Jahrhundert. Entstehung, Entwicklung und Ausbildung bis 1595/1602*, 2 vols (Veröffentlichungen aus dem Archiv der Stadt Freiburg im Breisgau, 29) (Freiburg im Breisgau/Würzburg, 1994), 1, pp. 331, 333.

[27] ADHR, C 674; Scott, *Regional Identity and Economic Change*, p. 113.

[28] Christian Dietrich, *Die Stadt Zürich und ihre Landgemeinden während der Bauernunruhen von 1489 bis 1525* (Europäische Hochschulschriften, 3rd series, 229) (Frankfurt am Main/Bern/New York, 1985), pp. 44, 53, 90.

Austrian Sundgau as embodying the third central-place system adumbrated by Walter Christaller, namely, the socio-political principle (although Christaller himself barely elaborated on it). It is based on the principle of the separateness of human communities, by which they are more firmly knit together and protected against outside influences hostile towards them.[29] The principle presumes a capital located at the core of the settlement network, and around it a circle of satellite places, administrative seats, and at the edge of the region thinly settled or even uninhabited terrain. We may safely ignore the fact that Christaller regarded the old German march communities (*Markgenossenschaften*) as part of this system, and recognize instead the astonishing parallels between the mediaeval system of administrative districts (*Ämter*) and the modern system of district courts (*Amtsgerichtsbezirke*), which Christaller regarded as an approximate realization of his principle: 'The leading idea of this administrative order is the creation of virtually complete districts, districts of practically equal area and population, in the center of which lies the most important place. The borders lie in the thinly settled regions and should follow closely the natural borders and barriers.'[30]

Yet we should not be misled by these congruences, however instructive they may appear. For the administrative principle, just as the market and traffic/transport principles, presupposes a centrally located capital of a higher order of importance, a role for which Ensisheim was manifestly unsuited either by its location or by its size (which hardly exceeded the other Outer Austrian administrative towns). Moreover, the number of central places according to the administrative principle which Christaller regarded as necessary to supply the area with central goods must increase dramatically.[31] But such a multiplication of central places of lesser importance never occurred in the Sundgau. Only in one respect does the separation or administrative principle offer a theoretical insight, inasmuch as the location of those central places whose importance ranks immediately below that of the capital itself is often pushed to the periphery of the hexagonal dispersion network—and that applies to a certain degree to Belfort.

---

[29] Christaller, *Die zentralen Orte*, p. 82; idem, *Central Places*, p. 77.

[30] Ibid., pp. 77–8 (I have retained the spelling of the American transl.); idem, *Die zentralen Orte*, p. 82.

[31] Ibid., p. 85; idem, *Central Places*, p. 80.

3. The third zone to be considered here, the Breisgau on the right bank of the Rhine, differs from the first two zones in two essential respects. On the one hand, the Breisgau was neither a consolidated area of lordship like the Sundgau, nor was it an area of seigneurial fragmentation like Upper and Lower Alsace. Here it was rather the case that two dynasties confronted each other, whose lordships largely comprised blocks of territory, but which at sensitive points intersected as slivers of land (see Map 10.3). Between Baden and Habsburg, on the other hand, a clear difference existed in terms of their attitude towards towns. The old urban foundations, going back to the dukes of Zähringen, were for the most part absorbed into Habsburg overlordship. The southern lands of the house of Baden—the margraviate of Hachberg and the so-called Margräflerland—remained by contrast poorly endowed with towns well into the sixteenth century. Indeed, the margraves were seen as hostile to towns *tout court.*

To compensate for this economic deficit, the margraves initially chose to establish new markets without urban charters. In 1418 the communes of Eichstetten and Emmendingen in the margraviate of Hachberg were granted privileges of weekly and annual markets. Whether this step was part and parcel of margrave Bernhard's expansionist policy at the expense of the Upper Rhenish towns (once lauded by Richard Fester as the beginnings of the Baden territorial state) can safely be left to one side.[32] At all events, the market privileges accorded to Eichstetten and Emmendingen found no echo in Baden politics for nearly a century thereafter.[33] On the diplomatic front, as Konrad Krimm has argued, no conscious antagonism between Baden and Habsburg can be traced in the fifteenth century.[34] In those decades the Austrian territorial towns were much more exposed to market competition from villages under the jurisdiction of the Breisgau

[32] Richard Fester, 'Markgraf Bernhard I. und die Anfänge des badischen Territorialstaates', *Neujahrsblätter der Badischen Historischen Kommission*, 6 (1896), pp. 111–12; Tom Scott, *Freiburg and the Breisgau. Town-Country Relations in the Age of Reformation and Peasants' War* (Oxford, 1986), p. 23.

[33] Idem, *Regional Identity and Economic Change*, pp. 137–42. The market privileges granted in 1442 to Sulzburg, which lay at the edge of the Markgräflerland, are very much the exception. They should be seen in conjunction with the boom in silver-mining, which led to supply shortages as the population rose.

[34] Konrad Krimm, *Baden und Habsburg um die Mitte des 15. Jahrhunderts. Fürstlicher Dienst und Reichsgewalt im späten Mittelalter* (Veröffentlichungen der Kommission für geschichtliche Landeskunde in Baden-Württemberg, B 89) (Stuttgart, 1976).

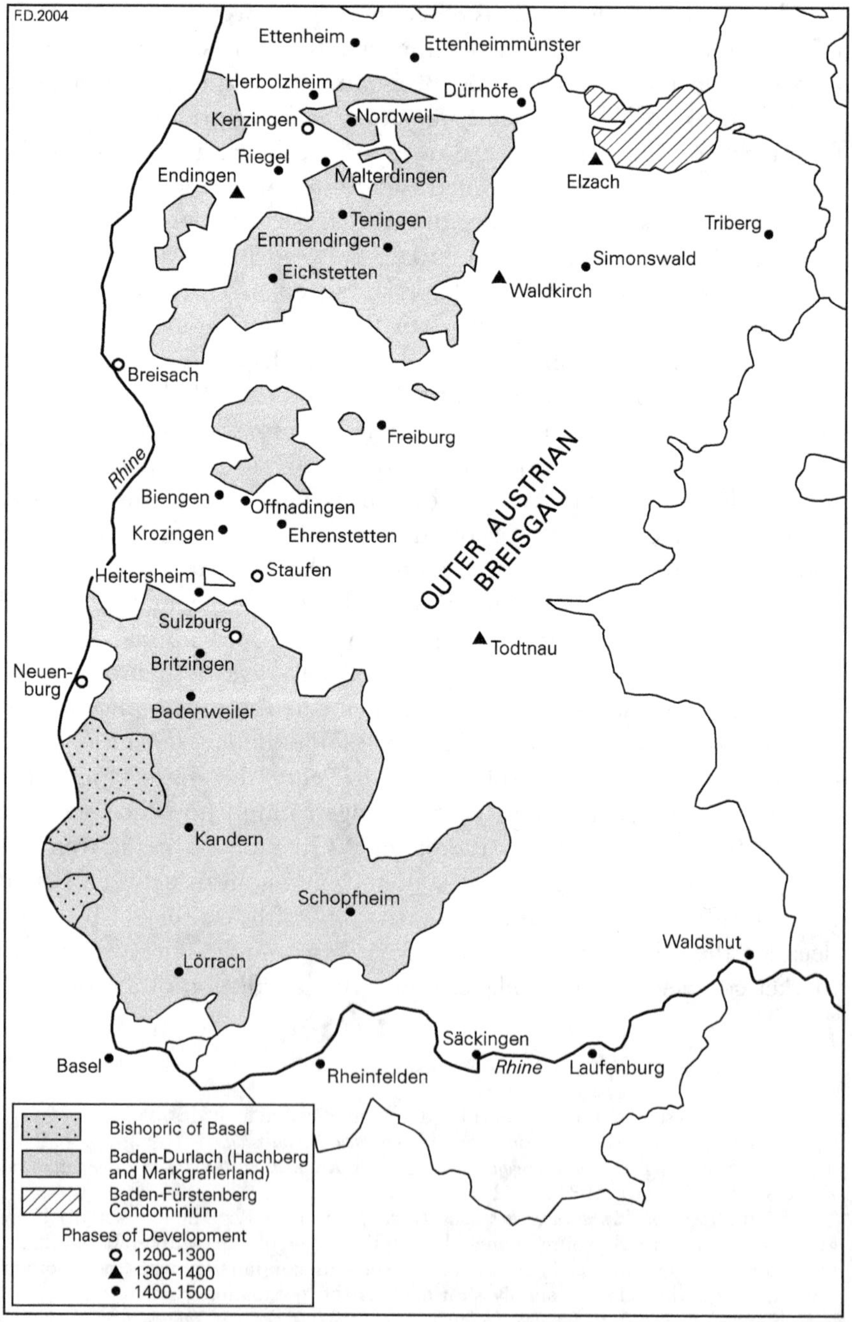

Map 10.3. Towns and Markets in the Breisgau.

nobility. Up to 1500 Offnadingen, Biengen, Ehrenstetten, and Heitersheim—all in the hands of Habsburg vassals—received market privileges; that applies under different circumstances to Badenweiler as well, for the castle settlement of the counts of Freiburg, which received a market charter in 1418, only fell to Baden on their extinction in 1444.

These village markets can hardly have amounted to more than pinpricks for the older market settlements. Neuenburg, by contrast, sandwiched in an exposed position between margravial territory and the course of the Rhine, was threatened with economic haemorrhaging for want of sufficient hinterland of its own. A foretaste of this predicament was provided by the long-running tensions between Neuenburg and margrave Rudolf IV of Hachberg that led in 1462 (for a brief time) to an arbitration accord brokered by Basel.[35] In the sixteenth century the tables were turned, as Neuenburg's haberdashers and craftsmen began to complain of increased stallage charges when they visited margravial annual markets and church-ales. In reprisal the Neuenburg council took the not very clever decision to raise steeply the tariffs for margravial peasants, who supplied the urban market with produce! As a result, the town was soon threatened with a complete boycott of its market.[36]

In the northern Breisgau, where the territorial boundaries were much less clearly delineated, relations between Baden and Habsburg took a somewhat different form. From the early sixteenth century onwards the Austrian towns of Waldkirch, Kenzingen, and Endingen came to repeated blows with the margravial communes of Emmendingen, Eichstetten, and Malterdingen. What at first sight appeared to be a straightforward conflict between privileged towns and competing market-places over hinterlands and market catchment areas transpired on closer inspection to be a longer-term struggle over access to and the usufruct of an important artery of trade. The trigger had been provided by the establishment of a weekly market in Malterdingen in 1510, which immediately provoked protests from Endingen and Waldkirch, who feared not only an infringement of their market franchise (*Bannmeile*) but also a diversion of transit trade

[35] Stadtarchiv Neuenburg, AA A 77, 16 Nov. 1462; *Oberrheinische Stadtrechte*, 2: *Schwäbische Rechte*, 3: *Neuenburg am Rhein*, ed. Walther Merk (Heidelberg, 1913), pp. 62–8.

[36] Scott, *Regional Identity and Economic Change*, pp. 127–9.

from their markets. In the decades that followed the conflict drew in many more protagonists, until even the Upper Austrian government in Innsbruck intervened in the affair.

As a counter-measure, the Austrian towns in the meantime had raised the toll-rates for margravial visitors to their markets—with much the same results as in Neuenburg. When a commission of enquiry was set up by Innsbruck in 1568 to investigate the events thoroughly, it was confronted with a new customs-post at Teningen on the river Elz, which was intended to catch goods being shipped northwards from Freiburg via Kenzingen to the Rhine. But the tolls, it emerged, only had to be paid by Austrian subjects, since Baden for decades had pursued a deliberate policy of undercutting tolls or granting complete exemption, which was designed to benefit its own subjects and to attract trade to the margravial markets, which were located advantageously from the point of view of commercial traffic. Although the customs-post at Teningen was temporarily suspended at the insistence of the Austrian authorities, it was re-established in 1577.[37]

The famine and dearth of the early 1570s could only make an intractable situation worse. Both Baden and Austria were concerned to prohibit the export of grain and to impose monopsony (that is, in this context, the obligation to visit only their own markets) upon their subjects. This policy of market protection turned out to be particularly fateful for the Markgräflerland, because the margravial subjects were accustomed to delivering their produce not only to domestic but also to foreign markets, above all Basel. We may dispense with an account of the highly complicated chain of events.[38] What matters is that the Baden and Austrian local officials during the negotiations repeatedly warned of the danger of a war of attrition. They realized straight away that reciprocal blockades and isolationist measures could only lead to staking everything on one card. Neither the towns of the Habsburg Breisgau nor the margravial market-places could afford to turn their backs on each other. They had to find a path as best they could between the Scylla of domination and the Charybdis of competition.

The reasons for the differing course of the conflicts in the northern

[37] Ibid., pp. 129–35, 149.
[38] Ibid., pp. 135–49.

and southern Breisgau in the later sixteenth century can in the end only be explained by considerations of location. Despite overlapping hinterlands, the margraves had no compunction in promoting both Emmendingen and Malterdingen as market-places within Hachberg territory—finally raising Emmendingen to a town in 1590—because they both lay on a line of communication between the Black Forest and the Rhine valley, namely the river Elz. By means of targeted toll concessions Baden hoped to leave the Austrian towns on the Elz, Waldkirch and Kenzingen, high and dry. From the flow of goods sufficient revenues accrued to the margravial exchequer for Baden to contemplate with equanimity the gradual decline of the market at Eichstetten, whose location was strategically much less favourable, and whose function as a central place chiefly resided in supplying the margravial communes in the Kaiserstuhl. Here fiscal, not commercial, considerations were paramount. In the Markgräflerland, by contrast, Baden was primarily interested in securing the sale of its agrarian produce. The promotion of new markets would have contributed little to that goal, since the possibility of diverting commercial traffic from foreign markets hardly arose, given the existence of a consolidated territory, except in the case of Neuenburg and perhaps Staufen. In any case, the Markgräflerland was sufficiently provided with weekly and annual markets at Schopfheim, Kandern, and Lörrach—barring the exceptional case of Sulzburg, where the margraves toyed with the idea of establishing a staple for goods in everyday demand.[39]

In the third zone, therefore, the market principle was in part overlaid by the traffic/transport principle. In contrast to the first zone, however, the traffic principle was revealed as too weak to suppress competition from subordinate central places within such a narrow canvas, not in the first instance on account of a clash of seigneurial interests (that would rather have been the case on the left bank of the Rhine), but because the economic significance of the Breisgau was clearly inferior to that of Alsace, and because its agrarian sector derived a much smaller proportion of its revenues from supra-regional trade.[40]

---

[39] Ibid., p. 150.

[40] For the case of the Freiburg merchant Marx Hoff see Steven W. Rowan (ed.), 'Die Jahresrechnungen eines Freiburger Kaufmanns 1487/88. Ein Beitrag zur Handelsgeschichte des Oberrheins, mit einem Nachwort von Berent Schwineköper',

III

If, in conclusion, we attempt to place these findings in a wider context, several peculiarities must strike us. Only in the most general terms can we speak of a uniform urban landscape on the southern Upper Rhine—for instance, that Alsace was densely settled and highly urbanized in comparison with Lorraine or the French interior west of Vosges, both sparsely endowed with urban settlements. The epistemological value of this verdict is, however, slight. What counts is that this urban landscape devolved into three zones, whose structures recall the three central-place systems which since the days of Walter Christaller have been part of the historical geographer's repertoire. Despite justified reservations about applying this theory without further ado to the Middle Ages and the early modern period, the principle of central places possesses the undeniable advantage of absolving us from having to differentiate between towns, dwarf towns, market-places, or village markets in terms of their constitutional status or settlement geography. What is decisive is rather the 'surplus of importance' which attaches to them, in other words, how they relate to each other in terms of the goods on offer or the distribution of resources. A strict separation between town and market/village as functional categories becomes otiose, and has been deliberately bracketed in my argument. This central-place approach, moreover, opens a window to understanding why the term urban landscape may mislead in the context of the Upper Rhine. If we return to Franz Irsigler's distinction between urbanized and urban landscapes, then only the first zone of the Vosges foothills qualifies in any sense as an urbanized landscape. But this landscape, despite the high percentage of towns as a proportion of the total population, was an area of commercialized agriculture, whose 'urban quality' remained pretty modest. In legal and constitutional terms we may be dealing with towns, on occasion even with imperial free cities, but functionally

in Erich Maschke and Jürgen Sydow (eds), *Stadt und Umland* (Veröffentlichungen der Kommission für geschichtliche Landeskunde in Baden-Württemberg, B 82) (Stuttgart, 1974), pp. 227–77. For further reflections on the towns of the Breisgau see now Tom Scott, 'Städte und Märkte im spätmittelalterlichen Breisgau zwischen wirtschaftlicher Konkurrenz und Umlandsicherung', in Ursula Huggle and Thomas Zotz (eds), *Burgen, Märkte, kleine Städte. Mittelalterliche Herrschaftsbildung am südlichen Oberrhein, Das Markgräflerland*, 2 (2003), pp. 164–81.

speaking they were mostly jumped-up villages with a hardly perceptible 'surplus of importance' over against their hinterlands. As components of an urban network (to use the English term on account of its greater conceptual precision), only the entrepôts along the Ill would qualify by virtue of their function as distribution-points within an area of regular dispersion.

On both banks of the Rhine—and this compromises the notion of an urban network still further—the gulf between towns with sub-regional central-place functions (whether radial or axial) and the profusion of small urban settlements is particularly marked. Within the band of 4,000 to 6,000 inhabitants there fall on the left bank of the Rhine in Upper Alsace Colmar, in Lower Alsace Sélestat, Haguenau, and Wissembourg, on the right bank Freiburg and perhaps Offenburg. The remaining towns hardly reached 2,000 inhabitants. The only exceptions are Belfort and Mulhouse on the left bank, and Breisach on the right bank, which may at times have exceeded this threshold. Population size as such is not the issue here—and on no account should be equated with central-place ranking—but rather the connection with seemingly no intermediate stage between the very few medium-sized towns and the very numerous dwarf towns and market-places. Should this be regarded as a predictable regular dispersion, or rather as an imbalance in the provision of central places? Elsewhere I have argued that Christaller's ranking order may readily be applied in our period to the large and medium-sized towns, but threatens to break down in the face of a profusion of overlapping dwarf towns, so that one is obliged to have recourse to other models of centrality, an issue which will not be pursued in the present essay.[41] It should simply be pointed out that Freiburg, despite its repeated and plangently expressed grievances about rural competition in the fifteenth century, was hardly affected by the conflict between Baden and Habsburg in the sixteenth century, as the council once smugly observed.[42]

As urban landscapes zones 2 and 3 satisfy Irsigler's categories, inasmuch as the rural area retained a considerable weight of its own. But the many quasi-urban settlements only correspond inexactly to a central-place dispersion. On the right bank of the Rhine they owe

[41] Scott, *Regional Identity and Economic Change*, pp. 95–9.
[42] Ibid., p. 146. The same seems to have applied to Breisach.

their foundation and development to seigneurial or fiscal interests, which were directly at odds with an optimal central-place dispersion in terms of economic geography. Seigneurial interests also explain why competition between the small towns and markets did not promote, but rather retarded, economic growth. A genuine network of mutually complementary centres, as Jan de Vries has argued for parts of the northern Netherlands in his specialization model, could not emerge. There so-called *vlekken* existed as local entrepôts side by side with peasant villages engaged in agriculture. From an urban perspective, these new rural markets at the outset represented a threat to market privileges, but in the longer term they contributed to a tangible surge in economic growth, which also redounded to the towns' advantage.[43]

On the Upper Rhine, by contrast, the economy experienced the distortions already described. In saying that I am not retreating from my view, recently echoed by Rolf Kießling for Upper Swabia, that market foundations on the Upper Rhine up to 1500 should be regarded as the next stage in European economic growth after the wave of urban foundations in the high Middle Ages.[44] This assessment has recently been endorsed in principle by the researches of Stephan Epstein, for whom the profusion of new regional fairs and annual markets at the very time of late mediaeval demographic collapse and supposed economic crisis is a sign of economic concentration and specialization, and therewith growth, throughout Europe as a whole.[45]

After 1500 on the Upper Rhine, in Meinrad Schaab's phrase, a positive euphoria of market foundations continued into the eighteenth century, which gave rise to a mutually paralyzing mass of tiny central places.[46] What produced the paralysis was simply the bundle of

---

[43] Jan de Vries, *The Dutch Rural Economy in the Golden Age, 1500–1700* (New Haven, CT/London, 1974), pp. 7–11, 125–7, 155–7.

[44] Scott, *Regional Identity and Economic Change*, pp. 123 f.; Kießling, 'Zentralitätstheorie', p. 33.

[45] Stephan R. Epstein, *Freedom and Growth. The Rise of States and Markets in Europe, 1300–1750* (Routledge Explorations in Economic History, 17) (London/New York, 2000), pp. 74–88; idem, 'Regional Fairs, Institutional Innovation and Economic Growth in Late Medieval Europe', *Economic History Review*, 2nd series, 47 (1994), pp. 459–82.

[46] Meinrad Schaab, 'Städtlein, Burg-, Amts- und Marktflecken Südwestdeutschlands in Spätmittelalter und früher Neuzeit', in Emil Meynen (ed.), *Zentralität als Problem*

immunities and privileges which the central places claimed exclusively for themselves. The erection of such institutional barriers stood in the way of regional market integration, or of an efficient urban network, for the fragmentation of territories and the profusion of seigneurial market privileges increased negotiation, enforcement, and exaction costs.[47] Only intervention by the state (or principality, in the German context) was capable of overcoming jealously guarded autonomies in favour of an urban network of central-place settlements differentiated by function.[48] That was achieved in Swabia by means of a commercial *arrondissement* on the part of the metropolises.[49] On the Upper Rhine, a victim of territorial fragmentation and in the age of princely 'good police' increasingly relegated to the economic periphery, few steps in this direction were undertaken.

The degree of urbanization, therefore, is an inadequate pointer to the potential for economic development, particularly when the urban landscape consisted largely of small and dwarf towns.[50] Despite its advantageous location, range of resources, and complementary economic zones the Upper Rhine never succeeded in treading the path towards proto-industrialization, whose preconditions, after all, are commonly taken to have involved a considerable urban density and already-developed urban guild manufactures.[51] In comparison with its neighbours Württemberg and northern Switzerland, the Upper Rhine in the early modern period must indeed be regarded as backward. It also seems to contradict developments in Swabia and parts of Altbayern, where the small towns and markets created the frame-

---

der mittelalterlichen Stadtgeschichtsforschung (Städteforschung. Veröffentlichungen des Instituts für vergleichende Städtegeschichte in Münster, A 8) (Cologne/Weimar/Vienna, 1979), p. 265.

47 Epstein, *Freedom and Growth*, p. 8.

48 Idem, 'Introduction. Town and Country in Europe, 1300–1800', in idem (ed.), *Town and Country in Europe, 1300–1800* (Themes in International Urban History, 5) (Cambridge, 2001), pp. 18–19. In it he questions the thesis that the potential for conflict revolved around freedom of trade and the mobility of capital: see Charles Tilly and Wim P. Blockmans (eds), *Cities and the Rise of States in Europe, A.D. 1000 to 1800* (Boulder, CO, 1994).

49 On the divergent development in Altbayern, where the small towns suffered from a loss of centrality, see Carl A. Hoffmann, 'Territorialstadt und landesherrliche Politik in Altbayern. Aspekte des Verhältnisses in der Frühen Neuzeit', in Flachenecker and Kießling, *Städtelandschaften*, pp. 97–8.

50 See Epstein, 'Introduction', p. 11.

51 Idem, *Freedom and Growth*, pp. 108–10.

work for proto-industrialization, which from the seventeenth century was based in rural guilds specially established for that purpose.[52]

Against this background a heretical question may in conclusion be permitted, namely, whether in certain circumstances the existence of an urbanized landscape may not lead to a dead-end. We should be wary of thinking that seigneurial and fiscal considerations alone were to blame. Rather, we need to investigate which economic structures conduced to different outcomes in various types of urban landscape. At all events, we can be sure that the terms 'urban landscape' or 'urban network' contain no inherent explanatory capacity; even as descriptors they are neither unequivocal nor unambiguous.

---

[52] Kießling, 'Ländliches Gewerbe', pp. 62 f.; idem, 'Oberschwaben', pp. 32, 49; idem, 'Städtebünde', p. 108; idem, 'Zentralitätstheorie', p. 27.

CHAPTER ELEVEN

THE TERRITORIAL POLICY OF FREIBURG IM BREISGAU IN THE LATER MIDDLE AGES

The local government policy in the Federal Republic over the last decade of incorporating outlying communes under the umbrella of urban centres has been driven by various and frequently controversial motives.* Freiburg im Breisgau notoriously offers one particularly expansionist example. But in the case of Freiburg it should not be forgotten that a comparable extension of its territory had already taken place in the fifteenth century. Within the space of one hundred years the Austrian territorial town accumulated a block of rural possessions which remained intact until the nineteenth century, and which was only exceeded in size in the post-war period. The reasons behind the late mediaeval expansion are no less contradictory and complex than the contemporary, but local research has only occasionally and inadequately turned its attention to Freiburg's territorial policy in the later Middle Ages.

It may strike one as extraordinary that a territorial town, despite its dependence on Austria which should have robbed it of any room for political manoeuvre, was in any position to build up and retain an urban territory. In this respect, though, Freiburg did not stand alone within Outer Austria. In the Breisgau Breisach took second place behind Freiburg, while in the Black Forest both Villingen and Bräunlingen succeeded in acquiring a jurisdictionally subordinate hinterland. Among the scattered Austrian lordships in Swabia, moreover, Riedlingen and Ehingen in the Danube valley both possessed small urban territories.[1]

---

* Archives are cited by the following abbreviations:
GAOb: Gemeindearchiv Oberried
StAFr: Stadtarchiv Freiburg im Breisgau
TLA: Tiroler Landesarchiv, Innsbruck

[1] See Paul Revellio, 'Villingen, Bräunlingen und die Herrschaft Triberg', in Friedrich Metz (ed.), *Vorderösterreich. Eine geschichtliche Landeskunde*, 2nd edn (Freiburg im Breisgau, 1967), pp. 467–89; Franz Herberhold, 'Die österreichischen Donaustädte', ibid., pp. 705–28; Clemens Bauer, 'Ehingen an der Donau als vorderösterreichische Stadt', ibid., pp. 741–52.

This list, however, ignores the Austrian towns in Upper Alsace and the Sundgau, but their omission helps to explain how towns on the right bank of the Rhine could have succeeded. The much older Austrian possessions in Alsace constituted a consolidated whole (apart from a few exceptions such as the Val de Lièpvre). There the territorial fragmentation was lacking which in the rest of Outer Austria created a need for political and strategic security, achievable by territorial expansion. In addition, the Habsburgs from the outset administered their Austrian possessions along territorial lines: the lordships in Upper Alsace and the Sundgau were divided into bailiwicks, whose seat of administration was located in the district town (*Amtsstadt*). In this fashion the political and constitutional differences between town and country were largely ironed out: the towns were not constitutionally separated from their surrounding countryside. Much the same applies to Württemberg and to the margraviates of Baden where the smaller district towns rarely succeeded in establishing themselves as autonomous communes distinct from their hinterland.

The situation in the Breisgau, by contrast, was entirely different. Here the Habsburgs' acquisition of lordships was both late and scattered. They were never able to consolidate their possessions on the right bank of the Rhine, since they came up against the insuperable obstacle of the margravial lordships of Hachberg and Rötteln-Sausenberg-Badenweiler. Accordingly, the configuration of seigneurial rule developed differently.[2] In contradistinction to the striking gulf in Alsace between the imperial cities of the Decapolis and subordinate district towns, in the Breisgau two forms of territorial towns emerged: simple dependent towns under feudal seigneurs, such as Staufen, Waldkirch, Kenzingen, or Burkheim; and then the territorial towns proper (directly under Austrian territorial sovereignty), Freiburg, Breisach, Neuenburg, and Endingen. This distinction was recognized in the territorial Diets, where only those towns without feudal overlords enjoyed rights of attendance and participation as members of the territorial Estates (*Landstandschaft*). These observations make plain that the four Breisgau territorial towns occupied a privileged position within the Outer Austrian community of subjects that

---

[2] See Hans Erich Feine, 'Die Territorialbildung der Habsburger im deutschen Südwesten vornehmlich im späten Mittelalter', *Zeitschrift der Savigny-Stiftung für Rechtsgeschichte, Germanistische Abteilung*, 67 (1950), pp. 176–308.

allowed them much greater room for manoeuvre and exercise of influence than the remaining Austrian dependent towns. Freiburg in particular was bound to exercise political responsibility and leadership as the mightiest town of Outer Austria, as long as the seat of government remained in the otherwise largely insignificant district town of Ensisheim. This alerts us to the fact that Freiburg's territorial policy could also lie in Austria's interest, if it contributed to the strengthening of the town's position of power. In assessing Freiburg's acquisitions policy in the 1490s this factor deserves particular emphasis, but has largely been overlooked or misunderstood in the literature so far.

That should not be taken to mean that the town seized upon its emancipation from the counts of Freiburg and its transfer to Austria in 1368 as an opportunity to launch a deliberate territorial policy. The roots of this policy also risk being misconstrued if we focus simply on the progressive acquisition of territory. The term territorial policy should not be applied narrowly to imply that it only embraced the purchase of villages and estates. The town's influence over its surrounding countryside took many forms on many levels, ranging from alliances, rights of access, to treaties of outburghership.[3] Above all, territorial policy cannot be seen in a vacuum, but should rather be set in the context of the town's wider political interests, of which it was the ultimate and most radical expression. Even viewing Freiburg's territorial policy within the web of town-country relations can mislead, since the latter were themselves shaped and conditioned by the situation of the town after 1368. What changes in Freiburg's situation as a whole resulted from its acceptance of Austrian territorial sovereignty?

Emancipation from the counts did indeed bring political advantages to the town, since it gained appreciable room for manoeuvre within the Austrian community of subjects, especially as the territorial ruler himself resided in distant Innsbruck or even Vienna, but it signalled a financial catastrophe. The enormous sums that the town had to raise for its discharge as well as the costs of the war of liberation

[3] Wolfgang Leiser, *'Sie dienen auch jetzt noch aber fremden Göttern.' Der Freiburger Herrschaftswechsel 1368* (Veröffentlichungen des Alemannischen Instituts, 25) (Freiburg im Breisgau, 1968), p. 15. See also Tom Scott, *Freiburg and the Breisgau. Town-Country Relations in the Age of Reformation and Peasants' War* (Oxford, 1986).

were by no means covered by the Austrian indemnity, which the dukes in any case were only able to pay in instalments after contracting numerous mortgages.[4] The loans which Freiburg was obliged to pay, particularly from citizens of Basel, had led within five years to a mountain of debt totalling around 120,000 fl., an altogether stupendous figure for the time.[5] The annual interest charges and repayment of capital weighed upon the civic budget throughout the entire fifteenth century. Not until the mid-sixteenth century could Freiburg once again count itself financially reasonably solvent.[6] The burden of debt paralyzed the economy of the town as a whole. High

---

[4] Freiburg had to buy the lordship of Badenweiler for 25,000 fl. as compensation to the counts, pay 5,000 marks of silver for the ransom of its prisoners and hand over another 15,000 marks to the counts in cash. Initially, only 1,800 marks of the last sum could be paid, with sixty citizens having to stand surety for the outstanding 13,200 marks. Johannes Lahusen, 'Die Urkunden über Freiburgs i. Br. Übergang an Österreich 1368', *Mitteilungen des Instituts für österreichische Geschichtsforschung*, 34 (1913), p. 120. Cf. Feine, 'Territorialbildung', p. 248; Leiser, *Herrschaftswechsel*, p. 19. According to the then prevailing exchange rate a total debt of around 145,000 fl. was reached. In recognition of its acknowledgement of Austrian sovereignty the town was promised 32,000 fl. by the Habsburgs (strictly, 30,000 fl., with another 2,000 fl. as interest). By 1377 this sum had been paid, barring a final 2,400 fl. TLA, Schatzarchiv, Urk. I. 2342 (13 Aug. 1375): receipt for 5,600 fl.; ibid., 2340 (7 Dec. 1377): receipt for 2,000 fl. (I am grateful to Dr Konrad Ruser (Freiburg) for this information.) The data given by Martin Wellmer, 'Der vorderösterreichische Breisgau', in Metz, *Vorderösterreich*, p. 280 should be correspondingly corrected. On these issues see now fundamentally Willy Schulze, 'Herrschaftswechsel und städtische Verschuldung. Bemerkungen zur finanziellen Lage Freiburgs im späten Mittelalter', *Zeitschrift des Breisgau-Geschichtsvereins ('Schau-ins-Land')*, 111 (1992), pp. 25–46; and idem, 'Der Freiburger Herrschaftswechsel 1368 als finanzielle Großtransaktion', ibid., 114 (1995), pp. 27–55.

[5] Between 1365 and 1370 Freiburg raised 3,842 marks of silver; £4,765 Rappen pence; and 86,148 fl., a total capital debt of 118,730 fl. This capital bore 5%, giving an annual interest charge of 6,000 fl. After 1370 further sums were raised, but also the first repayments undertaken. But throughout the 15th century the burden of interest payments never fell below 6,000 fl. *per annum*. See StAFr, B 1 255: Hermann Flamm, 'Skizze einer Geschichte der Anleihepolitik der Stadt Freiburg im Breisgau bis zum Ausgang des Mittelalters', pp. 1a–2a. The burden of debt corresponds fairly exactly to the shortfall between payments to the counts and the Austrian indemnity.

[6] See Norbert Ohler, 'Zum Haushalt der Stadt Freiburg im Breisgau im 16. und 17. Jahrhundert', *Zeitschrift des Breisgau-Geschichtsvereins ('Schau-ins-Land')*, 94/95 (1976/77), pp. 253–89; idem, 'Strukturen des Finanzhaushalts der Stadt Freiburg i. Br. in der frühen Neuzeit', *Zeitschrift für die Geschichte des Oberrheins*, 125 (1977), pp. 97–140; idem, 'Freiburg i. Br. im 16. und 17. Jahrhundert. Kreditaufnahme und Geldanlage der Stadt', in Hans Fenske, Wolfgang Reinhard, and Ernst Schulin (eds), *Historia Integra. Festschrift für Erich Hassinger zum 70. Geburtstag* (Berlin, 1977), pp. 155–71. See also Scott, *Freiburg and the Breisgau*, pp. 114–15.

direct and indirect taxation drove citizens to emigrate and deterred potential immigrants; a Keynesian policy of economic expansion was out of the question because any capital for investment was largely eaten up by debt repayment and interest charges. That the town did not go bankrupt (unlike a number of German towns in the fifteenth century) is testimony to its fierce will to survive.[7]

The town's debt was so damaging because its economic vitality was also on the wane. The efflorescence of the thirteenth and fourteenth centuries had developed on the back of extensive long-distance trade, which in turn rested upon the yield of silver-mining on the Schauinsland. From the mid-fourteenth century both yields and investment were dwindling, above all on account of the increasing technical difficulties and costs of extraction.[8] The incipient economic decline led to a crippling loss of population, which reduced the taxable capacity of the remaining inhabitants and therewith additionally hampered the debt repayment. The merchants who had set their commercial stamp upon the town retreated with growing frequency to the countryside, where they were absorbed into the lower nobility,[9] leaving behind them the mass of ordinary craftsmen to face a deteriorating economic livelihood. As a result, the town sank back to the level of a middling artisan community, whose economy was increasingly dominated by the interests of the guilds, who had gained tangible political power for the first time in 1392 and who were able in the course of the fifteenth century to establish themselves as the leading political force within the town.

In contrast to the age of long-distance trade Freiburg now lived increasingly from the exchange of goods with the surrounding countryside; craft goods were traded against agrarian produce at the town's

---

[7] Idem, 'Relations between Freiburg im Breisgau and the Surrounding Countryside in the Age of South-West German Agrarian Unrest before the Peasants' War' (Ph.D. Cambridge, 1973), pp. 85–153, which extensively corrects the older account by Hermann Flamm, *Der wirtschaftliche Niedergang Freiburgs i. Br. und die Lage des städtischen Grundeigentums im 14. und 15. Jahrhundert* (Volkswirtschaftliche Abhandlungen der badischen Hochschulen, 8, supplement 3) (Karlsruhe, 1905).

[8] Albrecht Schlageter, 'Der mittelalterliche Bergbau im Schauinslandrevier', *Zeitschrift des Breisgau-Geschichtsvereins ('Schau-ins-Land')*, 88 (1970), pp. 157–61; Paul Priesner, *Die Geschichte der Gemeinde Hofsgrund (Schauinsland)*, 1: *Der Bergbau im Schauinsland von 1340 bis 1954* (Freiburg im Breisgau, 1982).

[9] See Hermann Nehlsen, *Die Freiburger Familie Snewlin. Rechts- und sozialgeschichtliche Studien zur Entwicklung des mittelalterlichen Bürgertums* (Veröffentlichungen aus dem Archiv der Stadt Freiburg im Breisgau, 9) (Freiburg im Breisgau, 1967).

market. Relations with the town's immediate hinterland therefore took on a new importance and underwent significant change after 1368. Even before that date the growth of population and shortage of resources had obviously led to the town's penetration of the surrounding countryside. The extensive civic forests, which still largely exist today, stem essentially from acquisitions of the fourteenth century.[10] In addition, individual burghers and institutions acquired estates and revenues in the countryside—the most striking example being the Holy Ghost Hospital. The attraction of the burgeoning town prompted surrounding nobles to purchase citizen's rights, and acquire town residences, where they could lead a convivial social life away from their draughty, rat-infested castles on the land. But peasants too could acquire burgher's rights if their lords consented; many rural subjects of the counts of Freiburg swore a burgher's oath and therewith came under the town's protection.

After its liberation from the counts Freiburg had above all to maintain and strengthen its political influence over its hinterland. But it would be quite erroneous to suppose that this policy initially or primarily involved the construction of a dependent territory. Rather, the town was concerned to restore relations with the nobility, which had come under great strain during the war of liberation, since the majority of the Breisgau nobility had fought on count Egon's side against the town. The nobility, after all, dominated the countryside and could cut off the town's livelihood at will by preventing their subjects supplying Freiburg with produce. This was graphically demonstrated in 1476 as the council was contemplating a thoroughgoing revision and reform of the civic administration. In the constant search for new sources of revenue the council proposed to tax the nobility more heavily by upping the annual composition-fee which they paid for their citizen's rights (*Satzbürgerrecht*). But the Outer Austrian governor Wilhelm von Rappoltstein, himself a member of a distinguished Alsatian noble dynasty, pointed out that the nobility might take revenge by severing the town's arteries. The council accordingly desisted from its plan: 'That the nobles might cause their subjects (*arme Leute*) to cease delivering produce to the town, which gave rise

[10] Helmut Brandl, *Der Stadtwald von Freiburg. Eine forst- und wirtschaftsgeschichtliche Untersuchung über die Beziehung zwischen Waldnutzung und wirtschaftlicher Entwicklung der Stadt Freiburg vom Mittelalter bis zur Gegenwart* (Veröffentlichungen aus dem Archiv der Stadt Freiburg im Breisgau, 12) (Freiburg im Breisgau, 1970).

to all sorts of fears of a decline in our affairs.'[11] In reality, the town could not dispense with its nobility. The constitution of 1392 had provided that the mayor must always be a nobleman; a portion of the council had to be supplied by nobles, although in the course of the fifteenth century it became increasingly difficult to hold them to this obligation. But there were also tangible advantages for the town in maintaining good relations with the nobility. The noble outburghers made a significant contribution to the town's revenues through the composition-fee and the wine excise. Their military service was placed at the town's disposal during the many campaigns of the fifteenth century. And in general their burgher's rights as such constituted an important political link to the town's hinterland, although the acceptance of peasant outburghers often soured relations between the town and the nobility.

The acquisition of peasant outburghers (paleburghers) was the first direct step in extending the town's sphere of influence over its hinterland, but it had been initiated well before 1368. With the creation of consolidated territories in the fifteenth century, especially the efforts by the margraves of Baden, the acceptance of peasant outburghers ran into increasing difficulties, since their status implied that they were exempted from the legal and fiscal community of the village and subject instead to urban financial and military obligations. At the time of its transfer to Austria Freiburg had had to promise the margraves and other lords of the Breisgau to dispose of its outburghers.[12] Nevertheless, Freiburg—and to a lesser extent Breisach—was able to retain its peasant outburghers throughout the fifteenth century despite protracted legal battles. In this respect Freiburg was altogether the exception among south-west German territorial towns.[13]

Why should Freiburg have clung so resolutely to its outburghers, given that they only led to growing conflict with the neighbouring village lords? Yet the outburghers were a means of propping up the

---

[11] StAFr, B 5 XIIIa, 4, fo. 30r–v (9 Dec. 1476): *so möchten die edellut mit iren armen luten bestellen, das sy die statt mit fruchten zufüren vermitten, und stünd allerhand sorgen und abgangs uff den dingen.*

[12] Johann Heinrich Schreiber (ed.), *Urkundenbuch der Stadt Freiburg im Breisgau*, 2 vols (Freiburg im Breisgau, 1828–29), 1, pp. 516–19.

[13] Scott, 'Relations', pp. 217 ff. See now also idem, 'Städte und Märkte im spätmittelalterlichen Breisgau zwischen wirtschaftlicher Konkurrenz und Umlandsicherung', in Ursula Huggle and Thomas Zotz (eds), *Burgen, Märkte, kleine Städte. Mittelalterliche Herrschaftsbildung am südlichen Oberrhein, Das Markgräflerland*, 2 (2003), pp. 168–9.

town's much weakened demographic, financial, and military situation as long as Freiburg was unable to stabilize its oppidan population and economy, quite apart from the fact that Freiburg thereby acquired a certain degree of support in the countryside. The town's ability to keep hold of its outburghers into the sixteenth century, however, was bought at the cost of treating them on a par with seigneurial serfs.[14] Even so, between 1505 and 1549 the town was forced to sell its three largest outburgher communities—Waltershofen, Merdingen, and Neuershausen—to the village lords (who were all themselves noble outburghers of the town) in return for sizeable compensation, thereby abandoning its jurisdictional authority over them. Nevertheless, a considerable number of outburghers remained in other villages of the Outer Austrian Breisgau, until the town resolved to get rid of them altogether at the end of the sixteenth century.[15] By that time the focus of the town's territorial policy had long since shifted from the acceptance of peasant outburghers to the acquisition of a landed territory.

The relationship of the town with its hinterland should not be judged solely in the light of economic and strategic criteria. The switch from long-distance trade to exchange with its immediate market area placed much more emphasis on the hinterland in terms of economy and its location within a transport network. In this respect it was fatal for the town that its economic decline coincided with a burgeoning rural economy, which only served to exacerbate the former. As early as 1446 the town had complained 'how the town of Freiburg has suffered a marked decline on account of all trade and crafts spreading in the countryside'.[16] This grievance, which was iterated throughout the fifteenth and sixteenth centuries with increasing frequency, was regularly tabled by the Breisgau towns at the territorial Diets.[17] The great harm to the civic market and urban toll receipts was attested by the town in a submission to archduke

[14] See Claudia Ulbrich, *Leibherrschaft am Oberrhein im Spätmittelalter* (Veröffentlichungen des Max-Planck-Instituts für Geschichte, 58) (Göttingen, 1979), pp. 198–9.

[15] Ibid., p. 201.

[16] StAFr, A 1 VII b (14), 1443 (*recte*: 1446), folder D: *wie ein statt fryburg . . . mercklich zü abgang komen sigen durch das, das alle gewerb und handtwerck uff dem land geuffet werden.*

[17] StAFr, C 1 Landstände 1, 1453–1517: Grievances of the third Estate, n.d. (after 1504), fo. 1v; cf. Schreiber, *Urkundenbuch*, 2, p. 677 (1499).

Sigismund in 1486: 'Our markets decline, all trade, salt, iron, cloth, and other commodities subject to the civic weights and measures, all crafts and bath-houses are increasing around us, so that the common man cannot make a livelihood.'[18]

The Freiburg market was also threatened by competition from new country markets, particularly those in the margraviate of Baden.[19] Although these village markets, held once a week, were on their own in no position to encroach upon the much visited Freiburg market held every weekday, taken in the round they did represent a serious challenge—a series of small pinpricks, as it were, which together tore open a gaping wound. The shortfall in customs and market revenues was made even worse by the construction of new turnpikes from the Rhine valley over the Black Forest, which evaded the toll-bars on roads controlled by Freiburg and bypassed the civic market. In transport terms Freiburg did not lie on a north-south axis, for the road followed the Rhine on its left bank in Alsace, but rather on an east-west axis which led through the Dreisam valley via the Höllsteige and Wagensteig to Donaueschingen and Villingen. But in 1467 a new road suitable for carts was driven through the Simonswald, which linked the margraviate of Hachberg with Furtwangen and the eastern Black Forest. Freiburg protested vociferously that 'thereby a palpable decline in tolls and transit-dues had been inflicted on our gracious lordship of Austria and the common weal of this town'.[20] Not until 1483 did Freiburg and Villingen succeed after many attempts in destroying and barring this route for a protracted period.[21]

But that did little to remove the danger of such competition. In 1496 a new road through the Prech valley to Hornberg was built;[22] and in the sixteenth century there were frequent attempts not only to convert the drover's path through the Simonswald once again into a cart-track, but also to lay a second road through the Glotter

[18] StAFr, B 5 XI, 5/3, fo. 71r: *unser merckt gond ab, alle gewerb, salcz, ysen, tüch, und ander kouff fronwagen, alle handtwerk und badstuben werden umb uns gemeret, und mag sich der gemain man nit enthalten.*

[19] Scott, 'Relations', pp. 113 f.; see now in general idem, *Regional Identity and Economic Change. The Upper Rhine, 1450–1600* (Oxford, 1997), pp. 125–49.

[20] StAFr, A 1 VI b (9), 1473–84, folder A: *dadurch vorab unser gnedigen herrschaft von Österrich und ein gemein nucz diser stat mercklicher abgang an zöllen und gevellen zu gefügt worden.*

[21] StAFr, A 1 VI b (18), 10 Aug. 1484; (19), 31 Aug. 1484; (20), 29 Sept. 1484.

[22] StAFr, A 1 VI b (29), 2 Aug. 1496.

valley to St Peter.[23] It is quite understandable, therefore, that the town was obliged to turn its attention with increased urgency to the control of its existentially vital hinterland.

With that we have arrived at the nub of Freiburg's territorial policy in the later Middle Ages. Once again, it needs to be stressed that the town's territorial aspirations after 1368 were not absorbed by a single comprehensive and consistently applied policy of territorial purchases. This emerges from a systematic enumeration, which divides the acquisitions into three separate categories:

1. Rounding off the town's civic territory through the incorporation of neighbouring suburbs and villages. That includes:
   a) In 1412 purchase of the village of Adelhausen as a mortgage from Austria, i.e. the acquisition of that part of the village which lay outwith the town's boundaries, though another part of the village, known as old Adelhausen, had passed to Austria in 1368 along with the town. This mortgage was briefly redeemed in 1456 and transferred to a third party, but was finally restored to Freiburg in 1459. With that the town took possession of the extensive soke of Adelhausen with considerable forest, over which it became embroiled in a sharp dispute with the abbey of Günterstal.[24]
   b) In 1510 acquisition of the jurisdictional rights and subjects of old Adelhausen from Bartholome Snewlin after almost a century of wrangling. Therewith the town could at last combine jurisdictional authority over its southern suburbs in one hand, although it was always at pains to respect the particular situation of the mortgaged village of Adelhausen by instituting separate village courts for the Wiehre and old Adelhausen on one hand and the village of Adelhausen on the other.[25]
   c) In 1457 purchase of the manor and village of Herdern from the Freiburg commandery of the Teutonic Order for 2,550 fl. This purchase brought legal complications in its wake, for

[23] StAFr, B 5 XI, 12, fo. 100v–101r, 104r–v.

[24] See Tom Scott, 'Zu den Rechts- und Besitzverhältnissen eines Freiburger Vorortes. Das Dorf Adelhausen im 15. Jahrhundert', *Zeitschrift des Breisgau-Geschichtsvereins ('Schau-ins-Land')*, 101 (1982), pp. 97–106.

[25] Ibid., p. 99.

supreme ownership lay with the counts of Fürstenberg, who maintained that the Teutonic Knights had taken on the fief without their permission. Although Herdern remained Freiburg's, a bitter legal quarrel broke out in the early 1460s between its inhabitants and the council, whom they accused of various infringements of their ancient village rights. Not until 1538 did Freiburg succeed in acquiring full rights of ownership from Fürstenberg for 575 fl. Thereupon the path was finally cleared for Herdern to be incorporated into the town as a suburb with equal rights.[26]

2. The acquisition of villages beyond the town's immediate civic territory. That includes:
   a) In 1381 the purchase of Betzenhausen for 18 marks of silver (approximately 135 fl.). The village was not incorporated into the urban community, but remained part of Freiburg's landed territory. Its inhabitants were denied burgher's rights and admission to the civic guilds. Instead, they were treated as feudal subjects, had to perform labour-services in the Mooswald, and did not even enjoy preferential toll-rates.[27]
   b) In 1496 acquisition of three mortgaged margravial villages, Opfingen, Wolfenweiler, and Haslach, from Beatrix von Munzingen for 2,900 fl., of which only 1,700 fl. were paid out; the outstanding 1,200 fl. were transformed into an annual *rente* of 60 fl. These villages, however, did not remain long under Freiburg's control, for in 1503 the mortgage was redeemed, and the villages reverted to the overlordship of the margraves of Baden.[28]
   c) In 1543 Freiburg bought the lordship of Kirchhofen for 11,000 fl. from the heirs of Hans Christoph von Hattstatt. Within two years the town had sold it on to the imperial councillor Dr Andreas Könritz.[29]

---

[26] Idem, 'Relations', pp. 188 f.; idem, *Freiburg and the Breisgau*, pp. 40, 98–9; Ulbrich, *Leibherrschaft*, pp. 194 f.

[27] Scott, 'Relations', pp. 187 f.; idem, *Freiburg and the Breisgau*, pp. 39–40.

[28] StAFr, B 5 XIIIa, 4, fo. 34v; Scott, 'Relations', pp. 193 f.; idem, *Freiburg and the Breisgau*, pp. 40–1.

[29] StAFr, A 1 XIX Kirchhofen (3), 30 May 1543; C 1 Fremde Orte, Kirchhofen 12; Statistisches Landesamt Baden-Württemberg (ed.), *Freiburg im Breisgau. Stadtkreis und Landkreis. Amtliche Kreisbeschreibung*, 2 vols (Freiburg im Breisgau, 1965–74), 2, 1, p. 574.

d) In 1582 Freiburg bought a share of the village of Horben for 2,600 fl. and thereafter extended its rights to the point where by the beginning of the eighteenth century it had brought the entire village under its landlordship.[30]
e) Finally, in 1587 Freiburg bought the village of Lehen from the heirs of the lords of Stadion for 24,000 fl. That marked the end of Freiburg's rather heterogeneous acquisition of villages, whose focus had lain chiefly in the sixteenth century.[31]

3. The construction of a landed territory in the Dreisam valley (see Map 11.1).

At the outset it is remarkable how long Freiburg hesitated in taking such an obvious step in view of its precarious situation. The destruction of the robber barons' strongholds of Birchiberg, and Falkenstein in the Dreisam valley by the town between 1379 and 1391[32] (the wilde Schneeburg had been razed at the beginning of the fourteenth century and its land acquired in 1365)[33] did not form the starting-point for the construction of a territory, as happened in other towns.[34]

Not until 1462 did the first purchase occur, when the council resolved to buy the entire lordship of the abbey of St Märgen for 4,800 fl., which subsequently constituted the bailiwicks of St Märgen, Wagensteig, and Zarten. The following year the council rounded off its jurisdictional authority by purchasing the rights of stewardship from Hans von Landeck for a further 1,000 fl.[35] But it took another thirty years before the town decided to close the gap in its possessions between Zarten and the civic territory. Between 1491 and 1495 the village and castle of Kirchzarten were bought from David von

[30] StAFr, A 1 VIII a δ (23), 3 Jan. 1582; *Amtliche Kreisbeschreibung*, 2, 1, p. 478.
[31] StAFr, A 1 VIII a ε (19), 2 Nov. 1587; *Amtliche Kreisbeschreibung*, 2, 2, p. 630.
[32] Schreiber, *Urkundenbuch*, 2, pp. 16–22; ibid., pp. 59–83.
[33] Schreiber, *Urkundenbuch*, 1, pp. 203–6; Fritz Armbruster, 'Die Freiburger Talvogtei im Dreisamtal', in Metz, *Vorderösterreich*, p. 367.
[34] As, for example, in Braunschweig. See Heinz Germer, *Die Landgebietspolitik der Stadt Braunschweig bis zum Ausgang des 15. Jahrhunderts* (Studien und Vorarbeiten zum Historischen Atlas von Niedersachsen, 16) (Göttingen, 1937), pp. 14, 18.
[35] Fritz Armbruster, 'Die Freiburger Talvogtei im Dreisamtal. Studien zur Entwicklung und zur Verfassungsgeschichte bis zum Jahre 1661' (Diss. jur. Freiburg im Breisgau, 1950); Scott, 'Relations', p. 195; idem, *Freiburg and the Breisgau*, p. 42; Wolfgang Müller, 'Studien zur Geschichte der Klöster St. Märgen und Allerheiligen, Freiburg im Breisgau', *Freiburger Diözesan-Archiv*, 89 (1969), pp. 53–4.

Blumeneck and Konrad von Halfingen; in 1493 the jurisdictional lordship over Himmelreich from Martin von Blumeneck; in 1499 the Atten valley as an Austrian mortgage from the abbey of St Peter; and finally in 1502 the three Erlenhof farms and the annual toll at Zarten from the counts of Fürstenberg. These purchases came in total to 3,285 fl.[36] The Birkenreute estate, which the town had sought to buy in 1462, only came into civic ownership in 1556 for the inflationary sum of 4,050 fl.[37]

These lands were brought together as an administrative entity, the so-called Valley Bailiwick, which survived until the creation of the grand duchy of Baden in 1806. But the lands never constituted a unified territory, and the town apparently undertook no further efforts to close the politically sensitive gap at Ebnet. Nevertheless, the establishment of the Valley Bailiwick created the essential foundation for control of the Dreisam valley and access to the Black Forest. This significant acquisition was considerably strengthened in 1495/96 by taking over the stewardship of the two priories of Oberried. The priory of Oberried *in suburbio* held the landlordship of the Kappel valley, while the priory of Oberried *in Nigra silva*—in the St Wilhelm valley—controlled the entire area of Oberried between Geroldstal and Hofsgrund.[38] Together these territories formed a large block above Kirchzarten, which was never integrated into the Valley Bailiwick, but whose stewardship allowed the town to exert considerable influence at the heart of its strategic interests (see Map 11.1).

How should these three separate strands in the town's territorial policy be interpreted? Since Freiburg's territorial policy was not unique in the later Middle Ages, a comparison with other towns may give clues to its origins and aims. From her investigation of Lübeck and Zürich Elisabeth Raiser has derived a typology of the main phases of development in urban territorial policy. She identifies five stages:

---

[36] Scott, 'Relations', pp. 195 f.; idem, *Freiburg and the Breisgau*, p. 44; StAFr, A 1 VI d (94), 28 June 1502.

[37] Max Weber, 'Die Kirchzartner Geschichte', in Günther Haselier (ed.), *Kirchzarten. Geographie—Geschichte—Gegenwart* (Kirchzarten, 1966), p. 245.

[38] StAFr, B 5 XIIIa, 4a, fo. 32r–v; Scott, *Freiburg and the Breisgau*, pp. 44–5. See GAOb, Plan der Gemarkungen Oberried, St. Wilhelm, Zastler und Weilersbach, 1830. I am grateful to Paul Priesner for supplying me with a copy of this map.

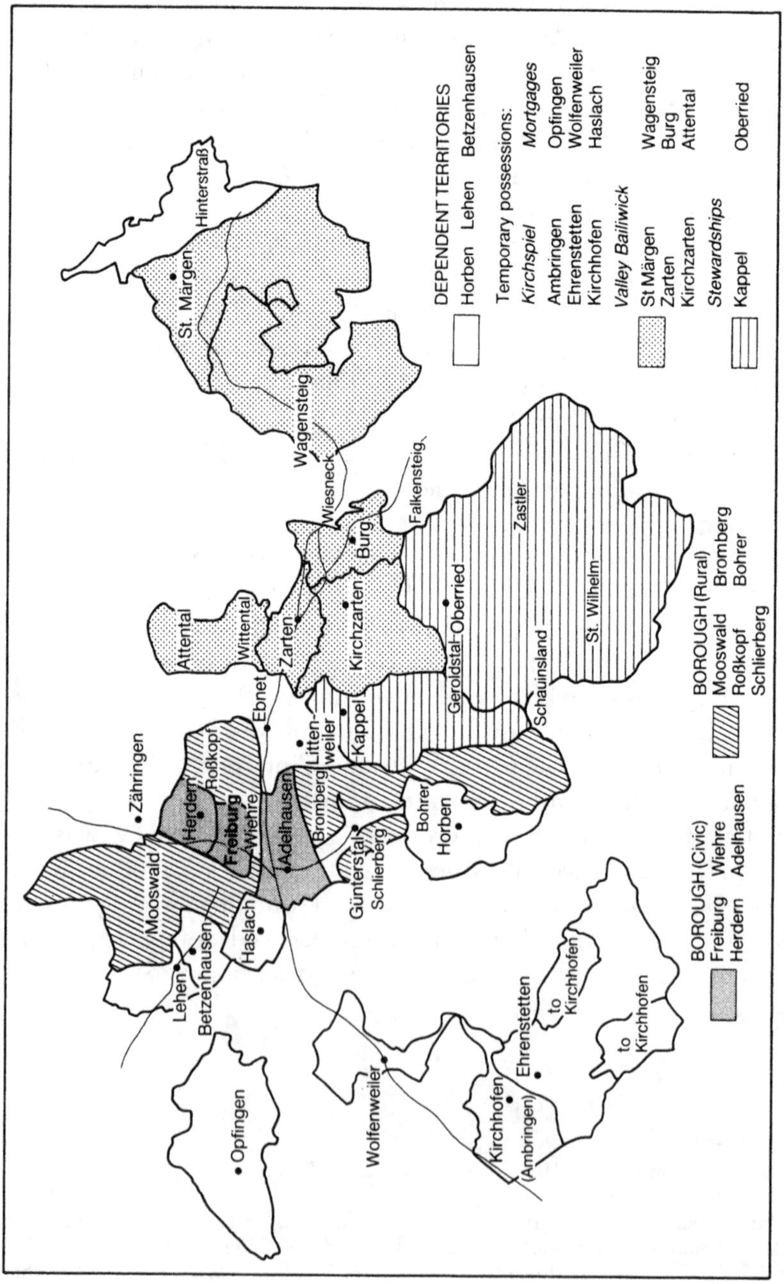

Map 11.1. Freiburg's territorial development to 1600.

1. Extension of the urban common and forest (*Stadt-* or *Feldmark*).
2. Acquisitions beyond the town of estates and revenues by individual burghers or institutions (in contrast to a deliberate policy of acquisitions directed by the council).
3. Opportunity purchases by the town (the council) itself.
4. A deliberate policy of territorial expansion by the town.
5. Extension and consolidation of the acquired territory or rights of overlordship by the town.[39]

If we apply these criteria to Freiburg, we can detect straight away a large degree of congruence in chronological terms. The first two phases can already be observed in Freiburg before 1368. Opportunity purchases by contrast only occur in the late fourteenth century, above all in the case of Betzenhausen. Subsequent purchases of villages retain something of this character. That a territorial policy properly speaking only begins thereafter is entirely confirmed by Freiburg's experience: the acquisitions in the Dreisam valley took place between 1462 and 1502 (or 1556); moreover, they were accomplished relatively quickly, so that by the sixteenth century all that remained was to consolidate the territory by administrative standardization. Thereafter no changes of substance occurred either in the extent of the territory or in its administration.

At first glance, therefore, Freiburg's territorial policy displays nothing surprising or deviant. But on closer inspection considerable doubts arise. It is simple enough to explain the rounding off of its civic territory, even if the acquisition of rights in Adelhausen threw up legal complications. In the case of Herdern, however, other motives were at work. Unlike Betzenhausen, Herdern was a prosperous village, whose inhabitants derived their livelihood not only from viticulture and tillage but also from the cultivation of the much rarer and more precious crop of saffron.[40] That fiscal reasons lay behind the purchase is demonstrated by Freiburg's efforts from 1463 onwards to alter the old weights and measures, to collect all the court-fines, and to introduce the higher-rate toll paid by foreigners.[41] The resentment

[39] Elisabeth Raiser, *Städtische Territorialpolitik im Mittelalter. Eine vergleichende Untersuchung über verschiedene Formen am Beispiel Lübecks und Zürichs* (Historische Studien, 406) (Lübeck/Hamburg, 1969), pp. 52–3.

[40] Schreiber, *Urkundenbuch*, 2, p. 446.

[41] StAFr, A 1 VIII a γ (43), *circa* 1460; Scott, *Freiburg and the Breisgau*, pp. 98–9.

which these steps occasioned led to renewed unrest in 1481.[42] In the case of villages beyond the civic territory it is striking that the purchases make little chronological sense, and seem for a long time to have had no further consequences. Betzenhausen was obviously an opportunity purchase. The village was too small and insignificant to bring the town much advantage; it could hardly have formed the nucleus of a landed territory in the Freiburg basin (*Freiburger Becken*). It had belonged to Freiburg citizens from the beginning of the fourteenth century;[43] in 1381 it had already been offered for sale once, and the modest purchase price allowed the town to seize the opportunity despite its high indebtedness.

That the town was not primarily concerned to extend its influence westwards can be seen from the short-term acceptance of the margravial villages of Opfingen, Wolfenweiler, and Haslach. This acquisition, the result of a disputed inheritance, followed upon the king Maximilian's express command, for he wanted to use Freiburg as a trustee until the case was settled. The town itself had considerable reservations, as a note by the then town clerk Ulrich Zasius makes clear:

> The council has been approached and solicited to take on the mortgage of Opfingen, Wolfenweiler, and Haslach. The council discussed the matter and weighed many things, gain or loss, advantage or disadvantage, usefulness or burden, fire, warfare; that His Royal Majesty might consider us mightier than we are, etc, and took many other aspects into account. And it was resolved with the aldermen, old and new councillors, to take it on.[44]

The fear that Maximilian might have overestimated the financial load-capacity of the town was accompanied by a reluctance to become involved with the margraves of Baden. The acquisition of the three villages occurred just at the point where the town's purchases in the Dreisam valley were reaching their climax. If the town had evinced a genuine interest in westwards expansion, it would surely have bent all its efforts to seize the opportunity of retaining the mortgage.

---

[42] StAFr, A 1 VIII a γ (56), 1481–2; Scott, *Freiburg and the Breisgau*, p. 99.

[43] *Amtliche Kreisbeschreibung*, 1, 2, p. 873.

[44] StAFr, B 5 XIIIa, 4a, fo. 34v: *Es ist an ein rat getragen und geworben, die pfandschaft opfingen, wolfenweiler, hasla an sich ze lösen; das ward in eim rat von geredt und menigerley ermessen, gwin und verlust, vor und nachteil, nutz und bswärd, brunst, kriegslöff, königliche maiestät uns mächtiger möcht achten, dann wir wären, etc., und vil andre stuck betracht. Und ist mit ächtwer, nuw und alten räten erkent, den anzenemen.*

The acquisition of Kirchhofen is even more bizarre, as perhaps the council realized, disposing of the village after a mere two years. I am inclined to regard the brief ownership of Kirchhofen as an opportunity purchase, particularly since the town's finances were on the mend from 1540 onwards, so that speculative transactions of this kind could be contemplated. Admittedly, Freiburg had contrived to maintain a sizeable outburgher community in the so-called Parish (*Kirchspiel*), comprising Kirchhofen, Ambringen, and Ehrenstetten, so that acquiring rights of lordship may have been intended to bolster the protection of its subjects. The acquisition of Horben and Lehen seems to have followed the logic of *arrondissement*, which need not surprise us. We should recall, though, that from around 1550 the town was accumulating sometimes quite considerable surpluses in the civic budget for the first time in two centuries, so that the purchase of the two villages may have been intended as a capital investment. According to Norbert Ohler's recent researches, the town in this period astonishingly never invested its surpluses but simply carried them forward in the accounts from year to year.[45]

The reasons for the construction of a territory in the Dreisam valley seem in the light of the economic and transport interests of the town so transparent that researchers hitherto have assumed that the town was following a targeted and consistent policy. This view is in need of urgent revision. There is no question that the town's general situation made territorial expansion in the Dreisam valley desirable, but it would be unwise to conclude that the town always acted on the logic of its own best insight. It is essential to judge its territorial policy not only in the light of Freiburg's subjective requirements but equally in the light of its objective possibilities. From this perspective the establishment of the Valley Bailiwick in the Dreisam valley takes on a quite different character.

In the first place, it is noticeable that the acquisition of St Märgen's landlordship took place a mere five years after the purchase of Herdern. Between 1457 and 1463, at a time when the urban economy had reached its nadir, the town expended 8,300 fl. on territorial acquisitions, a total which exceeded the town's annual income

[45] Ohler, 'Haushalt der Stadt Freiburg'; idem, 'Strukturen des Finanzhaushalts'; idem, 'Freiburg i. Br. im 16. und 17. Jahrhundert'.

by some margin. If one includes the buying back of the mortgaged village of Adelhausen in 1459, which together with the magistrate's office and seigneurial recognition-fee (*Herrschaftszoll*) as further mortgages amounted to 2,000 fl.,[46] then the town had within a very short space of time raised a quite unprecedented sum for territorial acquisitions. This may strengthen the suspicion that the town was making a deliberate choice to buy its way out of its precarious situation, notwithstanding the danger of incurring additional high debts. While this conjecture cannot be ruled out (despite the fact that the acquisition of St Märgen and Herdern served different ends), the purchase of the monastery's lands would not have occurred when it did, had not St Märgen itself been mired in a deep financial crisis. In 1462 St Märgen stood on the verge of bankruptcy and was compelled to satisfy its creditors by making immediate payments.[47]

Selling its landlordship offered the only way out, and the town did not hesitate to seize this unique opportunity. That St Märgen was acting against its will emerges from the subsequent court case, in which it tried to retrieve what it had so irresponsibly surrendered.[48] Understandably enough, the town had no intention of letting go. A settlement was not achieved until 1490, brought about by a committee of Freiburg guildsmen, whereby the town was finally granted full title to its St Märgen possessions, but the abbey was to receive compensatory damages for several infringements of its privileges, including the illegal appropriation of title-deeds to the St Märgen estates.[49]

In buying the rights of stewardship from Hans von Landeck in 1463, moreover, the town was using the opportunity to sideline a sworn political opponent (as Wolfgang Müller has convincingly demonstrated), rather than pursuing purely territorial goals. Hans von Landeck, who was fighting a bitter legal battle with the town over its peasant outburghers under his jurisdictional lordship,[50] had joined a feud by the elector Palatine (perhaps in order to neutralize the purchase of St Märgen's landlordship), which threatened to spill over into the Breisgau. Buying the stewardship from von Landeck, who

---

46 Scott, 'Adelhausen', p. 98 and n. 14.
47 Idem, 'Relations', p. 198; idem, *Freiburg and the Breisgau*, p. 42.
48 Armbruster, 'Talvogtei', Dissertation, p. 93.
49 StAFr, A 1 VIII a ζ (89), 31 March 1490.
50 StAFr, A 1 XII d (18), 1451–72; Scott, *Freiburg and the Breisgau*, pp. 84–5.

controlled the important stronghold of Wiesneck near Kirchzarten, therefore served just as much to ward off a pressing strategic danger at the heart of Freiburg's territorial interests as to secure the long-term integrity of the still unconsolidated territory.[51] It is in any case noteworthy that after this portentous start the town let thirty years elapse before resuming the expansion of its territory. The continuing legal dispute with St Märgen undoubtedly acted as a brake. In the meantime the town energetically set about mastering its internal problems by means of a carefully implemented policy of economic protection, which could certainly complement its territorial policy without ever becoming its main pillar.

It would, however, be equally wrong to assume that the purchase of lands in the Dreisam valley, which began in 1491 and was thereafter pursued resolutely, was simply a matter of course for the town. That is exactly what it was not. In his dissertation on the Valley Bailiwick, useful enough in its time, Fritz Armbruster ascribed to the town's policy a radical consistency which is latterly supposed to have elicited the indignation and mistrust of king Maximilian. Armbruster believed above all that the purchase of Kirchzarten provoked particular hostility on Maximilian's part.[52] While it is true that the king expressed reservations, these were not directed against the purchase as such, but against its procedure. The king argued on two counts. First, that David von Blumeneck, his councillor, should not be deprived of his share of the proceeds from the sale of one-third of a total of two-thirds of the lands which Konrad von Halfingen, the other seller, was proposing to surrender to the town.[53] Second, the king voiced his displeasure that the town had acquired a fortified castle without his explicit permission; such an action was illegitimate for a territorial town.[54] The quarrel between von Blumeneck and von Halfingen was resolved quickly in 1493.[55] And in 1495 a Freiburg delegation, which had travelled to the imperial Diet at Worms to seek a series of economic and political privileges from the king, received confirmation and sealed attestation of the purchase of the castle and village of Kirchzarten without a quibble.[56]

---

[51] Müller, 'St. Märgen', pp. 53–4.
[52] Armbruster, 'Talvogtei', Dissertation, pp. 90–1.
[53] StAFr, A 1 VIII a ζ (92), 1 Aug. and 9 Sept. 1491.
[54] Ibid.; Leiser, *Herrschaftswechsel*, p. 22.
[55] StAFr, A 1 VIII a ζ (95), 12 March 1493; (97), 24 May 1493.
[56] StAFr, B 1 2, fo. 18v–24r; cf. B 2 3, pp. 127–30.

The purchase of Kirchzarten shows exactly how far the town was dependent on the current financial embarrassment of the sellers. The same David von Blumeneck, together with his brother Rudolf, had sold their jointly held lordship of Lenzkirch—presumably for lack of money—to the counts of Fürstenberg for 6,600 fl.; this transaction also comprehended some estate revenues at Birken in the Dreisam valley as well as the annual toll at Zarten. It was precisely these latter—the three Erlenhof farms and the annual toll—which Fürstenberg sold on to Freiburg eleven years later for 450 gold fl.[57] It would be safe to conclude, therefore, that these acquisitions were triggered indirectly by the von Blumeneck brothers' financial predicament rather than being the result of a deliberate strategy on the part of the town.

Let us return to Maximilian's attitude. The notion that the king fundamentally disavowed the town's attempts to achieve security by acquiring rural estates is, in the light of the arguments advanced here, entirely absurd. Maximilian, after all, had called upon the town to take over the mortgage of the three margravial villages in 1495! At that point reservations were expressed by the council, not by the king. It must also be stressed that in the 1490s Maximilian made every effort to help overcome the town's weakened economic and financial situation by approving a series of important reforms. He sanctioned the reduction of the town's debt and the scaling back of the convents' immunities; and he encouraged steps to reinvigorate the urban economy, including the foundation of a third annual fair in 1516.[58] Moreover, in 1510 he issued a patent of protection for the town's peasant outburghers, although by then it should have been evident enough that they had become an anomaly.[59] One should also not forget that in 1498 Maximilian summoned the only imperial Diet in the town's history to Freiburg. These manifestations of his favour by no means derived from the king's ostensible preference for Freiburg, as an older tradition of local research liked to

[57] *Fürstenbergisches Urkundenbuch*, 4, ed. Siegmund Riezler and Franz Ludwig Baumann (Tübingen, 1879), p. 121; StAFr, A 1 VI d (94), 28 June 1502. It cannot be ruled out that the von Blumeneck sold their possessions in the Dreisam valley to the house of Fürstenberg in order to avert the danger of their falling into Freiburg's hands.

[58] Schreiber, *Urkundenbuch*, 2, pp. 582–8; StAFr, A 1 I d (52), 20 April 1516.

[59] StAFr, A 1 XII d (49), 13 March 1510.

maintain, but from concrete political-strategic interests. Through his marriage to Mary of Burgundy, the daughter of Charles the Bold, Outer Austria on Maximilian's accession in 1490 for the first time since the beginning of the fifteenth century acquired a key position within Habsburg dynastic policy. Since Freiburg was by far and away the most important town of Outer Austria, it lay entirely in the king's interest to bolster the town's power, even through the construction of a landed territory.

The result of this investigation can be summarized in the following theses:

1. Freiburg's territorial policy in the fifteenth century stemmed from the town's general need to shore itself up economically and politically over against its hinterland.
2. Within this overall policy several different directions can be discerned, with the construction of a rural dependency representing only one aspect. The construction was neither so straightforward nor so self-evident as a one-sided consideration of the subjective interests of the town might suggest.
3. The construction of a landed territory did not replace the other aspects of Freiburg's *rayonnement* into the surrounding countryside—its links to the nobility, the holding of peasant outburghers—but rather complemented and completed them.
4. We can agree with Elisabeth Raiser that late mediaeval towns were prepared to pay very sizeable sums for their landed territories if the aim was to buttress the economic and trade-route interests of the commune. The towns showed relatively little interest in the financial return from their territories, and were not concerned to recast the legal condition of their subjects to their own advantage.[60] The hands-off administration of the Valley Bailiwick in the sixteenth century demonstrates this for Freiburg quite clearly.[61] The contrast with its treatment of Herdern a century earlier is particularly striking.

---

[60] Raiser, *Städtische Territorialpolitik*, p. 20.

[61] Scott, 'Relations', pp. 200 f.; idem, *Freiburg and the Breisgau*, pp. 99–100; cf. Armbruster, 'Talvogtei', Dissertation, p. 105. The town did make efforts in the 16th century, however, to exclude foreign seigneurial rights in the Valley Bailiwick, in order to create a *territorium clausum*. Ulbrich, *Leibherrschaft*, pp. 208 ff., 213.

5. The construction of a landed territory is a hallmark of the guild-controlled towns, organized into craft associations, who were dependent on the exchange of goods with their immediate hinterland.[62] But Freiburg's territorial policy should not be too closely connected with the victory of the guilds, especially after their restoration in 1459. As early as 1316—long before the transfer to Austrian sovereignty and the economic decline of the town—Freiburg paid fifty marks of silver to prevent a road being built through the Simonswald.[63]

We can only assess Freiburg's territorial policy correctly if we do not seek to comprehend it solely in terms of its own internal logic, but as a component of Freiburg's late mediaeval history in general. It is only the contradictions, difficulties, and ambivalences of the concrete situation which produced them that render Freiburg's territorial aspirations in the late Middle Ages historically plausible.[64]

---

[62] Raiser, *Städtische Territorialpolitik*, p. 30.

[63] StAFr, A 1 VI b (1), 25 May 1316; cf. Friedrich Hefele (ed.), *Freiburger Urkundenbuch*, 3 (Freiburg im Breisgau, 1957), pp. 305–6.

[64] For completeness' sake, mention should be made of the work by Adolf Keller, *Die Eingemeindungen von Freiburg im Breisgau* (Freiburg im Breisgau, 1942), which never appeared in print and exists only as a proof copy in the town archive of Freiburg im Breisgau. Although the work deals with the incorporation of communes around 1900, the circumstances of the late Middle Ages are briefly sketched.

For further reflections on urban territorial policy see now Tom Scott, 'Town and Country in Germany, 1350–1600', in S. R. Epstein (ed.), *Town and Country in Europe, 1300–1800* (Themes in International Urban History, 5) (Cambridge, 2001), pp. 209–16 [repr. in this volume].

PART III

REGIONS AND LOCAL IDENTITIES

CHAPTER TWELVE

ALSACE AS AN ECONOMIC BRIDGING LANDSCAPE IN THE FIFTEENTH AND SIXTEENTH CENTURIES

I

'Bridging landscape' (*Brückenlandschaft*) is a term with unfortunate connotations, both linguistically and ideologically. Under the banner of European unification a bridging landscape may take on a linking, intermediary, or even reconciling role, but in the historiography of the last hundred years it has more often approximated to a bridgehead, that is, a landscape which projects a specific cultural identity into foreign territory, or, put another way, which seeks to restore the unity of what historically has been alienated and torn asunder, notwithstanding political *faits accomplis*. On the Upper Rhine it is scarcely necessary to advert to the problematic character of the term. It is unlikely to be an accident that the term bridging landscape finds no echo in French; there the Upper Rhine is described as a 'crossroads' (*carrefour*), and the district on the left bank of the Rhine as an 'interval landscape' (*pays d'Entre-Deux*), both relatively neutral expressions. Even in English the term bridging landscape strikes a slightly odd note.

In modern regional planning the Upper Rhine is usually comprehended in its entirety as a bridging landscape—see the various planning authorities that span the Rhine, all consciously invoking a regional identity. To prise a part-landscape such as Alsace from this setting and to affirm it as a landscape in its own right seems to contradict this approach, but given the economic development of Alsace in the later Middle Ages as a cultural landscape (*Kulturlandschaft*) it may yet be justified. An accurate assessment, however, requires us first of all to analyze the national historiographies of Germany and France in the twentieth century, which approached Alsace with altogether divergent perspectives and intentions.

German-nationalist historiography on the Upper Rhine, associated in the first instance with such names as Friedrich Metz[1] and Hektor

[1] Friedrich Metz, *Land und Leute. Gesammelte Beiträge zur deutschen Landes- und Volkskunde* (Stuttgart, 1961).

Ammann,[2] regarded Alsace (and also Lorraine) for self-evident reasons as a component of Germanic civilization, a claim which was to achieve fulfilment in their own lifetime in ominous fashion. But the debate over the Germanic identity of the left bank of the Rhine stretches back, as is well known, into the age of humanism, most obviously in the dispute between Jakob Wimpfeling and Thomas Murner.[3] In fact, the issue had been contentious from the very foundation of the empire, manifest in the distinction between *Gallia* and *Germania*.[4] It is worth stressing this tediously familiar tradition once again to illustrate that from the German vantage-point Alsace's affiliation to Germany (or to the empire) always rested on a cultural and linguistic community—sixty years ago some would have added an ethnic-racial community (*Volksgemeinschaft*). Only subordinately were the natural-topographical divisions (*naturräumliche Gliederung*) a defining feature. Yet in the interwar years it was this latter perspective which representatives of historical regional studies (*geschichtliche Landeskunde*) began to emphasize. First and foremost one thinks of the Institute of Historical Regional Studies at the University of Bonn, which from its foundation in 1920 had under the leadership of Hermann Aubin sought in numerous publications to construct a cultural morphology of the Rhineland that would embrace people (*Volk*), settlement, and space.[5] The inspiration for this approach was geopolitics, a branch

---

[2] See Emil Meynen, 'Hektor Ammann', *Berichte zur deutschen Landeskunde*, 43 (1969), pp. 41–72; Dietrich Hauck, *Hektor Ammann (1894–1967). Investigador de la Historia Económica Europea* (Publicaciones del Instituto Tecnológico y de Estudios Superiores de Monterrey, 12) (Monterrey, Mexico, 1970).

[3] See most recently Francis Rapp, 'Autour de l'identité régionale alsacienne au Moyen Âge', in Rainer Babel and Jean-Marie Moeglin (eds), *Identité régionale et conscience nationale en France et en Allemagne du Moyen Âge à l'époque moderne* (*Francia. Forschungen zur westeuropäischen Geschichte*, Beiheft 39) (Sigmaringen, 1997), pp. 289–91; Dieter Mertens, '"Landesbewußtsein" am Oberrhein zur Zeit des Humanismus', in Franz Quarthal and Gerhard Faix (eds), *Die Habsburger im deutschen Südwesten. Neue Forschungen zur Geschichte Vorderösterreichs* (Stuttgart, 2000), pp. 206 f., 210–14.

[4] Rüdiger Schnell, 'Deutsche Literatur und deutsches Nationalbewußtsein in Spätmittelalter und Früher Neuzeit', in Joachim Ehlers (ed.), *Ansätze und Diskontinuität deutscher Nationsbildung im Mittelalter* (Nationes. Historische und philosophische Untersuchungen zur Entstehung der europäischen Nationen im Mittelalter, 8) (Sigmaringen, 1989), pp. 247–319.

[5] Franz Irsigler, 'Raumkonzepte in der historischen Forschung', in Alfred Heit (ed.), *Zwischen Gallia und Germania, Frankreich und Deutschland. Konstanz und Wandel raumbestimmender Kräfte. Vorträge auf dem 26. Deutschen Historikertag* (Trierer Historische Forschungen, 12) (Trier, 1987), pp. 17 f. A critical survey of this direction of research is offered by Peter Schöttler, 'The Rhine as an Object of Historical Controversy

of science that had flourished from the end of the nineteenth century, and which held that the physical and topographical environment profoundly influenced human beings' cultural behaviour. In France, the concept of the historical landscape derived from geopolitics was successfully deployed by geographers such as Paul Vidal de la Blache.[6] In Germany, however, the concept was elaborated in fateful fashion by Friedrich Ratzel, whom we have to thank for coining the term *Lebensraum*.[7] On the Upper Rhine its most prominent advocate was Friedrich Metz, who in the course of several conferences of the West German Research Association (*Westdeutsche Forschungsgemeinschaft*) deployed historical regional studies to bolster national-racial territorial claims to the left bank of Rhine.[8]

That French historiography was in thrall to an equally partisan view of the Upper Rhine as a settlement and cultural landscape—albeit with the intention of retreating into its shell rather than embracing expansionism—has been largely overlooked by scholars on account of its lesser resonance and deployment. But even today eminent French geographers cherish assumptions of whose ideological colouring they seem not to be fully aware. The most recent textbook on the historical geography of France, written by Xavier de Planhol (acknowledged as an expert on Anatolia), contains the assertion that the Merovingians were obliged to construct their Alsatian duchy around the fertile slopes between the course of the river Ill and the foothills of the Vosges, because they were cut off in the west by mountains empty of settlers and in the east by low-lying forests and marshlands which were difficult to traverse.[9] This statement contains echoes of what Tourneur-Aumont in 1919, reflecting the spirit of the Versailles Treaty, had declared in a lapidary phrase: *Les Vosges*

in the Inter-War Years. Towards a History of Frontier Mentalities', *History Workshop Journal*, 39 (1995), pp. 5 f.

[6] Paul Vidal de la Blache, 'Régions françaises', *Revue de Paris*, 15 Dec. 1910, pp. 821–49.

[7] Woodruff D. Smith, 'Friedrich Ratzel and the Origins of Lebensraum', *German Studies Review*, 3 (1980), pp. 51–68; Karl-Georg Faber, 'Zur Vorgeschichte der Geopolitik. Staat, Nation und Lebensraum im Denken deutscher Geographen vor 1914', in Heinz Dollinger, Horst Gründer, and Alwin Hanschmidt (eds), *Weltpolitik, Europagedanke, Regionalismus. Festschrift für Heinz Gollwitzer zum 65. Geburtstag* (Münster, 1982), pp. 389–406.

[8] Schöttler, 'The Rhine', p. 8.

[9] Xavier de Planhol (with Paul Claval), *An Historical Geography of France* (Cambridge Studies in Historical Geography, 21) (Cambridge/Paris, 1994), p. 173.

favorisent le retour dans la plaine. Il y a entre la montagne et la plaine une intimité. Le Rhin n'y participe pas. La plaine est plus vosgienne que rhénane.[10]

Tourneur-Aumont's essay, it is true, was entitled *L'Alsace et l'Alemanie. Origine et place de la tradition germanique dans la civilisation alsacienne*, but its contents leave no doubt that the author was inclined to accord the *tradition germanique* only a very modest role in Alsatian civilization. It is even more disquieting to recall that Lucien Febvre himself, the subsequent co-founder of the journal *Annales* and after 1919 director of the Institute of Modern History at the newly established French University of Strasbourg, cited this passage approvingly in his survey of historical geography, *La terre et l'évolution humaine.*[11] By the time his book *Le Rhin* appeared in 1931, however, Febvre had modified his stance, giving pride of place to human agency in the formation of a historical landscape instead of a static geographical analysis. Accordingly, he argued that the Rhine had only become a frontier in the sixteenth century; in the Middle Ages the Upper Rhine area remained a historical landscape whose evolution derived from the common bonds of urban density and urban culture.[12]

After the war, Alsatian regional studies largely shook off the previous resentments—one need only mention the names of Francis Rapp, François-Joseph Fuchs, and Odile Kammerer—but at the same time struck out in a new direction, which emphasized the links between the left bank of the Rhine across the Vosges to the French interior. Here, too, there are subliminal echoes of Tourneur-Aumont, since the latter had never denied, for all his much-vaunted intimacy between mountain and plain, that the Vosges were to be seen as a clasp, not a barrier: *Les Vosges se sont constamment associées à l'histoire d'Alsace non comme un monde étranger, comme une barrière, répulsive, mais comme une partie vivante.*[13]

The researches of Rapp and Kammerer have entirely confirmed

---

[10] Jean-Médéric Tourneur-Aumont, 'L'Alsace et l'Alemanie. Origine et place de la tradition germanique dans la civilisation alsacienne (Études de géographie historique)', *Annales de l'Est,* 33 (1919), pp. 75–6.

[11] Lucien Febvre, *La terre et l'évolution humaine. Introduction géographique à l'histoire,* 2nd edn (Paris, 1938), p. 367.

[12] Albert Demangeon and Lucien Febvre, *Le Rhin* (Strasbourg, 1931) (2nd edn with the title *Le Rhin. Problèmes d'histoire et d'économie* (Paris, 1935)). On it see Schöttler, 'The Rhine', pp. 11 f.

[13] Tourneur-Aumont, 'L'Alsace et l'Alemanie', p. 153.

this view of the late mediaeval economy. Rapp points to the lively traffic through the Vosges passes, which served the exchange of goods between the Upper Rhine and Lorraine; even the improvement of the Gotthard pass hardly impinged upon these mercantile connections.[14] Odile Kammerer, distinguished through her study of the merchants of St-Nicolas-de-Port near Nancy, has extrapolated this view to assert: *Ces montagnes à vaches, surtout le versant lorrain, loin d'être une frontière, représentaient avant la XVIe siècle une véritable colonne vertébrale pour la région mosello-rhénane.*[15] Yet she avoids the danger of walking the Vosges as a nationalist ridge, unlike Tourneur-Aumont, by observing that towns and merchants on *both* banks of the Rhine participated in this exchange, not simply as partners but indeed as 'economic accomplices' of the Lorraine trading cities. It is also to Odile Kammerer's credit that she has turned her back upon the older French historical geography by highlighting the opportunities for cross-passage on the Upper Rhine, some of which can be traced back to Roman times.[16] The Rhine, in her phrase, was quite unsuited as a frontier.[17]

It would be fascinating to complete this survey by interrogating Swiss historiography on the Upper Rhine as a bridging landscape. (Hektor Ammann, although a Swiss by birth, counts as a German-nationalist historian.) But the topic, it seems, has largely been ignored by Swiss historians, apart from some casual remarks by Hans Conrad Peyer.[18] The situation is quite different with the *Hochrhein* (the Rhine

---

[14] Francis Rapp, 'Routes et voies de communication à travers les Vosges du XIIe au début du XVIe siècle', in *Les Pays de l'Entre-Deux au Moyen Âge. Questions d'histoire des territoires d'Empire entre Meuse, Rhône et Rhin* (Actes du 113e Congrès National des Sociétés Savantes, Strasbourg 1988, Section d'Histoire Médiévale et de Philologie) (Paris, 1990), pp. 195–207.

[15] Odile Kammerer, 'Le carrefour alsacien-lorrain dans le grand commerce des XVe et XVIe siècles', in Jean-Marie Cauchies (ed.), *Aspects de la vie économique des pays bourguignons (1384–1599). Dépression ou prosperité?* (Publications du Centre Européen d'Études Bourguignonnes (XIVe–XVIe s.), 27: Rencontres de Douai, 25 au 28 septembre 1986) (Basel, 1987), p. 84.

[16] Odile Kammerer, 'Échanges et marchands à la fin du Moyen Âge dans l'Oberrhein', in *Le marchand au Moyen Âge* (Société des Historiens Médiévistes de l'Enseignement Public, 19e Congrès, Reims 1988) (Nantes, 1992), pp. 137–53.

[17] Eadem, 'Der Oberrhein im Mittelalter. Zur Grenze nicht tauglich', *Alemannisches Jahrbuch*, 1993/94, pp. 125–32; cf. eadem, 'Le Haut-Rhin entre Bâle et Strasbourg. A-t-il été une frontière médiévale?', in *Les Pays de l'Entre-Deux*, pp. 171–93.

[18] Hans Conrad Peyer, 'Gewässer und Grenzen in der Schweizer Geschichte', in idem, *Gewässer, Grenzen und Märkte in der Schweizer Geschichte* (Mitteilungen der

above Basel), as we can see from Helmut Maurer's brilliant essay on Swabians and Swiss in the Middle Ages.[19] There is no question, though, that in economic terms north-west Switzerland belonged to the Upper Rhine region, a point to which we shall return in the context of the Rappen coinage league.

II

There are also obstacles in the path of a scientific approach to Alsace as a bridging landscape. Central-place theories turn out to be only partially capable of comprehending the specific characteristics of the region. Radial centrality, based on the work of Walter Christaller, follows the marketing principle.[20] According to it, a hierarchy of centres of differing importance developed in response to the intensity of economic exchanges between the central place and its surrounding hinterland. This pattern of distribution may hold good at the level of metropolises—Basel's space in the fifteenth and sixteenth century measured by Christaller's categories stood in a directly proportional relationship to Strasbourg's—but in the case of the middling and small towns it produces overlaps and zones of conflict which cannot be accommodated theoretically.[21] Alsace's urban density corresponds rather to an axial centrality, which is the hallmark of transit landscapes and arteries of traffic. There the degree of importance of central places does not derive from their market function, but from their role as distribution-points within a linear transport network. As a consequence, their hinterlands were shaped not as circles but as lozenges.[22] This transport or traffic principle seems to apply to Alsace

---

Antiquarischen Gesellschaft in Zürich, 48, 3 [= Neujahrsblatt 143]) (Zürich, 1979), pp. 5–17.

[19] Helmut Maurer, *Schweizer und Schwaben. Ihre Begegnung und ihr Auseinanderleben am Bodensee im Spätmittelalter* (Konstanzer Universitätsreden, 136), 2nd edn (Konstanz, 1991).

[20] Walter Christaller, *Die zentralen Orte in Süddeutschland. Eine ökonomisch-geographische Untersuchung über die Gesetzmäßigkeit der Verteilung und Entwicklung der Siedlungen mit städtischer Funktion* (Jena, 1933; repr. Darmstadt, 1968). Engl. as *Central Places in Southern Germany*, transl. Carlisle W. Baskin (Englewood Cliffs, NJ, 1966).

[21] Tom Scott, *Regional Identity and Economic Change. The Upper Rhine, 1450–1600* (Oxford, 1997), pp. 97 f.

[22] Christaller, *Die zentralen Orte*, pp. 57–8; idem, *Central Places*, pp. 53–4; idem, *Das Grundgerüst der räumlichen Ordnung in Europa. Die Systeme der europäischen Zentralen*

directly, if we call to mind the distribution-points along the river Ill at regular intervals, which served as entrepôts for the export of agrarian products (above all wine). But the principle is still insufficient to define Alsace as a bridging landscape, since it rests upon the existence of favourable transport opportunities. For the Upper Rhine that means in practical terms river transport and shipping on the Rhine and Ill, so that waterborne traffic takes precedence over landborne, and the east-west axis of commerce recedes before the north-south axis. Those who speak of Alsace as an exporting landscape are referring primarily to long-distance trade downriver via Frankfurt and Cologne to northern Germany and Scandinavia. Yet a bridging landscape is not defined by long-distance trade, but by regional trade. The latter—with Swabia or Switzerland—has largely been ignored in research, apart from Hektor Ammann's many studies, which however lack a theoretical dimension.

Central-place theories have failed to construct an adequate methodological approach to regional trade beyond the immediate hinterland. Either they posit an inner-regional model (the market principle) or a supraregional (the transport or traffic principle). A further critique is unnecessary here since we can simply refer to Franz Irsigler's many essays on the subject.[23] It is none the less striking that the term bridging landscape never occurs in any comprehensive typology of space; indeed it is at direct odds with the commonly invoked gradient between core and periphery. What is required is an *inter-regional* model, which embraces connections *between* neighbouring zones. This can be found in my view in the principle of complementarity. Recently this principle has been deployed in an exemplary analysis of the economic relations between Swabia and northern Switzerland. In his investigation of the grain market around Lake Constance after the Thirty Years War Frank Göttmann has revealed the growing specialization of complementary economic zones, whereby Swabian grain producers adjusted to demand from northern Swiss towns, which for their part turned increasingly to overland trade and cottage industries alongside cattle-rearing.[24] That did not result in

Orte (Frankfurter Geographische Hefte, 24, 1) (Frankfurt am Main, 1950), pp. 8–12. Cf. Paul M. Hohenberg and Lynn Hollen Lees, *The Making of Urban Europe 1000–1950* (Cambridge, MA/London, 1985), pp. 62 f.

[23] Irsigler, 'Raumkonzepte', pp. 22 f. (with further bibliographical references).

[24] Frank Göttmann, *Getreidemarkt am Bodensee. Raum—Wirtschaft—Politik—Gesellschaft*

Swabia becoming a region of monoculture, but its economic performance was decisively conditioned by the interregional exchange of complementary commodities. This symbiosis, Göttmann argues, produced a dynamic of its own in terms of economic space (*raumwirtschaftliche Eigendynamik*).[25]

Those who search for a similar development on the Upper Rhine in the fifteenth and sixteenth century will be disappointed. Up to 1500 any putative economic complementarity was confined to bilateral relations between individual towns and their merchants, whose effects in no way shaped economic space. Nevertheless, the preconditions for an intensification of interregional economic links were certainly present, for Alsace was, as the well-known phrase had it, the bread-basket and the wine-barrel of Switzerland. It would be otiose to elaborate the extent and configuration of Alsace's commercial relations, since Hektor Ammann has traced them meticulously.[26] Rather, it is important to delineate the main tendencies.

Relations with Switzerland took pride of place. Northern Switzerland suffered from a permanent grain deficit, which was made up in part by imports from the Vaud, but principally by relying on the Sundgau. Alsatian wine, moreover, was exported to Zürich, Bern, Solothurn, and Luzern, in return for imports of cattle, cheese, and skins. But these commodities were also available in Alsace itself, so that in monetary terms an export surplus in agrarian produce arose. In the case of artisanal goods more of a balance may have been struck, since Alsace took woollen cloth from Fribourg, fustian from Basel, and linen from St Gallen, while the cloth-producing towns of Lower Alsace under Strasbourg's leadership sent their wares to many Swiss

---

(1650–1810) (Beiträge zur südwestdeutschen Wirtschafts- und Sozialgeschichte, 13) (St Katharinen, 1991).

[25] Ibid., p. 57. In the years of famine in the early 1570s the villages on the right bank of the Rhine in the Ortenau petitioned the magistracy of Strasbourg for doles of corn from its granary. These requests were usually granted. But it would be quite wrong to see this as an example of complementarity in Göttmann's sense. On these connections see François-Joseph Fuchs, 'L'espace économique rhénan et les relations commerciales de Strasbourg avec le sud-ouest de l'Allemagne au XVIe siècle', in Alfons Schäfer (ed.), *Festschrift für Günther Haselier aus Anlaß seines 60. Geburtstages am 19. April 1974* (Oberrheinische Studien, 3) (Bretten, 1975), pp. 310–17.

[26] Hektor Ammann, 'Von der Wirtschaftsgeltung des Elsaß im Mittelalter', *Alemannisches Jahrbuch*, 1955, pp. 95–202; idem, 'Elsässisch-schweizerische Wirtschaftsbeziehungen im Mittelalter', *Elsaß-Lothringisches Jahrbuch*, 7 (1928), pp. 36–61.

towns, and, using intermediaries from Fribourg, for instance, even as far as the Genevan fairs.[27] But these were predominantly cheap cloths, undyed grey cloths and ticking. The Lower Alsatian cloth industry never expanded beyond the orbit of regional trade.

On the other hand, Alsace had a decided need for imported salt. Although the bulk of imports was shipped by long-distance merchants as return cargo for wine from Tirol (Reichenhall, Hallein, later Hall in Tirol), the salt-pans of Château-Salins in neighbouring Lorraine supplied salt to Alsace.[28] In return, Alsatian wine was delivered to convents in the Vosges and to the ducal courts at Bar-le-Duc and Lunéville.[29] The most important link between Alsace and Lorraine until the close of the sixteenth century undoubtedly remained mining, which even experienced a new upswing after 1500. The Val de Lièpvre and the Val de Villé above Sélestat were in any case partly settled by Romance-speakers, and thanks to immigration by German miners there gradually developed a culturally mixed district. In the Val de Villé regalian mining rights were shared between the dukes of Lorraine, the Habsburgs, and the lords of Rappoltstein. Lorraine's stake was augmented, however, by further mining rights in the dukes' own territory west of the Vosges watershed, at La-Croix-aux-Mines.[30] In this respect, the crest of the Vosges did indeed constitute a clasp.

At certain points westwards and on a broad front southeastwards, therefore, Alsace fulfilled the role of a bridging landscape. How did things stand to the south-west into the Burgundian lands? Here the historiographies of Germany and France display a remarkable consensus. In the case of wine exports, even Hektor Ammann could declare: 'Alsace wine was able to penetrate only a short distance into this landscape bereft of wine, to supply convents such as Lure or Luxeuil, or towns such as Delle, Belfort, and Montbéliard, but thereafter the realm of Burgundian wine began.'[31] On the French side

[27] Idem, 'Wirtschaftsgeltung', p. 169.

[28] Ibid., p. 115; Marc Drouot, 'Le commerce du sel lorrain en Haute-Alsace, Sundgau et Brisgau', in *Trois provinces de l'Est. Lorraine, Alsace, Franche-Comté* (Publications de la Société Savante d'Alsace et des Régions de l'Est, grandes publications, 6) (Strasbourg/Paris, 1967), pp. 119–27.

[29] Ammann, 'Wirtschaftsgeltung', p. 118.

[30] Otto Stolz, 'Zur Geschichte des Bergbaus im Elsaß im 15. und 16. Jahrhundert', *Elsaß-Lothringisches Jahrbuch*, 18 (1939), pp. 132 f.

[31] Ammann, 'Wirtschaftsgeltung', p. 118.

the judgement was even more sobering. In his study of 1930, *La Porte de Bourgogne et d'Alsace*, André Gibert maintained that France could probably do without Alsatian wine and cloth—and vice-versa.[32] (International trade by Strasbourg merchants at the fairs of Lyon, or Geneva, is a quite separate issue.) Gibert allowed only one exception: the regional cattle-trade from the duchy of Burgundy and the Franche-Comté via the Belfort Gap to south-west Germany.[33] At the same time, Gibert was at pains to play down the importance of this trade artery by pointing to the alternative route via the Saône to Gray and thence to Lorraine, which was used by cattle-dealers from Frankfurt and Cologne.[34] We will return to the cattle trade below.

On the 'foreign margins' (*welsche Confinen*) of Alsace—to use an expression from south Tirol—in the southern foothills of the Vosges a second mining area grew up from the end of the fifteenth century in the Val de Rosemont around Giromagny, whose silver was principally shipped to Basel merchants.[35] The copper and lead ores which appeared alongside silver were all marketed on the Upper Rhine; none were exported to Burgundy, or to Lorraine, which had further mines under its own control on the headwaters of the Moselle around Bussang and Le Tillot on the far side of the Vosges crest.[36]

In describing the economic contacts between Alsace and its neighbours it is essential to distinguish between a permanent demand for goods and market-led demand. Exchange between areas of cereal cultivation and cattle-rearing was not subject to any secular transformation, but the demand for wine and cloth fluctuated between conjunctural peaks and troughs. Despite the victorious advance of Alsatian wine throughout Europe in the later Middle Ages it was exposed to increasing competition on its own doorstep, long before

---

[32] André Gibert, *La Porte de Bourgogne et d'Alsace (Trouée de Belfort). Étude géographique* (Paris, 1930), p. 292.

[33] Ibid., p. 293.

[34] Ibid., p. 292.

[35] Stolz, 'Zur Geschichte des Bergbaus', p. 158; Rudolf Metz, 'Bergbau und Hüttenwesen in den Vorlanden', in Friedrich Metz (ed.), *Vorderösterreich. Eine geschichtliche Landeskunde*, 2nd edn (Freiburg im Breisgau, 1967), pp. 167 f.; Alfred Bissegger, *Die Silberversorgung der Basler Münzstätte bis zum Ausgang des 18. Jahrhunderts* (Basel, 1917), p. 38.

[36] Gisbert Roos, 'Die geschichtliche Entwicklung des Bergbaus, insbesondere des Bergrechts im Elsaß und in Lothringen' (Diss. ing. Technical University Clausthal, 1974), p. 8.

it was eclipsed in north German markets by the newly fashionable wines from the Middle Rhine and Franconia, as well as by rising beer consumption.[37] Indeed, it was the very success of Alsatian wine which produced its own counter-reaction. After 1400 Zürich tried to counteract the market dominance of Alsatian wine by promoting indigenous viticulture and then by outright import bans. Its example was followed a century later by Bern, particularly after its conquest of the Vaud in 1536, which brought it extensive vineyards on Lake Geneva.[38] This protectionism may even have been stiffened by confessional antagonisms, for Alsatian wine came predominantly from territories which remained Catholic.[39] The sale of Lower Alsatian cloth at Swiss markets also seems to have declined in the fifteenth century. According to the notarial registers of Fribourg, edited by Hektor Ammann and evaluated by Philippe Dollinger, Strasbourg merchants (who as middlemen in addition imported English cloth and Baltic herring into Switzerland) could find no takers for their cloth after mid-century, although sales of fleeces remained constant.[40]

As an interim balance we might conclude that Alsace's economic *rayonnement* via bilateral trading links, that is, by agreements and contracts between the urban merchants themselves, was naturally exposed to fluctuations and setbacks. But if we approach the issue regionally, rather than bilaterally, then around 1500 the outlines of an economic association on the southern Upper Rhine can be discerned, whose levers were located in Alsace. This economic association was based on the coinage league of Rappen pence, to which we have already alluded.

---

[37] Klaus Militzer, 'Handel und Vertrieb rheinischer und elsässischer Weine über Köln im Spätmittelalter', in Alois Gerlach (ed.), *Weinbau, Weinhandel und Weinkultur. Sechstes Alzeyer Kolloquium* (Geschichtliche Landeskunde, 40) (Stuttgart, 1993), pp. 165–85.

[38] Ammann, 'Wirtschaftsgeltung', p. 112; idem, 'Elsässisch-schweizerische Wirtschaftsbeziehungen', pp. 51–2.

[39] Kammerer, 'Échanges et marchands', p. 140.

[40] Philippe Dollinger, 'Commerce et marchands strasbourgeois à Fribourg en Suisse au Moyen Âge', in idem, *Pages d'histoire. France et Allemagne médiévales, Alsace* (Collection de l'Institut des Hautes Études Alsaciennes, 25) (Paris, 1977), p. 105.

III

At first sight it may appear strange to attribute to a coinage association responsibility for economic and commercial concerns, since its main task lay in the regulation of currency relations between the owners of regalian rights. Coinage associations from their origins in the later Middle Ages should be seen as instruments of high politics and the exercise of lordship; they provided a specific substitute for the lack of an effective imperial currency ordinance. They had no economic functions as such. This can be easily demonstrated on the southern Upper Rhine by the first currency agreement of Rappen pence minters in Schaffhausen in 1377. Those who signed the accord were the Habsburgs for their mints in Switzerland, the Breisgau, and Alsace, then further lordships—the counts of Kyburg, the countess of Neuchâtel, and the barons of Krenkingen—and finally the four cities of Basel, Zürich, Bern, and Solothurn.[41] Only tangentially did the agreement reflect a geographically determined sense of solidarity; rather, what was decisive was the political necessity of striking a balance between the Habsburgs' struggle for power and the interests of the cities. In the longer term, however, as the Rappen coinage league grew closer together—that is, by restricting itself to a smaller area—issues of good police came to the fore, prompted by the existing matrix of relations between the cities themselves. Odile Kammerer has recently traced this matrix back to the period between 1250 and 1350, during which the movement for public peace (*Landfriede*) first created *des réseaux taisibles et conservateurs*, but which after 1300 gave way to *des réseaux créatifs* and *des ligues politiques*, a development illustrated in exemplary fashion by the Alsatian Decapolis, the league of ten cities founded in 1354.[42] Nevertheless, cooperation between cities and lordships on the Upper Rhine in economic affairs within the framework of a coinage association only occurred after a considerable elapse of time. It should properly be dated to the sixteenth cen-

---

[41] Julius Cahn, *Der Rappenmünzbund. Eine Studie zur Münz- und Geld-Geschichte des oberen Rheinthales* (Heidelberg, 1901), p. 25.

[42] Odile Kammerer, 'Réseaux de villes et conscience urbaine dans l'Oberrhein (milieu XIIIe siècle—milieu XIVe siècle)', *Francia. Forschungen zur westeuropäischen Geschichte*, 25, 1 (1998), pp. 123–76; see also eadem, *Entre Vosges et Forêt-Noire. Pouvoirs, Terroirs et Villes de l'Oberrhein 1250–1350* (Publications de la Sorbonne: Histoire Ancienne et Médiévale, 64) (Paris, 2001).

tury, long after the boundaries of its competence had finally been staked out. These were much more modest than those of 1377, stretching on the left bank of the Rhine from the *Landgraben* (the boundary between Upper and Lower Alsace) to the Ajoie/Elsgau, and on the right bank from the Breisgau to the Sisgau.[43] At the same time, however, this area largely corresponded to the natural-topographical divisions, and it also coincided with the area already embraced by the urban leagues of the fourteenth century.[44] Yet this should not encourage us to regard the extension of the Rappen league's competence as a result of any immanent dynamic, or teleology. Rather, it arose from the requirements of good police in an age which was exposed to increasing population pressure, price inflation, and more frequent dearth and famine. Functional needs, in other words, rather than natural-topographical structural features of the coinage area were decisive. That natural-topographical divisions none the less helped to provide a convenient framework for action need not be denied.

Willingness to cooperate in matters of good police was largely confined to the existential issue of food provisioning. The deliberations of the coinage association did not extend, for instance, to apprenticeship or craft ordinances. Moreover, the intensity of cooperation fluctuated according to whether the Rappen league members were dealing with goods for export or for import. Only when the demand for grain escalated in the years of scarcity around mid-century and especially between 1570 and 1574 did a common provisioning policy become an urgent necessity. Up to that point the customary surplus of grain (apart from times of crisis) had allowed unrestricted exports from Alsace to Switzerland, which were not subject to any regionally binding price tariff or ceiling on quantity. The Perpetual Accord (*Erbeinigung*) between the Confederation and the Habsburgs in 1511 had, after all, guaranteed free trade and no customs barriers.[45] But in 1570 in order to protect its own subjects the Outer Austrian government felt obliged to issue a mandate banning

[43] Cahn, *Rappenmünzbund*, p. 68; Scott, *Regional Identity and Economic Change*, pp. 179 f.

[44] See Konrad Ruser (ed.), *Die Urkunden und Akten der oberdeutschen Städtebünde vom 13. Jahrhundert bis 1549*, 2 vols (Göttingen, 1979–88).

[45] *Amtliche Sammlung der älteren Eidgenössischen Abschiede*, 3, 2, ed. Anton Philipp Segesser (Luzern, 1869), p. 1344.

supplies to the Basel market (the entrepôt supplying the north-west Swiss cantons), whose consequences ran counter to the regional provisioning of grain within the Rappen coinage league area.[46] In this, confessional antagonisms probably also played a role; at any rate, in the next few years strengthened cooperation between the Reformed cantons and their Protestant partners among the cities of Alsace can be observed.[47] In short, the permanent requirement for grain in northern Switzerland caused complementary economic relations with Alsace to fall back to the level of bilateral links at best. Even in the long term trade embargoes were powerless to prevent this type of exchange.

When it comes to meat, however, which the members of the Rappen league could not supply fully from their own animal husbandry, the commercial ties were much closer, as regular meetings and agreements testify. The willingness to conclude meat ordinances on a regional basis which transcended the various lordships was initially more pronounced in the cities than on the part of the Outer Austrian government in Ensisheim. At the very beginning of the sixteenth century Alsatian imperial cities and territorial towns had reached mutual agreement over a common meat tariff—in 1515 these included Mulhouse (which had just joined the Swiss Confederation as an associate member), Guebwiller, Rouffach, and Ensisheim; a year later Kaysersberg, Riquewihr, Kientzheim, and Ammerschwihr came to a similar compact.[48] The simultaneous attempt by Freiburg to have Austrian prohibitions on meat forestalling extended throughout the Rappen coinage league, however, was treated by the Ensisheim administration with cool reserve. The latter was prepared only to negotiate with neighbouring princes and lords; the cities as the largest consumers were entirely bracketed.[49] Not until the famine of 1527 did the administration see the light by agreeing to regional meat Diets under the auspices of the coinage association, and to these Diets Basel was at last invited. In the course of the century Upper Alsatian city members of the Rappen coinage league were even able to ensure that foreigners, such as Sélestat, situated north of the

[46] Scott, *Regional Identity and Economic Change*, p. 257.
[47] Ibid., pp. 261 f.
[48] Ibid., p. 204.
[49] Ibid., pp. 204–5. Generallandesarchiv Karlsruhe 79/1644, 7 July 1515.

Landgraben and a member of the Strasbourg coinage area, were admitted to the deliberations.[50] The Upper Alsatian cities could not over time withstand the pull of Strasbourg's market, since the Alsatian metropolis evinced both the demand and the purchasing power to drive meat prices up and sweep the market clean for its less powerful neighbours. This increasing pressure on regional markets derived not least from the burgeoning international cattle-trade after 1470 with Denmark, Poland, and Hungary.[51]

Given normal levels of demand Strasbourg imported oxen from Swabia and the Danube region off its own bat, but the larger cattle which were gradually dominating the European market could only be obtained from much further afield, in particular the Hungarian steppe. As long as this supply did not dry up, Strasbourg—the western terminus, as it were, of this international trade route—presented no real threat to the provisioning of the Rappen league members through regional trade with the south-west. But when Polish and Hungarian supplies suddenly collapsed in 1575 commercial relations on the Upper Rhine were thrown into turmoil. Until then the Rappen members had drawn their cattle from Burgundy, the Franche-Comté, and the Franches Montagnes in the Swiss Jura, with the famous cattle-market on the Ochsenfeld at Cernay on Outer Austrian territory in the Sundgau playing the pivotal role as entrepôt for neighbouring regions. As long as Cernay served the needs of local or regional trade, it remained a market of secondary importance. That at least had the advantage for members of the Rappen league that despite inflationary thrusts they could keep meat prices relatively stable and prohibit practices such as forestalling which distorted the market, even if the success of those policies was being increasingly called into question.

The crisis of the 1570s dealt a death-blow to this regional policy. The Cernay market increasingly became the object of general desire. From an interregional market it was transformed into a supraregional, indeed, international entrepôt. Merchants from Strasbourg and other south-west German cities descended in droves upon the Cernay market, negotiating delivery contracts with cattle-ranchers

---

[50] Scott, *Regional Identity and Economic Change*, pp. 220–1.

[51] Ian Blanchard, 'The Continental European Cattle Trade 1400–1600', *Economic History Review*, 2nd series, 39 (1986), pp. 427–60.

from Savoy and Lorraine.[52] They paid not the slightest heed to the provisions of the Rappen coinage league—be they price tariffs, market monopsony, or export embargoes. As a result, the latent tensions that had accompanied the Rappen coinage league from the outset came to the surface. A provisioning policy intended to benefit the members of the Rappen league alone could in the longer term simply not be sustained in a transit zone, to wit a bridging landscape, which is what southern Alsace was. The Cernay market would have had to accept its neighbours beyond the frontiers of the coinage association in perpetuity not only as suppliers but also as customers—for instance, merchants from the county of Montbéliard. Yet in the 1530s and 1540s the Ensisheim government was even hoping to extend the validity of the meat ordinances to the district west of the Rappen coinage league as far as the river Saône![53] The plan collapsed, and the government was obliged to allow the Montbéliard merchants free passage through Outer Austrian territory without a *laissez-passer* for the cattle which they had purchased at Cernay. No doubt the concern for self-provisioning made a protectionist stance understandable; but this hardly contributed to the prosperity of the Cernay market, which was dependent on supplies from neighbouring lordships. Only if the market had been thrown open by lifting all barriers to trade would it have been able to develop as a flourishing supraregional entrepôt. Such neoclassical economic thinking, of course, was quite alien to the authorities of the sixteenth century. By 1600 the policies of the Rappen coinage league, which in the meantime had been dissolved but which continued to function informally as an association serving the interests of good police, finally collapsed under their own weight. The rise of competing markets and the evasive action of merchants in seeking alternative trade routes provoked blockades and embargoes, which could only make an already intractable situation worse. After 1600 meetings to discuss a common meat-provisioning policy were finally abandoned.[54]

Although the Rappen coinage league ultimately failed as a forum

---

[52] Ibid., p. 443; Jean Vogt, 'Grandeur et décadence du marché de bétail de Cernay (Deuxième moitié du XVIe et début du XVIIe siècle)', *Annuaire de la Société d'Histoire des Régions de Thann-Guebwiller*, 1970–72, p. 133.

[53] Scott, *Regional Identity and Economic Change*, pp. 218–26.

[54] Ibid., pp. 237–43; Vogt, 'Grandeur et décadence', pp. 134–6.

for good police, we should not forget that its difficulties did not arise in the first instance from a lack of regional solidarity—that is to say, from the understandable differences in perspective between the commercial cities and the Outer Austrian government—but from the structural conflict of two regional principles, which the Rappen league members never learnt to resolve: interregional cooperation *versus* participation in supraregional trade. For, on the one hand, Upper Alsace and its southwestern neighbours were in terms of meat provisioning bound together by the clasp of complementarity, which the government in Ensisheim could not simply ignore, hence its heavy-handed efforts in the 1530s and 1540s to impose the provisions of the Rappen meat ordinances upon the county of Montbéliard and the Burgundian lands, without offering them any prospect of benefiting from the advantages which Rappen membership bestowed; on the other hand, Upper Alsace and the Belfort Gap were partners along an artery of long-distance trade, even if that trade was largely confined to meat supplies.

Shortly before the Rappen coinage league was dissolved in 1584, however, a remarkable *démarche* took place, which casts the economic *rayonnement* of the league southwestwards through the Burgundian Gate and therewith the key role of Alsace as a bridging landscape in an entirely new light. This was the application in 1577 by the Württemberg councillors in Montbéliard—in the name of count Friedrich, who was still a minor—to join the Rappen coinage league.[55] We need not pursue here the prehistory of this diplomatic overture, but political and legal considerations supplied the ostensible reason, since the Württemberg government had long been pondering whether to introduce a common currency for its territories on the left bank of the Rhine—Montbéliard, Horbourg, and Riquewihr—which was to have ranked *pari passu* with the Rappen penny.[56] The suggestion must strike us as all the more surprising given that the Württemberg councillors had dismissed out of hand all previous efforts by the Outer Austrian government to include the Württemberg county of

[55] Cahn, *Rappenmünzbund*, pp. 203–4; Scott, *Regional Identity and Economic Change*, p. 196.

[56] Jean-Marc Debard, *Les monnaies de la principauté de Montbéliard du XVIe au XVIIIe siècle. Essai de numismatique et d'histoire économique* (Annales Littéraires de l'Université de Besançon, 220: Cahiers d'Études Comtoises, 26) (Paris, 1980), pp. 32 f.

Montbéliard on the river Doubs in the deliberations of the Rappen Diets. Why the councillors were eager to join the Rappen coinage league rather than the currency area of the Besançon pound (*livre estevenante*) emerges from the negotiations themselves, in which count Friedrich bluntly confessed the true reasons for the submission: *Les fréquentations sont plus du ressor d'Allemaigne que de Bourgogne pour vin, bassine, et les tisserandz vendans en Allemagne.*[57]

Between the county of Montbéliard and the southern Upper Rhine, in other words, not only agrarian produce but also craft goods—pots and pans, cloth—were traded. It is obvious that Württemberg's *démarche* must be seen in the context of its exposed situation on the western margins of the empire, and also in the light of the danger of coinage debasement as a result of the circulation of Lorraine coins of lesser fineness. All the same, the existence of a lively exchange of goods cannot be doubted, and that fully justifies regarding southern Alsace as a bridging landscape.

This survey of the fluctuating fortunes of Alsace in the fifteenth and sixteenth centuries permits the clear conclusion that elements of economic complementarity with Switzerland, the Burgundian Gate, and Lorraine were certainly present. Whether this complementarity could reach its full potential depended, however, only partly upon natural-topographical divisions. Functional rather than structural circumstances were decisive, and these in turn were shaped by general political considerations and not simply by economic self-interest. Towards the end of the sixteenth century, as is well known, a front of stormy political weather had engulfed the west of the empire. The willingness of competing lordships on the Upper Rhine to work together was dwindling, while relations with France and Lorraine also fell victim to a diplomatic little ice age.[58] But Alsace did not lose its role as a bridging landscape; interregional economic links based on complementary needs were not destroyed, even if the Thirty Years War put an end to the political integrity of the Upper Rhine.[59]

---

[57] Ibid., p. 36.

[58] Scott, *Regional Identity and Economic Change*, pp. 277–81.

[59] See Debard's conclusion: *Le XVI*[e] *siècle est une sorte d'apothéose bâloise à Montbéliard, glacis de l'impérialisme helvétique. Bâle avait toutes sortes d'intérêts politiques et économiques dans la Porte de Bourgogne: dans les affaires minières du massif sud-vosgien, dans le contrôle plus au moins avoué du passage vers la Franche-Comté, à Héricourt et jusqu'à l'Isle-sur-le-Doubs.* Idem, *Monnaies*, p. 195; cf. Michel Billerey, 'Le Pays Montbéliard, carrefour historique entre l'Alsace, la Franche-Comté et la Suisse', in *Trois provinces de l'Est*, p. 315.

CHAPTER THIRTEEN

THE 'REVOLUTIONARY OF THE UPPER RHINE' AND OUTER AUSTRIA. VISIONS OF REFORM BETWEEN EMPIRE AND TERRITORY

One of the most striking and contentious reform tracts at the close of the Middle Ages is the 'Booklet of One Hundred Chapters' (*Büchli der hundert Capiteln*) of the so-called Revolutionary of the Upper Rhine. Recent research by Klaus Lauterbach has done much to increase our knowledge of the intellectual and religious context and of the authorship of this anonymous tract. On the basis of a reforming biblicism shaped by Wyclif, the Revolutionary of the Upper Rhine elaborated a vision of the future which was intended to reinvigorate the weakened power of the emperor by invoking guiding principles derived from Christianity and Scripture.[1] The core of this purified empire was to be Alsace—understood as shorthand for the entire stretch of the Upper Rhine from Bingen to Basel—of which the author was himself a native and which he describes in the most visionary terms. Alsace is lauded as an earthly paradise at the heart of Europe, whose endowment of people, cities, natural resources, and agriculture spills over like a cornucopia:

> Further let it be understood that of all the climes none is more fruitful in terms of cities and people than the eighth, that is the fairest Alsace, full enough of everything that mankind needs to live. The earth is golden. If one washes the earth in the Rhine, one finds the best gold. The mountains around Alsace are full of silver and precious stones, many towns and castles dwelt in by valiant people, fine produce, good wine and grain, meat and fish.[2]

[1] Klaus H. Lauterbach, *Geschichtsverständnis, Zeitdidaxe und Reformgedanke an der Wende zum sechzehnten Jahrhundert. Das oberrheinische 'Büchli der hundert Capiteln' im Kontext des spätmittelalterlichen Reformbiblizismus* (Forschungen zur oberrheinischen Landesgeschichte, 33) (Freiburg im Breisgau/Munich, 1985).

[2] Annelore Franke and Gerhard Zschäbitz (eds), *Das Buch der hundert Kapitel und der vierzig Statuten des sogenannten Oberrheinischen Revolutionärs* (Leipziger Übersetzungen und Abhandlungen zum Mittelalter, A 4) (Berlin, 1967), p. 229: *Witer so ist zů verston, das vnder allen climata ist kein fruchtbares mit stetten und lutten den das achte, das ist*

But a plague of locusts has descended upon this blessed land: the excessive number of clerical lords in the 'parsons' lane' (*Pfaffengasse*) of the empire inflict on the inhabitants great damage and abuse (*misbruch*) with their oppression (*beschwerung*), and that contravenes natural law.[3] The common man is not simply oppressed by the clergy, however; he is also exposed to legal chicanery by the secular lords. Even though the Booklet rarely contains concrete references to the Upper Rhine as a historical landscape, apart from empty phrases such as 'rose-garden' and 'garden of Europe', the author does cite five instances of perverting the course of justice, in order to back up his indictment:

> Is it not pitiable to note that the common man is held prisoner in his home, or in special cases thrown into the tower and fined, as has happened in many places in the Black Forest, about which the Bräunlingers are still aggrieved, likewise Munzingen and others such as the Tribergers? All complaining, in the case of Neuenburg, that the governor [of Outer Austria] took the mayor and councillors into custody and dragged them off to Ensisheim, likewise four [councillors] in Breisach, etc. All have voiced their protest but, as they maintain, have remained without justice.[4]

Among this catalogue of grievances it is striking that all the victims without exception were subjects of Outer Austria, which was under Habsburg rule. If one recalls that the incidents apparently occurred during the author's lifetime—or were still festering—it is hard to resist the conclusion that the Revolutionary had personal knowledge

---

das schonest Elsas, als vil alles des genůg, das der mensch leben sol. Der boden ist gulden. Wo man das ertrich weschet in dem Rin, do find man das best gold. Die berg vmb das Elsas sind vol silbers vnd edels gestein, vil stett vnd schlos vol strittbaren luten besetzt, schone frucht, gůt win vnd korn, fleisch vnd fisch.

[3] Ibid., pp. 220, 293, 323. On anticlericalism see Hans-Jürgen Goertz, *Pfaffenhaß und groß Geschrei. Die reformatorischen Bewegungen in Deutschland* (Munich, 1987); idem, *Antiklerikalismus und Reformation* (Göttingen, 1995).

[4] Franke and Zschäbitz, *Buch der hundert Kapitel*, p. 245: *Ist es nit erbermlich zů scriben, das man den armen man in sim huß soll fohen, sunder sach turnen vnd schetzen, so in vil orten vmb den Schwartzen Wald ist geschehen als noch die von Brunligen clagen, des glichen Muntzingen vnd andri als Triberger? Al clagende, wie die von Nuwenburg, die ein landvogt nam den burgenmeister mitt den retten vnd fůrt sy gon Ensheim, desglichen fier zů Brisach etc. Alle, so sy clagen vnd, wie sy sagen, rechtloß sindt verbliben* . . . They point to the connection with the Bundschuh revolts on the Upper Rhine, which erupted again in greater earnest in 1493, ibid., p. 245, n. 12, as does Lauterbach, *Geschichtsverständnis*, pp. 286, 212 n. 661, even though the legal infringements cited reflect if anything urban, not peasant, grievances. See below, n. 22.

of recent or still current Outer Austrian court cases. That provides important clues about the author's identity.

In an exceptionally meticulous chain of reasoning Klaus Lauterbach has put forward the Austrian nobleman and former imperial councillor of Maximilian, Mathias Wurm von Geudertheim, as author of the Booklet.[5] Despite scattered objections to this identification,[6] I consider Lauterbach's case to be well-nigh watertight. In considering Mathias Wurm's attitude towards Outer Austria it is significant that Wurm was appointed territorial clerk in Ensisheim by Maximilian in 1492, but was never able to take up the post on account of the prevaricating tactics of the governor at the time, baron Kaspar von Mörsberg.[7] In his Booklet the author comments:

> Likewise at the assembly in Worms [the imperial Diet of 1495] I requested all princes and emissaries of the Empire to allow me to redress the silent sins. Likewise I intend always to deliver one thousand Rhenish florins to the Exchequer and propose to do so according to Godly written law... And gave my opinion how that would be possible to lord Berthold [von Henneberg], the archbishop [of Mainz] in writing. He gave me a missive to the governor. The latter summoned me five times to Ensisheim, without issuing any instructions. But finally I desisted from my journeying [to Ensisheim] when I saw that no one in power was minded [to go] the correct way.[8]

---

[5] Ibid., pp. 284–8; idem, 'Der "Oberrheinische Revolutionär" und Mathias Wurm von Geudertheim. Neue Untersuchungen zur Verfasserfrage', *Deutsches Archiv für Erforschung des Mittelalters*, 45 (1989), pp. 109–72.

[6] Klaus Graf, 'Aspekte zum Regionalismus in Schwaben und am Oberrhein im Spätmittelalter', in Kurt Andermann (ed.), *Historiographie am Oberrhein im späten Mittelalter und in der frühen Neuzeit* (Oberrheinische Studien, 7) (Sigmaringen, 1988), p. 182. On Graf's reservations see Lauterbach, 'Der "Oberrheinische Revolutionär"', pp. 122, n. 73, 158 n. 240. Recently Graf has repeated his objections: 'Wurm was after all—unlike the Revolutionary—not a lawyer with a degree.' Klaus Graf, 'Das "Land" Schwaben im späten Mittelalter', in Peter Moraw (ed.), *Regionale Identität und soziale Gruppen im deutschen Mittelalter* (*Zeitschrift für historische Forschung*, Beiheft 14) (Berlin, 1992), p. 136, n. 40. See in contrast Lauterbach's remark, 'that Wurm... must have satisfied the necessary minimum legal requirements'. Lauterbach, 'Der "Oberrheinische Revolutionär"', p. 149 and n. 204.

[7] Ibid., p. 153.

[8] Franke and Zschäbitz, *Buch der hundert Kapitel*, pp. 204-5: *Desglichen han ich zu Wurms in der samlung* [Reichstag 1495] *aller fursten vnd des richs botten gebetten, mir zu gunnen, die stummen sund abzustellen. So wil ich der K. M. altag tusend rintschi gulden in die kammern liefern vnd wel das mit gottlichen geschribnen rechten thon... Vnd gab die meinung, wie es muglich wer, herr Berchtolden* [von Henneberg], *einem erzbischoff* [zu Mainz] *verzeichnet. Der gab mir ein geschrift an den landvogt. Der ließ mich zum funften mol gon Einsen kumen, sunder etlich abscheid ston. Doch zůlest lies ich ab mit mym nochreysen, wenn ich sach, das kein gewaltiger geneigt wer, den rechten weg* [zu gehen]... The silent sins are those

Nevertheless, Wurm and von Mörsberg were instructed by Maximilian in the wake of the Diet of Worms in 1495 to collect the Common Penny from the imperial Estates on the Upper Rhine, and from the Outer Austrian territorial Estates there.[9] On that account Wurm opened negotiations with the territorial Estates in Ensisheim; furthermore, he spent eighteen months visiting the imperial Estates on the Upper Rhine. In both instances, he may have got to know of the grievances of the common man at first hand.[10] Once that mission had been accomplished, Wurm served several more years at the emperor's court, where he was responsible for Outer Austrian affairs.[11] Although he had defended his reforming ideas with passion at Worms, Wurm's enthusiasm for Maximilian as a potential reforming emperor and new ruler of the globe subsequently cooled off entirely, since his chosen hero never became serious about thoroughgoing reforms to assist the empire as a polity.

Two sets of questions accordingly arise, whose analysis may cast light on Wurm's plans for reform, and on his relationship to the emperor and the empire. We will begin by investigating the aforementioned breaches of law on Outer Austrian territory in order to establish how far Wurm was aware of their causes and what conclusions he drew from them. In particular, the attitude of the Ensisheim government towards the incidents will be examined. Then we shall discuss Wurm's career in imperial service, and his views on the administration of the 'outer lands', where the territorial-dynastic rule of the Habsburgs and their overlordship in terms of imperial feudal law intersected or were inseparably interconnected. Finally, we shall reflect on whether Wurm's imperial political vision, which vested all his hopes in the emperor, can be squared with his experience of the constitutional realities of the Upper Rhine.

---

which hinder mankind from beseeching God for forgiveness, and in that sense make it dumb to God's voice; that included unjust and violent exercise of authority by lords. See now Klaus H. Lauterbach, 'Der oberrheinische Revolutionär—der Theoretiker aufständischer Bauern?', in Peter Blickle and Thomas Adam (eds), *Bundschuch. Untergrombach 1502, Das unruhige Reich und die Revolutionierbarkeit Europas* (Stuttgart, 2004), pp. 140–79, here at p. 164. I am deeply grateful to Klaus Lauterbach for his advice on these points.

[9] *Deutsche Reichstagsakten, mittlere Reihe*, 5: *Wormser Reichstag 1495*, 1, 2, ed. Heinz Angermeier (Göttingen, 1981), pp. 1218–22 (no. 1663); Lauterbach, *Geschichtsverständnis*, p. 298. The introduction to the calendar entry erroneously refers only to visiting the Alsatian imperial Estates.

[10] Ibid., p. 294.

[11] Ibid., pp. 288 ff.

I

Among the brief references to acts of violence against Outer Austrian subjects the arrest of Neuenburg and Breisach councillors and their abduction to Ensisheim by the territorial governor are undoubtedly the most striking. The incidents seem to be linked directly to the arbitrary rule of the governor Peter von Hagenbach at the time when several Habsburg territories on the Upper Rhine were mortgaged to Burgundy between 1469 and 1474. The execution of von Hagenbach outside Breisach's town gate put an abrupt end to his rule. It is known that in 1473 von Hagenbach had seized the mayor of Neuenburg, Ludwig Siegelmann, at a wedding in Alsace and had kept him in harsh detention in Ensisheim. The reason for this act of violence lay in von Hagenbach's aim of gaining control of the Breisgau territorial town, which had not been mortgaged to Burgundy, and whose extensive lands on the left bank of the Rhine had provoked repeated conflict with the neighbouring Alsace villages.[12] In the case of Breisach, the governor made no secret of his intention of forcing the town to its knees, for in the final months of the mortgage Burgundian mercenaries had wreaked such havoc that the population was moved to attempt a desperate coup against von Hagenbach.[13]

There are, however, considerable objections to linking the incidents described in the Booklet with the events of the Burgundian years. If Mathias Wurm had intended to invoke the Burgundian reign of terror as a warning, then he would have been obliged to

---

[12] Franz Joseph Mone (ed.), *Quellensammlung der badischen Landesgeschichte*, 3 (Karlsruhe, 1863), pp. 214 f.; *Basler Chroniken*, 2: *Johannis Knebel capellani ecclesiae Basiliensis diarium*, ed. Wilhelm Vischer and Heinrich Boos (Leipzig, 1880), pp. 62–4; Konstantin Schäfer, *Neuenburg. Die Geschichte einer preisgegebenen Stadt* (Neuenburg, 1963), pp. 108–10. See now Tom Scott, *Regional Identity and Economic Change. The Upper Rhine, 1450–1500* (Oxford, 1997), pp. 35–6 and idem, 'Städte und Märkte im spätmittelalterlichen Breisgau zwischen wirtschaftlicher Konkurrenz und Umlandsicherung', in Ursula Huggle and Thomas Zotz (eds), *Burgen, Märkte, kleine Städte. Mittelalterliche Herrschaftsbildung am südlichen Oberrhein, Das Markgräflerland*, 2 (2003), pp. 175–7.

[13] Hildburg Bräuer-Gramm, *Der Landvogt Peter von Hagenbach. Die burgundische Herrschaft am Oberrhein 1469–1474* (Göttinger Bausteine zur Geschichtswissenschaft, 27) (Göttingen, 1957), pp. 285 ff.; Günther Haselier, *Geschichte der Stadt Breisach am Rhein*, 1, 1 (Breisach, 1969), pp. 223 ff. See now fundamentally Claudius Sieber-Lehmann, *Spätmittelalterlicher Nationalismus. Die Burgunderkriege am Oberrhein und in der Eidgenossenschaft* (Veröffentlichungen des Max-Planck-Instituts für Geschichte, 116) (Göttingen, 1995).

mention the atrocity which von Hagenbach perpetrated against the citizens of the small territorial town of Thann as a means of intimidating the neighbouring imperial city of Mulhouse in 1473, whereby he had thirty citizens brought to the town hall square for summary execution (although in the end only four were actually handed over to the hangman).[14] During von Hagenbach's interrogation, moreover, the charges levelled against him made no mention of any arrest and abduction of the four Breisach councillors.[15] During his trial, which in any case flouted proper legal procedure, the judges were concerned to condemn von Hagenbach as quickly as possible, so that it would have made no sense to pass over such a flagrant breach of the law in silence.

Shortly after the end of Burgundian rule, however, a new dispute broke out in Neuenburg in 1476 over the seizure of a servant. The Outer Austrian governor, Wilhelm von Rappoltstein the elder, by then restored to office, demanded the servant's release in order to question him in person in Ensisheim and to punish him (his offence is not recorded). After two such summonses, which the council stubbornly ignored, the governor had several councillors arrested for perjury against their duty of loyalty to Austria. The case spread further afield to the neighbouring Breisgau towns; at the end of May 1476 Freiburg informed Villingen that the governor had released all but two of the councillors, but that one of them had been condemned to banishment, because he had declared during a session of the council that the matter would lead to a revolt (against the territorial ruler).[16] At the end of the year, the Freiburg council petitioned the Ensisheim government to grant the outlaw his wish to be allowed to take up residence in Freiburg.[17] Whether these events were known to the author of the Booklet cannot be determined; but their unfolding chimes better with Wurm's account than the troubles

[14] Bräuer-Gramm, *Hagenbach*, pp. 235 ff.; Haselier, *Breisach*, pp. 231 ff.; Sieber-Lehmann, *Spätmittelalterlicher Nationalismus*, pp. 61 ff.

[15] Hermann Heimpel, 'Das Verfahren gegen Peter von Hagenbach zu Breisach (1474). Ein Beitrag zur Geschichte des deutschen Strafprozesses', *Zeitschrift für die Geschichte des Oberrheins*, new series 51 (1942), pp. 321–57, esp. 326–7. On the trial see now Claudius Sieber-Lehmann, 'Eine bislang unbekannte Beschreibung des Prozesses gegen Peter von Hagenbach', *Basler Zeitschrift für Geschichte und Altertumskunde*, 93 (1993), pp. 141–54; idem, *Spätmittelalterlicher Nationalismus*, pp. 89–94.

[16] Stadtarchiv Freiburg im Breisgau [StAFr], B 5 XI, 4/10, fo. 8v.

[17] Ibid., fo. 28r.

over von Hagenbach, unless Wurm had conflated the arrest of the mayor in 1473 with that of the councillors three years later into a single occurrence.

Another incident in Neuenburg in 1491 is recorded by Sebastian Münster in his *Cosmographei*:

> In the year 1491 a revolt took place in this town on account of a mayor who had previously been tried by the [court of] XXIV and stripped of his honour but restored to grace by [arch]duke Sigismund, and for some time sat as a councillor again, even becoming mayor, which provoked great discontent. For he sought to take revenge on those who previously had declared him dishonourable. The town was divided among itself; some took the mayor's part, others were against him. In sum, it came to pass that the governor in Ensisheim had the magistrate taken captive by subterfuge and force, and taken away as a prisoner and brought to justice. There were many accusations raised against him but he died in custody before the case was decided.[18]

The description of the course of events seems entirely to match the brief references in Wurm, but it is far from echoing his intention. For if one is to believe Münster's account, what was at stake was less a violent assault by the governor on the authority of the Neuenburg council than a preventative step designed to spare the town further splits. The grievances were directed against the magistrate, not against the governor, although the latter had resorted to 'subterfuge and force'. The sparsity of sources makes it equally impossible to pass comment on the arrest of the Breisach councillors.

We are, by contrast, much better informed about Bräunlingen and Triberg. Archduke Sigismund of Tirol had mortgaged the Austrian outpost of Bräunlingen in the southern Baar, surrounded by Fürstenberg territory, to count Heinrich VI of Fürstenberg in 1460, against the wishes of his cousin, emperor Frederick III. Count Heinrich immediately had all the inhabitants swear loyalty to the house of Fürstenberg.

[18] Sebastian Münster, *Cosmographei* (Basel, 1550), fo. 795: *Anno 1491 erstund ein auffrhur in dieser Statt eins Burgermeisters halb/der vormahls von den 24 berechtigt/vnd von den Ehren erkannt/durch Hertzog Sigmunden wider restituiert vnd vber etliche zeit wider in Rhat genommen/auch zu Burgermeister gesetzt/das zu grossem vnfrieden erreicht. Dann er vnderstund sich zu rechen an denen die yhn vorhin von Ehren gebracht hatten. Es ward die Statt in ihr selb zertrennt/etliche hatten es mit dem Burgermeister/die andern waren wider jhn. In summa es kam dahin, daß der Landvogt von Einßheim mit list vnd gewalt den Schultheissen fieng/vnd gefengklichen hinweg furht/vnd jn berechtiget/da kam grosse klag wider jhn/aber er starb in der Gefengknuß vor außtrag der Sachen.* I would like to thank Klaus Lauterbach for drawing my attention to this passage.

But he was not content to leave it at that, for subsequent grievances voiced by the town claimed that he was bent upon reducing the Bräunlingers to serfs. In the late summer of 1489 the entire male population left the town and sought refuge in Villingen, at a time when the town's mortgage had become a live issue following the imperial outlawry of archduke Sigismund's (so-called 'evil') councillors, among them count Heinrich VII of Fürstenberg, who stood to inherit the estates of his childless cousin Heinrich VI. Fürstenberg thereupon sent a posse to Bräunlingen to seize all moveable goods. A settlement negotiated by the Swabian League brought the Bräunlingers little by way of relief—they were allowed to return home unimpeded, but with no right of compensation for the damage sustained—until in 1490 king Maximilian intervened in the conflict, since he was concerned to redeem the mortgage as soon as possible. To that end, he gave the town permission to cover the necessary purchase sum through loans, which Bräunlingen was able to raise with remarkable speed, in particular from Freiburg and Villingen. The king granted Bräunlingen tax-exemption until the debt had been discharged. In 1492 Bräunlingen was thus at last able to return to Austrian sovereignty.[19]

Wurm's comments are too scanty to establish a direct connection with Bräunlingen's dispute with Fürstenberg. The march of the Bräunlingers to Villingen and the seizure of their property must not be confused with forcible arrest and illegal money fines. Wurm also claims to know that the legal infringements in Bräunlingen were still continuing, although after the mortgage was redeemed no further instances of conflict—apart from the usual squabbles over rights of common—are recorded in the sources. For Bräunlingen the bitter dispute with Fürstenberg had a happy ending, brought about by the Austrian territorial ruler, which does not entirely accord with Wurm's own description of the permanently oppressed common man. At this juncture the question therefore needs to be posed whether Wurm was in fact concerned to give an accurate account of real incidents or whether we are not confronted with a piece of arbitrary historical reportage intended to highlight a general state of lawlessness and

---

[19] Siegmund Riezler (ed.), *Fürstenbergisches Urkundenbuch*, 7 vols (Tübingen, 1877–91), 4, pp. 93–9, 144–6 (nos 106, 107, 154); Johannes Baptist Hornung, *Geschichte der Stadt Bräunlingen* (Bräunlingen, 1964), pp. 213–24; Eugen Balzer, 'Historische Grundlagen', in Hermann Sernatinger, *'Anno 1489'. Ein Festspiel aus Bräunlingens Vergangenheit* (Stuttgart, 1905), pp. ix–xxiii.

injustice. The traditional picture of the Revolutionary of the Upper Rhine as a historical bungler and confused visionary, however, has been completely erased by Klaus Lauterbach's researches. By virtue of his career in Austrian service Wurm was very well informed, at least at certain times, about the situation on the Upper Rhine. He may even have had knowledge of cases referred for mediation to the Outer Austrian government, though we cannot know this for certain since he never took up office in Ensisheim.

In the case of Triberg we can trace serious resistance from 1488 onwards on the part of the subjects of this Austrian cameral lordship against its mortgagees, the lords of Lichtenfels. The unrest, which has left a rich archival deposit, was provoked by Wilhelm von Lichtenfels's attempts to apportion the cost of the frequently increased mortgage sum (for which he had advanced the necessary money) onto his subjects by increasing dues and imposing excessive court fines. In 1493 there was a first legal hearing in Ensisheim, which found against the Tribergers, so that two years later they laid their mounting grievances as cameral subjects directly before the king as territorial ruler in Innsbruck. Their complaints were chiefly directed against servile heriots and other exactions that branded them as serfs, since they claimed to be 'free lordly subjects' (*frey herrschafft leütt*). They objected, moreover, to arbitrary application of the law: their bailiff (*Obervogt*), Wilhelm von Lichtenfels the younger, was holding them captive on minor charges or throwing innocent subjects into prison, only releasing them on payment of a money fine. Although Hans von Landau replaced Wilhelm von Lichtenfels as mortgagee lord in 1501, he let the latter's son remain in post as bailiff. As a result, the situation in the following years was by no means defused; instead, it led to further disturbances, which were brought to a provisional close in 1504. None the less, the Tribergers' resistance continued thereafter unabated into the Peasants' War.[20]

The Triberg grievances therefore do chime to a large degree with Wurm's account; in any case, both the Outer Austrian and the Upper Austrian administration were sufficiently informed about the complaints of their cameral subjects. In contrast to the Bräunlingers,

[20] Claudia Ulbrich, 'Bäuerlicher Widerstand in Triberg', in Peter Blickle (ed.), *Aufruhr und Empörung? Studien zum bäuerlichen Widerstand im Alten Reich* (Munich, 1980), pp. 152–60. In addition to the sources cited by Ulbrich see StAFr, C 1 Fremde Orte: Triberg 23 (1501–1722) and 23a (1505).

whose situation had diplomatic or dynastic-territorial implications for the king, the Tribergers could hardly count on support from their territorial ruler. The arbitration judgement handed down in Innsbruck in 1495 largely confirmed the claims of the mortgagees, although the Tribergers as cameral subjects should have been assured of protection by their direct territorial overlord. Austria regarded the events at Triberg, it seems, as an internal matter, and was altogether hesitant to intervene against Wilhelm von Lichtenfels as mortgagee, since Maximilian was after all his debtor.

On the last case referred to by the Revolutionary we have few sources to hand. Whether Munzingen mounted strenuous resistance against its village lords, as can be extensively documented for the neighbouring village of Lehen against Gabriel von Bollschweil, is unclear. The jurisdictional lord (*Oberschultheiß*) of Munzingen, Kaspar von Blumeneck, is known to have perpetrated several acts of violence against subjects in a string of Breisgau villages under his control. One peasant from Buchheim, Martin Berner, was moved to petition the Freiburg council in 1512 to gain access to his vineyard in Munzingen at vintage-time, which von Blumeneck was blocking. That, though, does not amount to a general protest by the villagers of Munzingen as a whole. Nevertheless, the accusations of arbitrary seigneurial rule caused Albert Rosenkranz, the editor of the Bundschuh sources, to prick up his ears, for he claimed to espy a connection with the grievances expressed in the Lehen Bundschuh in 1513.[21] If one adds further scattered references by the Revolutionary to the tangled legal situation on the Upper Rhine, then there are indeed striking parallels with the programme of the Lehen Bundschuh, as Klaus Lauterbach has recently demonstrated.[22] The author of the Booklet leaves no doubt that an uprising will ensue if the oppression of the common man is not curtailed:

> I declare that if we do not adopt the hundred [Wurm's envisaged new judicial district], I tell you that the common man in the Black Forest

[21] Albert Rosenkranz, *Der Bundschuh. Die Erhebungen des südwestdeutschen Bauernstandes in den Jahren 1493–1517*, 2 vols (Schriften des Wissenschaftlichen Instituts der Elsaß-Lothringer im Reich, 12) (Heidelberg, 1927), 1, pp. 263, 266; 2, pp. 193–4, note d.

[22] Lauterbach, *Geschichtsverständnis*, p. 212, n. 661. The basis of Wurm's vision of the future is the commonweal, which does not occur in the Bundschuh revolts. Ibid., p. 216.

> will lay down . . . his flail or hoe and take up the iron rod to put an end to this arrogance and to make the Word of God the test of accountability.[23]

Altogether the impression remains that Mathias Wurm showed some understanding of the plight of the common man in Outer Austria and sought to expose the violent conduct of the governor or the dismissive attitude of the Ensisheim government. To test this further, we must now turn to Wurm's career and his relations with the Outer Austrian power-holders of his day.

II

Mathias Wurm was not alone in envisaging the renewal of the empire on the basis of a flourishing Alsace or Upper Rhine. In the early 1490s the then Outer Austrian governor, Kaspar von Mörsberg, from a Sundgau family that for generations had numbered among the most eager partisans of the Habsburgs and whom emperor Frederick III had raised to the nobility in 1488,[24] had formulated a similar plan. It, too, was intended to strengthen the dynastic position of the imperial house on the Upper Rhine. Von Mörsberg's principal goal was to ensure a leading role for the territorial nobility in the new Habsburg community of subjects, which was to combine dynastic-territorial lordship in the Sundgau and Breisgau on the one hand with the maintenance and extension of imperial feudal overlordship over the imperial Estates on the other. Thereby, as von Mörsberg trusted,

> His Imperial Majesty may make obedient to himself the count Palatine, the bishop of Strasbourg, the city of Strasbourg, the margrave of Baden,

[23] Franke and Zschäbitz, *Buch der hundert Kapitel*, p. 466: *Ich sag, wenn wir den sent nit halten, so sag ich vch, das der gemein man in dem Schwartzwald wirt . . . den pflegel oder howen hinlegen vnd die yssen rütten in die hend nemmen, dem vbermůt vnd* [= keinen] *bystand ze tun vnd das wort gottes zu einem verantwurten geben . . .* Lauterbach, *Geschichtsverständnis*, p. 209. On the hundred see now idem, 'Sendgericht, Missat und Feme im Werk des sogenannten "Oberrheinischen Revolutionärs"', *Zeitschrift der Savigny-Stiftung für Rechtsgeschichte, Germanistische Abteilung*, 118 (2001), pp. 185–221.

[24] Dieter Mertens, 'Reich und Elsaß zur Zeit Maximilians I. Untersuchungen zur Idee- und Landesgeschichte im Südwesten des Reichs am Ausgang des Mittelalters' (Diss. habil. Freiburg im Breisgau, 1977), pp. 164–72, esp. 168; Lauterbach, 'Der "Oberrheinische Revolutionär"', pp. 156–7.

> and make of the selfsame lands Alsace, Sundgau, Breisgau, along with the Black Forest a land that will, as I adjudge, beyond peradventure serve to bring about considerable and great improvement in the Holy Empire and the house of Austria, so that in my estimation one would be hard put to find many mightier kings, the power of whose kingdoms would be the equal of these lands' strength and all their fruitfulness.[25]

If von Mörsberg's plan had ever been put into practice it would indeed have fundamentally underpinned Habsburg pre-eminence on the Upper Rhine. As such, it affords striking parallels to Wurm's vision of a purified empire emanating from Alsace. But recent research has quite rightly pointed out that the governor and the erstwhile imperial councillor were starting from entirely different premisses. Whereas Kaspar von Mörsberg wished to lay the foundations of a consolidated Austrian dynastic power-block on the Upper Rhine, Mathias Wurm was not thinking in dynastic terms but within the context of imperial reform, which the emperor, backed by the historical and prophetic role of Alsace, was himself called upon to promote. Considerations of power politics, therefore, stood opposed to a vision of reform, heightened by biblical-ethical norms.[26] The Revolutionary was, after all, a harsh critic of Maximilian's politics on the Upper Rhine, precisely because the latter was pursuing Habsburg dynastic goals rather than the overarching reform of the empire.[27]

Drawing attention to the ideological gulf between the advocates of a dynastic and an imperial policy on the Upper Rhine must not be allowed to obscure the fact that Mathias Wurm had every reason to find fault with von Mörsberg's style of leadership and drive for dominance on practical grounds. Von Mörsberg, who in the service of his territorial overlord took as 'Burgundian' a stance as his late and unlamented predecessor Peter von Hagenbach (both Sundgau

[25] Mertens, 'Reich und Elsaß', p. 224, citing Tiroler Landesarchiv, Innsbruck, Maximiliana XIV, fo. 2r: . . . *sin K. M. im gehorsamen macht einen pfalzgroffen, ein bischoff von Stroßburg, ein stat von stroßburg, ein margroffen von baden vnd macht vß den selben landen Elsaß, Sundgov vnd brisgov vnd mit dem Swartzwald ein landt, do ich acht, einem mechtigen kunigenrich wol zu verglichen ist. Wan die also zu samen brocht wurden, das vnngezwifelt dem heiligen Rich vnd dem huß ostreich zu einem merglichen vnd hohen vffgang dienen vnd kumen wurd vnd loß mich beduncken, das man vil mechtiger kung finden solt, die da macht der kungrich glich nit haben, als die land an macht vnd mit aller fruchtbarkeit also sind.*

[26] Mertens, 'Reich und Elsaß', p. 225; Lauterbach, 'Der "Oberrheinische Revolutionär"', pp. 156–7.

[27] Ibid., p. 120; cf. Mertens, 'Reich und Elsaß', pp. 208–14.

careerists, as it happens), behaved so high-handedly in his dealings with the Outer Austrian Estates, especially the towns, that he soon earned their antipathy. An outstanding example of his lust for power can be seen in his strained relations with Freiburg im Breisgau, beginning with the council election of 1489. As laid down in the town's constitution of 1392, the governor (who had only just taken up office) presented himself in Freiburg in mid-June to attend the election. In doing so, however, he was accompanied by six Ensisheim councillors, rather than the two provided for in the constitution[28]—in effect, a deliberate display of defiance. After it had reminded him of the town's privileges, the council gave way, pointing out that next year he would know better. But von Mörsberg countered:

> It was his duty to uphold the authority of our gracious lord; whatever his Grace permitted, that he would tolerate. Earlier he had interpreted the constitution's provision for two [Ensisheim councillors] [to mean] that his Grace might well have more present. That is how he understood the constitution.[29]

Early next morning after the election of the mayor, but before the election of councillors, the governor enquired about the procedure for electing the guild captain, that is, the head of the guilds and commandant of the urban militia. He was told that the preceding year the governor then in office, Lazarus von Andlau, and the territorial clerk had acquiesced in the election of the guild captain by the twelve guildmasters according to ancient custom. Thereupon Kaspar von Mörsberg read out an archducal mandate of 18th May 1489, according to which Sigismund had disapproved of the indulgence of the previous governor (who had acted without his knowledge), and ordered that the election should be conducted by the old council in the presence of the Outer Austrian councillors.[30] The council was taken aback at this instruction, so recently issued, and refused its consent, since the mandate had not even been proclaimed to the guilds. Instead, the council planned to petition the archduke in person to warn him of the dangers of snaffling the guilds, which had

---

[28] Johann Heinrich Schreiber (ed.), *Urkundenbuch der Stadt Freiburg im Breisgau*, 2, 1 (Freiburg im Breisgau, 1829), p. 89 (no. 341).

[29] StAFr, B 5 I a, 2, fo. 58r: *Er wer schuldig, vnnserm gnedigen herrn siner gnaden oberkeit zů behalten; was siner gnad darinn zuließ, möcht er lÿden. Dauor hatt er gelutert, die saczung stünd vff zweyen, daby möcht sin gnad wol me haben. Also wölt er die saczung verston.*

[30] Ibid., fo. 58r–v; copy of the mandate ibid., fo. 59r.

brought the town such great advantage. Only after midday did the governor indicate that he was prepared to let the council elections proceed without a final resolution of the guildmaster question.[31]

From this stalemate the governor drew the consequences. Over the next few years the Freiburg council was made to feel his displeasure. The town clerk and later university professor, Dr Ulrich Zasius, described the aggressive behaviour of the governor in his 'Book of Disloyalty' (*Untreuebuch*), composed between 1494 and 1496, under the heading 'Enmity [*Unfruntlichkeit*] of lord Kaspar von Mörsberg, the governor'.[32] Only the most serious points of friction need be cited here. In Freiburg's legal quarrel with Konrad von Kranznau, village lord of Oberschaffhausen in the Kaiserstuhl, who had imprisoned the wife of the outburgher bailiff there,[33] von Mörsberg intervened on behalf of the nobleman, in order to make an example of the town:

> Item, in the Kranznau affair he spoke much more sternly and harshly against the honourable council than is proper. We were malefactors; we treated him with contempt as governor; we wished not to have him as governor; and we should know that he was displeased; he would not tolerate that we should come down hard upon the [common] folk, with many other harsh words of enmity; and he would see to it that we should treat him as governor.[34]

Moreover, despite repeated appeals, he had deliberately omitted to convey important business of the town to Maximilian. He had turned down the council's request to impose an excise upon the foreign mercenaries recruited by Maximilian, who were stationed in Freiburg, as a contribution to the cost of quartering them. At that, he had thundered: 'Item, he was so angry that he was trembling with rage,

[31] Ibid., fo. 58v.
[32] StAFr, B 5 III c 10, fo. 5r–7r.
[33] StAFr, B 5 XI, 5/5, fo. 18v.
[34] StAFr, B 5 III c 10, fo. 5r: *Item in der sach Crantznow hat er vil herter und strenger, denn gegen eim ersamen rat sin solt, geredt. Wir sien frâvel, verachtind inn als landvogt, habind inn nit fúr ein landvogt, und wir sóllen wissen, das es im misfall, werd und well nit liden, das wir also uber die lut fallind, mit vil andern unfruntlichen herten worten, und er welle machen, das man inn fúr landvogt halten múss*. As a reprisal the council had sent a troop of horse to the village to capture a handful of von Kranznau's peasants. The legal dispute is set out in detail in StAFr, B I 2, fo. 14r ff.: *Conradts von Crancznow handel, anfang und end.*

declaring that if four of five should have their heads knocked together, then whatever they decided, that would stand.'[35] He had deliberately disparaged the council and sought to put it in its place:

> Item, he held the council in such low regard that when he appeared before the council with a proposal, he had the governor's assistant clerk— the master of the mint [*Pfennigmeister*] in Thann, for instance— accompany him into the council chamber to sit and listen to the proceedings.[36]

During the controversial election in the cobblers' guild of Kaspar Rotenkopf to the council in 1496, the governor had summoned the guild to a fresh ballot behind the backs of the council. When the council heatedly protested he riposted: 'It was within his discretion, and claimed that the commons had pledged itself to him more than to the council.' The latter rejected this claim with annoyance:

> That it shall not commonly be allowed, for if the governor should have power to call the guilds together and mobilize the commons behind the council's back whenever he chooses, that would be alarming and burdensome to our gracious lordship, and to the town, for the times are out-of-joint.[37]

Following upon the precedent established in 1489 the governor attended the annual elections in the company of several attendants of inferior rank: 'But this governor often takes three, four, or five with him and indeed at times clerks, servants, and persons of no quality, which he seats beside him, to the great contempt of the council.'[38]

---

[35] StAFr, B 5 III c 10, fo. 5v: *Item er was so zornig, das er vor zorn zitret, und redt, vier oder funff stiessen die köpff zu samen, und was die rieten, das músd sin.*

[36] Ibid., fo. 6r: *Item er hat ein rat in so kleiner achtung, wenn er für rat kompt und etwas anbringen wil, so lat er des landvogts underschriber, etwe der pfennigmeister von Tann, mit im in rat gon, da sitzen und zů hören.*

[37] Ibid., fo. 6v: *Es stund im zu, und meindt, die gmeind het im mer gesworn dann ein rat . . . Das gmeinlich nit zů zelassen ist, dann sölt ein landvogt macht haben, die zunfft zebesameln vnd volk zů wegen ze bringen hinder eim rat, wenn er welt, das wer vnnser g. herschaft und der stat sorgklich und swår, denn die loff sind unglich.* On Rotenkopf see Tom Scott, *Freiburg and the Breisgau. Town-Country Relations in the Age of Reformation and Peasants' War* (Oxford, 1986), pp. 148–9. On his participation in the so-called 'Walzenmüller Revolt' see ibid., pp. 144–6 and, with corrections, idem, 'Der "Walzenmüller-Aufstand" 1492. Bürgeropposition und städtische Finanzen im spätmittelalterlichen Freiburg im Breisgau', *Zeitschrift des Breisgau-Geschichtsvereins ('Schau-ins-Land')*, 106 (1987), pp. 69–93.

[38] StAFr, B 5 III c 10, fo. 6v: *Aber diser landvogt nimpt oft drÿ, vier, funf mit im und dennocht zů ziten schriber, dienstlut und unachtbar personen, die er zů im setzt, das ein mercklich verachtung gegen eim rat ist.*

This detailed account of Freiburg's complaints serves as an example of how the governor deliberately patronized the Outer Austrian territorial towns. It conforms exactly to the line taken by von Mörsberg in his constitutional plan for the Upper Rhine, which accorded the nobility a leading role but which denied the towns any say in a region of urban density and a flourishing economy. With his aristocratic temperament Kaspar von Mörsberg regarded the towns at best as targets of an exploitative fiscal policy (not altogether unlike his territorial overlord Maximilian). There is an undeniable gulf between von Mörsberg's advocacy of a rigidly authoritarian stance and the blueprints of the Revolutionary of the Upper Rhine as a defender of the common man. The Freiburg grievances (which may have come to Wurm's ears) prompt one to think that Wurm's censure of the anonymous governor may have been directed at von Mörsberg himself, if one adds the latter's forcible arrest of the Neuenburg magistrate in 1491 into the equation. While this must remain pure speculation, it cannot be overlooked that Wurm in his encomium on fruitful Alsace extols the number and the wealth of its cities. Although he only touches upon the situation of the towns, his sympathy for the fate of the Outer Austrian Estates is altogether believable. He was clearly concerned to grant them a more positive role in the community of Habsburg subjects and not to degrade them to simple recipients, let alone victims, of seigneurial decrees. The author of the Booklet did accord the nobility an explicit political voice in the new imperial constitution—here he seems to echo von Mörsberg—but he had the lower nobility and gentry principally in mind, especially the imperial knights, who were to assist the emperor in their capacity as impartial judges and valiant military commanders.[39] The visible hostility towards towns displayed by Kaspar von Mörsberg finds no counterpart in Wurm's conception of the reform of the empire.

III

The reasons why von Mörsberg resisted Maximilian's instruction and rejected Wurm's appointment to the Ensisheim chancery are shrouded

[39] Franke and Zschäbitz, *Buch der hundert Kapitel*, pp. 251–4; Lauterbach, 'Der "Oberrheinische Revolutionär"', p. 157.

in mystery. A letter dating from 1494 reveals merely that the governor regarded Wurm as unsuitable, although he well knew that Wurm had emerged as a dedicated champion of a renewed empire at the imperial Diets.[40] Lauterbach points to the discrepancy between both men's political visions: Wurm's attempts to integrate all the imperial Estates into a new imperial constitution were certainly at odds with von Mörsberg's efforts to curtail the power of the Palatinate in order to boost Habsburg dynastic interests on the Upper and Middle Rhine.[41] Another reason may well lie in the contrast, already discussed, in their views of the correct treatment of Outer Austrian subjects, above all the third Estate. That the cool relations between two servants of the crown were influenced more by practical than by personal considerations is revealed by Maximilian's decision to appoint both von Mörsberg and Wurm in 1495 as collectors of the Common Penny on the Upper Rhine. In the ensuing negotiations with the Outer Austrian Estates, however, Wurm was to display quite a different aspect of his personality.

Shortly after New Year 1496 the three Estates of prelates, nobles, and towns and districts were summoned to Ensisheim to receive royal instructions for a muster of troops against France, and for the levying of the Common Penny.[42] The emissaries were as usual only prepared to discuss the issues if allowed to refer back to their superiors (*Hintersichbringen*), but the Breisgau towns already let it be known that they would not provide the 1,500 men demanded and gave a temporizing answer on the question of the Common Penny. After time for reflection had been granted, Freiburg used the pause to call a consultative meeting of the Breisgau and Black Forest towns, including, it seems, the four Forest Towns on the Rhine, which the governor at the Diet had approached separately, and which he had listed among the Sundgau Estates,[43] together with the captains (*Einungsmeister*) of the eight districts of the cameral lordship of Hauenstein in the Black Forest. At it the delegates expressed grave reservations:

[40] Ibid., p. 153.
[41] Ibid., p. 157.
[42] The negotiations over the Common Penny are described by Ulrich Zasius in his *Geschichtbuch* under the heading '*Was des gmeinen pfennigs halb gehandelt, erraten unnd abgeredt ist*'. StAFr, B I 2, fo. 70v–84r.
[43] Ibid., fo. 71v.

> The Common Penny, proposed by his Imperial Majesty's governor and secretary, was considered under many aspects and gave rise to widespread apprehension. For one thing, it was not being collected in common throughout the Empire, but was being blocked by many imperial members. For another, there was concern that the Common Penny would perhaps not be properly levied or deployed in the manner that was being proposed.[44]

The towns also took the view that as territorial towns they should pay less than the imperial cities. If the tax were to be imposed on all Estates of the empire equally, then they would be prepared to pay the Common Penny. But they then qualified their willingness still further by demanding that the proceeds should be retained within Outer Austria to pay off debts and to redeem mortgages.

At the second Diet, which the Estates attended with plenipotentiary powers, the delegates of every town were ordered to cast their votes singly, one after the other, rather than *unisono* as an Estate. However, they unanimously recited the wording of the agreed resolution instead. The governor was visibly enraged by this common front and announced further negotiations. At a district Diet of the Breisgau shortly afterwards, which had met in Freiburg on 28th March 1496 to discuss the foreign mercenaries (*wälsche Garde*), it transpired that the prelates and nobles of the Breisgau had in the meantime also composed identical replies. This, the governor hinted, had come to the ears of Maximilian, who had chosen to interpret their stance as a straight refusal by the Breisgau to pay the Common Penny at all. Who was responsible for wilfully twisting their actual response rapidly became clear to the towns:

> Their and our [i.e. the towns'] response, which reached His Imperial Majesty as a rumour that the Breisgau had refused the Common Penny point-blank (there was a widespread suspicion that the secretary Mathias Wurm had done it), was the reason for His Imperial Majesty's outrage, who thereupon sent a missive to the district, voicing his displeasure, which was read out in public on the aforementioned Monday [28th March].[45]

---

[44] Ibid., fo. 81r: *Der gmein pfennig der von k. Mt. landvogt und secretari fürgehept, ist in vil weg ermessen unnd statt daruff menicherley sorg. Für eins, das der nit gmeinlich in rich uffgehept, sonder durch vil des richs gespert werd. Für das ander, so mag gesorgt werden, das diser gmein pfennig villicht ordenlich nit fürgang noch verwendt werd, als für gehept ist.*

[45] Ibid., fo. 82r: *Sölich iro und unnser antwort, was der k. Mt. also ruch angebracht (was ein gross vermeinen, Mathias Wurm der secretari hets ton) uff meinung, das Brisgow hett den*

Affirming their willingness in principle to pay, the Estates sought to pour oil on troubled waters. For his part the governor confirmed that he had forwarded the nobles' response himself to the king without adulteration: 'He, too, was puzzled who had published this disobliging letter; therefore, as previously mentioned, suspicion fell unanimously on Mathias Wurm, who had sat there listening to this false supplication.'[46] After further discussion, the three Breisgau Estates finally agreed to the Common Penny being levied.

The dubious role played by the secretary Mathias Wurm in these negotiations is altogether striking. The fact alone that the Estates appear to have pointed the finger of suspicion deliberately at Wurm reveals that he was not regarded as trustworthy. Von Mörsberg, too, took exception to the king's secretary apparently acting on his own initiative; he presumably felt snubbed and deceived, and his authority infringed. Perhaps Wurm was wrongly accused; but it is noteworthy that the Estates did not target the governor, who had after all done nothing whatever to make himself popular. In the light of his own reform plans von Mörsberg had in any case the least call to hoodwink the nobility. But if one considers Wurm's stance in the context of his vision of imperial reform, then a possible explanation for his intervention with the king emerges. In his Booklet Wurm sets forth his proposals for imperial taxation in detail. It was to be levied on the basis of the tithe, or rather of the ounce (*Untz*), that is, five per cent of what every subject of the empire, regardless of their status, earned from their work. The sums were to be deposited by the parish priests in 'chests', specially designated for the purpose, of which a part was to be retained for the upkeep of the parish, and the rest paid over to the emperor.[47] In principle—although the method of collection obviously differed—Wurm's plan bears comparison with the Common Penny. Against this background, Wurm may have

---

gmeinen pfennig gantz abgeslagen, deshalb die k. Mt. entsetzt was, und tett gar ein ungnädig schrifft an die landschafft, die uff den obgemelten mentag offennlich gelesen ward.

[46] Ibid., fo. 82v: *inn verwundert och selbs, wer dis ungnädig schrifft usgepracht het, deshalb, wie obstat, ein einhelliger argwon uff Mathias Wurm fiel, der da sass und das hort, dis unwarlichen fürtrags.*

[47] Franke and Zschäbitz, *Buch der hundert Kapitel*, pp. 473–4, 527–8; Lauterbach, *Geschichtsverständnis*, pp. 236–7. In English usage the ounce can mean a twelfth or (more rarely) a sixteenth, but the Revolutionary is here invoking the measure described in the prophetic tradition of Japheth as father of Europe, namely one-twentieth.

regarded the prevarication of the territorial subjects of Maximilian on the Upper Rhine—at the very heart of the future empire—as a particular threat to his reforming vision, since raising an imperial tax from the imperial Estates was always going to be more difficult than from the Habsburg territorial Estates, who were obliged at all events to submit to the king as their territorial overlord.

For Wurm all sectional interests had to bow before the overarching imperial interest. To regard the Upper Rhine principally as the playground of Habsburg territorial policy, as did von Mörsberg, was far removed from Wurm's thinking; rather, the Austrian 'outer lands' on the Upper Rhine as the heart of the empire should be treated solely from the vantage-point of imperial politics. As a consequence, any reservations on the part of the Outer Austrian Estates concerning a supposedly excessive or inequitably apportioned tax had to take second place. That is not to deny that Wurm evinced genuine sympathy for the fate of the common man.[48] But he apparently had confidence that a new imperial constitution would create a system of justice which would put an end to such complaints. Therefore, the Outer Austrian territorial Estates must recognize the necessity of imperial taxation, without which the desired system of justice could not begin to be realized. That only goes to show once again how difficult all the authors of reform tracts at the close of the Middle Ages—and not just the Revolutionary of the Upper Rhine—found it to persuade their public of the advantages of the empire as a viable legal entity over against the emerging territorial principalities. Outer Austria showed itself remarkably loyal to the house of Habsburg in the early modern period (in contrast to the Inner Austrian duchies), but this loyalty was in the first instance directed towards the dynasty and territorial overlordship, not towards the empire; a pronounced 'imperial' consciousness among Outer Austrian subjects on the Upper Rhine, as earlier scholarship occasionally claimed to discern, is well-nigh impossible to detect.[49] Instead,

---

[48] The fact that after carrying out this task Wurm abruptly left the king's service on concocted grounds may indicate that he felt increasingly unable to reconcile his sympathy for the common man with his sworn duty to collect the Common Penny. See Lauterbach, 'Der "Oberrheinische Revolutionär"', pp. 155–6 and n. 233.

[49] It has frequently been noted that the Lehen Bundschuh expressly recognized the authority of both pope and emperor. But that overlooks the fact that Joß Fritz deployed this maxim simply as a recruiting slogan; it appears nowhere in the par-

a growing solidarity among the territorial Estates can already be observed in the fifteenth century, which was able to confront the somewhat neglected and marginalized Ensisheim administration. Under Freiburg's leadership, the Breisgau territorial Estates in particular developed a lively political activity, which may well date from the period when the Breisgau was the only Outer Austrian district on the Upper Rhine not to be mortgaged to Burgundy.[50] Wurm clearly underestimated or else mistook as a sign of disobedience the self-confident stance adopted by the Breisgau Estates during the negotiations over the Common Penny. Had he joined the Outer Austrian chancery Wurm would have been able to see at first hand how power was distributed between government and Estates. But this opportunity was denied him, with the result that he saw the attitude of the Estates as frustrating his main goal of a general imperial tax. If the Revolutionary is to be accused of being a stranger to reality—a final judgement on Mathias Wurm's personality and vision must await the forthcoming edition of the Booklet by Klaus Lauterbach—then the charge-sheet should mention his lack of feel for the political circumstances of the Upper Rhine (described by him in such glowing terms), which under Habsburg rule was caught in a hardly reconcilable tension between territory and empire. Wurm, however, did not think in terms of a political dialectic, but in the consciousness of a vision. He was captivated by the historical-prophetic traditions of the Upper Rhine, according to which the empire would be led towards a new age by the emperor of peace.

---

ticipants' demands. Moreover, it should be noted that in the general Bundschuh uprising four years later, which planned to unite the entire region of the Upper Rhine under one banner, all direct references to the pope and emperor vanished.

[50] See Scott, *Freiburg and the Breisgau*, pp. 24–5; Dieter Speck, *Die vorderösterreichischen Landstände. Entstehung, Entwicklung und Ausbildung bis 1595/1602*, 2 vols (Veröffentlichungen aus dem Archiv der Stadt Freiburg im Breisgau, 29) (Freiburg im Breisgau/Würzburg, 1994).

CHAPTER FOURTEEN

LIBERTY AND COMMUNITY IN MEDIEVAL SWITZERLAND

The seven-hundredth anniversary of the oath sworn on the Rütli meadow in August 1291 was celebrated with considerable ceremony throughout Switzerland in 1991. The deed of the men of Uri, Schwyz, and Nidwalden has been taken as the constitutive act of the Helvetic Confederation ever since it was immortalized in the White Book of Sarnen at the end of the fifteenth century. Anniversaries of events so deeply anchored in national consciousness and tradition are not best suited to encourage deeper reflection on the historical realities which they purport to represent. Yet the governments of the five Forest cantons (the three original confederates, together with Zug and Luzern) determined to commemorate the jubilee by sponsoring a handsome and profusely illustrated two-volume history of Inner Switzerland in the formative centuries with contributions by leading scholars.[1] It appeared in an edition of ten thousand copies, well timed for the Christmas gift-giving season. Those recipients who chose to read the work may well have been amazed at the wholesale demolition of their most cherished beliefs contained within its covers. Gone was the heroic struggle against the Habsburgs, vanished the ideal of alpine freedom: in their place stood a summary of recent Swiss historiography based on meticulous exposition of the sources. Rarely can professional scholarship have reached so broad an audience. The press reviews were long and detailed—but none engaged with the fundamental arguments. The time for a critical assessment has now come.

---

[1] *Innerschweiz und Frühe Eidgenossenschaft. Jubiläumsschrift 700 Jahre Eidgenossenschaft*, ed. Hansjakob Achermann, Josef Brülisauer, and Peter Hoppe (on behalf of Historischer Verein der Fünf Orte), 2 vols, 1: *Verfassung, Kirche, Kunst*; 2: *Gesellschaft, Alltag, Geschichtsbild* (Olten, 1990).

I

There is general agreement among recent historians that the origins of the Swiss Confederation lay in the search for public order. The provisions of the *Bundesbrief* of 1291 were clearly directed against feuding within the inner cantons, rather than the expression of collective defiance against the political authority of the Habsburgs.[2] The most trenchant exponent of this view in recent times has been Peter Blickle. The prevalence of feuding conducted by clans according to well-recognized conventions was a particular feature of Inner Switzerland in the thirteenth and fourteenth centuries, of which the feud between the Izeling and Gruoba dynasties in Uri around 1250 is perhaps the best-known example. What is so striking about these feuds, argues Blickle, is that they were perpetrated by men who by rights should have been barred from recourse of this kind. According to Otto Brunner's definition, only the nobility or corporations were permitted to deploy the feud in redress of wrongs other than murder. Yet it was precisely such feuds by powerful peasant families that seem to have been common in the interior of Switzerland. Because these feuds could rapidly suck in an entire territory, collective action to enforce public peace became an urgent necessity. As a result, feuding, in Blickle's words, became 'communalized', that is to say, the political association of the *Land* placed limits on feuding and the laws governing it: the territorial law codes (*Landrecht*) of the cantons were, in effect, peace ordinances (*Friedensrecht*). When the *Land* waged collective aggression, as with Schwyz against the abbey of Einsiedeln before and after 1300, that was no longer feuding but war.[3] By extension, peace-keeping became a matter of negotiation between *Länder*, stretching from the sworn association of 1291 right through to the Perpetual Defence and Land Law (*Ewiges Burg- und Landrecht*)

---

[2] Guy P. Marchal, 'Neue Aspekte der frühen Schweizer Geschichte', *Schweizerische Zeitschrift für Geschichte*, 41 (1991), p. 236. The term 'canton' is anachronistic (it came into usage in the fifteenth century as a borrowing from French): the Swiss term is *Ort* (place), for which there is no adequate political equivalent in English.

[3] Peter Blickle, 'Das Gesetz der Eidgenossen. Überlegungen zur Entstehung der Schweiz 1200–1400', *Historische Zeitschrift*, 255 (1992), p. 565, n. 13. On peasant feuding see now, however, the important study by Christine Reinle, *Bauernfehden. Studien zur Fehdeführung Nichtadliger im spätmittelalterlichen römisch-deutschen Reich, besonders in den bayerischen Herzogtümern* (*Vierteljahrschrift für Sozial- und Wirtschaftsgeschichte*, Beiheft 170) (Stuttgart, 2003).

concluded in 1411 between the three original signatories (Nidwalden having been joined by Obwalden to form Unterwalden) and Appenzell, Zürich, Glarus, Luzern, and Zug.[4] Why feuding should have been so endemic is far from clear. Blickle dismisses with savage humour the image of the Swiss as born fighters, 'mountainy men' jealous of their alpine liberty.[5] Peasants in many parts of western Germany, after all, carried weapons, and the Swiss were no exception. What inculcated a love of war, he conjectures, was not innate bloodthirstiness, but the need to defend an emerging political system which was communal and antifeudal.[6] However that may be, he recognized that, chronologically, the 'peace movement' for the suppression of feuding preceded any 'freedom movement' designed to secure communal autonomy.[7]

A clue to the nature of feuding may be obtained by looking at the activities of clans in the fourteenth century, for which the evidence is less sparse. Roger Sablonier has drawn attention to the continued rivalries and conflicts within the territorial elites even after the communes had begun to assert their political will. In 1382, to take a spectacular example, three members of the Hunwil family, the richest and most powerful dynasty in Unterwalden, were barred from office and effectively banished by the *Land* of Unterwalden. The opponents of the Hunwil in Obwalden (and of two other leading clans in Nidwalden, the Waltersberg and Tottikon), it transpired, were other members of the territorial elite—the Rüdli, Seili, Wirz, and von Zuben in Obwalden, and the Amstein in Nidwalden. At the beginning of the century they had all, except the Amstein, been peasants, but by mid-century they had advanced to local rural potentates (largely through engagement in cattle-ranching), and after 1381 came to monopolize the office of territorial magistrate (*Landammann*). As Sablonier concludes, the oppositional families saw that they could further their private economic interests by politicking against their established rivals: private feuding had been elevated to communal

[4] Peter Blickle, 'Friede und Verfassung. Voraussetzungen und Folgen der Eidgenossenschaft von 1291', in *Innerschweiz und Frühe Eidgenossenschaft*, 1, pp. 17 f., 21–4, 30; idem, 'Gesetz der Eidgenossen', pp. 565–9.

[5] Idem, 'Friede und Verfassung', pp. 15 f., 63.

[6] Ibid., p. 63.

[7] Ibid., p. 169.

level in a struggle over public office.[8] A similar pattern may already be discernible in the thirteenth century. In the case of Uri and Schwyz, for instance, public office had from the 1250s been exercised by the magistrates on behalf of the emperor, for both territories were immediately dependent on the empire (*reichsunmittelbar*).[9] In the generation before 1291, however, the imperial dignity was held by Rudolf of Habsburg, whose own dynasty controlled extensive patrimonial rights of landlordship, monastic stewardship and secular jurisdiction (*Vogteirecht*) throughout northern Switzerland. This interpenetration of imperial and dynastic authority furnishes the context for the events of 1291. In mid-April the heavily indebted Alsatian abbey of Murbach (of which the Habsburgs were stewards) sold its considerable possessions, mainly around Luzern and in Unterwalden, to king Rudolf. When Rudolf died three months later, a dangerous power vacuum arose. The confirmation of immediate status (with the practical benefits that promised for the local elites) depended on the election of a new king, but the electors chose as his successor count Adolf of Nassau, rather than duke Albrecht of Habsburg, who in fact delayed six years, until 1297, before confirming the abbey's status. Against that background, the magistrates, dempsters, and heads of clans renewed an earlier league to protect their liberties and estates, for these would be at risk if the inner cantons succumbed to private warfare in a scramble for office during the political uncertainty.[10] The price they paid for what was understandably presented as an assertion of *communal* liberties was, however, integration into a territorially binding rule of law, and the enfranchisement of some of the non-patrician families. No longer could the *Geschlechterverband*, the alliance of powerful families and clans, dispose so readily over who might be admitted to the legal-judicial *universitas*. None the less, the number of enfranchised families in Uri, Schwyz, and Unterwalden

---

[8] Roger Sablonier, 'Innerschweizer Gesellschaft im 14. Jahrhundert. Sozialstruktur und Wirtschaft', in *Innerschweiz und Frühe Eidgenossenschaft*, 2, pp. 32–5.

[9] Konrad Ruser, 'Die Talgemeinden des Valcamonica, des Frignano, der Leventina und des Blenio und die Entstehung der Schweizerischen Eidgenossenschaft', in Helmut Maurer (ed.), *Kommunale Bündnisse Oberitaliens und Oberdeutschlands im Vergleich* (Vorträge und Forschungen, 33) (Sigmaringen, 1987), p. 142. The situation in Unterwalden was more complex, for there the powerful Benedictine abbey of Engelberg was *reichsunmittelbar*, rather than the commune.

[10] Ibid., pp. 144–5.

continued to fall well short of the total (male) population.[11] The notion of local elites fearful of forfeiting the perquisites which their role as imperial (or Habsburg) agents might bestow collides head-on with the chronicle accounts, which describe both the *conjuratio* of 1291, and an earlier *conspiracio*[12] as directed against the Habsburg bailiffs, but the chronicles were constructing a heroic legend from the safe distance of the fifteenth century.[13]

II

An accurate assessment of the situation in the inner cantons at the end of the thirteenth century, therefore, turns upon two distinct, though related questions: how far had Inner Switzerland been penetrated by seigneurial relations before the confederation of 1291; and to what extent had it been the object of attempts to integrate the alpine communities into a web of territorial lordship? It is not now seriously assumed that the alpine valleys of Inner Switzerland had originally been populated by free men.[14] At the beginning of the thirteenth century rights of landlordship and jurisdiction were exercised throughout the inner cantons by an array of secular and ecclesiastical lords, stretching from gentry right up to the emperor. What constituted the formative experience of the Helvetic Confederation was the rapid erosion of these rights over the next two centuries.[15] Serfdom, moreover, was widespread, at least on the estates of the secular nobility, for by becoming the subject of a convent (*Gotteshausmann*) a peasant might discharge his personal, though not his tenurial, unfreedom. The salient feature of the erosion of seigneurialism was that in the majority of cases these rights passed to, or

[11] Ibid., p. 150. In Schwyz the judicial assembly of the commune was attended in 1281 by 53 families from no more than a handful of clans. In Uri and Unterwalden the figures were 70 and 30 respectively.

[12] The sworn association of 1291, as a public act, was intended, in Peter Blickle's view, to absorb and neutralize the private (and sectional?) conspiracy beforehand. Blickle, 'Friede und Verfassung', p. 36.

[13] On the historiographical legend, see Guy P. Marchal, 'Die "Alten Eidgenossen" im Wandel der Zeiten. Das Bild der frühen Eidgenossen im Traditionsbewußtsein und in der Identitätsvorstellung der Schweizer vom 15. bis ins 20. Jahrhundert', in *Innerschweiz und frühe Eidgenossenschaft*, 2, pp. 307–403.

[14] Blickle, 'Friede und Verfassung', p. 179.

[15] Ibid., p. 64.

were acquired by, the *universitas* of the rural community, the *Land* acting politically as an entity. For example, the imperial toll at Flüelen, held by the Attinghausen, a local clan prominent in 1291, was acquired, together with its estates, by the *Land* of Uri in the mid-fourteenth century. The territory also bought out the landlord rights of four convents, Rathausen, Kappel, Frauental, and Wettingen between 1359 and 1362, and in 1426 absorbed the remaining landed rights of the Fraumünster in Zürich, which had owned extensive estates in Uri.[16] Schwyz likewise bought out all the landlords within its territory in the fourteenth century, including the powerful abbey of Einsiedeln.[17]

For Unterwalden, faced with the imperial abbey of Engelberg, outright purchase was more difficult, but even there revocable leases were replaced by hereditary tenures.[18] Although their feudal power was undeniably weakened, the acquisition of landlord rights did not strip the ecclesiastical foundations of all their authority. Indeed, Sablonier has suggested that a distinction needs to be drawn between an inner zone where feudal rights effectively disappeared, and an outer zone, comprising the territories of Zug and Luzern, which remained open to seigneurial influence, not least that of the Habsburgs. In the outer zone, patterns of manorial organization (which had never existed in the remoter valleys) may have given way to feudal dominion no longer based on landlordship but on judicial and fiscal rights. In that process the communes may have been the beneficiaries as much as individual nobles or corporate urban lords.[19] Although the higher nobility disappeared from Inner Switzerland by the fourteenth century, a new group of ministerials, lesser nobles serving the emergent *Landesherrschaft*, might have established itself as local aristocrats, had the Habsburgs succeeded in imposing effective territorial overlordship.[20]

Why the Habsburgs failed to do so has never satisfactorily been explained. There is virtually no evidence that they were repulsed on account of any particular animosity towards their seigneurial rule by

---

[16] Ibid., pp. 74, 193.
[17] Ibid., pp. 77 f., 194.
[18] Ibid., p. 79.
[19] Sablonier, 'Innerschweizer Gesellschaft', pp. 114–16.
[20] Ibid., pp. 23–9; Marchal, 'Neue Aspekte', p. 242.

freedom-loving communes. Only for a brief period under Rudolf of Habsburg is there any sign of a deliberate assertion of rights. Even so, his main concern was to buttress his dynastic power-base in northern Switzerland through the purchase or inheritance of lands in the Thurgau and Aargau, and the acquisition of the stewardship of both Zürich minsters, rather than in the inner cantons, although he did attempt to extend and enforce bailiff's rights in Glarus, as well as in Luzern, Schwyz, and Unterwalden.[21] Yet after his accession to the German throne in 1273, Rudolf's attention was deflected towards the recently won Austrian duchies, while Switzerland was relatively neglected. A graphic example of the paucity of Habsburg rights in the core of Inner Switzerland is provided by the great cadastre (*Urbar*) compiled between 1303 and 1308. When its entries are plotted cartographically, what emerges is that the Habsburgs' judicial rights extend northwards from the lake of Lucerne, whilst the three inner cantons remain entirely blank![22] Does this imply that Habsburg seigneurialism had never made much impact on the three original confederate territories, or that their rights had already been repulsed by the early thirteenth century? Many rights, it is generally agreed, had already been mortgaged,[23] although that in itself should not be taken as a sign of weakness. The pawning of estates, revenues, and jurisdictions was used by German princes throughout the Middle Ages both to capitalize revenues and strategically to secure the loyalty and service of local nobilities, especially at the periphery of their domains.[24] In many cases, moreover, the terms of the mortgage explicitly excluded both *Steuer* and *Reise*, the rights of territorial taxation and military service, which were regarded as hallmarks of territorial sovereignty.[25] At all events, there was nothing random about the Habsburgs' mortgage policy. All the pawns were carefully registered, and were usually only granted to a homogenous section of the local

---

21 Blickle, 'Friede und Verfassung', p. 160.

22 Ibid., p. 161.

23 Ibid., p. 162.

24 On mortgages in general see the fundamental study by Götz Landwehr, *Die Verpfändung der deutschen Reichsstädte im Mittelalter* (Forschungen zur deutschen Rechtsgeschichte, 5) (Cologne/Vienna, 1967).

25 Franz Quarthal, 'Residenz, Verwaltung und Territorialbildung in den westlichen Herrschaftsgebieten der Habsburger während des Spätmittelalters', in Peter Rück (ed.), *Die Eidgenossen und ihre Nachbarn im Deutschen Reich des Mittelalters* (Marburg an der Lahn, 1991), pp. 78–9.

power elite. Whether the pawns might be redeemed depended much less on the Habsburgs' recurrent financial difficulties than on the ability of the *Pfandherren* to convert their vicarious authority into territorial jurisdictional rights to a point where the mortgages could not in practice be retrieved.[26]

In Inner Switzerland the pawns which fell into the hands of the local communes or the *Länder* were never reclaimed.[27] This might suggest that the Habsburgs simply lost interest once Uri had freed itself from their overlordship in 1231 and reverted to the empire, notwithstanding Uri's control of the northern approaches to the Gotthard pass. How plausible this argument might be turns on the economic and fiscal importance attributed to the Gotthard route over the Alps from its opening up in the early thirteenth century—until recently a topic which has enjoyed totemic status in Swiss historiography. Whether the Gotthard was in fact more frequented, at least until 1400, than the Graubünden passes, or, indeed, the Brenner (which was traversable by carts, not merely pack animals) had been thrown into doubt by Fritz Glauser's researches on the trade passing through Luzern.[28] More broadly, Werner Meyer has questioned whether the Habsburgs really had a strategic stake in the inner cantons. As a measure of territorial-political control, the number of princely strongholds was never very large, and those that are known to have existed disappeared between 1200 and 1350. That was not, as the White Book of Sarnen was later to affirm, the result of deliberate destruction (*Burgenbruch*) by local communes—Neu-Habsburg near Meggen being the only exception—but of apparent neglect, in marked contrast to their survival in eastern Switzerland, Graubünden, and Tirol.[29] Given their active engagement elsewhere in mining ven-

---

[26] Marchal, 'Neue Aspekte', pp. 239–40.

[27] Idem, 'Die schweizerische Geschichtsforschung und die österreichische Herrschaft: Ergebnisse und Fragen', in Rück, *Eidgenossen*, p. 23; for the case of Gersau see Blickle, 'Friede und Verfassung', pp. 65 f.

[28] Hans-Jörg Gilomen, 'Sozial- und Wirtschaftsgeschichte der Schweiz im Spätmittelalter', *Schweizerische Zeitschrift für Geschichte,* 41 (1991), p. 481. Blickle's argument that the Inner Swiss communes were not mortgaged because of the crucial importance of the Gotthard pass does not carry conviction. Blickle, 'Friede und Verfassung', p. 90. For Luzern see Fritz Glauser, 'Der internationale Gotthardtransit im Lichte des Luzerner Zentnerzolls von 1493–1505', *Schweizerische Zeitschrift für Geschichte,* 18 (1968), pp. 177–244. His argument, admittedly, is based on rather limited, and late, evidence—though its very lateness might be taken as bolstering it.

[29] Werner Meyer, 'Siedlung und Alltag. Die mittelalterliche Innerschweiz aus der Sicht des Archäologen', in *Innerschweiz und frühe Eidgenossenschaft,* 2, pp. 266, 271.

tures, Meyer wonders whether the lack of mineral resources in Inner Switzerland (apart from iron-ore near Melchsee-Frutt in Obwalden) may account for the Habsburgs' indifference towards the inner cantons.[30]

After 1291, Albrecht of Habsburg pursued with vigour the extension of the Habsburgs' rights of stewardship over convents and churches, as well as the consolidation of the civic overlordship of the larger towns, a policy only halted by his untimely death in 1308.[31] With the exception of the imbroglio with the abbey of Einsiedeln, these efforts were concentrated outside Sablonier's 'inner zone' of the inner cantons. Yet even the battle of Morgarten in 1315, Blickle contends, should not be seen as an anti-Habsburg triumph, for hostilities broke out over efforts to contain the long-running feud within Schwyz between the *Land* and the abbey, of whom the Habsburgs were stewards—a conflict less over frontiers than over economic resources.[32] The outcome was a renewal of the *conjuratio* of 1291, with the stipulation that *Länder* should not seek the protection of foreign lords (*i.e.* the Habsburgs) without each other's consent. Yet the terms of the truce after Morgarten recognized Habsburg rights and revenues in Inner Switzerland; in return, they had to promise to respect the judicial autonomy of the three original *Länder* (whose *Reichsunmittelbarkeit* had been confirmed and extended by Henry of Luxemburg) and not to infringe it by recourse to foreign courts.[33] The situation in Luzern, which entered into confederation with the three inner cantons in 1332, was rather more complex. The city council declared that its allegiance was contingent upon upholding the Habsburgs' seigneurial rights over the commune, although, as Blickle shrewdly observes, any intervention to safeguard those rights could be taken as active aggression, and hence as a breach of the peace which would entitle the confederates to oppose them.[34] Blickle believes that the council could only have taken such a momentous step if it had first gained the consent of the commons of Luzern. In that case, there would be good reason to interpret the council's

---

30 Ibid., p. 293.

31 Heinrich Koller, 'Die politische Grundhaltung der Habsburger und der Südwesten des Reichs', in Rück, *Eidgenossen*, pp. 51, 56–7.

32 Sablonier, 'Innerschweizer Gesellschaft', pp. 145, 150.

33 Blickle, 'Friede und Verfassung', pp. 37, 45, 59.

34 Ibid., p. 38.

decision as a response to popular pressure from the 'poor' (as in many other German cities at the time), rather than as the pursuit of a traditional animus towards either the Habsburgs or their bailiffs, the von Rothenburg.[35] This reading, however, is at odds with Glauser's recent analysis, which sees rivalry within the civic elite as the cause of conflict, rather than any polarity between a pro-confederate commons and a pro-Habsburg patriciate.[36] Over the next two generations, indeed, Luzern citizens were buying up rural estates—mostly Austrian fiefs—whilst the council was busily granting the surrounding peasantry citizen's rights.[37] The denouement—the crushing defeat of the Habsburg forces, with the loss of many Outer Austrian nobles, at the battle of Sempach in 1386—was brought about essentially by Luzern's outburgher policy, as Guy Marchal has argued,[38] and that can scarcely be viewed as the outflow of a consciously 'anti-feudal' policy directed against territorial sovereignty, Habsburg or otherwise.

In the case of Zürich, the city's knightly families were also bent upon acquiring seigneurial rights in the countryside in the fourteenth century, often themselves already mortgaged, both from the imperial bailiwick of Zürich and from the Habsburgs, though these rights usually comprised *Vogteien* (jurisdictions) rather than landed estates. But when, in turn, the city as a corporation began to buy out the selfsame urban nobles after mid-century, the latter evinced no reluctance in entering princely service, for instance as Habsburg bailiffs. The failure of the Habsburgs to reclaim their pawned *Vogteien* should, in this instance, be attributed to financial incapacity rather than strategic indifference,[39] for Zürich lay at the heart of the Habsburgs' efforts to retain their dwindling power in northern Switzerland in the later Middle Ages. Indeed, Marchal accuses Blickle of playing down to vanishing-point the strenuous policy of recuperations by the Habsburgs, and Zürich's willingness to ally with the dukes against

[35] Ibid., pp. 117–20.

[36] Fritz Glauser, 'Luzern und die Herrschaft Österreich 1326–1336. Ein Beitrag zur Entstehung des Luzerner Bundes von 1332', in *Luzern und die Eidgenossenschaft. Beiträge zur Stellung Luzerns in der politischen Landschaft von 1332, im jungen Bundesstaat und in der Schweiz von heute. Festschrift zum Jubiläum 'Luzern 650 Jahre im Bund'* (Luzern, 1982), pp. 9–135.

[37] Blickle, 'Friede und Verfassung', p. 140.

[38] Guy P. Marchal, *Sempach 1386. Von den Anfängen des Territorialstaates Luzern. Beiträge zur Frühgeschichte des Kantons Luzern* (Basel, 1986), esp. pp. 109–96.

[39] Blickle, 'Friede und Verfassung', pp. 135–6.

the rest of the confederation, during the fifteenth century.[40] At all events, recent research can agree that no clear lines of demarcation can be discerned between spheres of confederate and Austrian influence, not only in the fourteenth century, but even after Sempach. A sustained anti-Habsburg struggle radiating outwards from the lake of Lucerne has no basis in the sources. Instead, as Marchal insists, the process of state formation in Switzerland cannot be explained by communalization and 'defeudalization' alone: the Habsburgs as territorial lords played their part as well.[41]

III

The problems of feudal authority in Inner Switzerland, caught between imperial liberties and mortgaged jurisdictions, cannot of themselves, however, explain why the political organization of the Forest cantons should have developed along expressly *communal* lines. As Sablonier stresses, 'the increasing weight of local autonomy and self-determination in collective association (*Genossenschaft*) and commune (*Gemeinde*) is less to be understood as a "liberation" from lordship but rather as its specific substitute.'[42] In other words, what circumstances disposed the inhabitants of the alpine valleys to choose corporative-confederal (that is, horizontal) modes of maintaining public order in preference to vertical ones? The Inner Swiss valleys were by no means the first communities in western Europe to do so. A comparative glance at communal endeavours elsewhere may, therefore, help to clarify what, if anything, distinguished the situation in Switzerland.

Three impulses have commonly been identified in the development of rural communes: the settling of peasants on new 'colonial' lands on advantageous terms; the actual situation of mountain or upland communities, remote from political interference by seigneurs; and the specific characteristics of a pastoral economy. Needless to say, these explanations are not mutually exclusive, though historians are

---

[40] Marchal, 'Schweizerische Geschichtsforschung', p. 20. The charge is somewhat unfair, since Blickle's brief in *Innerschweiz und frühe Eidgenossenschaft* stopped at 1400.

[41] Marchal, 'Neue Aspekte', p. 237; idem, 'Schweizerische Geschichtsforschung', pp. 17, 20.

[42] Sablonier, 'Innerschweizer Gesellschaft', p. 216.

often hard put to say how they may have interacted. The classic instances of the preferential treatment of peasants are the resettlement of parts of Spain, especially Catalonia and Andalusia, with Christian subjects in the wake of the *Reconquista* from the Muslims,[43] and the planned colonization of the east-Elbian lands by *locatores* from the twelfth century onwards. Neither example offers any direct parallel with the situation in Switzerland. By contrast, the sturdy independence of 'mountainy men' (or, indeed, 'marshy men'—witness the peasants of Dithmarschen in Schleswig-Holstein) has been much invoked by historians, and not simply for Switzerland. Perhaps the most celebrated instance—because at once the earliest and the longest surviving—is that of Andorra, where some communal rights, first established in 1003, were extended after 1087 into virtual autonomy in the wake of collective defiance by six rural communes in the face of the count of Urgel's tax demands.[44] The development of (semi-)autonomous communes in mountain valleys can be traced throughout much of the Pyrenees and the Alps (the francophone areas of Provence, the Dauphiné, and Savoy, as well as germanophone districts), and even the Haute-Auvergne during the Middle Ages[45]—indeed, it has become a Braudelian archetype. It is salutary to be reminded by Chris Wickham, therefore, that mountain communities might equally well be subordinated to dominating and intense territorial lordship. As he concludes, 'mountain environments tend to encourage extreme political solutions' because of the lack of mediating power-structures.[46] In that case, the issue ceases to turn on some supposedly innate characteristic of mountain communities and becomes instead a question of why some 'mountainy men' were ruggedly free and others parlously unfree. Gérard Sivéry contends that it was indeed pastoralism which held the key to the ability of mountain communes to resist their local feudal lords, yet at the same time he is unwilling to concede that pastoralism was in itself sufficient to create autonomous communes, not least because stock-rearing was

[43] On Catalonia see most recently Paul Freedman, *The Origins of Peasant Servitude in Medieval Catalonia* (Cambridge, 1991), esp. pp. 61 ff.

[44] Gérard Sivéry, *Terroirs et Communautés Rurales dans l'Europe Occidentale au Moyen Âge* (Lille, 1990), p. 108.

[45] Ibid., p. 111.

[46] Christopher J. Wickham, *The Mountains and the City. The Tuscan Appennines in the Early Middle Ages* (Oxford, 1988), p. 135.

so often symbiotically linked to adjacent areas of tillage, which commonly were penetrated by feudal relations of dependence.[47] Although this explanation remains vague and ambivalent, it does at least point away from alleged structural features of mountain communities *per se* to their functional (and dynamic) role. It is precisely the changing pattern of economic exploitation which Wickham identifies as the explanation for the emergence of communes in his study of the Garfagnana, the region flanking the valley of the Serchio above Lucca in northwestern Tuscany. From the late twelfth century the Garfagnana developed a distinctive silvo-pastoral economy, based on chestnuts (for flour, rather than milling grain) and sheep flocks, which was predicated upon a market economy centred on the major Tuscan cities—not simply Lucca, but Pisa and Florence as well. In this system pastures and forests provided the main economic resource, and these tended to be owned collectively rather than individually. As a result, their management became a matter of incessant wrangling between communes—Wickham instances Barga and Gallicano competing over pasture on the Monte Gragno, which coincided exactly with the emergence of the commune of Gragno itself. Wickham is careful to make clear that collective economic decisions did not necessarily cause (political) communes to appear; nevertheless, the economic and political aspects of collective activity strongly conditioned each other.[48]

Wickham's Italian evidence is highly suggestive in the Swiss context, particularly on account of Karl Meyer's venerable argument that the emergence of cisalpine rural communes in the italophone valleys of Ticino in the late twelfth century paved the way for the transalpine communes of the next century.[49] His investigation of the Blenio and Leventina valleys south of the Gotthard revealed the existence of family kinship groupings who collectively held the usufruct of alps and forests, as well as sumptery rights on the alpine transit routes. Perhaps as much under the impact of population pressure as of export demand (this was a region largely of oviculture) the families came together to prevent the division of common land or its sale to

[47] Sivéry, *Terroirs et Communautés*, pp. 110 f., 117.

[48] Wickham, *Mountains and the City*, pp. 137–9, 142, 148.

[49] Karl Meyer, 'Italienische Einflüsse bei der Entstehung der Eidgenossenschaft', *Jahrbuch für schweizerische Geschichte*, 45 (1920), pp. 1–76.

outsiders. From these deliberations (*fabulae*) a general council had developed in both Blenio and Leventina by the early thirteenth century, which resolved quarrels over grazing between neighbouring communes.[50]

The evidence is not in doubt—but its interpretation is. Konrad Ruser points out that these communal associations required the sanction of the valleys' judicial overlords; aristocratic families retained their local rights, and both valleys remained under the control of the cathedral chapter of Milan throughout the period.[51] Yet while seigneurial rights of justice might be preserved, the 'commune' of Blenio was already buying out aristocratic and monastic lords' estates as early as 1188, in particular the usufruct of alpine grazing held by the lords of Torre and Giornico.[52] Ruser insists that what drove the communes forward was the need to control intra- and inner-communal violence over access to scarce resources, not a general struggle for freedom from overlordship (or from domination by rural peasant potentates, as he posits for the inner cantons).[53] But how far did the hollowing out of the lords' ownership of estates (in order to augment economic resources) have to go before it amounted, *de facto*, to the extinction of feudal authority altogether? Is not the consolidation of the inner cantons in large measure a history of expropriating *land*lords, as the example of Uri over against the four convents after 1359 testifies? In this context, Peter Bierbrauer's explanation of how the city of Bern was able to buy out feudal lords in its hinterland offers a pertinent analogy: 'The feudal lordships could pass into civic ownership because—to put it starkly—the peasants had already plundered their inventory.'[54]

The difficulty in applying Wickham's analysis to the inner can-

---

[50] See now Ruser, 'Talgemeinden', p. 140; Lothar Deplazes, *Alpen, Grenzen, Pässe im Gebiet Lukmanier-Piora (13.–16. Jahrhundert)* (Quellen und Forschungen zur Bündner Geschichte, 1) (Disentis, 1986), p. 15. The sources are now printed in *Materiali e Documenti Ticinesi*, series 3: *Blenio*, ed. Vittorio F. Raschèr, Lothar Deplazes, Guiseppe Chiesi, and Consuelo Johner-Pagnani, fasc. 2/3, March/December 1981 (Bellinzona, 1981), esp. pp. 83–101, doc. 18. See also Lothar Deplazes, 'Una lita fra due vicinanze bleniesi all'inizio del XIII secolo. Evoluzione del possesso fondario, comportamenti sociali, uso di violenza e mezzi di pacificazione', ibid., fasc. 3, pp. 105–9.

[51] Ruser, 'Talgemeinden', pp. 139, 141.

[52] Deplazes, *Alpen, Grenzen, Pässe*, p. 15.

[53] Ruser, 'Talgemeinden', p. 118.

[54] Peter Bierbrauer, 'Die Ausbildung bäuerlicher Landschaften im Raum der Eidgenossenschaft', *Parliaments, Estates and Representation*, 2 (1991), p. 99.

tons lies in the absence of any consensus about the correct chronological sequence between *commercial* pastoralism and communalism. No one disputes that the growth of communes in Inner Switzerland revolved around the issue of grazing rights: their origins, after all, lay in associations for the management of the common (*Alp-*, *Allmendgenossenschaften*).[55] But how far was this economy of small-scale pastoralists being transformed into one of 'ranchers' by the pressures of an export market? There is not even agreement on the extent of ovi- as opposed to boviculture in Inner Switzerland.[56] It is now thought that cattle as well as sheep were raised before 1300, but when a commercialized economy based on cows and horses for the markets of Lombardy displaced local pastoralism is a matter of debate. Most recent authorities argue for the fourteenth century, but Hans Conrad Peyer, whose views carry considerable weight, would date the shift no earlier than the late fifteenth century! The evidence of cattle exports to Lombardy in the fourteenth century may only hold good for Obwalden and Uri: the enormous sum of 10,535 fl. which Uri was prepared to pay for the estates of the four convents between 1359 and 1362[57] is perhaps only conceivable against a background of very profitable stock-rearing. But whatever the dating, it still falls too late to offer any explanation for the development of territorial communal associations (*Landschaften*) before 1300. (The alternative line of argument, that it was the monastic houses themselves which promoted large-scale pastoralism from as early as the eleventh century, Sablonier dismisses as fanciful.)[58]

IV

How far the inner cantons displayed a genuinely communal mentality—not merely collective but egalitarian—is another question altogether. The legal documents confirming Uri's immediate dependence on the empire after 1231, for instance, are sealed in the name of the *universitas*

---

55 Marchal, 'Neue Aspekte', pp. 243–4.

56 Sablonier, 'Innerschweizer Gesellschaft', p. 134, but at p. 224 he argues that there was no sheep-rearing there at all!

57 Marchal, 'Neue Aspekte', p. 244.

58 Sablonier, 'Innerschweizer Gesellschaft', p. 144.

de Urania; there is little doubt, moreover, that the status of *Reichsunmittelbarkeit* was the decisive precondition for the rise of the inner *Länder*'s political autonomy.[59] In formal terms, the *Land* was a political and judicial unity, its 'law of the land' enshrined in *Landbücher* and confirmed by its legislative body, the *Landgemeinde*, at its annual assembly or moot, where the commons of the territory swore a *Landeseid*. This pattern of 'communal parliamentarianism', as Blickle dubs it, developed, with minor variations, from the late thirteenth century onwards in Uri, Schwyz, and Nidwalden.[60] Blickle, however, goes further. In these political-constitutional manifestations of communal freedom he descries a principled commitment not only to liberty but to equality as well. In support he cites, *inter alia*, the law of the valley commune of Urseren (admittedly a fifteenth-century source) which sought to restrict the growth of individual wealth by preventing each household from importing more than four beef and dairy cattle, and by limiting the number of beasts each was allowed to drive onto the common grazing to eight.[61] He ponders further why the cattle trade over the Alps did not lead to the rise of economic dynasties of peasant magnates in Uri, Schwyz, Luzern, and Zürich on a par with those which developed in the long-distance trading cities of the Low Countries. He answers his own question by noting that herds were driven from toll-bar to toll-bar (*Sust*) not by the traders but by the communes themselves, who apportioned droving as equitably as possible among their members.[62]

Objective constraints—the lack of sufficient grazing, the collective ownership and management of (summer) pastures, the harshness of climate, the need to preserve public order in the face of endemic feuding—undoubtedly conduced to a political culture which elevated the community above the individual and the commonwealth (*Gemeinnutz*) above private interest (*Eigennutz*).[63] From his examination of the continuity of factionalism within the ruling elites of Inner Switzerland, however, Sablonier concludes that what was 'new' about the new elites after 1300 was that, with public sanctions against feuding firmly established, they ceased to base their social and political power on

---

59 Blickle, 'Friede und Verfassung', pp. 73, 89.
60 Ibid., pp. 93 f., 99, 104–5.
61 Ibid., p. 197.
62 Ibid., p. 198.
63 See idem, 'Gesetz der Eidgenossen', pp. 580–1.

the clan, but began to derive their economic power from commerce and credit transactions, whilst anchoring their political influence in confederal cooperation between cantons.[64] From this perspective, the commune provided the indispensable carapace—cover might be a less charitable term—for the pursuit of sectional advantage. The evidence which he offers stems, it is true, largely from the period after 1380. Yet even when these new dynasties died out, as many surprisingly did in the early fifteenth century, they were replaced by others. The 'principle' of elites, in other words, was confirmed, and indeed their 'peasant' character diminished as they became more dependent on mercenary service, pensions, territorial office-holding (in *Landvogteien*) and jurisdictional rights.[65] There is no room within the present review to assess in detail the arguments which Sablonier adduces for the existence of a highly complex and evolving agrarian economy in the Alps after 1300; in any case, the evidence will always remain patchy and inconclusive. Nevertheless, he encourages us to turn our gaze away from the high pastures (the alps proper) and from transhumance downwards to the changes taking place on the middling slopes of the valleys.[66] The aggression displayed by Schwyz towards the abbey of Einsiedeln—a *locus classicus* of the origins of the 'freedom-loving' confederates—was not, he suggests, a boundary dispute but a conflict over communally organized and shared pastures. Was the quarrel, he enquires, not so much with the abbey itself but with the abbey's peasants, who had been driven onto the shared pastures in undue numbers by Einsiedeln's curtailment of grazing in order to create commercially oriented vaccaries (*Schweighöfe*)?[67] Furthermore, should we interpret this commercialization as a deliberate policy of the abbey or of its reeves (*Meier*), leading peasants who leased pastures from the abbey in order to rent them out to burghers eager to invest in the profits of pastoralism? A close connection between reeves and citizens has certainly been demonstrated not only for Einsiedeln, but for the abbey of Murbach's manor of Luzern and the city, as well as for Engelberg and Luzern.[68] These

---

[64] Sablonier, 'Innerschweizer Gesellschaft', p. 36.
[65] Ibid., p. 38.
[66] See esp. his typology, ibid., pp. 208–11.
[67] Ibid., pp. 145–6, 150–1.
[68] Ibid., p. 152.

subtle, but profound, shifts in the rural alpine economy seem, therefore, ultimately to have been driven by urban interests—we are back in Wickham's world of the Garfagnana! What, in these circumstances, remains of a genuine sense of communal solidarity? Blickle's argument about the absence of ranchers does not even mention Unterwalden! Even droving over the alpine passes, Sablonier hints, was not quite what it seems. Certainly it was communally, and strictly, controlled, but at the same time it represented a peasant by-employment, whereby those who owned the pack-animals were not necessarily the drovers: the latter might be wage-labourers or servants.[69]

That Blickle and Sablonier should differ so markedly in their analysis of the social reality of the Inner Swiss communes may depend less on the vagaries of the evidence than on fundamentally differing assumptions about the nature of medieval rural society. In his analysis of the causes of peasant revolts in the late medieval empire, Blickle observes that historians fall into two camps: the 'individualists', who stress the autonomy of peasant production as the manorial system disintegrated, and the 'communalists', who affirm the importance of the commune as the 'structural principle' of rural society alongside feudal landlordship. The 'individualists' tend to see peasant revolts as a struggle over the distribution of economic resources, whereas the 'communalists' regard peasant uprisings as political movements with ideological ends.[70] With the appropriate adjustments this distinction applies with uncanny aptness to the 'individualist' Sablonier, whose brief was to investigate the underlying social and economic structure of the inner cantons, and to the 'communalist' Blickle, who was charged with analyzing the political and constitutional development of the early confederation. In that sense, therefore, the differences of interpretation seem almost *vorprogrammiert*. Would their conclusions have been radically different if they had swapped briefs? Whilst firmly in the 'individualist' camp, I would agree with Blickle that the categories do overlap—provided that we are clear that 'equality' in no way implied 'communism', the abandonment of private property rights by peasant farmers.

---

[69] Ibid., pp. 182–4.

[70] Peter Blickle, *Unruhen in der ständischen Gesellschaft 1300–1800* (*Enzyklopädie Deutscher Geschichte*, 1) (Munich, 1988), p. 103.

V

The identification of considerable disparities of wealth, status, and power within individual communes or the *Länder* as a whole does not, of course, invalidate the general observation that the Inner Swiss cantons in the later Middle Ages were engaged in a wider struggle for emancipation which may legitimately be termed communal, in the sense of anti-feudal. What marks Inner Switzerland off from other areas within the empire where similar communal movements in the countryside occurred, notably in parts of Swabia and the Black Forest, was the unique alliance of free peasant communes with cities. It was not the *Bundesbrief* of 1291 but the extension of the original confederation in the fourteenth century by a series of urban alliances which embraced Luzern (1332), Zürich (1351), Zug (1352), and Bern (1359) up to the *Pfaffenbrief* of 1370—that for the first time referred to the *Eidgenossenschaft* rather than separate *Eidgenossen*—which constituted the distinctive formation of the Helvetic Confederation. It was not a single act, therefore, but a cumulative process.[71] But underpinning this constitutional development lay a much more remarkable social emancipation, as thousands of peasants bought citizen's rights as outburghers of the northern Swiss cities. How they were able to do so demands investigation. Blickle argues in a broader context that the area between Lake Constance and the Alps offered more scope for the achievement of personal freedom than the districts north of the Rhine. The strict manorial law (*Hofrecht*) of Bavaria, or the profusion of monastic lordships throughout Swabia, found no real counterpart in Switzerland. Already in the great Habsburg *Urbar* after 1303 greater freedom of movement and marriage was recorded, more hereditary tenures registered, and less onerous feudal obligations, such as the heriot, listed for the peasants in Switzerland than in the Habsburg domains in Upper Germany; Blickle believes that was true of Switzerland in general.[72] From 1270 onwards Habsburg serfs were buying themselves free in considerable numbers.[73] And even where manumission was less feasible—the example of Unterwalden

---

[71] Idem, 'Friede und Verfassung', pp. 38–41; on this point see fundamentally Hans Conrad Peyer, *Verfassungsgeschichte der alten Schweiz* (Zürich, 1978).

[72] Blickle, 'Friede und Verfassung', p. 182.

[73] Ibid., p. 80.

faced with the abbey of Engelberg has been cited—hereditary leases came to replace revocable tenures. Bierbrauer has pointed to a similar pattern in his wide-ranging study of the alpine territories of Bern. Individual deeds of manumission proliferated in the Bernese Oberland: by 1312 around half the serfs of Saanen had bought their freedom; by the end of the century a great many in the Lower Simmental had done likewise.[74] Moreover, communes might cancel feudal obligations collectively: between 1312 and 1448 Saanen as a community bought out servile obligations, bailiff's dues and landlord rights; between 1393 and 1445 the Lower Simmental discharged all remaining personal and tenurial dues for forty times the annual render—the staggering sum of 7,171 fl.[75]

The erosion of feudal bonds undoubtedly created favourable conditions for peasants to acquire citizen's rights, but their ability, individually or collectively, to afford outburghership remains puzzling, since neither chronology nor geography permit any straightforward link with the prosperity allegedly bestowed by the burgeoning traffic across the alpine passes. What is true, however, is that outburghership lay as much in the cities' as in the peasants' interests. From the fourteenth century Bern pursued a vigorous outburgher policy, which brought around half the population of the Bernese Mittel- and Oberland into the subject status of rural citizens, obliged to pay taxes and render military service to the city. This policy was the principal means whereby Bern contrived to undermine the power of the local nobility and so construct a vast rural territory which from the fourteenth to the sixteenth century rivalled the county (later the duchy) of Württemberg in size.[76] In Zürich, peasant outburghers are recorded from the end of the thirteenth century. The city offered *Verburgrechtung* (as it was called—essentially a protective alliance) to

---

[74] Peter Bierbrauer, 'Freiheit und Gemeinde im Berner Oberland 1300–1700', *Archiv des Historischen Vereins des Kantons Bern*, 74 (1991), p. 100; idem, 'Ausbildung bäuerlicher Landschaften', p. 95.

[75] Idem, 'Freiheit und Gemeinde', p. 133; idem, 'Die ländliche Gemeinde im oberdeutsch-schweizerischen Raum', in Peter Blickle (ed.), *Landgemeinde und Stadtgemeinde in Europa. Ein struktureller Vergleich* (*Historische Zeitschrift*, Beiheft 13, new series) (Munich, 1991), p. 175; cf. Bierbrauer, 'Der Aufstieg der Gemeinde und die Entfeudalisierung der Gesellschaft im späten Mittelalter', in Peter Blickle and Johannes Kunisch (eds), *Kommunalisierung und Christianisierung. Voraussetzungen und Folgen der Reformation 1400–1600* (*Zeitschrift für Historische Forschung*, Beiheft 9) (Berlin, 1989), pp. 41–4.

[76] Bierbrauer, 'Freiheit und Gemeinde', pp. 89, 102–3.

nobles, monastic houses and peasants alike, though the latter often remained technically unfree. In the second half of the fourteenth century Zürich acquired nearly 700 peasant outburghers, compared with its urban population of around 5,000.[77] But the most spectacular example was Luzern, which in the 1380s alone is reckoned to have admitted 1,000 new outburghers.[78] The dislocation of seigneurial authority in the countryside which this engendered entirely justifies Guy Marchal's view that the battle of Sempach was fought over this issue, rather than over the territorial rights of the Habsburgs as such.

The spread of outburghership throughout northern Switzerland (it embraced Basel and Solothurn as well) was on a scale unmatched elsewhere in the empire, Blickle believes, with the possible exception of Strasbourg.[79] This statement needs to be qualified. There is evidence that Swabian cities such as Augsburg,[80] Kempten, and Isny[81] possessed sizeable numbers of outburghers in the fifteenth century, and within the Alemannic region the same applies to Konstanz[82] and Freiburg im Breisgau.[83]

What is less certain is whether in these instances outburghership was the necessary prelude to an active policy of territorial expansion, whereas in Switzerland it certainly was. Indeed, the northern Swiss cities built up rural dependencies more rapidly, less expensively and with fewer obstacles in their path than was the case anywhere in southern Germany.[84] As Bierbrauer repeats, the territorial policy of Bern, Zürich, or Luzern was not more successful than that of

---

[77] Blickle, 'Friede und Verfassung', pp. 137–9.

[78] Ibid., p. 143.

[79] Ibid., p. 186.

[80] See Rolf Kießling, 'Herrschaft—Markt—Landbesitz. Aspekte der Zentralität und der Stadt-Land-Beziehungen spätmittelalterlicher Städte an ostschwäbischen Beispielen', in Emil Meynen (ed.), *Zentralität als Problem der mittelalterlichen Stadtgeschichtsforschung* (Städteforschung. Veröffentlichungen des Instituts für vergleichende Städtegeschichte in Münster, A 8 (Cologne/Vienna, 1979), p. 162.

[81] Tom Scott (ed.), *Die Freiburger Enquete von 1476. Quellen zur Wirtschafts- und Verwaltungsgeschichte der Stadt Freiburg im Breisgau im fünfzehnten Jahrhundert* (Veröffentlichungen aus dem Archiv der Stadt Freiburg im Breisgau, 20) (Freiburg im Breisgau, 1986), pp. 11, 13, 16.

[82] Bernhard Kirchgässner, *Das Steuerwesen der Reichsstadt Konstanz 1418–1460. Aus der Wirtschafts- und Sozialgeschichte einer oberdeutschen Handelsstadt am Ausgang des Mittelalters* (Konstanzer Geschichts- und Rechtsquellen, 10) (Konstanz, 1960), p. 161.

[83] Tom Scott, *Freiburg and the Breisgau. Town-Country Relations in the Age of Reformation and Peasants' War* (Oxford, 1986), pp. 78–98, 155–6.

[84] Blickle, 'Friede und Verfassung', pp. 147–8.

Strasbourg, Nuremberg, or Augsburg because they were more powerful and ambitious, but because they were the beneficiaries of the weakening of feudal power which the peasants' initiative had wrought.[85]

The peculiarity of late medieval Switzerland was that the policy of territorial aggrandizement was not confined to the 'city-states'; it was pursued by the rural inner cantons as well. What is more, their territorial designs extended beyond the predictable extirpation of feudal overlords to preying upon their neighbouring confederates. When Schwyz at last succeeded in incorporating the subjects of the abbey of Einsiedeln into its *Landrecht* in 1414, the latter became subjects of Schwyz, not members of the commune of Schwyz (though other communes were granted full territorial rights). Schwyz also tried to take over the city of Zug (possibly abetted by the city's rural subjects).[86] In 1403 Uri extended its protection south of the Gotthard to the Leventina as a bulwark against Milanese expansion, but under the terms of the alliance the Leventina became the joint subject of Uri and Obwalden, rather than a member of their *Landrecht*; by contrast, the Urseren valley, on account of its strategically vital location controlling the north side of the Gotthard, was granted Uri's *Landrecht* a few years later.[87] Such behaviour by the *Länder* contravened the spirit, if not the letter, of the *Bundesbrief* of 1291; by the fifteenth century it had in fact become much harder for the inner cantons to act as territorial predators. Instead they sought to extend their influence by sharing in the administration of the mandated territories (*gemeine Herrschaften*), such as the Aargau.[88]

Admittedly, the territorial policy of the inner cantons paled beside the single-minded expansion of the city cantons, but both illustrate how problematic the concept of 'liberty' is when applied to medieval Switzerland. The rural dependents of the 'city-states' found in most cases that they had merely exchanged their bonds to noble seigneurs for subjection to urban patriciates, who used much the same array of feudal instruments to hold their peasants in check as the judicial and manorial lords they supplanted. The magistrates were, echoing Perry Anderson's description of the Italian city-states' treatment of

---

[85] Bierbrauer, 'Ausbildung bäuerlicher Landschaften', p. 102.
[86] Blickle, 'Friede und Verfassung', pp. 49–50.
[87] Ibid., p. 153.
[88] Ibid., pp. 151–2.

their *contadi*, usurpers, not destroyers, of feudal dominion, that is, power exerted by extra-economic coercion.[89] It is no wonder that Switzerland experienced by far the greatest incidence of peasant revolts in the late medieval empire, because cities such as Zürich, Bern, Luzern, and even lowly Solothurn were bent upon a ruthless and predatory territorial policy.[90]

Conflict intensified in the fifteenth century, as Zürich fell victim in 1489 to the Grüningen revolt, which wrested substantial concessions from the city council,[91] and Bern became embroiled with the subjects of the abbey of Interlaken in 1445. From that revolt sprang a general uprising of much of the Bernese Oberland, rallying in the so-called Evil League (*Böser Bund*), which, although defused by the city council's shrewd tactics, had its aftermath in a new revolutionary conspiracy of Interlaken's subjects around Brienz between 1446 and 1451.[92] The Bernese revolts are of particular interest because they reveal a peasants' view of liberty which could go beyond the defence of hard-won rights. The rebels in Brienz claimed to be acting according to God's will; more striking still, they had already invoked divine justice in 1400, when deciding that women should enjoy the same inheritance rights as men. This, Bierbrauer maintains, is the first recorded instance of the slogan that was to prove so potent in the Bundschuh revolts on the Upper Rhine at the end of the century and in the German Peasants' War itself being adopted in the countryside.[93] For the most part, however, Bern's rural subjects understood 'freedom' to consist in the corporative rights of communes, set down in sealed deeds, that is, liberties of the community rather than of the individual peasant.[94] Only those who were members of the commune (which entailed acceptance by majority vote,

[89] Perry Anderson, *Passages from Antiquity to Feudalism* (London, 1974), p. 192. The actual term 'usurpers' is, of course, Max Weber's.

[90] Bierbrauer, 'Ausbildung bäuerlicher Landschaften', p. 100.

[91] Christian Dietrich, *Die Stadt Zürich und ihre Landgemeinden während der Bauernunruhen von 1489 bis 1525* (Europäische Hochschulschriften, 3rd series, 229) (Frankfurt am Main/Bern/New York, 1985).

[92] Bierbrauer, 'Freiheit und Gemeinde', pp. 133, 153, 171–7. See André Holenstein, 'Obrigkeit und Untertan. Zur Geschichte der Untertanenhuldigung im bernischen Territorium (15.–18. Jahrhundert)', in Rudolf Endres (ed.), *Nürnberg und Bern, Zwei Reichsstädte und ihre Landgebiete* (Erlanger Forschungen, A 46) (Erlangen, 1990), pp. 261–82, esp. 272.

[93] Bierbrauer, 'Freiheit und Gemeinde', pp. 178–9.

[94] Ibid., pp. 204–5.

the swearing of an oath, and the payment of an admission fee) partook fully of communal liberty; *per contram*, those who married outside the community ran the risk of forfeiting their heirs' right to belong to the commune and to inherit property in it.[95]

The shock which then befell the peasantry in early modern Switzerland was all the ruder. Confronted with the intensification of state power in the city territories the peasants could not escape the awful truth that their corporative liberties were quite inadequate to ward off the encroachment of the state upon rural autonomies, and that their active participation in 'communal parliamentarianism' was destined to yield before the passive role of subjects.[96] The sense of their own emancipatory contribution to liberty was gradually overlaid by conformity to the state.[97] What was left was the legend of Wilhelm Tell—a legend so refracted that in both the Thun Affair of 1641 and the Swiss Peasants' War of 1653 a string of new 'Tells' sprang up to claim his mantle.[98]

---

[95] Ibid., pp. 204, 226.

[96] See in general André Holenstein, *Die Huldigung der Untertanen. Rechtskultur und Herrschaftsordnung (800–1800)* (Quellen und Forschungen zur Agrargeschichte, 36) (Stuttgart, 1990).

[97] Bierbrauer, 'Freiheit und Gemeinde', pp. 362–3.

[98] Ibid., p. 360.

CHAPTER FIFTEEN

SOUTH-WEST GERMAN SERFDOM IN COMPARATIVE PERSPECTIVE

Since the end of the nineteenth century a clear contrast has existed in German social and economic history between east-Elbian domanial lordship (*Gutsherrschaft*) and west German landlordship (*Grundherrschaft*). Although this distinction has been considerably toned down over the years, it is still argued that in eastern Europe serfdom in its intensified form was deployed as a reinforcement of commercial landlordship, whereas in western Germany with the collapse of classical manorialism rights of landlordship, jurisdictional lordship, and lordship over serfs fell apart. Landlordship developed into simple rental lordship; only when the latter began to falter as a result of the late mediaeval agrarian crisis were rights of servile lordship reactivated in areas where landlordship as a source of income had all but run its course. That applied to large parts of south-west Germany, which were marked by severe fragmentation of landlordly estates and seigneurial rights. In north-west Germany, by contrast, where noble landlordships were as a rule larger and more consolidated, recourse to lordship over serfs became otiose.[1]

This account may be accurate enough in its broad outlines. But recent research has reached a more differentiated picture of late mediaeval lordship over serfs in south-west Germany. The following remarks are not so much intended to trace the divergence of views as to place the phenomenon of lordship over serfs/serfdom in a broader context. The question to be addressed, therefore, is not principally why rights of servile lordship were reactivated in the south-west in contrast to other areas of Germany, but rather why recourse to lordship over serfs as an instrument of seigneurial rule occurred

[1] Friedrich Lütge, *Geschichte der deutschen Agrarverfassung vom frühen Mittelalter bis zum 19. Jahrhundert* (*Deutsche Agrargeschichte*, 3), 2nd edn (Stuttgart, 1967); Werner Rösener, *Agrargeschichte, Agrarverfassung und ländliche Gesellschaft im Mittelalter* (*Enzyklopädie Deutscher Geschichte*, 13) (Munich, 1992).

at a point when the personal dependence of bondmen and -women in most other parts of Europe had either long disappeared or else was on its last legs. As a result, it is hoped not only to cast light on south-west German serfdom as such but also to interrogate it as evidence in the debate on the transition from feudalism to capitalism, which has recently been taken up once more by Robert Brenner.

For Swabia, Peter Blickle and his pupils have painted a highly nuanced picture of lordship over serfs, which has been developed further for the Upper Rhine by Claudia Ulbrich. Two motives above all—which need not exclude each other—made recourse to lordship over serfs an obvious choice. By comparing the abbeys of Kempten and Ottobeuren in the Allgäu, Blickle can convincingly show that differences in the structure of agriculture and settlement determined the choice of seigneurial devices. Ottobeuren had a relatively uniform landlordship based on tillage, compact settlements, and nucleated villages, which allowed the abbey to capitalize upon its landlordly revenues. Kempten, by contrast, lay in a district of pastoralism, scattered settlements, and isolated farmsteads, and thus was unable to activate its rights of landlordship (which in any case were less consolidated) to the same extent. Instead, the abbey fell back upon rights of servile lordship, which led to repeated conflicts with its subjects. These first came to a head in a revolt in 1490/91, and later in the Peasants' War itself. Kempten's lordship over serfs, however, only achieved its fullest extent in the middle of the sixteenth century.[2]

This structural difference was matched elsewhere by a functional one. From the need to stem the landflight of their subjects and to counteract the collapse of their agrarian revenues, the abbeys of Schussenried in Swabia and St Blasien in the Black Forest (according to Blickle) deployed lordship over serfs as a means of tying their villeins not only tenurially but bodily more closely to the abbey, though in St Blasien's case this occurred half a century earlier than Schussenried. This decision coincided with the blossoming of the

[2] Peter Blickle, 'Leibherrschaft als Instrument der Territorialpolitik im Allgäu. Grundlagen der Landeshoheit der Klöster Kempten und Ottobeuren', in idem, *Studien zur geschichtlichen Bedeutung des deutschen Bauernstandes* (Quellen und Forschungen zur Agrargeschichte, 35) (Stuttgart/New York, 1989), pp. 3–18 [originally in Heinz Haushofer and Willi A. Boelcke (eds), *Wege und Forschungen der Agrargeschichte. Festschrift zum 65. Geburtstag von Günther Franz* (*Zeitschrift für Agrargeschichte und Agrarsoziologie*, special vol. 3) (Frankfurt am Main, 1967), pp. 51–66].

south-west German imperial free cities; once they had begun to decline economically and demographically, the pressure to intensify lordship over serfs eased.[3]

Furthermore, in the case of the Allgäu Blickle points to the use of lordship over serfs as an instrument of territorial policy, with the abbey of Kempten once again offering a prime example. According to the so-called 'custom of the Allgäu', up to the sixteenth century it was the lord of serfs who exercised jurisdictional and financial control of subjects, regardless of their place of residence. This led to a considerable regional dispersion of serfs, which stood in the way of constructing a consolidated seigneurial territory. In order to overcome this obstacle, lords of serfs exchanged subjects in droves well into the sixteenth century. That was only possible, however, on the basis of levelling down the differing legal status of subjects, whereby monastic free rent-paying peasants (*Freizinser*) were degraded into serfdom. In the Peasants' War this process gave rise to bitter complaints by subjects of the abbey of Kempten. Once the rounding off of territorial jurisdictions had been completed, lordship over serfs lost much of its oppressive character.[4] Other seigneurs, however, failed to deploy lordship over serfs successfully in this way. The abbey of St Blasien found its room for manoeuvre constricted by the Austrian bailiffs of the cameral lordship of Hauenstein, and as a result chose gradually to expand and underpin its lordship by making the lease of farms dependent on submitting to serfdom. After 1500 the abbey in particular compelled the male subjects of foreign lords who married female subjects of the abbey to accept term-leases, whereby their heirs by virtue of the custom of the 'poorer hand' (*ärgere Hand*) were obliged to inherit their farms as serfs of St Blasien. St Blasien, too, exchanged serfs, but never with the assiduity or the success of Kempten.[5] Elsewhere on the Upper Rhine, lords such as the city of Basel or the margraves of Baden preferred to buttress their territorial

[3] Peter Blickle, 'Agrarkrise und Leibeigenschaft im spätmittelalterlichen deutschen Südwesten', in idem, *Studien zur geschichtlichen Bedeutung*, pp. 19–35 [originally in Hermann Kellenbenz (ed.), *Agrarisches Nebengewerbe und Formen der Reagrarisierung im Spätmittelalter und 19./20. Jahrhundert* (Forschungen zur Sozial- und Wirtschaftsgeschichte, 21) (Stuttgart, 1975), pp. 39–55].

[4] Blickle, 'Leibherrschaft im Allgäu', *passim*.

[5] Claudia Ulbrich, *Leibherrschaft am Oberrhein im Spätmittelalter* (Veröffentlichungen des Max-Planck-Instituts für Geschichte, 58) (Göttingen, 1979), pp. 25–113.

integrity by preventing exogamous marriage (in French *formariage*; in German *ungenossame Ehe*), or by imposing restrictions on freedom of movement. The financial burdens which devolved upon their subjects were in such cases mostly trivial.[6]

By 1600 serfdom in south-west Germany had run its course. Once the late mediaeval agrarian crisis had been overcome its economic utility receded; with the territorialization of smaller lordships it had accomplished its political purpose. Yet serfdom was almost nowhere abolished; rather, it degenerated into a formula with no defamatory connotations as a means of controlling the grant of farmsteads. The renders based on it amounted to no more than recognition-fees. In a word: south-west German lordship over serfs/serfdom survived because it had outlived its purpose.

This line of argument is highly persuasive for the Swabian or Alemannic regions because it takes account of differing patterns of lordship and hallmarks of subjection. But if we look further afield corrections soon become necessary. Werner Troßbach, for example, has posed the question in the light of sources from Nassau and Hessen whether south-west German serfdom in the early modern period really was no more than a bagatelle.[7] Even for a narrowly defined south-west, he points to long-standing disputes over serfdom into the eighteenth century; these occurred in Hohenzollern-Hechingen, between Baden and the Palatinate, and above all in the county of Hauenstein (to which we shall return).[8] For Palatine lordships Kurt Andermann does indeed regard serfdom as a bagatelle (in accord with Blickle and his pupils), but stresses that it should be differentiated in at least three respects from its configuration in the Swabian and Alemannic lands.

1. There is no evidence that it was deployed either as an income substitute in the wake of the agrarian crisis or as an instrument of the intensification of lordship; if anything, it was an obstacle to the creation of a *territorium clausum*, so that during the fourteenth and fifteenth centuries there were frequent exchanges and sales of serfs. (There are parallels here to the situation in the abbacy of Kempten.)

[6] Ibid., pp. 139–80, 216–34, 278.

[7] Werner Troßbach, '"Südwestdeutsche Leibeigenschaft" in der Frühen Neuzeit—eine Bagatelle?', *Geschichte und Gesellschaft*, 8 (1981), pp. 69–90, esp. 86–8.

[8] Ibid., pp. 77, 79–83.

2. Serfdom does not embody a legally fixed or unalterable status of personal unfreedom. Whoever resided beyond the Palatinate—'dwelling under other lords' (*hinter anderen herrschaften sytzen*)—was a serf. Whoever returned to Palatine territory, however, was released from serfdom and was treated thenceforth as a full subject (*rechter Untertan*).

3. In the Palatinate no jurisdictional authority over serfs emerged, which might have manifested itself in restrictions on marriage or movement. Neighbouring territories, however, chose a different path. The bishopric of Speyer issued a mandate in 1470, whereby all subjects, and not just serfs, were stripped of their freedom of movement and the right of exogamous marriage. Only after the process of territorialization in this region of fragmented lordship had been more or less completed was serfdom finally regulated by concluding treaties of reciprocal freedom of movement.[9]

Recent historiography, therefore, presents a highly uneven picture of south-west German servile lordship and the subjection which it engendered. Peter Blickle already recognised this fact when remarking of the Allgäu 'that landlordship is not just landlordship, and lordship over serfs is not simply lordship over serfs; rather, they should both be seen within the coordinates of time and space'.[10] From that there arise in my view three sets of questions which may lead us towards an accurate assessment and classification of south-west German lordship over serfs/serfdom.

1. To what extent does this lordship over serfs (*Leibherrschaft*) constitute a relationship of authority and dependency of a new quality? Should this dependency be classed as a particular configuration of older forms of servility (*Eigenschaft*)?

2. Are there congruences between the regionally confined lordship over serfs in south-west Germany and forms of dependent tenancy (*Eigenbehörigkeit*), which can be found in other parts of western Germany?

3. In what does the unfreedom of bodily serfdom consist? On what does it rest, and what burdens are associated with it?

---

[9] Kurt Andermann, 'Leibeigenschaft im pfälzischen Oberrheingebiet während des späten Mittelalters und der frühen Neuzeit', *Zeitschrift für Historische Forschung*, 17 (1990), pp. 281–303.

[10] Blickle, 'Leibherrschaft im Allgäu', p. 17.

Ad 1. In German-language sources the word *Leibherrschaft* (lordship over serfs) does not occur; it is a term coined by mediaevalists. The term *Leibeigenschaft* (bodily serfdom) on the other hand can be traced at odd places in the sources back to the fourteenth century, but usually the simple term *Eigenschaft* (serfdom) is deployed. Rolf Köhn has demonstrated that the adjectival use preceded the nominal; in Swiss sources of the late fourteenth century the descriptor *leibeigen* (bodily unfree) appears before the abstract noun *Leibeigenschaft* (bodily serfdom).[11] Claudia Ulbrich has come to similar conclusions for the Upper Rhine.[12] But the identical subject, albeit expressed as 'unfreedom of the body', can be found in Swiss sources even earlier, and in this sense *Eigenschaft* (serfdom) crops up in the early thirteenth century in Gottfried von Straßburg's *Tristan und Isolde.*[13] The earliest references to the word *leibeigen* (bodily unfree) in the Palatinate, however, cannot be dated any earlier than 1443; serfs are described variously as 'poor folk' (*arme Leute*) or as servile (*eigen*)—the terms are interchangeable.[14]

In the Latin sources vague and frequently overlapping terms predominate: *servi, mancipia, homines proprii.* Against the commonplace assumption that legal differences in the personal status of subjects gradually receded after the high Middle Ages, Rolf Köhn has recently insisted on a differentiation within the category of unfreedom, namely between rent-payers (*Zinser*) and serfs:

> In comparison with bodily unfree *servi* the *censuales* enjoyed far-reaching privileges, particularly through freedom to choose their place of residence and occupation, exemption from *corvées*, and superior rights of possession and inheritance. They were also advantaged by being subject to slight restrictions on marriage, or none at all, and limited renders.[15]

Köhn relates this distinction to a supposedly similar differentiation in the Anglo-Norman kingdom between *nativus* and *villanus*, where

---

[11] Rolf Köhn, 'Wahrnehmung und Bezeichnung von Leibeigenschaft in Mittel- und Westeuropa vor dem 14. Jahrhundert', in Jürgen Miethke and Klaus Schreiner (eds), *Sozialer Wandel im Mittelalter. Wahrnehmungsformen, Erklärungsmuster, Regelungsmechanismen* (Sigmaringen, 1994), pp. 301–334, here at p. 315.

[12] Ulbrich, *Leibherrschaft*, p. 32.

[13] Köhn, 'Wahrnehmung', p. 316.

[14] Andermann, 'Leibeigenschaft', p. 288.

[15] Köhn, 'Wahrnehmung', p. 311.

the *villani* were in the majority, albeit with regional variations. He therefore asks whether the differential spread in the use of the terms *servus* and *villanus* depended upon regional linguistic usage, or whether it reflected different degrees of personal unfreedom in southern and Middle England. Köhn believes that an unambiguous answer cannot be given.[16] The dramatic consequences of this distinction for our understanding of personal unfreedom in Germany, however, entirely escape him, and I will return to the point.

Despite the myriad of confusing terms Köhn concludes that the distinction between rent-payers (*Zinser*) and serfs should be attributed to a hierarchy of differing proprietary rights, which he can trace back to the early twelfth century. In his chronicle of the abbey of Zwiefalten the monk Ortlieb distinguished between rent-payers who belonged to the abbey *proprie*, and the servile unfree, who were subject to the convent *ex toto iure proprietatis*.[17] This distinction, however, derives from a period when the manorial constitution and the *familia* of subjects which it embraced were still intact. It would be illegitimate to apply it without further ado to the late fifteenth century. Nevertheless, it sharpens our awareness of what the distinction between Kempten's free rent-payers and its serfs may actually have involved. The rent-payers, as is well known, complained before and during the Peasants' War that they had been forced into serfdom. It may thus appear that previously they had been free: they merely paid the abbey an annual recognition-fee and the heriot. Apart from that they were free to move, although this right had been contentious from the end of the fourteenth century.[18] While freedom of movement is generally taken as the hallmark of free men and women over against the unfree,[19] in Kempten's case the efforts to achieve territorial consolidation by imposing serfdom had been undertaken precisely because the monastery's bodily serfs had become distributed over such a wide area in the course of the fourteenth century. Palatine serfdom, too, demonstrates the possibility of serfs' enjoying limited freedom of movement. Originally the serfs of St Blasien were

[16] Ibid., p. 312.

[17] Ibid., p. 322.

[18] Peter Blickle and Heribert Besch (eds), 'Der Kemptener Leibeigenschaftsrodel', *Zeitschrift für bayerische Landesgeschichte*, 42 (1979), pp. 567–629, here at p. 571.

[19] See Köhn, 'Wahrnehmung', p. 327.

also free to move (and to inherit without restriction), so that these subjects, described as 'people of the monastery' (*Gotteshausleute*), enjoyed almost as many economic and social opportunities as its free men and women.[20] Not until the manorial roll of 1467 was freedom of movement rescinded.[21] In recent research there is now agreement that the status of the unfree cannot readily be deduced from certain legal distinguishing marks or from payment obligations. We should enquire, therefore, whether the Kempten rent-payers were completely personally free, even if they displayed none of the usual marks of unfreedom, or whether their dependence on the convent may not have been founded on other criteria. That this conjecture is not entirely wayward will emerge from our subsequent comments on the situation in France. If bodily serfdom consisted in a particular form of a more general and traditional personal unfreedom, rather than being a belated and separate development,[22] then two provisional hypotheses suggest themselves:

a) Reducing the term *Leibeigenschaft* to the form in which we encounter it in south-west Germany in the late Middle Ages obscures the fact that other forms of personal unfreedom or subjection may have existed in other parts of the empire.

b) The offensiveness of *Leibeigenschaft* may not derive from its actual restrictions and impediments, but rather from a change of ideological perspective.

Walter Müller has traced the roots of a principled rejection of bodily serfdom in the Peasants' War, drawing attention to older sources such as the Reformation of Emperor Sigismund alongside the more obvious Reforming influences in the shape of brotherly love and Christian equality.[23] Linguistically, though, it is striking, as

---

[20] Ulbrich, *Leibherrschaft*, p. 41.

[21] Josef Bader (ed.), 'Urkundenregeste über die ehemaligen sankt-blasischen Niedergerichte', *Zeitschrift für die Geschichte des Oberrheins*, 7 (1856), pp. 235–9.

[22] See Hannah Rabe, *Das Problem Leibeigenschaft. Eine Untersuchung über die Anfänge einer Ideologisierung und des verfassungsrechtlichen Wandels von Freiheit und Eigentum im deutschen Bauernkrieg* (*Vierteljahrschrift für Sozial- und Wirtschaftsgeschichte*, Beiheft 64) (Wiesbaden, 1977). For a critique which demolishes Rabe's interpretation of the sources but which regards the distinction between *Leibeigenschaft* and *Eigenschaft* as potentially fruitful, see the review by Peter Blickle in *Zeitschrift für bayerische Landesgeschichte*, 42 (1979), pp. 190–3.

[23] Walter Müller, 'Wurzeln und Bedeutung des grundsätzlichen Widerstandes gegen die Leibeigenschaft im Bauernkrieg 1525', *Schriften des Vereins für Geschichte des Bodensees und seiner Umgebung*, 93 (1975), pp. 1–41.

Andermann has shown for the Palatinate, that after the Peasants' War only bodily serfdom (*Leibeigenschaft*) retained its degrading connotations, whereas terms such as *Pirmins-*, *Peters-*, or *Königsleute*, which meant the same thing, never aroused such passions.[24]

Ad 2. Now that we are willing to entertain the notion that *Leibeigenschaft* may be viewed as a component of a more general serfdom (*Eigenschaft*), we may direct our attention beyond south-west Germany. In neighbouring areas such as Franconia and Hessen bodily serfdom indeed survived, although principally in ecclesiastical territories such as the bishopric of Würzburg or the abbacy of Fulda.[25] Servile dues, however, had largely become tenurialized and were seldom oppressive. The same applies to Westphalia, where peasants were in any case fully free to move. In Westphalia, however, 'remains of the old form of personal dependence' (in Werner Rösener's phrase)—that is, from the era of the manorial constitution—survived, which manifested themselves in so-called *Eigenbehörigkeit.* Taking on a farm in many ecclesiastical and secular territories—in the bishoprics of Osnabrück and Münster,[26] or in the counties of Ravensberg, Lippe, or Hoya-Diepholz—depended on the peasant's willingness to surrender himself to the unfree status of an *Eigenbehöriger*, a term which, very loosely, might be equated to the English copyholder. Therewith he was assured hereditary usufruct of the farm, though not possession, which involved a substantial heriot, originally half the moveable property, though this was later transformed into a simple money payment. How this north-west German copyhold differed from bodily serfdom may be illustrated in exemplary fashion by the county of Lippe, where both forms of unfree subjection existed side by side. There copyholders on taking over a farm had to pay an entry-fine, but the bodily serfs in addition had to pay a heriot. Moreover, the copyholders could only be sold with the farm, whereas the bodily serfs could be alienated without their farmsteads. Although the personal

[24] Andermann. 'Leibeigenschaft', pp. 302–3.

[25] Rösener, *Agrarwirtschaft*, p. 39. The quotation following is at ibid., p. 38.

[26] On Osnabrück and Münster see most recently Christoph Reinders-Düselder, 'Eigenbehörigkeit als soziale Praxis der Grundherrschaft in osnabrückischen und münsterischen Regionen', in Jan Klußmann (ed.), *Leibeigenschaft. Bäuerliche Unfreiheit in der frühen Neuzeit* (Potsdamer Studien zur Geschichte der ländlichen Gesellschaft, 3) (Cologne/Weimar/Vienna, 2003), pp. 77–98.

renders—chiefly heriots and quit-rents—had been transformed by 1600 into payments under property law, copyhold was intensified after the Thirty Years War on account of population losses. Between free men and copyholders a social distinction barely existed, yet they were not allowed to inherit from each other. All in all, copyhold in Lippe in the early modern period served not only as a source of revenue, but also as a direct instrument of seigneurial authority, exercised via occupation of a farm, or its usufruct.[27] The bishopric of Hildesheim was home to a similar form of subjection, whereby 'serfdom of the neck' (*Halseigenschaft*), as it was there called, entailed both heriots and merchets.[28] *Eigenbehörigkeit* represents an inferior form of *Meierrecht* (dependent tenancy), prevalent in much of northern Germany, which itself implied only a hereditary right of use. Servile dependence was attached to the property or the farm, which is why mediaevalists sometimes call it *Realleibeigenschaft*, that is, bodily serfdom vested tenurially.[29] I will return to this problematic term in a moment. Personal unfreedom in the early modern period was therefore by no means restricted to south-west Germany or to Switzerland. What is more rarely appreciated is that on the western fringes of the empire serfdom remained widespread. Not until the eighteenth century were serfs in Savoy, francophone Switzerland, and Lorraine emancipated. In the francophone areas at the time, they were not called *hommes de corps* (a perfectly familiar mediaeval term, corresponding directly to *Leibeigene*), but *mainmortables*, that is, those obliged to pay heriots. In Savoy serfdom could attach either to the soil or to the person, but there were no restrictions on marriage or movement.[30] In Lorraine, by contrast, exogamous marriage (*formariage*) was pursued through

[27] Bernd Hüllinghorst, '"Daß keine ärmere geplagte leute in der Graffschaft Lippe wohneten!" Die lippische Leibherrschaft im 17. Jahrhundert', in *Der Weserraum zwischen 1500 und 1650. Gesellschaft, Wirtschaft und Kultur in der Frühen Neuzeit* (*Materialien zur Kunst und Kulturgeschichte in Nord- und Westdeutschland*, 4) (Marburg, 1993), pp. 93, 96, 98, 101, 110.

[28] André Holenstein, *Bauern zwischen Bauernkrieg und Dreißigjährigem Krieg* (*Enzyklopädie Deutscher Geschichte*, 38) (Munich, 1996), p. 34. Walter Achilles, however, points out that all servile renders had been recast as dues upon property. Walter Achilles, *Landwirtschaft in der frühen Neuzeit* (*Enzyklopädie Deutscher Geschichte*, 10) (Munich, 1991), p. 30.

[29] Troßbach, '"Südwestdeutsche Leibeigenschaft"', p. 70.

[30] Paul Darmstädter, *Die Befreiung der Leibeigenen (mainmortables) in Savoyen, der Schweiz und Lothringen* (Abhandlungen aus dem staatswissenschaftlichen Seminar zu Strassburg i. E., 17) (Strasbourg, 1897), pp. 17, 20.

the courts.[31] In this context it is also worth pointing to the survival of bodily serfdom in the Franche-Comté. It is remarkable that serfdom only survived in those francophone frontier areas which in constitutional law had once belonged to the empire. Under the French crown serfdom (*servage*) is supposed to have disappeared by the thirteenth century.[32]

Ad 3. From what has already been said it emerges that neither bodily serfdom nor its hallmarks can be defined uniformly throughout the German lands. That is not to say that they are beyond historical analysis. Rather, we need to consider how far ties under the law of persons constitute the essence of servile dependence. Already doubts arise for south-west Germany. In the Palatinate, where (as we have seen) jurisdictional authority by means of serfdom never developed, *Leibeigenschaft* in the course of territorialization was defined not as a personal but as a residential constraint, which is why the term local serfdom (*Lokalleibeigenschaft*) is sometimes used to describe it.[33] In the margraviate of Baden *Leibeigenschaft* could likewise attach either to the person or to the place of residence. Over time, as Ulbrich has shown for the Upper Rhine, the personal character of *Leibeigenschaft* receded in the face of its residential character. What became decisive for the status of subjects was their territorial allegiance.[34]

---

[31] Ibid., pp. 165 f.

[32] Marc Bloch, *French Rural History. An Essay on its Basic Characteristics*, transl. Janet Sondheimer (Berkeley/Los Angeles, 1970), pp. 107 f. Following Jean Bart, Wolfgang Schmale has pointed out that the continuing use of the term *mainmorte* only amounted to a curtailment of the right of free inheritance and disposal of heriotable property. Wolfgang Schmale, 'Vergleichende Analyse der Seigneurie in Burgund und der Grundherrschaft in Kursachsen', in Jan Peters (ed.), *Gutsherrschaft als soziales Modell. Vergleichende Betrachtungen zur Funktionsweise frühneuzeitlicher Agrargesellschaften* (*Historische Zeitschrift*, Beiheft 18, new series) (Munich, 1995), pp. 103, 110. All that proves is that Burgundian subjection attached to the property, not the person, a development which for Marc Bloch is characteristic of France as a whole since the end of the Middle Ages. See Jean Bart, *La liberté ou la terre. La mainmorte en Bourgogne au siècle des Lumières* (Publications du Centre des Recherches Historiques de la Faculté du Droit et de Science Politique de l'Université de Dijon, 7) (Dijon, 1984). That serfdom survived much more widely in France than is commonly supposed is demonstrated by several essays in Paul Freedman and Monique Bourin (eds), *Forms of Servitude in Northern and Central Europe, Thirteenth—Sixteenth Centuries. Decline, Resistance and Expansion* (Turnhout, 2005).

[33] Andermann, 'Leibeigenschaft', pp. 293, 299. See also now idem, 'Leibeigenschaft am mittleren und nördlichen Oberrhein in der frühen Neuzeit', in Klußmann, *Leibeigenschaft*, pp. 63–75.

[34] Ulbrich, *Leibherrschaft*, pp. 227, 229, 278.

Yet it is necessary to caution against equating local serfdom exclusively with the development of the territorial state, as if it only appeared in the early modern period. In a court case in 1511 between the town of Freiburg and a village lord of the Breisgau, Gabriel von Bollschweil, concerning the town's peasant outburghers under his jurisdiction, the latter maintained that in the Breisgau serfdom existed under two distinct signs. On the one hand, it manifested itself as personal unfreedom inherited through the mother, on the other as an impersonal status which attached to all those who were subject to a particular lord. This legal status was cancelled automatically on emigration beyond the frontiers of the old landgraviate of the Breisgau.[35] Such territorial serfdom must have been of considerable antiquity, since the landgraviate of the Breisgau as a judicial district had long since declined into an empty formula. Local serfdom as the subordination of all residents under the judicial authority (*Zwing und Bann*) of the local or jurisdictional lord can also be found at times in Franconia during the fifteenth century.[36]

Where serfdom became the general hallmark of subjects, as in the larger territorial states of Baden or Württemberg, the end result was initially startling. As Heide Wunder has put it: 'Universal personal unfreedom became the precursor of general citizenship and therefore did not carry with it social discrimination.'[37] Serfdom as the precursor of citizenship requires us to sit up and take notice! That implies that serfdom was deployed as a comprehensive badge of subject status, a judgement which is not entirely borne out either by the researches of Wolfgang von Hippel on peasant emancipation in Württemberg, or by Christian Keitel's more recent study of the medieval origins of serfdom in the duchy.[38]

With tenurially-vested personal serfdom (*Realleibeigenschaft*), on the

[35] Tom Scott, *Freiburg and the Breisgau. Town-Country Relations in the Age of Reformation and Peasants' War* (Oxford, 1986), p. 79; Generallandesarchiv Karlsruhe, 229/8577.

[36] Müller, 'Wurzeln', p. 9.

[37] Heide Wunder, 'Serfdom in Later Medieval and Early Modern Germany', in Trevor H. Aston, Peter R. Coss, Christopher Dyer, and Joan Thirsk (eds), *Social Relations and Ideas. Essays in Honour of R. H. Hilton* (Cambridge, 1983), p. 258.

[38] Wolfgang von Hippel, *Die Bauernbefreiung im Königreich Württemberg*, 2 vols (Forschungen zur deutschen Sozialgeschichte, 1) (Boppard am Rhein, 1977); Christian Keitel, *Herrschaft über Land und Leute. Leibherrschaft und Territorialisierung in Württemberg 1246–1593* (Schriften zur südwestdeutschen Landeskunde, 28) (Leinfelden-Echterdingen, 2000).

other hand, matters are quite different. As our Westphalian examples have shown, *Realleibeigenschaft* amounted to an aggravated form of villeinage, which should nevertheless not be confused with earlier manorialism, since this villeinage did not imply that the villein was tied to the soil. Similar forms of this villeinage can also be observed in Bavaria, where succession to a farm presupposed voluntary submission to the landlord's servile authority (*Eigenschaft*). This legal status was cancelled on emigration or change of tenancy, and that was possible without let or hindrance at any time. By contrast, the services and renders arising from *Realleibeigenschaft* could often be quite burdensome: extensive *corvées* and high quit-rents or entry-fines. This intensified form of villeinage, described by Friedrich Lütge as 'Bavarian landlordship', also occurred in Salzburg. It is no surprise, therefore, that it is sometimes compared with east-Elbian or east-European hereditary subjection (*Erbuntertänigkeit*), particularly since in Bavaria *Hofmarken* emerged, that is, relatively small demesnes using direct labour, which can rightly be regarded as *Gutsherrschaften* (or, properly speaking, *Gutswirtschaften*) in miniature.[39] But it would be impermissible to boil down the situation in Bavaria to a mere manifestation of *Realleibeigenschaft*. By the time of the territorial law code of 1616 a distinction was clearly being drawn between *servitus personalis* (personal serfdom) and *servitus realis* (tenurially-vested serfdom). According to Renate Blickle, this reflects an older state of affairs; it was not the invention of hair-splitting lawyers. Bavarian territorial law may well have regarded serfs as being of inferior estate—they had to petition to change their civil status—but as subjects they cannot be distinguished from free men and women. That focuses our attention on the fact that the character of Bavarian serfdom was reflected less in the burden of taxes and services than in subjection to seigneurial authority, a feature which emerges clearly in the geographically distinct dispersion of forms of *Realleibeigenschaft*. In the south (where monastic lordship predominated) *Realleibeigenschaft* and landlordly rights over peasants' farms were elided, while in the west along the river Lech, where the territorial ruler stood forth both as bailiff and jurisdictional lord, *Realleibeigenschaft* consisted in local serfdom.[40] This seems

[39] Holenstein, *Bauern*, pp. 32 f.; Rösener, *Agrarwirtschaft*, pp. 38 f.; Achilles, *Landwirtschaft*, p. 31.

[40] Renate Blickle, 'Leibeigenschaft. Versuch über Zeitgenossenschaft in Wissenschaft

to qualify recent judgements, according to which lordship over serfs in Bavaria was reduced to a vestige, since the Bavarian dukes exercised jurisdictional lordship over half the peasantry.[41] In the west of Altbayern (Upper and Lower Bavaria) jurisdictional lordship was exercised as lordship over serfs, which aligns it to south-west German serfdom. That is remarkable in two respects. On the one hand, it means that lordship over serfs and serfdom cannot always be regarded as the obverse and reverse of the same coin. On the other, tenurially-vested personal serfdom makes clear that the continuation of servile subjection in areas of western Germany cannot altogether be equated with the continuation of serfdom in its south-west German configuration. The sharp distinction applied to the south-west between landlordship (as simple rental lordship with a diminutive seigneurial component) and bodily serfdom (as the intensified exercise of jurisdictional or territorial sovereignty) impedes an understanding of other forms of dependence which were anchored in landlordship, and which therefore describe a trajectory towards the subjection which we encounter in eastern Europe. Whether one should speak of *Realleibeigenschaft* as a form of personal dependence is another matter altogether; from a different perspective similar considerations could be applied to the so-called local or residential serfdom (*Lokalleibeigenschaft*).

While the burdens of south-west German serfdom were in the longer term largely confined to trivial renders, that is, recognition-fees (which need not on any account rule out an ideologically motivated rejection of this unfreedom), subjects of landlordship elsewhere in western Germany could still be the victims of palpable seigneurial demands. In all this it needs to be stressed once again that a correct evaluation of the distinguishing marks of subjection still causes difficulties for historians. In the case of *corvées*, for example, regional variations must always be taken into account.[42]

---

und Wirklichkeit, durchgeführt am Beispiel Altbayerns', in Peters, *Gutsherrschaft als Modell*, pp. 69–71, 74 f.

[41] Holenstein, *Bauern*, p. 32; Achilles, *Landwirtschaft*, p. 32. Within the model of *Realleibeigenschaft* this may well be an exceptional instance; elsewhere tenurially-vested dependence was largely disengaged from jurisdictional lordship over serfs.

[42] Troßbach, '"Südwestdeutsche Leibeigenschaft"', p. 84. For further reflections on the survival of *Leibeigenschaft* and its tenurialized character, which emphasize the parallels between Upper Swabia and Bavaria see now Tom Scott, 'South-West German Serfdom Reconsidered', in Freedman and Bourin, *Forms of Servitude*.

* * *

It is undoubtedly a drawback that discussion of the continuing existence of personal unfreedom in Germany has almost exclusively concentrated on a comparison with east-Elbian subjection, even if recent research has noted many transitional zones and formations. If one sets to one side Rolf Köhn's acute observations on serfdom in central and western Europe (which, however, only cover the period before the fifteenth century), then, as far as I can see, no broad comparison exists which would place lordship over serfs and serfdom in the territories of the empire in their European context. That is all the more regrettable since the recent debate over the transformation and decline of serfdom in western Europe has entirely bracketed developments in western Germany, and has confined itself to a comparison with the hereditary subjection (*Erbuntertänigkeit*) associated with east-European *Gutsherrschaft* or *Gutswirtschaft*. On closer inspection this turns out to be a fateful omission.

In a wide-ranging survey Robert Brenner has posed the question why in the late Middle Ages and early modern period in various European countries serfdom underwent a chronologically skewed process of configuration and erosion. In the following remarks the term unfreedom will be preferred to serfdom, in order not to preempt an interpretation or definition of the concept. Brenner's explanatory model for western Europe rests upon a binary distinction between regions of what he terms classical or decentralized feudalism, and territories subject to monarchical centralization, which was deployed to buttress centralized feudal lordship in the localities.[43] By the former he means those areas of the *seigneurie banale*, usurped political-legal authority in the hands of local feudal bosses, characteristic of many parts of central and southern France, and of northern Spain, described to us by a generation of French historians stretching from Duby and Le Roy Ladurie to Bonnassie. By the latter he means the state feudalism of the Anglo-Norman monarchy and the division of feudal suzerainty between the crown and the high nobility in Catalonia.

[43] Robert Brenner, 'The Rises and Declines of Serfdom in Medieval and Early Modern Europe', in Michael L. Bush (ed.), *Serfdom and Slavery. Studies in Legal Bondage* (London/New York, 1996), pp. 247–76.

The jurisdictional lords of the *seigneurie banale* were incapable of upholding the serfdom of their subjects in the long term, so that by the end of the thirteenth century it had in effect disappeared. This posed a threat to the social and economic pre-eminence of the French aristocracy, a threat which was only averted by horse-trading with the French crown. A deal was struck whereby the crown creamed off the peasants' surplus *not* by extra-economic coercion but by state taxation, in return for which the nobility was granted lucrative offices in the emergent fiscal state.

In England and Catalonia, by contrast, the feudal aristocracy was able to perpetuate and indeed revive serfdom in the early thirteenth century thanks to monarchical underpinning. But even in these two territories feudalism—understood as the shorthand term for extra-economic coercion—was incapable in the end of reproducing peasant servility because the consolidation of centralized monarchical power through the expansion of the royal courts, along with the development of an institutionalized exchequer, was bound to encroach upon the decentralized lordship of the feudal aristocracy, and indeed in certain circumstances could actively promote peasant emancipation.[44]

For completeness' sake it should be added that Brenner contrasts this dualist model for western Europe, which places the power of the crown centre-stage, with developments in eastern Europe, concluding:

> It was only lordly states which were explicitly constructed from the bottom up to reproduce serfdom, through institutions designed to overcome intra-lordly competition and secure lordly co-operation, that were capable of maintaining it in the long run. Such states did not emerge until the fifteenth century, classically in Eastern Europe.[45]

We will return to this verdict at the end. We need not dwell on the supposed origins of the differential pattern of serfdom in the feudal revolution around AD 1000, which gave rise to the *seigneurie banale*. If there was such a revolution—much disputed in the recent historical literature—then I would agree with Thomas Bisson that the term be used with caution.[46] I am myself strongly of the view that there

---

[44] Ibid., pp. 250 f.

[45] Ibid., p. 251.

[46] Thomas N. Bisson, 'The "Feudal Revolution"', *Past and Present*, 142 (1994), pp. 6–42.

are clear continuities between the colonate of the late Roman Empire and the manorial bondmen of high mediaeval Europe.

Much more important is Brenner's cavalier treatment of serfdom in France after the eleventh century. He refers throughout his essay to serfs and serfdom, thereby ignoring the fundamental distinction between *vilains* (*villani*) and *serfs* (*servi*). In the twelfth and thirteenth centuries, as Marc Bloch pointed out beyond peradventure more than fifty years ago, the *vilains* were regarded as free, because they were bound to their lords only by virtue of the tenements which they leased from them, and in all other respects were free to move. Of course, these *vilains* were subject to their landlords' manorial jurisdiction and the burdens which arose from it. The serfs, by contrast, who also held land from their lords, were unfree by virtue of their person (which is why they were often termed *hommes de corps*, that is, bodily subjects). Occasionally, in parts of south-west France, they were unfree by virtue of their place of residence. These bodily serfs—neifs, as they are properly called in English—enjoyed no freedom of movement or right to marry outside the manor (*formariage*). Furthermore, they had to pay a heriot (*mainmorte*) on death if there were no direct inheritors.[47] In France, the *serfs* originally outnumbered the *vilains*. As the amount of demesne land directly cultivated by the lords declined after the end of the thirteenth century, the number of serfs correspondingly declined, for it had been their labour-services which had worked the demesne. Where *servage* in this precise sense survived, it was increasingly regarded as socially degrading and legally disabling. But unfreedom, as we may call the general category of subjection, did not disappear. Instead, it became tenurialized, attached to landholding, so that the sources begin to speak of *serfs de la glèbe*, bondmen tied to the soil.[48] In effect, they were put on a par with the *vilains*, whose freedom, after all, had only consisted in the fact that they were tenurially rather than bodily bound to their lords. But even this tenurialized unfreedom eroded in the course of the later Middle Ages, albeit with some significant exceptions. In the duchy of Burgundy and in the Franche-Comté patents of manumission were still being granted to serfs in the sixteenth and seventeenth centuries. Because Brenner operates with an undifferentiated

[47] Bloch, *French Rural History*, pp. 84 f.
[48] Ibid., pp. 104 f.

concept of serfdom, these developments escape him, with unfortunate consequences, for they undermine the foundations of the very contrast between France on the one hand, and England and Catalonia on the other, which he is so eager to make.

That such nuances are far from trivial can be seen by directing our gaze across the Channel to England. Here, too, the distinction between villeins and serfs was of fundamental importance, except that the proportions were reversed. Of the three-fifths of English peasants who were unfree, villeins were clearly preponderant. Serfs, that is to say, neifs, made up, John Hatcher has calculated, at best a third of the total peasantry. Unlike France, in England both villeins and serfs were liable to pay heriots and merchets.[49] Rodney Hilton, certainly one of the most knowledgeable historians of English serfdom, maintained more than thirty years ago that by the middle of the thirteenth century the distinction between villeinage and neifty had been elided.[50] But his view must be questioned not only in the light of John Hatcher's reassessment, but also given the grievances and demands voiced a hundred years later by the rebels in the English Peasants' Revolt of 1381. At the famous confrontation at Smithfield on 15th June 1381 between Wat Tyler and king Richard II, Tyler demanded that bondage be abolished—both villeinage *and* neifty, clearly distinguished in the surviving sources.

The background to the Peasants' Revolt of 1381 bears out the continuing validity of the distinction. Already in 1377 the parliamentary Commons had petitioned against recalcitrant villeins who had succeeded in having manorial dues and obligations cancelled in the royal courts[51]—a most remarkable achievement given that the principal mark of unfreedom in England is supposed to have resided in the subjection of both villeins and serfs to the jurisdiction of the manor and their explicit exclusion from access to the sheriff courts at county level, where justice was dispensed in the name of the crown, and not in the name of feudal landlords. When the rebellion broke out four years later, the peasants demanded *both* the 'fran-

[49] John Hatcher, 'English Serfdom and Villeinage. Towards a Reassessment', *Past and Present*, 90 (1981), pp. 3–39, here at pp. 7, 13.

[50] Rodney Hilton, 'Freedom and Villeinage in England', *Past and Present*, 31 (1965), pp. 3–19, here at p. 19.

[51] R. B. Dobson (ed.), *The Peasants' Revolt of 1381*, 2nd edn (Houndmills, Hants/London, 1983), pp. 76–8.

chise of their bodies' *and* a 'change in the condition of their tenure'.[52] All they were offered was the suspension of personal bondage; villeinage was to be left intact.[53]

It would be rash, however, to conclude that the revolt was provoked principally by the ties and burdens of landlordship imposed on peasants holding tenures under manorial custom. The longer-term origins of the revolt, after all, lay in the Statute of Labourers of 1351. As a result of population loss caused by the Black Death, a shortage of labour had arisen, so that the crown was determined to stem the landflight of wage-labourers and to establish a wage tariff for servants both male and female. Accordingly, the Statute speaks of carters, shepherds, swineherds, mowers, and domestic servants, as well as fixing the wages of carpenters, masons, tilers, cobblers, tanners, furriers, tailors, and even goldsmiths.[54] Only day-labourers and craftsmen, therefore, were affected by its provisions; tenant farmers are nowhere mentioned.

The incidence of serfs (in the Latin sources also called *nativi de sanguine*, those unfree by blood)[55] breaking their contracts of employment by taking to their heels increased markedly after 1350; in many cases they may have been able to take over vacant holdings, some even without feudal obligations, and thus advance into the ranks of the possessing peasantry.[56] That the latter—in many cases villeins themselves—might view this mobility with apprehension is understandable enough: here were existing tenant farmers being robbed of their traditional labour reservoir in parts of the country where agriculture was already commercialized and market-integrated.

It is by no means easy to give a clear definition of this form of serfdom. Landless labourers and artisans are clearly not the same as neifs, those bodily unfree peasants tied into manorial jurisdiction, or,

---

[52] Michael L. Bush, 'Serfdom in Medieval and Modern Europe', in idem, *Serfdom and Slavery*, p. 201.

[53] Ibid., p. 202.

[54] Dobson, *Peasants' Revolt*, p. 51.

[55] Christopher Dyer, 'The Social and Economic Background to the Rural Revolt of 1381', in Rodney H. Hilton and Trevor H. Aston (eds), *The English Rising of 1381* (Cambridge, 1984), pp. 9–42, here at p. 15.

[56] Bush, 'Serfdom in Medieval and Modern Europe', p. 212; Christopher Dyer, 'The Rising of 1381 in Suffolk: Its Origins and Participants', *Proceedings of the Suffolk Institute of Archaeology and History*, 36 (1986), pp. 274–87; reprinted in idem, *Everyday Life in Medieval England* (London, 1994), pp. 221–39.

to remind ourselves of Brenner's diction, decentralized feudalism. Indeed, it presents something of an anomaly, as Alan Harding has recognized. In the century before the Peasants' Revolt, according to Harding, the royal courts in England had developed through their own jurisprudence a new category of servile obligation, for which neither then nor now has an agreed term been found. In Harding's words: 'The main struggle in 1381 was for civic, not tenurial, freedom, because the landlords had got a new public jurisdiction which allowed them to enforce service far more general than the obligations of villein tenure.'[57] From this perspective we might therefore call the new serfdom 'civic' or 'public' serfdom, though these are terms which Harding himself does not deploy. However ungainly the term civic serfdom, it at least makes clear that this was bondage enforced by public law, not serfdom as the outflow of private feudal jurisdictional lordship. And in the Peasants' Revolt it was this new civic serfdom which provoked resentment far greater than that occasioned by the restrictions of tenurial unfreedom, that is to say, villeinage, because the power of the state—centralized feudalism—now stood behind the decentralized feudal lords in their attempts to enforce servile labour-contracts. The reasons for the emergence of civic serfdom cannot be pursued here. I would simply point to England's commercialized agriculture, which was tied into an increasingly integrated national market.[58] That required a flexible labour-force, which would carry out wage-work on fixed-term service-contracts. The manorial economy of late mediaeval England had travelled a long way from the classical demesne under the old manorial constitution, and was manifesting the first signs of capitalist organization. Against this background civic serfdom displays certain similarities with the forced labour-contracts performed by peasants' children (*Gesindezwangdienst*) within the system of east-Elbian *Gutswirtschaft*. That confirms the recent consensus among historians, whereby the commercialization of English agriculture did not lead inexorably to the dissolution of serfdom.[59]

[57] Alan Harding, 'The Revolt against the Justices', in Hilton and Aston, *English Rising*, pp. 165–93, here at p. 187.

[58] See most recently Richard H. Britnell, *The Commercialisation of English Society 1000–1500* (Cambridge, 1993); Christopher Dyer, 'Market Towns and the Countryside in Late Medieval England', *Canadian Journal of History*, 31 (1996), pp. 17–35.

[59] Idem, 'Memories of Freedom. Attitudes towards Serfdom in England, 1200–1350', in Bush, *Serfdom and Slavery*, p. 277.

The development of civic serfdom in England presents grave difficulties for the plausibility of Brenner's thesis. It was most certainly the result of cooperation between centralized monarchical authority and decentralized feudal lordship in order to buttress the latter (as Brenner's typology suggests), but it occurred under diametrically opposed circumstances. The extended competence of the royal courts—of which civic serfdom is a manifestation—did not lead, as Brenner predicted, to the eventual erosion of the power of decentralized feudal lordship, let alone to the promotion of peasant emancipation. On the contrary, its intention and its effect were in the first instance quite the opposite. It is, of course, true that villeinage and neifty (and civic serfdom) did wither in England, though the reasons are still imperfectly understood. What is equally true, however, is that the decline took much longer than is commonly believed. At the time of Kett's Rebellion in Norfolk in 1549, a movement largely directed against enclosures and the creation of sheep-pastures, there were still references to 'bondy lands' (that is, lands held under villein tenure), and to bondmen (that is, bodily serfs).[60]

Because he fails to take account of these survivals, Brenner comes to misleading conclusions about the decline of serfdom in late mediaeval England. In particular, his failure to distinguish between villeinage and neifty leads him to place disproportionate emphasis on the burdens of tenurial unfreedom, since, as Richard Smith has recently reminded us, as early as the beginning of the thirteenth century villeins in England were gaining access to the royal courts and developing an extraordinary repertoire of stratagems to evade manorial restrictions or penalties on transfers of property and on inheritance.[61] Here a clear difference of situation and interest was visible: the villeins were concerned to protect their tenancies and to dispose freely over them; for wage-workers and artisans—civic serfs—by contrast the choice was different: they could simply run away.

Only by ignoring the peculiarities of the situation in England could Brenner suppose that it can properly be equated with the spread and survival of serfdom in Catalonia—both allegedly the outflow of

---

60 Bush, 'Serfdom in Medieval and Modern Europe', p. 202.

61 Richard M. Smith, 'The English Peasantry, 1250–1650', in Tom Scott (ed.), *The Peasantries of Europe from the Fourteenth to the Eighteenth Centuries* (London/New York, 1998), pp. 339–71, esp. 347 ff.

support from a strong centralized monarchy. Catalonia, indeed, displays even more oddities than England. Even the nomenclature of serfdom in Catalonia conspires to confuse. The Latin sources speak of *homines proprii*, but they were certainly not bodily serfs in any conventional sense. Although peasants were described as belonging to their lords or owing them homage, their dependence was grounded in the holding of land and its use. Where tenancies changed hands, an entry-fine was levied and the new tenant had to swear allegiance to his lord.[62] This brings Catalonian serfdom close to north German *Eigenbehörigkeit* or 'Bavarian landlordship', and one could with justice therefore speak of it as a tenurially-vested personal unfreedom in the manner of *Realleibeigenschaft*. In Catalonia personal, that is, bodily, serfdom and tenurial unfreedom were in effect collapsed into one, with that serfdom being regarded as personally degrading. Moreover, this serfdom provided the legal framework for maltreatment of serfs according to the notorious 'bad customs' (*mals usos*). Any resemblance of Catalonian serfdom to English villeinage must therefore be regarded as superficial, especially since tenurial leases without servile obligations attached were also widespread in Catalonia.[63]

Once again, the origins of Catalonian serfdom are highly controversial. It was certainly not an extension of an older Frankish subjugation, for Islamic expansion after the eighth century swept any such servile vestiges away.[64] Nor was it a consequence of the *seigneurie banale*, since the emergence of Catalonian unfreedom should, according to Paul Freedman, be dated to the thirteenth century, at a time when the crown of Aragon was enjoying its first flush of power.[65] Brenner, by contrast, believes that its origins lie further back in the twelfth century, when the Aragonese crown had yet to achieve its supremacy, and was still in thrall to its feudal nobility.[66] Moreover,

---

[62] Paul Freedman, *The Origins of Peasant Servitude in Medieval Catalonia* (Cambridge, 1991), pp. 91, 123 f.

[63] Ibid., p. 124.

[64] Ibid., p. 207; see also idem, 'Cowardice, Heroism and the Legendary Origins of Catalonia', *Past and Present*, 121 (1988), pp. 3–28.

[65] Idem, *Origins of Peasant Servitude*, pp. 207 f.

[66] Ibid., pp. 176, 208. Here Brenner, 'Rises and Declines', pp. 264 f. is following the arguments of Pierre Bonnassie, 'The Formation of Catalan Feudalism', in idem, *From Slavery to Feudalism in South Western Europe*, transl. Jean Birrell (Cambridge, 1991), pp. 156–63. On the position of the count-kings of Barcelona see Stephen P. Bensch, *Barcelona and its Rulers, 1096–1291* (Cambridge Studies in Medieval Life and Thought, 26) (Cambridge, 1995).

he sees here a parallel to developments in eastern Europe. But on this score Brenner's analysis, which is indebted to Bonnassie, has been overtaken by Freedman; although Brenner cites Freedman approvingly, he does not seem to have fully absorbed his arguments.

There is no space here to explore the reasons for the peculiarly brutal character of Catalonian lordship over serfs. Brenner is certainly right to point to the precarious balance of power between the Aragonese crown and the Catalonian high nobility. For the oppression of the peasantry on the estates of the secular aristocracy contrasted with the relatively favourable status of peasants on royal and ecclesiastical lands. I would suggest that the crown only had a limited interest in opposing the exploitation of peasants on noble estates because its revenues essentially derived from the profits of its Mediterranean commercial empire. Unlike the French crown, Aragonese monarchs were not dependent on the fiscal resilience of peasant husbandmen. Politically, it was also difficult for the crown to face down the nobility, since the beneficiaries of servile lordship sat in the Catalan *corts*, whose extensive legal privileges trammelled the power of the monarchs.[67] It was left to Catalan serfs to fight for their freedom for over twenty years after 1462 (with some tacit support from the crown), until they at last achieved manumission in 1486.[68]

The character of Catalonian serfdom and the very specific reasons for its survival into the late fifteenth century are so obviously alien to the situation of peasants in the commercialized agriculture of England and to the phenomenon of civic serfdom that it seems foolhardy to derive from them a model of centralized feudalism which can be counterposed to the decentralized feudalism of the *seigneurie banale*. These reservations are all the more justified since Brenner not only omits to distinguish between the variants of unfreedom, but also overlooks the varying reasons for the retention and survival of serfdom in both his models, even beyond the period in which it is supposed to have vanished.

Most regrettable of all is his insistence on clinging to a model of centralized feudalism which alone can explain the survival of serfdom into the fifteenth century in western Europe. For it was exactly

[67] Freedman, *Origins of Peasant Servitude*, pp. 179 ff.

[68] Idem, 'The German and Catalan Peasant Revolts', *American Historical Review*, 98 (1993), pp. 39–54.

in this period that personal unfreedom was reactivated in south-west Germany, that is to say, in a region that by virtue of its advanced fragmentation can at best be assigned to the model of decentralized feudalism, particularly since its configuration as intensified jurisdictional lordship does indeed echo the *seigneurie banale* of the high Middle Ages. Brenner avoids this problem by simply ignoring south-west German serfdom altogether.

Brenner's approach, therefore, casts no light on the questions posed at the outset. Our remarks so far have suggested, however, that they should be regarded as *des questions mal posées*. Forms of unfreedom, whether tenurial, personal, or territorial, were more prevalent in western Europe and survived for longer than is usually supposed. To look for monocausal explanations is to embark on a fool's errand. That a specific configuration of subjection in the form of personal unfreedom arose in south-west Germany must not be taken to suggest that it should be explained simply by regional peculiarities. Rather, we need to identify structural parallels with unfreedom in other western European areas and territories, beyond the issue of nomenclature. In this regard research on the Peasants' War may have created an obstacle to understanding, inasmuch as it has sought—reasonably enough—to uncover regionally specific reasons for the preponderance of grievances concerning serfdom in the areas seized by revolt. It is true, though, that this research has emphasised the ideological background as well.

Robert Brenner, as is well known, is committed to a materialist interpretation of history. Therefore he regards serfdom exclusively as a means of extra-economic coercion, designed to appropriate the peasants' surplus. If he had turned his attention to south-west Germany he would have seen both the political and the territorial motives which underlay the intensification of late mediaeval personal unfreedom, as well as laying bare the roots of an ideological resistance to serfdom, which at times was quite disproportionate to the actual material burdens of unfreedom. Peter Blickle has shown this in exemplary fashion for the monastery of Schussenried. There the abbey's subjects had succeeded after a revolt in 1439 in pushing through a treaty whereby the heriot was reduced from half the estate to the best head of cattle (for men) or best dress (for women). Despite this palpable easement its subjects in decades to come pressed for a change in their legal status. They were no longer prepared to tolerate being treated as serfs; instead, they demanded to have the status of 'free monastery subjects' (*freie Gotteshausleute*), a term which we encounter in many Upper German ecclesiastical lordships. This recasting of their status was indeed granted. As Blickle correctly remarks, it was but a small step to placing the emphasis on 'free', rather than 'subjects', in order to disavow in principle their servile dependence.[69]

The incident with the greatest resonance and ramifications, however, stems from the eighteenth century, to wit, the revolt of the subjects of the county of Hauenstein in the southern Black Forest, which culminated in the so-called Saltpetre Wars between 1725 and 1745. From the late Middle Ages onwards, the abbey of St Blasien had succeeded in extending its lordship over serfs to the Hauensteiners to the point where by 1740 around 70 per cent of the Hauensteiners were serfs of St Blasien. The material burdens which this status entailed were admittedly nugatory: a recognition-fee in the form of a Shrovetide fowl and three days' boonwork a year. Servile dues in any case only made up 11.5 per cent of the monastery's income.[70] When in 1719 a court case occasioned a rehearsal of the manorial roll of 1467, which still provided the legal basis for the abbey's claims upon its subjects, the clerk of St Blasien—presumably inadvertently—spoke of bodily serfdom (*Leibeigenschaft*) instead of serfdom (*Eigenschaft*). In the manorial roll itself only *Eigenschaft* was mentioned, but during the Thirty Years War monastic documents had added the prefix *Leib-* (bodily). This nomenclature, which struck the subjects as intolerable, had, nevertheless, been rescinded by emperor Leopold I in a decree in 1704.[71] On this nice linguistic distinction a battle over their freedom arose, which led to ruptures amongst the Hauensteiners themselves and to the formation of rival factions. When in 1738 the moderate faction finally agreed to purchase a general patent of manumission from the abbey for 58,000 fl., it was violently attacked by the radicals, since the move tacitly presupposed the existence of bodily serfdom (*Leibeigenschaft*). Thereupon a real civil war erupted in the southern Black Forest, which took seven years to resolve.[72]

[69] Peter Blickle, 'Von der Eigenschaft in die Freiheit. Ein Beitrag zu den realhistorischen Grundlagen der Freiheits- und Menschenrechte in Europa', in Günter Birtsch (ed.), *Grund- und Freiheitsrechte im Wandel von Gesellschaft und Geschichte. Beiträge zur Geschichte der Grund- und Freiheitsrechte vom Ausgang des Mittelalters bis zur Revolution von 1848* (Göttingen, 1981), p. 31.

[70] David M. Luebke, *His Majesty's Rebels. Communities, Factions and Rural Revolt in the Black Forest, 1725–1745* (Ithaca, NY/London, 1997), p. 43.

[71] Ibid., pp. 61 f.

[72] Ibid., pp. 74 f.

The events in the county of Hauenstein must of course be set in a wider context, which acknowledges the change in attitude towards human rights in the age of the Enlightenment. That issue will not be pursued here. The Saltpetre Wars do show, however, that at the end of the *ancien régime* resistance in principle to bodily unfreedom in the west of Germany was still acute, even if that serfdom had long sunk in material terms to the level of an insignificant imposition.

* * *

Let us in conclusion return to the questions raised at the outset concerning the correct classification of south-west German lordship over serfs and serfdom. Looked at in depth, south-west German bodily serfdom can be regarded as a particular development or concentration of an older and more general unfreedom as a result of local circumstances. Looked at in broad terms, however, it is not to be distinguished fundamentally from other forms of unfreedom in western Germany. The very fact that in certain conditions tenurial, residential, and bodily unfreedom might fall together, as well as the use of initially strange terminology such as *Realleibeigenschaft*, destroy any notion that it only existed in the south-west. The examples cited of Lippe and Altbayern show, moreover, that personal bodily unfreedom could exist simultaneously with other forms of unfreedom, in which neither form necessarily implied a legally inferior status over against free peasants. Both in its configuration and in its degree of burdensomeness we are dealing with a sliding scale of serfdom, chronologically as well as spatially.

That is not by any means to equate unfreedom with subjection as such. A rent-paying peasant or a hereditary leaseholder (peasants with allodial tenures are another matter) was subject to his lord without being unfree, although in south-west Germany the generalized diffusion of bodily serfdom—or rather, the rounding off of lordship over serfs—could on occasion lead to a *de facto* subjection to the state. The intensification of bodily unfreedom is of course primarily to be found where the exercise of seigneurial authority was most easily achieved by means of lordship over serfs. But this somewhat banal insight should not be taken to mean that forms of personal unfreedom disappeared wherever feudal lords could either buttress their authority by recourse to other legal instruments or else had abandoned seigneurial lordship altogether in favour of simple rent-extraction. It would make a splendid subject for debate whether tenurial unfreedom should be seen as a form of personal unfreedom at all. The confusion has its roots in too ready an equation between personal-landlordly (tenurial) ties on the one hand, and corporeal ties (bodily serfdom) on the other; a comparison with England, where villeins and neifs existed alongside each other as personally unfree, would quickly have disabused anyone of such a notion.

By emphasizing the survival of tenurial dependence in parts of northern and western Germany, moreover, we have cleared the way for a re-evaluation of the gradient between areas of *Gutsherrschaft* in the east and landlordship in the west. In the case of Brandenburg, for example, Lieselott Enders has insisted on differentiating the concept of bodily serfdom, which should be subdivided into three categories: 1. Simple subjection (*Untertänigkeit*), which was linked to taking over a farm and the consequent acknowledgement of landlordship and jurisdictional lordship; 2. Hereditary subjection (*Erbuntertänigkeit*), which weighed upon the heirs, although they could buy themselves free; 3. Bodily serfdom (*Leibeigenschaft*) in the narrower sense, which entailed inferior rights of possession (or occupation) and the obligation to perform unspecified labour-services. In Brandenburg all three forms of subjection existed, though simple subjection was common until the late sixteenth century. Only after the Thirty Years War did the harsher forms of subjection become widespread, with *Leibeigenschaft* being prescribed in the Uckermark (northern Brandenburg) as the general condition of the peasantry in response to pressure from the nobility in 1653.[73] From that it is clear that bodily serfdom in Brandenburg derived from the duties attaching to taking on a farm—tenurial dependence, in other words. It should therefore be placed in a spectrum which stretches from dependent tenancy (*Meierrecht*), widespread in northern Germany, through so-called copyhold (*Eigenbehörigkeit*) to a fully-fledged attachment to the soil (*Schollengebundenheit*). Deterioration in the conditions of tenure can also be observed in Mecklenburg, where hereditary possession in the form of *Zinshufen*

[73] Lieselott Enders, *Die Uckermark. Geschichte einer kurmärkischen Landschaft vom 12. bis zum 18. Jahrhundert* (Weimar, 1992), pp. 192 f., 336 f. See also Christoph Schmidt, *Leibeigenschaft im Ostseeraum. Versuch einer Typologie* (Cologne/Weimar/Vienna, 1997), pp. 8 f.

(rental hides) was transformed into term-leases on farms held in tenurial dependence (*Meierhöfe*).[74]

Enders's typology is extraordinarily suggestive. For what she makes plain is that *Leibeigenschaft* in the east, the debilitating, degrading, personal, and hereditary unfreedom of which Marxists have made so much, was the end-point of a development that had begun with forms of *tenurial*, not corporeal, unfreedom encountered not only in Brandenburg but in lands further to the west. From that two observations follow. First, not only is the river Elbe an unconvincing dividing-line between differing social structures in east and west, it is doubtful whether such a dividing-line existed at all, at least with any sharpness. Second, the origins of the so-called 'second serfdom' in the east—at least in the areas of German colonization—lie in the conditions imposed upon leaseholding tenants, and *not* in the labour-services demanded of bodily unfree serfs. This demonstrates once again that *Gutsherrschaft* as 'intensified seigneurialism' could precede *Gutswirtschaft* as 'intensified commercialized agriculture' by as much as two centuries. Brenner may be right that eastern societies were constructed 'from the bottom up' upon extra-economic coercion, but only if he is prepared to concede that the first steps involved an intensification of *tenurial* obligations and not the deployment of *corvées* and servile wage-labour contracts (the notorious *Gesindezwangdienst*). Whether Brenner is aware of this distinction remains unclear.

As a final heretical reflection one could ask why those north German areas in which *Meierrecht* and *Eigenbehörigkeit* were prevalent never experienced a comparable aggravation of tenurial subjection up to and including the strictest form of *Leibeigenschaft* in its east-European manifestation—or rather, why such a development did occur in a few areas, for instance eastern Holstein, but never materialized in neighbouring districts. A historian of south-west Germany should not interfere in the competence of other regional specialists, and convincing explanations for the manifestations of *Gutsherrschaft* in north-west Germany have indeed been advanced by Edgar Melton, Silke Göttsch, and Christoph Schmidt.[75] But when Schmidt claims

---

[74] Ibid., pp. 24 f.

[75] Edgar Melton, 'Gutsherrschaft in East Elbian Germany and Livonia 1500–1800. A Critique of the Model', *Central European History*, 21 (1988), pp. 315–49; Silke Göttsch, *'Alle für einen Mann ...' Leibeigene und Widerständigkeit in Schleswig-Holstein im 18. Jahrhundert* (Neumünster, 1991); Schmidt, *Leibeigenschaft*, pp. 20–38.

that in the west it was the *dispersion* of seigneurial authority which prevented the nobility from unilaterally imposing or reimposing serfdom, since both the monarch (the emperor) and the cities would oppose the nobles' access of power,[76] one can only retort that it was in the south-west of the empire, the region most exposed to monarchical influence and the area of greatest urban density, that bodily serfdom was reinvigorated—by princes, nobles, and indeed on occasion by cities. For the purposes of comparison, therefore, whether in east or west, south-west Germany should always be included in any analysis of lordship over serfs and bodily serfdom.

[76] Ibid., p. 138.

PLACES OF ORIGINAL PUBLICATION

1. *Archiv für Reformationsgeschichte*, 69 (1978), pp. 82–102 [part 1]; *ibid.*, 70 (1979), pp. 140–69 [part 2].
2. Hans R. Guggisberg and Gottfried G. Krodel (eds), *Die Reformation in Deutschland und Europa: Interpretationen und Debatten* (*Archiv für Reformationsgeschichte*, Sonderband) (Gütersloh, 1993), pp. 175–92.
3. 'Der "Butzenkrieg". Der Aufstand zu Rufach 1514', in Heinrich R. Schmidt, André Holenstein, and Andreas Würgler (eds), *Gemeinde, Reformation und Widerstand. Festschrift für Peter Blickle zum 60. Geburtstag* (Tübingen, 1998), pp. 355–69.
4. 'Freiburg und der Bundschuh', in Hans Schadek (ed.), *Der Kaiser in seiner Stadt. Maximilian I. und der Reichstag zu Freiburg 1498* (Freiburg im Breisgau, 1998), pp. 332–53.
5. 'Vom Bundschuh zum Bauernkrieg. Von der revolutionären Verschwörung zur Revolution des gemeinen Mannes', in Peter Blickle and Thomas Adam (eds), *Bundschuch. Untergrombach 1502, Das unruhige Reich und die Revolutionierbarkeit Europas* (Stuttgart, 2004), pp. 278–96.
6. 'Südwestdeutsche Städte im Bauernkrieg. Bündnisse zwischen Opportunismus und Solidarität', in Bernhard Kirchgässner and Hans-Peter Becht (eds), *Stadt und Revolution* (Veröffentlichungen des Südwestdeutschen Arbeitskreises für Stadtgeschichtsforschung, 27) (Stuttgart, 2001), pp. 9–36.
7. Bob Scribner (ed.), *Germany: A New Economic and Social History*, 1: *1450–1630* (London/New York/Sydney/Auckland, 1996), pp. 1–31.
8. S. R. Epstein (ed.), *Town and Country in Europe, 1300–1800* (Themes in International Urban History, 5) (Cambridge, 2001), pp. 202–28.
9. Peter Ainsworth and Tom Scott (eds), *Regions and Landscapes. Reality and Imagination in Late Medieval and Early Modern Europe* (Oxford/Bern/Berlin/Brussels/Frankfurt am Main/New York/Vienna, 2000), pp. 155–76.
10. 'Die oberrheinischen Mittel- und Kleinstädte im 15. und 16. Jahrhundert zwischen Dominanz und Konkurrenz', in Holger T. Gräf and Katrin Keller (eds), *Städtelandschaft, réseau urbain, urban network. Städte im regionalen Kontext in Spätmittelalter und Früher Neuzeit*

(Städteforschung. Veröffentlichungen des Instituts für vergleichende Städtegeschichte in Münster, A 62) (Cologne/Weimar/Vienna, 2004), pp. 47–64.

11. 'Die Territorialpolitik der Stadt Freiburg im Breisgau im ausgehenden Mittelalter', *Zeitschrift des Breisgau Geschichts-Vereins ('Schau-ins-Land')*, 102 (1983), pp. 7–24.
12. 'Das Elsaß als wirtschaftliche Brückenlandschaft im 15. und 16. Jahrhundert', in Konrad Krimm and Rainer Brüning (eds), *Zwischen Habsburg und Burgund. Der Oberrhein als europäische Landschaft im 15. Jahrhundert* (Oberrheinische Studien, 21) (Ostfildern, 2003), pp. 215–28.
13. 'Der "Oberrheinische Revolutionär" und Vorderösterreich. Reformvorstellungen zwischen Reich und Territorium', in Norbert Fischer and Marion Kobelt-Groch (eds), *Außenseiter zwischen Mittelalter und Neuzeit. Festschrift für Hans-Jürgen Goertz zum 60. Geburtstag* (Studies in Late Medieval and Reformation Thought, 61) (Leiden/New York/Cologne, 1997), pp. 47–63.
14. *German History*, 13 (1995), pp. 98–113.
15. 'Wandel und Beharrung der Untertänigkeit. Die südwestdeutsche Leibherrschaft/Leibeigenschaft in komparativer Sicht', in Markus Cerman and Robert Luft (eds), *Untertanen, Herrschaft und Staat in Böhmen und im 'Alten Reich'* (Veröffentlichungen des Collegium Carolinum, 99) (Munich, 2004), pp. 291–313.

INDEX OF NAMES AND PLACES

[The Index does not include names and places listed in the appendix to chapter 6: Source References and Commentary, pp. 172–86.]

INDEX OF SUBJECTS

STUDIES IN MEDIEVAL AND REFORMATION TRADITIONS

(*Formerly Studies in Medieval and Reformation Thought*)

Founded by Heiko A. Oberman†
Edited by Andrew Colin Gow

1. DOUGLASS, E.J.D. *Justification in Late Medieval Preaching.* 2nd ed. 1989
2. WILLIS, E.D. *Calvin's Catholic Christology.* 1966 *out of print*
3. POST, R.R. *The Modern Devotion.* 1968 *out of print*
4. STEINMETZ, D.C. *Misericordia Dei.* The Theology of Johannes von Staupitz. 1968 *out of print*
5. O'MALLEY, J.W. *Giles of Viterbo on Church and Reform.* 1968 *out of print*
6. OZMENT, S.E. *Homo Spiritualis.* The Anthropology of Tauler, Gerson and Luther. 1969
7. PASCOE, L.B. *Jean Gerson: Principles of Church Reform.* 1973 *out of print*
8. HENDRIX, S.H. *Ecclesia in Via.* Medieval Psalms Exegesis and the *Dictata super Psalterium* (1513-1515) of Martin Luther. 1974
9. TREXLER, R.C. *The Spiritual Power.* Republican Florence under Interdict. 1974
10. TRINKAUS, Ch. with OBERMAN, H.A. (eds.). *The Pursuit of Holiness.* 1974 *out of print*
11. SIDER, R.J. *Andreas Bodenstein von Karlstadt.* 1974
12. HAGEN, K. *A Theology of Testament in the Young Luther.* 1974
13. MOORE, Jr., W.L. *Annotatiunculae D. Iohanne Eckio Praelectore.* 1976
14. OBERMAN, H.A. with BRADY, Jr., Th.A. (eds.). *Itinerarium Italicum.* Dedicated to Paul Oskar Kristeller. 1975
15. KEMPFF, D. *A Bibliography of Calviniana.* 1959-1974. 1975 *out of print*
16. WINDHORST, C. *Täuferisches Taufverständnis.* 1976
17. KITTELSON, J.M. *Wolfgang Capito.* 1975
18. DONNELLY, J.P. *Calvinism and Scholasticism in Vermigli's Doctrine of Man and Grace.* 1976
19. LAMPING, A.J. *Ulrichus Velenus (Oldřich Velenský) and his Treatise against the Papacy.* 1976
20. BAYLOR, M.G. *Action and Person.* Conscience in Late Scholasticism and the Young Luther. 1977
21. COURTENAY, W.J. *Adam Wodeham.* 1978
22. BRADY, Jr., Th.A. *Ruling Class, Regime and Reformation at Strasbourg, 1520-1555.* 1978
23. KLAASSEN, W. *Michael Gaismair.* 1978
24. BERNSTEIN, A.E. *Pierre d'Ailly and the Blanchard Affair.* 1978
25. BUCER, M. *Correspondance.* Tome I (Jusqu'en 1524). Publié par J. Rott. 1979
26. POSTHUMUS MEYJES, G.H.M. *Jean Gerson et l'Assemblée de Vincennes (1329).* 1978
27. VIVES, J.L. *In Pseudodialecticos.* Ed. by Ch. Fantazzi. 1979
28. BORNERT, R. *La Réforme Protestante du Culte à Strasbourg au XVIe siècle (1523-1598).* 1981
29. CASTELLIO, S. *De Arte Dubitandi.* Ed. by E. Feist Hirsch. 1981
30. BUCER, M. *Opera Latina.* Vol I. Publié par C. Augustijn, P. Fraenkel, M. Lienhard. 1982
31. BÜSSER, F. *Wurzeln der Reformation in Zürich.* 1985 *out of print*
32. FARGE, J.K. *Orthodoxy and Reform in Early Reformation France.* 1985
33. 34. BUCER, M. *Etudes sur les relations de Bucer avec les Pays-Bas.* I. Etudes; II. Documents. Par J.V. Pollet. 1985
35. HELLER, H. *The Conquest of Poverty.* The Calvinist Revolt in Sixteenth Century France. 1986

36. MEERHOFF, K. *Rhétorique et poétique au XVIe siècle en France.* 1986
37. GERRITS, G. H. *Inter timorem et spem.* Gerard Zerbolt of Zutphen. 1986
38. POLIZIANO, A. *Lamia.* Ed. by A. Wesseling. 1986
39. BRAW, C. *Bücher im Staube.* Die Theologie Johann Arndts in ihrem Verhältnis zur Mystik. 1986
40. BUCER, M. *Opera Latina.* Vol. II. Enarratio in Evangelion Iohannis (1528, 1530, 1536). Publié par I. Backus. 1988
41. BUCER, M. *Opera Latina.* Vol. III. Martin Bucer and Matthew Parker: Flori-legium Patristicum. Edition critique. Publié par P. Fraenkel. 1988
42. BUCER, M. *Opera Latina.* Vol. IV. Consilium Theologicum Privatim Conscriptum. Publié par P. Fraenkel. 1988
43. BUCER, M. *Correspondance.* Tome II (1524-1526). Publié par J. Rott. 1989
44. RASMUSSEN, T. *Inimici Ecclesiae.* Das ekklesiologische Feindbild in Luthers "Dictata super Psalterium" (1513-1515) im Horizont der theologischen Tradition. 1989
45. POLLET, J. *Julius Pflug et la crise religieuse dans l'Allemagne du XVIe siècle.* Essai de synthèse biographique et théologique. 1990
46. BUBENHEIMER, U. *Thomas Müntzer.* Herkunft und Bildung. 1989
47. BAUMAN, C. *The Spiritual Legacy of Hans Denck.* Interpretation and Translation of Key Texts. 1991
48. OBERMAN, H.A. and JAMES, F.A., III (eds.). in cooperation with SAAK, E.L. *Via Augustini.* Augustine in the Later Middle Ages, Renaissance and Reformation: Essays in Honor of Damasus Trapp. 1991 *out of print*
49. SEIDEL MENCHI, S. *Erasmus als Ketzer.* Reformation und Inquisition im Italien des 16. Jahrhunderts. 1993
50. SCHILLING, H. *Religion, Political Culture, and the Emergence of Early Modern Society.* Essays in German and Dutch History. 1992
51. DYKEMA, P.A. and OBERMAN, H.A. (eds.). *Anticlericalism in Late Medieval and Early Modern Europe.* 2nd ed. 1994
52. 53. KRIEGER, Chr. and LIENHARD, M. (eds.). *Martin Bucer and Sixteenth Century Europe.* Actes du colloque de Strasbourg (28-31 août 1991). 1993
54. SCREECH, M.A. *Clément Marot: A Renaissance Poet discovers the World.* Lutheranism, Fabrism and Calvinism in the Royal Courts of France and of Navarre and in the Ducal Court of Ferrara. 1994
55. GOW, A.C. *The Red Jews: Antisemitism in an Apocalyptic Age, 1200-1600.* 1995
56. BUCER, M. *Correspondance.* Tome III (1527-1529). Publié par Chr. Krieger et J. Rott. 1989
57. SPIJKER, W. VAN 'T. *The Ecclesiastical Offices in the Thought of Martin Bucer.* Translated by J. Vriend (text) and L.D. Bierma (notes). 1996
58. GRAHAM, M.F. *The Uses of Reform.* 'Godly Discipline' and Popular Behavior in Scotland and Beyond, 1560-1610. 1996
59. AUGUSTIJN, C. *Erasmus. Der Humanist als Theologe und Kirchenreformer.* 1996
60. McCOOG S J, T.M. *The Society of Jesus in Ireland, Scotland, and England 1541-1588.* 'Our Way of Proceeding?' 1996
61. FISCHER, N. und KOBELT-GROCH, M. (Hrsg.). *Außenseiter zwischen Mittelalter und Neuzeit.* Festschrift für Hans-Jürgen Goertz zum 60. Geburtstag. 1997
62. NIEDEN, M. *Organum Deitatis.* Die Christologie des Thomas de Vio Cajetan. 1997
63. BAST, R.J. *Honor Your Fathers.* Catechisms and the Emergence of a Patriarchal Ideology in Germany, 1400-1600. 1997
64. ROBBINS, K.C. *City on the Ocean Sea: La Rochelle, 1530-1650.* Urban Society, Religion, and Politics on the French Atlantic Frontier. 1997
65. BLICKLE, P. *From the Communal Reformation to the Revolution of the Common Man.* 1998
66. FELMBERG, B.A.R. *Die Ablaßtheorie Kardinal Cajetans (1469-1534).* 1998

67. CUNEO, P.F. *Art and Politics in Early Modern Germany.* Jörg Breu the Elder and the Fashioning of Political Identity, ca. 1475-1536. 1998
68. BRADY, Jr., Th.A. *Communities, Politics, and Reformation in Early Modern Europe.* 1998
69. McKEE, E.A. *The Writings of Katharina Schütz Zell.* 1. The Life and Thought of a Sixteenth-Century Reformer. 2. A Critical Edition. 1998
70. BOSTICK, C.V. *The Antichrist and the Lollards.* Apocalyticism in Late Medieval and Reformation England. 1998
71. BOYLE, M. O'ROURKE. *Senses of Touch.* Human Dignity and Deformity from Michelangelo to Calvin. 1998
72. TYLER, J.J. *Lord of the Sacred City.* The *Episcopus Exclusus* in Late Medieval and Early Modern Germany. 1999
74. WITT, R.G. *'In the Footsteps of the Ancients'.* The Origins of Humanism from Lovato to Bruni. 2000
77. TAYLOR, L.J. *Heresy and Orthodoxy in Sixteenth-Century Paris.* François le Picart and the Beginnings of the Catholic Reformation. 1999
78. BUCER, M. *Briefwechsel/Correspondance.* Band IV (Januar-September 1530). Herausgegeben und bearbeitet von R. Friedrich, B. Hamm und A. Puchta. 2000
79. MANETSCH, S.M. *Theodore Beza and the Quest for Peace in France, 1572-1598.* 2000
80. GODMAN, P. *The Saint as Censor.* Robert Bellarmine between Inquisition and Index. 2000
81. SCRIBNER, R.W. *Religion and Culture in Germany (1400-1800).* Ed. L. Roper. 2001
82. KOOI, C. *Liberty and Religion.* Church and State in Leiden's Reformation, 1572-1620. 2000
83. BUCER, M. *Opera Latina.* Vol. V. Defensio adversus axioma catholicum id est criminationem R.P. Roberti Episcopi Abrincensis (1534). Ed. W.I.P. Hazlett. 2000
84. BOER, W. DE. *The Conquest of the Soul.* Confession, Discipline, and Public Order in Counter-Reformation Milan. 2001
85. EHRSTINE, G. *Theater, culture, and community in Reformation Bern, 1523-1555.* 2001
86. CATTERALL, D. *Community Without Borders.* Scot Migrants and the Changing Face of Power in the Dutch Republic, c. 1600-1700. 2002
87. BOWD, S.D. *Reform Before the Reformation.* Vincenzo Querini and the Religious Renaissance in Italy. 2002
88. PELC, M. *Illustrium Imagines.* Das Porträtbuch der Renaissance. 2002
89. SAAK, E.L. *High Way to Heaven.* The Augustinian Platform between Reform and Reformation, 1292-1524. 2002
90. WITTNEBEN, E.L. *Bonagratia von Bergamo*, Franziskanerjurist und Wortführer seines Ordens im Streit mit Papst Johannes XXII. 2003
91. ZIKA, C. *Exorcising our Demons,* Magic, Witchcraft and Visual Culture in Early Modern Europe. 2002
92. MATTOX, M.L. "*Defender of the Most Holy Matriarchs*", Martin Luther's Interpretation of the Women of Genesis in the *Enarrationes in Genesin*, 1535-45. 2003
93. LANGHOLM, O. *The Merchant in the Confessional,* Trade and Price in the Pre-Reformation Penitential Handbooks. 2003
94. BACKUS, I. *Historical Method and Confessional Identity in the Era of the Reformation (1378-1615).* 2003
95. FOGGIE, J.P. *Renaissance Religion in Urban Scotland.* The Dominican Order, 1450-1560. 2003
96. LÖWE, J.A. *Richard Smyth and the Language of Orthodoxy.* Re-imagining Tudor Catholic Polemicism. 2003
97. HERWAARDEN, J. VAN. *Between Saint James and Erasmus.* Studies in Late-Medieval Religious Life: Devotion and Pilgrimage in The Netherlands. 2003
98. PETRY, Y. *Gender, Kabbalah and the Reformation.* The Mystical Theology of Guillaume Postel (1510–1581). 2004

99. EISERMANN, F., SCHLOTHEUBER, E. und HONEMANN, V. *Studien und Texte zur literarischen und materiellen Kultur der Frauenklöster im späten Mittelalter.* Ergebnisse eines Arbeitsgesprächs in der Herzog August Bibliothek Wolfenbüttel, 24.-26. Febr. 1999. 2004
100. WITCOMBE, C.L.C.E. *Copyright in the Renaissance.* Prints and the *Privilegio* in Sixteenth-Century Venice and Rome. 2004
101. BUCER, M. *Briefwechsel/Correspondance.* Band V (September 1530-Mai 1531). Herausgegeben und bearbeitet von R. Friedrich, B. Hamm, A. Puchta und R. Liebenberg. 2004
102. MALONE, C.M. *Façade as Spectacle: Ritual and Ideology at Wells Cathedral.* 2004
103. KAUFHOLD, M. (ed.) *Politische Reflexion in der Welt des späten Mittelalters / Political Thought in the Age of Scholasticism.* Essays in Honour of Jürgen Miethke. 2004
104. BLICK, S. and TEKIPPE, R. (eds.). *Art and Architecture of Late Medieval Pilgrimage in Northern Europe and the British Isles.* 2004
105. PASCOE, L.B., S.J. *Church and Reform.* Bishops, Theologians, and Canon Lawyers in the Thought of Pierre d'Ailly (1351-1420). 2005
106. SCOTT, T. *Town, Country, and Regions in Reformation Germany.* 2005
107. GROSJEAN, A.N.L. and MURDOCH, S. (eds.). *Scottish Communities Abroad in the Early Modern Period.* 2005